Neurobiology in the Treatment of Eating Disorders

WILEY SERIES ON
CLINICAL AND NEUROBIOLOGICAL
ADVANCES IN PSYCHIATRY

Series Editors: J.A. den Boer and H.G.M. Westenberg

Recent years have witnessed major advances in the study of neuroscience which have increased our understanding of the relationship between cerebral processes and behavioural, cognitive and emotional disorders. This series aims to monitor important research developments in the field of biological psychiatry and their relevance to clinical practice.

Volume 1: **Advances in the Neurobiology of Schizophrenia**
Edited by J.A. den Boer, H.G.M. Westenberg and H.M. van Praag

Volume 2: **Advances in the Neurobiology of Anxiety Disorders**
Edited by H.G.M. Westenberg, J.A. den Boer and D.L. Murphy

Volume 3: **Depression: Neurobiological, Psychopathological and Therapeutic Advances**
Edited by A. Honig and H.M. van Praag

Volume 4: **Neurobiology in the Treatment of Eating Disorders**
Edited by H. W. Hoek, J. L. Treasure and M. A. Katzman

Neurobiology in the Treatment of Eating Disorders

Edited by

HANS WIJBRAND HOEK

Department of Research, Psychiatric Institute, The Hague, and Leiden University, The Netherlands

JANET L. TREASURE

Head, Eating Disorder Unit, Bethlem and Maudsley Trust, London, UK

MELANIE A. KATZMAN

New York Hospital-Cornell Medical Center, New York, and Eating Disorder Unit, Bethlem and Maudsley Trust, London, UK

JOHN WILEY & SONS

Chichester · New York · Weinheim · Brisbane · Singapore · Toronto

Baffins Lane, Chichester,
West Sussex PO19 1UD, England

National 01243 779777
International (+44) 1243 779777
e-mail (for orders and customer service enquiries):
cs-books@wiley.co.uk
Visit our Home Page on http://www.wiley.co.uk
or http://www.wiley.com

Other Wiley Editorial Offices

John Wiley & Sons, Inc., 605 Third Avenue,
New York, NY 10158-0012, USA

WILEY-VCH Verlag GmbH, Pappelallee 3,
D-69469 Weinheim, Germany

Jacaranda Wiley Ltd, 33 Park Road, Milton,
Queensland 4064, Australia

John Wiley & Sons (Asia) Pte Ltd, 2 Clementi Loop #02-01,
Jin Xing Distripark, Singapore 129809

John Wiley & Sons (Canada) Ltd, 22 Worcester Road,
Rexdale, Ontario M9W 1L1, Canada

Library of Congress Cataloging-in-Publication Data

Neurobiology in the treatment of eating disorders / edited by Hans Hoek, Janet Treasure, and Melanie Katzman.
p. cm. — (Wiley series on clinical and neurobiological advances in psychiatry ; v. 4)
Includes bibliographical references and index.
ISBN 0-471-98102-8 (cased : alk. paper)
1. Eating disorders—Physiological aspects. 2. Neuropsychology. 3. Neurobiology. 4. Eating disorders—Treatment. I. Hoek, Hans. II. Treasure, Janet. III. Katzman, Melanie. IV. Series.
[DNLM: 1. Eating Disorders—therapy. 2. Eating Disorders–etiology. 3. Eating Disorders—psychology. 4. Neurobiology–methods. 5. Psychophysiology–methods. WM 175 N494 1998]
RC552.E18N39 1998
616.85′ 26–dc21
DNLM/DLC 97–48993
for Library of Congress CIP

British Library Cataloguing in Publication Data

A catalogue record for this book is available from the British Library

ISBN 0-471-98102-8

Typeset in 10/12pt Times by Techset Composition Ltd, Salisbury, UK
Printed and bound in Great Britain by Bookcraft (Bath) Ltd, Midsomer Norton, Somerset.
This book is printed on acid-free paper responsibly manufactured from sustainable forestry, in which at least two trees are planted for each one used for paper production.

DEDICATION

To

Jacquoline, Marijn, Tim and Jorinde
Tom, Jean and Sam
Russell, Wyndam and Harper

Contents

Contributors

David B. Allison
Fordham University, Obesity Research Center, St. Luke's-Roosevelt Hospital Center, 1090 Amsterdam Ave, New York, NY 10025, USA

Pierre J.V. Beumont
Department of Psychological Medicine, University of Sydney, NSW 2006, Australia

Rachel Bryant Waugh
Department of Psychological Medicine, Great Ormond Street Hospital, Great Ormond Street, London WC1 3JH, UK

Suzzanne Byrnes
University of Sydney, Repat General Hospital, Concord, Sydney, NSW 2139, Australia

Deborah Christie
Department of Psychological Medicine, Great Ormond Street Hospital, Great Ormond Street, London WC1 3JH, UK

Frances Connan
University of London, Institute of Psychiatry, Department of Psychology, De Crespigny Park, London SE5 8AF, UK

Zoë R. Ellison
The Maudsley Hospital, Denmark Hill, London SE5 8AZ, UK

Jackie Foong
The Maudsley Hospital, Denmark Hill, London SE5 8AZ, UK

Eric F. van Furth
Eating Disorder Unit, Robert-Fleury Stichting, PO Box 422, 2260 AK Leidschendam, The Netherlands

Christopher Gillberg
Department of Child and Adolescent Psychiatry, Sahlgren University Hospital, University of Göteborg, 413 45 Göteborg, Sweden

Isky Gordon
Department of Radiology, Great Ormond Street Hospital, Great Ormond Street, London WC1 3JH, UK

Richard A. Gordon
Bard College, Annandale-on-Hudson, New York, NY 12504, USA

Wolfgang Herzog
Medizinische Klinik und Poliklinik, Universität Heidelberg, Bergheimer Strasse 58, 69115 Heidelberg, Germany

Hans Wijbrand Hoek
Psychiatric Institute, The Hague and Leiden University, Albardastraat 100, 2555 VZ, The Hague, The Netherlands

Daphne van Hoeken
Psychiatric Institute, The Hague and Leiden University, Albardastraat 100, 2555 VZ, The Hague, The Netherlands

Melanie A. Katzman
The Eating Disorder Outpatient Unit, The Maudsley Hospital, Denmark Hill, London SE5 8AZ, UK

Walter H. Kaye
Department of Psychiatry, Western Psychiatric Institute and Clinic, University of Pittsburgh School of Medicine, Pittsburgh, PA 15213, USA

Bryan Lask
Department of Psychological Medicine, Great Ormond Street Hospital, Great Ormond Street, London WC1 3JH, UK

Michele D. Levine
Western Psychiatric Institute and Clinic, University of Pittsburgh School of Medicine, Pittsburgh, PA 15213, USA

Lisa R. Lilenfeld
Department of Psychiatry, Western Psychiatric Institute and Clinic, University of Pittsburgh School of Medicine, Pittsburgh, PA 15213, USA

Alexander R. Lucas
Mayo Clinic, 200 First Street SW, Rochester, MN 55905, USA

Marsha D. Marcus
Western Psychiatric Institute and Clinic, University of Pittsburgh School of Medicine, Pittsburgh, PA 15213, USA

Laurel E.S. Mayer
Department of Psychiatry, College of Physicians and Surgeons, Columbia University, 722 West 168th Street, New York, NY 10032, USA

Caroline Meyer
Department of Psychology, University of Southampton, Southampton SO17 1BJ, UK

Julie S. Nathan
Fordham University, Obesity Research Center, St. Luke's-Roosevelt Hospital Center, 1090 Amsterdam Ave, New York, NY 10025, USA

John B. Owen
School of Agricultural and Forest Sciences, University of Wales Bangor, Bangor, Gwynedd LL57 2UW, UK

Robert L. Palmer
Department of Psychiatry, University of Leicester, Leicester General Hospital, Gwendolen Road, Leicester LE5 4PW, UK

Maria Råstam
Department of Child and Adolescent Psychiatry, Sahlgren University Hospital, University of Göteborg, 413 45 Göteborg, Sweden

Janice Russell
University of Sydney, Repat General Hospital, Concord, Sydney, NSW 2139, Australia

Ulrike Schmidt
The Eating Disorder Outpatient Unit, The Maudsley Hospital, Denmark Hill, London SE5 8AZ, UK

Lucy Serpell
The Eating Disorder Outpatient Unit, The Maudsley Hospital, Denmark Hill, London SE5 8AZ, UK

Timo Specht
Medizinische Klinik und Poliklinik, Universität Heidelberg, Bergheimer Strasse 58, 69115 Heidelberg, Germany

Janet L. Treasure
The Eating Disorder Outpatient Unit, The Maudsley Hospital, Denmark Hill, London SE5 8AZ, UK

Glenn Waller
Department of Psychology, University of Southampton, Southampton SO17 1BJ, UK

B. Timothy Walsh
Department of Psychiatry, College of Physicians and Surgeons, Columbia University, 722 West 168th Street, New York, NY 10032, USA

Anne Waters
Department of Psychology, University of Southampton, Southampton SO17 1BJ, UK

Geoffrey Wolff
The Eating Disorder Outpatient Unit, The Maudsley Hospital, Denmark Hill, London SE5 8AZ, UK

Stephan Zipfel
Medizinische Klinik und Poliklinik, Universität Heidelberg, Bergheimer Strasse 58, 69115 Heidelberg, Germany

Preface

This book is part of a series of volumes on the neurobiology of severe mental disorders. Although there are many other books on eating disorders, we were intrigued and excited by the potential role for a book dealing with the neurobiology of the diseases, and we thought that it would be a challenging project for both authors and readers.

The aim of this book is to incorporate recent advances in biological sciences with our concepts of the aetiology and treatment of eating disorders. It is often difficult to house the knowledge from scientific research and clinical practice in the same chapters. As a result the two disciplines have not optimally cross-fertilized each other. We wanted to make accessible to clinicians the latest findings in the neurosciences and offer specific suggestions on how to incorporate these data in a treatment setting.

The editors are practising clinicians who set their work in the context of biopsychosocial model. Janet Treasure is an English psychiatrist trained also in internal medicine and neuroendocrinology. Melanie Katzman is an American psychologist, who is known for her work on coping strategies, but also on feminist and cultural issues. Hans Wijbrand Hoek is a Dutch psychiatrist with a background in social psychiatry and psychiatric epidemiology. We thought that it was an advantage to have three editors with different theoretical and cultural backgrounds to work towards the construction of a new biopsychosocial model. We aimed wherever possible to include authors from a variety of different countries.

The book is divided into three domains. Part I offers an overview on the clinical heterogeneity and instruments to measure eating disorders. In the chapters on epidemiology and aetiology, biological, psychological and social models have been described. Part II focuses on the advances in neurobiological research. In part III the authors focus on evidence-based care. At the beginning of each section the editors provide a short introduction which integrates the important concepts, new advances and implications for clinical practice. In order to make it a comprehensive and cohesive volume we have asked the contributors to organize their chapters along the following dimensions:

- To start with a summary of the research literature and recent advances
- To explore implications for current clinical practice. How would you incorporate this knowledge in a discourse with your patients?
- To suggest implications for future research
- To conclude with personal opinions, concepts and ideas that need further development, basically their prophesies for the future.

In addition we asked all contributors to provide a one page chart that distils their key message into a series of bullet points. By creating an easily understood, one page summary we hope to encourage teachers and clinicians to share the latest information with patients, students, and families. These charts, which appear before the references in each chapter, have also been gathered together in an Appendix, not only for ease of reference but also to enable them to be conveniently copied for use as handouts in classes or information sheets as part of the therapy.

The metaphor of the blind men examining various parts of the elephant has frequently been used as an apposite description of much of the research into eating disorders. There has been a tendency for each of us to take a part and examine it in detail but there has been difficulty in taking the wider view. We hope that this book unites the many 'explorers of the elephant' and provides a forum to bring their knowledge to all around them.

Hans Wijbrand Hoek
Janet L. Treasure
Melanie A. Katzman

Acknowledgements

Hans Wijbrand would like to thank Judith Rodenburg and Henriëtte Faas for their valuable assistance and moral support. Janet and Melanie would like to thank Gill Todd, for providing the clinical platform upon which the curiosity to understand more is built, and Janice May, for her tireless dancing digits on the keyboard. Melanie also acknowledges Russell Makowsky who did not dare inquire 'another book?' and Wyndam and Harper Makowsky who are busy writing their own 'texts'.

Finally, this book on integration require international intergration and co-operation at top speed. Thank you to all of the contributors who complied with our accelerated time schedule and the staff at John Wiley & Sons who made sure that we achieved our debut in New York.

I Introduction and Aetiology

Introduction

H. W. HOEK

Persons with eating disorders are best understood and treated according to a biopsychosocial model. Part I of this book with its focus on neurobiology and treatment starts with general chapters that approach this topic from a broader perspective. In six chapters the authors describe the phenomenology, measurement, epidemiology and aetiology of eating disorders.

Richard Gordon reflects on the history of eating disorders. Interest in eating disorders has increased rapidly since the 1960s and 1970s. For some time, people thought that anorexia nervosa was a modern illness. However, eating disorders, particularly anorexia nervosa, have been well known since the latter half of the 19th century; anorexia was first identified by Gull in London and Lasegue in Paris in the early 1870s. The medical literature contained descriptions of conditions similar to anorexia nervosa for at least two centuries prior to the writings of Gull and Lasegue. Even in the Middle Ages one comes across descriptions of so-called 'holy anorexics'. It has been suggested that the most crucial difference between saintly fasters and modern anorexics is the vast difference in their motivation: the former were seeking religious and moral perfection whereas the latter pursue a secular goal, namely an ideal body shape. In view of the long history of case descriptions of eating disorders, one must conclude that at least anorexia nervosa is not a modern illness. Gordon concludes that biological factors enter into the eating disorders both as predispositions and as sequelae; eating disorders can be seen as resulting from the clash of psychocultural stresses with biological realities.

Beumont describes the current state of our knowledge of psychopathology and phenomenology of eating disorders and the behavioural disturbance involved. Eating disorders, like most illnesses in psychiatry, are syndromes defined by clinical features. One could consider eating disorders as a spectrum of dysfunctional eating, extending along three related behavioural parameters: restriction, purging and overeating. The eating disorders can be grouped into two clusters: one in which behaviours directed towards losing weight are constant or frequently recurring features (anorexia and bulimia nervosa) and another in which attempts to lose weight are less prominent (binge eating disorder and obesity).

Nathan and Allison advocate a multidimensional approach to the assessment of eating disorders. They give a thorough overview of current psychological and physical methods for the assessment of persons with eating disorders. To plan appropriate treatment one needs to understand the (psycho)pathology, including comorbidity and physical disturbances of an individual patient. The evaluator should keep the goal of the assessment in mind and consider how the data obtained from the chosen measures can be used to develop an effective intervention or to test the desired hypothesis. Gillberg and Råstam warn us against beginning the assessment of a new case with preconceived prototypical notions about underlying causes and advise us to keep an open mind.

In their search for factors that influence the frequency of eating disorders van Hoeken and colleagues review the epidemiological studies. The incidence rate of eating disorders in females 15–24 years old, the most vulnerable group, seems to have gradually increased over the past 50 years. While most studies on neurobiology and treatment use clinical samples for obvious reasons, it is important to realize that they constitute only a minority of all patients with eating disorders. Only 6% of all community cases with bulimia nervosa do receive mental health care. We still know very little about specific risk factors for eating disorders. For example, although dieting behaviour seems to play a role in the pathogenesis of an eating disorder, only a small proportion of all dieters in the community develop an eating disorder.

In the two concluding chapters on aetiology the authors summarize the four previous chapters of Part I and prepare the way for the two other parts of this book. In their chapter on the aetiology of anorexia nervosa Gillberg and Råstam conclude that models based only on either biological, psychological or social factors can provide only partial explanations. In some cases anorexia nervosa is associated with strong genetic determinants; in other cases it might be triggered by major life events and in such cases biological factors might be less important in the aetiology.

In discussing the aetiology of bulimia nervosa Palmer argues that although enduring aspects of human biology are important, social factors may be even more important. Social factors are more likely to explain the rapid increase in the registered incidence of bulimia nervosa. Motivated eating restraint is the usual entry to the pathway of the disorder. Motivated eating restraint together with low self esteem form the background of bulimia nervosa. Certain risk factors may be associated with bulimia nervosa, like negative self evaluation in childhood, premorbid perfectionism, low parental contact or parental arguments, criticism and high expectations. However, it seems less likely that these risk factors would lead to this disorder in a culture where there is little pressure to be slim.

The authors describe advances in research and different models which have proved to be useful in clinical practice. All authors consider both anorexia nervosa and bulimia nervosa more or less as multifactorally determined disorders. It is clear from their writings and the literature that—as for other psychiatric disorders—it will take a long time until the ultimate goal, namely primary prevention of these severe mental disorders, is reached. However, our rapid progress in knowledge of eating disorders is also clear.

1 Concepts of Eating Disorders: A Historical Reflection

R. A. GORDON
Bard College, Annandale-on-Hudson, NY, USA

Eating disorders, anorexia nervosa and bulimia nervosa, have been the subject of intense interest in recent years. From a small trickle of research on these disorders even as recently as the 1960s, the number of publications in scientific journals has grown to a torrent, making it all but impossible for even the specialized clinician to keep abreast of developments in the field. Epidemiological studies from the US (Lucas *et al.* 1991), Scotland (Eagles *et al.* 1995), Switzerland (Willi and Grossman 1983) and Japan (Nadaoka *et al.* 1996) have documented significant increases in incidence of these conditions through the 1970s, 80s and 90s (see chapter 4). Moreover, while it was at one time assumed that eating disorders were found only in Western (or highly Westernized) societies, a spate of recent reports have indicated that they are now appearing in significant numbers in diverse locales such as Hong Kong (Lee *et al.* 1993), India (Khandelwal *et al.* 1995) and South Africa (Szabo *et al.* 1995), societies which were once considered to be immune to the factors that would give rise to them. Once considered to be limited to individuals of upper-class socioeconomic status in the US and Europe, it now appears that eating disorders are manifesting themselves over a broader part of the socioeconomic spectrum as well (Gard and Freeman 1996).

While many hypotheses about the etiology of eating disorders have been entertained, it is generally accepted that a precise understanding of their causes remains elusive (see chapters 5 and 6). It seems clear, however, that numerous factors contribute to their development, including individual personality, family dynamics, genetic and biological predispositions, and sociocultural factors. The latter are of particular importance in understanding why eating disorders have become more common in the latter half of the 20th century. It is the purpose of this chapter to provide an historical and sociocultural perspective on eating disorders, one that will hopefully throw light on the intense interest that they have generated both in psychiatric research and the popular imagination. In addition, it is hoped that this account will provide a wider context for understanding some of the challenges that the clinician faces in his or her interaction with the eating disordered patient.

Neurobiology in the Treatment of Eating Disorders.
Edited by H.W. Hoek, J.L. Treasure and M.A. Katzman.

A BRIEF HISTORY

As medical entities, eating disorders, particularly anorexia nervosa, have been well known since the latter half of the 19th century, when anorexia was first identified by Gull in London and Lasegue in Paris in the early 1870s. There is also reason to believe that patterns of behavior resembling eating disorders were in existence for centuries prior to their 'discovery' in 1873, but in forms that were not typically construed as illnesses. For example, numerous women during the late medieval period who were later sanctified by the church exhibited behavior that was in many respects strikingly parallel to what we would now describe as anorexia nervosa. These 'holy anorexics', as they were called by the historian Rudolph Bell (1985) in his controversial book on the subject, may or may not have been deserving of such a label, and a lively debate has subsequently developed about their psychiatric status (Bynum 1987; Brumberg 1988). It has been suggested that the most crucial difference between saintly fasters and modern anorexics is the vast difference in their motivations, namely that the former were seeking religious and moral perfection whereas the latter pursue a secular goal, namely a particular ideal body shape. This analysis may be excessively dichotomous, however, in that contemporary anorexic women may also be seen as engaging in a moral struggle for perfection, purity and transcendence that has a distinctly ascetic dimension (Rampling 1985). Thus, despite an obviously great gulf between medieval and contemporary culture, the one being saturated with a religious vocabulary and the other a secular one, there may indeed be considerable parallels between the self-starvers of the medieval world and the anorexics of today. It could be argued that both were women caught in periods of intense cultural ambiguity regarding gender roles, in which the aspiration of women to greater social power and status were viewed with ambivalence at best by the entrenched bastions of male power (Bynum 1987). Such an analysis is in line with recent sociocultural interpretations of eating disorders, which have placed increasing importance on the relevance of the politics of gender to an understanding of the waxing and waning of these conditions in historical time (Silverstein and Perlick 1995).

The 'high period' of such holy fasting was between the 12th and 15th centuries, at which point the pattern seemed to go into something of a decline (Bell 1985). But in the 17th, 18th and 19th centuries, another pattern emerged, that of the notorious 'fasting girls', who ultimately provoked intense public controversy as well as a debate between the scientific and religious communities as to their credibility (Brumberg 1988). Most of these young women had none of the religious stature of the figures written about by Rudolph Bell, which included such notable spiritual virtuosos as Catherine of Siena. They were typically poor and uneducated young women, whose inability to eat was exploited by their families as well as by church authorities and unscrupulous entrepreneurs who encouraged, for example, charging admission to witness their fasting. Nevertheless, they may have some place in a discussion of the prehistory of anorexia nervosa, if only to indicate the manipulative power of fasting and the ability of food refusal to elicit both public spectacle as well as scientific controversy (Vandereycken and van Deth 1994).

In addition to these spiritual and quasi-spiritual manifestations of the disorder, conditions similar to anorexia nervosa were described in the medical literature for at least two centuries prior to the writings of Gull and Lasegue. The earliest recognizable, although somewhat inchoate, medical description of anorexia nervosa is widely attributed to Thomas Morton, who described two cases, one female and one male, in his Treatise on Consumption (Silverman 1985). There were other references to conditions that involved psychogenic weight loss in the 18th and early 19th centuries, but these bore varying degrees of resemblance to anorexia nervosa (Vandereycken and van Deth 1990; Parry-Jones 1985). However, most contemporary observers are in agreement that the illness that we now recognize as anorexia nervosa was not fully described until the publications of Gull and Lasegue. In particular Gull (1874), who coined the name anorexia nervosa, offered several case histories in which he placed particular emphasis on the physical emaciation of the anorexic patient as well as her sometimes remarkable degree of energy and activity, in light of her undernourishment. Despite his attributing the cause of anorexia nervosa to a 'morbid mental state' and therefore the explicit recognition of the role that psychogenic factors played in the disorder, many observers have remarked on how little interest Gull showed in the actual psychological situation of his patients (Brumberg 1988). It was quite different with the French neurologist Lasegue (1873), who made numerous important observations not only about the psychological state of the anorexic patient but also her social interactions, particularly with members of her own family. Indeed, Lasegue made the trenchant comment, one which would evoke widespread support among contemporary clinicians who work with eating disorders from a family perspective, that 'It must not cause surprise to find me thus always placing in parallel the morbid condition of the . . . subject and preoccupations of those who surround her. These two circumstances are intimately connected, and we should acquire an erroneous idea of the disease by confining ourselves to an examination of the patient.' But while Lasegue's remarks were centered on the family, it could be argued that his perceptions of the importance of social factors opened the door to a sociocultural interpretation as well.

Following the writings of Gull and Lasegue numerous papers appeared about anorexia nervosa until the first decade of the 20th century, with major figures of late 19th century psychiatry, such as Sigmund Freud and Gilles de la Tourette, taking an interest in it (Sours 1980). However, for about the first three to four decades of the 20th century, psychiatric interest in anorexia nervosa in the English-speaking world went into abeyance. It is unclear whether this was due to an actual decline in the prevalence of the condition after a rise at the end of the 19th century, or perhaps was the result of other factors. Prominent among these was the interest in endocrine wasting diseases such as Simmond's pituitary cachexia, which was first identified in 1914, and the resulting misdiagnosis and inappropriate treatment of an unknown number of anorexic patients for the next twenty years (Sours 1980). The confounding of anorexia nervosa with panhypopituitarism was not clarified until the late 1930s when workers such as Ryle (1936) and Richardson (1939) differentiated anorexia nervosa from Simmond's disease and argued for the importance of psychological factors and their impact on endocrine function.

Moreover, despite the overall impression that the prevalence of anorexia nervosa was low in the first half of the 20th century, Silverstein *et al.* (1986), through a study of newspaper accounts as well as scattered remarks of prominent physicians, identified an 'epidemic of self-starvation' among women, and particularly among female college students, in the US during the 1920s. Given the prominence of a thin female body ideal (the 'flapper') as well as the turbulence that surrounded issues of female identity, achievement and sexuality during this period, perhaps there was a proliferation of subclinical eating disorders that in some sense resembled a similar increase in the 1970s and 1980s in Great Britain (Button and Whitehouse 1981) and the United States (Thompson and Schwartz 1982). This is a subject worthy of further inquiry by medical historians. Whatever the outcome of such research, any proliferation of eating disorder symptomatology that may have taken place during the 1920s apparently did not result in a sharp increase in hospital admissions. But then again, it is at least possible that a considerable number of anorexic patients were being misdiagnosed.

Following the clarification of the distinction between anorexia nervosa and purely endocrine disorders, the discussion of anorexia nervosa as a psychiatric disorder began again in earnest in the 1940s. During the 1940s and 50s, psychiatric thinking about anorexia nervosa in the US was dominated by a psychoanalytic model, which stressed the anorexic's fears about sexuality and more particularly a now notorious notion that the food refusal of the anorexic was due to the defense against a specific fantasy of oral impregnation. This hypothesis, which originated in a publication that cited two case histories (Waller *et al.* 1940), now seems to have been relegated to the dustbin of psychiatric history, although it continued to be extraordinarily influential through the 1940s and 50s both in the United States and to a lesser extent in Europe. Treatment based on this model was one of psychoanalytic interpretation of unconscious motives, also generally considered now to be unhelpful if not singularly harmful to this particular patient population (Bruch 1978).

Despite an increase in psychiatric publications during the 1940s and 50s, the phenomenon of anorexia nervosa continued to be viewed, in the words of Hill (1977), as a 'curiosity and a rarity' prior to around 1970. Psychiatric residents were told that one was likely only to see a few cases during a lifetime of practice. But the awareness of eating disorders began to change, beginning in the 1960s and then accelerating into the 1970s and 80s. A symposium held in Germany in 1965 included contributions from numerous researchers from Europe and the US and one paper from Japan as well, which suggested that the condition has been becoming more prevalent there since the Second World War (Meyer and Feldmann, 1965). A major breakthrough into a more modern perspective on anorexia nervosa came in the form of Hilde Bruch's publications on the subject, which had begun in the 1960s, culminating in her 1973 book, *Eating Disorders: Obesity, Anorexia and the Person Within*. In the latter work, Bruch severely criticized psychoanalytic 'drive' formulations and suggested a broader-based developmental perspective. Her new theoretical framework emphasized transactions between the individual and her family environment and placed a considerable emphasis on the distortions that arose as a result of these transactions in the anorexic's perception of her body image and her internal feeling states. At the center of the anorexic's psychopathology was a 'relentless pursuit of thinness' as well as an 'all-pervasive sense of ineffectiveness'. These considerations, particularly the focus on thinness, played a considerable role in the new diagnostic formulations for anorexia nervosa that emerged in the Diagnostic and Statistical Manual (DSM-III) (American Psychiatric Association 1980), which placed central emphases on a 'disturbance in body image' and an 'intense fear of becoming obese' (see also chapter 2).

The work of Bruch and others represented a significant advance in the clinical understanding of anorexia nervosa, but the new diagnostic formulations of the DSM-III may have narrowed the frame of discussion about the illness as well. In particular, the DSM incorporated Bruch's emphasis on the importance of body image and the pursuit of thinness, but in seeking symptom definitions that could be operationally defined, it may have subtly discounted the broader psychocultural context delineated by Bruch and writers such as the English psychiatrist Arthur Crisp (1980). In particular, Bruch saw the pursuit of thinness as a concrete manifestation of the anorexic's failed quest for autonomy and what she called the 'search for a self-respecting identity'. These in turn could be related to developmental deficits that resulted from an environment that failed to adequately support the need for self-initiated activity and that encouraged slavish adherence to external expectations. By placing the exclusive emphasis on the fear of weight gain and body image issues, the DSM approach may have discounted such issues, which may ultimately be more fundamental.

In this connection, recent critiques have suggested that an exclusive focus on thinness to the exclusion of other motives for self-starvation may be itself culture-bound. Reports of eating disorders by observers in Hong Kong (Lee *et al.* 1993) and India (Khandelwal *et al.* 1995) have indicated that body image concerns are not central for many patients, even though the number of cases of anorexia nervosa may be increasing in these areas. These accounts have suggested the possibility that the 'discovery' of the centrality of body image symptomatology in anorexia nervosa in the 1970s may itself have been influenced by cultural factors. The pursuit of thinness may have been the particular form in which broader issues regarding female identity conflicts have been (and continue to be) expressed in Western nations. However, the broader cultural issues raised by anorexia nervosa are those of the conflicts in identity and expectations experienced by women in cultural transition (Katzman and Lee 1997). Self-starvation, but not necessarily a preoccupation with thinness, appears to be an extreme response of young women who are acutely vulnerable to these conflicts.

To return to the historical account, the early 1980s were a period of explosive growth in research on eating disorders. A watershed event was the appearance of the *International Journal of Eating Disorders* in 1982. In the same year, Garfinkel and Garner (1982) published a major work on anorexia nervosa (*Anorexia Nervosa: A Multidimensional Approach*), which synthesized the research of preceding years and presented an influential formulation of the multidimensional etiology of eating disorders. Garner and Garfinkel pointed to the growing research evidence that suggested an increase in the prevalence of the condition, a phenomenon that, based on their own studies of changing body image ideals and the high prevalence of eating disorders in ballet students, they attributed to sociocultural factors. The 1980s also saw a proliferation of interest in bulimia nervosa, which had been first described in a paper by Boskind-Lodahl (1976) but later defined in more formal clinical terms by Russell (1979). Bulimia had been known for some time as a syndrome occurring within anorexia nervosa, but its appearance as an eating disorder in patients whose weight was in the normal range was deemed to be a new phenomenon. By the mid-1980s, it had become clear that bulimia nervosa was probably at least four times as prevalent as anorexia nervosa (Pope *et al.* 1984). Several reports indicated that it was occurring at what were described as epidemic rates on college campuses in the United States (Halmi *et al.* 1981) and systematic surveys as well as informal reports indicated that it had become quite common in France and Germany, as well (Aimez and Ohayon 1988; Habermas 1990). With the development of the more stringent diagnostic criteria of the DSM-III-R (APA 1980), which stipulated frequency criteria for binge-eating episodes, it became clear that some of the studies from the early 80s had overestimated the prevalence of bulimia somewhat. Nevertheless, more conservative estimates of the prevalence of bulimia of clinical severity in the populations at risk (e.g. females of college age) were still in the range of 2%, suggesting that the disorder was still four times as prevalent as anorexia nervosa (Pyle *et al.* 1991).

FROM GULL AND LASEGUE TO HILDE BRUCH: A CHANGING SYMPTOMATOLOGY?

In a reflection on the history of anorexia nervosa, Gerald Russell (1985) proposed that from the time of Gull and Lasegue to the age of Hilde Bruch and beyond, there have been significant changes in the nature of anorexia nervosa. The first of these, he suggested, is the simple fact that the disorder had increased so remarkably in frequency of occurrence. Russell pointed to epidemiological studies by Theander (1970), that had documented a steady increase in the number of cases in southern Sweden in the 1940s, 50s and 60s, as well to research indicating an increase in the disorder in the US, London, and north-east Scotland. These epidemiological findings cited by Russell, which were based on studies published in the 1970s, have been buttressed by more recent studies that were cited earlier in this chapter. The most detailed and sweeping of these was that of Lucas and his colleagues (Lucas *et al.* 1991), whose studies in the Rochester, MN area spanned five decades from the 1930s to the 1980s. While there was a slight increase in the incidence of anorexia nervosa from the 1930s to the 1940s, the incidence dropped to a low point in the 1950s, only to rise again from the 1960s and 70s, with a particularly dramatic acceleration in the 1980s. Lucas suggested that by 1985 anorexia nervosa had become the third most common disorder among female adolescents in the US, the first being asthma and the second obesity. While the assertion that the prevalence of anorexia nervosa has increased has not gone unchallenged (William and King 1987; Fombonne 1995), most contemporary observers seem to agree that the increase has been a real one.

Russell hypothesized that the dramatically increased frequency of anorexia nervosa in the second half of the 20th century could most likely be attributed to the sociocultural factors, especially, in his view, the demands created by the extremely thin female body ideal. But a correlate of the impact of these pressures was, Russell suggested, an actual change in the nature of the symptomatology of anorexia nervosa itself. While Gull and Lasegue had described a disorder unmistakably familiar in many respects to a contemporary observer, one crucial element that had been missing from the early descriptions was the psychopathology of thinness. In Russell's view, it was unlikely that 'keen clinical observers' such as Gull and Lasegue would have missed such a prominent feature of these disorders as they present themselves to clinicians now. Rather, the psychopathology of body image and the pursuit of thinness represented essential changes in the content of the disorder. These new elements represent the capacity of culture to mold the symptomatology of a disease, even though the core of the disorder remained constant. Such 'pathoplasticity', Russell asserted, is not unusual, particularly for psychiatric disorders which are subject to an uncommon degree of cultural influence. In fact, the very factors that had made the disorder more common, as indicated by prevalence studies, had also contributed to transforming its symptomatology.

Russell's third point was that along with changes in the essential psychopathology of anorexia nervosa, a new element had emerged, that is, the dramatic increase in bulimic expressions of the illness. Russell himself had coined the term 'bulimia nervosa' in 1979 to refer to a subgroup of eating disordered patients whose preoccupation with body weight and shape was similar to those of anorexic patients, but who compulsively gorged, vomited, abused laxatives, and otherwise attempted to compensate for the loss of control that they had experienced over their eating behavior. These patients were not necessarily or even typically underweight. Particularly notable was the fact that while this disorder was even less known than anorexia nervosa as little as a decade preceding the publication of Russell's paper, the number of individuals suffering from these symptoms in the late 1970s and 80s appeared to far outnumber those the number with classical 'restricting' anorexia nervosa. As a small addendum, it should be pointed out that there is a general consensus that bulimia nervosa, while related to anorexia nervosa, is a distinct clinical entity. Strictly speaking, then, Russell's formulation refers to both the increased presence of bulimic symptoms *within* anorexia nervosa as well as the dramatic appearance of bulimia nervosa as a distinct syndrome.

Gull and Lasegue had rarely mentioned anything resembling bulimia in their early descriptions of anorexia nervosa, and in fact it was not until the 1940s and 50s that bulimic symptoms began to be regularly mentioned in reports on series of cases of anorexia nervosa. Bulimia nervosa, while having historical antecedents, seems to be a new disorder, which, in the words of Stunkard, seems to have 'burst from the blue upon modern society' (Stunkard 1990; Russell 1997). In an effort to come to grips with this historical transformation in the symptomatology of eating disorders, Casper (1983) points to the possibility that the ever-growing cultural concern with overweight, which gradually assumed center stage in the psychopathology of anorexia nervosa in the middle of the 20th century, may have been the culprit. In particular, she suggests that the greater availability of low-cost food and the trends toward overweight in the population, coupled with the increasing influence of the fashionable ideal of thinness, may have caught a number of vulnerable individuals in a set of contradictory pressures that ultimately transformed the nature of anorexia nervosa. Specifically, she proposes that a new type of woman may have been recruited into the psychopathology of anorexia nervosa, one who had a history of overweight as well as tendencies towards difficulties with affect and impulse control. Such an individual may have internalized the culture's increasingly differentiated stigma of overweight as a reprehensible and shameful loss of control while at the same time adopting an overvalued concept of thinness, which came to represent the opposite qualities of moral purity and personal efficacy.

Indeed, it could be argued that the tension between the increasing weight of the population, which has been documented to be quite dramatic in recent studies conducted in the US (Kuczmarski *et al.* 1994), and the insistent demands for weight loss, driven by a host of social forces including appearance standards and health concerns, constitute the central dynamic of the contemporary proliferation of eating disorders (Gordon 1990). This conflict would be most acutely experienced by women, owing to the particularly stringent appearance standards for females as well as an equally skewed (from the standpoint of gender) stigmatization of obesity (Crocker *et al.* 1993).

THE ISSUE OF GENDER

Throughout history up until the present, one of the most striking facts about the prevalence of eating disorders has been the overwhelming predominance of women with these problems. What is remarkable is the consistency of this phenomenon, both historically and cross-culturally, including the pre-history of anorexia nervosa as well as the early modern history of the disorder in the late 19th century. The sex ratio of nine females for every male with anorexia nervosa seems to hold up virtually every epidemiological study, across several cultures. Despite the remarkable consistency of what is the most lopsided sex ratio of any psychiatric disorder, the role of gender in the causation of eating disorders remains one of the central puzzles in the questions of the genesis of these conditions.

There have been suggestions that one source of the sex difference in prevalence may lie in biological factors. One such speculation originates in the demonstration in animal research that female rats are able to tolerate food deprivation much longer than males (Hoyenga and Hoyenga 1979). One proposed explanation for this is evolutionary, namely, that it is in the interest of the survival of the species for females to be able to tolerate conditions of food deprivation during periods of famine (Beller 1977). Like other evolutionary explanations, this hypothesis is difficult to prove directly, but it has the appeal of providing a biological framework for a phenomenon that shows a remarkable degree of historical and cross-cultural consistency. Along somewhat different biological lines, the association of anorexia nervosa with puberty may have something to do with the relative complexity of female pubertal development from a hormonal standpoint, and therefore the vulnerability of these processes to disruption by factors such as emotional stress. Crisp (1980) suggests that the central role of fat development in female biological maturation is crucial in understanding the preponderance of weight and shape disorders in women.

As Crisp (1980) points out, though, it is impossible to understand how these biological predispositions culminate in eating disorders without taking into account the crucial shaping role of culture. In her widely read, popular work on anorexia nervosa, Bruch (1978) introduced the notion that sociocultural factors may well have been playing a role in the spread of the condition. In particular she pointed to 'the enormous emphasis that Fashion places on slimness'. Most sociocultural theory and research in the 1980s revolved around this notion. In particular, Garner and his colleagues published a highly influential study that documented a steady decrease in weight and an increasingly 'tubular' form in Miss America pageant winners and Playboy centerfolds over the period 1960 to 1979 (Garner *et al.* 1980). This change in the idealized female form seemed highly correlated with an increase in articles on dieting in popular magazines and appeared to correlate with the increase in eating disorders that had occurred over the same period as well. Buttressing these arguments, Garfinkel and Garner (1982) conducted an important study of dance students in Canada which documented a very high rate of disordered eating attitudes as well as unrecognized anorexia nervosa in this population, which is characterized by extraordinarily stringent norms of thinness. The implications of these studies appeared to be clear-cut. If women are exposed to particularly strong cultural pressures to achieve thinness, and if these expectations translate themselves into higher degrees of body dissatisfaction and dieting, then women as a whole would be expected to be far more vulnerable to eating disorders. What remained to be explained was why certain women would succumb to such pressures, while others (the majority, in fact) would be relatively immune, at least to developing an eating disorder.

The thesis of a powerful gender bias in cultural standards of body weight has had enormous influence, and it is difficult to contest its fundamental importance. However, there is a growing awareness that the sociocultural factors that make women vulnerable to eating disorders are probably more complex and profound than the pressure to conform reflexively to external standards of body shape. It is often forgotten that in addition to her comments on thinness, Bruch (1978) was concerned with more pervasive pressures that were encountered by young women in a period of dramatic changes in the female role. She noted that along with an increase in opportunities for contemporary young women came some subtle burdens: 'Growing girls can experience this liberation as a demand and feel that they have to do something outstanding. Many of my patients have expressed the feeling that they are overwhelmed by the vast number of potential opportunities available to them which they "ought" to fulfill, that there were too many choices and they had been afraid of not choosing correctly.' The fact that eating disorders have proliferated in a period of rapidly changing social expectations for women was relatively neglected in earlier sociocultural treatments of eating disorders, but is of central importance to a more comprehensive understanding of the role of gender (Gordon 1990). In fact, a good case can be made for the notion that those adolescents who experience the most wrenching discontinuities between their childhood cultural and family experience and the new demands encountered in adolescence—women who either come from more traditional families governed by conventional norms, or those who emigrate and experience particularly powerful cultural discontinuities—may be the ones who are most vulnerable to developing eating disorders (Katzman and Lee 1997).

It may seem paradoxical that in an era of feminism and expanding opportunities that women would experience a symptom that seems to bind them to the most traditional types of role expectations, that is, norms of physical appearance. This contradiction was noted in a review by Rodin *et al.* (1985) and has been the target of political interpretations by feminist writers. Thus Chernin (1981) and Wolf (1991) both argue that the social demand for thinness, as mediated by the fashion and beauty industries, intensified at just that point in history when women were beginning to make insistent claims for equality and autonomy. The demand that women 'reduce' their body size could be seen as a response of a still male-dominated and misogynist culture to the assertion of women of their rights to equal status in society. From this standpoint, the paradox of intensifying weight consciousness in an era of feminism is an understandable consequence of gender politics.

In an important and innovative historical study of these issues, Silverstein and Perlick (1995) have suggested that eating disorders have tended to emerge in just those periods of history in which the dislocations in the female role have created extraordinarily high levels of adolescent distress. These would include the late medieval period, the last half of the 19th century, and the late 20th century. What is particularly intriguing about their account is the linking of conflicts in female identity with cultural prescriptions about body shape in the 20th century. In a society still governed by sexist ideology, the curvaceous female body is associated stereotypically with low intelligence and subordinate status. Thus, thinness can really be understood as an avoidance of the 'traditional' implications of curvaceousness, and is particularly valued by women with high aspiration levels. Silverstein and Perlick suggest also that 'cosmetic' standards of the fashion industry, which are seen as the prime cause of eating disorders in traditional accounts, are really shaped by the values of non-traditional, achieving women.

FASHIONABLE ILLNESSES

The psychoanalytic anthropologist George Devereux (1980) suggested that certain psychiatric disorders achieve notoriety because of the way in which they capture the central psychological problems and dilemmas of a culture. Such 'ethnic disorders', as he called them, are exemplified in the classic 'exotic' syndromes of ethnopsychiatry, such as amok, latah, or koro, but they are also present, albeit more difficult to discern, in our own world. Eating disorders may be contemporary instances of ethnic disorders of Euro-American culture, but are now also manifesting themselves throughout the world. One of the defining features of an ethnic disorder is that as the syndrome becomes well known, it becomes a standardized or 'prescribed' template for the expression of psychological distress. In Devereux's provocative formulation, it is as if culture offers the following mandate: 'Don't go crazy, but if you do, do it this way.'

Public knowledge about eating disorders soared in the 1980s, owing to a number of factors. First, as the disorders became more prevalent, they became more familiar. A Gallup poll conducted in 1984 indicated that it had become common for respondents to know a sufferer. This was remarkable, in light of the virtual invisibility of eating disorders 10 or 20 years before (Rosenzwieg and Spruill 1987). Second, eating disorders were subject to unrelenting publicity through a deluge of articles in the popular press as well as television news specials and talk shows. A defining event in the public perception of anorexia nervosa was the death of Karen Carpenter, with pictures of her emaciated face haunting the front pages of newspapers and tabloids. The message of Carpenter's death seemed an ambivalent one, on the one hand reinforcing linkages of anorexia nervosa with stardom, but on the other sending a cautionary message about the potential lethality of the condition. Nevertheless, the relentless association of eating disorders with stardom continued throughout the 1980s and early 90s, in a culture that has apparently become addicted to public disclosure of pathology and tales of recovery. The voyeuristic curiosity about eating disorders seemed to reach its peak in the disclosures by the late Diana, Princess of Wales of her bulimia, and even after her death journalists do not seem to be able to resist making references to it.

Garfinkel and Garner (1982) were the first to point out the parallels between anorexia nervosa and the romantic metaphors associated with tuberculosis in the 19th century (Sontag 1978). The pale, wasting look of the latter was associated with a certain kind of perverse heroism to a 19th century romantic sensibility fascinated with early death, with 'consumption' by excessive energy, sensitivity and talent. The metaphors of anorexia nervosa, on the other hand, have a distinctly post-modern coloring and express such valued cultural themes as 'achievement', 'perfection', and 'control', as well as the heroic notion of self-denial in a culture of plenty. The confluence of loaded cultural imagery about anorexia nervosa lends it a powerful appeal as final common pathway for the discharge of psychological distress, particularly to those who have a readiness to incorporate such imagery into their self-destructive aims.

It is of interest to the clinician to ask what the impact is of the glamorization of anorexia nervosa on patients. Does it influence how patients think about themselves? Some insight into this question was provided in a study by Branch and Eurman (1981). These authors were struck by the apparent pride that their patients took in their thinness, despite the life-threatening nature of their condition. They wondered if the social reinforcement for thinness in contemporary culture might have an augmenting effect on the characteristically defiant posture of anorectic patients to treatment. Given these concerns they conducted a questionnaire inquiry to a number of family members and friends of the patients. Much to their surprise, they found more approval than disapproval from these significant others. In fact, while most expressed concern about the patient's medical conditions, they frequently described them with such terms as 'slender', 'neat', 'well-groomed', and 'fashionable'. Much more rarely, terms such as 'emaciated' and 'haggard' were utilized. While many respondents expressed frustration with regard to the patients' evasion of their efforts to help them, a number expressed admiration for the 'self-control' exhibited by patients. One commented that 'she is victorious'.

This study was carried out over 15 years go, and it is possible that, perhaps owing to the publicity about its lethality and intractability, the illness is now viewed more darkly. In a study of lay beliefs about eating disorders, Murray *et al.* (1990) found that a significant proportion of women in their sample reported that their knowledge about anorexia nervosa had led them to exercise caution about undertaking extremely stringent diets. Perhaps a growing awareness of the negative aspects of anorexia nervosa could also account for the findings in a recent survey (Heatherton *et al.* 1995) of college students of a significant decline in the prevalence of stringent fasting and carbohydrate-avoidant diets over the 10-year period from 1982 to 1992. In addition to the cautionary impact of the negative publicity about eating disorders, the appeal of the imagery of wasting diseases may also have undergone a significant decline in the age of acquired immune deficiency syndrome (AIDS). Nevertheless, clinical practice still suggests that anorexia nervosa may still have a certain cachet, particularly among adolescents. In the age of Kate Moss and the ultra-thin waif look, anorexia nervosa powerfully resonates as a symbol that somehow encompasses contradictory meanings of chic glamour, submissive sexuality, weightlessness (Tolman and Debold 1994) and yet the power of rebellion. With Kate Moss, the imagery of the child–woman, which had been a central element in representations of *femmes fatale* since the late 19th century when it first gained currency (Djikstra 1986), has once again emerged with a vengeance, but cloaked in a distinctly post-modern form. Fashion writers have protested that there is little evidence that waif models promote eating disorders, but clinicians may have a different set of insights into this question. Teenage anorexic patients will often come right out and tell the clinician that Kate Moss is their idol.

For bulimics, the popular imagery of their disorder has always been more negative, probably because vomiting is a behavior that most people find repugnant. While the 'control' exhibited by anorexics seems to elicit a kind of awe, the bulimic's binge eating is seen as distinctly shameful, evoking the specter of the addict. Even the ordinarily objective and empathic Hilde Bruch (1985) expressed irritation at what she perceived as the undisciplined behavior of bulimics in her last paper: 'They make an exhibitionistic display of their lack of control or discipline, in contrast to the adherence to discipline of the true anorexics... The modern bulimic is impressive by what looks like a deficit in the sense of responsibility... Though relatively uninvolved, they expect to share in the prestige of anorexia nervosa.'

These are harsh criticisms indeed, which would seem to aggravate rather than reduce inappropriate metaphors about the class distinctions between anorexics and bulimics. If there is one affect that is pervasive in bulimics when they first appear for treatment, it is their overwhelming sense of shame. In fact, a study by Habermas (1992), the results of which conform well with clinical experience, suggests that media accounts of the 'rich and famous' who are bulimic have the reverse effect than they may have for anorexia nervosa. Rather than glamorizing the disorder and thereby reinforcing it, they often serve to relieve the isolating burden of shame experienced by the patient and thereby make her more willing to seek treatment.

While bulimia has a more negative image than anorexia nervosa, publicity about the disorder may well contribute to its continued proliferation. A major shortcoming in most media presentations of eating disorders is the tendency to give priority to excruciatingly detailed descriptions of symptomatology. It has long been understood that patients with eating disorders are notoriously susceptible to incorporating weight control tricks into their behavioral repertoire. Particularly among bulimics, purging behaviors are often tried for the first time after exposure to someone else's description of them. In a letter to Cherry Boone O'Neill, whose autobiography contains elaborate symptomatic descriptions, a reader wrote: 'In some ways your story helped me to better understand myself but some of the techniques you used to lose weight were unknown to me and I borrowed them... I wish you hadn't gone into the details of your illness.' In light of these considerations, it would be wise for media accounts of eating disorders to place far less emphasis on symptomatology, and rather address issues related to causation and recovery (Gordon 1995).

THE FUTURE OF SOCIOCULTURAL RESEARCH ON EATING DISORDERS

Has the current wave of eating disorders in Western countries already crested? A suggestion to this effect was made by Richard Pyle and his colleagues in an ongoing cross-sectional study of bulimia nervosa in college students at the University of Minnesota (Pyle *et al.* 1991). Based on a series of cross-sectional assessments in which the number of students reporting a history of clinical bulimia went from 1% in 1980 to 3.2% in 1983 to 2.2% in 1986, these researchers concluded that 'the prevalence for this disorder may have peaked and may be declining.' Similar conclusions were reached by Heatherton *et al.* (1995) in their 10-year cross-sectional study of students at Harvard College. While bulimia nervosa still represented a significant problem, with the estimated number of students meeting diagnostic criteria declining from 7.2% in 1982 to 5.1% in 1992, Heatherton noted that the prevalence of extreme dieting practices, especially fasting and the use of 'low-calorie, low-carbohydrate' diets, had undergone a significant decline over the period. In their place, students in the 1990s expressed a preference for 'low-fat' diets, in line with the widespread prescriptions of an increasingly health-conscious culture. Furthermore, significantly fewer women perceived themselves as overweight or wanting to lose 10 pounds (4.5 kg), despite the fact that female students were on the average 5 pounds (2.22 kg) heavier over the decade. Is it possible that, given the increased awareness of the risks of extreme dieting associated with eating disorders as well as the negative associations of extreme thinness with AIDS and heroin chic, that eating disorder symptoms will show a correlated decline?

It is still far too early to say, in the absence of more extensive research, whether the findings of these studies reflect general trends. If they do, we should not necessarily be surprised. The fashionability and prevalence of certain psychiatric symptom patterns wax and wane over time (Gordon 1990). Witness the fate of that 'epidemic disorder' of the *fin-de-siècle*, conversion hysteria. Conversion symptoms still exist in contemporary societies, but with increasing rarity in urban populations, particularly among middle-class psychiatric patients. Were one to attempt to perform a study of conversion disorder in a contemporary clinical setting, one would be hard-pressed to generate a research sample. The same cannot be said, unfortunately, for eating disorders. And yet, despite the shifting prevalence in the templates of distress, we should not overlook the persistence of the problems underlying the eating disorders, conversion disorder, depression and numerous other syndromes: the acute distress associated with unresolved issues regarding female identity in a period of wrenching cultural upheaval in the female social role. The female body remains the vehicle through which these tensions are expressed.

If in fact the prevalence of eating disorders in Europe and the US has leveled off, it is equally striking that they have emerged in significant numbers in societies in which they were previously either non-existent or unknown, particularly in countries such as India and China as well as in several African and Latin American nations. This phenomenon, although striking, is not altogether surprising. As Western consumer culture becomes increasingly globalized, so do the norms of Western body ideals become increasingly pervasive through the ever expanding power of a multinational fashion industry. In addition, the change in the female role associated with urbanization and Westernization in formerly Third World areas is if anything potentially more wrenching and conflictual than is the case in the Western world. On a clinical level, these tensions are particularly evident in women from non-Western societies who come from extremely traditional backgrounds (Mumford *et al.* 1991). As suggested in this chapter, this is the fertile cultural soil on which an epidemic of eating disorders is likely to emerge. Future research on cultural factors in eating disorders will greatly benefit from a focus on cross-cultural issues, and particularly on the emergence of such symptoms in individuals who might be said to be in a process of 'cultural crossing' or transition.

IMPLICATIONS FOR CLINICAL PRACTICE

What are the implications of a sociocultural analysis of eating disorders for the clinical context? As clinicians we have a strong tendency, by virtue of our training and orientation, to view our patients strictly as individuals. Furthermore, our notions of disease are such that we tend to view our patients as afflicted with an objective condition that hopefully will yield to one or another technical procedures. This is particularly likely to be true if we are approaching the patient from a biomedical perspective. How then can cultural considerations come into play in our work? Many clinicians, when confronted with a sociocultural analysis of eating disorders, simply throw up their hands in despair. If cultural influences are important, how, one asks, can one hope to influence such forces in the consulting room? We are, after all, clinicians, not social change agents.

These questions are not irrelevant, but they are predicated on a kind of splitting of the person into 'social', 'psychological' or 'biological' matrices The sociocultural analysis proposed in the model that has been described in this chapter suggests a way of thinking about cultural influences in a more integrated fashion. Thus, to the extent that the person with an eating disorder is influenced by, say, cultural mandates regarding thinness, these forces have been internalized and are therefore operating right there in front of one in the consulting room. We need not think of ourselves as explicitly dealing with the external forces during treatment, which of course we are not, but we will of necessity be dealing with them implicitly. We have no choice.

It is important to understand that the very concept of the diagnosis of an eating disorder is culturally influenced and the act of diagnosis itself is at least to some extent a cultural construction (Swartz 1987). For example, the DSM-IV criteria of anorexia nervosa stipulate, in addition to the criterion of 'refusal to maintain weight at or above a minimally normal weight for age and height', an 'intense fear of gaining weight or becoming fat, even though underweight' and a 'disturbance in the way in which one's body weight or shape is experienced, undue influence of body weight or shape on self-evaluation, or denial of the seriousness of the current low body weight'. Similarly, for bulimia nervosa, in addition to criteria for binge eating and vomiting (or other forms of compensation for bingeing), the DSM stipulates that 'self-evaluation is unduly influenced by body shape and weight'. It is virtually impossible to understand these criteria without reference to the cultural construction of thinness and the role that it has played in the history of the concept of anorexia nervosa. An 'intense fear of gaining weight' and an 'undue influence of body weight and shape on self-evaluation' may indeed be said to be virtually normative for women in Western culture at the present time.

This is not to deny that there are certain clinical boundaries that are crossed by the eating disordered patient who presents for treatment or evaluation. Certainly the physical criteria—the degree of weight loss and amenorrhea in anorexia nervosa—and the behavioral criteria (bingeing and purging) for bulimia nervosa would seem to have objective, biomedical status. Nevertheless, given the degree to which cultural factors are inextricably involved with the current proliferation of eating disorders, it is of considerable importance to the clinician to be aware of and sensitive towards these issues.

1. The degree of thinness evidenced by individuals with eating disorders is typically highly valued and will be relinquished only with great reluctance. It has become part and parcel of the patient's identity and is influenced by powerful cultural reinforcements. Therefore, it is a strategic error to treat a patient's overvaluation of thinness as merely evidence of 'denial' or 'resistance'. An appreciation of the role of culture in the overvaluation of thinness can lead us to a more sensitive and empathic comprehension of the situation of the patient and potentially to a far more positive therapeutic outcome as a result.
2. Clinicians need to be aware of the public dialog about eating disorders, which may very well have influenced patients. To have anorexia nervosa or bulimia nervosa is no longer a completely private issue. To the extent that patients view their condition as a matter of status or achievement, and to the extent that cultural messages have reinforced these ideas, patients may have a further rationale, in addition to their quest for autonomy, to avoid treatment. How a contemporary patient feels about her eating disorder and precisely how she has responded to the cultural reflections about eating disorders is a potentially important component of a clinical assessment. Many patients are particularly sensitive to the notion that they have a disorder that reflects 'narcissism' or 'vanity'. Despite the importance of cultural norms about weight in the genesis of eating disorders, such notions represent a reductionistic misinterpretation and to that extent will not be helpful.
3. The politics of eating disorders are tied in with the politics of gender. By this statement, I mean that it is important for therapists to be able to empathize with the intricate linkages between the forces giving rise to eating disorders and the situation of women in contemporary culture. The history of eating disorders that was briefly recapitulated in this chapter shows that self-starvation, despite its diversity of cultural transformations, has always been intimately tied to gender, and the present period is no exception. To understand our clinical interventions as inevitably tied into issues affecting women, and as being one moment of a much larger historical arc, can only enhance our effectiveness.

CULTURE, PSYCHE AND SOMA

The biologically oriented researcher or clinician who reads this volume may well ask why an opening chapter addresses issues of history and culture that seem far removed from his or her concerns. More than thirty years ago, Kaufman and Heiman (1964) published a volume entitled *Evolution of Psychosomatic Concepts: Anorexia Nervosa: A Paradigm.* While we would not necessarily use this language today to describe anorexia nervosa, eating disorders can be seen as primary instances of disorders which reflect a confluence of sociocultural, individual psychological, and biological determinants. While this may be said of other psychiatric disorders as well, it is especially the case for the eating disorders. Biological factors enter into the eating disorders both as predispositions (e.g. genetic factors, predisposition for anxiety and mood symptoms, possibly altered serotonin metabolism) as well as sequelae (e.g. altered endocrine functions that normalize with weight restoration, dysregulated electrolyte function). Eating disorders may be seen as resulting from the clash of psychocultural stresses (conflicting demands of the female role, unrealistically stringent cultural body ideals, family and interpersonal turbulence) with biological realities (e.g. the expanding weights of the population, the limits of weight loss and the psychobiological constraints of dieting). These disorders exemplify the need for a new psychiatric paradigm that truly integrates these seemingly remote levels of analysis, and without which a comprehensive approach to the treatment of the eating-disordered patient will remain elusive.

CLINICAL IMPLICATIONS

- Eating disorders have a long history, and it is only within the past 100 years or so that they have been approached in exclusively medical terms. The expression and construction of eating disorders has always been heavily influenced by sociocultural factors, and the present is no exception.
- To remain sensitive to the human complexities of our patients, clinicians need to maintain an awareness of the wider social contexts that give rise to eating disorders. A focus on critical biological factors in the eating disorders need not and should not preempt such an awareness.
- Contemporary eating disorders are strongly colored by norms of weight and their impact on body image experience. It is important for clinicians to maintain an awareness about how such norms influence patients, as well as how public representations and discussion of eating disorders may influence patients's own perceptions of themselves, both positive and negative.

Continued

- Gender, and particularly female experience, plays a critical role in the genesis of eating disorders. In fact, issues in female identity and role expectations may well be more fundamental than 'cosmetic' concerns about body image. Clinician awareness of such factors are key to an effective therapeutic relationship.

RESEARCH IMPLICATIONS

- Ongoing research into the epidemiology of disordered eating behavior and particularly to how changes in symptomatology are correlated with changes in dieting practices, body image norms and related factors.
- Further cross-cultural research is needed, especially into the emergence of eating disorders in non-Euro/American cultural contexts as well the changing body image ideals and altered expectations and aspirations of women.
- It would be extremely useful to have further studies of the public imagery of eating disorders and particularly on how such imagery affects patient self concept or identity.

REFERENCES

Aimez, P. and Ohayon, M. (1988). Enquete epidemiologiques sur les criteres DSM III de la boulimie (Epidemiological inquiry into the DSM-III criteria for bulimia). *Annales Medico Psychologiques*, **146**, 677–687.

American Psychiatric Association (1980). *DSM-III*. American Psychiatric Association, Washington.

Bell, R. (1985). *Holy Anorexia*. University of Chicago Press, Chicago.

Beller, A. (1977). *Fat and Thin; A Natural History of Obesity*. McGraw Hill, New York.

Boskind-Lodahl, M. (1976). Cinderella's stepsisters: A feminist analysis of anorexia nervosa and bulimia. *Signs: A Journal of Women, Culture and Society*, **2**, 342–376.

Branch, C.H. and Eurman, L.J. (1981). Social attitudes toward patients with anorexia nervosa. *Am. J. Psychiatr.*, **137**, 631–632.

Bruch, H. (1973). *Eating Disorders: Obesity, Anorexia and the Person Within*. Basic Books, New York.

Bruch, H. (1978). *The Golden Cage*. Vintage, New York.

Bruch, H. (1985). Four decades of eating disorders. In *Handbook for the Psychotherapy of Anorexia Nervosa and Bulimia* (eds D.M. Garner and P.E. Garfinkel). pp. 7–18, Guilford, New York.

Brumberg, J.J. (1988). *Fasting Girls: The Emergence of Anorexia Nervosa as a Modern Disease*. Harvard University Press, Cambridge.

Button, E.J. and Whitehouse, A. (1981). Subclinical anorexia nervosa. *Psychol. Med.*, **II**, 509–516.

Bynum, C. (1987). *Holy Feast and Holy Fast: The Religious Significance of Food to Medieval Women*, University of California Press, Berkeley.

Casper, R. (1983). On the emergence of bulimia nervosa as a syndrome. *Int. J. Eat. Dis.*, **2**, 3–16.

Chernin, K. (1981). *The Obsession: Reflections on the Tyranny of Slenderness*. Harper and Row, New York.

Crisp, A.H. (1980). *Anorexia Nervosa: Let Me Be*. Academic Press, London.

Crocker, J., Cornwell, B. and Major, B. (1993). The stigma of overweight: Affective consequences of attributional ambiguity. *J. Pers. Soc. Psychol.*, **64**, 60–70.

Devereux, G. (1980). Normal and abnormal, in *Basic Problems in Ethnopsychiatry*. University of Chicago Press, Chicago.

Djikstra, A. (1986). *Idols of Perversity: Fantasies of Feminine Evil in Fin-De-Siècle Culture*. Oxford University Press, New York.

Eagles, J.M., Johnston, M.I., Hunter, D., Lobban, M. and Millar, H.R. (1995). Increasing incidence of anorexia nervosa in the female population of Northeast Scotland. *Am. J. Psychiatr.*, **152**, 1266–1271.

Fombonne, E. (1995). Anorexia nervosa: no evidence of an increase. *Brit. J. Psychiatr.*, **166**, 462–471.

Gard, M.C.E. and Freeman, C.P. (1996). The dismantling of a myth: A review of eating disorders and socioeconomic status. *Int. J. Eat. Dis.*, **20**, 1–12.

Garfinkel, P.E. and Garner, D.M. (1982). *Anorexia Nervosa: A Multidimensional Approach*. Brunner Mazel, New York.

Garner, D.M., Garfinkel, P.E., Schwartz, D. and Thompson, M. (1980). Cultural expectations of thinness in women. *Psych. Rep.*, **47**, 483–491.

Gordon, R.A. (1990). *Anorexia and Bulimia: Anatomy of a Social Epidemic*. Basil Blackwell, Oxford.

Gordon, R.A. (1995). Eating disorders and the media, *Eat. Dis.: J. of Treatment and Prevention*, **3**, 282–286.

Gull, W.W. (1874). Anorexia nervosa. *Trans. Clin. Soc.*, **7**, 22–28. Reprinted in *Evolution of Psychosomatic Concepts: Anorexia Nervosa: A Paradigm* (eds R.M. Kaufman and M. Heiman). International Universities Press, New York, 1964.

Habermas, T. W. (1990). Ravenous Hunger. *The Historical Context of Bulimia Nervosa*. Fischer, Frankfurt.

Habermas, T. (1992). Possible effects of the popular and medical recognition of bulimia nervosa. *Br. J. Med. Psych.*, **65**, 59–66.

Halmi, K.A., Falk, J.R. and Schwartz, E. (1981). Binge-eating and vomiting: A survey of a college population, *J. Psychol. Med.*, **11**, 697–706.

Heatherton, T.F., Nichols, P., Mahamedi, A.M. and Keel, P. (1995). Body weight, dieting and eating disorders symptoms among college students, 1982 to 1992. *Am. J. Psychiatr.*, **152**, 1623–1629.

Hill, O.W. (1977). Epidemiologic aspects of anorexia nervosa. *Adv. Psychosom. Med.*, **9**, 48–62.

Hoyenga, K.B. and Hoyenga, K.T. (1979). *The Question of Sex Differences*. Boston, Little Brown.

Katzman, M.A. and Lee, S. (1997). Beyond body image: the integration of feminist and transcultural theories in the understanding of self-starvation. *Int. J. Eat. Dis.*, **22**, 385–394.

Kaufman, R.M. and Heiman, M. (eds) (1964). *Evolution of Psychosomatic Concepts: Anorexia Nervosa: A Paradigm*. International Universities Press, New York.

Khandelwal, S.K., Sharan, P. and Saxena, S. (1995). Eating disorders: An Indian perspective, *Int. J. Soc. Psych.*, **41**, 132–146.

Kuczmarski, R.J., Flegal, K.M., Campbell, S.M. and Johnson, C.L. (1994). Increasing prevalence of overweight among US adults; The National Health and Nutrition Examination Surveys, 1960 to 1991. *J. Am. Med. Assoc.*, **272**, 205–210.

Lasegue, C. (1873). De l'anorexie hysterique. *Arch. Gen. de Med.*, **385**. Reprinted in *Evolution of Psychosomatic Concepts: Anorexia Nervosa: A Paradigm* (eds R.M. Kaufman and M. Heiman). International Universities Press, New York, 1964.

Lee, S., Ho, T.P. and Hsu, L.K.G. (1993). Fat phobic and non-fat phobic anorexia nervosa: a comparative study of 70 Chinese patients in Hong Kong. *Psych. Med.*, **23**, 999–1017.

Lucas, A.R., Beard, C.M., O'Fallon, W.M. and Kurland, L.T. (1991). 50-year trends in the incidence of anorexia nervosa in Rochester, Minn.: A population-based study. *Am. J. Psychiatr.*, **148**, 917–922.

Meyer, J.E. and Feldmann, H. (eds) (1965). *Anorexia Nervosa*. Verlag, Stuttgart.

Mumford, D.B., Whitehouse, A.M. and Platts, M. (1991). Sociocultural correlates of eating disorders among Asian schoolgirls in Bradford. *Br. J. Psychiatr.*, **158**, 222–228.

Murray, S., Touyz, S. and Beumont, P. (1990). Knowledge about eating disorders in the community. *Int. J. Eat. Dis.*, **9**, 87–95.

Nadaoka, T., Oiji, A., Takahashi, S., Morioka, Y., Kashiwakura, M. and Totsuka, S. (1996). An epidemiological study of eating disorders in a northern area of Japan. *Acta Psychiatrica Scand.*, **93**, 305–310.

Parry-Jones, W.L.I. (1985). Archival exploration of anorexia nervosa. *J. Psychiatr. Res.*, **2–3**, 95–100.

Pope, H.G., Hudson, J.I. and Yurgelun-Todd, D. (1984). Prevalence of anorexia nervosa and bulimia in three student populations. *Int. J. Eat. Dis.*, **3**, 45–51.

Pyle, R.L., Neuman, P.A., Halvorson, P.A. and Mitchell, J.E. (1991). An ongoing cross-sectional study of the prevalence of eating disorders in Freshman college students. *Int. J. Eat. Dis.*, **10**, 667–677.

Rampling, D. (1985). Ascetic ideals and anorexia nervosa. *J. Psych. Res.*, **19**, 89–94.

Richardson, H.B. (1939). Simmonds disease and anorexia nervosa. *Arch. Int. Med.*, **63**, 1–28.

Rodin, J., Silberstein, L. and Striegel-Moore, R. (1985). Women and weight: a normative discontent. *Nebraska Symposium on Motivation*, **32**, 267–307.

Rosenzweig, M. and Spruill, J. (1987). Twenty years after Twiggy: a retrospective investigation of bulimic-like behaviors. *Int. J. Eat. Dis.*, **6**, 59–66.

Russell, G.F.M. (1979). Bulimia nervosa; an ominous variant of anorexia nervosa. *Psychol. Med.*, **9**, 429–448.

Russell, G.F.M. (1985). The changing nature of anorexia nervosa: An introduction to the conference. *J. Psychiatr. Res.*, **19**, 101–109.

Russell, G.F.M. (1997). The history of bulimia nervosa, in *Handbook for Treatment for Eating Disorders* 2nd edn, (eds D.M. Garner and P.E. Garfinkel). pp. 11–24. Guilford, New York.

Ryle, J.A. (1936). Anorexia nervosa. *Lancet*, **2**, 892–894.

Silverman, J.A. (1985). Richard Morton, 1637–1698, limner of anorexia nervosa: his life and times—a tercentenary essay, *J. Psychiatr. Res.*, **19**, 83–88.

Silverstein, B. and Perlick, D. (1995). *The Cost of Competence: Why Inequality Causes Depression, Eating Disorders and Illness in Women*. Oxford University Press, New York.

Silverstein, B., Peterson, B. and Perdue, L. (1986). Some correlates of the thin standard of bodily attractiveness for women. *Int. J. Eat. Dis.*, **5**, 895–905.

Sontag, S. (1978). *Illness as Metaphor*. Farrar, Strauss, and Giroux, New York.

Sours, J.A. (1980). *Starving to Death in a Sea of Objects*. Jason Aronson, New York.

Stunkard, A. (1990). A description of eating disorders in 1932, *Am. J. Psychiatr.*, **149**, 263–268.

Swartz, L. (1987). Illness negotiation: The case of eating disorders. *Soc. Sci. Med.*, **24**, 613–618.

Szabo, C., Berk, M., Tiou, E. and Allwood, C.W. (1995). Eating disorders in black South African females. *S. Afr. Med. J.*, **85**, 588–590.

Theander, S. (1970). Anorexia nervosa: a psychiatric investigation of 94 female patients. *Acta Psychiatrica Scand. (Suppl.)*, **214**, 1–194.
Thompson, M.G. and Schwartz, A.M. (1982). Life adjustment of women with anorexia nervosa and anorexic-like behavior. *Int. J. Eat. Dis.*, **1**, 47–60.
Tolman, D.L. and Debold, E. (1994). Conflicts of body and image: female adolescents, desire and no-body body, In *Feminist Perspectives on Eating Disorders* (eds P. Fallon, M.A. Katzman and S.C. Wooley), pp. 301–317. Guilford, New York.
Vandereycken, W. and van Deth, R. (1994). *From Fasting Saints to Anorexic Girls. The History of Self-Starvation*. New York University Press, New York.
Waller, J.V., Kaufman, R. and Deutsch, D. (1940). Anorexia nervosa: a psychosomatic entity. *J. Psychosom. Med.*, **2**, 3–16.
Willi, J. and Grossman, S. (1983). Epidemiology of anorexia nervosa in a defined region of Switzerland. *Am. J. Psychiatr.*, **140**, 564–567.
William, P. and King, M. (1987). The 'epidemic' of anorexia nervosa: another medical myth? *Lancet*, 205–207.
Wolf, N. (1991). *The Beauty Myth: How Images of Beauty are Used Against Women*. William Morrow, New York.

2 The Behavioural Disturbance, Psychopathology, and Phenomenology of Eating Disorders

P. J. V. BEUMONT
Department of Psychological Medicine, University of Sydney, Sydney, Australia

EATING DISORDERS AND THE SPECTRUM OF DYSFUNCTIONAL EATING

Eating disorders, like most illnesses in psychiatry, are syndromes defined by clinical features. They may cause physical morbidity, but there is no good evidence that they arise from an underlying physical disease, despite past and current attempts to establish that this is so. Their aetiology is unknown, although somatic, psychological, and social factors are thought to be involved. Whether these factors are really causative, or merely predisposing, or themselves the result of the illness, is unclear. The contention that their aetiology is multidimensional (Garfinkel and Garner 1982) is more useful to hide what we do not know than state what we do.

As their name implies, eating disorders have in common a dysfunction of eating. The current diagnostic terms (anorexia nervosa, bulimia nervosa, binge eating disorder, and obesity) arose historically rather than from scientific studies or logical reasoning. They are based on different concepts: weight for obesity and anorexia nervosa; behaviour for binge eating disorder, bulimia and anorexia nervosa. The system is clearly inadequate. A large proportion of patients considered ill enough to warrant hospital admission do not fulfil the criteria of any of the current diagnoses; the proportion of such atypical cases in the community is probably even higher; an individual sufferer may fulfil one set of diagnostic criteria on one occasion, and another on the next; the group may be better categorized using parameters other than those of the current classification; and symptoms are not consistent with the current diagnostic terms (Beumont *et al.* 1994a,b, 1995c; Schweiger and Fichter 1997). Rather than attempt to overcome these inconsistencies by tinkering yet again with the criteria of DSM-IV or ICD-10, it is better to think of the eating disorders as a spectrum of dysfunctional eating, along three related behavioural parameters: restriction, purging and overeating. Each of these parameters includes various specific behavioural abnormalities. They need to be seen in relation to groupings of underweight, normal weight, and overweight. (Our team made a proposal similar to this a few years ago, suggesting the parameters of underweight, purging and binge eating (Beumont *et al.* 1994a).

Neurobiology in the Treatment of Eating Disorders.
Edited by H.W. Hoek, J.L. Treasure and M.A. Katzman.

RESTRICTION

Restriction includes changing food choices so as to avoid high energy foods, reducing the amount eaten, avoiding meals, intermittent semi-starvation, and the total refusal of all food. The last is usually but not invariably the result of progressive restriction, rather than a sudden complete abstinence as in self-starvation for political motives.

The kinds of foods avoided have changed as dieting fads have come and gone. In the 1960s simple carbohydrates were singled out, leading to erroneous claims of specific carbohydrate avoidance. More recently fats have been shunned, and some patients now are quite willing to accept simple carbohydrates, but limit themselves to a diet deficient in fats and proteins (Beumont *et al.* 1981). Vegetarianism, undertaken for anorexic rather than altruistic reasons, has become the most common eating perversion seen in eating disorder patients (O'Connor *et al.* 1987). What is often not recognized is that fluid intake may also be restricted, or even totally refused. On the other hand, some patients overload on water so as to bring about a feeling of fullness, or to disguise the progression of their emaciation, sometimes to the extent of water intoxication (Bhanji and Mattingley 1988). Many patients report that they have tried to diet on previous occasions without effect, and that now they have somehow found the power to succeed. Paradoxically, it seemed easier to reduce food drastically rather than just eat smaller amounts.

Eating is distorted in characteristic ways that may be observed and documented objectively, using a measure such as the Eating Behaviour Rating Scale (Wilson *et al.* 1989). Patients frequently show obsessive–compulsive, ritualistic behaviours in respect to eating. They may limit their intake in a ritualistic way (no meal to have more than 3 g of fat; or only allowed 500 Calories per day; or eat according to a rigid plan, e.g. three spoons of cereal, three teaspoonfuls of yoghurt, four bites of an apple), and adhere rigidly to the routine for several months. (When they break the pattern, and take even an extra orange, they may term the episode a binge, hence it is always important to explore what the patient is actually describing, lest we attribute inappropriate significance to specific behaviours.) The obsessionality is perhaps most marked in patients who also over-exercise (see below): they may set up a whole series of debting behaviours, carefully balancing food intake against energy expenditure. This is often done with meticulous care: weighing each portion of food, determining its caloric content per gram by consulting a food guide, calculating the precise number of Calories in the serving, and then comparing it with the exact energy expenditure per minute of a person of their size performing a given amount of exercise. Some patients will allow themselves to eat only as much food as is necessary to replace the energy expended since their last meal (or preferably a little less); others will exercise for as long as is necessary to burn off the energy taken in their last meal (or a little more) (Touyz *et al.* 1987). At times, the obsessionality reaches bizarre proportions: a patient who calculated from the microbe count of Sydney tap water that it contained about 3 Calories/litre, and adjusted her food intake accordingly; another who always used gloves when working on the office word processor lest some previous clerk might have been eating chocolate while typing, and left a stray Calorie on the keyboard.

At table, anorexia nervosa patients cut their food into minute portions; shuffle it around the plate, hiding energy-rich portions behind lettuce leaves or bulky vegetables; secrete food into their serviettes or clothes; scrape the butter off bread; dissect all the visible fat from meat or fish; add excessive condiments; use inappropriate utensils (a teaspoon for dessert); eat painfully slowly; drink too much (or too little) fluid; silently count the Calories in the meal set before them. If allowed to serve themselves, they take ridiculously small portions. Sometimes they talk continuously so as to avoid eating; more often, they remain mute, staring glumly at their dishes. These behaviours result in conflict with the family and that, together with the patient's increasing anxiety about food, leads her to avoid eating in company. She takes different meals from those of other family members, and eats at different times, often very late at night and only after hours of procrastination. On the other hand, such is their preoccupation with food, they may spend hours reading recipe books, cook high energy cakes for other members of the family, and eventually take over the responsibility of buying the food and preparing the family's meals, although they will eat hardly anything themselves.

OVERACTIVITY

Overactivity is usually considered together with restrictive behaviour. It may take two forms: excessive exercising deliberately undertaken to induce weight loss, that occurs in a rather large minority of patients, and a constant, agitated restlessness, that is found in almost all patients when they are severely emaciated but before they are so debilitated as to be lethargic (Beumont *et al.* 1994c).

The early phase of overactivity is insidious in onset. The girl has often been a keen sportsperson or ballet dancer in the past, encouraged by parents who gain vicarious gratification from her successes. Coaches and ballet mistresses have much to answer for: they direct their young pupils to lose weight so as to improve their performance. A state-sponsored high school in Sydney that caters for students aspiring to the performing arts has ballet teachers who insist that their students keep their BMI (body mass index) below 17.5, the criterion figure for anorexia nervosa according to ICD-10 (World Health Organization 1992); a Canadian ballet school participated in a prevention programme, and considered girls whose weight was restored to a similarly low BMI as healthy (Garner *et al.* 1987). Increased exercise is often the first response to such admonitions: at first moderate, but soon excessive. In addition, there is a progressive reduction in food intake.

In other patients, the initial overactivity is surreptitious, such as going up and down stairs repeatedly on the pretext of fetching different items, or getting off public transport several stops before the destination so that they may walk the rest of the way. Patients may follow the advice given in some girls' magazines; 'Never sit if you can stand; never stand if you can walk; never walk if you can run'. In many instances, the activity is strenuous physical exercise in the form of aerobic classes, jogging, swimming, and floor exercises such as sit-ups and touching the toes. Or a combination of all of these, as in the patient who protested that she attended only three aerobic exercise classes a week, but omitted that she ran there and back, 90 minutes each way! Characteristically, exercise is solitary, has a strongly obsessive character, and is performed in a regular and rigid sequence. Patients feel guilty if they do not exercise, whatever the reason. They become angry if anyone tries to prevent them, but may come to dread the times when they have the opportunity to exercise because its driven quality is so unpleasant. As mentioned previously, exercising and eating are often linked by debting behaviours: the patient earns the right to eat by undertaking prescribed activities; or conversely, she pays for some self-indulgence with an extra exercise session.

The second kind of overactivity is an automatic response of which the patient may genuinely be unaware. It is a persistent restlessness that occurs in most patients once they have become severely emaciated. It is often associated with a sleep disturbance, is beyond voluntary control, and may be the analogue of the ceaseless activity seen in laboratory animals when they are deprived of food (Epling and Pierce 1996). It persists until the patient's condition deteriorates to the point of weakness and lassitude.

VOMITING, LAXATIVE ABUSE, AND OTHER PURGING BEHAVIOURS

Purging behaviours are also varied. The most common is self-induced vomiting. Some patients use ipecacuanha syrup, detergent, or salt water to elicit vomiting, but most, at least at first, promote vomiting by manoeuvres such as inserting a finger into the throat to induce the gag reflex; hence Russell's sign, the occurrence of calluses on the knuckles. Later, vomiting becomes almost automatic, so that the patient vomits at will and, often with genuine lack of awareness of the distortion, claims she is no longer inducing it. Rumination, or the regurgitation of food, also occurs, as does chewing food and then spitting it out. These behaviours are less effective in reducing energy intake than the patients think, as a significant proportion of the kilojoules is absorbed before the food is ejected.

Even less effective, and certainly more dangerous, is the abuse of laxatives to bring about weight loss. Sometimes patients deny laxative abuse, because they are not using proprietary products, but rather herbal remedies. The distinction is unimportant because these two types of laxatives are essentially similar. In any case, all that is effected by their use is a loss of water from the large bowel, with no decrease in energy reserves, and hence they are completely ineffective in producing lasting weight loss. Their dangers, which are significant, arise from disturbance to the body's biochemistry, that may progress to affect both kidney and liver function, and to the destruction of the myenteric nerve complex controlling the large bowel. Rectal prolapse is a common result in chronic patients.

Patients give differing accounts of the onset of purging. Sometimes, persistent food restriction eventually leads to episodes of reactive hyperphagia or bulimia, and vomiting is first used as a compensatory manoeuvre. Just as frequently, vomiting is used deliberately to induce weight loss without a prior binge. The patient may then allow herself to eat in a less restrictive manner, or even to binge eat, because she now knows that she can dispose of the food she has ingested.

Diuretics are also abused by some patients, with undesirable consequences on the biochemical status. Although not actually purging behaviours, two other instances of drug abuse are best mentioned in this context. The first is the use of appetite suppressants, usually of the amphetamine class, and the second is the manipulation of insulin dosage by patients with insulin-dependent diabetes mellitus who also have an eating disorder.

BULIMIA, GORGING OR BINGE EATING

Overeating presents in several different ways. Most characteristic is bulimia. The word derives from the Greek *βουλιμος*, or ox-hunger, similar to the Dutch *vreten*, to feed as an animal; the German *fressen*, to devour like a beast; the French *paître* or *brouter*, to graze like a sheep or a cow; and English 'feed' (intransitive) for an animal, as opposed to eat for a human. Unfortunately, the term bulimia is often used incorrectly, to indicate purging, and it has been supplanted in respect to its true meaning by binge eating. This may lead to confusion as with the emaciated anorexic patient who comes to use purging in addition to restriction to induce weight loss, and is then incorrectly diagnosed as having developed bulimia nervosa, despite the absence of any overeating episodes. In most instances, bulimia arises from a background of long-continued attempts to lose weight by restraining eating. The persistent dietary restriction is eventually interrupted by episodes of uncontrolled, reactive hyperphagia (bulimia). Compensatory behaviours invariably follow, usually including vomiting or laxative abuse, but sometimes limited to self-starvation and excessive exercise. Bulimia is defined in DSM-IV (American Psychiatric Association 1994) as ingesting, within a period of 2 hours or less, an amount of food definitely larger than most people would eat in a similar period and under similar circumstances, combined with a feeling of loss of control over eating during the episode. In addition, the bulimic episode usually occurs in secret. Like most definitions, this one is inaccurate. All the features mentioned are not invariable. The bulimic episode may take the form of continuous picking behaviour, undertaken over several hours, a titbit of this and a titbit of that. Usually the food eaten is high calorie, fatty and sweet food, but sometimes the binge is on low energy foods (Abraham and Beumont 1982). Whether the episode does really entail the ingestion of a large amount of food is also controversial. Many patients talk of a binge when in fact they are referring to an episode when they ate more food than the limit they have set for themselves. This limit may be so low that the so-called binge is in fact a smaller quantity of food than a normal, average meal. Because of this discrepancy, the Eating Disorder Examination

(Cooper and Fairburn 1987) distinguishes between subjective and objective binges, but this distinction is difficult to make and puts the onus of judgement on the observer by not providing objective criteria. The observer's judgement is likely to be biased by his or her own attitudes and experience. Thus a young, female, weight-conscious psychologist is likely to consider as excessive a meal which a middle-aged, physically active, *bon vivant* family doctor might recognize as appropriate to his own family of strapping adolescents.

It is also difficult to apportion correctly the relative importance of the actual amount eaten against the feeling of loss of control. Garner (1993a) argues that the patient who feels a complete lack of control when taking a normal or even an inadequate amount of food might be considered more disturbed psychologically than one who becomes distressed over a truly enormous meal. Further, how can one possibly judge what is normal for the circumstances? Bulimic patients usually alternate between phases of severe restriction and those of bulimia. It is hardly surprising that when they do eat, they are so ravenously hungry that they consume a large amount. Much the same behaviour is seen in hunter-gathering societies when the community has made a big kill, after a period when resources were scant.

Bulimia patients are usually secretive about their bulimic episodes, so that overeating and purging may have been present for years without other family members being aware of the disturbance. Others leave obvious signs (stacks of empty food containers in the kitchen or plastic bags filled with vomitus under the bed) so that one must conclude that they wish to be exposed, perhaps to declare the level of their distress. Occasionally, patients binge in front of their mother or spouse, using it to manipulate ('See what you've made me do!'). Episodes of bulimia are often impulsive, but sometimes they are carefully planned. Food is stored for a time when the patient will be able to gorge without interruption. Binge foods are selected because they are easy to swallow and regurgitate. They are commonly the fatty, sweet, high-energy foods that patients deny themselves at other times. Sometimes the amount of food eaten is enormous: 30 times the recommended daily allowance of Calories in a single binge. Usually, the intake is more moderate, about 3000 Calories. It is always important to ascertain whether the amount eaten in an alleged binge is indeed excessive; often restricted eaters or anorexia nervosa patients label any break in their pattern of restrained eating as a binge. (A useful strategy to distinguish true or objective bulimia from episodes of subjective binge eating is to refer to gorging rather than bingeing when questioning the patient: the patient with subjective binges recognizes that she is not gorging.) Patients tend to eat very rapidly during a binge, stuffing in a large amount of food within a few minutes. Chronic patients binge eat at a slower rate, savouring their food, or even continuously picking at food. Patients may seek to resist the urge to eat by taking appetite suppressants or other stimulants. They avoid situations in which they are likely to be exposed to food, and find it difficult to exert control over their eating. They choose not to go out for a meal with friends, or to a party. This avoidance adds to their social handicap and helps establish a vicious cycle of bulimia, purging, and social withdrawal (Abraham and Beumont 1982).

OVEREATING

Not all persons who overeat are bulimic, although they may inappropriately describe their eating as binge eating. Just as drinking too much alcohol does not necessarily imply that the drinker is an addictive alcoholic, so eating too much is not necessarily associated with bulimia. Overeating is simply eating more than one's body requires for normal functioning, expenditure on activity, and maintenance of energy reserves. If one is very active physically, one may eat large amounts but not overeat. It is not so much that overeaters have a genuine loss of control over the eating, but rather that they eat more than they wish to, or perhaps should, for a variety of social (occupation), psychological (unhappiness, boredom) or even hedonistic (I like food) reasons. Overeating causes obesity, and obesity is a significant health problem as it is associated with much physical morbidity. Many obese persons are not concerned about their overeating. Making them appropriately concerned is a medical responsibility, but it must be undertaken with honesty and delicacy. The overwhelming evidence from the literature is that weight loss programmes do not bring about permanent changes to weight; they contribute to much personal guilt and unhappiness on the part of the patient; and that better health results are more likely to accrue from programmes that promote change in lifestyle (more healthy food choice, increased exercise) than those directed at losing weight (Garner 1993b).

IMPLICATIONS FOR THE CURRENT CLASSIFICATION SCHEME

Against the background of a spectrum of dysfunctional eating, the eating disorders may be categorized into rational groups. In anorexia nervosa, restriction is a major feature, whether or not it is accompanied by purging behaviours. Weight loss below a criterion value is a *sine qua non*. The DSM-IV subdivision of restricting versus purging anorexia refers to a distinction that is backed by clinician observation (Beumont *et al.* 1976) and that is important in treatment: the purging anorexia nervosa patient is at a greater risk of physical morbidity and death than the restricter. However, using the term binge eating as an alternative label for the purging group (DSM-IV) would be unfortunate. Some anorexic patients actually binge (Beumont and Abraham 1983), but more often the anorexic patient describes any occasion of near-normal eating as bulimic. Bulimia nervosa is also associated with restriction, although the association is not as tight as in anorexia nervosa. This has been recognized since Russell's (1979) description of it as an ominous variant of anorexia nervosa, and his comment that these patients had prior episodes of overt or cryptic anorexia nervosa. The distinction between bulimia nervosa with or without prior anorexia nervosa has been the subject of several reports, but has not proved heuristic. Many bulimia patients are currently restricting, or have done so previously, but fall short of the weight criterion for anorexia nervosa. Further, many bulimia patients purge, but this is not invariable, as recognized in the DSM-IV categorization of purging and non-purging bulimia. Because restriction is important to anorexia and bulimia nervosa, and to the *formes frustes* of these conditions (anorexic-like patients not yet thin enough, or bulimic-like patients whose episodes are not sufficiently frequent to fulfil the diagnostic criteria: ED NOS), the term 'dieting disorders' may be appropriate to distinguish them from other eating disorders.

Then there are conditions in which restriction is not entailed, or in which phases of restriction may occur from time to time over a cycle of several months, but are not consistent. These include the DSM-IV experimental category of binge eating disorder (restriction not usually apparent), obesity with concern and psychological distress (typically a history of repeated episodes of restriction to lose weight over several months, and then rapid regaining of weight) and obese patients who eat too much and apparently do not care. These conditions, which vary greatly in presentation, are defined more easily by their physical effects (obesity) than by the behaviours involved. Psychological distress may or may not be present. Perhaps these conditions are better considered as personal predicaments rather than illness entities (Beumont 1988).

Finally, there is a group of truly atypical presentations: the schizophrenic patient who refuses food for fear of poison; the retarded, depressed patient; the patients with hypochondriacal concerns about bowel function; Prader–Willi patients with obesity; the true anorexia associated with neoplastic disease. The physical and psychological mechanism involved in these conditions may be relevant to understanding illnesses such as anorexia and bulimia nervosa, and the spectrum of obesity, but their aetiology is much more clearly and restrictively defined.

PSYCHOPATHOLOGY

THE CORE PSYCHOPATHOLOGY OF ANOREXIA AND BULIMIA NERVOSA, AND ITS RELATION TO CULTURAL VALUES

Dysfunctional eating in anorexia and bulimia nervosa is associated with a variety of psychological symptoms. These may be assigned to a core, constituting the specific psychopathology of these illnesses, or to a more generalized group of related psychological disturbances.

The core psychopathology consists of the cognitions and attitudes that relate to the behavioural disorders in the previous section. These cognitions and attitudes derive from one central disturbance that is difficult to define. It is an intense preoccupation with weight and shape, a never-ending quest to be thin and to avoid being fat (well-depicted in the German term *Magersucht*), an undue salience to weight and shape so that these become the most important things in the patient's experience, sometimes even more important than life itself. (*Ka mate, ka mate*; *ka ora, ka ora*: This is death, this is death; this is life, this is life: Maori *Haka*; a New Zealander's or a South African's attachment to Rugby Football is only lukewarm compared to the attachment anorexia nervosa patients have to their anorexic attitudes and beliefs.) Anorexia patients are overwhelmed by concerns about their bodies; they protest that they feel themselves to be obese even when actually emaciated. They are preoccupied with plans to further reduce their weight, or at least to avoid ever gaining weight. They are genuinely terrified at the prospect of being overweight. Their attitudes reflect the widespread concern about weight and shape in our community, particularly in young women and adolescent girls, but exaggerated to the extreme.

Such beliefs and attitudes have been considered variously as a manifestation of hysteria (Janet 1929), a phobia of weight gain (Crisp 1967), an obsession (Palmer and Jones 1939), or even a delusion (Nicolle 1939). Perhaps they are best grouped together and conceptualized as an overvalued idea. From where does it derive? Clues are provided by the demography and the historical background of anorexia nervosa. Although the illness does occur in boys and men (Beumont *et al.* 1972; Touyz *et al.* 1993), prepubertal children (Lask and Bryant-Waugh 1993) and middle-aged and elderly women (Russell and Gilbert 1992), it is predominantly an illness of adolescent girls and young women. Despite occasional claims to the contrary (Nasser 1997), anorexia nervosa is a culturally bound syndrome, bound to Westernized and developed societies. Its origin was in western Europe (van Deth and Vandereycken 1988), and shortly after it spread to North America (Brumberg 1988), Australia (Vandereycken and Beumont 1990), and then more recently in southern and eastern Europe (Habermas 1994). It is becoming more common in developed, westernized East Asian societies (Japan, Hong Kong and Singapore), and also occurs among the more prosperous in developing African and Asian (Buhrich 1981) communities. In all these societies, there is a subculture of anorexic values among young women, just as there is a subculture of illegal drug usage, or fundamentalist Christianity. This subculture of self-starvation has a long history in the Western tradition, whether for religious reasons, asceticism, narcissism, or sometimes simply to attract notoriety (Bell 1985; van Deth and Vandereycken 1988; Bynum 1987; Beumont 1991).

The predominance of females among sufferers of anorexia (and bulimia) nervosa patients has been ascribed to social factors by feminist authors (Orbach 1986). Girls and women are judged by society on their appearance more than on their performance, in contrast to boys and men. Their bodies are a matter of public interest, and they are required to fulfil contradictory roles in society (Russell and Beumont 1995). Fashions for thinness as the ideal female shape have coincided with the three major epidemics of anorexia nervosa that are apparent from reviewing the literature, e.g. in the 1870s and 1880s, the 1920s, and since the 1960s. The prevalence of the illness has been shown to correlate with such bizarre elements as the body measures of centrefold models in the magazine *Playboy*.

However, there is also a biological factor that should not be overlooked. As boys go through puberty, they begin to produce large amounts of testosterone and build up muscle bulk. A youth of 19 eats about 20% more food than a growing boy of 10, but does not become obese because the Calories are required to supply the extra energy needed by the muscles, and the increase in body strength. Men do have a crisis period of weight control later in life, when their level of physical activity decreases in the context of a more sedentary life style, but it is relatively rare for boys to become overweight in their adolescent years. In contrast, when girls pass through puberty, they stop growing and require less energy input. Because they do not build up bulky muscles, the average girl of 19 eats about 12% less than she did at 10, but nevertheless her fat reserves increase (Lenter 1981). Whereas the average fat content in the composition of prepubertal boys and girls is much the same, that of postpubertal girls is about twice that of postpubertal boys (28% versus 15%) (Mitchell and Truswell 1987). This crisis of weight control in girls occurs at a critical time in psychosocial development (i.e. when the young person is establishing a role among peers as important as her role within the family, is attracting and being attracted to young men, and is seeking approval from society at large rather than only from her intimate family). It is inconceivable to think that this coincidence of weight control and psychosocial challenges is not relevant to the occurrence of anorexia nervosa in girls and young women in this age group.

RELATED PSYCHOPATHOLOGY

Other psychopathological features are superimposed on this core concern. Many of these are known to result from semistarvation irrespective of its cause (Keys *et al.* 1950): they include depressed mood, irritability, social withdrawal, loss of sexual libido, preoccupation with food, obsessional ruminations and rituals; progressing to lassitude, anxiety and restlessness, and eventually to reduced alertness and poor concentration. The dysphoric mood is so common that it is best considered an integral part of the illness rather than warranting a separate diagnosis.

Severe obsessional symptoms, often going beyond those described above in the section about dysfunctional eating, are also common in anorexia nervosa patients (Beumont *et al.* 1995a). The illness is generally associated with premorbid perfectionism, introversion, poor peer relations, and low self-esteem. Characteristically, the patient is described as having been a perfect child, always biddable and helpful, whose refusal to eat is all the more extraordinary because of her previous compliance. As the patient becomes increasingly preoccupied with food and dieting, she tends to withdraw from peer relationships, concentrating on study or work with exacting intensity and to the exclusion of other interests. These features are not invariable, and some patients remain extroverted and interactive.

Patients react to attempts to reverse their abnormal behaviour with anger, deception and manipulation, all inconsistent with their previous behavioural standards. With chronicity, they become absorbed by their illness, interacting with it as with another ego and increasingly dependent on close family or therapist. Regression, invalidism and social isolation come to dominate the picture.

Separation anxiety and difficulties with identity are often obvious. There is sometimes a pathogenic secret, such as a recollection of sexual or other physical abuse, that results in low self-esteem and intense feelings of shame. Starving is a means of assuaging the pain and gaining control over sexual development (Beumont *et al.* 1995b). The patient holds onto her emaciation as a form of self-realization, and identifies with her wasted body. A number of themes have been postulated to explain the occurrence of the illness. One such is the suggestion that it represents a rejection of fellatio (Waller *et al.* 1940), another that it is related to a preoccupation with death (Jackson and Davidson 1989). Although such explanations sometimes appear appropriate in particular instances, they are irrelevant to the majority of patients.

A distortion of body perception has been proposed as characteristic of anorexia nervosa, receiving strong endorsement from Bruch (1962) in her seminal papers. It is now realized that this distortion is not invariable, and that it is found in many other groups besides anorexia nervosa patients, such as pregnant women and obese subjects. Moreover, with careful questioning it is possible to elicit different facets of the abnormality. Anorexia nervosa patients are able to distinguish between how they actually see themselves (often realistically) and how they feel they look (usually as if they were obese). If asked to portray their ideal body shape, they pick a profile similar to their current emaciated state. If asked to portray a normal shape, they underestimate and give too slight a figure (Touyz *et al.* 1985).

In bulimia nervosa, binge episodes may be precipitated by various factors: anxiety, tension, or boredom; drinking alcohol or smoking cannabis; feeling insecure about going out on a date; being tired from overwork (Abraham and Beumont 1982). Only rarely do patients concede that hunger has led them to binge, even though they may have fasted for 24 hours before overeating. The actual bulimic episode is often described in the following terms: increasing frustration progressing to feelings of anxiety, then craving for food; capitulation to the craving, and self-indulgent gratification from the massive amounts of cafeteria-type foods ingested; guilt about having overeaten, often with real physical discomfort; relief from inducing vomiting, followed by feeling relaxed and satisfied. Some patients compare the experience to that of masturbation, and admit that sometimes they resort to binge eating in order to cope with ongoing stresses, just as an alcoholic turns back to drink. Counter-regulation is important: once they have started to eat, they might as well go the whole hog, and gorge themselves until they are sick (Abraham and Beumont 1982).

Mood disturbance is so common in bulimia nervosa that it has been proposed that it is a form of depressive illness (Hudson and Pope 1990). A careful analysis of the histories of bulimia nervosa patients was not consistent with this suggestion. The eating disorder usually precedes the depression (Laessle *et al.* 1987), and patients frequently relate their unhappiness to their eating problems ('If only I didn't have such a problem with eating, I would be perfectly happy'). The mental state of bulimia nervosa patients is characterized by feelings of anxiety and tension, helplessness and failure. Some report past sexual and physical abuse: these experiences contribute to their low self-esteem. Self-mutilation and thoughts of suicide are common, as are alcohol and drug misuse (Lacey 1995). Patients with these problems are likely to have a concomitant personality disorder.

In distinction from anorexia nervosa patients, those with bulimia nervosa are more likely to see themselves as overweight, in addition to feeling it. Their ideal is much thinner than their current shape, although their judgement of normality is more realistic than that of anorexia nervosa patients (Touyz *et al.* 1985). These findings are consistent with the disparagement of their bodies that is commonly present in bulimia nervosa subjects: patients express extreme self-loathing.

Obese patients are a very heterogenous group, and hence their psychopathology is more variable than that of anorexia and bulimia nervosa patients. In a substantial proportion, particularly young women with early onset obesity, many of the features described in bulimia nervosa are also present. The patients give a history of repeatedly attempting to lose weight, but with limited success. After each attempt, they regain weight, usually to a higher level than that they were at previously. Counter-regulation occurs, so that once they break their self-imposed diet, they feel they might as well eat as much as they can. Guilt, body disparagement and self-loathing may be prominent. Size and shape acquire undue salience in their lives, self-confidence and self-esteem are low, and dysthymia, avoidance of all situations in which their bodies are exposed, and social withdrawal are all present. Eventually, some obese patients of this grouping give up trying, and withdraw into a state of chronic depression, partial isolation, and progressively increasing weight.

PHENOMENOLOGY OF THE EATING DISORDERS

The editors of this book originally asked me to address the issue of phenomenology. In fact, their actual requirement was rather different, hence the preceding sections on behavioural disturbance and psychopathology. Nevertheless, the phenomenology of anorexia and bulimia nervosa is an interesting issue that has not been previously explored, so I will undertake a short foray into that territory.

What is phenomenology? The term has been much abused in psychiatry. It is often used to imply the objective description of the symptoms and signs of psychiatric illness, a synonym for clinical psychopathology as contrasted with that other psychopathology which derives from psychoanalytic theory. Actually, phenomenology has a distinct and specific meaning quite different to objective psychopathology (Beumont 1992). Kant taught that we never know the true nature of things, only our own sensations and the activities of our minds. He distinguished between realities or the true source of experiences, which he termed noumena, and the things that we experience, phenomena. Dilthey contrasted the natural sciences, in which we seek to *explain* facts, from the science of mind, whose goal is merely to *understand* the experience. These ideas were applied to clinical psychiatry and psychology by Karl Jaspers in the first decades of the 20th century (Mendelson 1989).

The objective manifestations of mental life are the matter of objective psychopathology, to be comprehended in the same ways as the data of other sciences. For the subjective phenomenon of mental life we need a different approach, one that is objective but that is directed at the subjective. This approach is phenomenology (Jaspers 1923). Unlike interpretive psychology, that concerns itself with the content of thinking and the alleged unconscious, phenomenology concerns itself only with the form of conscious thought. In order to properly understand conscious mental events in other people, one must listen carefully to what they say, then think oneself into their experience. By doing so we realize, for instance, that the actual experience of a person who has a delusion does not correspond with the definition of a delusion. It is not having an incredible false belief, unique among one's own social and religious group, held with extraordinary conviction, and impervious to contradiction. Clearly, a patient cannot experience his own belief as false, nor his conviction about the truthfulness as unreasonable. From the phenomenological viewpoint, a delusion is a primary experience involving the nature of judgement, the acquisition of a new type of certainty, outside the constraints of proof. It is incorrigible because proof is not relevant: one knows it is true. Logic has nothing to do with it. If the evidence is contrary to this truth, the evidence must be discarded.

To understand the core anorexic experience in phenomenological terms might well be beneficial for patient and therapist alike. For this purpose, it is necessary that the therapist listens carefully to what the patient says, and explores diligently by empathic questions so as to feel into her situation and understand the events of her mental life. The following extract from the record of a group of anorexia and bulimia nervosa patients presents some basic data from which a phenomenological account might be derived.

THERAPIST: Shirley, you say that you are attending for therapy because you want to get better, and that you realize you must eat normally in order to be better. What is it that stops you?

SHIRLEY: I'm afraid. I'm afraid that I'd like eating too much. No, more than that. I know I'd like it too much. If I let myself go, I'll overeat and I'll become as fat as when I was a child. I feel I've got to control it, keep eating under control.

KAYLYN: Do you feel guilty when you eat?

SHIRLEY: Yes. It's like doing something I know I shouldn't. I know I should eat, because that's being normal, but if I try to eat, then I feel guilty. The only way I can do it is by keeping to a rigid pattern, then I know it won't get out of control. And when the time comes to go to bed, I might give myself a chocolate as a reward, because I'm safe then. I've avoided all the temptations of the day to overeat.

KAYLYN: It's like that for me too. I feel I must keep absolute control. If I let myself go just a little bit outside that control, if I eat something I haven't given myself permission to eat, I've blown it altogether. I might as well pig out and stuff myself. Then I'll make myself vomit and vomit until I'm cleared out again.

THERAPIST: What do you feel when that happens? What do you feel when you decide to binge?

KAYLYN: Well, I suppose I get excited. I feel terrible because I've broken my promise to myself and eaten something I said I wouldn't. Then I feel, what the heck, I might as well go for it. I sort of get excited. It's doing something I really shouldn't do, but I want to. I sort of enjoy it. When I've finished bingeing I feel terribly guilty, I feel disgusting. But then I vomit and I feel much better. And somehow the binge and the vomit has made me more relaxed than when the whole thing started. Maybe I know that I've now done it, and won't be tempted to do it again for a few days.

DIANE: You lucky thing! When I was bulimic I used to binge and binge many times every day. One just went straight on to another.

THERAPIST: So you felt quite out of control?

DIANE: Yeah. Being bulimic is being out of control . . . but so is being anorexic. When Shirley says she has to control her eating, that is really not so. She's kidding herself. What is really happening is that her anorexia is controlling her. That's what I came to realize. The more I felt I had to be in control of my eating, the more I felt I was being controlled so that I'd limit my eating.

KARLIE: I don't know, I just felt good at not eating. Not eating was something I could do. It was great. It was just part of me, part of my identity.

SHIRLEY: Yes, yes. That's what I feel too. If I gave it away I'd be nothing.

KARLIE: I was so frightened of being fat. I suppose I know I'm not really fat. I can see that the other girls here are thin, and I guess I'm like them. But I feel I'm fat.

NICOLE: That's not true. They try to tell us here that we're not fat, but I know I am. They want us to be like other girls, but that's fat. They've got it wrong. I know if I can't get into a size 6 dress, I'm overweight. (*Sizes 10–16 are the sizes appropriate to healthy young women in Australia.*)

ROBYN: I don't really worry whether I'm fat or not, I'm just terrified about food. I dreamt the other night that I was chased by a piece of chocolate cake. It had funny little legs, and it was saying: Eat me, eat me. I know it sounds cute, but it was really scary. Then last night I dreamt we had a Maori nurse here. She was really big, like a rugby player. And she caught me and made me eat chocolate biscuits!

SHELLY: I don't worry about eating, or about being fat. I used to, but I don't now. It's exercising that bugs me. I've got to be active. If I'm not, I feel so guilty that I can't stand it. When my parents brought me here from Canberra, I couldn't stand being locked up in the car for 3 hours. I screamed until they let me get out at Goulbourn, and I ran around the oval three times before I would get into the car again.

THERAPIST: So all you want to do is exercise?

SHELLY: No. I don't want to do it. I have to do it because I feel so bad. I hate exercising, I just wish I could get away from it. When I come home from school, I dread going up to my bedroom. I know that when I get there, the exercise will be waiting. I'll have to do 1000 sit-ups. When I go to get something from the other side of the living room, I walk in a zigzag way to cross the room, so that I get as much activity as I can. When I go upstairs, I take two steps up, then one down, so that I climb half as many steps again as are actually there. If I go to fetch the newspaper from the front gate, I go out the back door, so that I have to run right round the house before I can walk down the drive.

DIANE: How does that make you feel?

SHELLY: I feel I'm going crazy, it upsets me so much. And it makes my parents mad. I understand how they feel and I wish they could stop me, but if they try, I just get angry, I'll swear at them and actually hit them.

THERAPIST: What about you, Joanne?

JOANNE: It isn't like any of that for me. I've never been overweight, never thought I needed to lose weight. My anorexia started last year, when my parents decided to get divorced. My whole family disintegrated, and we were all so unhappy. Then I caught a bug and lost a little weight. I thought, gee, this is something I can control. I can't stop my family falling apart, but I can control my eating. I felt good about not eating. I was sort of hurting myself, so what was happening around me wasn't so hurtful. I felt I was a kind of ascetic, like an Indian yogi. And then I couldn't stop, I couldn't make myself eat, although I knew I was far too thin and that I was feeling ill.

Nicole's comment provides an entrée to the patients' experiences: the acceptance of a belief system that distorts the reality of normal weight and shape. According to these attitudes, it follows that eating is bad and indulgent (Shirley); not eating is good (Karlie). There is an element of asceticism, or even more, of punishing oneself by not eating (Joanne), and on the contrary, of being wicked in allowing oneself to eat (Shirley). One can only earn the right for any indulgence by previous great restraint. One may need to calculate what one eats exactly by balancing energy expenditure from exercise against energy ingested in food (Touyz *et al.* 1987). If restraint breaks down so that one eats ravenously (has a bulimic episode), one may enjoy it and feel relief (Kaylyn), but eventually guilt follows. By controlling eating one feels in control of one's life (Shirley, Joanne). But actually that is nonsense: Diane realized that eating or not eating has come to control all their lives. Their own sense of control is spurious. Patients appreciate that they are drifting into an Alice-in-Wonderland world, but still cannot resist it (Joanne). And just as for Alice, so for them, the experience becomes increasingly frightening: loss of control over eating (Shirley), of becoming bulimic, of being fat (Karlie), are recurrent fears, but so is the iron grasp of anorexic behaviours, such as the demon of obsessive exercise that lurks in Shelly's bedroom.

The issue of body shape is a good illustration of the multivarious ways that the so-called symptom of body image distortion is actually experienced by patients. Some see the ideal 'slender' (scrawny) figure of fashion models as normal, hence average size girls are fat, and they too are fat if they are of average size. Others recognize extreme thinness as being abnormal, and may see it in others, but find it difficult to see in themselves. Yet others realize they are excessively thin, but nevertheless *feel* as if they were fat, particularly after eating even a small amount of food, which fills their shrunken stomachs. Only a minority actually see themselves as fat when they are emaciated, and often that alleged perception is little more than deliberate denial of what they know to be true. As the deluded patient is too devoted to his delusion to be able to give it up, so may the anorexic patient be too wedded to her anorexic cognitions to allow them to be challenged.

Mood alternates from satisfaction and self-congratulation at one's ability to be restrained, to not indulge, to be different from other girls in being sylph-like, a real princess; to guilt that every mouthful eaten is contaminating, a sign of weakness and gluttony, an unpardonable sin. Becoming fat is the worst of all possible fates: it is better to be dead than fat. As one may move from a perfectionism that is fuelled by a desire for success to one which is driven by a fear of failure (Slade 1997), so the anorexic patient moves from behaviours undertaken in the pursuit of being slender to behaviours driven by the terror of gaining weight.

Eventually the patient may come to realize that she has no control, and that the illness itself controls her life. This realization is too late. She is no longer able to escape, and feels trapped. It is easier to maintain her resistance to changing her behaviour, rather than fighting a battle she is sure to lose against the overpowering illness. She knows she cannot change, just as many nicotine addicts believe they can never stop smoking. Commitment to treatment does not arise only from an acceptance that her eating behaviours are unhealthy. It involves admitting that the cherished attitudes and beliefs that have become basic to her whole life are faulty and must be discarded. Anorexia nervosa has replaced her family, her friends, her ambitions, her eagerness for new experiences: it is all she has left. It requires great courage to reject an illness which has become the object of the most intense relationship in her life, and to challenge it while still unsure that it can be beaten, or that anything else in life will ever replace it. No wonder eating disorder patients, and particularly those with anorexia nervosa, experience so much difficulty in getting better.

CONCLUSIONS

The eating disorders may be grouped into two clusters: one in which behaviours to lose weight are constant or frequently recurring features (anorexia and bulimia nervosa, the dieting disorders), and another in which attempts to lose weight are less prominent, although there may well be a desire to be thinner (binge eating disorder and obesity). The psychopathology of the former group is remarkably consistent and fairly well understood. That of the latter group is variable and only poorly understood.

A thorough understanding of the objective psychopathology of an individual patient with a dieting disorder is necessary so as to avoid misdiagnosis and to plan appropriate treatment. It is important to identify themes such as overexercising or laxative abuse as these require special attention if they are to be halted: merely insisting that the patient eats more is inadequate. Similarly, more general issues such as low self-confidence and self-esteem (the two are not synonymous), depression, obsessionality, prior sexual abuse, require appropriate therapy. Concentrating exclusively on the eating disorder will not be effective if these other factors are neglected. The dieting disorders are pathoplastic, and their well-documented history illustrates how they have evolved over the last 150 years. Keeping up to date with clinical observations is just as important as keeping up with research. Anyone nowadays who speaks of patients as having a specific phobia of carbohydrates is simply misinformed. Understanding of the other eating disorders is inadequate, and clinicians should concentrate on clarifying the clinical features of these conditions.

Phenomenology, the objective study of subjective, conscious mental events, provides a means for clinicians to share patients' experiences in a way that will help to focus treatment. The ultimate goal of therapy is to emancipate the patient from the vicious grip of the illness, with its morbid preoccupations and fears. Only then can she return to the lovely, independent and healthy person that she is capable of being.

CLINICAL IMPLICATIONS

- The eating disorders can be categorised into two clusters: one in which behaviours to lose weight are prominent (anorexia nervosa and bulimia

Continued

nervosa) and another in which attempts to lose weight are less of a focus (binge eating disorder and obesity).

- One must understand the individual with a diet disorder fully, simply insisting that a person eats more will be inadequate.
- Issues such as low self esteem, depression, obsessionality, and prior sexual abuse all require appropriate therapy.
- Keeping up to date with clinical observations is as important as keeping up with the research developments as the eating disorders are pathoplastic and evolving.

RESEARCH IMPLICATIONS

- There is a need for more research on the psychopathology of binge eating disorder, because it is less understood than that of anorexia nervosa or bulimia nervosa.

REFERENCES

Abraham, S.F. and Beumont, P.J.V. (1982). How patients describe bulimia or binge eating. *Psychological Medicine*, **12**, 625–635.

American Psychiatric Association (1994). *Diagnostic and Statistical Manual of Mental Disorders*, 4th edn. APA, Washington.

Bell, R.M. (1985). *Holy Anorexia*. University of Chicago Press, Chicago.

Beumont, P.J.V. (1988). Bulimia: is it an illness entity? *International Journal of Eating Disorders*, **7**, 167–176.

Beumont, P.J.V. (1991). The history of eating and dieting disorders. *Clinics of Applied Nutrition*, **1**(3), 9–20.

Beumont, P.J.V. (1992). Phenomenology and the history of psychiatry. *Australian and New Zealand Journal of Psychiatry*, **26**, 532–545.

Beumont, P.J.V. and Abraham, S.F. (1983). Episodes of ravenous overeating or bulimia: their occurrence in patients with anorexia nervosa and with other forms of disordered eating, in *Anorexia Nervosa: Recent Developments in Research* (eds P.D. Darby, P.E. Garfinkel, D.M. Garner and D.V. Coscina), pp. 129–136. Alan R Lisk, New York. (Proceedings of the Toronto Workshop on Anorexia Nervosa, 1982.)

Beumont, P.J.V., Beardwood, C.J. and Russell, G.F.M. (1972). The occurrence of the syndrome of anorexia nervosa in male subjects. *Psychological Medicine*, **2**, 216–231.

Beumont, P.J.V., George, G.C.W. and Smart, D.E. (1976). 'Dieters' and 'vomiters and purgers' in anorexia nervosa. *Psychological Medicine*, **6**, 617–622.

Beumont, P.J.V., Chambers, T., Rouse, L. and Abraham, S.F. (1981). The diet composition and nutritional knowledge of patients with anorexia nervosa. *Journal of Human Nutrition*, **35**, 265–273.

Beumont, P.J.V., Garner, D. and Touyz, S.W. (1994a). Diagnoses of eating or dieting disorders; What may we learn from past mistakes? *International Journal of Eating Disorders*, **16**(4), 349–362.

Beumont, P.J.V., Garner, D. and Touyz, S.W. (1994b). Comments on the proposed criteria for eating disorders in DSM IV. *Eating Disorders Review*, **2**, 63–75.

Beumont, P.J.V., Arthur, B., Russell, J.D. and Touyz, S.W. (1994c). Excessive physical activity in dieting disorder patients: proposals for a supervised exercise programme. *International Journal of Eating Disorders*, **15**, 21–36.

Beumont, C., Beumont, P.J.V. and Touyz, S.W. (1995a). The association of eating disorders and obsessive compulsive disorders, in *Adult Health and Lifestyle: A Health Psychology Perspective* (eds R.F. Soames Job and D. Kenny), Proceedings of the Behavioural Medicine Conference, Sydney, October 1993.

Beumont, P.J.V., Russell, J. and Touyz, S.W. (1995b). Psychological concerns in the maintenance of dieting disorders, in *Handbook of Eating Disorders: Theory, Treatment and Research* (eds G. Szmukler, C. Dare and J. Treasure), pp. 221–241. John Wiley, London.

Beumont, P.J.V., Kopec-Schrader, E. and Touyz, S.W. (1995c). Defining subgroups of dieting disorder patients by means of the Eating Disorders Examination. *British Journal of Psychiatry*, **166**, 472–474.

Bhanji, S. and Mattingley, D. (1988). *Medical Aspects of Anorexia Nervosa*. Wright (Butterworth Scientific), London.

Bruch, H. (1962). Perceptual and conceptual disturbances in anorexia nervosa, *Psychosomatic Medicine*, **24**, 187–194.

Brumberg, J.J. (1988). *Fasting Girls: The Emergence of Anorexia Nervosa as a Modern Disease*. Harvard University Press, Cambridge, Massachusetts.

Buhrich, N. (1981). Frequency of presentation of anorexia nervosa in Malaysia. *Australian and New Zealand Journal of Psychiatry*, **15**, 153–155.

Bynum, C.W. (1987). *Holy Feast and Holy Fast. The Religious Significance of Food to Medieval Women*. University of California Press, Berkeley and Los Angeles.

Cooper, Z. and Fairburn, C.G. (1987). The Eating Disorders Examination: A semi-structured interview for the assessment of the specific psychopathology of eating disorders. *International Journal of Eating Disorders*, **6**, 1–8.

Crisp, A. (1967). Anorexia nervosa. *Hospital Medicine*, **5**, 713–718.

Epling, W.F. and Pierce, W.D. (1996). *Activity Anorexia: Theory, Research, and Treatment*. Lawrence Erlbaum Associates, Mahwah, New Jersey.

Garfinkel, P.E. and Garner, D.M. (1982). *Anorexia Nervosa: A Multidimensional Perspective*. Brunner/Mazel, Montreal.

Garner, D.M. (1993a). Binge eating in anorexia nervosa, in *Binge Eating: Nature, Assessment and Treatment* (eds C.G. Fairburn and G.T. Wilson), pp. 50–76. Guildford Press, New York.

Garner, D.M. (1993b). Confronting the failure of behavioural and dietary treatments for obesity, *Clinical Psychology Review*, **11**, 729–780.

Garner, D.M., Garfinkel, P.E., Rochert, W. and Olmsted, M.P. (1987). A prospective study of eating disturbances in the ballet. *Psychotherapy and Psychosomatics*, **48**, 170–175.

Habermas, T. (1994). *Zur Geschichte der Magersucht. Eine Medizinpsychologische Rekonstruktion*, pp. 107–126. Fischer Taschenbuch Verlag GmbH, Frankfurt am Main.

Hudson, J.I. and Pope, H.G. Jr (1990). Psychopharmacological treatment for bulimia, in *Bulimia Nervosa, Basic Research, Diagnosis and Treatment* (ed. Fichter, M.M.), pp. 331–334. John Wiley & Sons, Chichester.

Jackson, C. and Davidson, P. (1989). *Appetite for Death*. Boolarong Press, Brisbane.

Janet, P. (1929). *The Major Symptoms of Hysteria*. MacMillan, New York.

Jaspers, K. (1923). *General Psychopathology*. Translated from the German original of 1923 by Hoenig, J. and Hamilton, M.W. The University Press, Manchester.

Keys, A., Brozek, J., Henschel, A., Mickelsen, O. and Taylor, H.L. (1950). *The Biology of Human Starvation*. University of Minnesota Press, Minneapolis.

Lacey, H. (1995). Inpatient treatment of multi-impulsive bulimia nervosa, in *Eating Disorders and Obesity, A Comprehensive Handbook*, (eds Brownell, K.D. and Fairburn, C.G.) pp. 361–368. Guildford Press, New York.

Laessle, R.G., Kittl, S., Fichter, M.M., Wittchen, H.V. and Pirke, K.M. (1987). Major affective disorder in anorexia nervosa and bulimia. A descriptive diagnostic study. *British Journal of Psychiatry*, **151**, 785–790.

Lask, B. and Bryant-Waugh, R. (1993). *Childhood Onset Anorexia Nervosa and Related Disorders*. Lawrence Erlbaum Associates, Hove.
Lenter, C. (1981). *Geigy Scientific Tables,* 8th edn, p. 233. Ciba-Geigy, Basle.
Mendelson, G. (1989). Phenomenology, in *Textbook of Psychiatry* (ed. Beumont, P.J.V. [with Hampshire, R.]). Blackwell Scientific Publications, Melbourne.
Mitchell, P.B. and Truswell, A.S. (1987). Body composition in anorexia nervosa and starvation, in *Handbook of Eating Disorders, Part 1: Anorexia and Bulimia Nervosa*, p. 47. Elsevier, Amsterdam.
Nasser, M. (1997). *Culture and Weight Consciousness*. Routledge, London.
Nicolle, G. (1939). Pre-psychotic anorexia. *Proceedings of the Royal Society of Medicine*, **32**, 153–163.
O'Connor, M.A., Touyz, S.W., Dunn, S. and Beumont, P.J.V. (1987). Vegetarianism in anorexia nervosa: a review of 116 consecutive cases. *The Medical Journal of Australia*, **147**, 540–542.
Orbach, S. (1986). *Hunger Strike. The Anorectic's Struggle as a Metaphor for an Age*. Faber and Faber, London.
Palmer, H.D. and Jones, M.S. (1939). Anorexia nervosa as a manifestation of compulsive neurosis: a study of psychogenic factors. *Archives of Neurology and Psychiatry*, **41**, 856–871.
Russell, G.F.M. (1979). Bulimia nervosa: an ominous variant of anorexia nervosa. *Psychological Medicine*, **9**, 429–448.
Russell, J. and Gilbert, M. (1992). Is anorexia tardive a discrete diagnostic entity? *Australian and New Zealand Journal of Psychiatry*, **26**, 429–435.
Russell, J. and Beumont, P.J.V. (1995). Risk and prevention in eating disorders, in *Handbook of Studies on Preventive Psychiatry* (eds B. Raphael and G.D. Burrows), pp. 459–476. Elsevier, Amsterdam.
Schweiger, U. and Fichter, M. (1997). Eating disorders: clinical presentation, classification and etiologic models, in *Clinical Psychiatry* (ed. Baillière Tindall), in press.
Slade, P. (1997). Perfectionism: drive to succeed or fear of failure? Draft paper for submission: personal communication.
Touyz, S., Collins, J.K., Cowie, I. and Beumont, P.J.V. (1985). Body shape perception in bulimia and anorexia nervosa. *International Journal of Eating Disorders*, **4**, 259–266.
Touyz, S., Beumont, P.J.V. and Hook, S. (1987). Exercise anorexia. A new dimension anorexia nervosa, in *The Handbook of Eating Disorders, Part 1, Anorexia and Bulimia Nervosa* (eds P.J.V. Beumont, G.D. Burrows and R. Casper), pp. 143–157. Elsevier North Holland Biomedical Press, Amsterdam.
Touyz, S.W., Kopec-Schrader, E.M. and Beumont, P.J.V. (1993). Anorexia nervosa in males: a report of 12 cases. *Australian and New Zealand Journal of Psychiatry*, **27**, 512–517.
Vandereycken, W. and Beumont, P.J.V. (1990). The first Australian case description of anorexia nervosa, *Australian and New Zealand Journal of Psychiatry*, **24**, 109–112.
van Deth, R. and Vandereycken, W. (1988). *Van Vastenworder Tot Magersucht: Anorexia Nervosa in Historisch Perspectief*. Boom Meppel, Amsterdam.
Waller, J.V., Kaufman, M.R. and Deutsch, F. (1940). *Psychosomatic Medicine*, **2**, 3–16. Reprinted as Anorexia nervosa: a psychosomatic entity, in *Evolution of Psychosomatic Concepts. Anorexia Nervosa: A Paradigm*, pp. 245–273. International Universities Press, New York.
Wilson, A.J., Touyz, S.W., Dunn, S.M. and Beumont, P.J.V. (1989). The eating behaviour rating scale (EBRS). A measure of eating pathology in anorexia nervosa. *International Journal of Eating Disorders*, **8**, 583–592.
World Health Organization (1992). *The ICD-10 Classification of Mental and Behavioural Disorders*. WHO, Geneva.

3 Psychological and Physical Assessment of Persons with Eating Disorders

J. S. NATHAN and D. B. ALLISON
Fordham University, Obesity Research Center, St. Luke's-Roosevelt Hospital Center, Columbia University, NY, USA

INTRODUCTION

The two most well-established eating disorders, anorexia nervosa (AN) and bulimia nervosa (BN), occur primarily in females during adolescence and young adulthood. The psychopathology of both are complex and varied in form. The former is characterized by a failure to maintain a normal body weight, while the latter is characterized by recurrent episodes of binge eating and extreme weight control behaviors such as self-induced vomiting and laxative misuse. Disturbances regarding body weight and shape are core features of both disorders.

In contrast to previous diagnostic criteria, the Diagnostic and Statistical Manual, 4th Edition (DSM-IV; American Psychiatric Association 1994) subdivides AN into a restricting type and binge-eating/purging type. Data suggest each subtype has a different psychological and medical profile. Restricting anorexics tend to be highly controlled, rigid, and often obsessive (Wilson *et al.* 1996), whereas those who binge and purge tend to have higher rates of impulsivity and stronger personal and family histories of obesity (Strober 1980). Diagnostic criteria for BN also have been modified from previous editions of the DSM. The first change emphasizes the sense of lack of control of overeating during the binge episodes. The second change subtypes BN into a purging type and nonpurging type. A patient cannot be dually diagnosed with AN and BN, so that an emaciated individual who is bingeing and purging will be diagnosed with AN, bulimia subtype. The priority given to AN has important therapeutic implications, given the need for immediate weight gain in this population (Halmi 1994). The prognosis also may be very different for the two groups. BN often can be treated successfully with good probability for complete recovery (Fairburn *et al.* 1995). AN, however, remains resistant to successful long-term treatment (Hsu 1991).

At the broadest levels, this chapter focuses on the assessment of (1) body composition, (2) energy regulation, and (3) psychopathology among persons with eating disorders. Within the section on body composition, high tech methods (i.e. those reserved for laboratory settings and research studies) and low tech methods (i.e. those relatively less expensive) are reviewed. Within the section on energy

Neurobiology in the Treatment of Eating Disorders.
Edited by H.W. Hoek, J.L. Treasure and M.A. Katzman.

regulation, methods used to assess energy expenditure and energy intake among persons with eating disorders are summarized. Finally, within the section on psychopathology, behavior symptoms that define the core features of eating disorders are presented first, followed by procedures for assessing common secondary psychopathology associated with eating disorders. Assessment of personality characteristics among persons with eating disorders, an area that has been overlooked comparatively in the literature, will be addressed last.

Because of space constraints, only the most commonly used and/or most psychometrically sound measures have been included. The coverage is not intended to be exhaustive. For additional descriptions of assessment measures pertaining to eating disorder psychopathology, see Schlundt and Johnson (1990), Thompson (1990, 1995), and Morey and Kurtz (1995).

ASSESSING BODY COMPOSITION

WHY ASSESS BODY COMPOSITION?

Body composition refers to the amount and distribution of the constituents of one's body mass. Body composition can be conceptualized, measured, studied, and deranged at the atomic, molecular, cellular, tissue-system, or whole body level (Wang *et al.* 1992). The assessment of body composition can be important for several reasons. First, body composition plays a role in characterizing the nature and degree of undernutrition in individuals with AN. For example, although marathon runners and patients with AN may have similar BMIs (see below for an explanation of BMI) they are clearly distinguishable groups by the markedly greater lean body mass of the marathon runners (Russell *et al.* 1994). Second, alterations in body composition subsequent to the development of eating disorders may mediate some of the morbidity and mortality of the disorder (Siegel *et al.* 1995). Finally, by assessing body composition changes with treatment, the clinician is better able to monitor treatment safety and progress (e.g. Russell *et al.* 1994).

In this section, body composition measurement techniques are divided into two categories: 'high-tech' and 'low-tech' methods. The former are generally reserved for laboratory-based research studies of small to moderate numbers of subjects. These techniques will be reviewed briefly. The latter techniques are applicable to the field and the clinic and will be reviewed in somewhat greater detail.

'HIGH-TECH' METHODS

Selected techniques will be reviewed in a cursory manner. For more details, see Heymsfield *et al.* (1995a), Roche *et al.* (1996), or Heyward (1996).

In vivo neutron activation analysis (IVNA)

IVNA allows assessment of body composition on the atomic level. It has the advantage of resting on relatively few assumptions (Heymsfield *et al.* 1995a). However, its current use tends to be limited because of its high cost, moderate radiation dose (in most cases), and the fact that only a few IVNA facilities exist world-wide.

Total body potassium (TBK) counting

TBK counting is a classic technique for estimating fat, fat free mass (FFM), and body cell mass (Forbes 1987). It relies on the fact that, in humans, naturally occurring ^{40}K constitutes 0.0118% of TBK and that TBK constitutes an approximately constant fraction of the FFM and body cell mass (Pierson *et al.* 1974). This latter assumption may not be reasonable in disease states including eating disorders. This method requires no radiation exposure but does require large and expensive equipment.

Total body water (TBW)

TBW can be assessed by isotope dilution. These isotopes can be either non-radioactive stable isotopes (e.g. deuterium) or radioactive isotopes (e.g. tritium). This method for estimating fat and FFM relies on the assumption that a constant fraction of the FFM is water. Again, these assumptions may not be met perfectly in eating disordered patients because of variations in hydration due to menstruation, starvation, and various forms of 'purging' (Heymsfield *et al.* 1995a).

Hydrodensitometry/under-water weighing (UWW)

Using Archimedes' principle, UWW can determine body density (BD) (Heymsfield *et al.* 1995a). Once BD is determined, FFM can be estimated as:

$$\text{FFM} = \text{Weight}\left[1 - \left(\frac{4.95}{\text{BD}} - 4.50\right)\right]$$

This technique requires an underwater weighing tank.

Dual energy X-ray absorptiometry (DXA)

DXA can measure the bone mineral, fat, and lean soft tissue of individuals by evaluating the differential attenuation of two different energy level X-rays as they pass through the body. The method is easy, painless, provides a minimal radiation dose, and yields highly precise measurements. The bone mineral measurement can be especially important as AN may result in long-term losses of bone mass (Bachrach *et al.* 1991; Crosby *et al.* 1985; Newton *et al.* 1993).

Imaging techniques

Imaging techniques such as computed tomography (CT) and magnetic resonance imaging (MRI) can provide unparalleled information about both the quantity and organization (i.e. regional distribution) of body composition. Unfortunately, these methods tend to be expensive, time-consuming, and, in the case of CT, to provide a moderate dose of radiation.

'LOW-TECH' METHODS

For most clinicians, epidemiologists, and others needing to study large numbers of subjects, methods that involve little cost, equipment, and radiation are required. These techniques are reviewed below.

Body mass index (BMI)

The Belgian astronomer, statistician, and epidemiologist Quetelet observed that, among adults, the average weight appeared to be proportional to the square of height. Thus, he initiated the use of kg/m^2 as an index of relative body weight. This is now generally referred to as the body mass index or BMI. BMI tends to be highly related to weight and minimally correlated with height. Heymsfield *et al.* (1995b) reviewed 26 studies reporting the correlation between BMI and a more direct measure of body fat. Correlations ranged from 0.45 to 0.99 with a median of 0.71. Similar correlations have been found among anorexics (Hannan *et al.* 1995). It is important to realize, however, that BMI taps both fat and lean mass. It therefore has weak discriminant validity and might be considered more of a 'marker' than a 'measure' of adiposity.

To provide some perspective, a BMI of approximately 28 or greater generally is taken to indicate obesity (Sichieri *et al.* 1991). BMIs between 20 and 25 are quite common and generally believed to be healthy. BMIs between 10 and 12 appear to represent the lower limit of human survival (Henry 1994). It is not uncommon for hospitalized anorexic patients to achieve BMIs of 15 or lower.

Bio-impedance analysis (BIA)

BIA is basically a way to estimate TBW. It is based on the principle that adipose tissue contains very little water and is a good insulator whereas lean body mass contains substantial water (and electrolytes) and is a good conductor. Thus, there is an inverse correlation between impedance and FFM. BIA is an increasingly used tool and has a number of major strengths (Yanovski *et al.* 1996). It is easy to use (many are portable), completely safe, painless, and can be implemented in minutes. A number of BIA machines exist and can often be purchased for less than $2000. Correlations between adiposity as measured by BIA and DXA (a reasonable 'reference' method) tend to average about 0.80 (Heymsfield *et al.* 1995b) suggesting good validity. Questions have been raised about BIA's ability to measure reliably change in body composition with gain or loss (Birmingham *et al.* 1996). However, most data suggest that it is adequate for this purpose (Kushner *et al.* 1996).

Infrared interactance (IRI)

IRI or near infrared interactance (NRI) are based on the principle that the proportion of infrared energy absorbed is related to the composition of the object through which it passes (Gemperline and Webber 1989). Like BIA, IRI is easy to use, completely safe, painless, and can be implemented in minutes. Some machines are inexpensive and portable. The validity of IRI can vary greatly with the type of machine. Recently a number of studies have provided some validation of IRI results among eating disordered subjects and other populations. Results suggest that IRI is highly reliable (Schreiner *et al.* 1995). However, reports of the validity vary and generally suggest poor performance relative to skinfolds or BIA (Fuller *et al.* 1996; Flynn *et al.* 1995; Yasukawa *et al.* 1995; Williams *et al.* 1995; Brooke-Wavell *et al.* 1995).

Anthropometry

Anthropometry consists of physical measurements of the body including skinfolds and circumferences. When using anthropometry it is crucial that the individual taking the measurements has substantial training and experience. Precise descriptions of proper methods for anthropometry can be found in Lohman *et al.* (1988) or in a recent video produced by the National Center for Health Statistics (National Center for Health Statistics 1996). Methods to convert skinfold readings to estimates of total body fat exist (Steinkamp *et al.* 1965; Jackson and Pollock, 1978; Jackson *et al.* 1980).

The use of anthropometry has several advantages. It is safe and inexpensive. Moreover, there are substantial normative data with which one can compare one's results. Finally, anthropometry is one of the few 'low-tech' methods that can inform one about fat distribution. Despite these advantages, anthropometry (primarily the use of skinfolds) has two major disadvantages. First, skinfolds only assess subcutaneous body fat. Second, it is very difficult to get reliable and valid data from all but the most trained and experienced technicians. In the hands of a less trained individual, skinfolds yield data of very dubious quality.

ASSESSING ENERGY EXPENDITURE

WHY ASSESS ENERGY EXPENDITURE?

The assessment of energy expenditure (EE) has two major uses. First, such measurements are often of critical importance in research studies to define underfeeding or overfeeding or measure metabolic responses to selected manipulations. Second, EE defines energy needs. It is by determining energy needs that one can calculate the amount of energy intake an individual requires to maintain body weight or to lose or gain weight at a safe rate (Seale 1995; Salisbury *et al.* 1995).

METHODS FOR FREE LIVING SITUATIONS

The measurement of EE among free-living individuals is exceptionally difficult. Methods are reviewed in detail by Shelton and Klesges (1995), Murgatroyd *et al.* (1993), and Schoeller and Racette (1990).

Questionnaires

The least expensive method of measuring EE in free-living situations is to have subjects complete a questionnaire or record their physical activities in an activity log (Paffenbarger *et al.* 1993). The activities performed are then converted to estimates of EE either by use of standard or subject-specific energy (Racette *et al.* 1995). Claims for the validity of these self-report methods have been made (Paffenbarger *et al.* 1993). However, when validated against measures that do not rely on self-reports, these methods appear to yield questionable results particularly among groups concerned with weight issues (Lichtman *et al.* 1992).

Doubly labeled water (DLW)

The DLW method of assessing EE originally was developed for use in small animals by Lifson *et al.* (1955). Schoeller (1988) later showed how this method could be adapted for use in humans and it has since become the 'gold standard'. Schoeller's work has revolutionized the field. For the first time, it is possible to assess accurately EE in free-living individuals without relying on self-reports. This ability has led to the realization that data on EE and energy intake from self-reports are prone to enormous errors of both a random and systematic nature (Schoeller 1990, 1995).

The use of DLW to assess EE uses the differential excretion rates of two stable isotopes (deuterium and ^{18}oxygen). From this, one can calculate EE. DLW is completely safe and simple to employ. It yields measurements that are highly reliable and valid (Schoeller *et al.* 1986). However, DLW has one major disadvantage. Specifically, between the price of the isotopes and the cost of mass spectrometry analyses, the cost per person usually is somewhere around $500.

Actometers and heart rate monitors

There are various physical activity recorders and heart rate monitors that can be used to estimate EE (Haskell *et al.* 1993; Shelton and Klesges 1995). These devices are generally modestly priced but require the cooperation of the individual, which may make their use questionable among individuals with severe psychopathology. However, when used correctly, the better actometers may yield useful information with validity coefficients greater than 0.80 (e.g. Bouten *et al.* 1994). Heart rate monitors appear to be valid but to have low precision (Livingstone *et al.* 1990).

METHODS FOR CONFINED POPULATIONS

In confined populations, there are two major ways of measuring EE, indirect calorimetry and balance studies (Rosenbaum *et al.* 1996). In indirect calorimetry, the subject lives in a sealed room for some period of time (e.g. one or several days). The room is equipped with gas analyzers (Heymsfield *et al.* 1994) which allows one to determine the subject's oxygen consumption and, therefore, EE. This method is highly accurate. However, it has several limitations. First, there are only about a dozen room calorimeters nationwide, making access rather limited. Second, because of the limited availability and the expense of construction and operation, the use of calorimeters tends to be rather expensive. Third, because subjects are confined to the equivalent of a small hotel room this method often suppresses physical activity and therefore underestimates free-living EE (Rosenbaum *et al.* 1996).

In balance studies, one simply titrates the amount of food required to maintain an individual's body weight and then determines the caloric content of this food. This value must equal EE by the first law of thermodynamics. This method requires little in the way of sophisticated equipment and yields highly accurate results (Rosenbaum *et al.* 1996). Unfortunately, from a clinical point of view, it may be of limited utility. This is because an answer comes by achieving weight maintenance whereas the question one often is starting with is 'How much energy is required to achieve weight maintenance?'

ESTIMATION PROCEDURES

The simplest approach to obtaining a value for an individual's EE is to estimate, rather than measure it. Typically, these approaches involve the use of some published prediction equation. The validity of such prediction equations depends on a number of factors including: (1) the representativeness of the derivation sample; (2) the size of the derivation sample; and (3) the predictor variables included in the model. Under the very best circumstances, reasonably good predictions can be obtained (e.g. Astrup *et al.* 1990) as, for example, when the predictors include body composition and resting metabolic rate measurements. However, subjects with eating disorders may differ in important ways from other groups making many published equations questionable for use in this population (Schebendach *et al.*

1995). Moreover, there is substantial interindividual variability in EE among individuals even after accounting for many commonly included variables, making accurate prediction very difficult (Salisbury *et al.* 1995; Goran 1995).

ASSESSING ENERGY INTAKE

WHY ASSESS ENERGY INTAKE?

As with EE, the assessment of energy intake (EI) has two major uses. First, such measurements allow one to study the nature of the eating disorder(s) in question for a group or individual. Second, one can use this as a means to monitor treatment progress.

METHODS FOR FREE-LIVING SITUATIONS

For obvious reasons, the greatest interest in the assessment of food intake is an assessment of habitual food intake in free-living situations. Unfortunately, it is in this arena that few good methods for measuring food intake exist. Traditionally, it has been common to measure food intake through the use of some type of self-report measure such as a food diary or food frequency questionnaire (Wolper *et al.* 1995). Unfortunately, recent evidence suggests the information yielded by these methods is, at best, fraught with large random errors and, at worst, subject to large biases and systematic errors (Schoeller 1990, 1995; Howat *et al.* 1994; Heymsfield *et al.* 1995b). It frequently is claimed that methods of training in interviewing strategies can be used to reduce the measurement errors in these instruments (c.f. Buzzard and Willett 1994). Moreover, it is claimed these instruments show good validity. However, frequently they are validated against other self-report instruments which are themselves highly questionable. Finally, sometimes it is claimed that because these measurements are fraught with substantial error, statistically significant associations that are observed among these measurements and other variables cannot be attributed to measurement error because the poorer measurement can only attenuate rather than create associations. Unfortunately, this is true only when the measurement error is random and the variables measured with error are not being used as covariates in a multivariate analysis. In the case of food intake measurements, neither of these assumptions are universally valid or, in many cases, even plausible. Therefore, it is the opinion of the current authors that the measurement of food intake in free-living situations by self-report instruments is a practice that is somewhere between dubious and useless.

An alternative to the use of self-report instruments to assess habitual food intake is the use of DLW. As described previously, DLW yields an accurate measurement of EE. Because EI must equal EE plus change in energy stores, by the first law of thermodynamics, if one can measure EE and change in energy stores, one can calculate EI. DLW (a measure of EE) can be combined with repeated body composition assessments (a measurement of change in energy storage) to determine EI. This method has been shown to yield highly reliable and valid measurements. In this context, there are two major limitations to the use of DLW. First, as stated earlier, DLW can be rather expensive. Second, DLW only yields the total caloric intake over a period of time, not the composition of the diet or the pattern of food intake.

LABORATORY-BASED PROCEDURES

Finally, it is possible to study food intake in laboratories. Some studies that have assessed food intake patterns in laboratory settings among individuals with eating disorders include (Hadigan *et al.* 1992; Kaye *et al.* 1992; Weltzin *et al.* 1991; Sunday and Halmi 1996). It is beyond the scope of this chapter to review all laboratory-based methods for studying food intake. For a detailed review, see Westerterp-Plantenga *et al.* (1994). Such methods can include assessment of eating rate, composition of foods chosen, amount eaten, response to caloric preloads of varying degree, and subjective feelings and sensations that precede, accompany, or follow eating.

Laboratory studies of food intake have enormous advantages. One can measure accurately food intake that generally cannot be measured accurately in other ways. Moreover, one has the ability to manipulate the environmental circumstances and observe the results of these manipulations allowing one to assess the causality of putative influential factors. However, the assessment of eating in the laboratory has at least one major disadvantage. Specifically, the issue of external validity and generalizability remains open to question. It frequently is claimed that studies of eating behavior in the laboratory are unlikely to provide us the kind of information we need about eating behavior in the natural setting (Meiselman 1992). However, several authors have challenged this criticism (e.g. Kissileff *et al.* 1986). Although issues of external validity always will remain when studying eating in the laboratory, it does appear some of these issues may be less of a concern than initially believed. For example, it was previously thought it would be impossible to study bingeing and purging in the laboratory because, due to the secretive nature of these behaviors, subjects would not exhibit them in the laboratory. In contrast, several investigators have studied successfully bingeing and purging behavior in the laboratory (Kissileff *et al.* 1986), indicating that, when conditions are set up properly, even complex 'secretive' behaviors may be studied effectively in controlled experimental settings.

The treatment and nature of eating disorders involves both physical and psychological components. Therefore, no consideration of assessment of eating disorders can be complete without a consideration of both components. Heretofore we have focused on the physical aspects of eating disorders. We now turn our attention to the psychological components.

ASSESSING CORE PSYCHOPATHOLOGY

WHY ASSESS CORE SYMPTOMS?

Persons with eating disorders present with a diversity of pathological thoughts and behaviors. Assessing these symptoms can provide a conception of the problem and a means of evaluating treatment outcome, measure symptom severity, and aid in yielding diagnoses. Such information is integral to the establishment of an effective treatment program (Knibbs 1993). The following section is divided into two parts. In the first part, extreme weight control behaviors and undercontrolled eating are described. Selected methods for the assessment of each are reviewed. The second part, which reviews psychopathology related to body image, follows a similar format.

WEIGHT-CONTROL BEHAVIORS

DSM-IV criteria characterize BN by inappropriate compensatory behavior in order to prevent weight gain (including self-induced vomiting, laxative abuse, misuse of diet pills, emetics, intense exercise, etc.). Determining the intensity of the dieting efforts and types of compensatory behaviors employed may provide insight into an underlying psychopathologic condition (Garner 1995). When dieting first began, its course over the duration of the illness, and the frequency of weight control behaviors should be obtained in order to determine the severity of the disorder (Garner 1995).

UNDERCONTROLLED EATING

A hallmark feature of BN, also occurring among 50% of individuals with AN, is binge eating (Garner 1995). For purposes of clinical diagnosis, the most widely adhered to definition of binge eating is provided by the DSM-IV. Binge eating is characterized by: (1) the consumption of a large amount of food that is inappropriate given the circumstances, and (2) the experience of loss of control. Data suggest that many individuals with eating disorders do not experience a sense of loss of control and that the amount of food consumed during a binge varies widely (Garner 1995). Garner, therefore, recommends following the system proposed in the Eating Disorder Examination (below), in which episodes of overeating are divided into four types based on the amount of food eaten (large or small) and loss of control (present or absent). Determining the presence, age of onset, frequency, duration, and circumstances surrounding the bingeing episodes is critical to diagnosis and treatment planning. For a more complete description of the parameters of binge eating, readers are referred to Pike *et al.* (1995).

Bingeing typically occurs in private, and the tremendous stigma associated with it may result in the tendency for individuals to underreport or even deny the behavior (Pike *et al.* 1995). It seems male bulimics, however, may be less disturbed by their binge eating (Carlat and Camargo 1991) and therefore may be accurate reporters. Given the wide range in the definition of a binge, Pike *et al.* recommend that the specific criteria necessary for defining episodes of bingeing and purging are made explicit to individuals in order to increase the validity of self-report.

METHODS FOR ASSESSING WEIGHT CONTROL BEHAVIORS AND UNDERCONTROLLED EATING

Interviews

Clinical interviews are widely used to explore the complex features of eating disorders (Cooper and Fairburn 1987). Interviews afford the opportunity to help individuals with concepts they may not understand and cannot operationally define (e.g. binge eating and loss of control). Moreover, interviewers are able to clarify ambiguous responses that could be misinterpreted. Despite the advantages of using investigator-based interviews for assessing eating disorder symptoms, certain disadvantages limit their practicality. Training is required in the technique of interviewing, the constructs being assessed, and the rules governing the ratings, which may be expensive and time consuming. Second, many interviews are unwieldy and take between 30 and 90 minutes to administer. Interviews also are personally intrusive (Fairburn and Beglin 1994), and admitting to behaviors deemed socially inappropriate by society (e.g. bingeing and self-induced vomiting) may be extremely difficult.

Below is a review of the more widely used and/or more psychometrically sound interviews. Psychometric data are summarized in Table 3.1.

The Eating Disorder Examination (12th edition)
(EDE-12; Fairburn and Cooper 1993)

The EDE may be the most well-validated and widely used semistructured interview for eating disorders. Originally developed to assess the specific psychopathology of eating disorders and to evaluate treatment outcome, the EDE now may be used to arrive at a DSM-IV eating disorder diagnosis. The EDE-12 yields four subscale scores: restraint, eating concern, weight concern, and shape concern. See Fairburn and Cooper (1993) for items that comprise each subscale. The EDE-12 also yields a global score that provides an overall measure of the severity of the eating disorder. The interview takes 30 minutes to 1 hour to complete.

The Structured Interview for Anorexia and Bulimia
(SIAB; Fichter *et al.* 1989)

The SIAB is a semistructured interview divided into two parts. The first part, the SIAB-P assesses the psychopathology of the eating disordered patients. It consists of 62 items, all included for diagnostic classification purposes or as a result of

Table 3.1. Summary of selected measured for assessing eating disorders

		Reliability			Validity	
Name of Instrument	Author(s)	Internal consistency[1]	Test–retest	Interrater	Concurrent	Discriminant
Clinical Interviews						
Eating Disorder Examination (12th Edition) (EDE-12)	Fairburn and Cooper (1993)	5 subscales: 0.67–0.90		Subscale scores[2]: 0.83–0.99 Individual items: 0.69–1.00	Weight concern subscale: *r* with BSQ: 0.78 Shape concern subscale: *r* with BSQ: 0.82 *Dietary Restraint subscale:* *r* with Eating Record: −0.39	
Structured Interview for Anorexia and Bulimia (SIAB)	Fichter *et al.* (1989)	SIAB-P past: 0.87 present: 0.93 SIAB-FAM past: 0.78 present: 0.77		SIAB-P[3] past: 0.96 present: 0.94 SIAB-FAM past: 0.84 present: 0.89	SIAB bulimic behavior: *r* with EDE total: 0.43 *r* with EDE bulimia scale: 0.53 SIAB depression: *r* with EDE total: 0.30 *r* with EDE restraint scale: 0.38	

Yale–Brown–Cornell Eating Disorder Scale (YBC-EDS)	Mazure *et al.* (1994)	Total score: 0.87–0.90 Subtotals preoccupation: 0.81–0.83 ritual: 0.78–0.83		Total Score[4]: 0.99 Subtotals preoccupation: > 0.99 ritual: 0.98	*r* with DEBQ: 0.42 *r* with EDI scales: Drive for Thinness: 0.47 Body Dissatisfaction: 0.47 Bulimia: 0.60	*r* with BDI: 0.63 *r* with SCL-90: 0.57
Questionnaires						
Eating Disorder Inventory-2 (EDI-2)	Garner (1991)	Original EDI scales: 0.65–0.93 3 new scales: 0.70–0.80 (Asceticism scale = 0.40)	1 wk: 0.67–0.95 3 wks: 0.65–0.92 1 yr: 0.41–0.75	Not relevant	Eight original subscales with scores on EAT: 0.26–0.71 Eating and weight-related subscales with the Restraint Scale: 0.44–0.61	Subscales assessing general psychological characteristics correlate more highly with general measures of psycho-pathology, and less with measures that assess eating and dieting behaviors[6]
Setting Conditions for Anorexia Nervosa Scale (SCANS)	Slade *et al.* (1986)	Subscales: 0.66–0.84		Not relevant	Significant association shown between D and P scales and the EAT and the EAT-26[6]	

continued overleaf

Table 3.1. *(continued)*

Name of Instrument	Author(s)	Reliability: Internal consistency[1]	Reliability: Test–retest	Reliability: Interrater	Validity: Concurrent	Validity: Discriminant
Mizes Anorectic Cognitions Scale (MACS)	Mizes (1991); Mizes and Klesges (1989)	Subscales: 0.75–0.89 Total score: 0.91	2 mos: 0.78	Not relevant	*r* with BULIT: 0.69 *r* with EAT: 0.64 *r* with EDI: 0.80	*r* with WRAT scales: Spelling: 0.01 Arithmetic: 0.00
Eating Habits Questionnaire (EHQ)	Coker and Roger (1990)	Total score: 0.89	4 wks: 0.95	Not relevant	*r* with BITE: 0.85 *r* with EAT: 0.73	
Eating Symptoms Inventory (ESI)	Whitaker *et al.* (1989)	ESI Symptom Count: boys: 0.54 girls: 0.76		Not relevant	*r* with EAT: boys: 0.36 girls: 0.56	
Kids' Eating Disorder Survey (KEDS)	Childress *et al.* (1993)	Total score: 0.73	4 mos: 0.83	Not relevant		
Eating Attitudes TEST (EAT)	Garner and Garfinkel (1979)	Total score: anorexics: 0.79 total population: 0.94	2–3 wks: 0.84	Not relevant	*r* with EDI scales: Drive for Thinness: 0.81 Body Dissatisfaction: 0.50 *r* with BULIT: 0.67 *r* with MAC: 0.64 *r* with BITE: 0.70	*r* with EDI scales: Ineffectiveness: 0.35 Perfectionism: 0.40 Maturity Fears: 0.12

Children's Eating Attitude Test (chEAT)	Maloney *et al.* (1988)	Total score: 0.76	3 wks: grade 3: 0.84 grade 4: 0.88 grade 5: 0.75 grade 6: 0.85	Not relevant		
Bulimia Test-Revised (BULIT-R)	Smith and Thelen (1984); Thelen *et al.* (1991)	Total: 0.97	2 mos: 0.95	Not relevant	*r* with Binge Scale: 0.85 *r* with BULIT: 0.99	*r* with body weight: 0.24 *r* with BDI: 0.48
Eating Questionnaire-Revised (EQ-R)	Williamson *et al.* (1989a)	Total: 0.87	2 wks: 0.90	Not relevant	*r* with EAT: 0.59 *r* with BULIT: 0.80	*r* with body weight: 0.22 *r* with BDI: 0.33
Bulimic Investigatory Test-Edinburgh (BITE)	Henderson and Freeman (1987)	Symptom Subscale: 0.96 Severity Subscale: 0.62	1 wk: 0.86 15 wks: 0.68	Not relevant	*r* with EAT: 0.70 *r* with EDI scales: Drive for Thinness: 0.59 Bulimia: 0.69	*r* with EDI scales: Perfectionism: 0.14 Interpersonal Distrust: 0.23
Binge Scale Questionnaire (BSQ)	Hawkins and Clement (1980)	Total score: 0.68	1 mo: 0.88	Not relevant	*r* with BULIT-R: 0.93	
Binge Eating Scale (BES)	Gormally *et al.* (1982)	All item-total correlations significant[5]		Not relevant	BES scores were significantly different across interview-rated severity levels of binge eating[6]	

continued overleaf

Table 3.1. *(continued)*

		Reliability			Validity	
Name of Instrument	Author(s)	Internal consistency[1]	Test–retest	Interrater	Concurrent	Discriminant
Questionnaire on Eating and Weight Patterns Revised (QEWP-R)	Spitzer *et al.* (1993)	Samples: weight control: 0.75 community: 0.79		Not relevant		
Body Image Measures						
Eating Disorders Inventory-Body Dissatisfaction Scale	1. Garner *et al.* (1983) 2. Shore and Porter (1990) 3. Wood *et al.* (1993)	1. Anorexics: 0.90 2. Adolescents (11–18) males: 0.86 females: 0.91 3. Children (8–10) males: 0.72 females: 0.84	3 wks: >0.81 1 year: >0.70	Not relevant	*r* with BSQ: 0.78	Correlates more highly with other measures that assess eating and diet behaviors, and less with measures that assess general psycho-pathology[6]

Body Shape Questionnaire (BSQ)	Cooper *et al.* (1987)		3 wks: 0.88	Not relevant	Nonclinical samples: *r* with BDDE: 0.77 *r* with MBSRQ subscales: Appearance Evaluation: −0.67 Body Areas Satisfaction: −0.66	
Extended Satisfaction with Life Scale-Physical Appearance Scale	Alfonso and Allison (1993)	Total: 0.91	2 wks: 0.83	Not relevant	*r* with RSE: 0.32	Correlation with other subscales substantially lower than α reliability[6]
Body Image Avoidance Questionnaire (BIAQ)	Rosen *et al.* (1991)	Total: 0.89	2 wks: 0.87	Not relevant	*r* with BSQ: 0.78 *r* with EDE subscales: Shape Concern: 0.68 Weight Concern: 0.63	
Self-Image Questionnaire for Young Adolescents-Body Image Subscale	Petersen *et al.* (1984)	Boys: 0.81 Girls: 0.77	1 year: 0.60 2 years: 0.44	Not relevant	*r* with RSE: Boys: 0.54 Girls: 0.28	Impulse Control Scale with RSE: 0.34

continued overleaf

Table 3.1. *(continued)*

		Reliability			Validity	
Name of Instrument	Author(s)	Internal consistency[1]	Test–retest	Interrater	Concurrent	Discriminant
Figure Rating Scale (FRS)	Stunkard *et al.* (1983)	Not applicable	2 wks: 0.89–0.92	Females: 0.79–0.89 Males: 0.64–0.90	*r* with BMI: 0.63–0.92	
Body Image Assessment (BIA) procedure	Williamson *et al.* (1989b)	Not applicable	1–8 wks: CBS: 0.90 IBS: 0.71			
BIA-Children (BIA-C) and Preadolescents (BIA-P)	Veron-Guidry and Williamson (1996)	not applicable	1 wk: CBS: 0.79 IBS: 0.67 CBS-IBS: 0.67		*r* with ChEAT: CBS: 0.09 IBS: −0.22 CBS-IBS: 0.33	
Body Rating Scales	Sherman *et al.* (1995)	Not applicable		BRS17: 0.54 BRS11: 0.64	*r* with BMI: BRS17: 0.59 BRS11: 0.78	

Note. The authors acknowledge the seminal work of Cronbach describing the various forms of validity and how all forms can be conceived of as forms of construct validity. Nevertheless, for purposes of this paper, we found it useful to limit our report to convergent and discriminant validity, which are commonly described types.

For reliabilities, [1]Cronbach's alpha; [2]Pearson product moment correlations; [3]Kendall's coefficient; [4]Intraclass correlation coefficients; [5]No traditional method of internal consistency was found.

For validities, [6]No traditional measure of validity was found; if blank, no studies were found.

D and P scales = dissatisfaction and loss of control and perfectionism; WRAT = Wide Range Achievement Test; BDI = Beck Depression Inventory; BDDE = Body Dysmorphic Disorder Examination; RSE = Rosenberg Self-Esteem Scale; BMI = Body mass index; CBS = Current body size; IBS = Ideal body size; CBS-IBS = body dysphoria score; BRS11 = for 11-year-olds; BRS17 = for 17-year-olds factor analyses. The second part, the SIAB-FAM, assesses family interaction and family pathology. This part consists of 25 items derived via factor analyses. The SIAB, which targets a wide range of psychopathology, is useful for comparing groups who have AN and BN. The SIAB can be used in clinical and research settings to yield present and lifetime diagnoses for eating disorders based on DSM-III-R criteria. The instrument also can be used to evaluate the ongoing effects of psychological and pharmacological treatments of eating disorders. The SIAB requires extensive training and may take up to 1 hour to administer.

The Yale–Brown–Cornell Eating Disorder Scale
(YBC-EDS; Mazure *et al.* 1994)

The YBC-EDS is an adaptation of the Yale–Brown–Cornell Obsessive–Compulsive Scale (CY-BOCS; Goodman *et al.* 1989a,b), an instrument used in the assessment of obsessive–compulsive disorder (OCD). The YBC-EDS identifies a wide range of eating-related rituals and/or preoccupations frequently found in eating disordered patients. It permits interviewers to determine the target symptoms specific to each individual and then assess the degree of impairment associated with each patient's unique symptomatology. The YBC-EDS evaluates the severity of preoccupations and rituals experienced by patients by rating the time occupied by symptoms, distress caused by the symptoms, degree of control over symptoms, and overall impairment of functioning due to symptoms.

The YBC-EDS consists of a 65-item symptom checklist and 19 questions. Although the thoughts and behaviors included in the YBC-EDS symptom checklist are fairly extensive, patients may add any eating-related thoughts or behaviors not part of the checklist. Four core questions are asked regarding preoccupations and four regarding rituals, yielding a preoccupation subtotal, ritual subtotal, and YBC-EDS total score. A provisional score assessing the patient's motivation for change is an important predictor of treatment outcome (Sunday *et al.* 1995). The interview takes between 20 and 30 minutes to administer.

A slightly modified version of the EDE

Although no published reports were found of structured interviews developed specifically for use with eating-disordered children under 14 years, the EDI was modified to address this population. The pilot study is described in detail by Bryant-Waugh *et al.* (1996). There are some main differences between the child version of the EDE and the original. First, questions that demanded subjects to place a value of importance on weight and body shape were replaced with a sort task. Second, because young children often cannot skip meals, questions assessing actual behavior on the original EDE were reworded to assess intent (e.g. 'would you have done X if you could have?'). Third, items requiring subjects to think abstractly were reworded to make it easier for children to understand and additional probes were permitted when necessary. Finally, interviewers and children developed a timetable of prior events for the child to refer to throughout the interview. Even with this aide, children often found it difficult to remember the chronology of events reliably. Given the problems in administration and coding, further research should be conducted before this version of the EDE can be endorsed fully.

Self-report measures

Several circumstances in which a self-report measure may be more useful are: (1) during an epidemiologic investigation in which a large number of people need to be assessed; (2) when the individual feels uneasy about admitting his or her behaviors to others; and (3) when trained interviewers are unavailable. Self-report measures have the advantages of being relatively inexpensive, brief, easily administered and objectively scored.

Due to the ambiguous behaviors being assessed, self-report measures tend to be less accurate than interview methods. Individuals with eating disorders who find their symptoms reassuring and ego-syntonic may distort deliberately their self-report when it suits their purposes to do so (Vitousek and Manke 1994). Williamson (1990) cautions against the use of one self-report inventory for diagnosing an eating disorder. Instead, a pattern of test scores, along with interview data, yield the most accurate assessment. Widely used and/or psychometrically sound self-report measures are reviewed below, and psychometric data are summarized in Table 3.1. For additional information see Thompson (1990, 1992, 1995) and Pike *et al.* (1995).

The Eating Disorder Inventory-2 (EDI-2; Garner 1991)

The EDI-2 is among the most widely used self-report measures designed to assess symptoms relevant to both AN and BN. The EDI is useful in clinical and research settings as a screening instrument to detect at-risk populations, diagnose eating disorders, evaluate treatment outcome, and differentiate severity levels or subtypes of AN and BN. Subscales of the EDI measure ascetism, impulse regulation, social insecurity, attitudes and behaviors toward weight, body shape and eating, and more general psychological characteristics of eating disorder patients, such as ineffectiveness, perfectionism, and interpersonal distrust. EDI-2 contains 91 items designed to be answered on a six-point rating scale ranging from 'always' to 'never' and takes about 20 minutes to complete. Norms are available for eating disorder patients, nonpatient college females and males, and adolescents (Garner 1991; Shore and Porter 1990).

The Eating Disorder Examination-Questionnaire (EDE-Q; Fairburn and Beglin 1994)

The EDE-Q is a self-report instrument adapted from the EDE. Designed to be very similar to the EDE, the questionnaire is easy to fill in and takes less than 15 minutes to complete. Unlike the interview format, key terms are not defined and there are no detailed guidelines for how to rate the items. While there is little discrepancy between the two formats regarding self-induced vomiting, laxative abuse and dietary restraint, there is less agreement with respect to more ambiguous terms such as binge eating. Higher ratings tend to be generated by the self-report method, suggesting that results be interpreted cautiously.

The Setting Conditions for Anorexia Nervosa Scale (SCANS; Slade *et al.* 1986)

SCANS is designed for screening individuals at risk of developing an eating disorder. A 40-item self-report inventory, it includes five scales which assess dissatisfaction and loss of control, social and personal anxiety, perfectionism, adolescent problems, and need for weight control. Subjects are required to respond to a five-point Likert scale (ranging from 'very often' to 'never' or 'very satisfied' to 'very dissatisfied'). The entire test takes between 10 and 20 minutes and can be scored manually within ten minutes. A computerized version is also available (Butler *et al.* 1988).

The Mizes Anorectic Cognitions Scale (MACS; Mizes and Klesges 1989)

The MACS was developed specifically to measure cognitions relevant to AN and BN. A 33-item questionnaire designed to be answered on a five-point Likert-type scale ranging from 'strongly disagree' to 'strongly agree', the MAC yields a total score and three empirically derived factors: (1) rigid weight and eating regulation; (2) weight and eating behavior as the basis of approval from others; and (3) self-worth based on excessive self-control (Mizes and Klesges 1989). It has been used as a treatment outcome measure (Kettlewell *et al.* 1992) and may have use as a screening instrument for detecting at-risk populations. The MAC takes approximately 15 minutes to complete.

The Eating Habits Questionnaire (EHQ; Coker and Roger 1990)

The EHQ is a 57-item self-report questionnaire designed to discriminate between subjects with and without eating disorders and to identify subjects in the general population at-risk for developing an eating disorder. The EHQ can be used to stratify subjects in the normal population along a continuum, enabling clinicians to identify sub-clinical cases. It may, however, be more sensitive to distinguishing bulimic patients from those with anorexia. The scale may be useful in long-term studies of the etiology and development of eating disorders. The EHQ appears to have three factors labeled 'Concern with Weight and Dieting', 'Restraint', and 'Overeating'. Items are posed in a dichotomized (true/false) forced-choice format, and the entire scale takes about 25 minutes to complete.

The Eating Symptoms Inventory (ESI; Whitaker *et al.* 1989)

The ESI is another self-report questionnaire developed to assess the core features of AN and BN. Although developed for use with DSM-III diagnostic criteria, the instrument can be adapted for use with DSM-IV criteria for eating disorders. The ESI also yields a continuous measure of severity, referred to as the ESI Symptom Count, which is derived from certain items.

The Kids' Eating Disorder Survey (KEDS; Childress *et al.* 1993)

The KEDS is a simpler and shorter version of the EDI developed specifically for use with young children. It was normed on a large middle school sample (children 9–16 years). A 14-item self-report measure which assesses attitudes and behaviors related to AN and BN, the KEDS may be a useful screening tool to identify at risk children or children with current eating disorders. Responses are rated on a three-point scale ('yes', 'no', and 'don't know') and a set of eight child figure drawings are provided to assess body and weight dissatisfaction. The figures were adapted from adult drawings developed by Stunkard *et al.* (1983). The KEDS takes about 10–15 minutes to complete.

Self-report measures specific to anorexia nervosa

The Eating Attitudes Test (EAT; Garner and Garfinkel 1979)

The EAT is probably the most widely used rating scale in the study of AN. It can be used to measure a range of attitudes and behaviors, identify at-risk individuals, and evaluate treatment outcome. Although it has been found to differentiate eating disorder groups from normal controls (Gross *et al.* 1986; Williamson *et al.* 1993), it has not been found to discriminate between AN and BN. The EAT is available in a 40-item and a 26-item version (EAT-26; Garner *et al.* 1982) and each item is answered on a six-point Likert scale (1 = never; 6 = always). The EAT takes less than 10 minutes to administer. It has not been used in published studies with children under 15 years, probably because it is incomprehensible to young children (Maloney *et al.* 1988). Vacc and Rhyne (1987) developed an adapted language version of the EAT (A-EAT), and a version adapted for use with children (chEAT; Maloney *et al.* 1988) is described below.

The Children's Eating Attitude Test (chEAT; Maloney *et al.* 1988)

The chEAT was adapted from the EAT-26 for use with children aged 8–13 years. Those questions on the EAT-26 too hard for children to understand were simplified (e.g. 'terrified' was changed to 'scared' and 'preoccupied with' to 'think a lot about'). Studies indicate the chEAT has the same accuracy and validity as the EAT, suggesting the instrument is a reliable and valid means of assessing eating attitudes and dieting behavior in young children. Although the chEAT is not a diagnostic instrument, it can yield a rich clinical profile regarding young children's food preoccupations, dieting patterns and eating attitudes. It is noteworthy that the chEAT can be administered orally, which may make it suitable for children with reading disabilities. It takes about 35 minutes to administer.

Self-report measures specific to bulimia nervosa

The Bulimia Test-Revised (BULIT-R; Thelen *et al.* 1991)

The BULIT-R is a 28-item scale useful for diagnosing BN, measuring treatment outcome, and assessing symptom severity. It provides clear instructions and can be completed in about 10 minutes. The BULIT-R is written at the eleventh grade reading level.

The Eating Questionnaire-Revised (EQ-R; Williamson *et al.* 1989a)

The EQ-R is a 15-item scale designed as a symptom checklist for bulimia as defined by the DSM-III (American Psychiatric Association 1987). It may be used to assess binge eating, purgative habits, and loss of control over eating, yielding a score that measures the overall severity of bulimic symptoms. It can be completed in less than 5 minutes, and questions are written at a seventh grade reading level.

The Bulimic Investigatory Test, Edinburgh
(BITE; Henderson and Freeman 1987)

The BITE was developed to detect binge eating and measure the cognitive and behavioral features of bulimia. A 33-item self-report instrument, it is useful in clinical and research settings as a measure of symptom severity and treatment outcome. Although the authors suggest a total score of 25 is indicative of a severely disordered eating pattern, Waller (1992) notes this score may not detect adequately anorexics with bulimic symptoms. The BITE takes under 10 minutes to complete, and is written at a fourth grade reading level.

METHODS SPECIFIC TO BINGEING AND PURGING

Binge eating and purging can be assessed via laboratory observations, self-monitoring procedures, self-report instruments, and interviews. According to Pike *et al.* (1995), the EDE is the most comprehensive and investigated measure of binge eating and purging, yielding the most precise information. Despite the advantages of interviews such as the EDE and SCID, self-report measures are the most common means of assessing binge eating and purging. Because of the anonymity, individuals may be more likely to answer questions more honestly (Pike *et al.* 1995). The most widely employed self-report measures are described below.

The Binge Scale Questionnaire (BSQ; Hawkins and Clement 1980)

The BSQ is a nine-item questionnaire that assesses the behavioral and attitudinal aspects of binge eating and vomiting. It has been used as a brief screening instrument and as a measure of severity. It does not assess specific frequencies of binges or purging efforts.

The Binge Eating Scale (BES; Gormally *et al.* 1982)

The BES is a 16-item questionnaire that measures the behavioral, affective and cognitive aspects associated with binge eating episodes. It has been used widely in clinical research studies in order to categorize patient samples according to severity of binge eating (LaPorte 1992; Marcus *et al.* 1988).

The Questionnaire on Eating and Weight Patterns-Revised
(QEWP-R; Spitzer *et al.* 1993, cited in Yanovski, 1993)

The QEWP-R is a 28-item questionnaire that assesses binge eating and purging. It is a criterion-based instrument that assesses the essential diagnostic criteria for purging and nonpurging bulimia as enumerated in the DSM-IV. It also provides rules for whether to diagnose binge eating disorder (BED) or BN. See Pike *et al.* (1995) for more details.

BODY IMAGE DISTURBANCE

Psychopathology related to body shape or weight has long been recognized as a core feature in the development, maintenance, and prognosis of AN and BN (Bruch 1962). In fact, weight or shape must be the predominant or even the sole criterion for judging self-worth (American Psychiatric Association 1994). Data suggest individuals suffering from BN tend to overestimate their current body size and underestimate their ideal body size relative to control subjects (Cooper and Taylor 1988). Data pertaining to body image disturbances in AN have yielded inconsistent results, with conclusions both supporting and rejecting evidence for body size overestimation relative to control subjects (Cash and Brown 1987; Hsu and Sobkiewicz 1991).

Researchers have recognized two domains of body image: (1) the attitudinal component, which refers to thoughts, feelings, and behavioral reactions to one's own body; and (2) the perceptual component, which focuses on the accuracy with which one perceives various body parts. Although widely used, there are a number of methodological problems regarding perceptual measures (Thompson 1995). First, the perceptual index seems to be confounded by the nature of the instructional protocol. Questions with an affective slant (e.g. 'How large do you feel?') seem to yield larger estimates than cognitive questions (e.g. 'How large do you think you look?') (Thompson 1992). Second, the perceptual component does not seem to correlate highly with subjective levels of dissatisfaction (Altabe and Thompson

1992). Finally, perceptual size estimations seem to be affected by the individual's actual size (Penner *et al.* 1991), indicating the importance of controlling for actual body size when evaluating body image.

When compared to European Americans, African–Americans tend to choose silhouettes that more accurately estimate their actual body size (Hesse-Biber 1996). Caucasian women, in contrast, seem to choose significantly thinner ideal body sizes and often feel heavier, in relation to their ideals (Powell and Kahn 1995). In addition, data suggest that some children as young as 6 years old are dissatisfied with their bodies and prefer thinness (Lask and Bryant-Waugh 1993), suggesting that the early stages of eating disorders may develop before puberty. This necessitates the use of reliable and valid assessment devices for measuring these constructs in young children.

METHODS FOR ASSESSING BODY IMAGE DISTURBANCE

Approaches to assessing body image distortion and dissatisfaction can be placed into several categories: (1) self-report questionnaires; (2) silhouettes of differing body sizes; (3) distorting image techniques; and (4) visual size estimation tasks. The latter two categories ask individuals: (1) to estimate overall body size using images of their own bodies in a mirror or camera; and (2) to use a pulley to adjust two lights on a horizontal bar to estimate the width or depth of specific body regions, respectively. Further validation is required before applying these as body image assessment techniques (Knibbs 1993). They have yielded inconsistent results and appear to be insensitive to variations in body image over time. Therefore, they will not be reviewed here. For more comprehensive summaries of these techniques, see Thompson (1990) and Slade (1985).

The number of available measures to assess body image dissatisfaction approaches a total of almost 100 (Thompson 1995). Therefore, only widely used scales and techniques will be discussed. Readers are referred to Thompson (1990, 1995) and Slade (1985) for a more detailed review.

Questionnaires

Self-report questionnaires may be the most widely used method for assessing body image (Ben-Tovim and Walker 1991).

The Body Dissatisfaction Scale

The Body Dissatisfaction Scale of the EDI-2 may be the most widely used questionnaire measure. It includes seven items for which subjects indicate their degree of agreement (via a six-point scale) with nine statements about body parts being too large. This instrument is reliable for use with adolescents (Shore and Porter 1990) and, with some revisions, with children as young as 8 years of age (Wood *et al.* 1993).

The Body Shape Questionnaire (BSQ; Cooper *et al.* 1987)

The BSQ is a 34-item self-report inventory developed to assess global body dissatisfaction in patients with AN and BN. Each item represents a thought or feeling about one's body, and subjects rate how often they have felt that way in the last month using a six-point frequency scale. The BSQ may be most useful in research settings for treatment planning and monitoring treatment effects (Schlundt and Johnson 1990).

The Extended Satisfaction with Life Scale
(ESWLS-PA; Alfonso and Allison 1993)

The ESWLS-PA is designed to measure satisfaction in various life domains. It contains a Physical Appearance subscale that yields a global measure of body image satisfaction. The subscale consists of five items, and individuals are asked to rate their degree of agreement (or disagreement) with each item on a seven-point Likert-type scale. Questions pertain to individuals' present lives. It is suggested that individuals should be reading at least at the seventh grade level in order to understand the ESWLS (Alfonso *et al.* 1996).

The Self-Image Questionnaire for Young Adolescents (Peterson *et al.* 1984)

The Self-Image Questionnaire for Young Adolescents, an adaptation of the Offer Self-Image Questionnaire (OSIQ; Offer *et al.* 1981) is designed for use with children between the ages of 10 and 15 years. Standardized on over 300 sixth-grade students, it measures several dimensions of self-image in young adolescents. The 11-item Body Image subscale, specifically, assesses positive feelings toward the body. The scale has demonstrated good reliability and validity (Petersen *et al.* 1984).

The Body Image Avoidance Questionnaire (BIAQ; Rosen *et al.* 1991)

The BIAQ is a 19-item measure of behavioral tendencies that are associated with body image disturbance in women. Specifically, it measures the frequency with which eating disorder patients avoid situations that provoke concern about physical appearance, such as avoidance of tight-fitting clothes, social outings, and physical intimacy. The instrument contains four scales (clothing, social activities, eating restraint, and grooming/weighings). Although the BIAQ has demonstrated adequate psychometric properties, it needs to be validated with men before using it with male samples.

Figures/silhouettes

Silhouettes, also widely used, evaluate attitudes towards visual representations of the body. Individuals are presented with a series of silhouettes that vary systematically from very thin to quite obese and are asked to choose two figures, one that best represents their current size and one that represents their ideal size. Some studies use outlines of parts (Buree *et al.* 1984), while others use silhouettes of the whole body. Most are very simple and quick to administer, which may make them especially suitable for a younger age group. It is noteworthy that most figural stimuli have Caucasian features which may make them unsuitable for use with all ethnic groups (Allison *et al.* 1997).

The Figure Rating Scale
(FRS; Stunkard *et al.* 1983; Thompson and Altabe 1991)

The FRS is normed on over 300 undergraduate students and has been used with a wide age range of subjects. Subjects select from nine male or female schematic figures, which vary in size from underweight to overweight, yielding a measure of overall satisfaction. The psychometric properties of the FRS are better known than many others, demonstrating adequate reliability and validity.

The Body Image Assessment (BIA; Williamson *et al.* 1989b)

The BIA procedure was developed based on the self-ideal discrepancy as a measure of body dissatisfaction. Subjects are instructed to select from nine body silhouettes, and estimates of current body size, ideal body size, and the self-ideal discrepancy are obtained. Studies using the BIA procedure have provided evidence for its reliability and validity. Veron-Guidry and Williamson (1996) modified BIA for use with children as young as 8 years old (BIA-C) and pre-adolescents (BIA-P). Nine cards with body image silhouettes are placed randomly on a table or desk in front of the subject/patient. The subject is told to point to the body shape that looks most like him or her and to the body shape that he or she would most want to look like. The body dysphoria score is derived from the difference between the two numbers. The entire procedure takes less than 5 minutes.

The Body Rating Scales (Sherman *et al.* 1995)

The Body Rating Scales are another set of figural stimuli developed for use with preadolescent (BRS11) and adolescent (BRS17) females. Both the BRS17 and BRS11 consist of nine figures ranging from thin to fat. The main difference between the two is the more mature appearance of the BRS17 figures. Both appear to be reliable and valid measures of body image satisfaction.

ASSESSING GENERAL PSYCHOPATHOLOGY

WHY ASSESS ASSOCIATED PSYCHOPATHOLOGY?

Eating disorders have been found to be associated with interpersonal sensitivity, interpersonal and family problems, and a number of clinical (Axis I) and personality (Axis II) disorders (Wilson *et al.* 1996). Secondary psychopathology associated with eating disorders may impair patients' abilities to adhere to treatment plans and commit to behavior changes necessary for recovery (Deep *et al.* 1995). Adequately assessing these areas, therefore, may provide insight into the factors contributing to or maintaining the eating disorder, which is important from the perspective of treatment planning (Williamson 1990). It is also important to consider the presence and severity of comorbid disorders in planning research designs (e.g. for randomizing subjects to groups, setting exclusion criteria, and measuring and controlling for covariates).

Below is a description of these disorders and their prevalence rates in the eating disorder population. In this section, Axis I disorders associated with eating disorders are reviewed first, followed by methods for assessing Axis I disorders. Afterwards, a similar approach is taken for the assessment of Axis II disorders. We do not mean to suggest that these disorders do (or do not) share a common etiology with eating disorders. Rather, we simply provide this as descriptive information so the evaluator has a sense of what to expect when administering instruments to persons with certain types of eating disorders.

AXIS I DISORDERS

Affective disorders seem to be the most common comorbid diagnosis (Braun *et al.* 1994). Major depression has been reported to co-occur with acute anorexia, with prevalence rates ranging from 21 to 91% (Kaye *et al.* 1993) and bulimia, with prevalence rates ranging from 36 to 70% (Halmi 1994). Lifetime major depression has been found to be more common among patients who have both anorexia and bulimia (Braun *et al.* 1994; Laessle *et al.* 1989), and clinical depression rates as high as 56% have been found in samples of children with early onset anorexia (Fosson *et al.* 1987).

Eating disorders have been associated with high rates of anxiety disorders (Mash and Barkley 1996), with the strongest relationship seemingly between obsessive–compulsive disorder (OCD) and AN (Strober 1980; Braun *et al.* 1994; Wilson *et al.* 1996; Formea and Burns 1995). In patients with AN, OCD may exist at as high a rate as 26% (Halmi 1994). OCD often predates the eating disorder and continues throughout the patient's lifetime (Mash and Barkley 1996). Recently, evidence has been found for co-occurrence between OCD and BN (Formea and Burns 1995). It has been suggested that patients who have comorbid OCD present with a higher degree of disturbed behavior and attitudes concerning eating than do patients without these tendencies (Vitousek and Manke 1994).

Eating disorders and substance abuse also co-occur (Wilson *et al.* 1996). Prevalence rates ranging from 6.7 to 23% have been reported in patients with AN (Wilson 1991) and 9 to 55% reported in patients with BN. Bulimics are significantly more likely than anorexic restrictors to abuse substances (Braun *et al.* 1994). Higher levels of substance abuse have been found in the binge-eating/purging subtype of AN (20%) as compared with the restricting subtype

(0%) (Laessle *et al.* 1987). It is noteworthy that males seem to have more comorbid substance abuse disorders than females (Schneider and Agras 1987; Powers and Spratt 1994). This knowledge may be important given the denial often associated with drug use and in determining order of intervention (i.e. whether to remedy first the emaciation, personality disorder, or drug addiction).

Social phobia is another Axis I disorder that commonly co-occurs in persons with eating disorders. In persons with AN, social phobia may exist at as high a rate as 34% (Halmi 1994). The precise incidence of social phobia in bulimics has yet to be determined. However, data suggest that the prevalence of social phobia in eating disorder patients far exceeds that in the general population (Schneider *et al.* 1992). Social phobia most commonly precedes the eating disorder, and many patients with social phobia also have a history of major depression (Braun *et al.* 1994).

METHODS FOR ASSESSING AXIS I DISORDERS

Self-report measures

General psychological tests provide a multidimensional profile of psychopathology that may be relevant to understanding the eating disorder (Schlundt and Johnson 1990). Many tests exist that would serve this purpose adequately; to present them all is beyond the scope of this chapter. The most widely used standardized inventories are summarized below and in Table 3.2. See Morey and Kurtz (1995) and Schlundt and Johnson (1990) for more details.

The Minnesota Multiphasic Personality Inventory (MMPI-1; Hathaway and McKinley 1983)

The MMPI-1 is one of the most widely used and studied personality tests for measuring areas of psychological disturbance. The MMPI is commonly used for making diagnoses, screening patients at intake, and as a research tool for investigating psychopathology. Research suggests that women with eating disorders commonly display clinical elevations on several scales of the MMPI (Pryor and Wiederman 1996). Restricting anorectics have demonstrated clinical elevations on Scale 2 (Depression), with a general profile indicative of depression, anxiety and social withdrawal (Casper *et al.* 1992). Profiles of binge-eating/purging anorexics generally indicate greater psychopathology (Vitousek and Manke 1994).

Pryor and Wiederman investigated the usefulness of the MMPI-2 (Butcher *et al.* 1989) in the distinction of women with AN from women with BN. Mean profiles for each group were remarkably similar, suggesting the MMPI-2 may not yield clinical information beyond what could be obtained from an intake interview.

The Symptom Checklist-90 (SCL-90; Derogatis *et al.* 1977)

The SCL-90 asks patients to rate the severity of psychological or somatic complaints on a five-point distress scale. Like the MMPI, the SCL-90 provides

Table 3.2 Sample instruments for assessing comorbid psychopathology

Instruments	Reference	Advantages	Disadvantages
Axis I measures			
Minnesota Multiphasic Personality Inventory	Hathaway and McKinley (1983)	1. One of the most extensively used and investigated 2. Validity scales able to detect when individuals are trying to make themselves look better or worse	1. Takes a considerable amount of time to complete 2. Age of test norms may make interpretation difficult
Symptom Checklist-90	Derogatis (1977)	1. Easy to administer and score 2. Provides a quick overview of areas of distress 3. Good for comparing severity of different cases	1. Does not yield much specific information to use in treatment planning 2. The nine subscales may lack discriminant validity
Beck Depression Inventory	Beck and Steer (1984)	1. Measures severity of depression quite precisely 2. Can be administered repeatedly to monitor changes over time	1. Consistent order of the items (from least to most severe) may make it susceptible to a defensive response set
Children's Depression Inventory	Kovacs (1985)	1. Most widely used self-report measure for children ages 7 to 17 2. Economical and easy to administer 3. Useful in treatment-outcome studies	1. Cognitive skills at different ages may influence the child's interpretation of the questions 2. Validity data are equivocal 3. Should not be used alone to select research patients
Leyton Obsessional Inventory	Cooper (1970)	1. Has good test-retest reliability 2. Has a version that is appropriate for use with children and adolescents (LOI-CV)	1. Relies on a card-sorting task that can be unwieldy and time-consuming 2. Developed with 'perfectionist' mothers rather than OCD patients, it emphasizes domestic topics

Maudsley Obsessional Inventory	Hodgson and Rachman (1977)	1. Useful in behavior therapy studies and research on obsessional complaints in nonclinical samples	1. Constructed as a symptom inventory, it may favor particular types of obsessions and compulsions
Structured Clinical Interview for DSM-IV	First *et al.* (1996a)	1. Offers the widest coverage of Axis I disorders 2. Facilitates diagnosis and treatment planning	1. Training, supervision, clinical experience, and familiarity with DSM-IV criteria are imperative to conducting an accurate interview 2. Further studies are necessary to establish reliability with minority populations
Diagnostic Interview Schedule	Robins *et al.* (1989)	1. Can be administered by paraprofessionals with little training 2. Translated and validated in Spanish 3. Has self-administered versions	1. Does not offer ratings of severity for symptoms in the clinical range 2. Interviewers often must make complex judgments regarding the etiology of specific symptoms
Yale–Brown Obsessive–Compulsive Scale	Goodman *et al.* (1989a,b)	1. Assesses severity of obsessions and compulsions, regardless of type 2. Sensitive to treatment induced change	1. May not be useful in discriminating severity of OCD from severity of depression or anxiety in patients with OCD with comorbid depression
Axis II measures			
Millon Clinical Multiaxial Inventory	Millon (1982)	1. Comparable to other personality tests in terms of reliability and validity 2. Final item pool and scale composition refined through internal consistency methods and external criterion checks	1. Criticized for extensive item overlap among different scales 2. Very difficult to score by hand

continued overleaf

Table 3.2 *(continued)*

Instruments	Reference	Advantages	Disadvantages
Structured Clinical Interview for DSM-IV Personality Disorders	First *et al.* (1996b)	1. When used with SCID-I, provides a broad assessment of Axis I and Axis II disorders 2. Needs relatively little training to administer 3. Availability of the SCID-II-Q, an item-by-item screening questionnaire of Axis II criteria	1. Lack of large-scale reliability studies 2. Face validity of the items makes it vulnerable to response styles
Personality measures			
Multidimensional Perfectionism Scales	Hewitt and Flett (1991); Frost *et al.* (1990)	1. Takes into account the multidimensional nature of perfectionism 2. Reliability, validity, and factor structure have been demonstrated in clinical and nonclinical samples	1. Constructed and normed on an all-female college student sample (Frost *et al.* 1990)
Barratt Impulsiveness Scale	Patton *et al.* (1995)	1. Revised extensively to define impulsiveness within the broader structure of personality traits 2. Internally consistent across populations	1. Cognitive items load on all the factors, which may make it inappropriate for use with younger children
Rosenberg Self-Esteem Scale	Rosenberg (1962)	1. Psychometric properties have found considerable support 2. Brief (10-item) measure of global self-esteem	1. Disagreement concerning the factorial nature of the scale
Multidimensional Self-Concept Scale	Bracken (1992)	1. Standardization sample closely matches US population demographic characteristics 2. Has demonstrated good reliability and validity	1. Because it is fairly new, research is limited 2. Developmental issues suggest limitations in the use of any one instrument with children of all ages

screening for a broad range of psychological problems. The scale is easy to administer and takes less than 30 minutes to complete. Research using the SCL-90 suggests eating disordered patients express significantly more psychopathology than normal controls (Ordman and Kirschenbaum 1986). Bulimic patients, in particular, seem to show more psychological distress in almost all areas (Williamson *et al.* 1985; Weiss and Ebert 1983). Binge eating, for example, correlates with elevated levels of somatization, OCD, and depression (Marcus *et al.* 1988). When compared to patients seeking help for other psychological disorders, no particular area of distress stands out.

The Beck Depression Inventory, Revised (BDI; Beck *et al.* 1979)

The BDI may be the most widely used screening instrument for depression. It contains 21 items and takes only 5–10 minutes to complete. The BDI may be used with individuals as young as 13; a high school reading level is required. Because it quantifies the severity of depression, the BDI is useful in painting a clinical picture, assessing treatment outcome, testing research hypotheses, and selecting research subjects (Kovacs 1895). Individuals with eating disorders have scored higher than average on the BDI. The average score was 15.4 for a sample of bulimics (Williamson *et al.* 1985) and 28.6 for anorexics (Garfinkel *et al.* 1983). If patients score above 16, the pattern of responses should be reviewed to determine if thoughts of suicidal ideation are present.

The Children's Depression Inventory (CDI; Kovacs 1985)

The CDI is probably the best known of the self-report measures for children and adolescents. Derived from the BDI, it is a 27-item questionnaire that measures a broad range of depressive symptoms. Although developed for use with 7–17-year-olds, the wording of items is sometimes too hard for younger or less intelligent subjects to follow (Costello and Angold 1988). The CDI takes between 10 and 20 minutes to complete. It is most appropriate for use as an index of the severity of depression and as a measure of treatment efficacy (Kovacs 1985). A parallel parent version is available.

The Maudsley Obsessional–Compulsive Inventory
(MOCI; Hodgson and Rachman 1977)

The MOCI is a 30-item (true/false format) self-report measure of OCD symptoms that can be used in treatment studies. It targets two major complaints (checking and washing) and two minor types (slowness and doubting). The MOCI is used mostly in research on obsessional complaints in nonclinical samples (Richter *et al.* 1994).

The Leyton Obsessional Inventory (LOI; Cooper 1970)

The LOI is one of the oldest measures of OCD, but is not used as frequently in current research as it was in the past (Richter *et al.* 1994). A child version of the LOI, The Leyton Obsessional Inventory-Child Version (LOI-CV; Berg *et al.* 1986), however, may be appropriate for use with children and adolescents 12–16 years old. Both versions of the LOI have demonstrated good reliability and validity.

Clinical interviews

Interviews afford the opportunity to ask probing questions, check ambiguous responses, and obtain chronological data (including age of onset), yielding a more thorough profile of the patient. Given the denial often associated with the eating disorder population (Vitousek *et al.* 1991), results from interviews should be interpreted cautiously. Commonly used interviews to measure Axis I disorders are summarized below and in Table 3.2.

The Structured Clinical Interview for DSM-IV (SCID; First *et al.* 1996a)

The SCID is a criterion-based interview, the only measure developed to correspond exactly to DSM-IV criteria. It covers all Axis I and Axis II disorders, referred to as SCID-I and SCID-II, respectively. The interview can take as long as 150 minutes to complete, although an individual who presents with little psychopathology can be completed more quickly. The interview follows a flowchart format. Questions are asked based on each criterion and the interviewer proceeds to the next only if the patient demonstrates some degree of the symptom on the present item. Studies comparing groups based on SCID diagnoses consistently support its ability to discriminate among all the identified mental disorders, suggesting adequate reliability and validity (Segal *et al.* 1994).

The Diagnostic Interview Schedule, Version III-Revised (DIS-III-R; Robins *et al.* 1989)

The DIS-III-R is a highly structured interview developed to assess current and past episodes of common psychological disorders. It was designed to be used by non-professionals and is the only interview adequately validated for use with Hispanic populations (Rogers 1995). Questions must be read verbatim, and a training manual is provided which specifies how to code the clinical ratings of specific items (Robins *et al.* 1991). The DIS may be self-administered via a computerized version or an abridged paper-and-pencil version (DISSA or DIS Self-Administered; Kovess and Fournier 1990). These versions only cover depressive disorders, anxiety disorders and alcoholism.

The Yale-Brown Obsessive–Compulsive Scale
(Y-BOCS; Goodman *et al.* 1989a,b)

The Y-BOCS is a semistructured interview that takes a process-oriented approach to assessing obsessive–compulsive symptoms. The basic scale consists of 10 items and a checklist of 58 typical past and present obsessions and compulsions. Interviewers ask individuals about various aspects of obsessive–compulsive symptoms (e.g. pervasive slowness, pathological doubting, indecisiveness and avoidance are rated). For individuals under 16 years of age, the child version of the Y-BOCS may be more appropriate (CY-YBOCS; Goodman *et al.* 1989a,b). See Richter *et al.* (1994) for more details.

Currently, a number of well-established psychological interviews are available for assessing children. The reliability estimates for interviews administered to children are generally lower than those for adults. The reason for this is not understood completely, and may reflect in part children's lesser ability to report accurately and clearly their feelings and symptoms (Rogers 1995). In order to assess reliably what children disclose during interviews, the data should be corroborated by interviewing parents and conducting standardized observations (Harrington 1992). According to Rogers, four major diagnostic interviews for children are The Schedule of Affective Disorders and Schizophrenia for School-Age Children (K-SADS; Chambers *et al.* 1985); Diagnostic Interview Schedule for Children (DISC; Costello *et al.* 1984); Children's Assessment Schedule (CAS; Hodges *et al.* 1982); and Diagnostic Interview for Children and Adolescents (DICA; Herjanic and Reich 1982). All four were developed for use with children between the ages of 6 and 18, utilize parent-informant interviews along with the child interviews, and yield diagnoses based on the DSM. Each interview was developed for a different purpose and has its own advantages and disadvantages. For more details, see Rogers (1995).

AXIS II DISORDERS

Eating disorders co-occur with a number of personality disorders (Braun *et al.* 1994; Vitousek and Manke 1994; Casper *et al.* 1992). Although the effects of co-occurring personality disorders in eating disorder patients are uncertain, data suggest such comorbidity may be associated with a poorer prognosis (Skodol *et al.* 1993). Severe personality disturbances may affect length and difficulty of treatment for eating disorder patients, making diagnosis of these disorders important for planning interventions (Morey and Kurtz 1995).

Braun *et al.* (1994) found AN to be associated strongly with the Cluster C (anxious cluster) personality disorders. Prevalence rates were 23% and 32% in anorectic restrictors and anorectic bulimics, respectively. Braun *et al.* also found 38% of the anorectic bulimics displayed Cluster B, the impulsive cluster of personality disorders: antisocial, borderline, histrionic, and narcissistic.

Data suggest bulimic patients have considerable comorbidity with Axis II personality disorders. Prevalence rates range from 28 to 77%, with a predominance of Cluster

B disorders (Skodol *et al.* 1993; Braun *et al.* 1994). Skodol *et al.* found BN to co-occur highly with schizotypal and borderline personality disorders, with the strongest association with the latter. Prevalence rates range, however, from as little as 2% to over 50% (Skodol *et al.* 1993). Overall, lifetime, but not current, bulimia seems to be associated with the Cluster C disorders, particularly avoidant personality disorder.

METHODS TO ASSESS AXIS II DISORDERS

Questionnaires

The Millon Clinical Multiaxial Inventory (MCMI; Millon 1982)

The MCMI is one of the more commonly used self-report measures for assessing personality disorders. It is a 175-item, true–false psychological inventory intended to be used with clinical patients. The scales are clustered into three groups: personality scales, severe personality patterns, and clinical syndromes. Research using the MCMI with bulimics has shown significantly elevated scores on the Dependent, Avoidant, and Schizoid scales when compared to normal controls (Tisdale *et al.* 1990). Most bulimic patients in this group also met criteria for a dependent personality style. Patients with AN and BN have shown elevated scores on the Borderline scale, with proportions of the sample ranging from 32% (Sansone *et al.* 1989) to 79% (Kennedy *et al.* 1990). Despite its widespread use, certain aspects of the MCMI have been criticized, such as the extensive item overlap among different scales (Retzlaff and Gilbertini 1987).

The SCID-II

The SCID-II is a supplementary version of the SCID-I (described above) which provides DSM-IV diagnoses of personality disorders. The SCID-II has been found to yield highly reliable diagnoses for most Axis II disorders (Segal *et al.* 1994). Like the SCID-I, it is based solely on the DSM-IV criteria for mental disorders. Although the SCID is a structured interview, interviewers can probe and restate questions, challenge the respondent, and clarify ambiguous responses in order to determine whether a particular symptom is present.

PERFECTIONISM, IMPULSIVITY, AND OTHER CLINICALLY RELEVANT TRAITS

For clinical and research purposes, it may be important to assess normal personality characteristics among individuals with eating disorders (Morey and Kurtz 1995). Research suggests that these traits, taken to the extreme, may be linked with emotional distress and psychopathology (DiLalla *et al.* 1993). Below is a brief discussion of personality traits of interest to explore. Instruments to measure these are summarized in Table 3.2.

Perfectionism

Eating-disordered individuals have been described as neurotic perfectionists (Mitzman *et al.* 1994). They tend to set unattainable standards for themselves, view mistakes as disastrous, and view achievements as unsatisfying (Lask and Bryant-Waugh 1992). It is important to assess the attitudes and experiences associated with perfectionism that may be linked specifically to the eating disorder. Perfectionism often is measured by the Perfectionism subscale of the EDI. This scale consists of six items that emphasize personal standard setting and parental expectations. Newer scales, however, have been developed that take into account the multidimensional nature of perfectionism. Two groups have developed Multidimensional Perfectionism Scales; both are reviewed briefly below.

Multidimensional Perfectionism Scale (MPS; Frost *et al.* 1990)

The MPS is a 35-item self-report questionnaire that emphasizes the intrapersonal nature of the construct of perfectionism. The MPS yields six subscale scores (Concern over Mistakes, Personal Standards, Parental Expectations, Parental Criticism, Doubts about Actions, and Organization) and an overall perfectionism score. Originally normed on an all-female college student sample, the scale has demonstrated to be reliable with a mixed-gender sample and academically talented children in the sixth grade (Parker and Stumpf 1995).

Multidimensional Perfectionism Scale (MPS; Hewitt and Flett 1991)

The MPS is a 45-item scale that identifies three dimensions of perfectionism (self-oriented, other-oriented, and socially prescribed). Subjects respond to a seven-point Likert-type scale; as opposed to the MPS (Frost *et al.* 1991), this instrument has a strong interpersonal focus. Both are reliable and valid measures of different dimensions of perfectionism (Frost *et al.* 1993).

Impulsivity

Bulimics often are noted most for their impulsive and self-defeating style (Halmi 1994; Vitousek and Manke 1994). This is not limited to the way they binge and purge but is reflected in their higher rates of alcohol and drug abuse, shoplifting, sexual promiscuity, and suicidal gestures. Studies suggest impulsivity may lead to a lack of intimate relationships (Wilson *et al.* 1996). Given the high rate of suicidal threats, impulsivity is important to assess.

The Barratt Impulsiveness Scale Version II (BIS-II; Patton *et al.* 1995)

The BIS-II is a 30-item, four-point self-report measure of impulsiveness. Factor analysis suggests six primary factors and three second-order factors, including: motor impulsiveness, nonplanning impulsiveness, and attentional impulsiveness.

Cognitive processes seem to underlie all the items. The scale is useful for measuring impulsiveness among selected patient populations (Patton *et al.* 1995).

The Multidimensional Personality Questionnaire (MPQ; Tellegen 1982)

The MPQ is a 300-item self-report instrument which describes 11 primary personality dimensions. The MPQ assesses impulsivity/control, aggression, achievement, social potency, and social closeness, to name a few.

Self-image

Despite the tendency for AN patients to be competent and accomplished, self-image in these individuals is often significantly lower than that of the normal population (Bers and Quinlan 1992). The inability to recognize innate talents and competencies may hinder the treatment progress of any patient. Several scales have been developed to assess self-image.

The Rosenberg Self-Esteem Scale (RSE; Rosenberg 1979)

The RSE is probably the most widely used self-report scale designed to measure global self-esteem (Shevlin *et al.* 1995). Respondents are asked to rate the 10 items on a four-point scale. The RSE has received support as one of the most valid, unidimensional measures of global self-esteem (Blascovich and Tomaka 1991) and data support the scale's internal consistency and temporal stability.

A multidimensional perspective of self-concept also has received empirical support (Bracken 1992).

The Multidimensional Self-Concept Scale (MSCS; Bracken 1992)

The MSCS was designed specifically for use with children and adolescents between 9 and 19 years. A 150-item self-report inventory, the MSCS is designed to assess individuals' self-perceptions across six contexts: social, competence, affect, academic, family, and physical. It has been standardized on a national sample of children in all regions of the US ($N = 2501$). Although research with the MSCS is limited, preliminary data suggests it will be a promising assessment tool.

CONCLUSION

Assessments play an integral role in the development of individualized treatment plans when working with eating disorder patients, testing hypotheses, and characterizing groups and individuals. This chapter, in advocating a multidimensional approach to assessment, has summarized a wide variety of approaches. In determining which method or instrument to use, the age of the patient, comfort level, and degree of rapport with the assessor should be taken into consideration. The evaluator should keep in mind the goal of the assessment and how the data obtained from the chosen measures can be used to develop an effective intervention (Hayes *et al.* 1987) or test the desired hypothesis.

There are limited data on the relative prevalence and clinical features of eating disorders among 'special' populations (e.g. children, elderly, males and ethnic minorities). The proportion of male AN cases is between 4 and 8% and males account for 10–15% of all bulimics in community-based studies (Carlat and Camargo 1991; Mash and Barkley 1996). Although most studies have found that males and females have similar presenting symptoms, Turnbull *et al.* (1987) found the standard tests used for measuring eating disorders would not have identified the bulimic males in their sample. Males with BN may go underdiagnosed due to clinical descriptions that have focused on young women (Schneider and Agras 1987).

Eating disorders seem to be spreading among the African–American population (Hesse-Biber 1996) and among non-Western cultures as well (Lee *et al.* 1997). Yet, there are a limited number of measures valid for use in these populations. The literature on very late onset eating disorders, while uncommon, is also sparse (Beck *et al.* 1996). Elderly patients may be more reluctant to speak about psychological issues, eating habits, or sexual issues. In older individuals, serious medical illnesses become more common (Palmer 1973) and may contribute to the weight loss (Lee *et al.* 1996). Diagnosing eating disorders in the elderly relies on subjective clinical interpretation and instruments normed on younger populations.

Eating disorders have been reported among children as young as 8 years (Lask and Bryant-Waugh 1992). Children with early onset AN may have different features compared to adults (e.g. there is a higher proportion of boys and an absence of body image distortion) (Lask and Bryant-Waugh 1992). Given the marked difference in cognitive development between children and adolescents, the use of age-specific instruments may be required. Future research might include developing instruments which are suitable for the pre-pubertal anorectic population and tools which identify children at-risk for developing eating disorders.

Readers may note the dearth of assessment instruments found that were developed specifically for use with 'special' populations. Research and theoretical discussions concerning these subgroups also remain scarce. Although the clinical features may be similar in many respects, instruments normed on female, white adolescents may not be equally valid and reliable for all groups (Carlat and Camargo 1991). In general, there seems to be a need for more culturally sensitive assessment techniques for all minority populations.

ACKNOWLEDGMENTS

Supported in part by NIH grants P30DK26687, RO1DK51716, and R29DK47526.

We gratefully acknowledge Drs Suzanne Sunday and Myles Faith for their support and valuable comments.

CLINICAL IMPLICATIONS

- Assesments play an integral role in the development of individualized treatment plans.
- The age of the patient, comfort level and degree of rapport with the assessor must be taken into consideration when designing a multi-dimensional approach to assessment.
- The evaluator should be clear on the goal of the assessment and how the data can be used to develop effective interventions.
- Available tools are rarely designed for males, as a result men go undiagnosed with our current instruments.
- Although eating disorders exist in non-western populations, in older persons and in African-American populations, there are limited numbers of valid measures available.
- Diagnoses of eating disorders in the elderly may be compounded by physical ailment and must be done with caution.
- Age specific measures must be used with children who exhibit different cognitive development than adolescents.

RESEARCH IMPLICATIONS

- More culturally sensitive assessment techniques are needed for all minority populations.
- There is a need for tools which identify children at risk for eating disorders.

REFERENCES

Alfonso, V.C. and Allison, D.B. (1993, August). Further development of the Extended Satisfaction with Life Scale. Paper presented at the American Psychological Association, Toronto.

Alfonso, V.C., Allison, D.B., Rader, D.E. and Gorman, B.S. (1996). The Extended Satisfaction with Life Scale: development and psychometric properties. *Soc. Indic. Res.*, **38**, 275–301.

Allison, D.B., Edlen-Nezin, L. and Clay-Williams, G. (1997). Obesity among African-American women: Prevalence, consequences, causes, and developing research. *Women's Health*, **3** (394), 243–274.

Altabe, M.N. and Thompson, J.K. (1992). Size estimation vs. figural ratings of body image disturbance: Relation to body dissatisfaction and eating dysfunction. *Int. J. Eat. Dis.*, **11**, 397–402.

American Psychiatric Association (1987). Diagnostic and statistical manual of mental disorders (3rd Rev. edn). Washington, DC: American Psychiatric Association.

American Psychiatric Association (1994). Diagnostic and statistical manual of mental disorders (4th edn). Washington, DC: American Psychiatric Association.

Astrup, A., Thorbek, G., Lind, J. and Isaksson, B. (1990). Prediction of 24-h energy expenditure and its components from physical characteristics and body composition in normal-weight humans. *Am. J. Clin. Nutr.*, **52**, 777–783.

Axtell, A. and Newlon, B.J. (1993). An analysis of Adlerian life themes of bulimic women. *Indiv. Psychol. J. Adlerian Theory Res. Prac.*, **49**, 58–67.

Bachrach, L.K., Katzman, D.K., Litt, I.F., Guido, D. and Marcus, R. (1991). Recovery from osteopenia in adolescent girls with anorexia nervosa. *J. Clin. Endocrinol. Metab.*, **72**, 602–606.

Beck, A.T., Rush, A.J., Shaw, B.F. and Emery, G. (1979). *Cognitive Therapy for Depression*. New York: Guilford.

Beck, D., Casper R. and Andersen, A. (1996). Truly late onset of eating disorders: A study of 11 cases averaging 60 years of age at presentation. *Int. J. Eat. Disorders,* **20**, 389–395.

Beck, A.T. and Steer, R.A. (1984). Internal consistencies of the original and revised Beck Depression Inventory. *J. Clin. Psychology*, **40**, 1365–1367.

Ben-Tovin, D.I. and Walker, M.K. (1991). Women's body attitudes: A review of measurement techniques. *Int. J. Eat. Disorders*, **10**, 155–167.

Berg, C.Z., Rapoport, J.L. and Flament, M. (1986). The Leyton Obsessional Inventory–Child Version. *J. Am. Acad. Child Adolesc. Psychiatry*, **25**, 84–91.

Bers, S.A. and Quinlan, D.M. (1992). Perceived-competence deficit in anorexia nervosa. *J. Abnorm. Psychol.*, **101**, 423–431.

Birmingham, C.L., Jones, P.J., Orphanidou, C., Bakan, R., Cleator, I.G., Goldner, E.M. and Phang, P.T. (1996). The reliability of bioelectrical impedance analysis for measuring changes in body composition of patients with anorexia nervosa. *Int. J. Eat. Dis.*, **19**, 311–315.

Blascovich, J. and Tomaka, J. (1991). Measures of self-esteem. In J.P. Robinson, P.R. Shaver and L.S. Wrightsman (eds), *Measures of Personality and Social Psychological Attitudes* (pp. 115–160). London: Academic Press.

Bouten, C.V., Westerterp, K.R., Verduin, M. and Janssen, J.D. (1994). Assessment of energy expenditure for physical activity using a triaxial accelerometer. *Med. Sci. Sports Exerc.*, **26**, 1516–1523.

Bracken, B.A. (1992). *Multidimensional Self Concept Scale*. Austin, TX: Pro-Ed.

Braun, D.L., Sunday, S.R. and Halmi, K.A. (1994). Psychiatric comorbidity in patients with eating disorders. *Psychol. Med.*, **24**, 859–867.

Brooke-Wavell, K., Jones, P.R., Norgan, N.G. and Hardman, A.E. (1995). Evaluation of near infrared interactance for assessment of subcutaneous and total body fat. *Eur. J. Clin. Nutr.*, **49**, 57–65.

Brown, T.A., Cash, T.F. and Mikulka, P.J. (1990). Attitudinal body-image assessment: Factor analysis of the Body Self-Relations Questionnaire. *J. Pers. Assess.*, **55**, 135–144.

Bruch, H. (1962). Perceptual and conceptual disturbances in anorexia nervosa. *Psychosom. Med.*, **24**, 187–194.

Bryant-Waugh, R.J., Cooper, P.J., Taylor, C.L. and Lask, B.D. (1996). The use of the Eating Disorder Examination with children: a pilot study. *Int. J. Eat. Dis.*, **19**(4), 391–397.

Buree, B., Papageorgis, D. and Solyom, L. (1984). Body image perception and preference in anorexia nervosa. *Can. J. Psychiatry*, **29**, 557–563.

Butcher, J.N., Dahlstrom, W.G., Graham, J.R., Tellegen, A. and Kaemmer, B. (1989). *Minnesota Multiphasic Personality Inventory-2 (MMPI-2): Manual for Administration and Scoring*. Minneapolis: University of Minnesota Press.

Butler, N., Newton, T. and Slade, P.D. (1988). Validation of a computerized version of the SCANS questionnaire. *Int. J. Eat. Dis.*, **8**, 239–241.

Buzzard, I.M. and Willett, W.C. (eds). (1994). First international conference on dietary assessment methods: assessing diets to improve world health. *Am. J. Clin. Nutr.*, **59**, 143S–306S.

Carlat, D.J. and Camargo, C.A. (1991). Review of bulimia nervosa in males. *Am. J. Psychiatry*, **148**, 831–841.

Cash, T.F. and Brown, T.A. (1987). Body image in anorexia and bulimia nervosa: a review of the literature. *Behav. Modif.*, **11**, 487–521.

Casper, R.C., Hedeker, D. and McClough, J.F. (1992). Personality dimensions in eating disorders and their relevance of subtyping. *J. Am. Acad. Child Adol. Psychiatry*, **31**, 830–840.

Chambers, W.J., Puig-Antich, J., Hirsch, M., Paez, P., Ambrosini, P.J., Tabrizi, M.A. and Davies, M. (1985). The assessment of affective disorders in children and adolescents by semistructured interview: test–retest reliability of the Schedule for Affective Disorders and Schizophrenia for School-Aged Children, present episode version. *Arch. Gen. Psychiatry*, **42**, 696–702.

Childress, A.C., Brewerton, T.D., Hodges, E.L. and Jarrel, M. (1993). The Kids' Eating Disorders Survey (KEDS): a study of middle school students. *J. Am. Acad. Child Adol. Psychiatry*, **32**(4), 843–850.

Coker, S. and Roger, D. (1990). The construction and preliminary validation of a scale for measuring eating disorders. *Psychosom. Res.*, **34**, 223–231.

Cooper, J. (1970). The Leyton Obsessional Inventory. *Psychol. Med.*, **1**, 48–64.

Cooper, P.J., Taylor, M.J., Cooper, Z. and Fairburn, C.G. (1987). The development and validation of the Body Shape Questionnaire. *Int. J. Eat. Disorders*, **6**, 485–494.

Cooper, P.J. and Taylor, J.J. (1988). Body image disturbance in bulimia nervosa. *Brit. J. Psychiatry*, **153**, 32–36.

Cooper, Z. and Fairburn, C.G. (1987). The Eating Disorder Examination: a semi-structured interview for the assessment of the specific psychopathology of eating disorders. *Int. J. Eat. Dis.*, **6**, 1–8.

Costello, E.J. and Angold, A. (1988). Scales to assess child and adolescent depression: Checklists, screens, and nets. *J. Am. Acad. Child Adol. Psychiatry*, **27**(6), 726–737.

Costello, A.J., Edelbrock, C.S., Dulcan, M.K., Kalas, R. and Klaric, S.H. (1984). *Development and Testing of the NIMH Diagnostic Interview Schedule for Children on a Clinical Population: Final Report*. Rockville, MD: Center for Epidemiological Studies, National Institute of Mental Health.

Crosby, L.O., Kaplan, F.S., Pertschuk, M.J. and Mullen, J.L. (1985). The effect of anorexia nervosa on bone morphometry in young women. *Clin. Orthop.*, **201**, 271–277.

Deep, A.L., Nagy, L.M., Weltzin, T.E., Rao, R. and Kaye, W.H. (1995). Premorbid onset of psychopathology in long-term recovered anorexia nervosa. *Int. J. Eat. Disorders*, **17**, 291–297.

Derogatis, L.R. (1977). *Symptom Checklist-90 Manual*. Johns Hopkins University Press, Baltimore.

DiLalla, D.L., Gottesman, I.I., Carey, G. and Vogler, G.P. (1993). Joint factor structure of the Multidimensional Personality Questionnaire and the MMPI in a psychiatric and high-risk sample. *Psychol. Assess.*, **5**, 207–215.

Fairburn, C.G. and Beglin, S.J. (1994). Assessment of eating disorders: Interview or self-report questionnaire? *Int. J. Eat. Dis.*, **16**(4), 363–370.

Fairburn, C.G. and Cooper, Z. (1993). The Eating Disorder Examination (12th edn). In C.G. Fairburn and C.T. Wilson (eds), *Binge Eating. Nature, Assessment and Treatment* (pp. 317–360). London: Guilford.

Fairburn, C.G., Norman, P.A., Welch, S.L., O'Connor, M.E., Doll, H.A. and Peveler, P.C. (1995). A prospective study of outcome in bulimia nervosa and the long-term effects of three psychological treatments. *Arch. Gen. Psychiatry*. **52**(4), 304–312.

Farrow, J.A. (1992). The adolescent male with an eating disorder. *Pediatr. Ann.*, **21**, 769–774.

Fichter, M.M., Elton, M., Engel, K., Meyer, A., Poustka, F., Mall, H and von der Heydte, S. (1989). The Structure Interview for Anorexia and Bulimia Nervosa (SIAB): development and characteristics of a (semi-)standardized instrument. In M.M. Fichter (ed.), *Bulimia Nervosa: Basic Research, Diagnosis, and Therapy* (pp. 57–70). New York: Wiley.

Fichter, M.M., Elton, M., Engel, K., Meyer, A., Mall, H. and Poustka, F. (1991). Structured Interview for Anorexia and Bulimia Nervosa (SIAB): development of a new instrument for the assessment of eating disorders. *Int. J. Eat. Dis.*, **10**, 571–592.

First, M.B., Spitzer, R.L., Gibbon, M. and Williams, J.B.W. (1996a). *Structured Clinical Interview for DSM-IV Axis I Disorders-Patient Edition (SCID-I/P, Version 2.0)*. Washington, DC: American Psychiatric Association.

First, M.B., Spitzer, R.L., Gibbon, M., Williams, J.B.W. and Benjamin, L. (1996b). *Structured Clinical Interview for DSM-IV Axis II Personality Disorders (SCID-II)*. Washington, DC: American Psychiatric Association.

Flynn, M.A., Nolph, G.B. and Krause, G. (1995). Comparison of body composition measured by total body potassium and infrared interactance. *J. Am. Coll. Nutr.*, **14**, 652–655.

Forbes, G.B. (1987). *Human Body Composition: Growth, Aging, Nutrition, and Activity.* New York: Springer-Verlag.

Formea, G.M. and Burns, G.L. (1995). Relation between the syndromes of bulimia nervosa and obsessive compulsive disorder. *J. Psychopathol. Behav. Assess.*, **17**(2), 167–176.

Fornari, V., Kaplan, M., Sandbert, D.E., Matthews, M., Skolnick, N. and Katz, J.L. (1992). Depressive and anxiety disorders in anorexia nervosa and bulimia nervosa. *Int. J. Eat. Dis.*, **12**, 21–29.

Fosson, A., Knibbs, J., Bryant-Waugh, R. and Lask, B. (1987). Early onset anorexia nervosa. *Arch. Dis. Child.*, **62**, 114–118.

Frost, R.O., Marten, P., Lahart, C. and Rosenblate, R. (1990). The dimensions of perfectionism. *Cogn. Ther. Res.*, **14**, 449–468.

Frost, R.O., Heimberg, R. G., Holt, C. S., Mattia, J. I. and Neubauer, A. L. (1993). A comparison of two measures of perfectionism. *Pers. Indiv. Differences*, **14**, 119–126.

Frost, R.O., Heimberg, R.G., Holt, C.S., Mattia, J.I. and Neubauer, L. (1993). A comparison of two measures of perfectionism. *Pers. Indiv. Diff.*, **14**, 119–126.

Fuller, N.J., Sawyer, M.B., Laskey, M.A., Paxton, P. and Elia, M. (1996). Prediction of body composition in elderly men over 75 years of age. *Ann. Hum. Biol.*, **23**, 127–147.

Garfinkel, P.E., Garner, M., Rose, J., Darby, P.L., Brandes, J.S., O'Hanlon, K. and Walsh, N. (1983). A comparison of characteristics in the families of patients with anorexia and normal controls. *Psychol. Med.*, **13**, 821–828.

Garner, D.M. (1991). *Eating Disorder Inventory-2 Manual.* Florida: Psychological Assessment Resources, Inc.

Garner, D.M. (1995). Measurement of eating disorder psychopathology. In K.D. Brownell and C.G. Fairburn (eds), *Eating Disorders and Obesity: A Comprehensive Handbook* (pp. 117–121). New York: The Guilford Press.

Garner, D.M. and Garfinkel, P.E. (1979). The Eating Attitudes Test: An index of the symptoms of anorexia nervosa. *Psychol. Med.*, **9**, 273–279.

Garner, D.M., Olmsted, M.P., Bohr, Y. and Garfinkel, P.E. (1982). The Eating Attitudes Test: Psychometric features and clinical correlates. *Psychol. Med.*, **12**, 871–878.

Garner, D.M., Olmsted, M.P. and Polivy, J. (1983). Development and validation of a multidimensional Eating Disorder Inventory for anorexia nervosa and bulimia. *Int. J. Eat. Disorders*, **2**, 15–34.

Gemperline, P.J. and Webber, L.D. (1989). Raw material testing using soft independent modeling of class analogy of near-infrared reflectance spectra. *Anal. Chem.*, **61**, 138–144.

Goodman, W.K., Price, L.H., Rasmussen, S.A., Mazure, C., Fleischmann, R., Hill, C.L., Heninger, G.R. and Charney, D.S. (1989a). The Yale–Brown Obsessive–Compulsive Scale, I: development, use, and reliability. *Arch. Gen. Psychiatry*, **46**, 1006–1011.

Goodman, W.K., Price, L.H., Rasmussen, S.A., Mazure, C., Delgado, P., Heninger, G.R. and Charney, D.S. (1989b). The Yale–Brown Obsessive–Compulsive Scale, II. Validity. *Arch. Gen. Psychiatry*, **46**, 1012–1016.

Gormally, J., Black, S., Daston, S. and Rardin, D. (1982). The assessment of binge eating severity among obese persons. *Addict. Behav.*, **7**, 47–55.

Goran, M.I. (1995). Variation in total energy expenditure in humans. *Obes. Res.*, **3** Suppl 1, 59–66.

Green, B., Shirk, S., Hanze, D. and Wanstrath, J. (1994). The Children's Global Assessment Scale in clinical practice: An empirical evaluation. *J. Acad. Child Adol. Psychiatry*, **33**(8), 1158–1164.

Gross, J., Rosen, J.C., Leitenberg, H. and Willmuth, M. (1986). Validity of Eating Attitudes Test and the Eating Disorder Inventory in bulimia nervosa. *J. Consult. Clin. Psychol.*, **54**, 875–876.

Hadigan, C.M., Walsh, B.T., Devlin, M.J., LaChausee, J.L. and Kissileff, H.R. (1992). Behavioral assessment of satiety in bulimia nervosa. *Appetite*, **18**, 233–241.

Halmi, K.A. (1994). A multimodal model for understanding and treating eating disorders. *J. Women's Health*, **3**(6), 487–493.

Halmi, K.A., Eckert, E., Marchi, P., Sampugnaro, V., Apple, R. and Cohen, J. (1991). Comorbidity of psychiatric diagnoses in anorexia nervosa. *Arch. Gen. Psychiatry*, **146**, 1585–1591.

Hannan, W.J., Wrate, R.M., Cowen, S.J. and Freeman, C.P. (1995). Body mass index as an estimate of body fat. *Int. J. Eat. Dis.*, **18**, 91–97.

Harrington, R.C. (1992). The natural history and treatment of child and adolescent affective disorders. *J. Child Psychol. Psychiatry*, **33**, 1287–1302.

Haskell, W.L., Yee, M.C., Evans, A. and Irby, P.J. (1993). Simultaneous measurement of heart rate and body motion to quantitate physical activity. *Med. Sci. Sports Exerc.*, **25**, 109–115.

Hathaway, S.R., Hawkins, R.C. and Clement, P.F. (1980). Development and construct validation of a self-report measure of binge eating tendencies. *Addict. Behav.*, **5**, 219–226.

Hathaway, S.R. and McKinley, J. (1983). The Minnesota Multiphasic Personality Inventory Manual. New York: Psychological Corporation.

Hawkins, R.C. and Clement, P.F. (1980). Development and construct validation of a self-report measure of binge eating tendencies. *Addictive Behaviors*, **5**, 219–226.

Hayes, S.C., Nelson, R.O. and Jarrett, R.B. (1987). The treatment utility of assessment: a functional approach to evaluating assessment quality. *Am. Psychol.*, **42**, 963–974.

Henderson, M. and Freeman, C.P. (1987). A self-rating scale for bulimia: 'The BITE.' *Br. J. Psychiatry*, **150**, 18–24.

Henry, C.J.K. (1994). Variability in adult body size: uses in defining the limits of human survival. In S.J. Ulijaszek and C.G.N. Mascie-Taylor (eds), *Anthropometry: The Individual and the Population* (pp. 117–129). London: Cambridge University Press.

Herjanic, B. and Reich, W. (1982). Development of a structured psychiatric interview for children: Agreement between children and parent on individual symptoms. *J. Abnorm. Child Psychol.*, **10**, 307–324.

Hesse-Biber, S. (1996). *Am I Thin Enough Yet?* New York: Oxford University Press.

Hewitt, P.L. and Flett, G.L. (1991). Perfectionism in the self and social contexts: Conceptualization, assessment, and association with psychopathology. *J. Pers. Soc. Psychol.*, **60**, 456–470.

Heymsfield, S.B., Allison, D.B., Pi-Sunyer, F.X. and Sun, Y. (1994). Columbia Respiratory Chamber-Indirect Calorimeter: a new airflow and modeling approach. *Med. Biol. Eng. Comput.*, **32**, 406–410.

Heymsfield, S.B., Allison, D.B., Heshka, S. and Person, R.N., Jr (1995a). Assessment of human body composition. In D.B. Allison (ed.), *Handbook of Assessment Methods for Eating Behaviors and Weight-Related Problems* (pp. 303–346). New York: Sage Publications.

Heymsfield, S.B., Darby, P.C., Muhlheim, L.S., Gallager, D., Wolper, C. and Allison, D.B. (1995b). The calorie: myth, measurement, and reality. *Am. J. Clin. Nutr.*, **62** 1034S–1041S.

Heyward, V.H. (1996). Evaluation of body composition. *Sports Med.*, **22**, 146–156.

Hodges, K., Kline, J., Stern, L., Cytryn, L. and McKnew, D. (1982). The development of a Child Assessment Interview for research and clinical use. *J. Abnorm. Child Psychol.*, **10**, 173–189.

Hodgson, R.J. and Rachman, S. (1977). Obsessional–compulsive complaints. *Behav. Res. Ther.*, **15**, 389–395.

Howat, P.M., Mohan, R., Champagne, C., Monlezun, C., Wozniak, P. and Bray, G.A. (1994). Validity and reliability of reported dietary intake data. *J. Am. Diet Assoc.*, **94**, 169–173.

Hsu, L.K.G. (1991). Outcome studies in patients with eating disorders. In S.M. Mirin, J.T. Gossett, and M.C. Grob (eds), *Psychiatric Treatment Advances in Outcome Research* (pp. 159–180). American Psychiatric Press, New York.

Hsu, L.K.G. and Sobkiewicz, T.A. (1991). Body image disturbance: Time to abandon the concept for eating disorders. *Int. J. Eat. Dis.*, **10**, 15–30.

Jackson, A.S., Pollock, M.L. and Ward, A. (1980). Generalized equations for predicting body density of women. *Med. Sci. Sports Exerc.*, **12**, 175–182.

Jackson, A.S. and Pollock, M.L. (1978). Generalized equations for predicting bone density of men. *Br. J. Nutr.*, **40**, 497–504.

Katz, J.L. (1987). Eating disorder and affective disorder: Relatives or merely chance acquaintances? *Compr. Psychiatry*, **28**, 220–228.

Kaye, W.H., Wiltzin, T.E., McKee, M., McConaha, C., Hansen, D. and Hsu, L.K. (1992). Laboratory assessment of feeding behavior in bulimia nervosa and healthy women: methods for developing a human-feeding laboratory. *Am. J. Clin. Nutr.*, **55**, 372–380.

Kaye, W.H., Weltzin, T.E. and Hsu, L.K.G. (1993). Relationship between anorexia nervosa and obsessive compulsive behaviors. *Psychiatric Ann.*, **23**, 365–373.

Kazdin, A.E. (1981). Assessment techniques for childhood depression. *J. Am. Acad. Child Psychiatry*, **20**, 358–375.

Kennedy, S.H., McVey, G. and Katz, R. (1990). Personality disorders in anorexia nervosa and bulimia nervosa. *J. Psychiatric Res.*, **24**, 259–269.

Kettlewell, P.W., Mizes, J.S. and Wasylyshyn, N.A. (1992). A cognitive-behavioral group treatment of bulimia. *Behav. Ther.*, **23**, 657–670.

Kissileff, H.R. (1992). Where should human eating be studied and what should be measured? *Appetite*, **19**, 61–68.

Kissileff, H.R., Walsh, B.T., Kral, J.G. and Cassidy, S.M. (1986). Laboratory studies of eating behavior in women with bulimia. *Physiol. Behav.*, **38**, 563–570.

Knibbs, J. (1993). Behaviour Therapy. In B. Lask and R. Bryant-Waugh (eds), *Childhood Onset Anorexia Nervosa and Related Eating Disorders* (pp. 163–176). London: Psychology Press.

Kovacs, M. (1985). The Children's Depression Inventory (CDI). *Psychopharmacol. Bull.*, **21**(4), 995–998.

Kovess, V. and Fournier, L. (1990). The DISSA: An abridged self-administered version of the DIS. *Soc. Psychiatry Psychiatr. Epidemiol.*, **25**, 179–186.

Kushner, R.F., Gudivaka, R and Schoeller, D.A. (1996). Clinical characteristics influencing bioeletrical impedance analysis measurements. *Am. J. Clin. Nutr.*, **64**(3 Suppl), 423S–427S.

Laessle, R.G., Kittl, S., Fichter, M., Wittchen, H.U. and Pirke, K.M. (1987). Major affective disorder in anorexia nervosa and bulimia: A descriptive diagnostic study. *Br. J. Psychiatry*, **151**, 785–789.

Laessle, R.G., Witchen, H.U., Fichter, M.M. and Pirke, K.M. (1989). The significance of subgroups of bulimia and anorexia nervosa: Lifetime frequency of psychiatric disorders. *Int. J. Eat. Dis.*, **8**, 569–574.

Laporte, D.J. (1992). Treatment response in obese binge eaters: preliminary results using a very low calorie diet (VLCD) and behavior therapy. *Addict. Behav.*, **17**, 247–257.

Lask, B. and Bryant-Waugh, R. (1992). Early-onset anorexia nervosa and related eating disorders. *J. Child Psychol. Psychiatry*, **33**(1), 281–300.

Lask, B. and Bryant-Waugh, R. (1993). *Childhood Onset Anorexia Nervosa and Related Eating Disorders*. London: Psychology Press.

Lee, S., Lee, A.M., Leung, T. and Yu, H. (1997). Psychometric properties of the Eating Disorders Inventory (EDI-1) in a nonclinical Chinese population in Hong Kong. *Int. J. Eat. Disorders*, **21**, 187–194.

Livingstone, M.B., Prentice, A.M., Coward, W.A., Ceesay, S.M., Strain, J.J., McKenna, P.G., Nevin, G.B., Barker, M.E. and Hickey, R.J. (1990). Simultaneous measurement of free-living energy expenditure by the doubly labeled water method and heart-rate monitoring. *Am. J. Clin. Nutr.*, **52**, 59–65.

Lichtman, S., Pisarska, K., Berman, E.R., Pestone, M., Dowling, H., Offenbacher, E., Weisel, H., Heshka, S., Matthews, D. and Heymsfield, S.B. (1992). Discrepancy between self-reported and actual caloric intake and exercise in obese subjects. *N. Engl. J. Med.*, **327**, 1839–1848.

Lifson, N., Gordon, G.B. and McClintock, R. (1955). Measurement of total carbon dioxide production by means of D_2O. *J. Appl. Physiol.*, **7**, 704–710.

Lohman, T.G., Roche, A.F. and Reynaldo, M. (eds) (1988). *Anthropometric Standardization Reference Manual* (pp. 131–136). Champaign: Human Kinetics Publishers.

Maloney, M.J., McGuire, J.B. and Daniels, S.R. (1988). Reliability testing of a children's version of the Eating Attitude Test. *J. Am. Acad. Child Adol. Psychiatry*, **27**(5), 541–543.

Marcus, M.D., Wing, R.R. and Hopkins, J. (1988). Obese binge eaters: Affect, cognitions, and response to behavioral weight control. *J. Consult. Clin. Psychol.*, **56**, 433–439.

Margo, J.L. (1987). *Anorexia nervosa in males: A comparison with female patients. Br. J. Psychiatry*, **151**, 80–83.

Mash, E.J. and Barkley, R.A. (1996). *Child Psychopathology*, Guilford Press, New York.

Mazure, C.M., Halmi, K.A., Sunday, S.R., Romano, F.J. and Einhorn, A.M. (1994). The Yale–Brown–Cornell Eating Disorder Scale: development, use, reliability and validity. *J. Psychiatric Res.*, **28**(5), 425–445.

Meiselman, H.L. (1992). Methodology and theory in human eating research. *Appetite*, **19**, 49–55.

Millon, T. (1982). *Millon Clinical Multiaxial Inventory Manual* (2nd edn). Minneapolis: National Computer Systems.

Mitzman, S.F., Slade, P. and Dewey, M.E. (1994). Preliminary development of a questionnaire designed to measure neurotic perfectionism in the eating disorders. *J. Clin. Psychol.*, **50**(4), 516–520.

Mizes, S. (1988). Controlled comparison of bulimics and noneating disordered controls on the MMPI-168. *Int. J. Eat. Dis*, **7**, 425–428.

Mizes, J.S. (1991). Construct validation and factor stability of the Anorectic Cognitions Questionnaire. *Addictive Behaviors,* **16**, 59–93.

Mizes, J.S. and Klesges, R.C. (1989). Validity, reliability, and factor structure of the Anorectic Cognitions Questionnaire. *Addict. Behav.*, **14**, 589–594.

Morey, L.C. and Kurtz, J.E. (1995). Assessment of general personality and psychopathology among persons with eating and weight-related concerns. In D.B. Allison (ed.), *Handbook of Assessment Methods for Eating Behaviors and Weight-Related Problems* (pp. 1–22). New York: Sage Publications.

Murgatroyd, P.R., Shetty, P.S. and Prentice, A.M. (1993). Techniques for the measurement of human energy expenditure: a practical guide. *Int. Obes. Related Metabol. Dis.*, **17**, 549–568.

National Center for Health Statistics (1996). *NHANES III Anthropometric Procedures Video* (Stock Number 017-022-0133505). Hyattsville, MD: Government Printing Office.

Newton, J.R., Freeman, C.P., Hannan, W.J. and Cowen, S. (1993). Osteoporosis and normal weight bulimia nervosa–which patients are at risk? *J. Psychosom. Res.*, **37**, 239–247.

Norman, D.K. and Herzog, D.B. (1983). Bulimia, anorexia nervosa, and anorexia nervosa with bulimia: A comparative analysis of MMPI profiles. *Int. J. Eat. Dis.*, **2**, 43–52.

Offer, D., Ostrov, E. and Howard, K.I. (1981). *The Adolescent: A Psychological Self-Portrait*. New York: Basic Books.

Ordman, A.M. and Kirschenbaum, D.S. (1986). Bulimia: assessment of eating, psychological adjustment, and familial characteristics. *Int. J. Eat. Dis.*, **5**, 865–878.

Paffenbarger, R.S., Blair, S.N., Lee, I.M. and Hyde, R.T. (1993). Measurement of physical activity to assess health effects in free-living populations. *Med. Sci. Sports Exerc.*, **25**, 60–70.

Palmer, E. (1973). Benign chronic gastric ulcer and weight loss. *Am. Fam. Physician*, **8**, 109–111.

Parker, W.D. and Stumpf, H. (1995). An examination of the Multidimensional Perfectionism Scale with a sample of academically talented children. *J. Psychoed. Assess.*, **13**, 372–383.

Parmer, J.C. (1991). Bulimia and object relations: MMPI and Rorschach variables. *J. Pers. Assess.*, **56**, 266–276.

Patton, J.H., Stanford, M.S. and Barratt, E.S. (1995). Factor structure of the Barratt Impulsiveness Scale. *J. Clin. Psychol.*, **51**, 768–774.

Penner, L.A., Thompson, J.K. and Coovert, D.L. (1991). Size estimation among anorexics: much ado about very little? *J. Ab. Psychol.*, **100**, 90–93.

Petersen, A.C., Schulenberg, J.E., Abramowitz, R.H., Offer, D. and Jarcho, H.D. (1984). A self-image questionnaire for young adolescents (SIQYA): reliability and validity studies. *J. Youth Adol.*, **13**, 93–111.

Pierson, R.N., Jr, Lin, D.H.Y. and Phillips, R.A. (1974). Total-body potassium in health: effects of age, sex, height, and fat. *Am. J. Physiol.*, **226**, 106–121.

Pike, K.M., Loeb, K. and Walsh, B.T. (1995). Binge eating and purging. In D.B. Allison (ed.), *Handbook of Assessment Methods for Eating Behaviors and Weight-Related Problems* (pp. 303–346). New York: Sage Publications.

Powell, A.D. and Kahn, A.S. (1995). Racial differences in women's desires to be thin. *Int. J. Eat. Dis.*, **17**, 191–195.

Powers, P.S. and Spratt, E.G. (1994). Males and females with eating disorders. *Eat. Dis.: J. Treatm. Prev.*, **2**, 197–213.

Pryor, T. and Wiederman, N.W. (1996). Use of the MMPI-2 in the outpatient assessment of women with anorexia nervosa or bulimia nervosa. *J. Pers. Assess.*, **66**(2), 363–373.

Racette, S.B., Schoeller, D.A. and Kushner, R.F. (1995). Comparison of heart rate and physical activity recall with doubly labeled water in obese women. *Med. Sci. Sports Exerc.*, **27**, 126–133.

Retzlaff, P. and Gilbertini, M. (1987). Factor structure of the MCMI basic personality scales and common-item artifact. *J. Pers. Assess.*, **51**, 588–594.

Richter, M.A., Cox, B.J. and Direnfeld, D.M. (1994). A comparison of three assessment instruments for obsessive–compulsive symptoms. *J. Behav. Ther. Exper. Psychiatry*, **25**, 143–147.

Robins, L.N., Helzer, J.E., Cottler, L.B. and Goldring, E. (1989). *NIMH Diagnostic Interview Schedule, Version III-Revised.* St. Louis, MO: Washington School of Medicine.

Robins, L.N., Cottler, L.B., and Keating, S. (1991). *NIMH Diagnostic Interview Schedule, Version III-Revised (DIS-III-R): Question-by-question specifications.* Washington University School of Medicine, St. Louis, MO.

Roche, A.F., Heymsfield, S.B. and Lohman, T.G. (1996). *Human Body Composition.* USA: Human Kinetics.

Rogers, R. (1995). *Diagnostic and Structured Interviewing: A Handbook for Psychologists.* USA: Psychological Assessment Resources, Inc.

Rosen, J.C., Srebnik, D., Saltzberg, E. and Wendt, S. (1991). Development of a body image avoidance questionnaire. *Psychol. Assess.: J. Consult. Clin. Psychol.*, **3**, 32–37.

Rosen, J.C., Reiter, J. and Orosan, P. (1995). Assessment of body image in eating disorders with the Body Dysmorphic Disorder Examination. *Behav. Res. Ther.*, **33**(1), 77–84.

Rosenbaum, M., Ravussin, E., Matthews, D.E., Gilker, C., Ferraro, R., Heymsfield, S.B., Hirsch, J. and Leibel, R.L. (1996). A comparative study of different means of assessing long-term energy expenditure in humans. *Am. J. Physiol.*, **270**, R496–504.

Rosenberg, M. (1979). *Conceiving the Self.* New York: Basic Books.

Russell, J.D., Mira, M., Allen, B.J., Stewart, P.M., Vizzard, J., Arthur, B. and Beumont, P.J. (1994). Protein repletion and treatment in anorexia nervosa. *Am. J. Clin. Nutr.*, **60**, 794–795.

Salisbury, J.J., Levine, A.S., Crow, S.J. and Mitchell, J.E. (1995). Refeeding, metabolic rate, and weight gain in anorexia nervosa: a review. *Int. J. Eat. Dis.*, **17**, 337–345.

Sansone, R.A., Fine, M.A., Seufere, S. and Bovenzi, J. (1989). The prevalence of borderline personality symptomatology among women with eating disorders. *J. Clin. Psychol.*, **45**, 603–610.

Schebendach, J., Golden, N.H., Jacobson, M.S., *et al.* (1995). Indirect calorimetry in the nutritional management of eating disorders. *Int. J. Eat. Dis.*, **17**, 59–66.

Schlundt, D.G. and Johnson, W.G. (1990). *Eating Disorders; Assessment and Treatment.* Boston: Allyn and Bacon.

Schneider, J.A. and Agras, W.S. (1987). Bulimia in males: A matched comparison with females. *Int. J. Eat. Dis.*, **2**, 235–242.

Schneider, F.R., Johnson, J., Hornig, C.D., Liebowitz, M.R. and Weissman, M.M. (1992). Social phobia: comorbidity and morbidity in an epidemiologic sample. *Arch. Gen. Psychiatry*, **1**, 282–288.

Schoeller, D.A. (1988). Measurement of energy expenditure in free-living humans by using doubly labeled water. *J. Nutr.*, **118**, 1278–1289.

Schoeller, D.A. (1990). How accurate is self-reported dietary energy intake? *Nutr. Rev.*, **48**, 373–379.

Schoeller, D.A. (1995). Limitations in the assessment of dietary energy intake by self-report. *Metab.: Clin. Exper.*, **44**, 18–22.

Schoeller, D.A. and Racette, S.B. (1990). A review of field techniques for the assessment of energy expenditure. *J. Nutr.*, **120** Suppl 11, 1492–1495.

Schoeller, D.A., Ravussin, E., Schutz, Y., Acheson, K.J., Baertschi, P. and Jequier, E. (1986). Energy expenditure by doubly labeled water: validation in humans and proposed calculation. *Am. J. Physiol.*, **250**, R823–R830.

Schreiner, P.J., Pitkaniemi, J., Pekkanen, J. and Salomaa, V.V. (1995). Reliability of near-infrared interactance body fat assessment relative to standard anthropometric techniques. *J. Clin. Epidemiol.*, **48**, 1361–1367.

Scott, R.L. and Baroffio, J.R. (1986). An MMPI analysis of similarities and differences in three classifications of eating disorders: anorexia nervosa, bulimia, and morbid obesity. *J. Clin. Psychol.*, **42**, 708–713.

Seale, J.L. (1995). Energy expenditure measurements in relation to energy requirements. *Am. J. Clin. Nutr.*, **62**, 1042S–1046S.

Segal, D.L., Hersen, M. and Van Hasselt, V.B. (1994). Reliability of the Structured Clinical Interview for DSM-III-R: An evaluative review. *Compr. Psychiatry*, **35**, 316–327.

Shaffer, D., Gould, M.S., Brasic, J., Ambrosini, P., Fisher, P., Bird, H. and Aluwahlia, S. (1983). A Children's Global Assessment Scale (CGAS). *Arch. Gen. Psychiatry*, **40**, 1228–1231.

Shelton, M.L. and Klesges, R.C. (1995). Measures of physical activity and exercise. In Allison, D.B. (ed.), *Handbook of Assessment Methods for Eating Behaviors and Weight-Related Problems* (pp. 303–346). New York: Sage Publications.

Sherman, D.K., Iacono, W.G. and Donnelly, J.M. (1995). Development and validation of body rating scales for adolescent females. *Int. J. Eat. Disorders,* **18**, 327–333.

Shevlin, M.E., Bunting, B.P. and Lewis, C.A. (1995). Confirmatory factor analysis of the Rosenberg Self-Esteem Scale. *Psychol. Rep.*, **76**, 707–710.

Shore, R.A. and Porter, J.E. (1990). Normative and reliability data for 11 to 18 years olds on the Eating Disorder Inventory. *Int. J. Eat. Dis.*, **9**, 201–207.

Sichieri, R., Everhart, J.E. and Hubbard, V.S. (1991). Relative weight classifications in the assessment of underweight and overweight in the United States. *Int. J. Obes.*, **16**, 303–312.

Siegel, J.H., Hardoff, D., Golden, N.H. and Shenker, I.R. (1995). Medical complications in male adolescents with anorexia nervosa. *J. Adol. Health*, **16**, 448–453.

Skodol, A.E., Oldham, J.M., Hyler, S.E., Kellman, H.D., Doidge, N. and Davies, M. (1993). Comorbidity of DSM-III-R eating disorders and personality disorders. *Int. J. Eat. Dis.*, **14**, 403–416.

Slade, P.D. (1985). A review of body-image studies in anorexia nervosa and bulimia nervosa. *J. Psychiatric Res.*, **19**, 255–265.

Slade, P.D., Phil, M. and Dewey, M.E. (1986). Development and preliminary validation of SCANS: A screening instrument for identifying individuals at risk for developing anorexia and bulimia nervosa. *Int. J. Eat. Dis.*, **5**(3), 517–538.

Smith, M.C. and Thelen, M.H. (1984). Development and validation of a test for bulimia. *J. Consult. Clin. Psychology*, **52**, 863–872.

Spitzer, R.L., Yanovski, S.Z., and Marcus, M.D. (1993). *The Questionnaire on Eating and Weight Patterns-Revised (QEWP-R, 1993)*. (Available from the New York State Psychiatric Institute, 722 West 168th Street, New York, NY 10032.)

Stanford, M.S. and Barratt, E.S. (1995). Factor structure of the Barratt Impulsiveness Scale. *J. Clin. Psychol.*, **51**(6), 768–774.

Steinkamp, R.C., Cohen, N.L., Siri, S.W.E., Sargent, T.W. and Walsh, H.E. (1965). Measures of body fat and related factors in normal adults: I. Introduction and methodology. *J. Chronic Dis.*, **18**, 1279–1289.

Stunkard, A., Sorenson, T. and Schlusinger, F. (1983). Use of the Danish Adoption Register for the study of obesity and thinness. In S. Kety, L.P. Rowland, R.L. Sidman and S.W. Matthysse (eds), *The Genetics of Neurological and Psychiatric Disorders* (pp. 115–120). New York: Raven.

Strober, M. (1980). Personality and symptomatological features in young, nonchronic anorexia nervosa patients. *J. Psychosom. Res.*, **24**, 353–359.

Sullivan, P.F. (1995). Mortality in anorexia nervosa. *Am. J. Psychiatry*, **152**(7), 1073–1074.

Sunday, S.R., Halmi, K.A. and Einhorn, A. (1995). The Yale–Brown–Cornell Eating Disorder Scale: A new scale to assess eating disorder symptomatology. *Int. J. Eat. Dis.*, **18**(3), 237–245.

Sunday, S.R. and Halmi, K.A. (1996). Micro- and macroanalyses of patterns within a meal in anorexia and bulimia nervosa. *Appetite*, **26**, 21–36.

Telegen, A. (1982). *Brief manual for the Multidimensional Personality Questionnaire*. Unpublished manuscript, University of Minnesota.

Thelen, M.H., Farmer, J., Wonderlich, S. and Smith, M. (1991). A revision of the Bulimia Test: The BULIT-R. *Psychol. Assess.*, **3**, 119–124.

Thompson, J.K. (1990). *Body Image Disturbance: Assessment and Treatment*. New Jersey: Pergamon.

Thompson, J.K. (1992). Body image: Extent of disturbance, associated features, theoretical models, assessment methodologies, intervention strategies, and a proposal for a new DSM-IV diagnostic category—body image disorder. In M. Hersa, R.M. Eisler, and P.M. Miller (eds), *Progress in Behavior Modification* (pp. 3–54). Illinois: Sycamore.

Thompson, J.K. (1995). Assessment of body image. In D.B. Allison (ed.), *Handbook of Assessment Methods for Eating Behaviors and Weight-Related Problems* (pp. 119–148). New York: Sage Publications.

Thompson, J.K. and Altabe, M.N. (1991). Psychometric qualities of the Figure Rating Scale. *Int. J. Eat. Disorders*, **10**, 615–619.

Tisdale, M.J., Pendleton, L. and Marler, M.R. (1990). MCMI characteristics of DSM-III-R bulimics. *J. Pers. Assess.*, **55**, 477–483.

Turnbull, J.D., Freeman, C.P.L., Barry, F. *et al.* (1987). Physical and psychological characteristics of five male bulimics. *Brit. J. Psychiatr.*, **150**, 25–29.

Vacc, N.A. and Rhyne, M. (1987). The Eating Attitudes Test: Development of an adapted language form for children. *Percept. Mot. Skills*, **65**, 335–336.

Veron-Guidry, S. and Williamson, D.A. (1996). Development of a body image assessment procedure for children and adolescents. *Int. J. Eat. Dis.*, **20**(3), 287–293.

Vitousek, K. and Manke, F. (1994). Personality variables and disorders in anorexia nervosa and bulimia nervosa. *J. Ab. Psychol.*, **103**(1), 137–147.

Vitousek, K.B., Daly, J. and Heiser, C. (1991). Reconstructing the internal world of the eating-disordered individual: overcoming distortion in self-report. *Int. J. Eat. Dis.*, **10**, 647–666.

Waller, G. (1992). Bulimic attitudes in different disorders: Clinical utility of the BITE. *Int. J. Eat. Dis.*, **11**, 73–78.

Wang, J., Pierson, R.N. and Heymsfield, S.B. (1992). The five level model: A new approach to organizing body composition research. *Am. J. Clin. Nutr.*, **56**, 19–28.

Weiss, S.R. and Ebert, M.H. (1983). Psychological and behavioral characteristics of normal-weight bulimics and normal-weight controls. *Psychosom. Med.*, **45**, 293–303.

Weltzin, T.E., Hsu, L.K., Pollice, C. and Kaye, W.H. (1991). Feeding patterns in bulimia nervosa. *Biol. Psychiatry*, **30**, 1093–1110.

Westerterp-Plantenga, M.S., Fredrix, E.W.H.M. and Steffens, A.B. (eds) (1994). *Food Intake and Energy Expenditure*. Boca Raton, FL: CRC Press.

Whitaker, A., Davies, M., Shaffer, D., Johnson, J., Abrams, S., Walsh, B.T. and Kalikow, K. (1989). The struggle to be thin: A survey of anorexic and bulimic symptoms in a non-referred adolescent population. *Psychol. Med.*, **19**, 143–163.

Williams, D.P., Going, S.B., Milliken, L.A., Hall, M.C. and Lohman, T.G. (1995). Practical techniques for assessing body composition in middle-aged and older adults. *Med. Sci. Sports Exerc.*, **27**, 776–783.

Williams, G.J., Power, K.G., Miller, H.R., Freeman, C.P., Yellowlees, A., Dowds, T., Walker, M. and Parry-Jones, W.L. (1994). Development and validation of the Stirling Eating Disorder Scales. *Int. J. Eat. Dis.*, **16**, 35–43.

Williamson, D.A. (1990). *Assessment of Eating Disorders*. New York: Pergamon.

Williamson, D.A., Kelley, M.L., Davis, C.J., Ruggiero, L. and Blouin, D. (1985). Psychopathology of eating disorders: a controlled comparison of bulimic, obese, and normal subjects. *J. Consult. Clin. Psychol.*, **53**, 161–166.

Williamson, D.A., Davis, C.J., Goreczny, A.J., Bennett, S.M. and Watkins, P.C. (1989a). The Eating Questionnaire-Revised: a new symptom checklist for bulimia. In P.A. Keller and L.G. Ritt (eds), *Innovations in Clinical Practice: A Sourcebook* (pp. 321–326). Florida: Professional Resource Exchange, Inc.

Williamson, D.A., Davis, C.J., Bennett, S.M., Goreczny, A.J. and Gleaves, D.H. (1989b). Development of a simple procedure for body image assessment. *Behav. Assess.*, **11**, 433–446.

Williamson, D.A., Cubic, B.A. and Gleaves, D.H. (1993). Equivalence of body image disturbances in anorexia and bulimia nervosa. *J. Ab. Psychol.*, **102**, 1–4.

Wilson, G.T. (1991). The addiction model of eating disorders: a critical analysis. *Adv. Behav. Res. Ther.*, **13**, 27–72.

Wilson, G.T., Heffernan, K. and Black, C.M. (1996). Eating disorders. In E.J. Mash and R.A. Barkley (eds), *Child Psychopathology* (pp. 541–571). New York: The Guilford Press.

Wolper, C., Heshka, S. and Heymsfield, S.B. (1995). Measuring food intake: an overview. In D.B. Allison (ed.), *Handbook of Assessment Methods for Eating Behaviors and Weight-Related Problems* (pp. 215–240). New York: Sage Publications.

Wood, K.C., Becker, J.A. and Thompson, J.K. (1993). Reliability of body image assessment for young children (ages 8–10). Unpublished manuscript.

Yanovski, S.Z. (1993). Binge eating disorder: Current knowledge and future directions. *Obes. Res.*, **1**, 308–324.

Yanovski, S.Z., Hubbard, V.S., Lukaski, H.C. and Heymsfield, S.B. (1996). Introduction. *Am. J. Clin. Nutr.*, **64**, 387S.

Yasukawa, M., Horvath, S.M., Oishi, K., Kimura, M., Williams, R. and Maeshima, T. (1995). Total body fat estimations by near-infrared interactance, A-mode ultrasound, and underwater weighing. *Appl. Hum. Sci.*, **14**, 183–189.

4 Epidemiology

D. VAN HOEKEN[1], A. R. LUCAS[2] and H. W. HOEK[1]
[1] *The Hague Psychiatric Institute, The Hague, The Netherlands and* [2] *Mayo Clinic, Rochester, MN, USA*

INTRODUCTION

Epidemiology is the study of the distribution of diseases or disorders in populations, searching for factors that influence the frequency of disease. Populations are groups defined by a common feature, and the features distinguishing a population with a higher disease rate from another with a lower disease rate often give important clues as to aetiology. Furthermore, epidemiological information facilitates treatment planning on the basis of the community, rather than the individual. The purposes of epidemiological studies can be summarized as follows (Weissman 1987; Shepherd 1991):

- to describe the occurrence of disorders
- to determine the factors which are associated with the onset of the disorders
- to control the distribution of disorders.

Epidemiological research of eating disorders is still at the stage of determining the incidence and prevalence rates of the disorders within populations and comparing the rates among different population groups (Hsu 1990). Incidence and prevalence rates are the basic measures of disease frequency. The incidence is defined as the number of new cases in the population in a specified period of time (usually 1 year), and is commonly expressed as the rate per 100 000 of the population per year. The rates cited as incidence rates of eating disorders do not represent the onset of an eating disorder, but only report the moment of detection. The prevalence is defined as the total number of cases in the population at a specific point in time. The 1-year period prevalence rate is the (point) prevalence rate per 100 000 of the population + the annual incidence rate. The prevalence rate is most useful for planning facilities, as it indicates the demand for care. Differences in prevalence rates between groups suggest possible aetiological differences. However, prevalent cases reflect the disease itself as well as all concomitants it has created in the individual since the inception of the disease. Incidence rate differences between groups are much better, less confounding clues to aetiology/risk factors than prevalence rate differences, because they refer to recently started disease (Eaton *et al.* 1995). Rates are 'crude' if they have not been adjusted for other variables, such as age or sex.

Neurobiology in the Treatment of Eating Disorders.
Edited by H.W. Hoek, J.L. Treasure and M.A. Katzman.

Szmukler (1985) and Hoek (1993) provide thorough overviews of the methodological problems of epidemiological studies of eating disorders. Incidence and prevalence rates are derived from two integers, a numerator and a denominator. The study of these usually poses a number of problems. For the numerator the problem concerns the definition of what constitutes a 'case', while for the denominator the problem lies in the selection of a population or in drawing a probability sample of it, such that each member of the population has an equal chance of being included.

Regarding the definition of a case, the issues are the choice of a classification system and the choice of a detection method. Almost all recent studies have defined a case as fulfilling diagnostic criteria defined by some widely accepted classification system, such as the Diagnostic and Statistic Manual of Mental Disorders (DSM) (e.g. American Psychiatric Association (APA) 1994) or the International Classification of Diseases (ICD) (e.g. World Health Organization (WHO) 1995). These criteria achieve a reasonable degree of precision for clinical cases, but will exclude subclinical cases, which are important for the study of possible causal factors. Sometimes statistics are provided for both strictly defined as well as broadly defined cases. The criteria are not absolute but reached by consensus, and they are subject to change over time. Until recently, most studies used the DSM-III-R (APA 1987) criteria for the definition of a case of anorexia nervosa or bulimia nervosa. More recent studies use the DSM-IV (APA 1994) criteria for the definition of a case of eating disorder, sometimes including cases of binge eating disorder (BED) according to the newly proposed criteria. After the scene for case definition has been set by choosing a particular classification system, the choices of the specific case finding method and instrument(s) ultimately determine case detection and thus case definition.

Concerning the selection of a population, problems specific to the eating disorders are their low prevalence and the tendency of eating disorder subjects to conceal their illness and avoid professional help (Hsu 1996). These make it necessary to study a very large number of subjects from the general population in order to reach enough differential power for the cases. It is generally accepted among researchers that a face to face clinical interview is required to elicit reliably the main features of an eating disorder (Fairburn and Beglin 1990). However, it is practically impossible to use such a highly time- and cost-intensive method for screening a large population, particularly so for the study of incidence, which requires longitudinal monitoring of a population. Several strategies have been used to circumvent this problem, in particular case register and other record-based studies, two-stage studies, and studies of special populations.

Case register and other (mainly hospital-) record-based studies rely on external data entry to estimate the prevalence or incidence of an eating disorder. The limitations of these record-based studies are considerable (Hsu 1990, 1996). Case registers include only patients who have come into the mental health care system. The validity of their findings depends on their diagnostic accuracy and coverage of cases. They fail to detect those in care of non-psychiatric systems. To overcome the latter problem, most studies also use other sources for case detection, such as hospital records or information from caregivers. This still leaves out those who have never entered the health care system or have not been diagnosed as having an eating disorder. Hospital record studies report only on in-patients. Patients who only receive out-patient care will therefore be missed. Furthermore, treated cases are not representative of all cases. A proportion of mild cases or cases with 'only' one disease would not seek treatment. Thus, there is a tendency for those in treatment to have comorbid conditions. This tendency is called Berkson's bias (Eaton *et al.* 1995). It has been shown to be true for bulimia nervosa (Fairburn *et al.* 1996). Findings from case registers/hospital records are of more value to treatment planning than for generating hypotheses on the aetiology of disease, because there is no direct access to the subjects and the additional information that is available is usually limited and of a demographic nature only.

Two-stage studies refer to a study design in which first a large population is screened for the likelihood of an eating disorder by means of a screening questionnaire, identifying an at-risk population (first stage), after which definite cases are established using a personal interview on subjects from this at-risk population as well as on a randomly selected sample of those not at risk (second stage) (Williams *et al.* 1980). Methodological problems of two-stage studies are poor response rates to, and selectivity/specificity of, the screening instrument, and the often restricted size of the interviewed groups, particularly of those not at risk (Fairburn and Beglin 1990). The limitations of prevalence studies which only use a questionnaire, are considerable, even when they use a test of high sensitivity and specificity. Because of the low prevalence of eating disorders in the general population, a test will be of low efficiency in terms of its 'positive predictive value', that is, the proportion of those identified as cases by the test, who turn out to be true cases, will be small (Williams *et al.* 1982).

Studies of special populations address a particular segment of the general population, selected *a priori* for being at increased risk, such as female high school/university students, athletes or a particular age cohort. The major methodological problem associated with this type of study is the specificity of the findings to the selected subset of the general population.

Both two-stage studies and studies of special populations have the potential for providing information relevant to aetiology, because there is direct access to the subjects and the availability of additional information is not restricted by a predetermined registration system.

The epidemiology of eating disorders has been reviewed before (Consoli and Jeammet 1984; Pyle 1985; Szmukler 1985; Connors and Johnson 1987; Hsu 1990, 1996; Fairburn and Beglin 1990; Hoek 1993). In the great majority of studies younger female patients are the main or even sole focus of attention. The reason for this is that they constitute over 90% of all eating disorder cases. In this chapter, attention will also be paid to epidemiological information on less typical eating disorder cases, such as males and older patients. This chapter is based on the 1993 review by Hoek and will update this and the other reviews.

THE DISTRIBUTION OF EATING DISORDERS

In the following paragraphs only studies using strict definitions of anorexia nervosa or bulimia nervosa (meeting Russell, DSM, or ICD criteria for eating disorders) are discussed. In DSM-IV (APA 1994) a third diagnostic category was added to anorexia nervosa and bulimia nervosa: the eating disorders-not otherwise specified (ED-NOS). This is a mixed category, including a heterogeneity of patients who do not meet all criteria for anorexia nervosa or bulimia nervosa but who do have symptoms severe enough to qualify them as having a clinically significant eating disorder. This heterogeneity makes it an unattractive category for the search on possible aetiological factors, and it is rarely included in incidence studies. In DSM-IV a provision was made for a separate possible eating disorder category, the binge eating disorder (BED). It is felt that these often obese patients have treatment needs that require more than the 'mere' treatment of overweight by dietary measures, coming close to those for bulimia nervosa. Because this 'category' is becoming more known, clinics are faced with a new surge of patients, for which they have yet neither standard treatment programmes nor treatment capacity. Because of the recency and mixed nature of the diagnostic (provisional) categories, no reliable epidemiological information is available on the eating disorders not-otherwise-specified and binge eating disorder as yet. Therefore this overview is restricted to studies of the incidence and prevalence of anorexia nervosa and bulimia nervosa.

INCIDENCE OF EATING DISORDERS

Because the incidence rates of eating disorders are low, and the detection of an eating disorder case is highly time and cost intensive, studies on their incidence in the general population are lacking. Therefore, the incidence rates have been based on cases presenting to health care.

Anorexia nervosa

The incidence studies of anorexia nervosa have used psychiatric case registers (Kendell *et al.* 1973; Jones *et al.* 1980; Hoek and Brook 1985; Szmukler *et al.* 1986; Møller-Madsen and Nystrup 1992), medical records of hospitals in a circumscribed area (Theander 1970; Willi *et al.* 1990), a registration by general practitioners (Hoek 1991; Hoek *et al.* 1995; Turnbull *et al.* 1996), or medical records of health care providers in a community (Lucas *et al.* 1991).

Psychiatric case registers contain cases treated in mental health care settings (in- and outpatients), while medical record studies identify in-patients of hospitals, including those in psychiatric, medical and paediatric departments. General practitioner registers contain incidence and prevalence information on those patients that consulted with, and were identified as eating disordered, by their GP.

Table 4.1 summarizes the results of the studies on the incidence of anorexia nervosa that report overall rates for a general population sample. Available inci-

Table 4.1. Incidence of anorexia nervosa per year per 100 000 population

Study	Region	Source	Period	Incidence
Theander 1970	Southern Sweden	Hospital records	1931–1940	0.10
			1941–1950	0.20
			1951–1960	0.45
			(1931–1960)	0.24
Jones *et al.* 1980	Monroe County	Case register + hospital records	1960–1969	0.37
			1970–1976	0.64
Willi *et al.* 1990	Zurich	Hospital records	1956–1958	0.38
			1963–1965	0.55
			1973–1975	1.12
			1983–1985	1.43
Kendell *et al.* 1973	NE Scotland	Case register	1960–1969	1.60
Szmukler *et al.* 1986	NE Scotland	Case register	1978–1982	4.06
Kendell *et al.* 1973	Camberwell	Case register	1965–1971	0.66
Hoek and Brook 1985	Assen	Case register	1974–1982	5.0
Møller-Madsen and Nystrup 1992	Denmark	Case-register	1970	0.42
			1988	1.36
			1989	1.17
Lucas *et al.* 1991	Rochester, MN	Medical records	1935–1984	8.2
Hoek *et al.* 1995	Netherlands	General practitioners	1985–1989	8.1
Turnbull *et al.* 1996	England, Wales	General practitioners	1993	4.2

dence rate information on subgroups of the populations (e.g. young women) will be given in the text. The overall rates vary considerably, ranging from 0.10 in a hospital-records-based study in Sweden in the 1930s to 8.2 in a medical-records-based study in the USA, both per 100 000 population per year.

The rate of 8.2 per 100 000 population per year was found in the Mayo Clinic study by Lucas *et al.* (1991), covering the period of 1935–1984. For females aged 15–19 years they report a rate of 69.4 per 100 000 population per year. They had access to all medical records of health care providers in a community, whether these represented office visits or episodes of hospitalization, and they included the records of general practitioners and specialists in the community. Furthermore, Lucas and colleagues not only studied the registered incidence of diagnosed anorexia nervosa, but also the possible non-detected cases. To this purpose, not only records of patients with a clinical diagnosis of anorexia nervosa were screened, but records mentioning amenorrhoea, oligomenorrhoea, starvation, weight loss or other related diagnostic terms as well.

Hoek *et al.* (1995) and Turnbull *et al.* (1996) have studied the incidence at the primary care level. In the study by Hoek and colleagues, general practitioners using DSM-III-R criteria have recorded the rate of eating disorders in a large (1985: $N = 151\,781$), representative sample (1.1%) of the Dutch population. The incidence rate of anorexia nervosa was 8.1 during the period 1985–1989, with a highest rate of 79.6 for females aged 15 to 19 years (Hoek *et al.* 1995). During this period 63% of the incidence cases were referred to mental health care, accounting for an incidence rate of anorexia nervosa in mental health care of 5.1 per year per 100 000 population. Turnbull and colleagues searched the General Practice Research Database (GPRD), covering 550 general practitioners and 4 million patients, for first diagnoses of anorexia nervosa or bulimia nervosa in the period 1988–1993. The type of classification system used by the general practitioners working with the GPRD was not given, but a randomly selected subset of cases was checked with DSM-IV criteria, from which estimates for adjusted incidence rates were made. They found a raw overall age- and sex-adjusted incidence rate of 4.2 per 100 000 population in 1993, and an estimated incidence rate adjusted for false positives (minus 40%) of 2.5. For females 10–19 years they reported an incidence of 34.1 per 100 000 population per year.

Although it is clear that eating disorders occur in men as well as in women, few studies report incidence rates for males. This makes it difficult to evaluate the size of the problem in males. The majority of male incidence rates reported was below 0.5 per 100 000 population per year (Jones *et al.* 1980: 0.09; Nielsen 1990: 0.17; Turnbull *et al.* 1996: 0.2), with the exception of Lucas *et al.* (1991) who reported a male incidence rate of 1.8. The rather high overall and sex-specific rates found by Lucas and colleagues may be the result of their particular case finding method, in which medical records including those not detected as eating disorder cases were screened on a number of diagnostic terms. Making eating disorder diagnoses on records of patients not detected as such could indicate that medical specialists not working in the field of eating disorders underdiagnose eating disorders, and this could particularly be the case in males. In those studies where it is reported, the female to male ratio is around 11 : 1 (Szmukler *et al.* 1986: 12 : 1; Nielsen 1990: 11.8 : 1; Lucas *et al.* 1991: 8.1 : 1; Hoek *et al.* 1995: 10.5 : 1), with the exception of Turnbull *et al.* (1996), who reported a ratio of 39.5 : 1. The surprisingly high ratio found by Turnbull and colleagues may have a number of causes: it may be that general practitioners do not recognize male eating disorder patients as well as female patients and/or male patients may consult their general practitioners less often, or it may be an artefact of the low number of males detected as a case. Turnbull and colleagues detected only three male cases. Had four been found, the ratio would have been 23.8 : 1; had they found five, the ratio would have been 19.0 : 1, and so on.

The majority of the eating disorder patients are young females. Few studies report age-specific rates beyond the age of 35. As was the case for males, for older patients too this makes it difficult to evaluate the size of the problem. In the study by Nielsen (1990) only 3% of the women with a first psychiatric admission for anorexia nervosa were 40 or more years old. Jörgensen (1992) gives an incidence rate of 0.6 per 100 000 population per year for women aged 25 and over. On an overall female rate of 14.7 per 100 000 population per year, Hoek *et al.* (1995) report a detection rate in primary care of 2.3 for women aged 35 and over. Turnbull *et al.* (1996) report an incidence rate of 0.4 for persons (male and female) aged 40 and over versus an overall rate of 4.2. On an overall incidence rate of 8.2 per 100 000 population per year, Lucas *et al.* (1991) report a rate of 3.2 for 40–49-year-olds, 1.1 for 50–59-year-olds, and 0.0 for people aged 60 and over.

There has been considerable debate whether the incidence of eating disorders is—or has been—on the rise (Williams and King 1987; Willi *et al.* 1990; Hsu 1990, 1996; Lucas *et al.* 1991; Møller-Madsen and Nystrup 1992; Hoek 1993, 1995; Fombonne 1995a,b, 1996; Munk-Jørgensen *et al.* 1995). Figure 4.1 shows a graphic representation of the incidence of anorexia nervosa registered in mental health care and hospitals as given in the studies from Table 4.1, with the exception of the studies by Lucas *et al.* (1991) and Turnbull *et al.* (1996). The latter were excluded because they used more extensive case-finding methods, which would contaminate the comparison. For the study by Hoek *et al.* (1995), the incidence was used of patients detected in primary care that were referred to mental health care. Several of the studies cover a period of more than one year. In the figure, the mid-point of the study-period is chosen to depict the average 1-year incidence rate over the study period.

Figure 4.1 shows an equivocal picture. Since the 1970s, the number of incidence studies have increased. Excluding the three studies in the upper right hand corner, it would appear that these case register studies show at most a slight increase over time of incident anorexia nervosa cases. The studies in the 1980s show widely diverging incidence rates. It is unclear what this reflects. Most likely, there is a

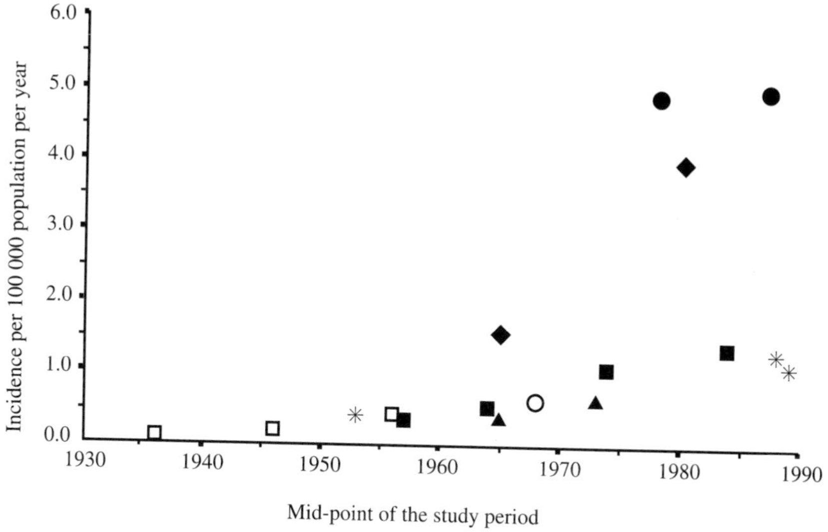

Figure 4.1. Registered incidence of anorexia nervosa per year per 100 000 population in different regions: (*) Denmark; (●) The Netherlands; (○) England; (◆) Scotland; (■) Switzerland; (▲) USA (Monroe Co. NY); (□) Sweden (see Table 4.1)

methodological explanation for this difference. It might be due to variations in registration policy such as including day-patients (Munk-Jørgensen *et al.* 1995), demographic differences between the populations, faulty inclusion of readmissions, the particular methods of detection used, or the availability of services (Williams and King 1987; Fombonne 1995a). Fombonne (1995a,b), who examined 16 published studies mentioning incidence rates, concluded that although some studies showed an increase, no study ruled out plausible alternative explanations, and there were just as many studies, generally based on larger samples, showing no upward trend. As state of the art, it may be concluded that the notion of an increased incidence of anorexia nervosa over time is not supported by current epidemiological data.

However, several studies do provide evidence that there is a rise in registered incidence of anorexia nervosa specific for young women (Williams and King 1987; Nielsen 1990; Lucas *et al.* 1991; Munk-Jørgensen *et al.* 1995). Munk-Jørgensen and colleagues stressed the sensitivity of this type of study to minor changes in absolute numbers and in methods, and emphasized the value of very long study periods, such as that of Lucas *et al.* (1991). Lucas *et al.* (1991) found that the age-adjusted incidence rates of anorexia nervosa in females 15–24 years old showed a highly significant linear increasing trend from 1935 to 1984 (Figure 4.2). This age group represented 61% of the female cases. The rates for older women remained relatively constant. Among males anorexia nervosa remained rare with no appreciable change in the rates over time. The incidence rates among female residents

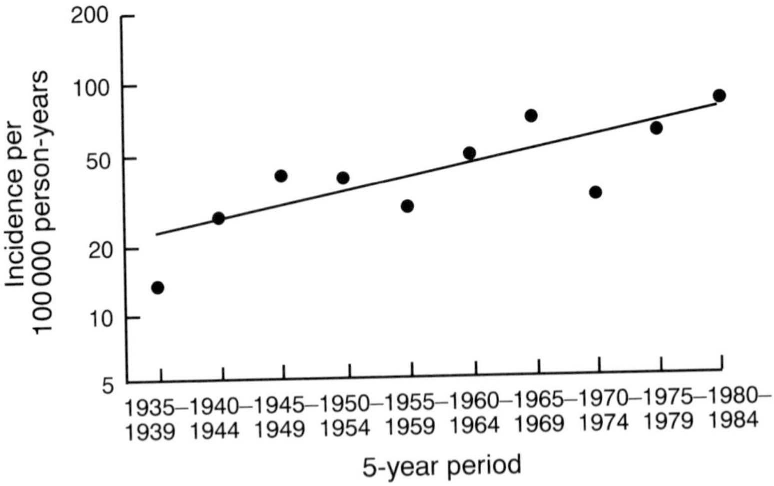

Figure 4.2. Age-specific incidence rates (plotted on a log scale) for anorexia nervosa, by 5-year periods, in 15–24-year-old female residents of Rochester, MN. Observed = circles, predicted = line. From *American Journal of Psychiatry*, **148**, 917–922, 1991, Copyright 1991, the American Psychiatric Association. Reprinted by permission

fell from 16.6 per 100 000 persons-years in the 1935–1939 period to a low of 7.0 in 1950–1954 and increased to 26.3 in 1980–1984. It should be taken into account that the diagnostic certainty in the period 1935–1939 has been low: of the 14 cases with anorexia nervosa only two are definite cases, 10 are probable and two are possible cases (Lucas *et al.* 1988).

All these studies will grossly underestimate the true incidence, because not all cases will be referred to mental health care or become hospitalized. Despite the doubts whether there is a true increase in incidence, the higher incidence rates of registered cases in the 1980s imply at least that there is an increased demand for health care facilities for anorexia nervosa.

Bulimia nervosa

Incidence studies of bulimia nervosa have hardly been conducted. The most obvious reason is the lack of criteria for bulimia nervosa in the past. Most case registers have been using the ICD, which has not been providing a separate code for bulimia nervosa. Bulimia nervosa has been distinguished as a separate disorder by Russell in 1979 and DSM-III in 1980 (APA 1980). Therefore it is impossible to examine trends in the incidence of bulimia nervosa or a possible shift from anorexia nervosa to bulimia nervosa, which might have influenced the previously described incidence figures of anorexia nervosa.

Cullberg and Engström-Lindberg (1988) have asked secondary and primary care personnel for information about patients on the possibility of eating disorders during 1984–1985. They have found a 1-year incidence rate for bulimia nervosa of 3.9 per 100 000 population. This figure has been derived from only six cases (three cases per year). From a fall and spring survey Drewnowski *et al.* (1988) report a high incidence rate of 4.2 cases per 100 female college freshmen per year, but the study has some methodological shortcomings, such as a low response rate and the fact that respondents were not interviewed.

Using information from psychiatric case registers, psychiatric and somatic medical records, and primary care physicians, Pagsberg and Wang (1994) assessed the epidemiology of eating disorders on the island of Bornholm, Denmark. Potential cases were included when they fulfilled ICD-10 criteria. They observed stable incidence rates for the period 1970–1984 (average annual incidence rates of 1.5 per 100 000 females and of 5.3 per 100 000 females aged 10–24 years), but significantly higher rates for the period 1985–1989 (average annual incidence rates of 6.0 per 100 000 females and 17.6 per 100 000 females aged 10–24 years). The maximum incidence rate of bulimia nervosa occurred in 1989, when it was 45 per 100 000 females aged 10–24 years.

Soundy *et al.* (1995) determined the trend in incidence of bulimia nervosa in Rochester, Minnesota for the 11-year period 1980–1990. Identifying cases of bulimia nervosa prior to 1980 among Rochester residents was deemed to be unreliable because the diagnostic term bulimia nervosa did not exist until Russell defined it in his 1979 publication. Before then the term 'bulimia' in medical records designated symptoms of heterogeneous conditions manifested by overeating, but not the syndrome as it is known today. Soundy and colleagues used methodology similar to that in the long-term anorexia nervosa study by Lucas *et al.* (1991). They have screened not only the records of patients with a clinical diagnosis of bulimia nervosa, but also those mentioning (psychogenic) feeding disturbance, rumination syndrome, polyphagia/hyperphagia/excess eating, adverse effects of cathartics/emetics, nutritional sialosis, cyclic vomiting/psychogenic gastrointestinal disorder, and adverse effects of diuretics. They identified 103 Rochester residents (100 female and 3 male) who fulfilled DSM-III-R diagnostic criteria for bulimia nervosa. The overall age- and sex-adjusted annual incidence was 13.5 per 100 000 population. The annual age-adjusted incidence rates were 26.5 per 100 000 population for females and 0.8 per 100 000 population for males. Yearly incidence rates rose sharply from 7.4 per 100 000 females in 1980 to 49.7 in 1983, and then remained relatively constant around 30 per 100 000 females. Among 15–19-year-old females the incidence was 125.1 per 100 000 population, among 20–24-year-old females the incidence was 82.7, and among 25–29-year-old females the incidence was 45.9. Russell (1997) reviewed the study of Soundy *et al.* (1995) and also a prevalence study by Kendler *et al.* (1991) concluding that bulimia nervosa was rare before the 1970s, and that the disease appeared suddenly in the late 1970s in significant numbers.

General practitioners using DSM-III-R criteria have studied the incidence rate of bulimia nervosa in a large representative sample of the Dutch population (Hoek *et al.* 1995). The incidence rate was 11.5 per 100 000 population per year ($N = 85$ cases) during 1985–1989. Of all bulimia nervosa cases, only three were male, giving an incidence rate of 0.8 per 100 000 males per year, and a female to male ratio of 26.8 : 1 (unadjusted for age). For women aged 35 and over, the incidence rate was 8.3. There was a non-significant trend for the incidence rates of bulimia nervosa to increase by 15% each year (rate ratio: 1.15; 95% confidence interval 0.99–1.33). During 1985–1989 53% of the incident cases were referred to mental health care, accounting for an incidence rate of bulimia nervosa in mental health care of 6.0 per year per 100 000 population. These incidence rates of bulimia nervosa can only serve as minimum estimates of the true incidence rate. Because of the lack of data, the greater taboo around bulimia nervosa and its smaller perceptibility compared to anorexia nervosa, the true incidence rate of bulimia nervosa seems still as much a secret as the syndrome itself is for many patients.

In Great Britain, Turnbull *et al.* (1996) screened the General Practice Research Database (GPRD), covering a large, representative sample of the English and Welsh population, for first diagnoses of anorexia nervosa and bulimia nervosa. For bulimia nervosa they found a raw overall age- and sex-adjusted incidence rate of 12.2 per 100 000 population in 1993 ($N = 301$ cases), and an estimated incidence rate adjusted for false negatives and false positives of 6.7. Of the 301 detected cases, only six were male, giving an incidence rate of 0.5 per 100 000 males per year, and a female to male ratio of 46.8 : 1 (unadjusted for age). For people aged 40 and over, the incidence rate was 1.7 per 100 000 population per year. They noted a highly significant, threefold increase in bulimia nervosa incidence rates for women aged 10–39 in the period 1988–1993, increasing from 14.6 in 1988 to 51.7 in 1993. This was in contrast to rather constant incidence rates for anorexia nervosa for the same period in the same study. It is not unlikely that an increased awareness of the symptoms both in general practitioners and in the general population have paved the way for a better recognition and more 'coming out' of bulimia nervosa patients. After all, this is a relatively new diagnosis, having been designed a separate diagnostic category starting with DSM-III (APA 1980).

PREVALENCE OF EATING DISORDERS

In contrast to the incidence studies, more prevalence studies have been carried out on bulimia nervosa than on anorexia nervosa. Register-based prevalence figures are of limited value, because they represent only detected cases in inpatient, and occasionally in outpatient, psychiatric care. As will be discussed in more detail later on, the treated cases represent only a minority of all eating disorder cases. General-population-based prevalence studies of eating disorders are often conducted in high-risk populations, like schoolgirls or female students. At present a two-stage screening survey is the most widely accepted procedure for case identification (Williams *et al.* 1980). Register-based prevalence studies and prevalence studies using questionnaires only will not be discussed here.

Anorexia nervosa

The often cited prevalence rate of 1% for anorexia nervosa has been derived from a study by Crisp *et al.* (1976), but this citation is a biased figure, because it only reflects findings at private schools and not at state schools. Table 4.2 summarizes the two-stage surveys of anorexia nervosa in young females (Button and Whitehouse 1981; Szmukler 1983; Eisler and Szmukler 1985; King 1986, 1989; Meadows *et al.* 1986; Johnson-Sabine *et al.* 1988; Whitehouse and Button 1988; Råstam *et al.* 1989; Whitaker *et al.* 1990; Rathner and Messner 1993; Whitehouse *et al.* 1992; Wlodarczyk-Bisaga and Dolan 1996).

Six studies have investigated teenage schoolgirls, being the population most at risk for developing anorexia nervosa. Button and Whitehouse (1981) and Whitehouse and Button (1988) studied full-time students at a college of technology, Meadows *et al.* (1986) did a postal survey in two general practices and King (1986) and Whitehouse *et al.* (1992) studied female consecutive series of patients, attending their family doctor. Most studies have screened their populations with the Eating Attitude Test (EAT; Garner and Garfinkel 1979). Råstam *et al.* (1989) initially used growth charts and a questionnaire and Whitehouse *et al.* (1992) used a short questionnaire on weight and dietary practices during the first stage.

All studies have succeeded in obtaining high response rates of 85% or more, except Meadows *et al.* (1986), who reached a response rate of 70%. In the second

Table 4.2. Two-stage surveys of prevalence of anorexia nervosa in young females

	Subjects			Methods		
Study	Source	Age	*N*	Screening	Criteria	Prevalence %
Button and Whitehouse (1981)	College students	16–22	446	EAT	Feighner	0.2
Szmukler (1983)	Private schools	14–19	1331	EAT	Russell	0.8
	State schools	14–19	1676	EAT	Russell	0.2
King (1989)	General practice	16–35	539	EAT	Russell	0
Meadows *et al.* (1986)	General practice	18–22	584	EAT	DSM-III	0.2*
Johnson-Sabine *et al.* (1988)	Schoolgirls	14–16	1010	EAT	Russell	0
Råstam *et al.* (1989)	Schoolgirls	15	2136	growth chart + questionnaire	DSM-III	0.47
					DSM-IIIR	0.23
Whitaker *et al.* (1990)	High school girls	13–18	2544	EAT	DSM-III	0.3
Whitehouse *et al.* (1992)	General practice	16–35	540	questionnaire	DSM-IIIR	0.2
Rathner and Messner (1993)	Schoolgirls + case register	11–20	517	EAT	DSM-IIIR	0.58
Wlodarczyk-Bisaga and Dolan (1996)	Schoolgirls	14–16	747	EAT	DSM-IIIR	0

* Not found by screening (EAT score below threshold).

stages of the studies trained researchers interviewed subjects who were probable cases using DSM-III or DSM-III-R criteria or the criteria of Feighner *et al.* (1972) or of Russell (1970).

Johnson-Sabine *et al.* (1988) and King (1986) did not discover cases, which fulfilled Russell criteria; using DSM-III-R criteria, the same held for Wlodarczyk-Bisaga and Dolan (1996). The other two-stage surveys found, following strict criteria, a prevalence rate for anorexia nervosa of between 0.2 and 0.8% of young females. Most studies found much higher prevalence rates for partial syndromes of anorexia nervosa. These rates are possibly minimum estimates. Johnson-Sabine *et al.* (1988) found two cases of anorexia nervosa among non-responders. Meadows *et al.* (1986) detected their only case of anorexia nervosa because she was referred to the authors. At the screening, she had scored below threshold on the EAT.

Three other studies are worth mentioning, because they are not confined to high-risk populations and give prevalence figures for the entire population. These studies did not use a two-stage procedure for case finding. In a general practice study, Hoek (1991) found a point-prevalence rate of 18.4 per 100 000 of the total population. In the high-risk group of 15–29-year-old females, a 1-year prevalence rate of 0.16% was found. From their extensive screening of medical records in Rochester, MN, Lucas *et al.* (1991) recorded an overall sex- and age-adjusted point prevalence of 0.15% on 1 January 1985. The age-adjusted rates were 0.27% for all females, and 0.02% for all males, giving a female-to-male ratio of 12 : 1 on the prevalence date. For 15–19-year-old girls, the point prevalence on 1 January 1985 was 0.48%. Pagsberg and Wang (1994) also studied the epidemiology of eating disorders with an extensive screening procedure, including a psychiatric case register containing information on in-patients, out-patient records, hospital records of patients in somatic departments, and patients in primary care. For the period 1973–1987 they reported a 1-year prevalence rate for anorexia nervosa of 23.5 per 100 000 population for all females, and of 32.2 per 100 000 population for the high-risk group of 10–24-year-old females. They detected one male anorexia nervosa patient. The age at onset for all cases, including bulimia nervosa patients, ranged from 9 to 54 years.

Bulimia nervosa

In 1990 Fairburn and Beglin gave a review of the prevalence studies on bulimia nervosa. This landmark review yielded the generally accepted prevalence rate of 1% of young females with bulimia nervosa according to DSM criteria. We will report and update their review of more than 50 prevalence studies.

Fairburn and Beglin divided the prevalence studies into three groups on the basis of the method of case detection employed (see Table 4.3). The first group contained the majority of the studies on the prevalence of bulimia nervosa, in which diagnoses were based exclusively on subject responses to self-report questionnaires. Fairburn and Beglin discuss three important limitations of these studies. Firstly, the samples were selected, secondly, most studies have obtained unsatisfactory

Table 4.3. Review of prevalence studies on bulimia nervosa by Fairburn and Beglin (1990)

Diagnosis	Self-report questionnaires				Interview, preliminary studies				Interview, more sophisticated studies			
	Prevalence %			No of studies	Prevalence %			No of studies	Prevalence %			No of studies
	Mean	SD	Range		Mean	SD	Range		Mean	SD	Range	
DSM-III bulimia	9.0	4.3	3–19	20	1.9	1.9	0–5	4	1.5	1.0	1–3	4
DSM-III bulimia with weekly binge eating	3.6	2.0	0–7	13	–	–	–	0	–	–	–	–
DSM-III bulimia with weekly binge eating and purging	2.8	2.8	1–10	11	–	–	–	0	1.0	–	–	1
Bulimia nervosa diagnosed with Russell or DSM-III-R criteria	2.6	1.0	2–4	4	1.6	–	–	1	0.9	0.3	0–1	4

From *American Journal of Psychiatry*, **147**, 401–408, 1990, Copyright 1990, the American Psychiatric Association. Reprinted by permission.

response rates and thirdly, the methods of case detection employed were in most cases inadequate. As argued before, because of the low prevalence of eating disorders in the community, questionnaires have a low positive predictive value, even when a test with high sensitivity and specificity is used. The only conclusion to be drawn from these questionnaire studies, was that binge eating seems to be common among high-risk groups, like female students. Fairburn and Beglin refer to the studies in the second group as preliminary interview-based studies. These studies incorporated a two-stage design, self-report screening instruments and an interview to establish the definite diagnosis. These studies did not include a formal evaluation of the performance of the screening instruments. The studies of the first and second group will not be presented here, because of the limitations already discussed.

The third group contains the more sophisticated interview-based studies. Fairburn and Beglin reviewed eight studies in this group of two types. Six used a two-stage design, including a test of the efficiency of the screening instruments (Szmukler 1983; King 1986; Williams *et al.* 1986; Schotte and Stunkard 1987; Freeman and Henderson 1988; Johnson-Sabine *et al.* 1988). In the other two it was attempted to interview the entire sample (Rand and Kuldau 1992; Drewnowski *et al.* 1988). The more sophisticated studies are impressively consistent in finding that bulimia nervosa appears to have a prevalence rate of about 1% among adolescent and young adult women. This figure may be an underestimation of the true rate, because eating disorders are over-represented among those who choose not to cooperate with prevalence studies (Fairburn and Beglin 1990).

Seven recent two-stage surveys have been conducted of which four are represented in Table 4.2 (Råstam *et al.* 1989; Whitaker *et al.* 1990; Whitehouse *et al.* 1992; Rathner and Messner 1993). Råstam *et al.* (1989) have found a prevalence of only 0.14% (three cases) among Swedish 15-year-old schoolgirls, which confirms the results from other epidemiological and clinical studies indicating that bulimia nervosa usually starts at ages over 15. Whitaker *et al.* (1990) observed a lifetime DSM-III prevalence of 4.2% among high-school girls. Whitehouse *et al.* (1992) report a prevalence of 1.5% of bulimia nervosa and of 5.4% of partial syndrome bulimia nervosa among 540 consecutive female general practice attendees. Rathner and Messner (1993) recorded only 0.87% subclinical cases of bulimia nervosa among 15 to 19-year-old schoolgirls.

Since the review by Fairburn and Beglin (1990) three more two-stage surveys have been reported (Bushnell *et al.* 1990; Szabó and Túry 1991; Wlodarczyk-Bisaga and Dolan 1996). Bushnell *et al.* (1990) have conducted a prevalence study in a general population of 1498 adults using the Diagnostic Interview Schedule (DIS) by lay-interviewers at the first stage and an interview by a clinician at the second stage. They have reported a point-prevalence of 1% and a lifetime prevalence of 2.6% of DSM-III bulimia among women aged 18–44. In Hungary, Szabó and Túry (1991), using a two-stage design, found a prevalence rate of 1.3% among female college students. The response rate in this study was low (39.6%) and only subjects who came for therapeutic assistance were interviewed. In Poland,

Wlodarczyk-Bisaga and Dolan (1996), using a two-stage design, did not find any clinical cases of DSM-III-R bulimia nervosa in a group of 14–16-year-old schoolgirls. This again confirms the clinical impression that bulimia nervosa usually starts at ages over 15. They did find a point prevalence of 2.34% for subclinical eating disorders, representing subjects who showed grossly disturbed eating behaviours and attitudes towards weight but not meeting the DSM-III-R criteria for specific eating disorders.

Three studies not using a two-stage procedure for case finding are reported here as well, because they give prevalence figures for the entire population and not just for the high-risk group of young females. In a study of incident cases reported by general practitioners, Hoek (1991) has found a point-prevalence rate of 20.4 per 100 000 of the total population. In the group of 15–29-year-old females, a 1-year prevalence rate of 0.17% was found. Garfinkel *et al.* (1995) assessed eating disorders in a random, stratified, non-clinical community sample, using a structured interview for the whole sample. They reported a lifetime prevalence for bulimia nervosa of 1.1% in women and of 0.1% in men aged 15–65, using DSM-III-R criteria. Pagsberg and Wang (1994), while using an extensive screening procedure for eating disorder patients in psychiatric and medical care, unfortunately did not provide prevalence figures for the entire population. They reported a 1-year prevalence rate of 0.054% per 100 000 population for the high-risk group of 10–24-year-old females in the period 1977–1986. No male bulimia nervosa patients were found. The age at onset for all cases, including anorexia nervosa patients, ranged from 9 to 54 years. Soundy *et al.* (1995) conducted a study on bulimia nervosa in Rochester, MN, with an extensive case-finding method similar to the one used for anorexia nervosa reported by Lucas *et al.* (1991). They did not attempt to determine prevalence rates for bulimia nervosa because of unreliable information about how long symptoms had persisted and the long duration (mean 39.8 months) of symptoms before diagnosis.

SUMMARY OF INCIDENCE AND PREVALENCE

Considering that the case-finding methods of Lucas *et al.* (1991), Pagsberg and Wang (1994), Soundy *et al.* (1995), Hoek *et al.* (1995) and Turnbull *et al.* (1996) were probably the most complete, and assuming that even these give an underestimate of the true incidence, as state of the art we might conclude that the incidence of anorexia nervosa is at least 8 per 100 000 population per year and the incidence of bulimia nervosa is at least 13 per 100 000 population per year. The incidence rate in females 15–24 years old, the most vulnerable group, has increased during the past 50 years. Summarizing the two-stage surveys of community populations, an average 1-year prevalence of anorexia nervosa, using strict diagnostic criteria, was found of 0.28% of young females. Although Soundy *et al.* (1995) caution for the possibility of unreliable information, figures of a lifetime prevalence rate of bulimia nervosa of 1% in women and of 0.1% in men seem accurate.

A MODEL OF THE PATHWAY TO CARE

Despite their different nature, it would be interesting to combine the different rates in one model to discuss the morbidity at different levels of care. Goldberg and Huxley (1980) have described a model of the pathway to psychiatric care. Table 4.4 shows three levels of morbidity and the two filters between them and also presents the prevalence rates per 100 000 young females at the different levels. The figures represent the 1-year period prevalence. The 1-year period prevalence = point prevalence + annual incidence rate. Goldberg and Huxley (1980) in Britain, and Hoek (1983) in the Netherlands, have estimated the morbidity of all psychiatric disorders. They show that only a small percentage of the total psychiatric morbidity comes into psychiatric care.

Each level in the model of Table 4.4 represents a different population of subjects. In order to move from one level to the next, it is necessary to pass through a filter.

Level-1 represents the community. Our knowledge concerning this level is derived from the two-stage surveys of eating disorders. We have calculated above that the mean point-prevalence rate for anorexia nervosa is 280 and for bulimia nervosa 1000 per 100 000 young females. We do not know the incidence rates in the community. Hoek (1991) has found that the incidence of anorexia nervosa was about one-third of the point prevalence and of bulimia nervosa half of the point prevalence in primary care. If we use these primary care figures as estimates for the community, the 1-year prevalence rates in the community are 370 for anorexia nervosa and 1500 for bulimia nervosa.

Level-2 consists of those patients identified as 'psychiatrically ill' by their doctor, attending primary care physicians. These patients collectively represent psychiatric morbidity as it is seen from the vantage point of the primary care physician, and they are referred to as the 'conspicuous psychiatric morbidity' of general medical practice. The rates in Table 4.4 are derived from the general practice study by Hoek (1991).

The first filter is represented by the doctors' ability to detect eating disorders among patients who consult them. Seventy percent of women consult their family doctor in the course of one year in the British National Health Service (Goldberg and Huxley 1980). We do not know how many people with eating disorders consult

Table 4.4. One year period prevalence rates per 100 000 young females at different levels of care

Level of morbidity	Characteristic of filter	Anorexia nervosa	Bulimia nervosa
1. Community		370	1500
→ filter 1: detection of disorder			
2. Detected in primary care		160	170
→ filter 2: referral to psychiatrist			
3. Total in mental health care		127	87

their primary care physician for whatever reason. Most patients with marked psychiatric disorders, and the majority of those with mild disorders, do consult their doctors. Passage through this filter is determined by characteristics of both doctor and patient.

When it is assumed that at least 70% of the women with an eating disorder visit their general practitioner for any kind of medical or psychological problem during the course of one year, this would yield 260 consults of women with anorexia nervosa and 1050 consults of women with bulimia nervosa per year. Table 4.4 indicates that the majority (62%) of patients with anorexia nervosa in primary care has been detected by the general practitioner (160 out of 260). Of all bulimia nervosa patients in primary care only 16% (170 out of 1050) has been recognized by the general practitioner. Mattingly and Bhanji (1982) found that in one-third of their patients anorexia nervosa as diagnosis was not considered by the general practitioners. Among 50 cases of DSM-III-R bulimia nervosa identified in the community Welch and Fairburn (1992) found that only six (12%) were receiving treatment. Several other studies show that general practitioners have problems detecting eating disorders (Dhondt *et al.* 1989; Hoek 1991; Bryant-Waugh 1991). It is probably more difficult to detect eating disorders than other psychiatric disorders, because eating disorders are characterized by taboo and denial. Hoek (1991) concludes that especially bulimia nervosa patients with normal weight might be difficult to detect.

Patients attending outpatient and in-patient services of mental health care represent level-3. In countries like the Netherlands and UK, the primary care physician is critically placed to determine who will be referred for psychiatric outpatient care, and the general practitioner will therefore be thought of as the second filter. Table 4.4 shows that this second filter lets through more anorexia than bulimia nervosa patients. The rates for eating disorders have been derived from the number of patients referred by the general practitioner according to the study by Hoek (1991) and are consistent with the case-register study by Hoek and Brook (1985).

Being aware of the methodological differences and problems of the studies described, we might conclude from Table 4.4 that roughly calculated nearly half of the anorexia nervosa patients are detected by their general practitioner and most of these detected patients are referred to mental health care. In contrast, only a small minority of the community cases with bulimia nervosa appears to be detected in primary care and of these, only half will be referred to mental health care.

RISK FACTORS

Besides indicating the extent of the problem by providing disease rates, epidemiological studies are also important for uncovering prognostic factors differentiating those who become ill from those who do not. These risk factors give clues to the aetiology of the disease and can be used to target prevention programmes.

The major areas on which risk factor research for eating disorders has focused are environmental pressures for thinness, parental psychopathology, and intra-individual characteristics, divided into biological risk and behaviour risk with symptom-related and non-symptom criteria (Leung *et al.* 1996).

Ideally, risk factors are uncovered in prospective follow-up studies of initially non-clinical populations, allowing the determination of differences that precede—not follow or accompany—the disease. As yet, there have only been a very limited number of studies with such a design. A second option is a study using a case–control design. Although they do not shed light on the direction (cause/consequence) of the differences found, they do stimulate causal modelling and thus aid in narrowing down the range of factors to be assessed in more decisive studies. Case–control studies assess differences between prevalent eating disorder cases and a control group of subjects, usually matched on age, gender and social class. Methodological difficulties involved in the interpretation of the results are the issues of directionality (cause/consequence) and of the reliability of retrospectively gathered information on premorbid differences.

PROSPECTIVE FOLLOW-UP STUDIES

King (1989), using the EAT questionnaire, followed up a group of 76 high-scoring patients from general practices at 12 and 18 months after initial assessment. He used only scores from the EAT questionnaire and no clinical interview to diagnose for caseness. The numbers of patients changing category from disorder-free to subclinical or clinical and vice versa were too low to allow the assessment of differentiating factors. It did appear that dieting often preceded an eating disorder (23% of the high-scoring dieters had developed bulimic symptoms at follow-up), but unfortunately none of the low EAT scorers were followed up to identify the factors that turned dieting into an eating disorder.

Patton *et al.* (1990) screened a large group of 15-year-old schoolgirls and selected a high scoring, an intermediate scoring and a low-scoring group for interview. Seventy-five percent were re-interviewed at 12 months. Here too, 21% of the original dieters had developed a partial or full eating disorder syndrome at follow-up. Higher weight, familial obesity and social stress correlated with dieting behaviour, but only a change in GHQ (General Health Questionnaire) scores differentiated dieters who became cases from dieters who did not become cases. Thus, general psychopathology seems to mediate the effect of dieting behaviour to result in the onset of an eating disorder.

Wlodarczyk-Bisaga and Dolan (1996) re-interviewed a high- and a low-risk group of 14–16-year-old schoolgirls, defined by their scores on the EAT, 10 months after initial assessment. Although over 10% had changed EAT category, the number of those classified as subclinical syndrome for the first time at follow-up (seven) was too low to draw firm conclusions.

These results are too inconclusive or too unspecific to advance the understanding of the causes of eating disorders or to use for targeting prevention programmes.

Although some other prospective follow-up studies have been conducted, these have suffered from methodological flaws (e.g. a large time gap between the questionnaire-based screen and the final determination of caseness by interview) deemed too great to consider their results.

CASE–CONTROL STUDIES

Under this heading, a great number of studies have been conducted. Only one study is presented here, which through its breadth encompasses a large number of the variables addressed in other studies. Other advantages over many of the other studies were that cases were not restricted to inpatients of tertiary care centres but were recruited from the community through general practitioner lists, that two types of control groups were used (healthy controls and 'controls' with other psychiatric conditions) instead of one, and that sophisticated analysis methods were used.

Fairburn *et al.* (1997) compared bulimia nervosa subjects with healthy control subjects without an eating disorder (general risk factors), and with subjects with other psychiatric disorders (specific risk factors), recruited from general practices in Oxfordshire, UK. After screening with self-report questionnaires, a retrospective risk-factor interview was carried out that addressed the period before the alleged onset of the eating disorders. This interview focused on biological, psychological, and social factors believed to place persons at risk for the development of eating disorders.

The general risk factor, separating bulimia nervosa cases from healthy controls, was a greater degree of exposure to the majority of personal vulnerability factors (e.g. childhood characteristics of negative self-evaluation or behavioural problems), environmental factors (e.g. parental problems or disruptive events) and dieting vulnerability factors (e.g. critical comments about shape, weight or eating by others). The higher the degree of exposure, the higher the risk of developing bulimia nervosa is. Parental problems, obesity risk, parental psychiatric disorders, sexual or physical abuse, and premorbid psychiatric disorder were the most strongly associated with caseness.

Specific factors, separating bulimia nervosa from other psychiatric disorders, were negative self-evaluation, parental alcoholism, low parental contact, and high parental expectations, critical comments by family about shape, weight, or eating, childhood and parental obesity, and a younger age at menarche. The results suggest that bulimia nervosa is most likely to develop in dieters who are at risk of obesity and of psychiatric disorder in general (Fairburn *et al.* 1997).

Methodological problems of this study were that it relied on retrospectively gathered data, that all information concerning the families was obtained from the patient and not from personal interviews of family members, and that the interviewer was not blind to case status (Halmi 1997).

Although risk factor studies have been conducted for anorexia nervosa, there is no study with a comparable design, addressing a wide range of variables and recruiting cases plus two types of controls from the community.

OTHER STUDIES

There are a number of publications that point out the possibility of psychosocial mechanisms in the development of eating disorders, including the impact of a culture of slimness and dieting and socio-economic factors.

It is commonly thought that anorexia nervosa is a western illness: there appears to be a developmental gradient across cultures, with predominance in industrialized, developed countries, linking the disorder to an affluent society (DiNicola 1990; Vandereycken and Hoek 1993; Hoek 1995). Transcultural studies provide evidence that anorexia nervosa is rare in non-western countries (Buhrich 1981; Ballot *et al.* 1981; Buchan and Gregory 1984; Famuyiwa 1988; Lee *et al.* 1989; King and Bhugra 1989; Dolan 1991; Davis and Yager 1992; Khandelwal *et al.* 1995). Non-western immigrants are more likely to develop an eating disorder than their peers in the homeland, like Arab college students in London (Nasser 1986), and Greek and Turkish girls in Germany (Fichter *et al.* 1988). There are also clinical reports of anorexia nervosa in immigrant families suggesting that immigration and acculturation stress are key factors triggering the illness (DiNicola 1990; Lacey and Dolan 1988; Mumford and Whitehouse 1988; Bhadrinath 1990; Bryant-Waugh and Lask 1991). Since World War II the Japanese health care system is facing increasing numbers of anorexia nervosa patients (Mizushima and Ishii 1983; Suematsu *et al.* 1985). Although all of these studies pertain to anorexia nervosa, it is believed that the same applies to bulimia nervosa.

However, none of the studies to date provide reliable population-based incidence/prevalence rates of eating disorders in non-western countries and/or cultures. Probably, a major reason for the lack of general population-based epidemiological data from non-western societies is the lack of advanced administrative structures, such as reliable population and mental health registers. Some epidemiological data are available from countries in eastern Europe that are considered to have a non-western culture (Szabó and Túry 1991; Rathner *et al.* 1995; Wlodarczyk-Bisaga and Dolan 1996). These suggest that, contrary to previous thought, eating disorders may be at least as prevalent in eastern Europe as in the West. In a recent overview of the effect of culture on eating disorders, Nasser (1997) concludes that anorexia nervosa is not a culture-bound syndrome. Thus, doubts are cast on the validity of the sociocultural theory for eating disorders that holds that eating disorders are promoted by a western culture favouring slimness as a beauty ideal for females, and by consequence are less prevalent in non-western cultures. A weakness of these studies is that it is assumed, not demonstrated, that the population under study has a non-western culture. The study by Wlodarczyk-Bisaga and Dolan (1996) demonstrated that the prevalence of abnormal eating attitudes and behaviours in adolescent Polish schoolgirls was not markedly different from that reported in North America and western Europe.

Hoek *et al.* (1995) report that the incidence of bulimia nervosa is three to five times higher in urbanized areas and cities than in rural areas, while anorexia nervosa is found with almost equal frequency in areas with different degrees of urbanization. The drift-hypothesis, relating urbanization differences to migration for educational reasons, is rejected because the differences remain after adjusting for age. If the hypothesis that there is an increased pressure to be slender in urbanized areas holds true, this would imply that anorexia nervosa is less sensitive to social factors than bulimia nervosa, has a much more biological origin and is more driven by other factors such as a tendency toward asceticism and compulsive behaviour.

Most psychiatric disorders show a higher prevalence in the lower socio-economic classes, and it is difficult to determine whether this is the result of the social selection process, or whether it is caused by social factors (Dohrenwend *et al.* 1992). For anorexia nervosa, there has been a traditional belief of an upper social class preponderance. However, Gard and Freeman (1996) have questioned this belief in a thorough examination of the studies considered exemplary for the alleged preponderance. They concluded that the 'evidence' in support of the preponderance of eating disorders in high socio-economic groups was based almost entirely on methodologically dubious studies on unrepresentative groups of patients. Studies using more sound methodology reported either insignificant relationships between eating disorders and socio-economic status, thus leaving the relationship between anorexia nervosa and high socio-economic status unproven, or rather a preponderance of eating disorders, particularly of bulimia nervosa, in low socio-economic groups.

Some occupations appear to run a greater potential risk of being linked to the development of an eating disorder (Vandereycken and Hoek 1993). Typical examples of these are professions within the world of fashion and ballet. We do not know whether this is a causal factor or rather the result of disturbed attitudes around body and shape. In other words, are pre-anorexics attracted by the ballet world, or are ballerinas more prone to develop anorexia (Vandereycken and Hoek 1993)? Hoek and Brook (1985) have found that anorexia nervosa patients did not differ that much in the level of education, compared to females of the same age group in the general population. However, the anorexia nervosa patients were very different from the general population by choosing much more often for general education than for vocational education.

When tying eating disorders to culture, the relationship may be interpreted in three ways (DiNicola 1990; Vandereycken and Hoek 1993): (1) The strong thesis of this connection is that culture acts as a causative factor by providing a blueprint for eating disordered behaviour; (2) the moderate thesis states that specific cultural factors trigger the eating disorder which is further determined by many other factors; and (3) the weak thesis considers culture as an envelope or context for the expression of the eating disorder.

The data supporting a socio-cultural approach are mainly correlational in nature, and do not provide specific evidence for causal models. We cannot say that cultural influences cause serious eating disorders. We might conclude that environmental factors seem to play an important role for the development of an eating disorder to a vulnerable individual. The vulnerability may be determined by psychological and biological factors of the individual and early environmental features.

COMMENTS

The value of epidemiology lies in its particular methodology that gives rise to population-based disease rates and ratios. When properly established, these rates and ratios provide a scientific basis on the community level for treatment planning and aetiological model building. Epidemiological information is needed to examine and extend on clinical observations. For example, although dieting precedes practically all cases of anorexia nervosa and bulimia nervosa, only a small proportion of all dieters develops an eating disorder. A prospective follow-up study of initially healthy dieters, sampled from the general population, may shed light on the mechanisms that turn dieting into an eating disorder.

The basic epidemiological measures are incidence and prevalence rates. For the purpose of treatment planning, there is an ongoing need for prevalence information at the local level. For reasons of time- and cost-efficiency, this is best done by monitoring existing health care consumption registers. Attention must be paid to changing consumption rates in relation to changes in health care recruitment and admission policy. When the adequacy or accuracy of case definition and registration is questioned, efforts are needed to improve registration.

For the purpose of aetiological model building, the mere determination of prevalence and incidence rates is not enough. Although more is becoming known on general and specific risk factors for the onset of an eating disorder, there still is an impressive gap. Furthermore, the developmental mechanisms of these factors are largely unknown. The general conclusion is that dieting behaviour plays a role in the pathogenesis of anorexia nervosa and bulimia nervosa. However, not all dieters proceed to develop an eating disorder. We need to find out what additional factors are necessary or sufficient to turn dieting into an eating disorder. This requires prospective follow-up studies, comparing adequately sized groups of subjects who are healthy at initial assessment and ill at follow-up with adequately sized control groups of subjects who remain healthy throughout.

Lucas (1981) elaborated the concept of a predisposition–environment interaction in the development of an eating disorder by using the biopsychosocial model. This model conceptualizes anorexia nervosa as a disease entity having roots in three spheres: the biological, the psychological, and the social. Specific early experiences and family influences may create modes of thinking and a self-concept that determine the psychological predisposition. Societal influences and expectations play their role in setting the social climate that is conducive to the development of an obsession with thinness. The biological vulnerability may be genetically determined and becomes activated by pubertal endocrine changes. Halmi (1994, 1997) expanded this model to bulimia nervosa, proposing that bulimia nervosa develops after the stress of dieting in an individual with antecedent conditions including a genetic and physiological vulnerability, psychological predispositions often affected by the family, and societal influences.

Future studies focusing on the onset of disorder are needed to illuminate the risk mechanisms. To circumvent the power and cost problems caused by the relatively low rates of eating disorders in the general population, a few suggestions for the design of economically feasible studies providing generalizable, reliable results on risk factors and mechanisms are given:

1. For high-risk groups, such as young females, dieters and participants in weight-restricted sports including ballet dancing, there is a need for prospective, follow-up designs using initially healthy subjects. Depending on the question to be answered, these could be matched on sex, age and socio-economic status with initially healthy intermediate risk and low-risk groups.
2. For lower risk groups, such as males or older persons, a prospective design is too cost inefficient and a case–control design is more appropriate. Cases should be collected at as low a level of entry into the health-care system as possible, preferably primary care. As controls same-sex probands and other same-sex persons matched for age and socio-economic status could be of use. To facilitate hypothesis testing and the exchange of knowledge and ideas, the formation of a multi-centre database of these rare cases would mean a great improvement.
3. For both prospective follow-up studies and case–control studies, a comprehensive assessment of biological, psychological, familial and social variables is needed. The factors and mechanisms studied should be based on findings from previous research such as that by Fairburn *et al.* (1997). To decide on the effect of weight- and shape-centred beauty ideals on the frequency of eating disorders, studies are needed that compare the distribution of eating disorders between groups differing in weight- and shape-related attitudes.

Finally, an issue to be solved for epidemiological studies on eating disorders is the reliance on a categorical approach of caseness, particularly for the 'newer' diagnoses of bulimia nervosa, the eating disorders-not otherwise specified, and binge eating disorder. By focusing on incident clinical cases and ignoring atypical or subclinical cases, aetiological reasoning may miss the crucial developmental elements in what have been called 'broad spectrum' disorders. For such disorders a dimensional approach may be more appropriate. Traditionally, epidemiological methodology has been more suited to the categorical approach. Here lies a challenge for both general methodologists and risk factor researchers in the field of eating disorders.

CLINICAL IMPLICATIONS

- Clinicians in secondary and tertiary care should be aware that they see only a selected minority of all persons with a clinically significant eating disorder.
- There is a tendency for those in treatment to have comorbid conditions.
- Although an eating disorder is usually preceded by dieting, not all dieters develop an eating disorder.
- There has been an enormous increase in the 'treated' incidence of eating disorders. However, from epidemiological studies there is no convincing evidence that eating disorders in general are on the rise; there does seem to be an increase for the most vulnerable group of females 15–24 years old over the past 50 years.
- General practitioners detect only about 12% of all bulimia nervosa cases, and about 45% Of all anorexia nervosa cases. As they often serve as gate-keepers to specialized care, they should receive better training in the recognition of eating disorders, particularly of bulimia nervosa.

RESEARCH IMPLICATIONS

- It is time to move beyond the study of the occurrence of eating disorders, and to undertake studies which focus on risk factors.
- This requires prospective follow-up studies on carefully chosen, initially healthy at-risk populations of sufficient size.
- In the search for etiological factors, it seems wise to adopt a 'broad-spectrum' approach to the assessment of eating disorder symptomatology, including a wide definition of atypical and/or subclinical criteria. This might result in specific risk factors of more narrowly defined subgroups of eating disorders.

REFERENCES

American Psychiatric Association (APA) (1980) *Diagnostic and Statistical Manual of Mental Disorders. 3rd Edition*. American Psychiatric Association, Washington DC.

American Psychiatric Association (APA) (1987) *Diagnostic and Statistical Manual of Mental Disorders. 3rd Edition Revised*. American Psychiatric Association, Washington DC.

American Psychiatric Association (APA) (1994) *Diagnostic and Statistical Manual of Mental Disorders. 4th Edition*. American Psychiatric Association, Washington DC.

Ballot, N.S., Delaney, N.E., Erskine, P.J., Langridge, P.J., Smit, K., Van Niekerk, M.S., Winters, Z.E. and Wright, N.C. (1981) Anorexia nervosa–a prevalence study. *South African Medical Journal*, **59**, 992–993.

Bhadrinath, B.R. (1990) Anorexia nervosa in adolescents of Asian extraction. *British Journal of Psychiatry*, **156**, 565–568.

Bryant-Waugh, R.J. (1991) Do doctors recognise eating disorders in children? Paper presented at *Symposium International: Les Troubles des Conduites Alimentaires* (International Symposium: Eating Disorders) April 1991, abstract 51 (Paris).

Bryant-Waugh, R.J. and Lask, B. (1991) Anorexia nervosa in a group of Asian children living in Britain. *British Journal of Psychiatry*, **158**, 229–233.

Buchan, T. and Gregory, L. D. (1984) Anorexia nervosa in a black Zimbabwean. *British Journal of Psychiatry*, **145**, 326–330.

Buhrich, N. (1981) Frequency of presentation of anorexia nervosa in Malaysia. *Australian and New Zealand Journal of Psychiatry*, **15**, 153–155.

Bushnell, J.A., Wells, J.E., Hornblow, A.R., Oakly-Browne, M.A. and Joyce, P. (1990) Prevalence of three bulimia syndromes in the general population. *Psychological Medicine*, **20**, 671–680.

Button, E.J. and Whitehouse, A. (1981) Subclinical anorexia nervosa. *Psychological Medicine*, **11**, 509–516.

Connors, M.E. and Johnson, C.L. (1987) Epidemiology of bulimia and bulimic behaviors. *Addictive Behaviors*, **12**, 165–179.

Consoli, S. and Jeammet P. (1984) L'épidémiologie de l'anorexie mentale. *Sem. Hôpital Paris*, **60**, 2139–2143.

Crisp, A.H., Palmer, R.L. and Kalucy, R.S. (1976) How common is anorexia nervosa? A prevalence study. *British Journal of Psychiatry*, **128**, 549–554.

Cullberg, J. and Engström-Lindberg, M. (1988) Prevalence and incidence of eating disorders in a suburban area. *Acta Psychiatrica Scandinavica*, **78**, 314–319.

Davis, C. and Yager, J. (1992) Transcultural aspects of eating disorders. A critical literature review. *Culture Medicine and Psychiatry*, **16**, 377–394.

Dhondt, A.D.F., Volman, H.G., Westerman, R.F., Weeda-Mannak, W.L. and Van der Horst, H.E. (1989) Bulimia nervosa: Hoe bekend is het ziektebeeld bij huisartsen? (Bulimia nervosa: how familiar are general practitioners with the syndrome?) *Medisch Contact*, **44**, 231–233.

DiNicola, V.F. (1990) Anorexia multiforme: self-starvation in historical and cultural context. Part II: anorexia nervosa as a culture-reactive syndrome. *Transcultural Psychiatric Research Review*, **27**, 245–286.

Dohrenwend, B.P., Levav, I., Shrout, P.E., Schwartz, S., Naveh, G., Link, B.G., Skodol, A.E. and Stueve, A. (1992) Socio-economic status and psychiatric disorders: the causation-selection issue. *Science*, **255**, 946–952.

Dolan, B.M. (1991) Cross-cultural aspects of anorexia nervosa and bulimia: a review. *International Journal of Eating Disorders*, **10**, 67–78.

Drewnowski, A., Yee, D.K. and Krahn, D.D. (1988) Bulimia in college women: incidence and recovery rates. *American Journal of Psychiatry*, **145**, 753–755.

Eaton, W.W., Tien, A.Y. and Poeschla, B.D. (1995) Epidemiology of schizophrenia. In *Advances in the Neurobiology of Schizophrenia* (eds J.A. Den Boer, H.G.M. Westenberg and H.M. Van Praag), pp. 27–57, Wiley & Sons, Chichester.

Eisler, I. and Szmukler, G.I. (1985) Social class as a confounding variable in the eating attitudes test. *Journal of Psychiatric Research*, **19**, 171–176.

Fairburn, C.G. and Beglin, S.J. (1990) Studies of the epidemiology of bulimia nervosa. *The American Journal of Psychiatry*, **147**, 401–408.

Fairburn, C.G., Welch, S.L., Norman, P.A., O'Connor, M.E. and Doll, H.A. (1996) Bias and bulimia nervosa: how typical are clinic cases? *American Journal of Psychiatry*, **153**, 386–391.

Fairburn, C.G., Welch, S.L., Doll, H.A., Davies, B.A. and O'Connor, M.E. (1997) Risk factors for bulimia nervosa. A community-based case-control study. *Archives of General Psychiatry*, **54**, 509–517.

Famuyiwa, O.O. (1988) Anorexia nervosa in two Nigerians. *Acta Psychiatrica Scandinavica*, **78**, 550–554.
Feighner, J.P., Robins, E., Guze, S.B., Woodruff, R.A., Winokur, G. and Munoz, R. (1972) Diagnostic criteria for use in psychiatric research. *Archives of General Psychiatry*, **26**, 57–63.
Fichter, M.M., Elton, M., Sourdi, L., Weyerer, S. and Koptagel-Ilal, G. (1988) Anorexia nervosa in Greek and Turkish adolescents. *European Archives of Psychiatry and Neurological Sciences*, **237**, 200–208.
Fombonne, E. (1995a) Anorexia nervosa. No evidence of an increase. *British Journal of Psychiatry*, **166**, 464–471.
Fombonne, E. (1995b) Eating disorders: Time trends and possible explanatory mechanisms. In *Psychosocial Disorders in Young People. Time Trends and Their Causes* (eds M. Rutter and D.J. Smith), pp. 616–685, Wiley & Sons, Chichester.
Fombonne, E. (1996) Is bulimia nervosa increasing in frequency? *International Journal of Eating Disorders*, **19**, 289–296.
Freeman, C.P.L. and Henderson, M. (1988) The BITE: indices of agreement. *British Journal of Psychiatry*, **152**, 575–577.
Gard, M.C.E. and Freeman, C.P. (1996) The dismantling of a myth: A review of eating disorders and socioeconomic status. *International Journal of Eating Disorders*, **20**, 1–12.
Garfinkel, P.E., Lin, E., Goering, P., Spegg, C., Goldbloom, D.S., Kennedy, S., Kaplan, A.S. and Woodside, D.B. (1995) Bulimia nervosa in a Canadian community sample: prevalence and comparison of subgroups. *American Journal of Psychiatry*, **152**, 1052–1058.
Garner, D.M. and Garfinkel, P.E. (1979) The Eating Attitudes Test: an index of the symptoms of anorexia nervosa. *Psychological Medicine*, **9**, 273–279.
Goldberg, D. and Huxley, P. (1980) *Mental Illness in the Community: The Pathway to Psychiatric Care*. London, Tavistock Publications.
Halmi, K.A. (1994) A multi-modal model for understanding and treating eating disorders. *Journal of Women's Health*, **3**, 487–493.
Halmi, K.A. (1997) Models to conceptualize risk factors for bulimia nervosa. *Archives of General Psychiatry*, **54**, 507–508.
Hoek, H.W. (1983) Psychiatrische morbiditeit in Nederland. (Psychiatric morbidity in The Netherlands.) *Tijdschrift voor Sociale Gezondheidszorg*, **61**, 805–807.
Hoek, H.W. (1991) The incidence and prevalence of anorexia nervosa and bulimia nervosa in primary care. *Psychological Medicine*, **21**, 455–460.
Hoek, H.W. (1993) Review of the epidemiological studies of eating disorders. *International Review of Psychiatry*, **5**, 61–74.
Hoek, H.W. (1995) Epidemiology of anorexia nervosa and bulimia nervosa in the Western world. *CME*, **13**, 501–508.
Hoek, H.W. and Brook, F.G. (1985) Patterns of care of anorexia nervosa. *Journal of Psychiatric Research*, **19**, 155–160.
Hoek, H.W., Bartelds, A.I.M., Bosveld, J.J.F., Van der Graaf, Y., Limpens, V.E.L., Maiwald, M. and Spaaij, C.J.K. (1995) Impact of urbanization on detection rates of eating disorders. *American Journal of Psychiatry*, **152**, 1272–1278.
Hsu, L.K.G. (1990) *Eating Disorders*. New York, The Guilford Press.
Hsu, L.K.G. (1996) Epidemiology of the eating disorders. *The Psychiatric Clinics of North America*, **19**, 681–700.
Johnson-Sabine, E., Wood, K., Patton, G., Mann, A. and Wakeling, A. (1988) Abnormal eating attitudes in London schoolgirls—a prospective epidemiological study: factors associated with abnormal response on screening questionnaires. *Psychological Medicine*, **18**, 615–622.
Jones, D.J., Fox, M.M., Babigian, H.M. and Hutton, H.E. (1980) Epidemiology of anorexia nervosa in Monroe County, New York: 1960–1976. *Psychosomatic Medicine*, **42**, 551–558.

Jörgensen, J. (1992) The epidemiology of eating disorders in Fyn county Denmark 1977–1986. *Acta Psychiatrica Scandinavica*, **85**, 30–34.

Kendell, R.E., Hall, D.J., Hailey, A. and Babigian, H.M. (1973) The epidemiology of anorexia nervosa. *Psychological Medicine*, **3**, 200–203.

Kendler, K.S., Maclean, C., Neale, M., Kessler, R., Heath, A. and Eaves, L. (1991) The genetic epidemiology of bulimia nervosa. *American Journal of Psychiatry*, **148**, 1627–1637.

Khandelwal, S.K., Sharan, P. and Saxena, S. (1995) Eating disorders: an Indian perspective. *International Journal of Social Psychiatry*, **41**, 132–146.

King, M.B. (1986) Eating disorders in general practice. *British Medical Journal*, **293**, 1412–1414.

King, M.B. (1989) Eating disorders in a general practice population. Prevalence, characteristics and follow-up at 12 to 18 months. *Psychological Medicine* suppl. **14**, 1–34.

King, M.B. and Bhugra, D. (1989) Eating disorders: lessons from a cross-cultural study. *Psychological Medicine*, **19**, 955–958.

Lacey, J.H. and Dolan, B.M. (1988) Bulimia in British Blacks and Asians: a catchment area study. *British Journal of Psychiatry*, **152**, 73–79.

Lee, S., Chiu, H.F.K. and Chen, C.-N. (1989) Anorexia nervosa in Hong Kong. Why not more in Chinese? *British Journal of Psychiatry*, **154**, 683–688.

Leung, F., Geller, J., and Katzman, M. A. (1996) Issues and concerns associated with different risk models for eating disorders. *International Journal of Eating Disorders*, **19**, 249–256.

Lucas, A.R. (1981) Toward the understanding of anorexia nervosa as a disease entity. *Mayo Clinic Proceedings*, **56**, 254–264.

Lucas, A.R., Beard, C.M., O'Fallon, W.M. and Kurland, L.T. (1988) Anorexia nervosa in Rochester, Minnesota: a 45-year study. *Mayo Clinic Proceedings*, **63**, 433–442.

Lucas, A.R., Beard, C.M., O'Fallon, W.M. and Kurland, L.T. (1991) 50-year trends in the incidence of anorexia nervosa in Rochester, Minn.: a population-based study. *American Journal of Psychiatry*, **148**, 917–922.

Mattingly, D. and Bhanji, S. (1982) The diagnosis of anorexia nervosa. *Journal of the Royal College of Physicians of London*, **16**, 191–194.

Meadows, G.N., Palmer, R.L., Newball, E.U.M. and Kenrick, J.M.T. (1986) Eating attitudes and disorder in young women: a general practice based survey. *Psychological Medicine*, **16**, 351–357.

Mizushima, N. and Ishii, Y. (1983) The epidemiology of anorexia nervosa in junior and senior highschool students in Ishikawa prefecture. *Shinshin-Igaku*, **23**, 311–319.

Møller-Madsen, S. and Nystrup, J. (1992) Incidence of anorexia nervosa in Denmark. *Acta Psychiatrica Scandinavica*, **86**, 197–200.

Mumford, D.B. and Whitehouse, A.M. (1988) Increased prevalence of bulimia nervosa among Asian schoolgirls. *British Medical Journal*, **297**, 718.

Munk-Jørgensen, P., Møller-Madsen, S., Nielsen, S. and Nystrup, J. (1995) Incidence of eating disorders in psychiatric hospitals and wards in Denmark, 1970–1993. *Acta Psychiatrica Scandinavica*, **92**, 91–96.

Nasser, M. (1986) Comparative study of the prevalence of abnormal eating attitudes among Arab female students of both London and Cairo Universities. *Psychological Medicine*, **16**, 621–625.

Nasser, M. (1997) *Culture and Weight Consciousness*. London, Routledge.

Nielsen, S. (1990) The epidemiology of anorexia nervosa in Denmark from 1973 to 1987: a nationwide register study of psychiatric admission. *Acta Psychiatrica Scandinavica*, **81**, 507–514.

Pagsberg, A.K. and Wang, A.R. (1994) Epidemiology of anorexia nervosa and bulimia nervosa in Bornholm County, Denmark, 1970–1989. *Acta Psychiatrica Scandinavica*, **90**, 259–265.

Patton, G.C., Johnson-Sabine, E., Wood, K., Mann, A.H. and Wakeling, A. (1990) Abnormal eating attitudes in London schoolgirls—a prospective epidemiological study: outcome at twelve month follow-up. *Psychological Medicine*, **20**, 383–394.

Pyle, R.L. (1985) The epidemiology of eating disorders. *Pediatrician*, **12**, 102–109.

Rand, C.S.W. and Kuldau, J.M. (1992) Epidemiology of bulimia and symptoms in a general population: sex, age, race and socioeconomic status. *International Journal of Eating Disorders*, **11**, 37–44.

Råstam, M., Gillberg, C. and Garton, M. (1989) Anorexia nervosa in a Swedish urban region, a population based study. *British Journal of Psychiatry*, **155**, 642–646.

Rathner, G. and Messner, K. (1993) Detection of eating disorders in a small rural town: an epidemiological study. *Psychological Medicine*, **23**, 175–184.

Rathner, G., Túry, F., Szabó, P., Geyer, M., Rumpold, G., Forgács, A., Söllner, W. and Plöttner, G. (1995) Prevalence of eating disorders and minor psychiatric morbidity in Central Europe before the political changes in 1989: a cross-cultural study. *Psychological Medicine*, **25**, 1027–1035.

Russell, G.F.M. (1970) Anorexia nervosa: its identity as an illness and its treatment. In *Modern trends in psychological medicine*, Vol 2 (ed. J. Harding-Price), pp. 131–164, Butterworth, London.

Russell, G.F.M. (1979) Bulimia nervosa: an ominous variant of anorexia nervosa. *Psychological Medicine*, **9**, 429–448.

Russell, G.F.M. (1997) The history of bulimia nervosa. In *Handbook of Treatment for Eating Disorders*, 2nd edn (eds D.M. Garner and P.E. Garfinkel). New York, The Guilford Press.

Schotte, D.E. and Stunkard, A.J. (1987) Bulimia vs bulimic behaviors on a college campus. *Journal of the American Medical Association*, **258**, 1213–1215.

Shepherd, M. (1991) Introduction to psychiatric epidemiology. In *The European handbook of psychiatry and mental health* (ed. A. Seva). Zaragoza, Spain, Prensas Universitarias de Zaragoza.

Soundy, T.J., Lucas, A.R., Suman, V.J. and Melton, L.J. III. (1995) Bulimia nervosa in Rochester, Minnesota from 1980 to 1990. *Psychological Medicine*, **25**, 1065–1071.

Suematsu, H., Ishikawa, H., Kuboki, T. and Ito, T. (1985) Statistical studies on anorexia nervosa in Japan: detailed clinical data on 1,011 patients. *Psychotherapy and Psychosomatics*, **43**, 96–103.

Szabó, P. and Túry, F. (1991) The prevalence of bulimia nervosa in a Hungarian college and secondary school population. *Psychotherapy and Psychosomatics*, **56**, 43–47.

Szmukler, G.I. (1983) Weight and food preoccupation in a population of English schoolgirls. In *Understanding Anorexia Nervosa and Bulimia: Report of 4th Ross Conference on Medical Research* (ed. G.I. Bargman), pp. 21–27, Ross, Columbus, Ohio.

Szmukler, G.I. (1985) The epidemiology of anorexia nervosa and bulimia. *Journal of Psychiatric Research*, **19**, 143–153.

Szmukler, G., McCance, C., McCrone, L. and Hunter, D. (1986) Anorexia nervosa: a psychiatric case register study from Aberdeen. *Psychological Medicine*, **16**, 49–58.

Theander, S. (1970) Anorexia nervosa: a psychiatric investigation of 94 female patients. *Acta Psychiatrica Scandinavica*, Supplement 214.

Turnbull, S., Ward, A., Treasure, J., Jick, H. and Derby L. (1996) The demand for eating disorder care. An epidemiological study using the General Practice Research Database. *British Journal of Psychiatry*, **169**, 705–712.

Vandereycken, W. and Hoek, H.W. (1993) Are eating disorders culture-bound syndromes? In *Psychobiology and Treatment of anorexia nervosa and bulimia nervosa* (ed. K.A. Halmi), pp. 19–36, American Psychopathological Association Series, Washington DC.

Weissman, M.M. (1987) Epidemiology overview. In *Psychiatry update: The American Psychiatric Association Review* Vol. 6 (eds R.E. Hales and R.J. Francis), pp. 574–588, American Psychiatric Press, Washington DC.

Welch, S. and Fairburn, C. (1992) Sampling bias and bulimia nervosa. Paper presented at Fifth International Conference on Eating Disorders April 1992, abstract 161 (New York).

Whitaker, A., Johnson, J., Shaffer, D., Rapoport, J.L., Kalikow, K., Walsh, B.T., Davies, M., Braiman, S. and Dolinsky, A. (1990) Uncommon troubles in young people: prevalence estimates of selected psychiatric disorders in a nonreferred adolescent population. *Archives of General Psychiatry*, **47**, 487–496.

Whitehouse, A.M. and Button, E.J. (1988) The prevalence of eating disorders in a UK college population: a reclassification of an earlier study. *International Journal of Eating Disorders*, **7**, 393–397.

Whitehouse, A.M., Cooper, P.J., Vize, C.V., Hill, C. and Vogel, L. (1992) Prevalence of eating disorders in three Cambridge general practices: hidden and conspicuous morbidity. *British Journal of General Practice*, **42**, 57–60.

Willi, J., Giacometti G. and Limacher, B. (1990) Update on the epidemiology of anorexia nervosa in a defined region of Switzerland. *The American Journal of Psychiatry*, **147**, 1514–1517.

Williams, P. and King, M. (1987). The 'epidemic' of anorexia nervosa: another medical myth? *The Lancet*, **i**, 205–207.

Williams, P., Tarnopolsky, A. and Hand, D. (1980) Case definition and case identification in psychiatric epidemiology: review and reassessment. *Psychological Medicine*, **10**, 101–114.

Williams, P., Hand, D. and Tarnopolsky, A. (1982) The problem of screening for uncommon disorders—a comment on the Eating Attitudes Test. *Psychological Medicine*, **12**, 431–434.

Williams, R.L., Schaefer, C.A., Shisslak, C.M., Gronwaldt, V.H. and Comerci, G.D. (1986) Eating attitudes and behaviors in adolescent women: discrimination of normals, dieters, and suspected bulimics using the Eating Attitudes Test and Eating Disorder Inventory. *International Journal of Eating Disorders*, **5**, 879–894.

Wlodarczyk-Bisaga, K. and Dolan, B. (1996) A two-stage epidemiological study of abnormal eating attitudes and their prospective risk factors in Polish schoolgirls. *Psychological Medicine*, **26**, 1021–1032.

World Health Organization (WHO) (1995) *International Classification of Diseases, 10th Edition*. World Health Organization, Geneva.

5 The Etiology of Anorexia Nervosa

C. GILLBERG and M. RÅSTAM
Department of Child and Adolescent Psychiatry, Sahlgren University Hospital, University of Göteborg, Sweden

INTRODUCTION

The etiology of anorexia nervosa (AN) is a much disputed topic, even now, more than 100 years after it was first described as a relatively homogeneous clinical entity. The range of suggested underlying pathologies has been enormous, and include exclusively psychological and exclusively biological factors and variations on the theme of nature–nurture interaction explanatory models.

This chapter reviews the evidence in the field of background factors in AN. The etiology of AN is still unknown, although it seems clear that this phenomenologically defined eating disorder is multiply determined and that it is unlikely that a single cause will ever be uncovered that accounts for all cases. The review therefore covers a whole host of associated factors that might be linked to the pathogenesis of the disorder, ranging from genetic and otherwise biological factors, to social and psychological correlates of AN.

CULTURAL FACTORS AND GENDER

AN is found in many different cultures and is certainly not confined to industrialized parts of the world (Hoek *et al.* 1995). It is less clear whether AN occurs in families comprising one or more individuals starving for reasons other than eating disorders. However, it does appear that AN is more common in countries where food and material prosperity abound.

Girls and women born in countries with a seemingly low prevalence of AN seem to have an increased risk of developing the disorder after moving to a high-frequency region (Fichter *et al.* 1988; Dolan *et al.* 1990).

It is often surmised that AN is caused by the present-day idealizing of a tall and thin female body. The extreme overrepresentation of females among individuals with AN would be supportive of such a notion. A hypothetical increase in the frequency of AN in parallel with the promotion of megastar models such as Twiggy has been proposed as supportive evidence. However, in spite of some reports of an increased rate of AN from the mid 1960s to the mid 1980s in certain regions (Lucas and Holub 1995), there is no consensus that AN prevalence generally has increased

Neurobiology in the Treatment of Eating Disorders.
Edited by H.W. Hoek, J.L. Treasure and M.A. Katzman.

over the corresponding time period (Fombonne 1995; Råstam and Gillberg 1996). Even so, there is reason to suspect that the female body image as flaunted by the media, may create a psychological environment in which AN is more likely to develop if there are underlying personality characteristics such as perfectionism and obsessive–compulsive traits (Steiner *et al.* 1995). In recent years there has also emerged a new male body ideal in the media with tallness, thinness, abdominal flatness and muscular arms and thighs. During this same period, young men have become increasingly engaged in body-building and often use anabolic steroids and diuretics. Many of these young men are reminiscent of young females with AN in their compulsive pursuit of more training and a specific body image. Nevertheless, the fact that role expectations have changed dramatically over the past three decades but the rate of AN in females has remained relatively stable, suggests that, to a considerable degree, it is the biology of being a women that confers a risk of developing AN.

Some private schools and certain ballet schools have reported a very high rate of AN (Crisp *et al.* 1976; Szmukler *et al.* 1985; McKenna 1989). This could be due to cultural imitation (one individual taking after the behaviour of another), individuals with obsessive–compulsive and perfectionist personality traits opting for certain schools, to an 'anorexogenic' milieu (hypothetically an authoritarian and weight- and food-emphasizing setting), or to other, currently unknown, factors. Incidentally, some recent studies have not found a high incidence of AN in ballet schools (Neumärker *et al.* 1998).

Males with AN have strikingly similar clinical symptoms when compared with females with the disorder (Vandereycken and Van den Broucke 1984; Margo 1987). Given such clear similarities, the very low prevalence among males suggests biological, social and intrapsychic determinants that can be conceived to be more active in females than in males (Steiger 1989). Males with AN tend to be less concerned than females with achieving smaller bodily proportions, while on the other hand tending to overvalue musculature and athleticism (Andersen 1984). Our own clinical experience suggests that young males with AN tend to have more schizoid personality problems than do young females, but, so far, no systematic study has been able to corroborate this impression.

ADOPTION

One English study (Holden 1991) and some case reports (Crisp and Toms 1972; Fry and Crisp 1989) suggest that AN may be slightly overrepresented among teenagers who have been adopted in childhood. The reason for a possible connection is unknown at present.

SOCIAL CLASS

For many years it was taken almost for granted that AN is a disorder of the upper classes (Dally 1969; Anderson and Hay 1985). Recent reports, including a population-based study (Pate *et al.* 1992; Råstam 1992), have not supported this notion.

Some studies (e.g. Råstam 1990) have found a tendency for young people with AN to come from families who are 'on the way up', that is who, within their social class, are in the upper section of that class. It is possible that such an observation could be linked to a generally higher level of ambition in such families.

AMBITION, SCHOOL, EDUCATION, REPORTS AND GRADES

A considerable proportion of all teenagers with AN (Dally 1969; Patton 1988; Mills and Medlicott 1992; Råstam 1992) are perfectionists and have great ambition in respect of school work and education. Given that IQ is not generally higher than in other young people (Gillberg *et al.* 1996), there may be a mismatch between demands and ambition on the one hand and actual capacity on the other, and this could contribute to the development of the eating disorder.

PUBERTY

Many authors (including Crisp 1975) have suggested that puberty in itself is one of the most important triggering factors in AN. It is clear that peak age of onset of AN is in the pubertal years (Casper 1996). Psychological and biological factors could be important, but specific studies of the relationship between puberty and the occurrence of AN have not been performed.

ACCOMMODATION, NOT ASSIMILATION

Hilde Bruch (1979), a US psychoanalyst with considerable clinical experience with patients suffering from AN, reported that affected individuals very often had had childhoods characterized by 'accommodation' rather than 'assimilation'. She made the point that the premorbid personality of individuals who developed AN was one characterized by imitation and passive acceptance of rules laid down by other people rather than by gradual modification and incorporation of general themes into the personality structure.

FAMILY FACTORS

Child and adolescent psychiatrists and psychologists have a long tradition in highlighting the importance of family factors in AN (Minuchin *et al.* 1978).

FAMILY RELATIONS

The concept of the so called anorexogenic family has attracted considerable attention in the past. There is little, if any, support for this notion (Lask and Bryant-Waugh 1992). Nevertheless, there is ample evidence that family relations may be strained and dysfunctional in AN (Humphrey 1988; Råstam and Gillberg 1991; Thienemann and Steiner 1993), but it is unclear whether the problems documented are an effect or cause of the eating disorder, or merely indicative of an unspecific correlate of psychiatric disorder generally (Steiger and Stotland 1995; Steiner *et al.* 1995).

PARENTAL AGE

One study suggests raised maternal and paternal age in a cohort of individuals with AN as compared with the general population (Råstam and Gillberg 1991), but it is clear that AN can occur in families with young parents as well as if one or both parents are older.

SIBLINGS

Siblings of patients with AN appear to be much more commonly affected by eating disorders than siblings of individuals without AN (Theander 1970; Strober *et al.* 1990). This could be taken to imply the importance of either psychosocial or genetic influences. In the light of findings from twin studies, many authors now interpret the possibly increased rate of AN among siblings as indicative of a genetic liability for the disorder. However, there is at least one study of a representative group of individuals with AN that does not support the general view that AN is more common in siblings of individuals with AN (Wentz Nilsson *et al.* 1997). The failure to replicate previous findings in this study might be due either to the population-based nature of the sample or to the fact that siblings were relatively young (and that further follow-up might indeed reveal an increased rate of eating disorders in the siblings of the AN group).

ABUSE IN THE FAMILY

The role of abuse, particularly sexual abuse, in the etiology of AN has received considerable attention in recent years. Connors and Morse (1993), in a review, found that about 30% of women diagnosed as suffering from an eating disorder also reported a history of sexual abuse, a finding similar to the rate of such abuse in the general female population. The figure is lower than in other psychiatric diagnostic groups. If there is a relationship between sexual abuse and eating disorder, it appears to be with bulimia nervosa, not AN (Root and Fallon 1988; Waller 1992).

THE IMPACT OF AN ON THE FAMILY

AN is a disorder that may have a very poor outcome. It seems reasonable to assume that it would have a considerable impact on other family members and on the family system. Surprisingly, in spite of the focus on the family in research on AN, little is known about the ways in which AN affects the family.

MAJOR LIFE EVENTS

Some studies suggest that major life events can trigger the onset of AN (Råstam and Gillberg 1992; Gowers *et al.* 1996). It is unclear as to whether such events can trigger AN only in individuals predisposed to eating disorders or if they can act on their own in causing the syndrome. Some support for the latter view is the preliminary finding that individuals with a triggering major life event appear to have a better outcome than those who do not (Gowers, personal communication 1995). Also, in the community-based study of AN in western Sweden, a subgroup with AN had major life events as the only plausible background factor (Råstam and Gillberg 1992).

GENETIC FACTORS

CHROMOSOMES IN AN

Chromosomes tend to be normal in AN, at least when examined using routine karyotyping and buccal smears for sex chromatine. A proposed association of AN with Turner syndrome was not supported in a population-based study (Råstam *et al.* 1991).

GENERAL GENETIC FACTORS

There are now several studies supporting the importance of genetic factors in the development of AN. As already mentioned, siblings of individuals with AN appear to be affected by AN much more often than other siblings (Strober *et al.* 1985). This, in itself, can be taken as supporting the notion of a genetic liability to AN. However, because of the similar psychosocial environment that siblings are exposed to, claims could equally be made that any sibling frequency increase could be accounted for by environment rather than by genes.

Twin studies (Holland *et al.* 1984, 1988; Treasure and Holland 1990) have demonstrated a higher rate of concordance for AN in monozygotic twin pairs as compared with same-sexed dizygotic twin pairs. This is strongly suggestive of a genetic factor operating in AN. However, the studies referred to have all been on clinical samples, and there is a risk of bias in such studies to the effect that more concordant monozygotic twin pairs may be reported. However, in an on-going population-based twin study of AN in Denmark, it seems clear that there is a significantly higher rate of concordance in monozygotic as compared with dizygotic twin pairs even in unselected samples (Kortegaard-Sandal *et al.* 1997, in progress).

SPECIFIC GENETIC FACTORS INCLUDING PSYCHIATRIC AND PERSONALITY DISORDERS AND PHYSICAL DISORDERS IN RELATIVES

It is unclear just what it is that might be inherited in AN. Is it the eating disorder, another psychiatric disorder, an underlying personality trait, or a specifically abnormal physical characteristic?

As has already been mentioned, there appears to be an increased risk of eating disorders in the relatives of patients with AN. However, it does not appear that AN as such is inherited, given that increased rates of other kinds of eating disorder (bulimia nervosa, eating disorder-not otherwise specified, and obesity) have also been reported in the families of individuals with AN.

Many authors have demonstrated a link with affective disorders in a substantial proportion of cases with AN (Cantwell *et al.* 1977; Hendren 1983; Strober and Katz 1988; Steiger *et al.* 1992; Råstam 1992; Råstam *et al.* 1995). Whether this should be interpreted as a genetic liability for affective disorder in AN, a comorbid problem with or without genetic roots or AN leading to starvation leading to depression is unclear. However, there is some support for the notion that depression in AN is not merely a result of starvation (Steiner *et al.* 1989). There have been several clinical studies suggesting a familial link between AN and affective disorders (Hudson *et al.* 1983; Strober *et al.* 1990; Toro *et al.* 1995). The study by Råstam (Råstam 1992; Wentz Nilsson *et al.* 1997) suggests that depression is an almost universal symptom in AN and that there is a subgroup with familial loading of affective disorder, indicating a possible genetic connection at least in this subgroup.

The study by Wentz Nilsson *et al.* (1997) found an increased rate of autistic-type symptoms—only rarely amounting to the full syndrome of autistic disorder or Asperger syndrome—in first-degree relatives of individuals with AN. Some earlier studies have found first-degree relatives to be emotionally reserved, conventional and compulsive (Strober *et al.* 1982; Casper 1990), findings which could be indicative of the same type of underlying heritable impairment of reciprocal social interaction.

The results of several different studies combine to suggest that there might be an AN subgroup with a genetic liability to the so called cluster C personality disorders (obsessive–compulsive, avoidant and dependant) and to obsessive–compulsive disorder (Casper 1990; Halmi *et al.* 1991; Gillberg *et al.* 1995; Wentz Nilsson *et al.* 1997). However, none of the studies published to date has been able to provide conclusive evidence, and the results of the twin studies provide only weak, if any, support for a *genetic* connection between AN and obsessive–compulsive disorder (Kortegaard-Sandal *et al.* 1997).

Recently, it has been suggested that what might be inherited in AN is a 'drive for thinness' or an unusual distribution of fat (Treasure 1995). Eating disorders are overrepresented among women with excessive fat distribution in the buttocks and thighs (Radke-Sharpe *et al.* 1990). This type of body characteristic is likely to be genetic–metabolic. A high body mass index (and index of body composition and of obesity) appears to confer a high risk for eating disorders, as does obesity per se. Body mass index is highly heritable (Rutherford *et al.* 1993). Taken together, these findings could be taken to indicate that what is inherited in AN is a relatively high body mass index, with a characteristic distribution of fat, plus a personality characterized by perfectionism and drive for thinness.

BRAIN DYSFUNCTION

With the exception of neuroendocrinology, there have been comparatively few studies examining the brain basis of AN. No consistent pattern can yet be discerned on the basis of the studies performed, even though some interesting trends are beginning to emerge. The following section provides a brief review of some recent findings in the field.

PRE- AND PERINATAL RISK FACTORS

Very few studies have detailed results of examination of the pre- and perinatal periods in AN. In the most detailed study to date of pre- and perinatal risk factors there was no difference between an AN group and an age-, sex-, and school-matched comparison group (Råstam 1992). This is not to say that pre- and perinatal events may not be of importance in the etiology of eating disorders in a subgroup of individuals, but such factors cannot account for a large proportion of the variance, at least not with regard to the etiology of AN.

NEUROENDOCRINOLOGICAL AND NEUROCHEMICAL FINDINGS

Many changes secondary to starvation in AN occur in the production and functioning of several hormones, particularly along the hypothalamic–pituitary–gonadal axis.

Female patients with AN, as they begin to lose weight, return to an infantile state of the hypothalamic–pituitary–gonadal axis. Even adrenarche, the secretion of androgen hormones (such as dehydroepiandrosterone) by the adrenal gland about 2 years prior to puberty, is reversed (Pirke and Platte 1995). During weight restoration, pubertal development is repeated, and the ovary undergoes a polycystic state. Repeated pubertal development is not specific to AN, but occurs also in weight gain after weight loss for other reasons (Vigersky and Loriaux 1977).

Osteoporosis is a common complication in AN (Seeman *et al.* 1992; Gillberg *et al.* 1994). This, most likely, is an effect of the suppression of gonadal hormones and of low intake of calcium and phosphate (Pirke and Platte 1995). However, the hypercortisolism that is present in a majority of cases, at least during starvation (Halmi 1987), is also believed to play a role. Hypercortisolism may also be responsible for (pseudo?) atrophy of the brain (Krieg *et al.* 1989) and cognitive deficits seen in some patients (Laessle *et al.* 1989).

Zinc deficiency is common in AN (Lask *et al.* 1993; Birmingham *et al.* 1994). It is unlikely that such deficiency is of any primary etiological importance in most cases, but it may contribute to chronicity in some individuals.

NEUROPHYSIOLOGICAL FINDINGS

A handful of studies have reported on EEG findings in AN. Although major abnormalities in the standard EEG are rare, Rothenberger *et al.* (1995) have found abnormalities (mostly so called vertex transients) in 56% of an adolescent patient group ($n = 100$) with AN (compared with 14% in a sample of 100 healthy adolescents). The observed deviations were mostly independent of body mass index. The results were interpreted as reflecting developmental deviation in AN and to signal a state of disinhibition.

Evoked response findings are equivocal. Miyamoto *et al.* (1992) recorded auditory brainstem responses (ABR) in AN before and after weight gain and in a normal comparison group. They found evidence of brainstem dysfunction (smaller amplitude of wave V) in the AN group that appeared to be independent of body mass index. A study of ABR and of auditory cortical responses indicated that patients with AN have difficulty modulating auditory stimuli in adequate ways, even after weight restoration (Rothenberger *et al.* 1986, 1991).

NEUROIMAGING FINDINGS

Computerized tomography (CT) and magnetic resonance imaging (MRI) studies have yielded contradictory results. Apparent atrophy is present in the brains of some underweight patients with AN according to CT scanning (Kohlmeyer *et al.* 1983; Hentschel *et al.* 1994). With weight gain, this (pseudo?) atrophy seems to be reversed.

Single positron emission CT (SPECT) studies are only now being published. In a recent study from our center, there was hypofrontality and hypoperfusion of the parietal lobes plus some degree of hypoperfusion of the temporal lobes in weight-restored AN cases 7 years after onset of the disorder (Råstam *et al.* 1997). Hypoperfusion of the temporal lobes was found in a British study of underweight AN adolescents, some of whom showed the same type of abnormality after weight restoration (Gordon *et al.* 1997).

NEUROPSYCHOLOGICAL FINDINGS

Neuropsychological tests appear to be only rarely performed in AN. IQ has been believed to be above normal in a majority of cases, but this was not supported by a community-based study comprising a reasonably large group of weight-restored individuals with AN (Gillberg *et al.* 1996). Interestingly, the object assembly subtest of the Wechsler Adult Intelligence Scale–Revised (WAIS) (Wechsler 1981) yielded significantly poorer results in the AN than in the comparison group in that study. Object assembly could be seen to reflect the ability to disregard detail and attend to 'wholes' and central coherence, and dysfunction on this test could, hypothetically, reflect right hemisphere dysfunction. Some evidence of right hemisphere dysfunction in the acute stage of AN was found by Casper and Heller (1991), using visuo-constructive, verbal fluency and chimeric face tasks.

SUMMARY OF STUDIES OF BRAIN DYSFUNCTION IN AN

Because of the scarcity of published studies, it is difficult to formulate a coherent hypothesis regarding the brain basis of AN. It appears that most of the findings of brain dysfunction in AN are secondary to starvation. However, there are indications that certain abnormalities (as reflected in EEG, ABR, SPECT and neuropsychological findings in particular) may reflect a premorbid disposition rather than starvation effects. If observed deviations remain after weight gain, this would support a more primary 'trait'. Nevertheless, it is impossible to exclude long-lasting effects of starvation, and only prospective studies (practically almost impossible to perform) would be able to settle these issues convincingly.

SUBGROUPS IN ANOREXIA NERVOSA ACCORDING TO BACKGROUND FACTORS

In the community-based study of adolescent onset AN in Göteborg, Sweden (Råstam and Gillberg 1992), attempts were made to classify all cases according to most likely etiology/pathogenesis/major background factors. Subgrouping was attempted on the basis of findings clearly separating the AN group from an age-, gender- and school-matched comparison group of individuals without AN. The results are schematically reviewed in Figure 5.1.

There was no clue as to underlying pathogenetic factors in almost one-third of the group with AN. About half of all cases had premorbid obsessive–compulsive problems, amounting to full-blown obsessive–compulsive personality disorder in about two in three of these. Major life events believed to have a direct triggering effect on the development of AN were present in about one in five of all cases.

In some individuals it appeared that multiple factors contributed to the precipitation of AN, and that each of these factors separately would not have been a sufficient condition. For instance, there was a group with obsessive–compulsive personality who had had considerable gastro-intestinal problems throughout

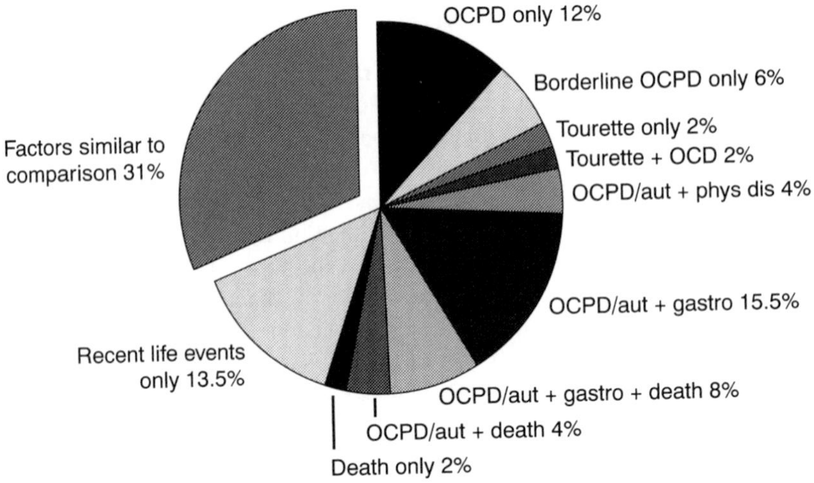

Figure 5.1. Background factors in anorexia nervosa

infancy and early childhood and who also had lost a parent or sibling through death. There was another group characterized by obsessive–compulsive personality and gastro-intestinal problems 'only', and yet another one with obsessive–compulsive problems and death of a first-degree relative.

CONCLUSIONS

It is clear that AN is associated with strong genetic determinants in some cases. However, whether or not the genetic liability is linked to specific personality traits, depression, drive for thinness, body mass index, body fat distribution, or some other factor particularly affecting feeding behavior, has yet to be determined. Further, the extent of the genetic contribution to AN in the general population remains to be established. It appears that in some cases AN can be triggered (caused?) by major life events. There is preliminary evidence that outcome may be better in such cases, possibly suggesting that genetic and other biological factors may be less important in this subgroup. However, in many cases of AN, etiology is unknown. There is still no support for the once widely held belief that family dysfunction is a major causative factor in AN.

It seems likely that AN is a multifactorially determined disorder that should always be seen and interpreted in a biopsychosocial perspective (Garfinkel and Garner 1982; Strober 1991; Garner 1993). Singularly biological, psychological or family-based models will probably never provide anything but partial explanations. Subgroups of individuals with AN almost definitely have etiologies that partly overlap, although some subgroups may not share any etiological variance with the others.

It will remain important to keep an open mind in respect of AN etiology and not begin the assessment of a new case with preconceived prototypical notions about underlying causes, be they biological, psychological or social.

CLINICAL IMPLICATIONS

- Anorexia is associated with strong genetic determinants in some cases.
- It appears that in some cases AN can be triggered by life events.
- In many cases of AN the aetiology is still unknown, yet it appears to be multifactorially determined and therefore should be interpreted from a biopsychosocial perspective.
- There is no support for the once widely held belief that family dysfunction is a major causative factor.
- It is important to begin an assessment of a new case with no preconceived notion about underlying causes.

RESEARCH IMPLICATIONS

- Singularly biological, psychosocial, or family based models will probably only provide partial explanations.
- Subgroups of individuals with AN will have aetiologies that partly overlap.

REFERENCES

Andersen, A.E. (1984) Anorexia nervosa and bulimia in adolescent males. *Pediatric Annals*, **13**, 901–904.

Anderson, A. and Hay, A. (1985) Racial and socio-economic influences in anorexia nervosa and bulimia. *International Journal of Eating Disorders*, **4**, 479–487.

Birmingham, C.L., Goldner, E.M. and Bakan, R. (1994) Controlled trial of zinc supplementation in anorexia nervosa. *International Journal of Eating Disorders*, **15**, 251–255.

Bruch, H. (1979) Developmental deviations in anorexia nervosa. *Israel Annual Psychiatry*, **17**, 255–261.

Cantwell, D.P., Sturzenberger, S., Burroughs, J., Salkin, B. and Green, J.K. (1977) Anorexia nervosa; an affective disorder? *Archives of General Psychiatry*, **37**, 1087–1093.

Casper, R.C. (1990) Personality features of women with good outcome from restricting anorexia nervosa. *Psychosomatic Medicine*, **52**, 156–170.

Casper, R.C. (1996) Outcome of anorexia nervosa with teenage onset. *Journal of Youth and Adolescence*, **25**, 413–418.

Casper, R.C. and Heller, W. (1991) 'La douce indifférence' and mood in anorexia nervosa: neuropsychological correlates. *Biological Psychiatry*, **15**, 15–23.

Connors, M.E. and Morse, W. (1993) Sexual abuse and eating disorders: a review. *International Journal of Eating Disorders*, **13**, 1–11.

Crisp, A.H. (1975) Anorexia nervosa. *British Journal of Psychiatry*, Spec. No. 9, 150–158.

Crisp, A.H. and Toms, D.A. (1972) Primary anorexia nervosa or weight phobia in the male: report on 13 cases. *British Medical Journal*, **1**, 334–338.

Crisp, A.H., Palmer, R.L. and Kalucy, R.S. (1976) How common is anorexia nervosa? A prevalence study. *British Journal of Psychiatry*, **128**, 549–554.

Dally, P. (1969) *Anorexia Nervosa*. London: William Heineman Medical Books.

Dolan, B., Lacey, J.H. and Evans, C. (1990) Eating behaviour and attitudes to weight and shape in British women from three ethnic groups. *British Journal of Psychiatry*, **157**, 523–528.

Fichter, M.M., Elton, M., Sourdi, L., Weyerer, S. and Koptagel-Ilal, G. (1988) Anorexia nervosa in Greek and Turkish adolescents. *European Archives of Psychiatry and Neurological Sciences*, **237**, 200–208.

Fombonne, E. (1995) Anorexia nervosa. No evidence of an increase [see comments] Comment in: *Br J Psychiatry* 1996 Feb; **168**(2): 251–2. *British Journal of Psychiatry*, **166**, 462–471.

Fry, R. and Crisp, A.H. (1989) Adoption and identity: a case of anorexia nervosa. *British Journal of Medical Psychology*, **62**, 143–152.

Garfinkel, P.E. and Garner, D.M. (1982) *Anorexia Nervosa: A Multidimensional Perspective*. New York: Brunner/Mazel.

Garner, D.M. (1993) Pathogenesis of anorexia nervosa. *Lancet*, **341**, 1631–1635.

Gillberg, C., Råstam, M. and Gillberg, I.C. (1994) Anorexia nervosa: Physical health and neurodevelopment at 16 and 21 years. *Developmental Medicine and Child Neurology*, **36**, 567–575.

Gillberg, I.C., Råstam, M. and Gillberg, C. (1995) Anorexia nervosa 6 years after onset. Part I. Personality disorders. *Comprehensive Psychiatry*, **36**, 61–69.

Gillberg, I.C., Gillberg, C., Råstam, M. and Johansson, M. (1996) The cognitive profile of anorexia nervosa. A comparative study including a community-based sample. *Comprehensive Psychiatry*, **37**, 23–30.

Gordon, I., Lask, B., Bryant-Waugh, R., Christie, D. and Timini, S. (1997) Childhood-onset anorexia nervosa: towards identifying a biological substrate. *International Journal of Eating Disorders*, **22**, 159–165.

Gowers, S.G., North, C.D., Byram, V. and Weaver, A.B. (1996) Life events precipitants of adolescent anorexia nervosa. *Journal of Child Psychology and Psychiatry*, **37**, 469–477.

Halmi, K.A. (1987) Anorexia nervosa and bulimia. *Annual Review of Medicine*, **38**, 378–380.

Halmi, K.A., Eckert, E., Marchi, P., Sampugnaro, V., Apple, R. and Cohen, J. (1991) Comorbidity of psychiatric diagnoses in anorexia nervosa. *Archives of General Psychiatry*, **48**, 712–718.

Hendren, R.L. (1983) Depression in anorexia nervosa. *Journal of the American Academy of Child Psychiatry*, **22**, 59–62.

Hentschel, F., Woerner, W. and Rothenberger, A. (1994) Hirnvolumenschwankungen bei Anorexia nervosa. *Klinische Neuroradiologies*, **4**, 19–26.

Hoek, H.W., Bartelds, A.I.M., Bosveld, J.J.F. *et al.* (1995) The impact of urbanization on the detection rates of eating disorders. *American Journal of Psychiatry*, **152**, 1272–1278.

Holden, N.L. (1991) Adoption and eating disorder: a high-risk group? *British Journal of Psychiatry*, **158**, 829–833.

Holland, A.J., Hall, A., Murray, R., Russell, G.F.M. and Crisp, A.H. (1984) Anorexia nervosa: A study of 34 twin pairs and one set of triplets. *British Journal of Psychiatry*, **145**, 414–419.

Holland, A.J., Sicotte, N. and Treasure, J. (1988) Anorexia nervosa: Evidence for a genetic basis. *Journal of Psychosomatic Research*, **32**, 561–571.

Hudson, J.I., Pope, H.G., Jonas, J.M. and Yurgelun-Todd, D. (1983) Phenomenologic relationship of eating disorders to major affective disorder. *Psychiatry Research*, **9**, 345–354.

Humphrey, L.L. (1988) Relationships with subtypes of anorexic, bulimic, and normal families. *Journal of the American Academy of Child and Adolescent Psychiatry*, **27**, 544–551.

Kohlmeyer, K., Lehmkuhl, G. and Poustka, F. (1983) Computed tomography of anorexia nervosa. *American Journal of Neuroradiology*, **4**, 437–438.

Kortegaard-Sandal, L., Hørder, K., Jørgensen, J. and Gillberg, C. (1997) Is anorexia nervosa a genetic disorder? Evidence from a population study of twins. In preparation.

Krieg, J., Lauer, C., Lensinger, G., Pahl, J., Schreiber, W., Pirke, K. and Moser, E.A. (1989) Brain morphology and regional cerebral blood flow in anorexia nervosa. *Biological Psychiatry*, **25**, 1041–1048.

Laessle, R.G., Krieg, J.C., Fichter, M.M. and Pirke, K.M. (1989) Cerebral atrophy and vigilance performance in patients with anorexia nervosa and bulimia nervosa. *Neuropsychobiology*, **21**, 187–191.

Lask, B. and Bryant-Waugh, R. (1992) Early-onset anorexia nervosa and related eating disorder. *Journal of Child Psychology and Psychiatry*, **33**, 281–300.

Lask, B., Fosson, A., Rolfe, U. and Thomas, S. (1993) Zinc deficiency and childhood-onset anorexia nervosa. *Journal of Clinical Psychiatry*, **54**, 63–66.

Lucas, A.R. and Holub, M.I. (1995) The incidence of anorexia nervosa in adolescent residents of Rochester, Minnesota, during a 50-year period. In Steinhausen, H.C. (ed.) *Eating Disorders in Adolescence*. New York: Walter de Gruyter.

Margo, J.L. (1987) Anorexia nervosa in males. A comparison with female patients. *British Journal of Psychiatry*, **151**, 80–83.

McKenna, M.S. (1989) Assessment of eating disordered patients. Special Issue: Eating disorders. *Psychiatric Annals*, **19**, 467–472.

Mills, I.H. and Medlicott, L. (1992) Anorexia nervosa as a compulsive behaviour disease. *Quarterly Journal of Medicine*. **New Series 84**, 507–522.

Minuchin, S., Rosman, B.L. and Baker, L. (1978) *Psychosomatic families; anorexia nervosa in context*. Cambridge, Massachusetts: Harvard University Press.

Miyamoto, H., Sakuma, K., Kumagai, K., Ichikawa, T. and Koizumi, J. (1992) Auditory brain stem response (ABR) in anorexia nervosa. *Japanese Journal of Psychiatry and Neurology*, **46**, 673–679.

Neumärker, K.J., Bettle, N., Bettle, O., Dudeck, U. and Neumärker, U. (1998) The Eating Attitudes Test: comparative analysis of female and male students at the Public Ballet School of Berlin. *European Child and Adolescent Psychiatry*, **7**, in press.

Pate, J., Pumariega, A., Hester, C. and Garner, D. (1992) Cross-cultural patterns in eating disorders: a review. *Journal of the American Academy of Child and Adolescent Psychiatry*, **31**, 802–809.

Patton, G.C. (1988) Mortality in eating disorders. *Psychological Medicine*, **18**, 947–951.

Pirke, K.M. and Platte, P. (1995) Neurobiology of eating disorders in adolescence. In Steinhausen, H.-C. (ed.) *Eating Disorders in Adolescence*, 171–189. New York: Walter de Gruyter.

Radke-Sharpe, N., Whitney-Saltiel, D. and Rodin, J. (1990) Fat distribution as a risk factor for weight and eating concerns. *International Journal of Eating Disorders*, **9**, 27–36.

Råstam, M. (1990) *Anorexia nervosa in Swedish urban teenagers*. M.D. Thesis. University of Göteborg.

Råstam, M. (1992) Anorexia nervosa in 51 Swedish children and adolescents. Premorbid problems and comorbidity. *Journal of the American Academy of Child and Adolescent Psychiatry*, **31**, 819–829.

Råstam, M. and Gillberg, C. (1991) The family background in anorexia nervosa; a population-based study. *Journal of the American Academy of Child and Adolescent Psychiatry*, **30**, 283–289.

Råstam, M. and Gillberg, C. (1992) Background factors in anorexia nervosa. A controlled study of 51 teenage cases including a population sample. *European Child and Adolescent Psychiatry*, **1**, 54–65.

Råstam, M. and Gillberg, C. (1996) Anorexia nervosa rates—conclusions for wrong reasons. Letter to the Editor. *British Journal of Psychiatry*, **168**, 251–252.

Råstam, M., Gillberg, C. and Wahlström, J. (1991) Chromosomes in anorexia nervosa. A study of 47 cases including a population-based group: a research note. *Journal of Child Psychology and Psychiatry*, **32**, 695–701.

Råstam, M., Gillberg, C. and Gillberg, I.C. (1995) Anorexia nervosa 6 years after onset. Part II. Comorbid psychiatric problems. *Comprehensive Psychiatry*, **36**, 70–76.

Råstam, M., Bjure, J., Vestergren, E., Uvebrant, P., Gillberg, I.C., Wentz Nilsson, E. and Gillberg, C. (1997) Regional Cerebral Blood Flow (rCBF) in anorexia nervosa. Submitted.

Root, M.P. and Fallon, P. (1988) The incidence of victimization experiences in a bulimic sample. *Journal of Interpersonal Violence*, **3**, 161–173.

Rothenberger, A., Lehmkuhl, G., Kohlmeyer, K., Blanz, B., Reiser, A. and Grote, I. (1986) Anorexia nervosa (AN) in adolescents—evoked potentials help to elucidate the biological background. In Gallai, V. (ed.) *Maturation of the CNS and Evoked Potentials*. 375–384. Amsterdam: Elsevier.

Rothenberger, A., Blanz, B. and Lehmkuhl, G. (1991) What happens to electrical brain activity when anorectic adolescents gain weight? *European Archives of Psychiatry and Clinical Neuroscience*, **240**, 144–147.

Rothenberger, A., Dumais-Huber, C., Moll, G. and Woerner, W. (1995) Psychophysiology of anorexia nervosa. In Steinhausen, H.-C. (ed.) *Eating Disorders in Adolescence*. New York: Walter de Gruyter.

Rutherford, J., McGuffin, P., Katza, R.J. and Murray, R.M. (1993) Genetic influences on eating attitudes in abnormal female twin population. *Psychological Medicine*, **23**, 425–436.

Seeman, E., Szmukler, G.I., Formica, C., Tsalamandris, C. and Mestrovic, R. (1992) Osteoporosis in anorexia nervosa: the influence of peak bone density, bone loss, oral contraceptive use, and exercise. *Journal of Bone and Mineral Research*, **7**, 1467–1474.

Steiger, H. (1989) Anorexia nervosa and bulimia in males: lessons from a low-risk population. *Canadian Journal of Psychiatry*, **34**, 419–424.

Steiger, H. and Stotland, S. (1995) Individual and family factors in adolescents with eating symptoms and syndromes. In Steinhausen, H.-C. (ed.) *Eating Disorders in Adolescence*. New York: Walter de Gruyter.

Steiger, H., Leung, F., Puentes-Neumann, G. and Gottheil, N. (1992) Psychosocial profiles of adolescent girls with varying degrees of eating and mood disturbances. *International Journal of Eating Disorders*, **11**, 121–131.

Steiner, H., Wilber, J.F., Prasad, C., Rogers, D. and Rosenkranz, R. (1989) Histidyl Proline Diketopiperazine (Cyclo [His-Pro]) in eating disorders. *Neuropeptides*, **14**, 185–189.

Steiner, H., Sanders, M. and Ryst, E. (1995) Precursors and risk factors of juvenile eating disorders. In Steinhausen, H.C. (ed.) *Eating Disorders in Adolescence*. New York: Walter de Gruyter.

Strober, M. (1991) Disorders of the self in anorexia nervosa: an organismic-developmental paradigm. In Johnson, C. (ed.) *Psychodynamic Treatment for Eating Disorders*. New York: Guilford Press.

Strober, M. and Katz, J. (1988) Depression in the eating disorders: A review and analysis of descriptive, family and biological factors. In Garner, D.M. and Garfinkel, P.E. (eds) *Diagnostic Issues in Anorexia Nervosa and Bulimia*. New York: Brunner/Mazel.

Strober, M., Salkin, B., Burroughs, J. and Morrell, W. (1982) Parental personality characteristics and family psychiatric morbidity. *Journal of Nervous and Mental Diseases*, **170**, 345–351.

Strober, M., Morrell, W., Burroughs, J., Salkin, B. and Jacobs, C. (1985) A controlled family study of anorexia nervosa. *Journal of Psychiatric Research*, **19**, 239–246.

Strober, M., Lampert, C., Morrell, W., Burroughs, J. and Jacobs, C. (1990) A controlled family study of anorexia nervosa: evidence of familial aggregation and lack of shared transmission with affective disorders. *International Journal of Eating Disorders*, **9**, 239–253.

Szmukler, G.I., Eisler, I., Gillies, C. and Hayward, M.E. (1985) The implications of anorexia nervosa in a ballet school. *Journal of Psychiatric Research*, **19**, 177–181.

Theander, S. (1970) Anorexia nervosa: a psychiatric investigation of 94 female patients. *Acta Psychiatrica Scandinavica*, Suppl. 214.

Thienemann, M. and Steiner, H. (1993) Family environment of eating disordered and depressed adolescents. *International Journal of Eating Disorders*, **14**, 43–48.

Toro, J., Nicolau, R., Cervera, M., Castro, J., Blecua, M.J., Zaragoza, M. and Toro, A. (1995) A clinical and phenomenological study of 185 Spanish adolescents with anorexia nervosa. *European Child and Adolescent Psychiatry*, **4**, 165–174.

Treasure, J. (1995) (April 24–27)) Families, food and feeding. Paper Read at the Eating Disorder '95 Conference. London.

Treasure, J. and Holland, A.J. (1990) Genetic vulnerability to eating disorders: evidence from twin and family studies. In Remschmidt, H. and Schmidt, M. (eds) *Anorexia Nervosa—Child and Youth Psychiatry: European Perspectives*. pp. 59–68. New York: Hogrefe and Huber Publishers.

Vandereycken, W. and Van den Broucke, S. (1984) Anorexia nervosa in males. *Acta Psychiatrica Scandinavica*, **70**, 447–454.

Vigersky, R.A. and Loriaux, D.L. (1977) Anorexia nervosa as a model of hypothalamic dysfunction. In Vigersky, R.A. (ed.) *Anorexia nervosa*. New York: Raven Press.

Waller, G. (1992) Sexual abuse and the severity of bulimic symptoms. *British Journal of Psychiatry*, **161**, 90–93.

Wechsler, D. (1981) *Manual for the Wechsler Adult Intelligence Scale–Revised*. San Antonio, TX: The Psychological Corporation.

Wentz Nilsson, E., Gillberg, C. and Råstam, M. (1997) Familial factors in anorexia nervosa. A community-based study. Submitted.

6 Aetiology of Bulimia Nervosa

R. L. PALMER
Department of Psychiatry, University of Leicester, Leicester, UK

Bulimia nervosa emerged into clear prominence only two decades ago. This is certainly so from the perspective of the psychiatric and psychological literature (Vandereycken 1994; Russell 1997). It remains an open question whether some all seeing viewpoint would reveal a different picture (Parry-Jones and Parry-Jones 1995). However, the best guess is that the recognition of bulimia nervosa and the like followed a substantial increase in the prevalence of a pattern of disordered behaviour which had hitherto been more of a rarity. Any discussion of the aetiology of bulimia nervosa must take this into account. Although enduring aspects of human biology or circumstance may be important, there must be some space for a factor or combination of factors which has come to operate recently in a way that was not the case before. Social factors are most likely to show such rapid change over time. Amongst these, motivated eating restraint seems to be the most probable candidate. Such restraint (usually as 'slimming' or 'dieting') characteristically forms the background of bulimia nervosa. There is at least anecdotal support for the idea that there have been changes in the prevalence of such behaviour over time and that levels have been especially high over recent decades (Gordon 1990).

AETIOLOGICAL FACTORS

There is, as yet, no fully satisfactory aetiological theory to account for bulimia nervosa. It is plausible that motivated eating restraint is likely to be the usual entry to the pathway toward the disorder. Factors which increase the risk of developing the disorder may do so by increasing the frequency or intensity of such restraint. However, once restraint is established other factors must somehow render the individual vulnerable to becoming frankly eating disordered. It is possible that further factors perpetuate bulimia nervosa once it has started. This chapter will examine possible factors in turn although the classification into different kinds is too neat and artificial. In reality each factor may well contribute at different stages and in complex ways. It will also discuss ways in which the various factors might operate together to produce and sustain the disorder.

Neurobiology in the Treatment of Eating Disorders.
Edited by H.W. Hoek, J.L. Treasure and M.A. Katzman.

EATING RESTRAINT

Of all the people who restrain their eating in pursuit of slimness, health or beauty, only a small proportion develop any significant eating disorder. However, of the people who develop bulimia nervosa almost all seem to have done so in the context of eating restraint. The near ubiquity of such restraint in the history of sufferers is apparent in practice and has been confirmed by systematic observations of clinical cases (Cooper *et al.* 1989; Polivy and Herman 1993). Furthermore, the risk of bulimia nervosa in a group seems to vary with the rate of weight concern and slimming behaviour. At the crudest level, it is young women who diet the most and young women who most often develop the disorder. Within groups, the role of weight concern (Killen *et al.* 1994) and slimming have been studied prospectively as a risk factor for developing bulimia nervosa and eating symptoms. The latter increased the risk by a factor of eight in a study of schoolgirls (Patton *et al.* 1990). It seems plausible that even that elevated risk may underestimate the extent of the association between eating restraint and bulimia (Hsu 1997).

In addition to this evidence from association, it is not difficult to construct a rationale for the role of eating restraint in the genesis of bulimia nervosa. Undereating in the presence of an intact appetite is likely to increase the drive to eat (this has been called the 'Dieter's Dilemma'). In circumstances where undereating is forced upon the individual by scarcity of food it would be advantageous to eat unusually large quantities when the chance to do so arose. Over evolutionary time, environmental circumstances are likely to have selected any mechanism which promoted such compensatory eating. Indeed there is evidence for such mechanisms. The classic 'Minnesota experiment' showed that even healthy male volunteers starved by external control develop many of the same preoccupations and experiences, including an increased urge to eat, as the predominantly female sufferers from eating disorders who impose such control upon themselves (Keys *et al.* 1950). Furthermore, laboratory experiments with restrained and non-restrained eaters show that although the former, by definition, tend to eat less in general, they may eat *more* once they have passed some threshold of eating. They tend to 'let go' in the face of prior consumption rather than eating less when they have eaten already (Herman and Polivy 1984; Polivy and Herman 1995). This has been called counter-regulation in contrast to the more straightforward regulation of the unrestrained eater. It is at least plausible that counter-regulation might play some part in the more exaggerated letting go and loss of control experienced with the bingeing of the bulimia sufferer. This role could include a contribution to both precipitation and perpetuation. The mechanisms involved in counter-regulation seem to be mainly cognitive (Polivy and Herman 1995) although there might also be some physiological component (Thompson *et al.* 1988).

Of course, it is possible to tell another plausible story about the association between eating restraint and bulimia nervosa. This would suggest that restraint is a response to binge eating rather than the other way around. Or that both undereating and overeating are manifestations of some primary problem in the regulation of consumption. These two alternative accounts seem less than compelling in the majority of cases of bulimia nervosa. However, they may be preferable in what seems to be the minority of cases where bingeing appears to have preceded restraint and in what may be the majority of cases of binge eating disorder (Mussell *et al.* 1995, 1997; Marcus 1997). The pathogenesis of the latter may well be different from that of bulimia nervosa in this respect. There is a real possibility that some primary problem of appetite and regulation is present in binge eating disorder and some cases of obesity. It could be that this is the case in bulimia nervosa also but it seems less necessary to invoke it. It is more parsimonious to suggest that it is eating restraint that disrupts the normal pattern of eating.

If eating restraint is involved in the perpetuation of bulimia nervosa, there are clear implications for treatment. Sufferers should be more likely to recover if they can bring themselves to lessen restraint and eat regularly and substantially. Successful treatment approaches characteristically include the shaping up of such an eating pattern (Fairburn *et al.* 1993; Freeman 1995) or its prescription (Lacey 1983). Clinical experience tends to support the view that the sufferer who insists upon continuing to diet is unlikely to stop bingeing for long. It is of interest that this may not be so in the treatment of binge eating disorder, since it has been shown that control of the eating disorder may be achieved in combination with calorie restriction (Marcus 1997).

WHAT MAKES SOME PEOPLE VULNERABLE?

Attempting to lose weight is very common and the pattern of the prevalence of dieting in a population may go a long way to explaining which *groups* of people are especially at risk for developing bulimia nervosa. Likewise it may explain why rates of disorder change over time. It is less useful in an attempt to understand why any one individual does or does not develop the disorder. As stated above, only a small minority of those who restrain their eating go on to develop any eating disorder. Why are some people vulnerable when others are apparently much less so?

One reason may involve factors which make individuals not only more likely to diet but also to diet with more determination. In doing so they might place themselves at greater risk. Another reason may be that the consequences of dieting might be different for some people.

THE MOTIVATION FOR EATING RESTRAINT

For most people eating restraint in the service of slimming is something which may be embarked upon with enthusiasm but which is readily abandoned when negative consequences accrue. The immediate rigours of restraint come to seem not to be worth the more distant pay off of slimness. Most attempts at slimming end in such arguably healthy failure, although not uncommonly the sequence of attempt and abandonment will be repeated. But for some it may seem worthwhile.

It is at least plausible to think that, compared to other people, adolescent girls and young women may slim more often and do so with more determination because weight and shape are experienced as especially important issues for them. Female development into adulthood is marked by notable changes in body shape and composition. These accrue powerful personal and social meanings. To be just the right size and shape may seem to promise confidence, well-being and acceptance at a time when such things are felt to be in short supply (Striegal-Moore 1993). This promise may be illusory and the idea of being 'just right' may be a chimera, but to try to achieve it is tempting and not to do so may feel like a failing. Cultural, peer and even family pressure to slim may encourage such feelings (Pike and Rodin 1991; Wilfey and Rodin 1995). A major case control study from Oxford found that bulimia sufferers were more likely than non-morbid controls to have family members who dieted and to recall teasing and comments about such matters (Fairburn *et al.* 1997). Furthermore, there is in most Western societies a wider culture which includes the active promotion of an unrealistic ideal of slender beauty and the peddling of products which purport to help those who would seek to attain it. The models of such culture—often models in the related sense also—may be *selected* as such because of natural attributes but the individual young woman may feel invited to *mould* herself in a way which is against her own natural form. The fashion industry and the media are sometimes blamed for causing eating disorders. This is a simplification because they reflect as much as they promote. However, they do make an important contribution to the context in which people decide to try to change themselves through slimming. The dieting industry thrives upon these attempts and arguably also upon their repeated failure.

There is some evidence that groups of people who are under exaggerated social pressure to be slim such as dancers and models have an increased risk of developing eating disorders including bulimia nervosa (Hamilton *et al.* 1985; Garner *et al.* 1987). Such groups may be thought of as experiencing a greater than average dose of the widespread social pressures. Other groups such as male wrestlers and jockeys are driven to eating restraint by quite other social forces but they too may be at increased risk of eating disorders resembling bulimia nervosa (King and Mezey 1987).

It seems that the Western culture which places such value on slimness in young women is becoming world wide in extent (Nasser 1997). It is likely to bring bulimia nervosa with it and there is some evidence for this, for instance, in Egypt (Nasser 1997). The tendency toward uniformity in a world wide culture which values slimness in young women is undoubtedly facilitated by an increasingly global economy and by the media. Why this nearly ubiquitous culture should promote this particular image is a matter for speculation. Grist for any speculative mill might include the association of slenderness with youth and with general fitness. In this respect, it is of interest that the degree of slimness which is characteristic of the iconic beauties of our age may not be associated with *reproductive* fitness. (A recent paper suggested that if the plaster mannequins used to model clothes in shops were to be real women they would not have enough body fat to sustain menstruation

(Rintala and Mustajoki 1992). This may also be the case for some of the flesh-and-blood models also.) It may be that the currently valued female shape reflects some amalgam of youth, general fitness and a partial rejection of reproductively potent femininity. This in turn could be related to the complexities and dilemmas of the demands upon women as their social roles and expectations change (Striegal-Moore 1993). However, such ideas are inevitably the result of post hoc theorizing. Many ideas are put forward and there is often no clear way of choosing between them. Nevertheless, it does seem that the current search for slenderness is being pursued against a background of increasing obesity (Williamson 1995). On average young women have become plumper over recent decades. There is an increasing tension between image and reality.

Actual obesity provides a rational motivation for eating restraint even though the long term results in terms of weight loss are so often disappointing (Garner and Wooley 1991). Obesity is associated with some health risks and furthermore is socially stigmatized (Stunkard and Sobal 1995). For many, the attraction of slenderness is augmented by a fear of fatness which is rooted in personal or family experience. The Oxford case–control study found that both personal childhood obesity and parental obesity were risk factors for bulimia nervosa (Fairburn *et al.* 1997).

Occasionally the motivation for restraint seems to be unconnected with weight and the search for slenderness or even physical health. Many clinicians have anecdotes of people who have become eating disordered in relation to exaggerated fears of food allergies or religious beliefs about the value of fasting. They may come to have disorders which fulfil diagnostic criteria for bulimia nervosa except that they lack weight concern. They have different motivations for their eating restraint but it seems a pity that they should be excluded from the diagnosis (Palmer 1993).

THE CONSEQUENCES OF RESTRAINT

As noted above, the usual consequence of eating restraint in people with an otherwise unimpaired appetite for food is an increase in hunger and food preoccupation. There may also be general dysphoria. When the restraint is motivated by beliefs and ideas, these may in turn be affected by such consequences. The dieter may feel greedy and lacking in will power and the religious faster may feel sinful. For both there may come to be something circular in their thinking with the consequences of their behaviour reinforcing its motivation. It may be that this circularity contributes to the perpetuation of the situation and, of course, some challenge to its components is part of cognitive behavioural therapy (Fairburn *et al.* 1993). Such circularity or positive feedback may lead to increasing instability, especially when compensatory behaviours such as vomiting or laxative abuse enter the picture.

Eating restraint has biological consequences as well as or as part of those that are describable in psychological terms. The mechanisms involved are poorly understood. However, there is evidence that dieting changes serotonergic function (Goodwin *et al.* 1987; Cowen *et al.* 1996). Furthermore, such changes are more evident in females than males. Women are not only more likely to diet but also have a physiology which responds differently. It is likely that other biological variation exists but this has not as yet been described.

It is at least plausible that antidepressant drugs act upon such mechanisms and this may be especially true of the selective serotonin reuptake inhibitors (SSRIs) such as fluoxetine (Goldbloom and Garfinkel 1990). However, evidence of efficacy in bulimia nervosa is not confined to drugs with a predominant effect upon 5-hydroxytryptamine (serotonin: HT) mechanisms (Walsh *et al.* 1991; Mitchell and de Zwaan 1993; Wakeling 1995). The modest positive effects of antidepressants may be mediated by quite other means. It is of interest that their utility does not depend upon the presence of comorbid major depression.

It is possible that many of the physiological consequences of eating restraint are universal or subject only to limited biological variation. However, just as the initial psychological motivation for restraint may be varied, the psychological interpretations put upon the experiences arising from restraint are likely to be more varied still. The psychology and psychogenesis of bulimia nervosa are likely to be complex. Nevertheless, much can be encompassed within the broad concept of self esteem.

SELF ESTEEM AND PERSONAL FACTORS

People suffering from bulimia nervosa characteristically have a low opinion of themselves. Their problems of self esteem are not always pervasive but they are often profound (Polivy and Herman 1993). Of course, it is possible that having a disorder like bulimia may in itself lead to such problems. A sufferer could feel a failure, or worse, for having allowed herself to become trapped in such a state. However, it is even more plausible that low self esteem may often precede the disorder and be a risk factor for its development as well as a factor in its perpetuation. Indeed, there is some limited prospective evidence that this is the case (Button *et al.* 1996). Retrospectively, the Oxford case–control study showed that bulimic subjects in the community were more likely to describe themselves in a way which led them to be rated as having a ‘negative self evaluation’ *in childhood* when compared to normal controls (Fairburn *et al.* 1997).

Once again, as with eating restraint, what is a demonstrable association between bulimia nervosa and low self esteem can be buttressed by a rational conjecture to form a plausible hypothesis. By definition, people setting out to restrain their eating in order to lose weight are dissatisfied with themselves—at the very least with their bodies. Commonly, dieting occurs at times of wider trouble and personal uncertainty. It seems likely that when the strongly motivated dieter encounters the ‘dieter’s dilemma’, her response may be importantly influenced by what she feels about herself in general. If her self esteem is reasonably good she may give up her attempt to slim for the time being or even permanently; she may judge it not worthwhile to continue. She will join the ranks of the healthily 'failed' dieters. However, if she feels badly about herself and perhaps worries that others share this low opinion, the whole venture may seem too important to give up. She then persists in her restraint and if she does give in to her urge to eat this may provoke even greater efforts to fight that urge which comes to feel increasingly out of control. Lapses may become binges and come to be invested with complex and ambivalent meaning. An unstable system of restraint and binge eating itself becomes a powerful generator of more such behaviour. It may also promote more extreme ideas and beliefs about weight and eating control (Cooper *et al.* 1989). Such a sequence could lower further the person's self esteem and lead to depression of mood.

Whilst the above account is largely conjectural, its individual elements have been observed in populations of bulimic subjects. Their personal backgrounds and life stories tend to contain more than their fair share of troubles and difficulties of a kind which might well affect the development of a healthy self esteem. Thus, bulimia nervosa sufferers have been shown to have had an excess of difficult childhood experiences such as parental conflict, criticism, over or under involvement and lack of affection (Fairburn *et al.* 1997). Furthermore, they are more likely than normal controls to have suffered sexual or physical abuse as children (Welch and Fairburn 1994; Wonderlich *et al.* 1996). They are also more likely to describe being the object of childhood bullying. All of these factors may make the individual more vulnerable as an adult, probably through promoting problems of self esteem.

Bulimia nervosa tends to arise disproportionately—although not exclusively—in women with disturbed and troubled backgrounds. Overall, the risk factors for bulimia nervosa are similar to those for many other psychiatric disorders and may be regarded in the main as potent but non-specific. Many of the factors mentioned above, such as childhood abuse and adversity, are risk factors for psychiatric disorder in general or at least for major depression. Once again the Oxford case–control study provides the best evidence to date (Fairburn *et al.* 1997). In that study, the community sample of bulimia nervosa sufferers were compared to a matched community sample of women suffering from other psychiatric disorders (predominantly depression) as well as with non-morbid women. Broadly the bulimic women resembled the depressed women on a range of personal and childhood variables which distinguished both groups from the women without psychiatric disorder. These included such issues as childhood shyness, school absence through anxiety, lack of childhood friends and parental depression. The specific variables which distinguished bulimic from depressed women were importantly those concerned with weight, eating and the risk of dieting. This suggests that it is the coincidence of such specific factors with a more general psychological vulnerability that is noxious.

However, there is some evidence that certain 'general' factors (i.e. factors unrelated to weight and eating) may have some special association with bulimia nervosa. These included the negative self evaluation in childhood mentioned above as well as premorbid perfectionism, low parental contact or parental arguments, criticism and high expectations (Fairburn *et al.* 1997). It is therefore possible that certain personal and family characteristics may be particularly related to bulimia nervosa even though they are not to do with weight and eating (Kendler *et al.* 1995). However, it is important to note that these risk factors have been identified in groups of women who live in a culture where weight, shape, fatness and figure are issues which are loaded with meaning and where slimming is commonplace. It seems unlikely that the presence of these risk factors would lead to this disorder in a radically different cultural context.

Overall, the family and childhood troubles of girls and young women who are to come to suffer from bulimia nervosa do resemble those who become disordered in other ways (Schmidt *et al.* 1993a). In this they seem somewhat different to those who suffer from anorexia nervosa who tend to report less overt family problems than would be expected of a psychologically disturbed group (Schmidt *et al.* 1993b).

Amongst other risk factors for bulimia nervosa are a parental history of depression or alcohol or drug abuse and a personal premorbid history of major depression. This raises the issue of the relationship between bulimia nervosa and other psychiatric disorders.

COMORBIDITY

Given what seems to be an important raft of shared risk factors, it is perhaps not surprising that the core symptoms of bulimia nervosa are commonly found with the core symptoms of other psychiatric disorders. Indeed, this is the case with full syndromes also. This coincidence of syndromes may produce mixed feelings in us. To a degree we may be reassured that our nosology carves nature at its joints and produces syndromes with some stability. However, extensive comorbidity must also lead us to question whether the details of our particular classifications are yet optimal and perhaps to anticipate the answer that they may not be.

One important issue concerns the relationship of bulimia nervosa with anorexia nervosa. Russell first described bulimia nervosa as a variant of anorexia but acknowledges that the two disorders have gradually come to be ‘partly separate’ (Russell 1979, 1997). It seems likely that the earliest formal description of bulimia nervosa was of people who had moved from a position of abstinent anorexia nervosa into bingeing when their capacity to sustain extreme restraint broke down. They were in a sense ‘failed’ anorectics. However, whereas almost all bulimia sufferers have a history of eating restraint, most have not taken this to a point where they have at any time fulfilled diagnostic criteria for anorexia nervosa. When an individual has a history of both anorexia and bulimia nervosa the former is much more likely to precede the latter than the other way around (Palmer and Robertson 1995). This consistent observation is in tune with a central role for eating restraint in bulimia nervosa.

In addition to low self esteem itself, bulimia nervosa sufferers characteristically have low mood, higher than average levels of depressive symptoms and a greater risk of showing full comorbid depressive syndromes and anxiety disorders (Cooper 1995; Bulik *et al.* 1996). Clinical experience suggests that some people develop the syndrome of bulimia nervosa as part of a major depressive disorder and that the bingeing remits if the depression is successfully treated. However, such cases seem to be few. In general, the depressive symptoms associated with bulimia nervosa tend to improve with remission of the eating disorder (Collings and King 1994; Fairburn *et al.* 1995). This suggests that they are a potentially understandable part of the same process and are not usually best thought of as primary. However, in terms of family history, there is some evidence of an association between bulimia nervosa and major depression (Kendler *et al.* 1991; Strober 1995). There is still much that is unclear about the relationship between bulimia and mood disorder.

A good deal has been written about the relationship between bulimia nervosa and alcohol and drug abuse. Some theorists emphasize apparent similarities but in general an addictive model of bulimia has not proved enlightening (Holderness *et al.* 1994; Wilson 1995). Nevertheless, the problems do occur together more often than would be expected by chance (Kendler *et al.* 1991; Higuchi *et al.* 1993) and when they do they may compound each other. Often they seem to coexist in the presence of personality disorder.

In clinical practice, bulimia nervosa seems to be associated with a comorbid axis II diagnosis in at least a substantial minority of cases (Herzog *et al.* 1992; Wonderlich 1995). In the main the disorders are of the so called cluster B (dramatic erratic types) and especially borderline personality disorder. However, two important questions arise about this association. Firstly, to what extent is it to be explained by the selection of doubly troubled people into clinical series? Secondly, to what extent are the features of 'personality disorder' a product of the instability of bulimia nervosa itself? Probably, the answer to both questions is somewhat but not completely. In considering the complex issues of personal development and style that get subsumed into the questionable concepts of personality and personality disorder, linear causation is unlikely. However, bulimia and personality disorder may well grow from common roots. When an individual has features of both they are likely to be especially troubled and probably especially difficult to help, although the evidence of poorer outcome is less consistent than might be anticipated (Rossiter *et al.* 1993; Wonderlich *et al.* 1994; Steiger and Stotland 1996). The concept of a multi-impulsive personality disorder which importantly includes individuals with bulimia nervosa and a range of other apparently impulsive behaviours, has been proposed but it is not as yet clear whether it does more than provide a neat name for this clinically challenging subgroup (Lacey and Evans 1986).

PRECIPITATION AND PERPETUATION

Given the presence of some mix of risk factors, there is still much that is mysterious or at best conjectural about how and why any individual comes to develop and then get stuck within the state of bulimia nervosa. It is plausible that motivated eating restraint together with low self esteem and the rest come together to trap the person in some kind of vicious circle. It is not difficult to develop an intuitive feel for the nature of this trap. Various diagrams full of boxes and arrows have been produced (Fairburn 1995). Such intuitions and graphics are useful in clinical practice. However, it is important to acknowledge that we remain ignorant of the details and indeed could still be mistaken about much of what we think we know. Perhaps the components of the trap are simply the normal regulatory mechanisms which take on this vicious character when pushed out of kilter by forceful restraint. Or perhaps some as yet unknown but crucial factor is operating. Many psychological mechanisms have been proposed and some have clinical or experimental support but none seems wholly satisfactory (Polivy and Herman 1993). Although plausible stories can be told, the detailed pathogenesis of bulimia nervosa remains obscure.

Little can be said with confidence about the process that leads from the presence of risk factors such as eating restraint and low self esteem to the full disorder. It is probable that onset often follows some sort of crisis of confidence and self esteem. Women with bulimia nervosa report having more life events in the year before onset than comparison women without disorder (Welch *et al.* 1997). Such events may be the final precipitant in many cases.

Once established, bulimia nervosa is characterized (by definition) by the presence of overvalued and sometimes extreme ideas about the importance of body size and shape. Such ideas provide the glue that binds the elements of the disorder together. They seem to play a major part in the perpetuation of the disorder. If they persist then the disorder is likely to recur even if behaviour is changed in the short term (Fairburn *et al.* 1995).

It is arguably inappropriate to look to successful treatments for evidence about aetiology. (That electroconvulsive therapy (ECT) is useful in severe depressive illness does not indicate that that disorder arises through lack of either electricity or convulsions.) Nevertheless it is tempting to think that therapeutic efficacy may say something about the perpetuation of bulimia nervosa. The evidence for what it is worth seems to go along with the picture drawn from other sources. Thus, the importance of eating restraint and the beliefs that are associated with it are at the heart of cognitive behaviour therapy (Fairburn *et al.* 1993). Likewise, it is reasonable to think that positive changes in self esteem may underlie the efficacy of interpersonal psychotherapy which pays little direct attention to eating and the like (Fairburn 1997). That both can be efficacious could be thought to support the idea of a vicious circle that can be broken at more than one point. Likewise the efficacy of a variety of antidepressants, even in the absence of comorbid depression, may provide some support for an undefined biological component (Mitchell and de Zwaan 1993; Wakeling 1995). However, such efficacy does not seem to be confined to serotonergic drugs and so does not provide any support for a specific role for this neurotransmitter above others.

BIOLOGICAL OBSERVATIONS

There are in the literature numerous observations of the physical and biological aspects of established bulimia nervosa. The jaded commentator might be tempted to see many as being the result of 'fishing trips' in which tests or observations are made to see what comes up rather than for any reason to do with theory or clinical observation. (Of course, such criticisms can also be made of other kinds of research and at least the biological researcher has the defence that some potentially interesting variables are simply not observable at all without special methods.) Nevertheless, many results of biological research are difficult to incorporate into a coherent aetiological story. There remains, however, the probability that potentially definable biological variation may make a crucial contribution to the pathogenesis of bulimia nervosa and especially to the differential vulnerability of individuals to the disorder. A chapter such as this written in a decade or two would probably be able to give a much more coherent account of these matters. Furthermore, to be fair, such an account might well owe much to the serendipitous findings of the 'fishing' alluded to above. However, for the moment, the picture is bitty and unsatisfactory (Pirke 1995).

One area of promise is genetic research which may, in the long run, not only define relevant genotypic variation, but also facilitate the study of how environmental and developmental issues interact with such variation to produce the phenotypic disorder. To date there is evidence to suggest some familial risk factor or factors for bulimia nervosa which are most likely genetic (Fichter and Noegel 1990; Hsu *et al.* 1990; Kendler *et al.* 1991; Treasure and Holland 1995). The nature of any genetically transmitted factor which increases the risk of bulimia remains unknown.

As stated above, serotonin mechanisms play a role in the consequences of eating restraint and they show sex differences. Serotonin is a likely candidate for abnormality in bulimia nervosa because it seems to have a role in normal satiety mechanisms (Goldbloom and Garfinkel 1990; Weltzin *et al.* 1994). However, definite neurotransmitter differences specific to bulimia nervosa have not been convincingly demonstrated. Areas of promise, in addition to serotonin, include the peptide transmitter PPY, cholecystokinin and the protein product of the obesity *ob* gene, leptin, which is postulated as playing a key role in what has been termed the 'lipostat' (Pirke 1995; Treasure *et al.* 1997).

There have been a number of reports of the results of brain scanning in bulimic subjects. Although less clear than the findings in low weight anorexia nervosa, studies using computed tomography (Kreig *et al.* 1989) and magnetic resonance imaging (Hoffman *et al.* 1989) have found differences between bulimics and controls, with the former tending to show sulcal widening and other evidence of diminished brain substance. Reduced metabolism of glucose has been demonstrated with positron emission tomography (Delvenne *et al.* 1997). The implications of these findings are unclear. It remains possible that they are direct and reversible effects of fluid and nutritional status and are without major pathogenic significance.

SYNTHESIS AND SPECULATION

Bulimia nervosa remains a disorder of uncertain aetiology in the sense that there is no single account that is able to specify necessary and sufficient conditions for its development. Nevertheless, some progress has been made in finding plausible causal issues for what is a fairly newly defined disorder. The best guess would seem to be that motivated eating restraint places some individuals at risk of entering a self sustaining pattern of behaviour and belief which leads to bulimia nervosa. There is a good deal of evidence about which groups of people are most at risk but less about which are the vulnerable individuals within these groups. Future research would do well to concentrate upon trying to define factors which raise or lower the risk of disorder in the presence of determined eating restraint. It is likely that such risk factors might be definable in either psychological or biological terms and indeed in both together. To use an old-fashioned term, 'constitutional' factors may well be promising. For instance, it may be that people who differ along a psychological dimension from controlled asceticism to erratic impulsivity are definably different in biological terms at least by the time that they are adult. When eating restraint is rare, those who do restrain are more likely to be drawn from the former and to engage in such behaviour for motives which are individual and internal. When eating restraint is widespread, the latter may succumb to external social pressure to slim. Is it not plausible that their response to restraint might be doubly different—that is for both psychological and biological reasons? Perhaps it was the recruitment of the more impulsive into the previously ascetic ranks of those who determinedly restrain their eating that led to the rise of bulimia nervosa a quarter of a century ago.

CLINICAL AND RESEARCH IMPLICATIONS

Personal versions of prevalent beliefs about weight and eating provide the motivation for eating restraint which is the usual first step on the pathway to the disorder.

- Primary prevention of bulimia nervosa would need to involve successful challenge of the widespread overvaluing of slimness and the belief that weight reduction can be easily achieved by dieting.
- Treatment requires that the sufferer lessens or abandons such restraint.

Restraint of eating leads to psychological and biological consequences.

- Further research should investigate the nature and range of these consequences. It is possible that relevant drugs might be produced if the biological consequences were better understood.

Continued

Such consequences may be different or be interpreted differently by people who are in some ways vulnerable.

- Such vulnerability includes low self esteem and a range of developmental experiences which have promoted it. Treatment needs to address such wider issues.
- There may be biological variation in response to eating restraint. Genetic research may help to elucidate this.
- There is certainly psychological variation. Research should examine further the risk factors and mechanisms that determine whether or not an individual develops disorder in the presence of a sustained attempt at eating restraint.

As the disorder develops the sufferer comes to have more unusual ideas linking weight and eating with wider personal issues. These tend to be exaggerated versions of the beliefs which prompted the eating restraint in the first place. Such ideas constitute the specific psychopathology of the disorder.

- Treatments which address directly this specific psychopathology (e.g. CBT) may be especially efficacious.

It is possible that a minority of bulimia nervosa sufferers and perhaps a majority of those with binge eating disorders have a disorder which is not based in restraint. They may have some primary problem of eating regulation.

- Future research needs to further define, describe and study this subgroup.

REFERENCES

Bulik, C.M., Sullivan, P.F., Carter, F.A. and Joyce, P.R. (1996) Lifetime anxiety disorders in women with bulimia nervosa. *Comprehensive Psychiatry*, **37**, 368–374.

Button, E.J., Sonuga-Barke, E.J.S., Davies, J. and Thompson, M. (1996) A prospective study of self-esteem in the prediction of eating problems in adolescent schoolgirls: questionnaire findings. *British Journal of Clinical Psychology*, **35**, 193–203.

Collings, S. and King, M. (1994) Ten year follow up of 50 patients with bulimia nervosa. *British Journal of Psychiatry*, **164**, 80–87.

Cooper, P.J. (1995) Eating disorders and their relationship to mood and anxiety disorders, in Brownell, K.D. and Fairburn, C.G. (editors) *Eating Disorders and Obesity; a Comprehensive Handbook*. Guilford Press: New York.

Cooper, Z., Cooper, P.J. and Fairburn, C.G. (1989) The validity of the Eating Disorders Examination and its subscales. *British Journal of Psychiatry*, **154**, 807–812.

Cowen, P.J., Clifford, E.M., Walsh, A.E.S., Williams, C. and Fairburn, C.G. (1996) Moderate dieting causes 5HT(2C) receptor supersensitivity. *Psychological Medicine*, **26**, 1155–1159.

Delvenne, V., Goldman, S., Simon, Y., de Maerteler, V. and Lotra, F. (1997) Brain hypometabolism of glucose in bulimia nervosa. *International Journal of Eating Disorders*, **21**, 313–320.

Fairburn, C.G. (1995) *Overcoming Binge Eating*. Guilford Press: New York.

Fairburn, C.G. (1997) Interpersonal psychotherapy for bulimia nervosa, in Garner, D.M. and Garfinkel, P.E. (editors) *Handbook for the Treatment of Eating Disorders*. Guilford Press: New York.

Fairburn, C.G., Marcus, M.D. and Wilson, G.T. (1993) Cognitive behaviour therapy for binge eating and bulimia nervosa: a comprehensive treatment manual, in Fairburn, C.G. and Wilson, G.T. (editors) *Binge Eating: Nature, Assessment and Treatment*. Guilford Press: New York.

Fairburn, C.G., Norman, P.A., Welch, S.L., O'Connor, M.E., Doll, H.A. and Peveler, R.C. (1995) A prospective study of outcome in bulimia nervosa and the long-term effects of three psychological treatments. *Archives of General Psychiatry*, **52**, 304–312.

Fairburn, C.G., Welch, S.L., Doll, H.A., Davies, B.A. and O'Connor, M.E. (1997) Risk factors for bulimia nervosa: a community-based case–control study. *Archives of General Psychiatry*, **54**, 509–517.

Fichter, M.M. and Noegel, R. (1990) Concordance for bulimia nervosa in twins. *International Journal of Eating Disorders*, **9**, 255–263.

Freeman, C.P.L. (1995) Cognitive therapy, in Szmukler, G., Dare, C. and Treasure, J. (editors) *Handbook of Eating Disorders*. John Wiley & Sons: Chichester.

Garner, D.M. and Garfinkel, P.E. (1980) Socio-cultural factors in the development of anorexia nervosa. *Psychological Medicine*, **10**, 647–656.

Garner, D.M. and Wooley, S.C. (1991) Confronting the failure of behavioural and dietary treatments for obesity. *Clinical Psychology Review*, **11**, 729–780.

Garner, D.M., Garfinkel, P.E., Rockert, W. and Olmsted, M.P. (1987) A prospective study of eating disturbances in the ballet. *Psychotherapy and Psychosomatics*, **48**, 170–175.

Goldbloom, D.S. and Garfinkel, P.E. (1990) The serotonic hypothesis of bulimia nervosa. *Canadian Journal of Psychiatry*, **35**, 741–744.

Goodwin, G.M., Fairburn, C.G. and Cowen, P.J. (1987) Dieting changes serotonergic function in women, not men: implications for the aetiology of anorexia nervosa. *Psychological Medicine*, **17**, 839–842.

Gordon, R. (1990) *Anorexia and Bulimia: Anatomy of a Social Epidemic*. Basil Blackwell: Cambridge, Mass.

Hamilton, L.H., Brooks-Gunn, J. and Warren, M.P. (1985) Sociocultural influences on eating disorders in professional female ballet dancers. *International Journal of Eating Disorders*, **4**, 465–477.

Herman, C.P. and Polivy, J. (1984) A boundary model for the regulation of eating, in Stunkard, A.J. and Stellar, E. (editors) *Eating and its Disorders*. Raven Press: New York.

Herzog, D.B., Keller, M.B., Lavori, P.W., Kenny, G.M. and Sacks, N.R. (1992) The prevalence of personality disorders in 210 women with eating disorders. *Journal of Clinical Psychiatry*, **53**, 147–152.

Higuchi, S., Suzuki, K., Yamada, K., Parish, K. and Kono, H. (1993) Alcoholics with eating disorders: prevalence and clinical course. *British Journal of Psychiatry*, **162**, 403–406.

Hoffman, G.W., Ellingwood, E.H., Rockwell, W.J., Herfkens, R.J., Nishita, J.K. and Guthrie, L.F. (1989) Cerebral atrophy in bulimia. *Biological Psychiatry*, **25**, 894–902.

Holderness, C.C., Brooks-Gunn, J. and Warren, M.P. (1994) Comorbidity of eating disorder and substance abuse—review of the literature. *International Journal of Eating Disorders*, **16**, 1–34.

Hsu, L.K.G. (1997) Can dieting cause an eating disorder? *Psychological Medicine*, **27**, 509–513.

Hsu, L.K.G., Chesler, B.E. and Santhouse, R. (1990) Bulimia nervosa in eleven sets of twins: a clinical report. *International Journal of Eating Disorders*, **9**, 275–282.

Kendler, K.S., MacLean, C., Neale, M., Kessler, R., Heath, A. and Eaves, L. (1991) The genetic epidemiology of bulimia nervosa. *American Journal of Psychiatry*, **148**, 1627–1637.

Kendler, K.S., Walters, E.E., Neale, M.C., Kessler, R.C., Heath, A.C. and Eaves, L.J. (1995) The structure of the genetic and environmental risk factors for six major psychiatric disorders in women. *Archives of General Psychiatry*, **52**, 374–383.

Keys, A., Brozek, J., Henschel, A., Mickelson, O. and Taylor, H.L. (1950) *The Biology of Human Starvation*. Minneapolis: University of Minnesota Press.

Killen, J.D., Taylor, C.B., Hayward, C., Wilson, D.M., Haydel, K.F., Hammer, L.D., Simmonds, B., Robinson, T.N., Litt, I., Vardy, A. and Kraemer, H. (1994) Pursuit of thinness and onset of eating disorder symptoms in a community sample of adolescent girls: a three year prospective analysis. *International Journal of Eating Disorders*, **16**, 227–238.

King, M. and Mezey, G. (1987) Eating behaviour in male racing jockeys. *Psychological Medicine*, **17**, 249–253.

Kreig, J.L., Lauer, C. and Pirke, K.M. (1989) Structural brain abnormalities in patients with bulimia. *Psychiatry Research*, **27**, 39–48.

Lacey, J.H. (1983) Bulimia nervosa, binge eating and psychogenic vomiting; a controlled treatment study and long term follow up. *British Medical Journal*, **286**, 1609–1613.

Lacey, J.H. and Evans, C.D.H. (1986) The impulsivist: a multi-impulsive personality disorder. *British Journal of Addiction*, **81**, 641–649.

Marcus, M.D. (1997) Adapting treatment for patients with binge-eating disorder, in Garner, D.M. and Garfinkel, P.E. (editors) *Handbook of Treatment for the Eating Disorders* (2nd Edition). Guilford: New York.

Marshall, P.D., Palmer, R.L. and Stretch, D. (1993) The description and measurement of abnormal beliefs in anorexia nervosa: a controlled study. *International Journal of Methods in Psychiatric Research*, **3**, 193–200.

Mitchell, J.E. and de Zwaan, M. (1993) Pharmacological treatment of binge eating, in Fairburn, C.G. and Wilson, G.T. (editors) *Binge Eating: Nature, Assessment and Treatment*. Guilford: New York.

Mussell, M.P., Mitchell, J.E., Weller, C.L., Raymond, N.C., Crow, S.J. and Crosby, R.D. (1995) Onset of binge eating, dieting, obesity and mood disorders among subjects seeking treatment for binge eating disorder. *International Journal of Eating Disorders*, **17**, 395–410.

Mussell, M.P., Mitchell, J.E., Fenna, C.J., Crosby, R.D., Miller, J.P. and Hoberman, H.M. (1997) A comparison of onset of binge eating and dieting in the development of bulimia nervosa. *International Journal of Eating Disorders*, **21**, 353–360.

Nasser, M. (1997) *Culture and Weight Consciousness*. Routledge: London.

Palmer, R.L. (1993) Weight concern should not be a necessary criterion for the eating disorders; a polemic. *International Journal of Eating Disorders*, **14**, 459–465.

Palmer, R.L. and Robertson, D.N. (1995) Outcome in anorexia nervosa and bulimia nervosa. *Current Opinion in Psychiatry*, **8**, 90–92.

Parry-Jones, B. and Parry-Jones, W.L. (1995) History of bulimia and bulimia nervosa, in Brownell, K.D. and Fairburn, C.G. (editors) *Eating Disorders and Obesity; A Comprehensive Handbook*. Guilford Press: New York.

Patton, G.C., Johnson-Sabine, E., Wood, K., Mann, A.H. and Wakeling, A. (1990) Abnormal eating attitudes in London schoolgirls—a prospective epidemiological study. *Psychological Medicine*, **20**, 383–394.

Pike, K.M. and Rodin, J. (1991) Mothers, daughters and disordered eating. *Journal of Abnormal Psychology*, **100**, 198–204.

Pirke, K.M. (1995) Physiology of bulimia nervosa, in Brownell, K.D. and Fairburn, C.G. (editors) *Eating Disorders and Obesity; A Comprehensive Handbook*. Guilford: New York.

Polivy, J. and Herman, C.P. (1993) Etiology of binge eating: psychological mechanisms, in Fairburn, C.G. and Wilson, G.T. (editors) *Binge Eating: Nature, Assessment and Treatment*. Guilford: New York.

Polivy, J. and Herman, C.P. (1995) Dieting and its relation to eating disorders, in Brownell, K.D. and Fairburn, C.G. (editors) *Eating Disorders and Obesity; A Comprehensive Handbook*. Guilford: New York.

Rintala, M. and Mustajoki, P. (1992) Could mannequins menstruate? *British Medical Journal*, **305**, 1575–1576.

Rossiter, E.M., Agras, W.S., Telch, C.F. and Schneider, A. (1993) Cluster B personality disorder characteristics predict outcome in the treatment of bulimia nervosa. *International Journal of Eating Disorders*, **13**, 349–358.

Russell, G.F.M. (1979) Bulimia nervosa: an ominous variant of anorexia nervosa. *Psychological Medicine*, **9**, 429–448.

Russell, G.F.M. (1997) The history of bulimia nervosa, in Garner D.M. and Garfinkel P.E. (editors) *Handbook of Treatment for the Eating Disorders*. Guilford Press: New York.

Schmidt U., Tiller J. and Treasure, J. (1993a) Psychosocial factors in the origins of bulimia nervosa. *International Review of Psychiatry*, **5**, 51–60.

Schmidt U., Tiller J. and Treasure J. (1993b) Setting the scene for the eating disorders: childhood care, classification and course of illness. *Psychological Medicine* **23**, 663–672.

Steiger, H. and Stotland, S. (1996) Prospective study of outcome of bulimics as a function of axis II comorbidity: long term response on eating and psychiatric symptoms. *International Journal of Eating Disorders*, **20**, 149–161.

Streigal-Moore, R.H. (1993) Etiology of binge eating: a developmental perspective, in Fairburn, C.G. and Wilson, G.T. (editors) *Binge Eating: Nature, Assessment and Treatment*. Guilford: New York.

Strober, M. (1995) Family-genetic influences on anorexia nervosa and bulimia nervosa, in Brownell, K.D. and Fairburn, C.G. (editors) *Eating Disorders and Obesity; A Comprehensive Handbook*. Guilford: New York.

Stunkard, A. and Sobal, B. (1995) Psychosocial consequences of obesity, in Brownell, K.D. and Fairburn, C.G. (editors) *Eating Disorders and Obesity; A Comprehensive Handbook*. Guilford: New York.

Treasure, J. and Holland, A. (1995) Genetic factors in eating disorders, in Szmukler, G., Dare, C. and Treasure, J. (editors) *Handbook of Eating Disorders*. John Wiley & Sons: Chichester.

Thompson, J., Palmer, R.L. and Petersen, S. (1988) Is there a physiological component to counterregulation? *International Journal of Eating Disorders*, **7**, 307–319.

Treasure, J., Collier, D. and Campbell, I.C. (1997) Ill fitting genes: the biology of weight and shape control in relation to body composition and eating disorders. *Psychological Medicine*, **27**, 505–508.

Vandereycken, W. (1994) Emergence of bulimia nervosa as a separate diagnostic entity: a review of the literature from 1960 to 1979. *International Journal of Eating Disorders*, **16**, 105–116.

Wakeling, A. (1995) Physical treatments, in Szmukler, G., Dare, C. and Treasure, J. (editors) *Handbook of Eating Disorders; Theory, Treatment and Research*. John Wiley & Sons: Chichester.

Walsh, B.T., Hadigan, C.M., Devlin, M.J., Gladis, M. and Roose, S.P. (1991) Long-term outcome of antidepressant treatment for bulimia nervosa. *American Journal of Psychiatry*, **148**, 1206–1212.

Welch, S.L. and Fairburn, C.G. (1994) Sexual abuse and bulimia nervosa: three integrated case–control comparisons. *American Journal of Psychiatry*, **151**, 402–407.

Welch, S.L., Doll, H.A. and Fairburn, C.G. (1997) Life events and the onset of bulimia nervosa: a controlled study. *Psychological Medicine*, **27**, 515–522.

Weltzin, T.E., Fernstrom, M.H. and Kaye, W.H. (1994) Serotonin and bulimia nervosa. *Nutrition Reviews*, **52**, 399–408.

Wilfey, D.E. and Rodin, J. (1995) Cultural influences on eating disorders, in Brownell, K.D. and Fairburn, C.G. (editors) *Eating Disorders and Obesity; A Comprehensive Handbook* Guilford: New York.

Williamson, D.F. (1995) Prevalence and demographics of obesity, in Brownell K.D. and Fairburn, C.G. (editors) *Eating Disorders and Obesity; A Comprehensive Handbook.* Guilford: New York.

Wilson, G.T. (1995) Eating disorders and addictive disorders, in Brownell, K.D. and Fairburn, C.G. (editors) *Eating Disorders and Obesity; A Comprehensive Handbook.* Guilford: New York.

Wonderlich, S.A. (1995) Personality and eating disorders, in Brownell, K.D. and Fairburn, C.G. (editors) *Eating Disorders and Obesity; A Comprehensive Handbook.* Guilford: New York.

Wonderlich, S.A., Fullerton, D., Swift, W.J. and Klein, M.H. (1994) Five year outcome from eating disorders: relevance of personality disorders. *International Journal of Eating Disorders*, **15**, 233–244.

Wonderlich, S.A., Wilsnack, R.W., Wilsnack, S.C. and Harris, T.R. (1996) Childhood sexual abuse and bulimic behaviour in a nationally representative sample. *American Journal of Public Health*, **86**, 1082–1086.

II Neurobiology

Introduction

J. TREASURE
The Eating Disorder Outpatient Unit, The Maudsley Hospital, London, UK

In this section we span time by dipping into developmental issues and try to build a biological understanding which ranges from the molecule to meaning. The chapter by Christie and colleagues from Great Ormond Street concentrates on children. The process of diagnosis in this age group is more complex. Anorexia nervosa is uncommon in children and there is a wider range of probable differential diagnosis including, for example, brain tumours. Also as the level of physical, cognitive and emotional development is less advanced the psychopathology may be atypical. Pervasive refusal syndrome, food avoidant emotional disorder, selective eating and functional dysphagia are additional diagnoses which need to be considered.

Starvation has profound effects on development. For example, a subject not mentioned in any of the chapters of this book and yet with direct implications for women with anorexia nervosa who conceive whilst still symptomatic are the effects of intra-uterine starvation on later development. Low birth weight at term (common in babies born to anorexic mothers) is associated with an increased adult risk of hypertension, coronary heart disease, non insulin dependant diabetes and autoimmune thyroid disease (Barker 1994). This work emphasizes how good nutrition is necessary to promote health throughout the life span.

Christie and colleagues document what is known about how starvation in the pubertal period (a classical feature of anorexia nervosa) affects later development. The reproductive system appears to be resilient to the interruption and regression caused by anorexia nervosa in that there have been reports of women aged 30 with primary amenorrhoea who achieve menarche. Nevertheless it is uncertain whether normal levels of fertility are achieved. Growth is more time limited and the effects of starvation can be irreversible and lead to stunting. It is uncertain whether anorexia nervosa occurring at this critical period can also prevent the attainment of optimal bone density and so increase the risk of osteoporosis. Starvation is known to also have effects on brain and cognitive development. The time at which anorexia occurs is the period in which there is active myelination of the brain and abstract cognitive processing begins. Lask and colleagues have used SPECT scanning on children and found reduced perfusion in the temporal lobe which persists after recovery. This may represent an interruption in normal brain development caused by the illness or it may be of aetiological relevance. It is uncertain whether anorexia nervosa interrupts normal cognitive development. For example, malnourished children from the third world have specific impairments in visuo-spatial ability. Although levels of academic achievement are high IQ scores fall in the average range which suggests that these women are out performing their potential probably because of their personality traits of persistence and low reward sensitivity (see below). For obvious reasons there has been very little in the way of analysis of body fluids or neuroendocrine probe tests in children.

The Great Ormond Street Group illustrate clearly how they integrate the biology of anorexia nervosa into treatment. Biology can shape the answers to distraught parents who ask 'Why my child?'; 'What did we do that was wrong?' Answers such as, 'There may be a genetic vulnerability which sensitizes the system to stress at puberty' can help alleviate the guilt which can paralyse all action and even lead to behaviours which serve to perpetuate the illness.

Physical measures such as pelvic ultrasonography or bone density scans can be important motivators for parents who find it difficult to grapple with the idea that their child might have emotional difficulties. For the child herself biology can provide concrete goals rather than the more abstract and distant statement 'You will die if you don't eat'. Also for the therapist physical factors can produce important markers of treatment effectiveness and outcome. Finally in this illness which has such a clear onset during an important phase of development the possibility of primary or secondary preventive strategies appears tantalizingly feasible. Christie mourns for the loss of the school nurse who might be able to detect cases before they had lost the 20% of weight that is common in those attending specialist clinics. Cross-cultural studies might open up the possibility of natural experiments. Do systems which retain a school nurse have a lower incidence of anorexia nervosa or are the cases less severe? These are fascinating questions.

Lilenfeld and Kaye gather the evidence for a genetic explanation of eating disorders. Monozygotic twins with anorexia nervosa ascertained from clinics are more likely than dizygotic twins to be concordant for the illness. This finding was not replicated in a study of a large sample of normal twins however the number of anorexic cases was small and the overall finding was that co-twins had a greater likelihood of developing anorexia nervosa. Higher levels of concordance of bulimia nervosa amongst monozygotic twins was also found. Anorexia nervosa and bulimia nervosa are both found more commonly amongst first degree relatives of probands with both types of eating disorder than would be expected. This suggests that there may be a shared transmissible vulnerability. On the other hand the link between eating disorders and affective disorders is probably not due to a single, shared aetiological factor between the two disorders. A similar conclusion is drawn from the pattern of associations between eating disorders and obsessive–compulsive disorder (OCD) and between bulimia nervosa and a family history of substance abuse. The conclusion is that there is probably not a strong genetic link between eating disorders and these additional types of axis I comorbidity but rather that there is independent familial transmission.

In contrast, the link between obsessional personality and restricting anorexia nervosa seems to be a familially determined vulnerability factor. It is possible that certain temperamental traits such as emotional restraint, avoidance of novelty, anxious worry, self doubt, compliancy, obsessionality, perfectionism and perseverance in the face of non-reward are what is genetically determined. These traits can manifest themselves as a variety of phenotypes including OCD personality disorder and restricting anorexia nervosa. These traits may themselves be manifestations of abnormalities in serotonin function.

In contrast, traits such as thrill seeking, excitability and dysphoria in the face of non-reward may shape the presentation towards bulimia nervosa. This may be underpinned by a variability in the sensitivity of brain systems to hedonic and rewarding aspects of food which in turn may determine whether unremitting starvation can be tolerated or whether this will be punctuated with breakthrough binging.

Owen takes us into a journey into the realm of 'new' biology in which Dolly the sheep and other clones or exotic breeds may give us the tools to tackle some of the puzzles that have tasked us over the years. His area of expertise is agriculture, an unusual contributor to an edition on anorexia nervosa! However farmers have interfered with nature for years to optimize aspects of the body composition of animals to suit the palate, purse and the ecosystem. Diet choice, physical activity, body composition are all highly genetically determined. Owen argues that eating disorders may result from a distorted or 'mis-read' reference set point for body composition. Owen surveys the animal kingdom looking for models which may have potential candidate genes. Several strains of domesticated animals such as pigs have analogous conditions to anorexia nervosa. He roams into the uncharted territory of the future to consider what implications there may be for management.

Beumont brings us back to basics in man where our level of knowledge is much less sophisticated. Unfortunately in man the act of studying and monitoring food intake so often serves to change it. New, less cumbersome methods of measuring metabolism may help clarify the picture. The hypothalamus has long been recognized to be a hub in the control of appetite both in terms of wanting (driven by hedonistic factors) and needing food to maintain a weight set point. A variety of neurotransmitters are involved in this network with leptin acting as a link between the central and peripheral systems. Beumont suggests that we reflect on other animal models in which there are physiologically driven changes in eating behaviour such as species who hibernate or who fast during reproductive periods as these may provide clues as to the aetiology of eating disorders.

The nervosa stem of the names we use for the eating disorders emphasizes that psychological strain has been thought to be a key component. Severe life events or difficulties are important antecedents to both forms of eating disorders. In addition, development stress such as parental neglect and abuse is a common precursor of bulimia nervosa. Multivariate analysis of a large sample of twins revealed that shared family environment explained a large proportion of the variance for bulimia nervosa. The chapter by Connan and Treasure illustrates how research from a variety of animal models of chronic stress can illuminate our understanding of eating disorders. Serotonin and the hypothalamic–pituitary axis are at the heart of the neurochemical systems that control stress and appetite. Several clinical implications follow from this. For example, a mixture of pharmotherapy and psychotherapy may provide optimal management for patients with bulimia nervosa associated with developmental stress. The success of selective serotonin reuptake inhibitor (SSRI) drugs may be related to their ability to moderate the over sensitized physiological response to stress. Once the arousal level is reduced it may be possible to introduce more adaptive coping strategies.

Ellison and Foong attempt to synthesize the developments in brain imaging. At the moment the field is somewhat difficult to digest and people seem to be grazing throughout all territories of the brain with no *a priori* hypotheses.

The earlier scanning techniques revealed there to be a loss of brain substance in anorexia nervosa which was not always reversed after weight gain. The reason for the apparent loss of brain tissue was not clear. One theoretical mechanism is receiving a great deal of attention in other psychiatric fields: Sapolsky 1996 suggests that long-term stress and high cortisol may damage the hippocampus, in particular, and lead to memory difficulties (see Connan and Treasure for further details). This theory remains controversial (O'Brien 1997) and it has not been specifically addressed in related to the eating disorders however some of the scanning studies with greatest definition have found that subcortical areas to be most affected in anorexia nervosa. A recent study by Lambe *et al.* (1997) in young adolescents found persistent structural effects after recovery. Such persistent damage to the brain may play a role in the maintenance of the disorder. It is difficult to establish how much of structural damage that is seen results from rather than predates the illness. In some studies between a quarter to a half of patients have abnormalities which appear to be congenital.

Many functional imaging studies have been empirical rather than hypothesis driven. Reductions in temporal lobe blood flow were found with SPECT scans in children but not in adults which suggests that there are developmental differences.

The findings from PET studies are difficult to interpret because it has been necessary to make compromises for ethical reasons leading to studies of small size with less than optimal comparison groups. Both SPECT and PET studies have found temporal lobe hypermetabolism (in particular on the left) in bulimia nervosa. Functional imaging with SPECT seems to suggest that eating in anorexia nervosa causes differential changes in all areas of the brain (inferior frontal cortex, parietal, occipital and temporal regions). Functional MRI scanning has accuracy, with fewer of the complications of radiation and validity. Specific changes in flow in the amygdala, insula and anterior cingulate area occur in response to images of high-Calorie food. These are areas which are associated with emotional processing.

Most research into the meaning of eating disorders has focused upon weight and shape. Meyer and colleagues have brought emotional issues back into the cognitive model. They suggest that the traditional model with its focus on physiological factors relating to starvation and hunger drives is too simple and they develop a model which incorporates the emotional reinforcers of overeating. For example, in their model eating can serve the function of avoiding distressing emotions. Not only do they open the door to the emotions but they allow the unconscious to make a comeback. Preconscious processing of abandonment and threat cues is associated with overeating. Eating may reduce the activation of schema relating to threats to self esteem.

In conclusion this section which lies at the heart of the book is vibrant with new information. However, the authors have all tried to set this knowledge into the context of clinical models and we hope that you will be able to merge this information into your clinical practice.

REFERENCES

Barker, D.J.P. (1994) *Mothers, Babies and Disease in Later Life*. BMJ Publishing Group, London.

Lambe, E.K., Katzman, D.K., Mikulis, D.J., Kennedy, S.H. and Zipursky, R.B. (1997) Cerebral gray matter volume deficits after weight recovery from anorexia nervosa. *Arch Gen Psychiatry*, **54**: 537–542.

O'Brien, J.T. (1997) The glucocorticoid cascade hypothesis in man. *Brit J Psych*, **170**: 199–201.

Sapolsky, R.M. (1996) Why stress is bad for your brain. *Science*, **273**: 749–750.

Scrimshaw, N.S. (1997) The relation between fetal nutrition and chronic disease in later life. *Brit Med J*, **315**: 825–826.

7 Genetic Studies of Anorexia and Bulimia Nervosa

L. R. LILENFELD and W. H. KAYE
Department of Psychiatry, University of Pittsburgh School of Medicine, Pittsburgh PA, USA

THE ROLE OF GENETIC STUDIES IN EATING DISORDERS

Genetic studies have become increasingly prominent in psychiatric research during the past two decades. Eating disorders have not traditionally been viewed as heritable illnesses; however, a spate of recent family and twin studies lend credence to the possible role of genetic transmission of vulnerability (e.g. Strober 1991; Kendler *et al.* 1995). Indeed, in the face of robust cultural factors shaping attitudes toward weight and shape, the relative rarity of severe forms of eating disorders suggests a major contribution to risk and pathogenesis mediated by genetic, biological, and environmental processes.

Genetic analysis of an illness requires that the traits under study be relatively homogeneous, easily identifiable conditions (Woodside 1993). Although the specific etiology of anorexia nervosa remains uncertain, this illness has been repeatedly demonstrated to have a certain psychopathology, characterized by obsessional thinking and rigid, inflexible behavior (Strober 1980). Bulimia nervosa presents as a less homogeneous disorder than does anorexia nervosa, although personality traits such as emotional lability have reliably been found among bulimic individuals (Vitousek and Manke 1994). Given that eating disorders, restricting-type anorexia nervosa in particular, express clinical phenotypes that have been clearly and consistently defined, they are as suitable for genetic study as other forms of psychopathology. Limitations of genetic studies with eating disorders include the relative rarity of the illness, and the likely role of multigenic, rather than single gene effects, as is the case with most psychiatric illnesses.

TWIN STUDIES

HERITABILITY

A major empirical and heuristic advantage of the twin study paradigm is its ability to decompose the variance in liability to illness into independent genetic and

Neurobiology in the Treatment of Eating Disorders.
Edited by H.W. Hoek, J.L. Treasure and M.A. Katzman.

environmental factors and to derive estimates of the magnitude of these effects. There have been few methodologically rigorous twin studies of eating disorders. Existing reports are summarized in Table 7.1. In the first such study of anorexia nervosa (Holland *et al.* 1984), twins were ascertained through three sources; referrals to the eating disorders treatment program at St George's Hospital in London, the Maudsley Hospital Twin Registry, and voluntary referral based on knowledge of the study. Zygosity was established by blood group in 15 of the 16 monozygotic (MZ) pairs and 10 of the 14 dizygotic (DZ) pairs. The majority of eating disorder diagnoses were based on direct interviews with the twins, and one or both parents. Among the 30 pairs, they found concordance rates of 56% (9 of 16) among MZ twin pairs compared to 7% (1 of 14) among DZ twin pairs, indicating a very strong hereditary component to the illness.

Two subsequent reports from this research team have provided updated analyses on larger, partially overlapping samples. Holland *et al.* (1988) reported on 45 twin pairs, including 10 pairs who were part of the earlier study. Of the 45 pairs, 27 were voluntary referrals and 18 were identified through local hospital clinics. MZ twins and concordant pairs were overrepresented among volunteers. Again, all diagnoses were made through structured interviews with the twins themselves and their parents. Among these 45 pairs, they found concordance rates of 56% (14 of 25) among MZ twin pairs compared to 5% (1 of 20) among DZ twin pairs, again indicating a very strong hereditary influence. Treasure and Holland (1989) reported on 59 twin pairs and an unspecified number of probands who were included in the prior two analyses. Proband-wise concordance for restricting-type anorexia nervosa was found to be substantially higher for MZ twins (66%) than for DZ twins (0%), extending findings from their previous studies. In contrast, there was no evidence of differential concordance among MZ and DZ twin pairs for bulimia nervosa, where concordance rates were 35% and 29%, respectively.

Two studies of bulimia nervosa report evidence of higher concordance among MZ than DZ twin pairs, however the sample sizes are too small to be conclusive. Fichter and Noegel (1990) obtained subjects from those responding to a survey on bulimia nervosa, from patients in an eating disorders clinic, and from hospitalized patients at a university psychiatric facility. Zygosity was determined only by physical similarity. Eating disorder diagnoses were based on responses to self-report questionnaires designed to allow for classification by DSM-III-R criteria. Pair-wise concordance was found to be 83% (5 of 6) in MZ twins and 27% (4 of 15) in DZ twins. In a smaller study of 11 twin pairs by Hsu *et al.* (1990), subjects were obtained from patients referred over a three-year period to the University of Pittsburgh Eating Disorders Clinic. Zygosity was based only on physical similarity and diagnoses were made by direct interviews with the subjects. Two of the 6 (33%) MZ pairs and 0 of the 5 (0%) DZ pairs were concordant for bulimia nervosa.

Heritability of both anorexia and bulimia nervosa was examined in a recent epidemiological study of 2163 female twins, ascertained through the population-based twin registry in the Commonwealth of Virginia. This sample consisted of 590 MZ and 440 DZ twin pairs, and three pairs of unknown zygosity. All assessments

Table 7.1. Twin studies

Study	Subjects (*n*)	Concordance rates (# of concordant twin pairs)	Heritability estimate
Holland *et al.* 1984	Anorexia nervosa (60)	56% MZ (9 of 16) 7% DZ (1 of 14)	0.54[a]
Holland *et al.* 1988	Anorexia nervosa (90)	56% MZ (14 of 25) 5% DZ (1 of 20)	0.80
Treasure and Holland 1989	Anorexia nervosa (62)	66% MZ (14 of 21) 0% DZ (0 of 10)	0.70
	Bulimia nervosa (62)	35% MZ (5 of 14) 29% DZ (5 of 17)	0.15
Fichter and Noegel 1990	Bulimia nervosa (42)	83% MZ (5 of 6) 27% DZ (4 of 15)	not estimated
Hsu *et al.* 1990	Bulimia nervosa (22)	33% MZ (2 of 6) 0% DZ (0 of 5)	not estimated
Kendler *et al.* 1991	Epidemiological female twin sample (total $n = 2163$);		0.55
	Narrowly defined bulimia nervosa ($n = 60$)	Narrow definition: 23% MZ 9% DZ	
	Broadly defined bulimia nervosa ($n = 123$)	Broad definition: 26% MZ 16% DZ	
Walters and Kendler 1995	Epidemiological female twin sample (total $n = 2163$);		not estimated
	Narrowly defined anorexia nervosa ($n = 35$)	Narrow definition: not reported	
	Broadly defined anorexia nervosa ($n = 80$)	Broad definition: 10% MZ 22% DZ	

[a] Broad heritability estimate based on Smith (1974).

were conducted through direct interviews with the Structured Clinical Interview for DSM-III-R (SCID; Spitzer *et al.* 1987) and blind reviews of the interviews by an experienced psychiatrist. Zygosity determinations were based on a series of standard questions concerning similarity and frequency of contact, shown to be >95% accurate (Walters and Kendler 1995), and in cases of uncertain zygosity, blood typing was performed. Walters and Kendler (1995) found much lower concordance rates among MZ twins than previous studies by Holland and colleagues; however, the numbers of twin pairs in which one twin had anorexia nervosa was extremely small, because of the epidemiological nature of the sample. Different definitions of anorexia nervosa were used in this study. The 'computer narrow' definition was a strict computer algorithm based solely on responses to DSM-III-R based SCID items; the 'clinical narrow' definition was a definite or probable diagnosis based on all available information; the 'clinical broad' definition was a definite, probable, or possible diagnosis based on all available information.

Depending upon the definition of anorexia nervosa used, probandwise concordance rates for MZ twins ranged from 0% (for computer narrow and clinical narrow definitions) to 10% (for clinical broad definition) for MZ twins, and from 22% (for clinical broad definition) to 40% (for computer narrow definition) for DZ twins. Traditional heritability estimates were not calculated because of the very low prevalence of anorexia nervosa in the general population and because the number of twins concordant for anorexia nervosa in this sample was very small. These factors are also likely to account for the unexpectedly higher concordance rates among DZ compared to MZ twin pairs.

On the other hand, the authors found that the risk for a cotwin having anorexia nervosa, given that her twin had anorexia nervosa, was between 5 and 50, depending upon the definition of anorexia nervosa used (Walters and Kendler 1995). In addition, these authors found that the risk of bulimia nervosa was also significantly elevated in the cotwin of an anorexic twin (risk = 2.6), even after controlling for comorbidity with the anorexia nervosa. Thus, this large, epidemiological study of female twins is suggestive of a heritable component to anorexia nervosa, and suggests that family–genetic factors may be shared, in common with bulimia nervosa. Finally, the risk of major depressive disorder in the cotwin of an anorexic twin was found to be doubled, even after controlling for the presence of major depressive disorder in the first twin.

In the same population-based female twin sample, Kendler *et al.* (1991) found concordance rates of 23% among MZ and 9% among DZ twin pairs for 'narrowly defined' bulimia nervosa (definite or probable cases), and concordance rates of 26% among MZ and 16% among DZ twin pairs for 'broadly defined' bulimia nervosa (definite, probable, or possible cases). The heritability estimate for bulimia nervosa from this study was 0.55. The risk for anorexia nervosa in the cotwin of a bulimic twin was 8.2. As with anorexia nervosa, this study supports the notion that genetic factors are likely to play some role in the liability to bulimia nervosa, and that some of these factors may be shared between the two eating disorder phenotypes.

ENVIRONMENT

Genetic studies can tell us just as much about the role of environmental factors as heritable factors in the pathogenesis of a disorder. Most twin studies of psychopathology have found that non-genetic sources of variance are accounted for mainly by non-shared environmental factors outside the family (Walters *et al.* 1992; Kendler *et al.* 1991). The twin study conducted by Kendler *et al.* (1995) supported this finding for all psychiatric illnesses examined in their large sample of female twins, with the exception of bulimia nervosa. That is, multivariate analyses pointed toward a substantial role for shared familial environment in the development of bulimia nervosa. Although this may not seem surprising, given the many descriptions of the family dynamics of eating disordered individuals (Strober and Humphrey 1987), this finding is at odds with almost all previous genetic research of other psychiatric illnesses.

Thus, the most important factors involved in the development of bulimia nervosa may be family environment and genetic factors. It is likely that some common set of familial factors may influence the risk for both types of eating disorders (Walters and Kendler 1995). Final expression of the clinical phenotype (i.e. anorexia nervosa versus bulimia nervosa) may be caused by complex relationships among personality or temperamental traits, familial environment, and genetic predisposition. In fact, heritable personality traits may have a profound influence on family interactions.

LIMITATIONS

There are potential limitations of genetic research that must be considered. One limitation of twin study methodology concerns the 'equal environments' assumption (Plomin *et al.* 1990), wherein it is assumed that the degree of environmental similarity is approximately the same for both types of twins. If this assumption is not valid, any excess resemblance of MZ twins compared to DZ twins which is ascribed to genetic factors could be partly or entirely attributable to environmental factors. Although an early analysis of their 1030 female twin pairs showed support for the validity of the equal environments assumption in a study of several psychiatric disorders (Kendler *et al.* 1993), a later analysis showed that this assumption may not be valid for bulimia nervosa specifically, and in fact, physical similarity may indeed influence twin resemblance for this disorder (Hettema *et al.* 1995). Thus, while the equal environments assumption may be valid for most psychiatric illnesses, its violation may lead to spuriously high heritability estimates for bulimia nervosa.

Another limitation to be considered is biased subject ascertainment. For instance, gathering subjects through voluntary referrals, as was the case in Holland *et al.* (1984, 1988), may overselect for MZ twins and concordance, a problem avoided in the more expensive and time-consuming epidemiologic approach taken by Kendler and colleagues. Finally, many of the existing twin studies of eating disorders have relatively small sample sizes. These limitations notwithstanding, the available twin study literature suggests an important role played by genetic and familial environmental factors in the pathogenesis of anorexia and bulimia nervosa.

FAMILY STUDIES

The clustering of a particular illness among the relatives of an individual with the illness is the hallmark of intergenerational familial transmission (Strober 1995). Increased rate of the illness among one's relatives compared to that of unrelated people in the population is suggestive of some mechanism of transmissibility of illness within families. However, evidence of familial aggregation does not imply that the origin of a disorder is genetic. Aggregation can result from shared genes or common environmental factors. Although family studies do not yield information about the amount of genetic variation, data from family studies can serve several purposes. One of the most important is to provide a better understanding of diagnostic heterogeneity. For instance, if the diagnostic subgroup under study breeds true within families, this would support the validity of the diagnostic group (Weissman *et al.* 1986).

FAMILIAL AGGREGATION OF EATING DISORDERS

Eating disorders have been found, in a number of studies, to aggregate in families. The controlled family studies of eating disorders to date are summarized in Table 7.2. Several have found increased rates of both eating disorders among the relatives of anorexia nervosa probands, as well as among the relatives of probands with bulimia nervosa, in comparison to rates among the relatives of controls (Gershon *et al.* 1984; Hudson *et al.* 1987a; Kassett *et al.* 1989; Strober *et al.* 1990), suggesting a shared transmissible vulnerability for both disorders.

In the first rigorously conducted family–genetic study of anorexia nervosa, Gershon *et al.* (1984) examined 99 first-degree relatives of 24 anorexic probands and 265 first-degree relatives of 44 nonpsychiatrically ill control subjects using the Schedule for Affective Disorders and Schizophrenia (Spitzer and Endicott 1978) and the Family History-Research Diagnostic Criteria (Andreasen *et al.* 1977). Approximately three-quarters of interviews were conducted blind to proband status and 54% of relatives were directly interviewed. They found rates of anorexia nervosa and bulimia among first-degree relatives of anorexic probands to be 2% and 4.4% respectively, compared to 0% and 1.3% among relatives of control probands.

Hudson *et al.* (1987a) conducted lifetime psychiatric assessments on 283 first-degree relatives of 69 bulimic probands, 149 relatives of 28 community control subjects, and 104 relatives of 24 probands with major depressive disorder. Diagnoses of relatives were based solely on family history information provided by the probands. No cases of eating disorders were detected among relatives of controls,

Table 7.2. Controlled studies of lifetime risk of eating disorders among first-degree relatives of eating disorder probands

Study	# Probands (# first-degree relatives)				Relatives interviewed	Diagnosis in proband relatives (%)			Diagnosis in control relatives (%)		
	AN	BN	NC	other controls		AN	BN	Total	AN	BN	Total
Gershon *et al.* 1984	24 (99)	–	43 (265)	–	Y	2.0	4.4	6.4	0	1.3	1.3
Hudson *et al.* 1987a	–	69 (283)	28 (149)	24 (104)	N	1.7	1.7	3.4	0	0	0
Logue *et al.* 1989	17 (75)	13 (57)	20 (107)	16 (75)	Y	0	0	0	0	0	0
Kassett *et al.* 1989	–	40 (185)	24 (118)	–	Y	2.2	9.6	11.8	0	3.5	3.5
Strober *et al.* 1990	97 (387)	–	–	183 (738)	Y	4.1	2.6	6.7	0	1.1	1.1
Halmi *et al.* 1991	62 (169)	–	62 (178)	–	Y	1.2	1.2	2.4	0	0	0
Stern *et al.* 1992	34 (153)	–	34 (140)	–	Y (1 parent only)	5.9	2.9	8.8	0	5.9	5.9
Lilenfeld *et al.* unpublished	26 (93)	47 (177)	44 (190)	–	Y	1.1	1.1, 2.3 (relatives of AN and BN probands respectively)	11.8[a], 19.8[a] (relatives of AN and BN probands respectively)	0	0	3.7[a]

AN = anorexia nervosa; BN = bulimia nervosa; NC = non-eating disordered control. [a] Includes anorexia nervosa, bulimia nervosa, and eating disorder-not otherwise specified diagnoses.

whereas the combined rate of anorexia nervosa and bulimia nervosa among relatives of probands was 3.4%.

Kassett *et al.* (1989) studied eating disorder risk among 185 first-degree relatives of 40 probands with DSM-III-R bulimia nervosa and 118 relatives of 24 normal controls. Diagnoses were made blind to proband status, and were based on direct interviews for 62% of relatives and family history information for the remaining relatives. The rate of anorexia nervosa and bulimia nervosa among relatives of probands was over three times that of relatives of controls.

Strober *et al.* (1990), in the largest family–genetic study of anorexia nervosa conducted thus far, examined 387 first-degree relatives (over the age of 12) of 97 anorexic probands, 269 relatives of 66 affective disorder probands, and 469 relatives of 117 non-mood disorder psychiatrically ill probands. Direct interviews were conducted with 79% of relatives and diagnostic information for relatives was assessed blindly, although interviewers were not fully blind to proband diagnosis. Strober *et al.* (1990) found that the rate of anorexia nervosa was 4.1% among relatives of anorexic probands, whereas no case of anorexia nervosa was detected among relatives of controls. The lifetime rate of bulimia nervosa was 2.6% among relatives of anorexic probands, a rate that did not differ substantially from the population risk of this disorder among females.

Finally, Kaye and his colleagues (Lilenfeld *et al.* in press) studied 93 first-degree relatives of 26 anorexic probands, 177 first-degree relatives of 47 bulimic probands, and 190 first-degree relatives of 44 non-eating disordered control women. All interviewers were blind to proband status, and direct interviews were conducted with approximately three-quarters of all relatives; the remaining relatives were assessed through family history interviews with all of their available relatives. Although we found no evidence of elevated rates of anorexia nervosa and bulimia nervosa among relatives, when all eating disorders were considered (i.e. including eating disorder-not otherwise specified diagnoses), rates were 11.8% and 19.8% among the first-degree relatives of anorexic probands and bulimic probands, respectively, compared to a rate of 3.7% among relatives of control women.

Some family studies have found no evidence of familial aggregation of eating disorders (Logue *et al.* 1989; Halmi *et al.* 1991; Stern *et al.* 1992). Logue *et al.* (1989) studied 30 eating disorder probands (six with restricting-type anorexia nervosa; 11 with binge eating/purging-type anorexia nervosa; and 13 with bulimia nervosa) and their 132 adult first-degree relatives, who were compared with 107 relatives of nonpsychiatrically ill control subjects and 75 relatives of depressed control subjects. Eighty percent of relatives were directly interviewed, but diagnostic assessment of relatives was not blind to proband status. Halmi *et al.* (1991) obtained information on 62 probands with anorexia nervosa and their 169 first-degree relatives, as well as 62 control women and their 178 first-degree relatives. The Diagnostic Interview Schedule, Version III (DIS; Robins *et al.* 1981) was conducted with parents of probands and the Family History Research Diagnostic Criteria (Andreasen *et al.* 1977) was conducted with mothers of anorexic probands and control subjects to obtain family history information. All assessments were conducted by interviewers who were blind to the hypotheses of the study. Stern *et al.* (1992) studied 34 anorexic probands and 34 control women. One parent of each proband was interviewed to obtain a personal (using the Research Diagnostic Criteria interview; Spitzer *et al.* 1978) and family (using the Family History Research Diagnostic Criteria; Andreasen *et al.* 1977) psychiatric history. Relatively small sample sizes may account for the negative findings in these studies.

Overall, evidence from family study data suggest an increased prevalence of eating disorders among the first-degree relatives of probands with eating disorders. While the exact relationship between anorexia nervosa and bulimia nervosa remains obscure, the possibility of their cross-transmission suggests the existence of a shared etiologic factor(s) between the two syndromes. Likewise, the precise nature and mechanism of the transmitted liability, and the circumstances under which it is expressed phenotypically, remain unknown.

COMORBIDITY

It is well recognized that both anorexia and bulimia nervosa are often accompanied by other psychiatric symptoms and syndromes, in particular depression, substance use disorders, anxiety, obsessive–compulsive disorder, and personality disorders. These comorbidities are substantially exaggerated by malnutrition and pathologic eating behaviors (e.g., Keys *et al.* 1950). However, in some patients they antedate weight loss or disordered eating, or persist after recovery of normal weight or abstinence from binge eating (Strober 1980; Srinivasagan *et al.* 1995; Pollice *et al.* 1997), indicating that they may not simply be consequences, or sequelae, of malnutrition or pathologic feeding behavior. Whether such symptoms enhance vulnerability to the development of eating disorders remains uncertain.

In the absence of high risk paradigms, unraveling the essential nature and mechanisms underlying eating disorder comorbidities is a challenging task. One potential strategy is use of the family study design in which patterns of familial aggregation of other disorders among first-degree relatives of probands are examined. Examination of these patterns in reference to the presence versus absence of proband diagnostic comorbidity allows for the testing of different hypotheses regarding the nature of associations between these phenotypically different forms of psychopathology.

As reviewed and summarized by Klein and Riso (1993), covariation among disorders arises from any number of sources: (1) both disorders are different manifestations of a shared underlying etiology (i.e. genetic factors with behaviorally diverse expressions); (2) the disorders have different causes, but the presence of one may increase the risk of the development of the other; (3) some independent disorder causes both disorders; (4) the disorders have some vulnerabilities in common and some which are specific to each disorder. Family study methodology is a particularly useful approach for understanding general mechanisms that underlie the frequent coexistence of two disorders (Klein and Riso 1993; Wickramaratne and Weissman 1993).

Mood disorders

Mood disorders are among the most well-studied comorbid conditions with respect to the question of shared or independent familial transmission with eating disorders. A substantial number of family studies have shown elevated lifetime rates of major mood disorders among relatives of individuals with eating disorders compared to relatives of non-eating disordered individuals (Winokur *et al.* 1980; Gershon *et al.* 1984; Hudson *et al.* 1983, 1987a; Rivinus *et al.* 1984; Bulik 1987; Logue *et al.* 1989; Kassett *et al.* 1989; Strober *et al.* 1990; Boumann and Yates 1994; Lilenfeld *et al.* in press). By contrast, two studies failed to detect familial aggregation of mood disorders among relatives of women with bulimia (Stern *et al.* 1984; Halmi *et al.* 1991). At least one of these negative findings, however, is likely to be explained by the investigators' failure to screen control subjects for mood disorders, which led to unusually high rates of mood disorders among the relatives of control women (Stern *et al.* 1984), thereby confounding the assessment of familial risk. Tables 7.3 and 7.4 summarize controlled studies of mood disorders among relatives of probands with anorexia nervosa and bulimia nervosa.

Across all studies, relative risks for unipolar and bipolar affective illness combined are in the range of 2 to 4.2; that is, the biological relatives of individuals with eating disorders are two to four times more likely to have lifetime diagnoses of mood disorders compared to the relatives of non-eating disordered individuals. The one exception to these findings is the study by Hudson *et al.* (1983), in which risks of over 20 were found for relatives of anorexic and bulimic probands. This figure may be spuriously inflated, however, because familial psychopathology was determined by hospital chart records, which may have underestimated the true risk of affective illness among the relatives of psychiatric control probands.

Several attempts have been made to determine the effects of proband comorbidity on familial risk for mood disorders. Specifically, probands with eating disorders have been stratified by the presence or absence of a comorbid mood disorder themselves, and rates of mood disorders among the relatives of these two groups have been compared. A summary of these studies are reported in Table 7.5. In reports by Strober *et al.* (1990) and Biederman *et al.* (1985), mood disorders were found to be elevated only among the relatives of those eating disorder probands who also had a concomitant mood disorder. In a report by Lilenfeld *et al.* (in press), similar findings were obtained for bulimia nervosa probands and their relatives, specifically. By contrast, other studies (Gershon *et al.* 1984; Logue *et al.* 1989) suggest that eating disorders may be a variant expression of affective disease. These studies have found similarly elevated rates of affective illness among the relatives of eating disorder probands, independent of comorbid affective status. Still other reports (Hudson *et al.* 1987a; Kassett *et al.* 1989) failed to yield clear support for either hypothesis. In the reports by Hudson *et al.* (1987a) and Kassett *et al.* (1989), rates of affective illness were higher among the relatives of bulimic probands with affective illness compared to the relatives of bulimic probands without affective illness; however, rates were also elevated among the relatives of bulimic probands

Table 7.3. Controlled studies of lifetime risk of mood disorders among first-degree relatives of anorexia nervosa probands

Study	# Probands (# first-degree relatives)	# Controls (# first-degree relatives)	Relatives interviewed	Diagnosis in proband's relatives (%)			Relative risk[a]
				Unipolar depression	Bipolar illness	Total	
Winokur *et al.* 1980	25 (192)	25 (177)	Y	20.4	6.8	27.2	2.1
Hudson *et al.* 1983	34 (99)	43[b] (265)	N	14.2	3.0	17.2	25.6
Gershon *et al.* 1984	24 (169)	87 (499)	Y	13.3[c]	8.3[c]	21.6[c]	3.2
Rivinus *et al.* 1984	40 (545)[d]	23 (277)[d]	N	16.1[c]	0.0[c]	16.1[c]	3.4
Logue *et al.* 1989	17 (75)	30 (107)	Y	14.7	–	14.7	2.9
Strober *et al.* 1990	97 (387)	183[e] (738)	Y	7.2	1.6	8.8	2.1
Halmi *et al.* 1991	62 (169)	62 (178)	Y	6.5	0.6	7.1	1.4
Lilenfeld *et al.* unpublished	26 (93)	44 (190)	Y	15.1	1.1	16.2	2.2

[a] Rate of illness in relatives of anorexic probands divided by rate of illness in relatives of normal control subjects, unless otherwise noted. [b] Personality disorder and schizophrenic control subjects, screened for mood and eating disorders. [c] With age correction. [d] Includes first- and second-degree relatives. [e] Mood disorder and other psychiatrically ill control subjects, screened for mood and eating disorders.

Table 7.4. Controlled studies of lifetime risk of mood disorders among first-degree relatives of bulimia nervosa probands

Study	# Probands (# first-degree relatives)	# Controls (# first-degree relatives)	Relatives interviewed	Diagnosis in relatives (%)			Relative risk[a]
				Unipolar depression	Bipolar illness	Total	
Hudson *et al.* 1983	55 (251)	87[b] (499)	N	15.1	1.2	16.3	23.3
Stern *et al.* 1984	27[c]	61[cd]	Y (1 parent only)	–	–	9.0	0.9
Hudson *et al.* 1987a	69 (283)	28[d] (149)	N	15.5	4.2	19.8	4.2
Bulik 1987	35[c]	35[c]	N	37.1	–	37.1	2.6
Logue *et al.* 1989	13 (57)	20 (107)	Y	10.5	–	10.5	2.1
Kassett *et al.* 1989	40 (185)	24 (118)	Y	22.0[e]	5.9	27.9[e]	3.2
Boumann and Yates 1994	25 (47)	25 (49)	N (reports on parents only)	28.0	–	28.0	2.8
Lilenfeld *et al.* unpublished	47 (177)	44 (190)	Y	15.8	0.6	16.4	2.2

[a] Rate of illness in relatives of bulimic probands divided by rate of illness in relatives of normal control subjects, unless otherwise noted. [b] Personality disorder and schizophrenic control subjects, screened for mood and eating disorders. [c] Unknown number of relatives. [d] Unscreened community control subjects. [e] With age correction.

Table 7.5. Risk of affective illness in first-degree relatives by affective status of probands

	Probands		Risk to relatives (%)		
Study	Affective status	*n*	Unipolar depression	Bipolar illness	Total
Gershon *et al.* 1984	AN + MAD	13	13.4[a]	10.1[a]	23.5[a]
	AN − MAD	11	13.1[a]	5.3[a]	18.4[a]
Biederman *et al.* 1985	AN + MAD	17	17.3	0.0	17.3
	AN − MAD	21	3.3	0.0	3.3
Hudson *et al.* 1987a	BN + MAD	46	–	–	36.2[a]
	BN − MAD	23	–	–	18.7[a]
Logue *et al.* 1989	ED + MAD	10	13.0	–	13.0
	ED − MAD	20	12.0	–	12.0
Kassett *et al.* 1989	BN + MAD	23	29.5[a]	5.3[a]	34.8[a]
	BN − MAD	17	12.5[a]	6.6[a]	19.1[a]
Strober *et al.* 1990	AN + MAD	28	14.4	3.6	18.0
	AN − MAD	69	4.3	0.7	5.1
Lilenfeld *et al.* unpublished	AN + MDD	12	19.0	–	19.0
	AN − MDD	14	17.1	–	17.1
	BN + MDD	26	20.2	–	20.2
	BN − MDD	21	12.3	–	12.3

AN = anorexia nervosa; BN = bulimia nervosa; ED = eating disorder (anorexia nervosa and bulimia nervosa combined); MAD = major affective disorder; MDD = major depressive disorder. [a] With age correction.

without affective illness compared to the relatives of control probands. Although there continues to be some debate in the field, the weight of evidence suggests that mood disorders and eating disorders frequently coexist, but this is not due to a single, shared etiologic factor between the two disorders.

Substance use disorders

It is particularly important to distinguish between anorexia nervosa and bulimia nervosa when studying the relationship between substance use disorders and eating disorders, in as much as alcohol and drug use disorders appear to be over-represented among individuals with bulimic symptomatology (i.e. bulimia nervosa and binge eating/purging-type anorexia nervosa) (Holderness *et al.* 1994; Lilenfeld and Kaye 1996).

A number of family studies have shown elevated lifetime rates of substance use disorders among relatives of individuals with bulimia nervosa compared to relatives of individuals with anorexia nervosa or relatives of non-eating disordered individuals (see review by Holderness *et al.* 1994). A summary of the controlled family studies of substance use disorders among relatives of anorexic and bulimic probands is reported in Tables 7.6 and 7.7.

As with mood disorders and eating disorders, only a handful of studies have investigated whether bulimia nervosa and substance use disorders represent alter-

Table 7.6. Controlled studies of lifetime risk of substance use disorders among first-degree relatives of anorexia nervosa probands

Study	# Probands (# first-degree relatives)	# Controls (# first-degree relatives)	Relatives interviewed	Diagnosis in relatives (%)					
				Alcohol abuse	Alcohol dependence	Drug abuse	Drug dependence	Total	Relative[a] risk
Rivinus *et al.* 1984	40 (545)[b]	23 (277)[b]	N	–	–	–	–	11.9[c]	1.7
Logue *et al.* 1989	17 (75)	20 (107)	Y	–	17.0[d]	4.0	–	21.0	0.8
Halmi *et al.* 1991	62 (169)	62 (178)	Y (parents only)	–	5.3[d]	–	1.2[e]	6.5	3.8
Stern *et al.* 1992	34 (153)	34 (140)	Y (1 parent only)	–	3.0[d]	–	3.0[e]	5.0	0.6
Lilenfeld *et al.* unpublished	26 (93)	44 (190)	Y	7.5	12.9	4.3	4.3	23.7	0.8

[a] Rate of illness in relatives of anorexic probands divided by rate of illness in relatives of normal control subjects. [b] Includes first- and second-degree relatives. [c] With age correction.
[d] Alcohol abuse and/or dependence. [e] Drug abuse and/or dependence.

Table 7.7. Controlled studies of lifetime risk of substance use disorders among first-degree relatives of bulimia nervosa probands

Study	# Probands (# first-degree relatives)	# Controls (# first-degree relatives)	Relatives interviewed	Diagnosis in relatives (%)				Total	Relative[a] risk
				Alcohol abuse	Alcohol dependence	Drug abuse	Drug dependence		
Stern *et al.* 1984	27 (368)[b]	27 (384)[b]	Y (1 parent only)	–	–	–	–	8.2	1.3
Hudson *et al.* 1987a	69 (283)	28 (149)	N	–	16.1[cd]	–	4.0[ce]	19.1[c]	2.1
Bulik 1987	35	35	N	–	48.6[d]	–	22.9[e]	–	2.4[d]; 1.3[e]
Logue *et al.* 1989	13 (57)	20 (107)	Y	–	21.0[d]	2.0	–	23.0	0.9
Kassett *et al.* 1989	40 (185)	24 (118)	Y	–	27.6[d]	11.9	–	39.5	2.0
Keck *et al.* 1990	66 (306)	28 (149)	N	–	8.6[cd]	–	3.4[ce]	12.0[c]	1.8
Boumann and Yates 1994	25 (47)	25 (49)	N (reports on parents only)	–	10.0[d]	–	–	10.0	2.5
Lilenfeld *et al.* unpublished	47 (177)	44 (190)	Y	10.7	19.2	9.6	7.9	36.7	1.2

[a] Rate of illness in relatives of bulimic probands divided by rate of illness in relatives of normal control subjects. [b] Includes first- and second-degree relatives. [c] With age correction. [d] Alcohol abuse and/or dependence. [e] Drug abuse and/or dependence.

native phenotypic expressions of a shared transmissible factor. The few well-controlled family studies to date have found elevated rates of substance use disorders only among the relatives of those bulimic probands who themselves had a substance use disorder.

Bulik (1991) reported that a subset of bulimic probands with comorbid alcohol abuse or dependence were more likely to have one or more relatives with a history of drug or alcohol abuse or dependence, compared to bulimic probands without alcohol abuse or dependence. Likewise, Mitchell *et al.* (1988) found that bulimic women with positive family histories of substance use disorders were more likely than bulimic women without such histories to have experienced drug problems themselves. The results of a study by the current authors are consistent with these findings. In this study, direct lifetime psychiatric history interviews were conducted with 47 women with DSM-III-R bulimia nervosa (20 with a lifetime history of alcohol and/or drug dependence and 27 without such a history), 44 non-eating disordered community control women, and the majority of the first-degree relatives of each of these groups. We found elevated rates of substance dependence *only* among the first-degree relatives of those women with bulimia nervosa *and* substance dependence (Kaye *et al.* 1996). In addition, similar findings of a lack of common familial transmission between alcohol dependence and bulimia nervosa were obtained from a large study of alcohol dependent probands and their relatives. Schuckit *et al.* (1996) conducted structured interviews of 2283 women and 1982 men participating in the Collaborative Study on the Genetics of Alcoholism. Lifetime rates of anorexia and bulimia nervosa were assessed through direct interviews with alcohol-dependent probands and their relatives, and comparison probands and their relatives. This study did not find a significantly higher rate of eating disorders among the relatives of primary alcoholics or among those of primary and secondary alcoholics combined than among the relatives of comparison subjects. The authors concluded that any relationship that might exist between bulimia nervosa and alcohol dependence is not likely to be due to a strong genetic link between the two disorders.

These family study findings converge with multivariate genetic modeling of the large population-based twin study data base investigated by Kendler and colleagues, in which it was found that bulimia nervosa and alcoholism were accounted for by distinct genetic factors (Kendler *et al.* 1995). Thus, genetic factors that were found to influence vulnerability to alcoholism in women did not alter the risk for the development of bulimia nervosa.

Anxiety disorders

Very little data exist regarding the rate or patterns of transmission of anxiety disorders among family members of probands with eating disorders, despite the fact that anxiety disorders are common among eating disorder probands themselves (Hudson *et al.* 1987b; Toner *et al.* 1988; Laessle *et al.* 1989; Fornari *et al.* 1992; Herzog *et al.* 1992b; Schwalberg *et al.* 1992; Smith *et al.* 1993; Bossert-Zaudig *et al.* 1993; Braun *et al.* 1994; Brewerton *et al.* 1995; Deep *et al.* 1995; Thiel *et al.* 1995; Garfinkel *et al.* 1995). The one exception is obsessive–compulsive disorder (OCD), in which three family studies (Halmi *et al.* 1991; Pasquale *et al.* 1994; Lilenfeld *et al.* in press) reported elevated rates of OCD among the relatives of probands with eating disorders. Halmi *et al.* (1991) found a rate of 11% among the mothers of probands with anorexia nervosa compared to a rate of 2% among the mothers of control women. Pasquale *et al.* (1994) assessed lifetime rates of OCD among the first-degree relatives of three proband groups: those with OCD, eating disorder, and mood disorder. They found that the first-degree relatives of probands with anorexia nervosa had a lifetime morbid risk for OCD of 3.2. Similarly, in a family study completed recently by the current authors, we found a morbid risk for OCD of 4.1 for relatives of anorexic probands and 3.0 for relatives of bulimic probands for OCD, compared to relatives of non-eating disordered, control women (Lilenfeld *et al.* in press). Thus, all three of these family studies have found OCD to occur at increased rates among family members of women with eating disorders.

The co-segregation of OCD and eating disorders within families has been investigated only in the family study by the current authors (Lilenfeld *et al.* in press). We found that OCD and eating disorders were independently transmitted in families; specifically, OCD was elevated primarily among the relatives of those eating disordered probands who themselves had OCD. Thus, although OCD and eating disorders frequently co-occur within individuals and within families, there is no evidence in this study of a shared etiological factor. This finding replicates most findings with mood disorders and substance use disorders, in which there was evidence of independent familial transmission from eating disorders.

Personality disorders

As with anxiety disorders, very little data exist regarding the rate or patterns of transmission of personality disorders among family members of probands with eating disorders, despite the fact that personality disorders are common among individuals with eating disorders (Levin and Hyler 1986; Piran *et al.* 1988; Gartner *et al.* 1989; Schmidt and Telch 1990; Wonderlich *et al.* 1990; Zanarini *et al.* 1990; Steiger *et al.* 1991; Råstam 1992; Ames-Frankel *et al.* 1992; Herzog *et al.* 1992a; Rossiter *et al.* 1993; Skodol *et al.* 1993; Gillberg *et al.* 1995; Kennedy *et al.* 1995). Specifically, obsessional traits are particularly common among restricting anorexic women (Strober 1980; Sohlberg and Strober 1994; Vitousek and Manke 1994), while a less consistent picture has been suggested from studies of bulimic women; although impulsivity and mood lability are among the most common features in this population (Vitousek and Manke, 1994). Whereas much has been written about personality disorders among women with eating disorders, only two studies, to our knowledge, have assessed personality disorders among the family members of individuals with eating disorders.

Carney *et al.* (1990) assessed personality disorders among women with bulimia nervosa, normal controls, and first-degree family members of both groups using the

Personality Disorder Questionnaire (Reich 1985). While they found significantly higher scores on almost all categories, especially borderline traits, among women with bulimia nervosa compared to control women, few differences were found among the first-degree relatives of these groups. In contrast to these findings, our group (Lilenfeld *et al.* in press) found elevated lifetime rates of obsessive–compulsive personality disorder among the relatives of anorexic probands only, whether or not the personality disorder was present in the proband herself; rates of obsessive–compulsive personality disorder were comparatively low among relatives of bulimic probands and control women probands. Thus, obsessional personality appears to be more or less specific to anorexic women, suggesting that such traits may constitute a familially determined vulnerability factor for restricting-type anorexia nervosa, and that obsessive–compulsive personality disorder and restricting-type anorexia nervosa may represent a continuum of phenotypic expressions of a similar genotype.

Cluster B personality disorders (antisocial, borderline, histrionic, narcissistic) are characterized by impulsivity and affective dysregulation. These traits and disorders have been found to often occur among bulimic, but not anorexic probands (DaCosta and Halmi 1992; Vitousek and Manke 1994). In the family study by the current authors (Lilenfeld *et al.* 1997), we found elevated rates of threshold and subthreshold Cluster B personality disorders among the relatives of bulimic probands (12%) compared to the relatives of control women probands (3%). A recent study by Bulik *et al.* (1997) found that borderline personality disorder was one of the most significant variables to discriminate between bulimic women with and without alcohol dependence. They concluded that the trait of impulsivity may be among the most important features which differentiates these two groups of bulimic women. Consistent with these findings, our group (Lilenfeld *et al.* 1997) found that cluster B personality disorders were more common among the first-degree relatives of bulimic women with comorbid substance dependence. Thus, impulsivity may be a familial risk factor for the 'multi-impulsive' type of bulimia nervosa, characterized by substance dependence, as well as other impulsive behaviors. These studies suggest that affective instability and impulsivity are particularly present in a subset of bulimic women who have substance dependence.

TEMPERAMENT AND PERSONALITY

Most genetic researchers doubt that there are specific genes for starvation or binge eating; instead, it is more likely that the most relevant heritable factors in the development of eating disorders are personality traits, such as harm avoidance and emotional restraint in anorexia nervosa and emotional lability and behavioral undercontrol in bulimia nervosa. The interaction of these premorbid personality traits and experimentation with dieting may 'release' the risk for an eating disorder in vulnerable individuals.

Few studies have examined such personality traits among the family members of eating disordered individuals. One exception is a study by Casper (1990), in which she administered the Multidimensional Personality Questionnaire (MPQ; Tellegen 1982) to recovered restricting-type anorexics, their sisters, and unrelated control women. The MPQ personality scales and higher order factors have been shown to have heritabilities ranging from 0.39–0.58 (Tellegen *et al.* 1988). Casper's (1990) findings pointed to low levels of positive emotionality and high levels of traditionalism and constraint among the previously anorexic women, even after an average of 6 years of recovery. Their sisters tended to score intermediately between the recovered anorexics and normal controls, suggesting the possibility of familially mediated traits of emotional constraint and conformity.

Restricting-type anorexia nervosa, in particular, is characterized by a stereotypic cluster of personality traits found with remarkable consistency. These temperamental traits include emotional restraint, avoidance of novelty, anxious worry and self-doubt, compliancy, obsessionality, perfectionism, and perseverance in the face of nonreward (Strober 1995; Pryor and Wiederman 1996). While many of these traits may be exaggerated by starvation (Keys *et al.* 1950), retrospective accounts indicate that they often predate the onset of the eating disorder and remain even after long-term weight restoration (Strober 1980; Srinivasagan *et al.* 1995; Pollice *et al.* 1997). Thus, this cluster of personality traits may be part of a genetically transmitted spectrum of temperamental risk factors for anorexia nervosa.

That this phenotypic personality structure may be related to underlying biological substrates, gains support from evidence of increased serotonergic activity in anorexic patients well after restoration to normal weight levels (Kaye *et al.* 1991), as well as strong evidence linking serotonergic mechanism to restraint of reward motivation for exploring novel environments, modulating feeling and sexual behavior, and regulating the sensitivity of neurobehavioral systems to stimulus events (Kaye *et al.* 1993). Thus, high levels of serotonergic activity in anorexia nervosa may play a role in the pathogenesis of the illness by shaping marked behavioral liabilities toward rigidity and constraint.

Although the presentation of bulimia nervosa is less consistent than that of restricting-type anorexia nervosa, certain common personality and behavioral traits may play an important biologically mediated etiological role in the development of the disorder. Bulimia nervosa, in contrast to anorexia nervosa, is usually characterized by traits such as thrill seeking and excitability, and a tendency toward marked dysphoria in response to rejection or nonreward (Strober 1995). These features may protect against sustained dietary restriction and, thus, predispose an individual to periodic lapses in control and eventual dietary chaos. One potentially fruitful avenue for genetic research is to examine possible heritable variations in the sensitivity of brain systems to the reward properties of feeding behavior. Such heritable variations may function as a diathesis facilitating the development and reinforcement of extreme eating patterns.

CONCLUSIONS

Eating disorders have not traditionally been viewed as heritable illnesses; however, results from twin studies suggest that at least half of the variance in the development of eating disorders is attributable to genetic factors. Although the majority of current evidence supports the notion that anorexia and bulimia nervosa have a strong familial component, the exact nature of the familially transmitted vulnerability is, as yet, unknown. In addition to elevated rates of eating pathology among relatives, some family studies have also found increased rates of mood disorders, substance use disorders, anxiety disorders, and personality disorders among these family members. Future family studies must seek to further understand the relationship of these disorders to anorexia nervosa and bulimia nervosa, as this may inform us about etiologic processes involved in the development of eating disorders. However, a focus on temperamental or personality traits in future genetic studies may be of greatest utility.

There may be shared, as well as separate, heritable factors of importance for the development of anorexia and bulimia nervosa. Specifically, a familial tendency toward obsessionality and restraint may be vulnerability factors for restricting-type anorexia nervosa; in contrast, impulsivity and affective instability may be familial vulnerability factors for certain forms of bulimia nervosa (e.g. the 'multi-impulsive' or substance dependent subtype). The findings from family studies may help tailor the focus of future genetic studies.

CLINICAL IMPLICATIONS

- An understanding of genetically determined premorbid personality traits, which may be etiologically related to the development of eating disorders, may influence the approach of clinicians in what potential areas of behavior and personality are targeted for change during treatment.
- An understanding of familial personality and behavioral traits which may be relevant in the etiology of eating disorders may influence the targets of change in family intervention approaches used by clinicians.
- The likelihood of genetically determined personality traits playing a role in the development of eating disorders may influence the assessment of such patients, both when gathering information about the patient as well as her family members.
- The convergence in the literature that eating disorders aggregate in families suggests that clinicians should assess for a history of these disorders in the families of these patients, as it may potentially influence the conceptualization and understanding of a particular case.

Continued

- The convergence in the literature that anxiety and mood disorders aggregate in families should encourage clinicians to be sure to assess for a history of such disorders in the families of eating disorder patients, as it may potentially influence the conceptualization and understanding of a particular case.

RESEARCH IMPLICATIONS

- Future genetic research on personality and temperamental traits, such as harm avoidance and emotional restraint in anorexia nervosa and emotional lability and impulsivity in bulimia nervosa, is needed to further our understanding of the personality traits that may function as risk factors in eating disorders.
- Evidence of familial aggregation of anxiety and mood disorders among the relatives of eating disordered probands exists and requires further study with larger family study samples in order to develop a greater understanding of potentially common underlying mechanisms which may explain the relationship between these disorders and eating disorders.
- The finding that anorexia nervosa and obsessive–compulsive personality disorder may share a similar underlying vulnerability is particularly worthy of future family and genetic methodological study.
- The relationship between bulimia nervosa and impulsive behavior is also worthy of future family and genetic methodological study.

REFERENCES

Ames-Frankel, J., Devlin, M.J., Walsh, B.T. *et al.* (1992) Personality disorder diagnoses in patients with bulimia nervosa: clinical correlates and changes with treatment. *Journal of Clinical Psychiatry* **53**: 90–96.

Andreasen, N.C., Endicott, J., Spitzer, R.L. and Winokur, G. (1977) The family history method using diagnostic criteria. *Archives of General Psychiatry* **34**: 1229–1235.

Biederman, J., Rivinus, T., Kemper K. *et al.* (1985) Depressive disorders in relatives of anorexia nervosa patients with and without a current episode of nonbipolar major depression. *American Journal of Psychiatry* **142**: 1495–1496.

Bossert-Zaudig, S., Zaudig, M., Junker, M. *et al.* (1993) Psychiatric comorbidity of bulimia nervosa inpatients: relationship to clinical variables and treatment outcome. *European Psychiatry* **8**: 15–23.

Boumann, C.E. and Yates, W.R. (1994) Risk factors for bulimia nervosa: A controlled study of parental psychiatric illness and divorce. *Addictive Behaviors* **19**: 667–675.

Braun, D.L., Sunday, S.R. and Halmi, K.A. (1994) Psychiatric comorbidity in patients with eating disorders. *Psychological Medicine* **24**: 859–867.

Brewerton, T.D., Lydiard, R.B., Herzog, D.B. *et al.* (1995) Comorbidity of Axis I psychiatric disorders in bulimia nervosa. *Journal of Clinical Psychiatry* **56**: 77–80.

Bulik, C.M. (1987) Drug and alcohol abuse by bulimic women and their families. *American Journal of Psychiatry* **144**: 1604–1606.

Bulik, C.M. (1991) Family histories of bulimic women with and without comorbid alcohol abuse or dependence. *American Journal of Psychiatry* **148**: 1267–1268.

Bulik, C.M., Sullivan, P.F., Joyce, P.R. and Carter, F.A. (1997) Lifetime comorbidity of alcohol dependence in women with bulimia nervosa. *Addictive Behavior* **22**: 437–446.

Carney, C.P., Yates, W.R. and Cizaldo, B. (1990) A controlled family study of personality in normal-weight bulimia nervosa. *International Journal of Eating Disorders* **9**: 659–665.

Casper, R.C. (1990) Personality features of women with good outcome from restricting anorexia nervosa. *Psychosomatic Medicine* **52**: 156–170.

DaCosta, M. and Halmi, K.A. (1992) Classifications of anorexia nervosa: question of subtypes. *International Journal of Eating Disorders* **11**: 305–313.

Deep, A.L., Nagy, L.M., Weltzin, T.E. *et al.* (1995) Premorbid onset of psychopathology in long-term recovered anorexia nervosa. *International Journal of Eating Disorders* **17**: 291–297.

Fichter, M.M. and Noegel, R. (1990) Concordance for bulimia nervosa in twins. *International Journal of Eating Disorders* **9**: 255–263.

Fornari, V., Kaplan, M., Sandberg, D.E. *et al.* (1992) Depressive and anxiety disorders in anorexia nervosa and bulimia nervosa. *International Journal of Eating Disorders* **1**: 21–29.

Garfinkel, P.E., Lin, E., Goering, P. *et al.* (1995) Bulimia nervosa in a Canadian community sample: prevalence and comparison of subgroups. *American Journal of Psychiatry* **152**: 1052–1058.

Garner, A.F., Marcus, R.N., Halmi, K. and Loranger, A.W. (1989) DSM-III-R personality disorders in patients with eating disorders. *American Journal of Psychiatry* **146**: 1585–1592.

Gershon, E.S., Schreiber, J.L., Hamovit, J.R. *et al.* (1984) Clinical findings in patients with anorexia nervosa and affective illness in their relatives. *American Journal of Psychiatry* **141**: 1419–1422.

Gillberg, C., Råstam, M. and Gillberg, C. (1995) Anorexia nervosa 6 years after onset: part I. Personality disorders. *Comprehensive Psychiatry* **36**: 61–69.

Halmi, K.A., Eckert, E., Marchi, P. *et al.* (1991) Comorbidity of psychiatric diagnoses in anorexia nervosa. *Archives of General Psychiatry* **48**: 712–718.

Herzog, D.B., Keller, M.B., Lavori, P.W. *et al.* (1992a) The prevalence of personality disorders in 210 women with eating disorders. *Journal of Clinical Psychiatry* **53**: 147–152.

Herzog, D.B., Keller, M.B., Sacks, N.R. *et al.* (1992b) Psychiatric comorbidity in treatment-seeking anorexics and bulimics. *Journal of the American Academy of Child and Adolescent Psychiatry* **31**: 810–818.

Hettema, J.M., Neale, M.C. and Kendler, K.S. (1995) Physical similarity and the equal-environment assumption in twin studies of psychiatric disorders. *Behavior Genetics* **25**: 327–335.

Holderness, C.C., Brooks-Gunn, J. and Warren, W.P. (1994) Co-morbidity of eating disorders and substance abuse; Review of the literature. *International Journal of Eating Disorders* **16**: 1–34.

Holland, A.J., Hall, A., Murray, R. *et al.* (1984) Anorexia nervosa: a study of 34 twin pairs. *British Journal of Psychiatry* **145**: 414–419.

Holland, A.J., Sicotte, N. and Treasure, J. (1988) Anorexia nervosa: evidence for a genetic basis. *Journal of Psychosomatic Research* **32**: 561–571.

Hsu, L.K.G., Chesler, B.E. and Santhouse, R. (1990) Bulimia nervosa in eleven sets of twins: a clinical report. *International Journal of Eating Disorders* **9**: 275–282.

Hudson, J.I., Pope, H.G., Jonas, J.M. *et al.* (1983) A family history study of anorexia nervosa and bulimia. *British Journal of Psychiatry* **142**: 133–138.

Hudson, J.I., Pope, H.G., Jonas, J.M. *et al.* (1987a) A controlled family history study of bulimia. *Psychological Medicine* **17**: 883–890.

Hudson, J.I., Pope, H.G., Yurgelun-Todd, D. *et al.* (1987b) A controlled study of the lifetime prevalence of affective and other psychiatric disorders in bulimic outpatients. *American Journal of Psychiatry* **144**: 1283–1287.

Kassett, J.A., Gershon, E.S., Maxwell, M.E. *et al.* (1989) Psychiatric disorders in the relatives of probands with bulimia nervosa. *American Journal of Psychiatry* **146**: 1468–1471.

Kaye, W.H., Gwirtsman, H.E., George, D.T. and Ebert, M.H. (1991) Altered serotonin activity in anorexia nervosa after long-term weight restoration. *Archives of General Psychiatry* **48**: 556–562.

Kaye, W.H., Weltzin, T. and Hsu, L.K.G. (1993) Relationship between anorexia nervosa and obsessive and compulsive behaviors. *Psychiatric Annals* **23**: 365–373.

Kaye, W.H., Lilenfeld, L.R., Plotnicov, K. *et al.* (1996) Bulimia nervosa and substance dependence: Association and family transmission. *Alcoholism: Clinical and Experimental Research* **20**: 878–881.

Keck, P.E., Pope, H.G., Hudson, J.I. *et al.* (1990) A controlled study of phenomenology and family history in outpatients with bulimia nervosa. *Comprehensive Psychiatry* **31**: 275–283.

Kendler, K.S., MacLean, C., Neale, M. *et al.* (1991) The genetic epidemiology of bulimia nervosa. *American Journal of Psychiatry* **148**: 1627–1637.

Kendler, K.S., Neale, M.C. and Kessler, R.C. (1993) A test of the equal-environment assumption in twin studies of psychiatric illness. *Behavior Genetics* **23**: 21–27.

Kendler, K.S., Walters, E.E., Neale, M.C. *et al.* (1995) The structure of the genetic and environmental risk factors for six major psychiatric disorders in women. *Archives of General Psychiatry* **52**: 374–383.

Kennedy, S.H., Katz, R., Rockert, W. *et al.* (1995) Assessment of personality disorders in anorexia nervosa and bulimia nervosa. *Journal of Nervous and Mental Disease* **183**: 358–364.

Keys, A., Brozek, J., Henschel, A. *et al.* (1950) *The Biology of Human Starvation*. Minneapolis: University of Minnesota Press.

Klein, D.N. and Riso, L.P. (1993) Psychiatric disorders: problems of boundaries and comorbidity. In Costello, C.G. (ed.) *Basic Issues in Psychopathology*. pp. 19–66. New York: Guilford Press.

Laessle, R.G., Wittchen, H.U., Fichter, M.M. and Pirke, K.M. (1989) The significance of subgroups of bulimia and anorexia nervosa: lifetime frequency of psychiatric disorders. *International Journal of Eating Disorders* **8**: 569–574.

Levin, A.P. and Hyler, S.E. (1986) DSM-III personality diagnosis in bulimia. *Comprehensive Psychiatry* **27**: 47–53.

Lilenfeld, L.R. and Kaye, W.H. (1996) The link between alcoholism and eating disorders. *Alcohol Health and Research World* **20**: 94–99.

Lilenfeld, L.R., Kaye, W.H., Greeno, C.G. *et al.* (1997) Psychiatric disorders in women with bulimia nervosa and their first-degree relatives: effects of comorbid substance dependence. *International Journal of Eating Disorders* **22**(3): 253–264.

Lilenfeld, L.R., Kaye, W.H., Greeno, C.G. *et al.* (in press). A controlled family study of anorexia nervosa and bulimia nervosa: psychiatric disorders in first-degree relatives and effects of proband comorbidity.

Logue, C.M., Crowe, R.R. and Bean, J.A. (1989) A family study of anorexia nervosa and bulimia. *British Journal of Psychiatry* **30**: 179–188.

Mitchell, J., Hatsukami, D., Pyle, R.L. and Eckert, E.D. (1988) Bulimia with and without a family history of drug abuse. *Addictive Behaviors* **13**: 245–251.

Pasquale, L., Sciuto, G., Cocchi, S. *et al.* (1994) A family study of obsessive compulsive, eating and mood disorders. *European Psychiatry* **9**: 33–38.

Piran, N., Lerner, P., Garfinkel, P.E. *et al.* (1988) Personality disorders in anorexic patients. *International Journal of Eating Disorders* **7**: 589–599.

Plomin, R., DeFries, J.C. and McClearn, G.E. (1990) *Behavioral Genetics: A Primer* (2nd edition). New York: W.H. Freeman and Company.

Pollice, C.P., Kaye, W.H., Greeno, C.G. and Weltzin, T.E. (1997) Relationship of depression, anxiety, and obsessionality to state of illness in anorexia nervosa. *International Journal of Eating Disorders* **21**: 367–376.

Pryor, T. and Wiederman, M.W. (1996) Measurement of nonclinical personality characteristics of women with anorexia nervosa and bulimia nervosa. *Journal of Personality Assessment* **67**: 414–421.

Råstam, M. (1992) Anorexia nervosa in 51 Swedish adolescents. *Journal of the American Academy of Child and Adolescent Psychiatry* **31**: 819–829.

Reich, J. (1985) Measurement of DSM-III, Axis II. *Comprehensive Psychiatry* **26**: 352–363.

Rivinus, T.M., Beiderman, J., Herzog, D.B. *et al.* (1984) Anorexia nervosa and affective disorders: a controlled family history study. *American Journal of Psychiatry* **141**: 1414–1418.

Robins, L., Helzer, U., Groughon, I. and Ratcliff, K. (1981) The NIMH diagnostic interview schedule: its history, characteristics and validity. *Archives of General Psychiatry* **38**: 381–389.

Rossiter, E.M., Agras, W.S., Telch, C.F. and Schneider, J.A. (1993) Cluster B personality disorder characteristics predict outcome in the treatment of bulimia nervosa. *International Journal of Eating Disorders* **13**: 349–357.

Schmidt, N.B. and Telch, M.J. (1990) Prevalence of personality disorders among bulimics, nonbulimic binge eaters, and normal controls. *Journal of Psychopathology and Behavioral Assessment* **12**: 169–185.

Schuckit, M.A., Tipp, J.E., Anthenelli, R.M. *et al.* (1996) Anorexia nervosa and bulimia nervosa in alcohol-dependent men and women and their relatives. *American Journal of Psychiatry* **153**: 74–82.

Schwalberg, M.D., Barlow, D.H., Alger, S.A. and Howard, L.J. (1992) Comparison of bulimics, obese binge eaters, social phobics, and individuals with panic disorder on comorbidity across DSM-III-R anxiety disorders. *Journal of Abnormal Psychology* **101**: 675–681.

Skodol, A.E., Oldham, J.M., Hyler, S.E. *et al.* (1993) Comorbidity of DSM-III-R eating disorders and personality disorders. *International Journal of Eating Disorders* **14**: 403–416.

Smith, C. (1974) Heritability of liability and concordance in monozygous twins. *Annals of Human Genetics* **26**: 454–466.

Smith, C., Feldman, S.S., Nasserbakht, A. and Steiner, H. (1993) Psychological characteristics and DSM-III-R diagnoses at 6-year follow-up of adolescent anorexia nervosa. *Journal of the American Academy of Child and Adolescent Psychiatry* **32**: 1237–1245.

Sohlberg, S. and Strober, M. (1994) Personality in anorexia nervosa: an update and a theoretical integration. *Acta Psychiatrica Scandinavica* **89**: 1–15.

Spitzer, R.L. and Endicott, J. (1978) *Schedule for Affective Disorders and Schizophrenia (Lifetime Version)*, 3rd Edition. New York: New York State Psychiatric Institute.

Spitzer, R.L., Endicott, J. and Robbins, E. (1978) Research diagnostic criteria: rationale and reliability. *Archives of General Psychiatry* **34**: 773–782.

Spitzer, R.L., Williams, J.B.W. and Gibbon, M. (1987) *Structured Clinical Interview for DSM-III-R (SCID)*. New York: New York State Psychiatric Institute, Biometrics Research.

Srinivasagan, N.M., Plotnicov, K.H., Greeno, C. *et al.* (1995) Persistent perfectionism, symmetry, and exactness in anorexia nervosa after long-term recovery. *American Journal of Psychiatry* **152**: 1630–1634.

Steiger, H., Liquornik, K., Chapman, J. and Hussain, N. (1991) Personality and family disturbances in eating-disorder patients: comparison of 'restricters' and 'bingers' to normal controls. *International Journal of Eating Disorders* **10**: 501–512.

Stern, S.L., Dixon, K.N., Nemer, E. *et al.* (1984) Affective disorder in the families of women with normal weight bulimia. *American Journal of Psychiatry* **141**: 1224–1227.

Stern, S.L., Dixon, K.N., Sansone, R.A. *et al.* (1992) Psychoactive substance use disorder in relatives of patients with anorexia nervosa. *Comprehensive Psychiatry* **33**: 207–212.

Strober, M. (1980) Personality and symptomatological features in young, nonchronic anorexia nervosa patients. *Journal of Psychosomatic Research* **24**: 353–359.

Strober, M. (1991) Family-genetic studies of eating disorders. *Journal of Clinical Psychiatry* **52**: 9–12.

Strober, M. (1995) Family-genetic perspectives on anorexia nervosa and bulimia nervosa. In Brownell, K.D. and Fairburn, C.G. (eds) *Eating Disorders and Obesity*. pp. 212–218. New York: The Guilford Press.

Strober, M. and Humphrey, L.L. (1987) Familial contributions to the etiology and course of anorexia nervosa and bulimia. *Journal of Consulting and Clinical Psychology* **55**: 654–659.

Strober, M., Lampert, C., Morrell, W. *et al.* (1990) A controlled family study of anorexia nervosa: evidence of familial aggregation and lack of shared transmission with affective disorders. *International Journal of Eating Disorders* **9**: 239–253.

Tellegen, A. (1982) Brief Manual for the Multidimensional Personality Questionnaire. Unpublished manuscript. University of Minnesota.

Tellegen, A., Bouchard, T.J., Wilcox, K.J. *et al.* (1988) Personality similarity in twins reared apart and together. *Journal of Personality and Social Psychology* **54**: 1031–1039.

Thiel, A., Broocks, A., Ohlmeier, M. *et al.* (1995) Obsessive–compulsive disorder among patients with anorexia nervosa and bulimia nervosa. *American Journal of Psychiatry* **152**: 72–75.

Toner, B.B., Garfinkel, P.E. and Garner, D.M. (1988) Affective and anxiety disorders in the long-term follow-up of anorexia nervosa. *International Journal of Psychiatry and Medicine* **18**: 357–364.

Treasure, J. and Holland, A.J. (1989) Genetic vulnerability to eating disorders: evidence from twin and family studies. In Remschmidt, H. and Schmidt, M.H. (eds) *Child and Youth Psychiatry: European Perspectives*. pp. 59–68. New York: Hogrefe and Huber.

Vitousek, K. and Manke, F. (1994) Personality variables and disorders in anorexia nervosa and bulimia nervosa. *Journal of Abnormal Psychology* **1**: 137–147.

Walters, E.E., Neale, M.C., Eaves, L.J. *et al.* (1992) Bulimia nervosa and major depression: a study of common genetic and environmental factors. *Psychological Medicine* **22**: 617–622.

Walters, E.E. and Kendler, K.S. (1995) Anorexia nervosa and anorexic-like syndromes in a population-based twin sample. *American Journal of Psychiatry* **152**: 64–71.

Weissman, M.M., Merikangas, K.R., John, K. *et al.* (1986) Family-genetic studies of psychiatric disorders: Developing technologies. *Archives of General Psychiatry* **43**: 1104–1116.

Wickramaratne, P.J. and Weissman, M.M. (1993) Using family studies to understand comorbidity. *European Archives of Psychiatry and Clinical Neuroscience* **243**: 150–157.

Winokur, A., March, V. and Mendels, J. (1980) Primary affective disorder in relatives of patients with anorexia nervosa. *American Journal of Psychiatry* **137**: 695–698.

Wonderlich, S.A., Swift, W.J., Slotnick, H.B. and Goodman S. (1990) DSM-III-R personality disorders in eating-disorder subtypes. *International Journal of Eating Disorders* **9**: 607–616.

Woodside, D.B. (1993) Genetic contributions to eating disorders. In Kaplan, A.S. and Garfinkel, P.E. (eds) *Medical Issues and the Eating Disorders: the Interface*. pp. 193–212. New York: Brunner/Magel Publishing Co.

Zanarini, M.M., Frankenburg, F.R., Pope, H.G. *et al.* (1990) Axis II comorbidity of normal-weight bulimia. *Comprehensive Psychiatry* **30**: 20–24.

8 Models of Eating Disturbances in Animals

J. B. OWEN
School of Agricultural and Forest Sciences, University of Wales Bangor, Bangor, UK

RELEVANCE OF ANIMAL MODELS

The use of animal models in tackling human problems has received a significant boost with the development of molecular biology, specifically the continuing delineation of the genome of the higher mammals. This has underlined the extensive homology that exists in terms of genetic loci and their constituent allelic DNA sequences, in spite of the chromosomal rearrangement that has occurred. For example, the locus of the gene obese (*ob*), first located on mouse chromosome 6, is present on human chromosome 7, and pig chromosome 18 (Sazaki *et al.* 1996).

The basis of similarity in disorders between animal models and the human subject largely lies in genetic relationship at the loci influencing the disorder. In relation to eating disorders, the value of animal models therefore depends on the extent and nature of the shared genetic basis. This includes the extent of the involvement of that part of the central nervous system, especially the brain, which makes humans unique amongst animals. If, as the classification of some eating disorders as psychiatric illness suggests, a significant element of eating disorder is a consequence of human consciousness and the stress involved in an appreciation of self-image, then animal models may be less relevant. If on the other hand human eating disorders belong to the more ancient conserved genetic component of the higher animal, shared by non-humans, then animal models may provide a powerful tool. Animal models are a more acceptable subject of some forms of experimental manipulation than human subjects themselves (Surwit and Williams 1996). For example, animal models are a fruitful subject for testing promising drugs for eating disorders (Mattei and Carlini 1996). It is also already apparent that transgenic model animals are becoming useful experimentally in relation to eating disorders (Stenzelpoore *et al.* 1994). There have also been several useful studies involving 'knockout' animals, with specific genes inactivated. For example genetically lean mice have resulted from targeted disruption of the RII β subunit of protein kinase A (Cummings *et al.* 1996). The cloning of cells from adult sheep at the Roslin Institute by Wilmut *et al.* (1997) could eventually provide a powerful experimental tool for separating the effects of nature from nurture in animal eating disorders.

Neurobiology in the Treatment of Eating Disorders.
Edited by H.W. Hoek, J.L. Treasure and M.A. Katzman.

THE NATURE AND POSSIBLE GENETIC BASIS OF EATING DISORDERS

Eating disorder traits occupy the extreme ends of normal continuous phenotypic variables, be they defined as body composition, body mass index (BMI) (body weight in kg)/(height in metres)^2 or voluntary food intake in relation to body weight (Price *et al.* 1990; Hebebrand and Remschmidt 1995). These extremes of phenotypic traits increasingly reflect major gene effects, as opposed to the basal polygenic effect, often underlying the less extreme deviations from the species mean (Owen 1996). In many body composition traits a small number of gene loci account for most of the variance, in contrast to that traditionally assumed under the polygenic model.

Obesity is classifiable into many components and depots and at the lower levels of the hierarchy of these components single gene effects often dominate the sub-component (Bouchard *et al.* 1993a; Bouchard 1995; Bouchard and Perusse 1996).

Anorexia nervosa is a striking phenotype with high heritability (Holland *et al.* 1989; Schepank 1991); it resembles some of the characteristics of phenotypes controlled by a single or very few loci. There are also many similarities between anorexia nervosa and bulimia nervosa (Kendler *et al.* 1991) which could stem from a common, substantial, genetic basis. So far no single gene effect on these conditions has been identified. However, if some component of obesity and anorexia stems from extreme manifestations of the same feature (or alleles of the same gene locus) of the appetite mechanism, this would imply a common causality. Indeed there are indications from animal models that such common underlying bases may exist. For instance serum leptin levels, coded by the *ob* gene, are not only involved in the aetiology of obesity but are also associated with low weight and percentage body fat in anorexic subjects as compared to normal controls. Leptin levels were correlated with weight, percentage body fat, and intrinsic growth factor-I (IGF-I) in women with anorexia nervosa, suggesting a role for the physiological regulation of leptin in anorexia nervosa (Herzog and Klibanski 1996). Similarly obesity, anorexia and bulimia are associated with the serotonin (5-hydroxytryptaniline; 5-HT) system (Blundell and Lawton 1995; Weltzin *et al.* 1994). Chipkevitch (1994) has also shown that structural lesions of the hypothalamus or other centres regulating food intake in animal models show symptoms that closely mimic anorexia nervosa.

There is therefore a possibility that the gene loci involved in the common human eating disorders are shared with other animals and that these loci are populated by similar (although not identical) allelic DNA sequences. These may involve regulatory genes affecting early development and thus have profound effects. Homologous alleles also can have markedly differential expression in different genetic backgrounds as shown later for the *ob* gene.

The view that the extremes of the distribution of body composition and food intake are not simply gradations in the normal biological variation but manifestations of major gene effects, requires further elucidation. It is possible to

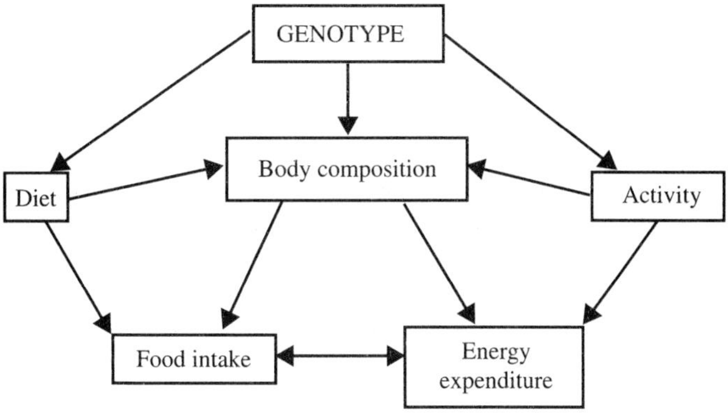

Figure 8.1. Control of voluntary food intake in the non-lactating animal

define an eating disorder as a discontinuous departure from the normal population variation in body composition achieved from a balance between energy intake, energy dissipation and energy storage shown in Figure 8.1. However the sufferers may enjoy periods of stability of body composition when their energy input and output are in balance at the extreme body composition. This implies a distorted or misread reference set-point for body composition.

APPETITE MECHANISM

Although the appetite mechanism is complex in that it has to combine strategic long-term homeostasis with short-term peripheral, meal by meal tactics, the roots of much of the disorder described in this chapter must lie largely in the central neurobiological systems located in the brain. The ventro-medial region of the hypothalamus appears to be the main centre for satiety and thermogenesis, co-ordinating and processing the information through the action of a variety of neuro-transmitters, neuro-modulators, pathways and receptors (Blundell and Halford 1994; Blundell *et al.* 1996).

The basic concept involves a genetically determined set-point for the orderly development of a mature body composition equilibrium, which the brain centre 'reads' and can achieve by effecting appropriate feed-back mechanisms, involving appetite and thermogenesis. Eating disorders may not only stem from such a misreading or slippage of the set-point reference but also from a malfunctioning of the feed-back corrective mechanisms. Following the early hypotheses of workers such as Hervey (1969), a search for humoral agents in satiated and fasted animals has been underway for some time and has confirmed the presence of fat-mobilizing, anorexigenic, and food-intake-stimulating substances in the blood and urine of pigs and rats (Wyllie and Owen 1978; Harris and Martin 1984; Hulsey and Martin 1992).

More recently the mouse obese (*ob*) gene and its protein product leptin, expressed in the white lipocytes, have provided an exciting new framework for the set-point hypothesis (Zhang *et al.* 1994). The expression of the *ob* gene seems to enable the sensing of fat cell status as well as influencing corrective food intake response. However, the differential effects in the human and in the mouse model underlie the commonly observed differential expression of homologous genes in contrasting genetic backgrounds, both within and between species, indicating that this is only the start of an unfolding story (Frederich *et al.* 1995; Masuzaki *et al.* 1995; Daniel and Herget 1996; Mizuno *et al.* 1996). The evidence of Barbato (1994) working with chickens, intensely selected for body weight, indicates a genetic basis for neurotransmitter levels in the hatching chick. This may be a rare within-experiment glimpse of the evolution of the appetite mechanism in a species noted for the early operation of discriminatory feeding behaviour.

ENVIRONMENTAL FACTORS

Several animal studies have helped to elucidate a major aspect in relation to eating disorders. The work first came into prominence with the 'cafeteria feeding' experiments where rats, that had perfectly normal appetite control on laboratory 'chow' diets, exhibited varying degrees of obesity when offered a variety of high-fat palatable 'cafeteria' feeds (Rothwell and Stock 1979). Some rats with dietary obesity genes Do_2 and Do_3, subjected to such diets, had normal weights indicating a genotype–environment interaction (West *et al.* 1994a,b, 1995). Humans as well as rats show a differential response to a high-fat diet, with some people showing resistance to obesity on high-fat diets (Blundell *et al.* 1996; Heitmann *et al.* 1995).

Blundell *et al.* (1996) have interpreted the results of their experiments as a differential response to dietary nutrients. On high carbohydrate diets the appetite mechanism works well, whereas with high-fat diets it does not. These results indicate the importance of considering the background environment over which the human genome evolved and in the light of work on extant human groups practising a traditional lifestyle well into modern times, e.g. Pima Indians (Ravussin *et al.* 1994). The major part of the diet of *Homo sapiens*, since his emergence as the modern human about 50 000 years ago, appears to have been plant-based with a relatively high fibre and complex carbohydrate content. The diet was also supplemented in some part with the flesh of wild animals, seemingly far leaner than modern domesticates, based on comparisons with modern wild and feral stock. Such a diet necessitated a sophisticated control mechanism for carbohydrate for good adaptation but it would have been no adaptive advantage for there to be limitation on high-fat components, likely to be scarce in the environment.

Under modern living conditions such genotypes are prone to obesity and diabetes. A striking animal model for this situation and the consequences of modern living conditions is the desert rodents described by Coleman (1978). These rodents are adapted to their desert environment due to their thrifty genotype and ability to withstand extreme seasonality of food supply without overeating. Such rodents when transferred to laboratory conditions overeat, become obese and often diabetic.

Similar results, primarily with laboratory rats, have indicated that whilst animals are on an appropriate diet (high carbohydrate and fibre) the appetite mechanism operates efficiently. Greenberg and Smith (1996) have shown that orosensory properties by themselves were an important effect in driving overfeeding.

Liebel *et al.* (1995) have confirmed similar mechanisms in human subjects, the strong defence of an apparent set-point of body composition both in lean and obese subjects when subjected to a regime of food consumption that changed body weight to above or below their normal set weight. Furthermore they showed that the homeostatic mechanism involved both a strong appetite and a thermogenic response to redress these imbalances.

At low exercise levels the mechanism is also less efficient resulting in a predisposition to obesity (Roberts 1995). There is also evidence that level of activity and diet composition interact in their effect on the appetite mechanism so that there is not a simple additive effect of these two factors (King and Blundell 1995).

The two extremes of eating disorder—obesity and anorexia—are intimately associated with diet choice and voluntary physical activity.

The well-documented animal models of obesity show a clear association of the condition with a preference for high-fat feeds and a voluntary low level of physical activity, as compared to controls. The studies in humans tend to confirm that these associations in the animal models are an accurate reflection of the human subject. The diet choice of anorexia nervosa subjects is the reverse of that characteristic of obese subjects, in that they avoid high energy feeds and actively seek those of low energy (Simon *et al.* 1993). Similarly anorexia nervosa is associated with hyperactivity as opposed to the relative indolence of obesity. Such animal models as are available for anorexia nervosa—the activity-based anorexia of wheel-running rodents and the anorexia of young nursing females of farm species, pig, mink, goat, sheep—also exhibit similar diet choice and hyperactivity. Diet choice and levels of habitual voluntary exercise thus jointly contribute a significant component of the extreme conditions that result in obesity and anorexia.

GENETIC BASIS OF DIET CHOICE AND VOLUNTARY PHYSICAL ACTIVITY

Animal experiments indicate that there is a major genetic basis to diet choice as illustrated by the strong inter-species and inter-breed differences in this respect. In *Drosophila* for instance, species differences in olfactory behaviour are controlled by gene(s) located on the 2nd chromosome (Higa and Fuyama 1993). It is not easy in many experiments on the higher animal models to dissociate the component due to maternal territory choice and maternal copying, from the individual's own genetic component in this respect. Ingenious experiments such as those of Ritchie

(1991), involved weaning from the dam before the start of foraging in ground squirrels, in an attempt to dissociate primary genetic from learning effects. These and similar experiments indicate that the early, mainly maternal, environment influences the earliness of adoption of the characteristic adult diet preference. However experiments on young mule deer (*Odocoileus hemonius*) that were artificially reared from birth, suggest that this may be more a matter of timing than of fundamental influence on long-term diet choice (Longhurst *et al.* 1968). The existence of a genetically programmed diet wisdom is now being exploited in the feeding practice of several farm species (Kyriakis *et al.* 1991a). In some instances this relates to quite precise matching of amino acid to needs in chickens, although there are significant differences in preferences between different chicken stocks (Noble *et al.* 1993). The wealth of evidence pertaining to human adoption studies (Sorenson and Stunkard 1994) indicates that, even with separation shortly after birth, children's BMI bears little relation to that of their adoptive parents. This also implies that early dietary habits are either not strongly related to the consequent BMI or that the child's inherited diet preference thwarts the effect of adoptive parental influence. Falciglia and Norton (1994) found a greater similarity in food preference between members of monozygotic twin pairs than between dizygotic twin pairs for several common food items including orange juice, broccoli, cottage cheese, chicken and sweetened cereal.

The information on the genetic basis of level of activity in animal models is scant. From human data Bouchard (1991) and Bouchard *et al.* (1993b) suggested, on the basis of twin and parent–child data, that the heritability of resting metabolic rate, thermic response to food and energy cost of sub-maximal exercise is as high as 0.4. They also concluded that the heritability of habitual physical activity is about 0.25. Several other studies (Astrup 1996; Ravussin 1995) have confirmed that people with a low metabolic rate (adjusted for weight and body composition) and with a low level of spontaneous physical activity, are prone to weight gain and obesity.

Several questions remain in terms of the interaction of eating disorders in relation to genetic and non-genetic factors. One is the extent to which diet choice (particularly energy density) and voluntary activity are the primary driving forces in some or all of these disorders or are they secondary manifestations of a more deep-seated genetic control of energy intake.

ANALOGOUS SYNDROMES AND POSSIBLE CANDIDATE GENES FROM ANIMAL MODELS

Table 8.1 summarizes some of the main possible candidate genes at animal model loci related to eating disorders in humans.

Table 8.1. Example candidate loci in animals that could encode proteins relevant to eating disorder traits

Locus or trait	Symbol	Chromosome		Homologue	Reference
Halothane-induced malignant hyperthermia (partially recessive)	*Hal*	Pig	6	19	Archibald (1991)
Ryanodin receptor	*Ryr*	Pig	6	19	Fries *et al.* (1992)
Double muscling (partially recessive)	*mh*	Cattle	2		Charlier *et al.* (1995)
Callipyge (dominant)	*CLPG*	Sheep	18		Cockett *et al.* (1996)
Fat deposition (QTL)		Pig	4		Andersson *et al.* (1994)
Obese (recessive)	*ob*	Mouse	6	7	Zhang *et al.* (1994)
Diabetes (recessive)	*db*	Mouse	4	1	Bahary *et al.* (1990)
Fatty (recessive)	*fa*	Rat	5	1	Truett *et al.* (1991)
Neuropeptide Y-receptor	*Y5*	Rat		4	Gerald *et al.* (1996)
Fat (recessive)	*fat*	Mouse	8	4	Coleman and Eicher (1990)
Tubby (recessive)	*tub*	Mouse	7	11	Coleman and Eicher (1990)
Dietary obese 1	*Do1*	Mouse	4	1	West *et al.* (1994a)
Dietary obese 2	*Do2*	Mouse	9	3	West *et al.* (1994b)
Dietary obese 3	*Do3*	Mouse	15	5	West *et al.* (1994b)
Agouti yellow (dominant)	A^y	Mouse	2	20	Bultman *et al.* (1992)
Adipose (dominant)	*Ad*	Mouse	7		Leiter (1993)

LABORATORY RODENTS

The mouse has been a fertile species for research due to its small size and it has often provided the main initial source of interesting candidate loci (Roberts and Greenberg 1996). Rats, and to a lesser extent, rabbits (Carroll *et al.* 1996) are also useful possible animal models, especially for the relation between anorexia and hyperactivity, as in voluntary wheel running (Morse *et al.* 1995; Rieg and Aravich 1994). This activity-based anorexia, sometimes triggered by nutritional stress, is a useful animal model of anorexia nervosa and may relate to similar anorexic, hyperactive, wasting syndromes in farm animal species, discussed below. It is interesting and possibly significant in the search for a candidate gene involved in anorexia nervosa, that such activity-based anorexia is alleviated by treatment with fluoxetine, an antidepressant that blocks serotonin uptake (Altemus *et al.* 1993, 1996). Stress has been implicated as a trigger in many animal models of eating disorders as in the human. Rat experiments have shown that hedonic responsiveness, as measured by consumption of sweet solutions, is reduced by exposure to mild unpredictable stress. This effect was not a secondary effect of weight-loss and was alleviated by antidepressant drugs (Willner *et al.* 1996). The effect of species and within-species genetic background on gene expression must be considered in terms of the final phenotype.

PIGS

Pigs may be a useful model for human eating disorders because the species is roughly comparable in body weight and has a similar digestive process, being omnivorous and simple-stomached (Andersson 1996). Looking at the species in terms of possible eating disorders we can see a gradation from: (a) the primitive wild pig, which is omnivorous, with an apparently well controlled appetite mechanism, allied to a relatively lean body to (b) the domesticated pig that was obese until the middle of the 20th century to (c) thereafter a progressively leaner animal bred to satisfy the modern meat consumer demand.

It is possible that the most frequent alleles at important body composition loci in the wild pig were quickly supplanted, post-domestication, by alleles leading to greater obesity leading to the then more desirable fatty carcass. The more recent intense selection for leanness has possibly not only revived the 'primitive' leanness alleles but also dredged up less desirable leanness alleles like the halothane gene with its well-known deleterious side effects.

An interesting condition in pigs is the 'thin sow' or 'wasting pig' syndrome (Maclean 1968; Morrowtesch and Andersson 1994). This syndrome is allied to nutritional or social stress and is widespread under some pig husbandry systems. Although some of the alleged sufferers are simply the victims of bad management, possibly complicated by internal parasite infection, poor housing and low nutrition, there were others that could not be explained in this way. These are usually young female pigs, often from lean hybrid strains, and there is some evidence of a genetic basis. The symptoms of these pigs bear a striking resemblance to those of human anorexia nervosa sufferers after due allowance for the human tendency to interpret the symptoms in terms of human psychology. One interesting feature is that the pig syndrome is frequently successfully treated with amperozide, a drug that influences the serotonin (5HT) system in the brain (Kyriakis *et al.* 1991b). Whether this is related to its appetite regulative function or to its reputed more general stress-reduction properties, is not yet clear.

Unfortunately for scientific study, the proportion of such pigs, as of human anorexics, is very small and it is not easy to assemble sufficient experimental material to get unequivocal results to make the search for a homologous genetic basis more than an interesting speculative avenue of investigation. However there are interesting analogous conditions in some other farm animal species, noted below.

A much researched leanness gene in pigs is the halothane gene that not only confers leanness but has many other, less desirable effects, as its full name 'inherited halothane-induced malignant hyperthermia' implies (Archibald 1991). These include effects on muscle quality, giving rise to pale soft exudative muscle and on susceptibility to stress.

SHEEP, GOATS AND MINK

Intractable anorexic conditions, analogous to the thin-sow syndrome noted above, have also been observed in young female goats, sheep and mink, usually in their first parity, for which there is no ready diagnosis (Owen 1990). For example in the 'nursing disease' in mink, emaciation and dehydration were the only consistent pathological features noted by Schneider and Hunter (1993) in a comparison of affected animals and their matched controls. They concluded that the disease was the extreme manifestation by susceptible animals of the energy-depletory stress of lactation; a rather similar conclusion to that reached for sufferers from the 'thin-sow syndrome' (Maclean 1968).

CATTLE AND SHEEP

The other class of interesting leanness models in the larger animals are the muscular hypertrophy (*mh*) genes with major effects on body composition. One is common in cattle of several breeds and possibly most highly developed in the Belgian Blue breed (Charlier *et al.* 1995). The other is the callipyge gene in sheep that has several unusual features in its inheritance. Although these bear some similarity to the halothane-gene there are some marked differences, particularly in relation to the effect of the gene on muscle composition and the resulting meat quality. The callipyge gene in sheep is an interesting one in that it demonstrates polar overdominance, where only heterozygous animals that inherited the callipyge gene from the sire actually express the phenotype (Cockett *et al.* 1996).

IMPLICATIONS FOR CLINICAL PRACTICE

As the genetic picture for eating disorders becomes clearer it becomes more evident that multifactorial polygenic composite traits are being teased out into their component traits, often influenced by only a few loci and with a much clearer non-genetic influence. The justification for a psychiatric classification of these disorders therefore becomes less appropriate and the disorders regarded as biologically based dysfunctions shared by many higher animals.

However, the way we regard eating disorders seems to have had a profound influence on their clinical treatment. To begin with, many of the patient's subjective feelings about the disorder may be the result not of mind over matter but of the way physiological disorder impacts on the brain. Subjects suffering the effect of plain starvation in prison camps or in controlled voluntary experiments, have reported many of the symptoms and feelings associated with eating disordered patients. The so-called human mental manifestations may therefore be secondary symptoms initiated by the primary biological causation.

The change in perception of eating disorders as biologically based and as involving the strongest feed-back reactions, could lead to a marked change in attitude for both patient and clinician. The notion that the sufferer is in any way weak-willed in relation to eating phenotype would be dispelled and treatments based on self-discipline would lose favour. Evidence from animal models and epidemiology shows that physiological factors such as hyperinsulinaemia underlie strong hunger reactions in the obese and can account for failure to stick to dieting (Heller 1994). The child study of familial trends in obesity, in the Belgian–Luxembourg obesity cluster, showed a strong genetic effect on population obesity traits, including such an early manifestation as heavier birthweights (Grinspoon *et al.* 1995).

This underlies the likelihood of genetically controlled physiological mechanisms acting in obesity that are almost impossible to thwart by will-power on any long-term basis. 'Calorie-counting' in such a context is doomed to failure. Indeed Owen *et al.* (1971) showed that pigs whose energy intake was restricted during a period of their early growth, not only showed compensatory intake but 'remembered' all the calories thus denied them when returned to *ad libitum* feeding, as compared to non-restricted controls. To make matters worse, not only is voluntary restriction of total energy eaten likely to be, at best, achievable only in the short term but the associated factors of diet composition and degree of activity are almost as incalcitrant to voluntary manipulation on a long-term basis. Anorexics and healthy humans are much more realistic in their appreciation of their inability to overeat, i.e. to gorge above their normal satiety level, than are most people about their ability to 'diet' or fast successfully. However most experimentation with animal models and human subjects points to the difficulty of sustaining both over and undereating in relation to the set-point. Overeating is restrained by immediate physiological discomfort culminating in vomiting, whereas undereating is restrained by complex physiological hunger reactions, many mediated through mental craving (Heller 1994).

Another aspect of the acceptance of the biological basis of eating disorders is the realism engendered in relation to cure prospects. So far the treatments of eating disorders have seldom shown reliable results in terms of long-term recovery (Eckert *et al.* 1995) and a realization of this fact could relieve many patients of the suffering of disappointing progress.

CONCLUSIONS AND FUTURE RESEARCH

In spite of the sobering reality of the disappointing progress in controlling eating disorders to date, the proper understanding of the genetic basis of eating disorders is currently improving quickly. Before long it may be possible to alleviate these disorders in a purposeful, well-based manner.

Eating disorders are currently increasing alarmingly in the Western developed nations (Goodrick *et al.* 1996). A closer look at the statistics shows that the variance of body weight is concurrently increasing at a faster than expected rate. This anomaly can be explained on a threshold basis since the trend to heavier mean body weight masks a substantial group that is relatively static in terms of body weight and a growing proportion of obese individuals and of a smaller proportion of anorexia and bulimia sufferers.

Evidence discussed in earlier sections of this chapter suggests that the appetite mechanism evolved under conditions that differ from modern times in two distinct respects. First of all, intake restriction was only necessary for the carbohydrate component of the diet since high energy (fat) components were always in deficit. Secondly, the appetite mechanism operated under conditions of a relatively high body activity level. Members of early hunter–gatherer societies could only satisfy their needs by considerable physical effort involved in food gathering, amongst other activities.

Since then, and particularly after the middle of the current century, these conditions have been rapidly eroded. First, a wide variety of foods have become freely and cheaply available to an increasing proportion of people in modern Western societies. In parallel, long periods of inactivity have become a norm for many people, much if not most of the time.

The removal of these environmental constraints on food-seeking has uncovered gene loci at which alleles disturb the proper functioning of the appetite mechanism. With the help of animal models, where homologous regions of the genome can be explored by direct experimentation, the genes responsible are being progressively discovered. This is particularly the case with obesity, whose multitude of forms and their causation are rapidly being elaborated. With anorexia nervosa and bulimia nervosa and other less specified eating disorders, the evidence for a genetic basis is increasing but as yet this has not been resolved at the level of single gene loci.

Research will continue to unravel more of the common elements of the genome of the higher animals and the major challenge to research will be how this knowledge can be applied. Knowing the genetic basis in itself will not cure human eating disorders, since artificial breeding as in farm animals, is not available for human societies.

Gene therapy, using the protein products coded by the genes or somatic gene-transfer to supplement the failing internal supply, may be a possible avenue. However, the complex interactions of genes and their protein products with other parts of the complex human body make it impossible at this stage to predict the outcome or its likely timing.

In relation to the distinction between males and females in the incidence of eating disorder, there is so far little evidence from animal models to help directly in illuminating human sex differences. However, the sex differences in animal body-fat content and the stress, nutritional and otherwise, involved at the start of the female's reproductive life, may provide parallels between human and non-human higher animal disorders.

CLINICAL AND RESEARCH IMPLICATIONS

- Evidence from animal models together with that on human patients, indicate that vulnerability to anorexia nervosa (AN) and several obesity syndromes show a significant genetic component.
- The degree of expression of the genetic predisposition depends on environmental triggers or stress factors that influence the timing and/or severity of the symptoms.

Continued

- This finding is consistent with the fact that both appetite control and stress response are subject to hypothalamus control.
- Both AN and obesity appear to stem from a mis-setting or mis-reading by the brain of the body composition target for different growth-stages, resulting in overshooting (obesity) or undershooting (emaciation as in AN).
- Animal models are increasingly suggesting suitable candidate genes by which these basal errors are compounded.

FUTURE RESEARCH

- Search for candidate genes influencing the range of body composition from emaciation to obesity across a number of appropriate animal species.
- Further elucidation of stress responses acting as triggers in animal models.

DIFFICULTIES

- Getting sufficient multiply affected families to carry out powerful linkage studies (QTLs) in humans and animal models.
- Distinguishing the results of primary genetic defects from secondary physiological effects of emaciation in AN subjects (vice versa in obese subjects).

FORMULATION

- These findings from animal models strengthen the need for more comprehensive case formulation procedures.
- These should include, in addition to routine measures of weight, height etc., as full a family history as possible of degree of leanness, stress susceptibility as well as related conditions such as alcohol abuse.

TREATMENT

- The indication of a significant genetic basis from animal models has several implications for treatment and establishing open communication with the patient.
- Patients will benefit from being classified as suffering from a basic metabolic dysfunction rather than an ill-defined, primarily psychiatric mental, condition. This will enable clinicians and patients to better understand and to cope with the secondary 'psychiatric' phenomena, minimising any possible guilt feeling by the patient.
- Animal models present an opportunity in the near future to identify genetic markers that will enable individuals to be classified as 'at risk'. This will allow targeted preventative measures to avoid potential risk factors (triggers), including extreme caution in indulgence in wilful 'dieting' that could trigger a catabolic spiral.

Continued

- Candidate genes from animal model work could also help to identify the lack of, or miscoded, proteins. These basic deficiencies could be rectified by direct administration of replacements or by somatic gene therapy.

OTHER EATING DISORDERS

- Bulimia nervosa and bingeing: There are as yet no reported direct equivalents of these conditions in animal models. Even if there were, they would be observable only in non-ruminant models, because of similarity to humans in their digestive anatomy. At first sight this could strengthen the argument that AN and Bulimia are distinctly separate entities, even though they coincide in a proportion of sufferers. However, there are many indirect evidential features that point to the possibility of a common aetiology, possibly genetic. If this is so then we may be observing a rather different degree and symptoms of closely related genetic disorders.
- Obesity: Many of the points made for AN above apply in some measure to the other side of the coin and the *ob* gene is one candidate for both conditions.

REFERENCES

Altemus, M., Glowa, J.R. and Murphy, D.L. (1993). Attenuation of food-restriction-induced running by chronic fluoxetine treatment, *Psychopharm. Bull.*, **29**, 397–400.

Altemus, M., Glowa, J.R., Galliven, E., Leong, Y.M. and Murphy, D.L. (1996). Effects of serotonergic agents on food-restriction-induced hyperactivity, *Pharmacol. Biochem. Behav.*, **53**, 123–131.

Andersson, L.B. (1996). Genes and Obesity, *Ann. Med.*, **28**, 5–7.

Andersson, L., Haley, C.S., Ellegren, H. *et al.* (1994). Genetic mapping for growth and fatness in pigs, *Science*, **263**, 1771–1774.

Archibald, A.L. (1991). Inherited halothane-induced malignant hyperthermia in pigs, In *Breeding for Disease Resistance in Farm Animals* (Eds. J.B. Owen and R.F.E. Axford), pp. 449–466, CAB International, Wallingford.

Astrup, A. (1996). Obesity and Metabolic Efficiency, *Ciba Found. Symp.*, **201**, 159–173.

Bahary, N., Leibel, R.L. and Friedman, J.M. (1990). Molecular mapping of the mouse *db* mutation, *Proc. Natl. Acad. Sci., USA*, **87**, 8642–8646.

Barbato, G.F. (1994). Genetic control of food intake in chickens, *J. Nutr.*, **124**, S1341–S1348.

Blundell, J.E. and Halford, J.C.G. (1994). Regulation of nutrient supply: the brain and appetite control, *Proc. Nutr. Soc.*, **53**, 407–418.

Blundell, J.E. and Lawton, C.L. (1995). Serotonin and dietary fat intake-effects of dexfenfluramine, *Metab. Clin. Exp.*, **44**, 33–37.

Blundell, J.E., Lawton, C.L., Cotton, J.R. and MacDiarmid, J.I. (1996). Control of human appetite—implications for the intake of dietary fat, *Ann. Rev. Nutr.*, **16**, 285–319.

Bouchard, C. (1991). Heredity and the path to overweight and obesity. *Med. Sci. Sports Exerc.*, **23**, 285–291.

Bouchard, C. (1995). Genetics of obesity—an update on molecular markers, *Int. J. Obes.*, **19**, S10–S13.

Bouchard, C. and Perusse, L. (1996). Current status of the human obesity map, *Obesity Research*, **4**, 81–90.

Bouchard, C., Despres, J.P. and Mauriege, P. (1993a). Genetic and non-genetic determinants of regional fat distribution, *Endocr. Rev.*, **14**, 72–93.

Bouchard, C., Perusse, L., Deriaz, O., Despres, J.P. and Tremblay, A. (1993b). Genetic influences on energy-expenditure in humans, *Crit. Rev. Food Sci. Nutr.*, **33**, 345–350.

Bultman, S.J., Michaud, E.J. and Woychik, R.P. (1992). Molecular characterisation of the mouse agouti locus, *Cell*, **71**, 1195–1204.

Carroll, J.F. *et al.* (1996) Hypertension, cardiac hypertrophy and neurohumoral activity in a new model of obesity. *Am. J. Physiol.—Heart and Circulatory Physiology*, **40**, H373–H378.

Charlier, C., Coppieters, W., Farnir, F. *et al.* (1995). The *mh* gene causing double-muscling in cattle maps to bovine chromosome-2. *Mamm. Genome*, **6**, 788–792.

Chipkevitch, E. (1994). Brain tumors and anorexia nervosa syndrome, *Brain Dev.*, **16**, 175–179.

Cockett, N.E., Jackson, S.P. and Shay, T.I. (1996). Polar overdominance at the ovine callipyge locus, *Science*, **273**, 236–238.

Coleman, D.L. (1978). Diabetes and obesity: thrifty mutants? *Nutr. Rev.*, **36**, 129–132.

Coleman, D.L. and Eicher, E.M. (1990). Fat (*fat*) and tubby (*tub*)—2 autosomal recessive mutations causing obesity syndromes in the mouse, *J. Hered.*, **81**, 424–427.

Cummings, D.E., Brandon, E.P., Planas, J.V., Motamed, K., Idzerda, R.L. and McKnight, G.S. (1996). Genetically lean mice result from targeted disruption of the RIIβ subunit of protein kinase A. *Nature*, **382**, 622–626.

Daniel, H. and Herget, M. (1996). Obese people and mice. *Ernahrungs-Umschau*, **43**, 4.

Eckert, E.D., Halmi, K.A., Marchi, P., Grove, W. and Crosby, R. (1995). 10-year follow-up of anorexia-nervosa—clinical course and outcome, *Psychol. Med.*, **25**, 143–156.

Falciglia, G.A. and Norton, P.A. (1994). Evidence for a genetic influence on preference for some foods, *J. Am. Diet. Assoc.*, **94**, 154–158.

Frederich, R.C., Hamann, A., Anderson, S., Lollmann, B., Lowell, B.B. and Flier, J.S. (1995). Leptin levels reflect body lipid-content in mice—evidence for diet-induced resistance to leptin action, *Nature Med.*, **1**, 1311–1314.

Fries, H.R., Pliska, V., Vogeli, P. and Strangzinger, G. (1992). Is the ryanodin receptor gene a major gene for meatiness in pigs. *Landwirtschaft-Schweitz*, **5**, 37–39.

Gerald, C. *et al.* (1996). A receptor subtype involved in neuropeptide-Y-induced food intake, *Nature*, **382**, 168–171.

Goodrick, G.K., Poston, W.S.C. and Foreyt, J.P. (1996). Methods for voluntary weight-loss and control—update 1996, *Nutrition*, **12**, 672–676.

Greenberg, D. and Smith, G.P. (1996). The controls of fat intake. *Psychosom. Med.*, **58**, 559–569.

Gregory, J., Foster, K., Tyler, H. and Wiseman, M. (1990). *The Dietary and Nutritional Survey of British Adults*, HMSO, London.

Grinspoon, S., Gulick, T., Askari, H. *et al.* (1995). Familial trends of obesity through 3 generations—the Belgian–Luxembourg child study, *Int. J. Obes.*, **19**, S5–S9.

Harris, R.B.S. and Martin, R.J. (1984). Specific depletion of body-fat in parabiotic partners of tube-fed obese rats, *Am. J. Physiol.*, **247**, R380–R386.

Hebebrand, J. and Remschmidt, H. (1995). Anorexia-nervosa viewed as an extreme weight condition—genetic implications, *Hum. Genet.*, **95**, 1–11.

Heitmann, B.L., Lissner, L., Sorensen, T.I.A. and Bengtsson, C. (1995). Dietary fat intake and weight gain in women genetically predisposed for obesity, *Am. J. Clin. Nutr.*, **61**, 1213–1217.

Heller, R.F. (1994). Hyperinsulinemic obesity and carbohydrate addiction—the missing link is the carbohydrate frequency factor, *Med. Hypotheses*, **42**, 307–312.

Hervey, G.R. (1969). Regulation of energy balance, *Nature*, **222**, 629–631.

Herzog, D. and Klibanski, A. (1996). Serum leptin levels in women with anorexia-nervosa, *J. Clin. Endocrinol. Metab.*, **81**, 3861–3863.

Higa, I. and Fuyama, Y. (1993). Genetics of food preference in *Drosophila sechellia.* 1. Responses to food attractants, *Genetica*, **88**, 129–136.

Holland, A.J., Sicotte, N. and Treasure, J. (1989). Anorexia nervosa: evidence for a genetic basis, *J. Psychosom. Res.*, **32**, 561–571.

Hulsey, M.G. and Martin, R.J. (1992). An anorectic agent from adipose tissue of overfed rats: effects on feeding behavior, *Physiol. Behav.*, **52**, 1141–1149.

Kendler, K.S., Maclean, C., Neale, M., Kessler, R., Heath, A. and Eaves, L. (1991). The genetic epidemiology of Bulimia Nervosa, *Am. J. Psychiatry*, **148**, 1627–1637.

King, N.A. and Blundell, J.E. (1995). High-fat foods overcome the energy-expenditure induced by high-intensity cycling or running, *Eur. J. Clin. Nutr.*, **49**, 114–123.

Kyriakis, I., Emmans, G.C., and Whittemore, C.T. (1991a). The ability of pigs to control their protein intake when fed in three different ways, *Physiol. Behav.*, **50**, 1197–1203.

Kyriakis, S.C., Olsson, N.G., Martinsson, K. and Bjork, A.K.K. (1991b). Observations on the action of Amperozide—are there social influences on sow-litter productivity?, *Research in Veterinary Science*, **51**, 169–173.

Leiter, E.H. (1993). Obesity genes and diabetes induction in the mouse, *Crit. Rev. Food Sci. Nutr.*, **33**, 333–338.

Liebel, R.L., Rosenbaum, M. and Hirsch, J. (1995). Changes in energy expenditure resulting from altered body weight, *New England J. Med.*, **332**, 621–628.

Longhurst, W.M., Oh, H.K., Jones, M. B. and Kepner, R.E. (1968). A basis for the palatability of deer forage plants, *North American Wildlife Natural Resource Conference Transactions*, **33**, 181–192.

Maclean, C.W. (1968). The thin sow problem, *Vet. Rec.*, **83**, 308–316.

Masuzaki, H., Ogawa, Y., Hosoda, K., Kawada, T., Fushiki, T. and Nakao, K. (1995). Augmented expression of the obese gene in the adipose tissue from rats fed high-fat diet. *Biochem. Biophys. Res. Commun.*, **216**, 355–358.

Mattei, R. and Carlini, E.A. (1996). A comparative study of the anorectic and behavioral effects of Fenproporex on male and female rats, *Braz. J. Med. Biol. Res.*, **29**, 1025–1030.

Mizuno, T.M., Bergen, H., Funabashi, T. *et al.* (1996). Obese gene expression—reduction by fasting and stimulation by insulin and glucose in lean mice and persistent elevation in acquired (diet induced) and genetic (yellow agouti) obesity, *Proc. Natl. Acad. Sci. USA*, **93**, 3434–3438.

Morrowtesch, J. and Andersson, G. (1994). Immunological and hematological characterizations of the wasting pig syndrome, *J. Anim. Sci.*, **72**, 976–983.

Morse, A.D., Russell, J.C., Hunt, T.W.M., Wood, G.O., Epling, W.F. and Pierce, W.D. (1995). Diurnal variation of intensive running in food-deprived rats, *Can. J. Physiol. Pharmacol.*, **73**, 1519–1523.

Noble, D.O., Picard, M.L., Dunnington, E.A., Uzu, G., Larsen, A.S. and Siegel, P.B. (1993). Food intake adjustments of chicks: short term reactions of genetic stocks to deficiencies in lysine, methionine or tryptophan, *Br. Poult. Sci.*, **34**, 725–735.

Owen, J.B. (1990). Weight control and appetite: nature over nurture, *Anim. Breed. Abstr.*, **58**, 583–591.

Owen, J.B. (1996). Effects of quantitative trait selection on the frequency of major genes in relation to the underlying additive polygenic breeding value, *EAAP Book of Abstracts*, No. 2: 16.

Owen, J.B., Ridgman, W.J. and Wyllie, D.W. (1971). The effect of food restriction on subsequent voluntary intake of pigs, *Anim. Prod.*, **13**, 537–546.

Price, R.A., Ness, R. and Laskarzewski, P. (1990). Common major gene inheritance of extreme overweight, *Hum. Biol.*, **62**, 747–765.

Ravussin, E. (1995). Metabolic differences and the development of obesity, *Metab. Clin. Exp.*, **44**, 12–14.

Ravussin, E., Bennett, P.H., Valencia, M.E., Schultz, L.O. and Esparaza, J. (1994). Effects of a traditional lifestyle on obesity in Pima Indians, *Diabetes Care*, **17**, 1067–1074.

Rieg, T.S. and Aravich, P.F. (1994). Systemic clonidine increases feeding and wheel running but does not affect rate of weight loss in rats subjected to activity-based anorexia, *Pharmacol. Biochem. Behav.*, **47**, 215–218.

Ritchie, M.E. (1991). Inheritance of optimal foraging behavior in Columbian ground-squirrels. *Ev. Ecol.*, **5**, 146–159.

Roberts, S.B. and Greenberg, A.S. (1996). The new obesity genes, *Nutr. Rev.*, **54**, 41–49.

Roberts, S.B. (1995). Abnormalities of energy expenditure and the development of obesity, *Obesity Research*, **3**, S155–S163.

Rothwell, N.J. and Stock, M.J. (1979). Regulation of energy balance in two models of reversible obesity in the rat, *J. Comp. Physiol. Psychol.*, **93**, 1024–1034.

Sazaki, S., Clutter, A.C. and Pomp, D. (1996). Assignment of the porcine obese (leptin) gene to chromosome 18 by linkage analysis of a new PCR-based polymorphism, *Mamm. Genome*, **7**, 471–472.

Schepank, H. (1991) Erbdeterminanten bei der Anorexia nervosa (Hereditary determinants of anorexia nervosa), *Zeitschrift fur Psychosomatische Medizin und Psychoanalyse*, **37**, 265–281.

Schneider, R.R. and Hunter, D.B. (1993). Nursing disease in mink—clinical and postmortem findings, *Vet. Pathol.*, **30**, 512–521.

Simon, Y., Bellisle, F., Monneuse, M., Samuel-Lajeunesse, B. and Drewnowski, A. (1993). Taste responsiveness in anorexia nervosa, *Br. J. Psychiatry*, **162**, 244–246.

Sorenson, T.I.A. and Stunkard, A.J. (1994). Overview of the adoption studies, in *The Genetics of Obesity* (Ed. C. Bouchard), pp. 49–61. CRC Press, Boca Raton, FL.

Stenzelpoore, M.P., Heinrichs, S.C., Rivest, S., Koob, G.F. and Vale, W.W. (1994). Overproduction of corticotropin-releasing factor in transgenic mice—a genetic model of anxiogenic behavior, *J. Neurosci.*, **14**, 2579–2584.

Surwit, R.S. and Williams, P.G. (1996). Animal models provide insight into psychosomatic factors in diabetes, *Psychosom. Med.*, **58**, 582–589.

Truett, G.E, Bahary, N., Friedman, J.M. and Leibel, R.L. (1991). The Zucker rat obesity gene fatty (*fa*) maps to rat chromosome-5 and is a homolog of the mouse diabetes (*db*) gene, *FASEB J.*, **5**, A708.

Weltzin, T.E., Fernstrom, M.H. and Kaye, W.H. (1994). Serotonin and bulimia nervosa, *Nutr. Rev.*, **52**, 399–408.

West, D.B., Waguespack, J., York, B., Goudey-Lefevre, J. and Price, R.A. (1994a). Genetics of dietary obesity in AKR/J × SWR/J mice: segregation of the trait and identification of a linked locus on chromosome 4, *Mamm. Genome*, **5**, 546–552.

West, D.B., Goudeylefevre, J., York, B. and Truett, G.E. (1994b). Dietary obesity linked to genetic loci on chromosome 9 and chromosome 15 in a polygenic mouse model, *J. Clin. Invest.*, **94**, 1410–1416.

West, D.B., Waguespack, J. and McCollister, S. (1995). Dietary obesity in the mouse-interactions of strain with diet composition, *Am. J. Physiol.—Regulatory Integrative and Comparative Physiology*, **37**, R658–R665.

Willner, P., Moreau, J.L., Nielsen, C.K., Papp, M. and Sluzewska, A. (1996). Decreased hedonic responsiveness following mild stress is not secondary to loss of body-weight. *Physiol. Behav.*, **60**, 129–134.

Wilmut, I., Schnieke, A.E., McWhir, J., Kind, A.J. and Campbell, K.H.S. (1997). Viable offspring derived from fetal and adult mammalian cells, *Nature*, **385**, 810–813.

Wyllie, D. and Owen, J.B. (1978) Anorexigenic substances and voluntary food intake in the pig, *Anim. Prod.*, **26**, 19–29.

Zhang, Y., Proenca, R., Maffei, M., Barone, M., Leopold, L. and Friedman, J.M. (1994). Positional cloning of the mouse obese gene and its human homologue, *Nature*, **372**, 425–432.

9 Stress, Eating and Neurobiology

F. CONNAN and J. L. TREASURE
Institute of Psychiatry, London, UK

INTRODUCTION

The aim of this chapter is to provide a review of the current research and hypotheses regarding the neurochemical mechanisms that underlie the eating disorders. Stress and a disturbance of eating behaviour are core features of both anorexia nervosa and bulimia nervosa. Therefore, in this chapter we review current research into stress and, in particular, focus on how it affects eating behaviour both in man and in animal models.

It is not currently possible to examine human brain chemistry directly, although new scanning techniques may facilitate this in time. We rely, therefore, at present, on indirect methods, such as measurements of cerebrospinal fluid (CSF), neuroendocrine challenge tests and extrapolation from animal models. There are several basic assumptions underlying these methods which may be flawed. For example, lumbar spine CSF may not reflect central CSF turnover and abnormal challenge tests of the hypothalamic–pituitary–adrenal axis may not be generalizable to dysfunctional neurotransmitter systems in other brain areas.

Furthermore, an animal model which resembles a clinical disorder in terms of phenotype and behaviour may not have the same underlying biology. Research in this area, therefore, requires cautious interpretation.

CORE CLINICAL FEATURES OF ANOREXIA NERVOSA AND BULIMIA NERVOSA

Russell (1995) has warned that many of our current definitions of anorexia nervosa are framed within contemporary Western culture and may not be generalizable to other times and places. He emphasizes the core features which are 'That the patient avoids food and induces weight loss by virtue of a range of psychosocial conflicts whose resolution she perceives to be within her reach through the achievement of thinness and/or the avoidance of fatness.' This reduces the key components of anorexia nervosa to a disruption of body weight/appetite control precipitated by stress.

The definition of bulimia nervosa shares with anorexia nervosa avoidance of food with the aim of reducing weight but includes oscillation between

Neurobiology in the Treatment of Eating Disorders.
Edited by H.W. Hoek, J.L. Treasure and M.A. Katzman.

consummatory behaviours and those related to weight loss. Psychological distress is thought to play a key role in the aetiology and maintenance of bulimia nervosa.

STRESS AND EATING DISORDERS

The onset of both anorexia nervosa and bulimia nervosa is usually preceded by a severe stressful life event or difficulty (Schmidt *et al.* 1997). Most commonly, this is an event which involves a disruption of the subject's social relationships with family and friends (Schmidt *et al.* 1997). The meaning of many of the events differed although, in approximately a fifth of patients with anorexia nervosa, the event contained a component of sexual disgust.

In addition, in cases of bulimia nervosa, there is usually a history of developmental stress. High levels of childhood adversity such as parental separation, neglect and abuse occur (Schmidt *et al.* 1993). This type of childhood history is much less common in restricting anorexia nervosa although it is usually present in the bulimic subtype. In an interesting study of cases of bulimia nervosa who had not presented for medical care the levels of developmental stress were higher than those seen in depression (Fairburn *et al.* 1997). In particular, there were higher levels of poor parenting (parental separation, arguments, criticism, high expectations, over/under-involvement and minimal affection) and parents also had higher levels of drug misuse and alcoholism. In a study of twins which was able to partial out genetic factors, it was found that family environmental factors are especially important in the development of bulimia nervosa (Kendler *et al.* 1995).

However, stress may only have an impact on an individual if it places strain on the coping resources. We have found that women with eating disorders tend to have a helpless response to both developmental and later stressful events (Troop and Treasure, 1997a,b). In particular, women with anorexia nervosa show an avoidant cognitive style whereas patients with bulimia nervosa, in contrast, tend to ruminate about their problems. Poor coping skills may lead to the stress becoming chronic which, in turn, alters physiological and psychological systems.

Several studies have focused on the role of stress and strain in the development of eating disorders but an area which has been neglected is whether treatment is able to bring about change. Is treatment which focuses on the developing of an understanding of the psychosocial conflict and which aims to produce a more adaptive coping response and hence less strain effective? The course of treatment of a 24-year-old woman who presented to our clinic with a three year history of anorexia is illustrated in Figure 9.1. Despite the patient's being very motivated to recover from her anorexia nervosa at the time of her first assessment no progress was made, indeed her weight fell in the initial sessions of outpatient treatment. The first phase of treatment involved patient and therapist developing a good alliance so that there was enough trust between them to facilitate the discussion of previously avoided, shameful issues. It is interesting to note that weight gain only occurred after there had been an active strategy to deal with this issue and the meaning of the

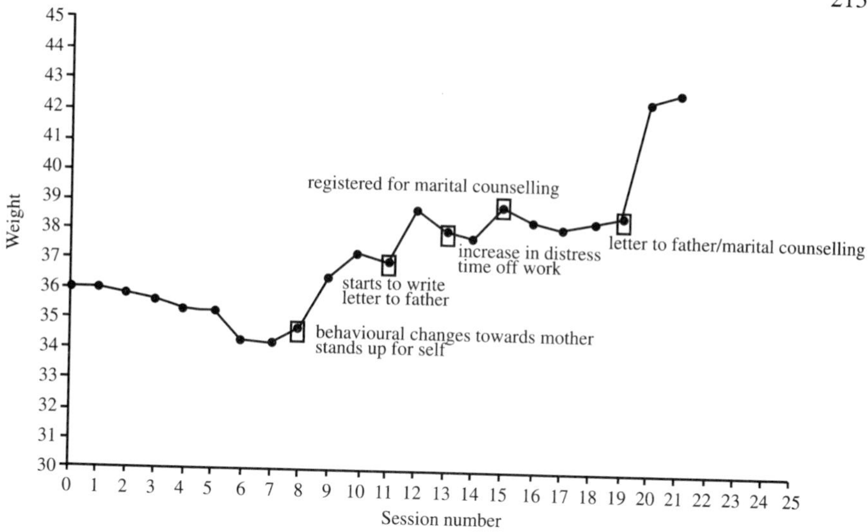

Figure 9.1. Course of treatment of a 24-year-old woman with anorexia

event was transformed from a shameful secret into a set-back that had been mastered.

THE NEUROBIOLOGY OF STRESS

Stress is a core feature of both types of eating disorder both as a triggering event and, in the case of bulimia nervosa, as a setting condition. We will, therefore, give a brief overview of the biology of both types of events. Further details are available in a recent review (Herbert 1997).

The stress response involves an integration of the serotonin (5-hydroxytryptamine; 5-HT) system, the limbic and hypothalamic peptide network, the pituitary and the adrenal glands. Cortisol is one of the key effectors in man. Dehydroepiandrosterone (DHEA) another steroid hormone secreted from the adrenal cortex can antagonize the effects of cortisol. Therefore, an alteration in the DHEA/cortisol ratio which varies with the developmental age or depending on the type of stress, can moderate the response.

There are numerous feedback loops and points of interaction within the stress system. Corticosteroids generate feedback inhibition to the hypothalamic–pituitary–adrenal (HPA) axis at the levels of the adrenal glands, the pituitary and the hypothalamus and limbic structures. The mechanisms and time frames of this negative feedback vary at different levels of the axis. The effects of corticosteroids on the brain are mediated by two receptor types. High affinity mineralocorticoid receptors (MR) are tonically occupied at basal levels of hormone and are thought to be involved in the control of circadian rhythmicity. Glucocorticoid receptors (GR) show lower affinity and are activated in response to increases in cortisol levels, induced, for example, by stress. Hippocampal GRs are transiently occupied in response to changes in glucocorticoid concentration and mediate fast feedback at this level. At the level of the pituitary, GRs are activated in response to mean glucocorticoid concentration over time and thus mediate delayed feedback (for a review see Checkley 1996). In animals the stress response differs depending on the predominant sensory input (interoceptive versus exteroceptive). The hypothalamic response to chronic emotional stress, such as low ranking and submission in a dominance hierarchy, appears to be characterized by release of corticotrophin releasing hormone (CRH), oxytocin and arginine vasopressin (AVP) (Romero and Sapolsky 1996). The latter has a synergistic action with CRH in activating the HPA axis. There are populations of hypothalamic neurones which synthesize only AVP or CRH, and a population in which they are co-localized. These different populations may be preferentially activated by different types of stress and, furthermore, susceptibility to glucocorticoid (GC) feedback inhibition may differ. For example, a subpopulation of CRH neurones have been identified which do not express GC receptors and are thus insensitive to GC feedback inhibition (Agnati *et al.* 1985). The AVP pathways may also be relatively resistant to GC feedback inhibition. Alternatively, AVP and CRH when released in large quantity may generate sufficient adrenocorticotrophin hormone (ACTH) sectretagogue activity to override GC feedback inhibition at the level of the pituitary.

The serotonergic system is activated by stress and it has been suggested that it may play a role in the resilience or vulnerability to the psychopathic results of stress (Deakin *et al.* 1991). These authors suggest that a failure of the 5-HT neurones in the raphe that project onto 5-HT_{1A} receptors in the hippocampus can lead to helplessness in animals and depression in man. In turn, cortisol moderates serotonergic function via increased formation of 5-HT, increased expression of 5-HT_2 receptors in the cerebral cortex and reduced 5-HT_{1A} expression in the hippocampus (McKittrick *et al.* 1995).

Gender differences in the response to stress have often been noted. Oestrogen increases the response of ACTH, cortisol and noradrenaline to psychosocial stress in men (Kirschbaum *et al.* 1996). CRH gene expression is modulated by oestrogen which may, in part, explain this sexual dimorphism (Vamvakopoulos and Chrousos 1993).

ANIMAL MODELS OF CHRONIC STRESS

It is usually only severe events and difficulties which have an impact over at least 2 weeks that lead to psychological stress in man. Therefore, any animal models need to involve this dimension of chronicity. Analogues of developmental adversity (a model for bulimia nervosa) and chronic stress (a model for both) have been developed in primates and in rodents.

The paradigms of developmental adversity usually involve some form of disruption in attachment relationships. The neurobiological underpinning of the formation of attachment bonds, in particular, the role of vasopressin and oxytocin has been reviewed by Insell (1997). Pair bonding in monogamous animals, the initiation of parental care and some aspects of the infants' attachment system are thought to be mediated by these neurohypophyseal hormones with oxytocin having the greater effect in females and vasopressin in males. Insell suggests that these various developmental forms of attachment behaviours may be manifestations of the same neurobiological pathway which are moderated by the social and endocrine context.

Disruption in attachment bonds leads to distress and a neurendocrinological response. Over-activity of the HPA axis occurs frequently in conjunction with an alteration in central 5-HT function. Usually, loss of appetite occurs as a secondary feature. The implications of such models for eating disorders have often been ignored.

DEVELOPMENTAL STRESS

RODENTS

Rats who had repeated short periods of separation from their mothers during infancy had long standing persistent changes in CRH neuronal systems, with elevated CRH in the median eminence, elevated CRH-mRNA expression in the amygdala and hypothalamus, elevated CRH in the cerebrospinal fluid and in the hypothalamo–hypophyseal portal blood (Ladd *et al.* 1996). These animals show a propensity to prefer alcohol to water. The stress response in these animals remained exaggerated into adulthood and the CRH receptor in the pituitary remained down regulated throughout life. Interestingly, treatment with a selective serotonin reuptake inhibitor (SSRI) reverses the neuroendocrine effects of early maternal separation in the rat (Nemeroff 1996 *et al.* 1997).

PRIMATES

A series of studies looking at rhesus monkeys has helped clarify the links between early experiences, neurobiology and later behaviour in higher mammals (Suomi 1997). This work has highlighted the effect of individual (possibly genetic) vulnerabilities as well as the effect of specific environmental experiences. The two often interact. Approximately 20% of the rhesus monkey study population, a so called 'high reactive' subgroup show increased arousal and behavioural disruption to novel stimuli. A second subgroup (5–10% of the total) show extreme impulsivity and have evidence of low central 5-HT turnover. Both of these types of monkey show less secure attachments. In the long term they have a poor social outcome and end up at the bottom of the ranking hierarchy. However, there is an interaction between these temperamental traits and maternal rearing style. If 'high reactive' infant monkeys are fostered by mothers who show high nurturant behaviours then they show very secure attachment behaviour and in adulthood hold positions at the top of the dominance hierarchy.

If infant monkeys are separated from their mothers, initially being hand reared and later brought up by peers, they show a typical insecure attachment pattern, are reluctant to explore novel situations and are more anxious. These animals have an exaggerated HPA and sympathetic nervous system (SNS) response to separation which persists during development. Maternal separation, therefore, produces an effect similar to that seen in the naturally 'high reactive' subgroup. In addition, peer reared monkeys are more impulsive and have lower CSF 5-hydroxyindoleacetic acid (5-HIAA) turnover. Socially, even when introduced to different groups, these animals fare poorly in the social ranking process.

Lesser degrees of maternal separation in more natural conditions can produce similar effects. For example, when the environment was manipulated so that mothers had to spend longer foraging for food, the offspring showed less secure attachments with 'high reactive' and impulsive behaviour and persistent elevations in CSF corticotrophin releasing factor. Long-lasting abnormalities in response to noradrenergic and serotonergic probes were also seen.

Suomi (1991) has described further fascinating developmental changes in the stress response produced by separation in primates. These changes may have important implications for eating disorders which develop during adolescence. The normal behavioural response to separation is an initial phase of agitation followed by passive withdrawal when the animal adopts a foetal-like posture (a huddle). This is associated with immediate activation of the HPA axis and increased noradrenergic turnover. Adolescent monkeys do not show the withdrawal and 'huddle' response, instead they continue to be agitated, frequently displaying idiosyncratic, stereotypic patterns of activity (e.g. repetitive pacing around their cage, or fiddling with the mesh front of their cage for hours at a time). Furthermore, the biochemical changes in the adolescents differ from that of all other age groups in that they have a long term increase in the cerebrospinal fluid levels of the serotonin metabolite 5-HIAA (Higley *et al.* 1990).

MODELS OF CHRONIC STRESS IN ADULT ANIMALS

One model of chronic stress in animals involves mixing unrelated groups in confined spaces. The animals compete for dominance over the resources. The defeated, subordinate animals change their behaviour. Feeding, activity, aggression and copulation are reduced. In rats this leads to dramatic weight loss and early mortality. The pathophysiology of this phenomenon has been investigated. These animals show chronic activation of the HPA axis and a large proportion are unable to respond to further stress. Subordinate animals have higher levels of 5-HIAA and alterations in 5-HT binding with reduced binding to 5-HT_{1A} receptors in the hippocampus and increased binding to 5-HT_2 receptors in the cortex (Blanchard and Blanchard 1990; McKittrick *et al.* 1995). The reduction in hippocampal 5-HT_{1A} receptors is thought to result from increased levels of corticosteriods acting on the mineralocorticoid type of receptor (Meijer and De Kloet 1995). Not only does chronic stress cause alterations in 5-HT receptors in the hippocampus, it also leads to dendritic shrinkage (Magarinos and McEwan 1995). Subordinate monkeys have been found to have degeneration in the hippocampus after persistent social stress (Salpolsky 1992). Prolonged exposure to high levels of cortisol in conditions such as Cushing's disorder, depression, and childhood sexual abuse in humans may also lead to hippocampal damage (for review see: Sapolsky 1996).

STRESS HORMONES IN ANOREXIA NERVOSA

The following is merely a summary of recent research and the interested reader is referred to a recent review by Licinio and colleagues (1996).

Underweight patients with anorexia nervosa have elevated indices of cortisol secretion shown by elevated plasma and urinary free cortisol, increased cortisol production rate relative to the clearance rate and a lack of suppression of plasma cortisol following dexamethasone. The adrenal has an exaggerated response to ACTH which suggests that the adrenal cortex is functionally hypertrophic.

This increased HPA activity appears to be driven by hypersecretion of CRH. CSF levels of CRH are increased (Kaye *et al.* 1987). Patients with anorexia nervosa have attenuated release of ACTH to CRH which suggests that feedback at the pituitary is intact but that this is overridden by an increased ACTH secretagogue drive (Cavagnini *et al.* 1986; Gold *et al.* 1986, Hotta *et al.* 1986). One possible explanation for this overactivity is that cortisol feedback to the brain is in some ways defective. This doesn't appear to be the case because RU486, a glucocorticoid antagonist, led to an increased release of both ACTH and cortisol. This effect was most marked in the afternoon (Kling *et al.* 1993). This suggests that it is the set-point for ACTH secretagogue release which is increased.

After short-term weight restoration, the release of ACTH by CRH remained diminished. Also, RU486 continued to produce an afternoon exaggerated release of ACTH and cortisol (Kling *et al.* 1993; Gold *et al.* 1986). Together these findings suggest that there is persistent activation of the HPA system in the face of intact feedback and that this is not an effect of starvation. On the other hand, CSF CRH levels had returned to normal (Kaye *et al.* 1988). After long-term weight recovery we have also found evidence of abnormalities in cortisol secretion. There are higher levels of cortisol in the afternoon and a lack of response to a meal (Ward *et al.* 1997). These findings suggest that there may be a persistent elevation in set-point for cortisol secretion in anorexia nervosa.

One explanation of these findings is that CRH activation of the HPA axis is augmented by release of a second ACTH secretagogue which is not attenuated by cortisol feedback at the pituitary. Vasopressin could be a candidate for this effect (Demitrack *et al.* 1989). Vasopressin is known to release ACTH in response to chronic difficulties (Romero and Sapolsky 1996). Patients with anorexia nervosa have increased central AVP in the acute state and after weight recovery (Gold *et al.* 1983). Oxytocin, which acts to oppose the actions of vasopressin, is reduced in acute anorexia nervosa (Demitrack *et al.* 1990). There is also evidence of a disruption in AVP function with loss of the normal pattern of AVP release in response to changes in osmolality (Gold *et al.* 1983). 1-desamino-D-arginine-vasopressin (DDAVP) failed to enhance ACTH or cortisol release in weight restored patients with anorexia nervosa (Foppiani *et al.* 1996). The authors interpreted this as evidence for down-regulation of DDAVP receptors which may be caused by tonically increased release of AVP.

STRESS HORMONES IN BULIMIA NERVOSA

There has been no consistency in reports on the hypothalamic–pituitary–adrenal axis in bulimia nervosa with some studies reporting pathophysiological changes similar to those seen in anorexia nervosa (Kennedy *et al.* 1989; Coiro *et al.* 1992) whereas others report normal values (Walsh *et al.* 1987; Fichter *et al.* 1990). These discrepancies may be caused by differences in nutrient intake. An alternative explanation is that it is only the patients who have experienced developmental adversity who show abnormalities in the HPA system. There appears to be abnormal regulation of cortisol secretion as cortisol levels did not show the expected fall during an intravenous glucose tolerance test (Coiro *et al.* 1992). The CSF levels of β-endorphin were significantly lower in patients with bulimia nervosa (Brewerton *et al.* 1992).

RELEVANCE OF THESE ANIMAL MODELS OF STRESS TO MAN

In Table 9.1 we have compared the various clinical conditions in which chronic stress is thought to play a role. Depression, anorexia nervosa and early adversity tend to show a similar pattern of neuroendocrine change, characterized by high levels of cortisol thought to be driven by increased activity above the pituitary level. This is in contrast to patients with post-traumatic stress disorder (PTSD) in which cortisol levels are low and there is enhanced negative feedback. The difference may be that the stressors involved in depression and anorexia nervosa are chronic, unlike the unusual single events that are characteristic of PTSD. Patients with borderline personality disorder frequently have adverse early experiences and it is interesting to note that in a pilot study, low levels of 5-HT synthesis were found (Leyton *et al.* 1997). Thus, the results obtained from primates may be applicable to man. This is of relevance to patients with bulimia nervosa as a large proportion also have features of a borderline personality and severe childhood adversity.

Table 9.1. The hypothalamic–pituitary–adrenal system in various human conditions

	Anorexia nervosa	Chronic adversity	Depression	PTSD
Evidence for increased central drive	Gold *et al.* 1986; Cavagnini *et al.* 1986; Hotta *et al.* 1986	De Bellis *et al.* 1994	Ur *et al.* 1992; Young *et al.* 1994	Bremner *et al.* 1997; Smith *et al.* 1989
Cortisol level	High (as above)	Normal: De Bellis *et al.* 1994 High: Lemieux & Coe 1995	High: as above	Low: Boscarino 1996; Yehuda *et al.* 1996

HOMEOSTATIC MECHANISMS FOR THE CONTROL OF WEIGHT AND APPETITE

There have been remarkable developments in our understanding of the mechanisms controlling appetite and weight in the last decade. Nutritional balance is achieved by a complex homeostatic network which is thought to be governed centrally within the hypothalamus. Here, central and peripheral components of the anabolic and catabolic networks are integrated to provide both long- and short-term control of body composition and appetite. Central effectors of this system include components of the HPA axis, serotonin and neuropeptide Y (NPY), whilst peripheral mechanisms include leptin, cortisol, insulin and the sympathetic nervous system. Certain effectors paradoxically participate in both the anabolic and catabolic networks, for example, cortisol activity is catabolic peripherally and anabolic centrally.

In bulimia nervosa homeostatic mechanisms appear to be functional. In the majority of cases weight is maintained within the normal range and attempts to self-starve are counterbalanced by episodes of excessive intake. However, in anorexia nervosa, persistent weight loss occurs without the appropriate re-feeding response, providing compelling evidence that homeostasis is lost. Thus, an understanding of normal homeostasis is necessary to facilitate understanding of the differing aetiologies of the eating disorders.

THE HPA AXIS, INSULIN AND NEUROPEPTIDE Y

Homeostasis is achieved by a balance of anabolic and catabolic systems within the hypothalamus. CRH is a key effector in the catabolic network of the hypothalamus and produces anorexia when injected into the hypothalamus of rats (Glowa and Gold 1991). CRF2 receptors in the ventromedial hypothalamus appear to be of particular significance in this system (Richard *et al.* 1996). Catabolic effects are mediated peripherally, at least in part, by release of cortisol and centrally, by direct inhibition of NPY synthesis (Van Huijsduijen *et al.* 1993).

NPY is a powerful anabolic effector which, when injected directly into the hypothalamus, increases food intake and fat storage (Stanley *et al*, 1986). When infused into the CNS of animals pair fed (thus avoiding the confounding effects of NPY induced hyperphagia) insulin and corticosteroid levels rise (Rohner-Jeanrenaud *et al.* 1996). This provides one of the links between the central and peripheral components of the anabolic system. Cortisol readily diffuses into the brain. Insulin enters via a saturable transport system. The ratio of cortisol to insulin modulates NPY mRNA levels and hence the expression of the peptide: a rise in cortisol increases NPY synthesis and a rise in insulin attenuates this effect (Strack *et al.* 1995). All of the effects of NPY infusions are abolished by adrenalectomy, in keeping with the findings that high levels of CRH inhibit NPY synthesis (Van Huijsduijen *et al.* 1993) and that cortisol facilitates NPY synthesis. There is a reciprocal interaction with the catabolic system as NPY stimulates the HPA axis via stimulation of CRH and AVP release (Liu *et al.* 1994).

In starvation, insulin levels fall, increasing the cortisol : insulin ratio and stimulating NPY release. NPY stimulates the HPA axis and the consequent rising levels of cortisol further stimulate NPY synthesis. This is a 'feed forward' system, generating an increasingly powerful anabolic drive. With re-feeding and increases in blood glucose, insulin levels rise, attenuating the central effects of cortisol and switching off NPY synthesis (Schwartz *et al.* 1995). Another important feedback loop involves leptin, levels of which rise in response to insulin and act centrally to inhibit NPY release (Stephens *et al.* 1995).

LEPTIN

Leptin is a new arrival as part of the system that controls appetite. It appears to be the missing link in the lipostat feedback system originally proposed by Kennedy (1957). The essence of the lipostat hypothesis is that body weight is held constant by means of a signal from fat stores which is relayed to the brain and controls appetite and food intake. The gene for leptin is expressed in fat tissue and is dysfunctional in the *ob* mouse which is phenotypically fat, infertile and inactive (Zhang *et al.* 1994). If leptin is given to *ob* mice their appetite decreases, metabolism increases, activity increases, weight falls, and they become fertile (Chehab 1996). A primary role of leptin may be to provide a signal to the hypothalamus that fat stores are sufficient for reproduction (Chehab *et al.* 1997).

SEROTONIN

Serotonin (5-HT) also plays an important role in the control of appetite (see Blundell and Hill 1991; Curzon 1990 for reviews). The situation is made complex by the existence of numerous receptor subtypes (the nomenclature of which has changed with time), which are widely dispersed at diverse brain sites. In addition, much of the experimental evidence is derived from indirect methods of assessment of serotonin function, using agonists and antagonists that lack good receptor subtype specificity. Enhancement of serotonergic function in humans and animals, using, for example D-fenfluramine, decreases appetite and increases satiety probably by an effect on 5-HT_{2C} receptors (known as 5-HT_{1C} at the time) (Hill and Blundell 1990, 1991). This effect is countered in humans by metergoline, a non-specific 5-HT receptor antagonist (Goodall and Silverstone 1988). In contrast, 5-HT_{1A} agonists increase feeding, presumably because this receptor subtype are autoreceptors and activation may thus reduce serotonergic activity (Dourish *et al.* 1987). Indeed, Dourish *et al.* (1987) found that 5-HT_{1A} agonists attenuate the appetite suppressant effects of D-fenfluramine. Mice bred to have no 5-HT_{2C} receptors are overweight and have an increased appetite (Tecott *et al.* 1995). *m*-Chlorophenylpiperazine (mCPP), a 5-HT agonist with high affinity for 5-HT_{2C} receptors, reduces food intake in wild type mice but not in those lacking the 5-HT_{2C} receptor. Interestingly, when mice lacking the 5-HT_{2C} receptor are pair fed with wild type mice, the mutant strain do not become obese, indicating that the effect of 5-HT_{2C} receptors is behavioural and not metabolic (Tecott *et al.* 1995). These findings are consistent with the observation that psychotropics such as clozapine, with 5-HT_{2C} antagonist activity, induce weight gain. In rhesus macaques oestrogen increases gene expression for tryptophan hydroxylase (TPH), decreases the expression of serotonin reuptake transporter (SERT) and decreases the expression for the 5-HT_{1A} autoreceptor, all of these would produce an overall increase in serotonin transmission (Pecins-Thompson *et al.* 1996; Pecins-Thompson and Bethea 1997). The effects of oestrogens upon 5-HT systems depend upon the age of the animal (Keck and Lakowski 1996; Lakowski 1997).

ANIMAL MODELS OF BULIMIA NERVOSA

Specific animal models with a focus on eating behaviour have also been developed. Specific models of bulimia nervosa have not been developed but many of the physiological preparations designed to test the homeostatic control of appetite and body weight are relevant. Any model which reduces intake leads to rebound over-consumption. The monograph *Hunger* by Le Magnen, 1985 describes much of the experimental work underpinning this hypothesis. A simple animal model of bulimia nervosa analogous to patients who vomit is an animal with a tube in the stomach draining gastric contents. An animal with this form of surgery rapidly increases its appetite, eating more and so maintaining its weight. A model of the non-purging subtype is provided by animals that are fasted for long periods: these animals quickly adjust the size of meal to the interval between meals.

ANIMAL MODELS OF ANOREXIA NERVOSA

In contrast, there are no simple models of anorexia nervosa because the condition contravenes normal physiological principles. Most of the models that have been developed include various combinations of stress, restricted food, and exercise—

all of which are of course key features of anorexia nervosa. The majority of relevant animal models involve rodent species (some of these are discussed further in Chapter 11). Large domestic animal models are available and are discussed more fully in Chapter 8 and in a recent article (Treasure and Owen 1997). In this chapter we discuss these models only in so far as they illustrate underlying pathophysiology. A summary of some of the key features of the animal models of anorexia are shown in Table 9.2.

Common to all of these animal models is stress, poor appetite and weight loss and an abnormal neuroendocrine stress response which can be moderated by drugs which affect 5-HT function. Interestingly, female animals appear to be most prone to develop these conditions.

Most interest has focused on the food deprivation/exercise model described by Epling and Pierce (1984) and Routtenberg and Kuznesoff (1967). In this model rats have free access to a running wheel but the availability of food is time limited. On such a regimen the animals persistently exercise despite being unable to eat enough to maintain their weight: some die as a consequence. Female rats in particular are prone to show this behaviour. Fichter and Pirke (1990) used a variation of this model in which food intake was adjusted to maintain the rats at a level of 70% of their body weight (the usual degree of weight loss in anorexia nervosa). They suggested that the semi-starved rats learned to exercise as this increased their serotonergic drive with resultant reduction of hunger, and thus reinforcing the exercise behaviour. They go further and suggest that pharmacological methods to decrease the hyperactivity in anorexia nervosa may help weight gain. Another rodent model of anorexia is that of immobilization stress (Dourish *et al.* 1987). Again, female animals are more profoundly affected. Many of the pathophysiological features are similar to the exercise/food deprivation model in that abnormal 5-HT and CRH function are implicated.

The pathophysiology of the 'anorexic' pigs is also similar in that there is an abnormal stress response which can be ameliorated by drugs which affect the 5-HT system. It is also interesting that a mutation of the calcium release channel (CRC) on the sarcoplasmic reticulum of skeletal muscle, the so called 'Halothane' gene, results in a phenotype characterized by leanness and sensitivity to stress (Fujji *et al.* 1991). These animals also have abnormal neuroendocrine stress responses and altered central levels of 5-HT.

Other animal models in which pathophysiology has not been so clearly defined are social rodents. For example, Demaret (1993) has suggested that some of the phenotypes expressed by the mole rat may be similar to that of anorexia nervosa. These creatures live under harsh desert conditions where two forms of adult females develop. One form is big and reproductive, the others are much smaller and do not reproduce but spend their time on 'helping' activities such as digging burrows. Chemical triggers are believed to give rise to these two forms and if social circumstances change, non-reproductive, small females may increase their size and become reproductive.

Table 9.2. The pathophysiology of various animal models of anorexia nervosa

	Exercise/food restriction rat	Immobilization stress	Wasting pig	Thin-sow disease	Halothane gene (Pietrain pigs)
Gender specificity	F (Fichter & Pirke 1995)	F (Kennet *et al.* 1986)		F	
HPA activity	Increased corticosterone (Fichter & Pirke 1995)	Condition reversed by CRH antagonist (Shibasaki *et al.*, 1988)	Decreased corticosterone (Albinsson & Andersson 1990)		Dysregulation of the stress response (Nyberg *et al.* 1988)
Central neurotransmitters	Increased 5-HT turnover (Fichter & Pirke 1995)				Decreased serotonin in the hippocampus and hypothalamus (Adeola *et al.* 1993)
5HT system	Behaviour reversed by 5-HT_{1C} agonist and increased with 5-HT depletion (Aravich *et al.* 1994; Fichter & Pirke 1995)	Behaviour reversed by 5-HT_{1A} agonist (Dourish *et al.*, 1987)	Behaviour reversed by 5-HT_2 antagonist (Kyriakis & Anderson 1989)	Behaviour reversed by 5-HT_2 antagonist (Kyriakis *et al.* 1991)	Behaviour reversed by 5-HT_2 antagonist (Nyberg *et al.* 1988)

STUDIES OF THE NEUROBIOLOGY RELATING TO EATING IN HUMANS

Our present methodologies do not allow us to measure hypothalamic function directly. Most of the evidence therefore, focuses on neuroendocrine probes to examine the serotonin system or measurement of peripheral hormones and metabolites.

Anorexia Nervosa

Interpretation of studies of the pathophysiology of anorexia nervosa is difficult as nutritional and menstrual status and weight are often confounding variables. That is, some of the apparently discrepant findings in the literature arise because observed findings may be a result, rather than a cause, of the illness. Thus, although animal data suggest that increased hypothalamic release of 5-HT may be a cause of anorexia nervosa (Morley *et al.* 1986), there are reports that in anorexia nervosa, plasma tryptophan levels are reduced (Coppen *et al.* 1976) as are CSF levels of 5-HIAA (Kaye *et al.* 1988). Interestingly, however, when compared with controls, long term (6 months or more) weight restored anorexic subjects have elevated concentrations of CSF 5-HIAA which showed an inverse correlation with previous lowest weight (Kaye *et al.* 1991). Brewerton (1995) suggests that reduced serotonergic function in those with severe weight loss is a state-dependent finding and that the increased function in fully recovered individuals may be a phase dependent finding arising from a rebound up-regulation of the system. Alternatively, elevated 5-HT function may be a trait phenomenon, in keeping with findings in animal models.

The same problems of data interpretation arise upon examination of the literature dealing with responses to neuroendocrine challenge. McBride *et al.* (1991) found reduced and delayed release of prolactin in response to D-fenfluramine in low weight women with eating disorders. A similar pattern of blunted prolactin release and additionally, blunted GH release, was seen in response to challenge with L-tryptophan (Goodwin *et al.* 1989) and *m*-chlorophenylpiperazine (mCPP) (Brewerton and Jimerson 1996). A subset of patients in the latter study were restudied after weight restoration when the results appeared to have normalized. O'Dwyer *et al.* (1996) gave D-fenfluramine to a group of long-term recovered anorexia nervosa patients and they found no differences between these patients and controls. However, the numbers were small and there was no placebo condition. As both 5-HT receptors and the response to 5-HT are affected by oestrogen, patients who biologically, and on self report, had recovered from anorexia nervosa were investigated with the hypothalamic gonadol axis clamped (Ward *et al.* 1997). There was no difference in the prolactin response to D-fenfluramine between these patients and controls. Thus, these clinical studies find that underweight anorexic subjects have a reduced neurendocrine effect to a 5-HT probe but this is reversed once there is biological and subjective recovery.

Different findings occurred with eating behaviour. Long-term recovered anorexia nervosa subjects did not reduce their meal size in response to D-fenfluramine (Ward *et al.* 1997). Brewerton and Jimerson (1996) also failed to find an mCPP induced reduction in meal size in underweight and short-term weight restored patients. This suggests that one of the serotonergic components of the food intake control system is underactive in anorexia nervosa and because it does not normalize with weight gain, it is possible that this represents a trait phenomenon. However, given that emotional and cognitive factors modulate biological control of single meal size, it is conceivable that serotonergic food intake control is functioning but is overridden by learned patterns of 'normal eating'.

Bulimia nervosa

Studies of anorexia nervosa are confounded by starvation. Similarly, studies of bulimia nervosa can be difficult to interpret because of the variabilty of weight loss, the variety of eating behaviours and the spectrum of comorbidity. The tryptophan long chain neutral amino acids (LNAA) ratio in bulimia nervosa is higher in patients with bulimia nervosa in both the fasting condition and after a meal (Pijl *et al.* 1995). Acute tryptophan depletion led to an increase in caloric intake and irritability in women with bulimia nervosa (Weltzin *et al.* 1995). This finding was not replicated in patients who had recovered from bulimia nervosa for a minimum of 6 months (Cowen *et al.* 1996). When neurotransmitter metabolites were measured in the CSF it was found that patients with bulimia nervosa with highest binge frequency had lower concentrations of 5-HIAA and homovanillic acid (HVA) (Jimerson *et al.* 1992). These findings suggest that a low turnover of 5-HT is linked to an increased severity of bulimia nervosa.

Platelet reuptake of 5-HT was significantly increased in bulimia nervosa, as was 5-HT induced platelet calcium mobilization (Okamoto *et al.* 1995) which could be interpreted to show that there is less active 5-HT available centrally (Goldbloom *et al.* 1990). In response to 5-HT neuroendocrine probes patients with bulimia nervosa have a blunted prolactin response to tryptophan, mCPP (Brewerton *et al.* 1992) and 5-hydroxytryptophan (Goldbloom *et al.* 1996). This suggests that 5-HT receptors are down-regulated. This may occur as a compensatory response to chronic over release of 5-HT. Alternatively, it may result from changes in steroid hormones for example: an increase in cortisol or a decrease in oestradiol which are known to have profound effects in modulating 5-HT function.

In conclusion, a blunted release of prolactin in response to various 5-HT system stimulants has been found in obesity and bulimia nervosa as well as in acute anorexia nervosa (see Table 9.3). It is difficult to interpret these various findings in the light of the appetite control system as the results are neither related to body weight nor to nutrient intake. One possible common feature of the conditions which are associated with blunted prolactin release may be chronic dieting (although the effectiveness of the dieting differs markedly with anorexia nervosa and obesity at opposite ends of the poles). On the other hand, normal dieting is associated with the opposite effect i.e. an enhanced release of prolactin. (However these effects were seen within a month and may not persist over the long term). Cowen and his group

Table 9.3. 5-HT challenge tests in varieties of eating behaviours

Obesity	Bulimia nervosa	Anorexia nervosa (underweight)	Anorexia nervosa (recovered)	Dieters
Blunt (D-fenfluramine)	Blunt (tryptophan, mCPP Brewerton *et al.* 1992; 5-hydroxytryptophan) Normal (buspirone Waller *et al.* 1996)	Blunt (DL-fenfluramine McBride *et al.* 1991; L-tryptophan Goodwin *et al.* 1989; mCPP Brewerton & Jimerson 1996)	Normal (D-fenfluramine O'Dwyer *et al.* 1996; Ward *et al.* 1997)	Enhance (L-tryptophan Goodwin *et al.* 1987; Anderson *et al.*, 1990; mCPP)

(1996) suggest that dieting causes a reduction in plasma tryptophan levels and thus, with less substrate available for 5-HT synthesis, 5-HT transmission decreases and 5-HT receptors are consequently up-regulated. They suggest that the reduced 5-HT increases appetite and so makes it difficult for dieters to maintain a restricted intake. However, given that 5-HT activity can either increase or decrease food intake depending upon the anatomical site and the type of receptor activated, and that central 5-HT activity is profoundly influenced by steroids such as corticosteroids, oestrogen (Fink and Sumner 1996) and progesterone (see below) any model of dysfunction of appetite and weight control in these pathological conditions will have to be very complex. Exercise may also be a confounding factor. For example: the physical hyperactivity in anorexia nervosa will cause lipolysis of inter-muscular lipid with resultant release of free fatty acids. These displace tryptophan from albumin causing an increase in free tryptophan and an increase in 5-HT turnover in the brain (Chaouloff *et al.* 1986; Blomstrand *et al.* 1988; Fischer *et al.* 1991). Yet again, depression, which is common to all the eating disorders, may be an alternative explanation for the serotonergic abnormalities described.

Leptin and human eating behaviour

In the majority of disorders of human weight control leptin appears to be normally controlled in that plasma leptin levels correlate well with body mass index (Considine *et al.* 1996). On the other hand CSF levels of leptin do not correlate as well with body mass index in obesity (Caro *et al.* 1996). This suggests that there may be a defect in the transporter receptor which carries leptin across the blood–brain barrier to sites where it is active in the hypothalamus (Caro *et al.* 1996). Thus, obese subjects may be partially resistant to leptin, the hypothalamus receiving a reduced leptin signal, which underestimates the amount of fat stored, and which, therefore, fails to trigger weight control systems to generate appropriate weight loss.

Patients with anorexia nervosa have low levels of plasma leptin (Hebebrand and Remschmidt 1995; Brown *et al.* 1996; Grinspoon *et al.* 1996), which suggests that the peripheral part of the lipostat system is functioning normally. Indeed, the absence of menstruation in anorexia nervosa also suggests that this part of the leptin/hypothalamic control system is functioning normally.

PUTATIVE NEUROCHEMICAL MODELS OF ANOREXIA NERVOSA

Given the central role of CRH and 5-HT in the appetite and stress response, both may be involved in the pathogenesis of the eating disorders. The serotonin system has come under scrutiny as a possible vulnerability factor for anorexia nervosa from many research workers. Treasure and Campbell (1994) examined how well the serotonin system could explain the clinical and psychopathological features of anorexia nervosa. The report from the Study Group of Anorexia Nervosa which focused on biological causal explanations of anorexia nervosa also concluded that the 5-HT system was a suitable case for further examination (Study Group on Anorexia Nervosa 1995). However, as discussed above, serotonergic abnormalities described in anorexia may arise secondary to starvation, or to oestrogen deficiency, cortisol excess or to co-existent depression. A recent preliminary study has found that patients with anorexia nervosa have an increased frequency of one of the alleles on the promoter region of the 5-HT_{2A} gene (Collier *et al.* 1997). It will be important to see whether these results can be replicated in other clinical groups.

Connan *et al.* (1998) recently formulated an hypothesis which focuses on the hypothalamic–pituitary–adrenal system. The studies on long-term recovered patients with anorexia nervosa suggest that there is underlying, possibly genetic, vulnerability in cortisol control with a raised set-point. Strain resulting from maladaptive adjustment to stress during adolescence in those with this vulnerability gives rise to an unusual hypothalamic neuroendocrine response which is characterized by release of CRH and AVP, increasing the set-point for cortisol. In this context the HPA axis may be rendered less sensitive to cortisol feedback inhibition. Puberty, a period of adaptation, generates a window of vulnerability in the system controlling body mass composition—a window of increased risk of expression of the disorder in genetically and psychologically predisposed individuals. These biological factors at puberty may contribute, not only to the timing of onset of anorexia nervosa, but also to the tendency for the disorder to present in females rather than males. At puberty males do not have to adjust the set-point of their lipostat system. In females, body composition changes markedly at puberty with the percentage of fat tissue increasing to between 17–25% of body weight. The vulnerability of the appetite and weight control system at the time of puberty may be increased by developmental changes such as the rapid rise in oestrogen levels or changes in adrenal activity such as dihydroepiandrosterone secretion. Oestrogen increases 5-HT_{2A} receptor expression and many of the components of the stress response. Thus, there may be a period of instability as the system adapts to these changes. High levels of exercise may override the deficit of 5-HT substrate that usually occurs with weight loss. Thus, persistent CRH release, which is not amenable to feedback, stimulates increased 5-HT activity and generates a catabolic spiral which overrides the normal homeostatic mechanisms. Thus, severe weight loss can occur without the appropriate anabolic response.

PUTATIVE NEUROCHEMICAL MODELS OF BULIMIA NERVOSA

The animal models of developmental stress appear to be especially pertinent to bulimia nervosa. The hyper-reactivity and impulsivity that result when monkeys are deprived of maternal care is analogous to the personality features characteristic of bulimia nervosa, in particular, borderline personality disorder. It follows from this that women who have such developmental adversity are likely to have abnormalities in their HPA axis and 5-HT system. This may predispose them to develop bulimia nervosa especially if the system is perturbed by an episode of dieting which in itself alters both 5-HT function and the HPA axis. Decreased tryptophan reduces 5-HT release which decreases satiety and so large amounts of food are eaten before satiation is achieved. Those with a higher weight set-point such as those with a family history of obesity are more at risk of dieting because of the social stigma arising because of their size. The homeostatic controls of appetite and weight control function normally and resist weight loss and a self perpetuating trap is formed. When the cognitive control of intake is successful nutrient levels fall and fat levels are depleted. This leads to a decrease in leptin and an increase in neuropeptide Y. The former causes a disruption in menstruation and the latter generates anabolic drive with an increase in appetite and reduction of metabolism (Treasure *et al.* 1997).

CLINICAL IMPLICATIONS

- The prolonged exposure to high levels of cortisol in anorexia nervosa may lead to damage of hippocampal neurons.
- It will be important in psychotherapeutic work to encourage effective problem solving and coping strategies so that the stress and strain caused by any difficulty is rapidly resolved. This will prevent the over-sensitive HPA system from perpetuating the catabolic spiral.
- SSRI drugs may be able to ameliorate the hyper-reactive stress response which is a vulnerability factor for the development of bulimia nervosa. However, psychotherapeutic work will be necessary to counteract the effect of maintaining factors such as prolonged emotional stress and strain.
- It may be possible to monitor the effectiveness of psychotherapy by measuring the level of cortisol. We might hypothesize a biphasic response in anorexia nervosa, involving an increase in cortisol release when the issues surrounding the psychosocial conflict are first addressed and a decrease in cortisol levels when these issues are resolved.

RESEARCH IMPLICATIONS

- There may be heterogeneity in bulimia nervosa: those with developmental stress may have persistent abnormalities in the HPA and 5-HT system. Those with a family history of obesity may have reduced central leptin.
- It may be possible to screen for vulnerability to anorexia nervosa by measuring plasma cortisols.
- The genetic vulnerability may involve components of the 5-HT system, and/or HPA axis.

REFERENCES

Adeola O., Ball, R.O., House, J.D. and O'Brien, P.J. (1993). Regional brain neurotransmitter concentrations in stress-susceptible pigs. *J. Anim. Sci.* **71**(4), 968–974.

Agnati, L., Fuxe K., Yu Z.-Y. *et al.* (1985). Morphometrical analysis of the distribution of corticotrophin releasing factor, glucocorticoid receptor and phenylethanolamine-*N*-methyltransferase immunoreactive structures in the paraventricular hypothalamic nucleus of the rat. *Neurosci. Lett.*, **54**, 147–152.

Albinsson, A.R. and Andersson, G.K. (1990). Subclinical characteristics of the wasting pig syndrome. *Res. Vet. Sci.*, **49**(1), 71–76.

Anderson, I.M., Parry-Billings, M., Newsholme, E.A. *et al.* (1990). Dieting reduces plasma tryptophan and alters brain 5-HT function in women. *Psychol. Med.* **20**(4), 785–791.

Aravich, P.F., Doerries, L.E. and Rieg, T.S. (1994). Exercise-induced weight loss in the rat and anorexia nervosa. *Appetite* **23**(2), 196.

Blanchard, D.C. and Blanchard, R.J. (1990). Behavioural correlates of chronic dominance-subordination relationships of male rats in a seminatural situation. *Neurosci. Biobehav. Rev.*, **14**, 455–462.

Blomstrand, E., Cesling, F and Newsholme, E.A. (1988). Changes in plasma concentrations of aromatic and branched chain amino acids during sustained exercise in man and their possible role in fatigue. *Act. Physiol. Scand.*, **133**, 115–121.

Blundell, J.E. and Hill, A.J. (1991). Serotonin, eating disorders and the satiety cascade. In *Serotonin-related Psychiatric Syndromes: Clinical Implications and Therapeutic Links* (eds. C.B. Cassano and H.S. Akiskal), pp. 125–129. Royal Society of Medicine, Services International Congress and Symposium. Series No: 165.

Boscarino, J.A. (1996). Posttraumatic stress disorder, exposure to combat, and lower plasma cortisol among Vietnam veterans: findings and clinical implications. *J. Consulting Clin. Psychol.*, **1**.

Bremner, J.D., Licinio, J., Darnell, A., Krystal, J.H., Owens, M.J., Southwick, S.M., Nemeroff, C.B. and Charney, D.S. (1997). Elevated CSF corticotropin-releasing factor concentrations in posttraumatic stress disorder. *Am. J. Psychiatry*, **154**(5), 624-629.

Brewerton, T.D. (1995). Towards a unified theory of serotonin disturbances in eating and related disorders. *Psychoneuroimmunology*, **20**, 561–590.

Brewerton, T.D. and Jimerson, D.C. (1996). Studies of serotonin function in anorexia nervosa. *Psychiatry-Res.*, **62**, 31–42.

Brewerton, T.D., Lydiard, R.B., *et al.* (1992a) CSF b-endorphin and dynorphin in bulimia nervosa. *Am. J. Psychiatry* **149**(8), 1086–1090.

Brewerton, T.D., Mueller, E.-A., *et al.* (1992b). Neuroendocrine responses to *m*-chlorophenylpiperazine and L-tryptophan in bulimia. *Arch. Gen. Psychiatry* **49**(11), 852–861.

Brown, N., Ward, A., Treasure, J., Campbell, I., Tiller, J., Caro, R. and Surwit, R. (1996). Leptin levels in anorexia nervosa (acute and long term recovered). *Int. J. Obesity*, **20**, (suppl. 4), 37.

Caro J.F., Kolaczynski J.W., Nyce M.R. *et al.* (1996). Decreased cerebrospinal-fluid/serum leptin ratio in obesity: a possible mechanism for leptin resistance [see comments]. Comment in: *Lancet*, **342**, 140–141.

Cavagnini, F., Invitti, C., Passamonti, M. and Polli, E. (1986). Response of ACTH and cortisol to corticotrophin releasing hormone in anorexia nervosa. *N. Engl. J. Med.*, **314**, 184–185.

Chaouloff, F., Kennett, G.A., Serrurier, B. *et al.* (1986). Amino acid analysis demonstrates that increased plasma free tryptophan causes increase of brain tryptophan during exercise in the rat. *J. Neurochem.*, **46**, 1647–1650.

Checkley, S. (1996). The neuroendocrinology of depression and chronic stress. *Br. Med. Bull.*, **52 (3)**, 597–617.

Chehab, F.F. (1996). A broader role for leptin [letter; comment]. *Nat. Med.*, **7**, 723–724.

Chehab, F.F., Mounzih, K., Lu, R. and Lim, M.E. (1997). Early onset of reproductive function in normal female mice treated with leptin. *Science*, **275**, 88–90.

Coiro, V., Volpi, R., Marchesi, C. *et al.* (1992). Abnormal growth-hormone and cortisol, but not thyroid-stimulating hormone, responses to an intravenous glucose-tolerance test in normal-weight, bulimic women. *Psychoneuroendocrinology*, **17**, 639–645.

Collier, D.A., Arrantz, M.J., Li, T., Mupita, D., Brown, N. and Treasure, J. (1997). Association between 5-HT_{2A} promoter polymorphism and anorexia nervosa. *Lancet*, **350**, 412.

Connan, F., Campbell, I.C. and Treasure J.L. (1998). Anorexia nervosa: submission to a stereotype or domination by a cause? (In prep.).

Considine, R., Sinha, M., Heiman, M. *et al.* (1996). Serum immunoreactive-leptin concentrations in normal-weight and obese humans. Comment in *N. Engl. J. Med.*, **334**, 292–2955.

Coppen, A.J., Gupta, R.K., Eccleston, E.G., Wood, K.M. and Wakeling, A. (1976). Plasma tryptophan in anorexia nervosa. *Lancet*, **1**, 961.

Cowen, P.J., Clifford, E.M., Williams, C., Walsh, A.E.S. and Fairburn, C.G. (1995). Why is dieting so difficult? *Nature* **376**, 557.

Cowen, P.J., Clifford, E.M., Williams, C., Walsh, A.E.S. and Fairburn C.G. (1996). Moderate dieting causes 5-HT_{2C} supersensitivity. *Psychol. Med.*, **26**, 1155–1159.

Curzon, G. (1990). Serotonin and appetite. *Ann. N. Y. Acad. Sci.*, **600**, 521–531.

Deakin, J.F.W. and Graeff, F.G. (1991). 5-HT and mechanisms of defence. *J. Psychopharmacol.* **B**: 305–315.

De Bellis, M.D., Chrounos, G.P., Dorn, L.D., Burke, L., Helmers, K., Kling, M.A., Trickett, P.K. and Putnam, F.W. (1994). Hypothalamic pituitary adrenal axis dysregulation in sexually abused girls with history of abuse. *J. Clin. Endocrinol. Metab.*, **78**, 249–255.

Demaret, A. (1993). Evolutionist hypotheses on anorexia nervosa, bulimia and nervous pregnancy. *Neuropsychiatrie de l'Enfrance* **41**, 254–259.

Demitrack, M.A., Lesem M., Brandt, H.A., Pigott, T.A., Jimerson, D.C., Altemus, M. and Gold, P.W. (1989). Neurohypophyseal dysfunction: implications for the pathophysiology of eating disorders. *Psychopharmacol. Bull.*, **25**, 439–443.

Demitrack, M.A., Lesem, M.D. and Listwak, S.J. (1990). CSF oxytocin in anorexia nervosa and bulimia nervosa clinical and pathophysiological considerations. *Am. J. Psych.*, **147**, 882–886.

Dourish, C.T., Kennett, G.A. and Curzon, G. (1987). The 5-HT($_{1A}$) agonists 8-OH-DPAT, buspirone, and ipsapirone attenuate stress-induced anorexia in rats. *J. Psychopharmacol.*, **1**, 23–30.

Epling, W.F. and Pierce, W.D. (1984). Activity-based anorexia in rats as a function of opportunity to run on an activity wheel. *Nutr. Behav.*, **2**, 37–49.

Fairburn, C.G., Welch, S.L., Doll, H.A., Davies, B.A. and O'Connor, M.E. (1997). Risk factors for bulimia nervosa – A community-based case-control study. *Arch. Gen. Psychiatry*, **54**, 509–517.

Fichter, M.M. and Pirke, K.M. (1990). Psychobiology of human starvation in anorexia nervosa. In: H. Remschmidt and M.H. Schmidt (Eds), *Anorexia Nervosa*, pp. 15–29. Hogrefe and Huber, Stuttgart.

Fichter, M.M., Pirke, K.M., Pollinger, J., Wolfram, G. and Brunner, E. (1990). Disturbances in the hypothalamo–pituitary–adrenal and other neuroendocrine axes in bulimia. *Biol. Psychiatry*, **27**, 1021–1037.

Fichter, M.M. and Pirke, K.M. (1995). Starvation models and eating disorders. In: *Handbook of Eating Disorders. Theory, treatment and research*. (eds G. Szmukler, C. Dare and J.L. Treasure) pp. 83–109. Wiley, Chichester.

Fink G. and Sumner, B.E. (1996). Oestrogen and mental state [letter]. *Nature*, **383**, 306.

Fischer, G., Hollman, W. and De Meirleir, K. (1991). Exercise changes in plasma tryptophan fraction and relationship with prolactin. *Intl. J. of Sports Med.*, **12**, 487–489.

Foppiani, L., Sessarego, P., Velenti, S., Falivene, M.R., Cuttica C.M. and Giusti, M. (1996). Lack of effect of desmopressin on ACTH and cortisol responses to ovine corticotrophin releasing hormone in anorexia nervosa. *Eur. J. Clin. Invest., 26*, 879–883.

Fujji, J., Otsu, K., Zorato, F. *et al.* (1991). Identification of a mutation in porcine ryanodine receptor associated with malignant hyperthermia. *Science*, **253**, 448–451.

Glowa J.R. and Gold P.W. (1991). Corticotrophin releasing hormone produces profound anorexigenic effects in the rhesus monkey. *Neuropeptides*, **18**, 55–61.

Gold, P.W., Kaye, W.H., Robertson, G.L. and Ebert, M. (1983). Abnormalities in plasma and cerebrospinal fluid vasopressin in patients with anorexia nervosa. *N. Eng. J. Med.*, **308**, 1117–1123.

Gold, P.W., Gwirstman, H., Avgerinos, P.C. *et al.* (1986). Abnormal pituitary adrenal function in anorexia nervosa: Pathophysiological mechanisms in underwight and weight corrected patients. *N. Eng. J. Med.*, **314**, 1335–1342.

Goldbloom, D.S. and Garfinkel, P.E. (1990). The serotonin hypothesis of bulimia nervosa: theory and evidence. *Can. J. Psychiatry* **35**(9), 741–744.

Goodall, E. and Silverstone, T. (1988). The interaction of metergoline, a 5-HT receptor blocker, and dexfenfluramine in human feeding. *Clin. Neuropharmacol.*, **11**, (S) 135–138.

Goodwin, G.M., Fairburn, C.G. and Cowen, P.J. (1987). The effects of dieting and weight loss on neuroendocrine responses to tryptophan, clonidine, and apomorphine in volunteers: important implications for neuroendocrine investigations in depression. *Arch. Gen. Psychiatry*, **44**(11), 952–957.

Goodwin, G.M., Shapiro, C.M., Bennie, J. *et al.* (1989). The neuroendocrine responses and psychological effects of infusion of L-tryptophan in anorexia nervosa. *Psychol Med.* **19**(4), 857–864.

Grinspoon, S., Gulick, T., Askari, H. *et al.* (1996). Serum leptin levels in women with anorexia nervosa. *J. Clin. Endocrinol. Metab.*, **81**, 3861–3863.

Hebebrand, J. and Remschmidt, H. (1995). Anorexia nervosa viewed as an extreme weight condition: genetic implications. *Hum. Genet.*, **95**, 1–11.

Herbert, J. (1997). Stress, the brain and mental illness. *Brit. Med. J.*, **315**, 530–535.

Higley, J.D., Suomi, S.J. and Linnoila M. (1990). Developmental influences on the serotonergic system and timidity in the non human primate In: E.F. Coccaro and D.L. Murphy. (eds) *Serotonin in Major Psychiatric Disorders*. American Psychiatric Press, Washington DC.

Hill, A.J. and Blundell, J.E. (1990). Sensitivity of the appetite control-system in obese subjects to nutritional and serotoninergic challenges. *Int. J. Of Obesity, 3*, 219–233.

Hill, A.J. and Blundell, J.E. (1991). Food selection, body weight and premenstrual syndrome (PMS). Effect of D-fenfluramine. (Abstr.) *Int. J. Obesity*, **15**, 215.

Hotta, M., Shibasaki, T., Masuda, A., Imaki, T., Demura, H., Ling, N. and Shizume, K. (1986). The response of plasma adrenocorticotrophin and cortisol to corticotrophin releasing hormone (CRH) and immunoreactive CRH in anorexia nervosa patients. *J. Clin. Endocrinol. Metab.*, **69**, 319–324.

Insell, T.R. (1997). Neurobiological basis of social attachment. *Am. J. Psychiatry*, **154**, 726–735

Jimerson, D.C., Lesem, M.D., Kaye, W.H. and Brewerton, T.D. (1992). Low serotonin and dopamine metabolite concentrations in cerebrospinal fluid from bulimic patients with frequent binge episodes. *Arch. Gen. Psychiatry*, **49**, 132–138.

Jimerson, D.C., Wolfe, B.E., Metzger, E.D., Finkelsetin, D.M., Cooper, T.B. and Levine, J.M. (1997). Decreased serotonin function in bulimia nervosa. *Arch. Gen. Psych.*, **54**, 529–534

Kaye, W.H., Berrettini, W.H., Gwirtsman, H.E. and Chretien, M. (1987). Reduced cerebrospinal fluid levels of immunoreactive pro-opiomelanocortin related peptides (including beta-endorphin) in anorexia nervosa. *Life Sci.*, **41**, 2147–2155.

Kaye, W.H., Berretini, W., Gwirstman, H.E. and George, D.T. (1990). Altered cerebrospinal fluid neuropeptide Y and peptide YY immunoreactivity in anorexia and bulimia nervosa. *Arch. Gen. Psychiatry*, **47**, 548–556.

Kaye, W.H., Gwirtsman, H.E., George, D.T. and Ebert, M.H., (1991). Altered serotonin activity in anorexia nervosa after long term weight restroration: Does elevated cerebrospinal fluid 5-hydroxyindoleacetic acid level correlate with rigid and obsessive behaviour? *Arch. Gen. Psychiatry*, **48**, 556–562.

Kaye, W.H., Gwirstman, H.E., Brewerton, T.D., George, D.T. and Wurtman, R.J. (1988). Bingeing behaviour and plasma amino acids: A possible involvement of brain serotonin in bulimia nervosa. *Psychiatry Res.*, **23**, 31–43.

Keck, B.J. and Lakowski, J.M. (1996). Age related assessment of $5HT_{1A}$ receptors following irreversible inactivation by *N*-thoxycarbony 1-2-ethoxy-1,2 dihydorxuquinoloine (EEDQ). *Brain Res.* **728**, 1130–1134.

Kendler, K.S., Walters, E.E., Neale, M.C., Kessler, R.C., Heath, A.C. and Eaves, L.J. (1995). The structure of the genetic and environmental risk factors for six major psychiatric disorders in women. *Arch. Gen. Psych.*, **52**, 374–383.

Kennedy, G.C. (1953). The role of depot fat in the hypothalamic control of food intake in the rat. Proceedings of the Royal Society, London. *Biology*, **140**, 579–592.

Kennedy, S.H., Garfinkel. P.E., Parienti, V., Costa, D. and Brown, G.M. (1989). Changes in melatonin levels but not cortisol levels are associated with depression in patients with eating disorders. *Arch. Gen. Psychiatry*, **46**, 73–78.

Kennet, G.A., Chaouloff, F., Marcou, M. and Curzon, G. (1986). Female rats are more vulnerable than males in an animal model of depression: the possible role of serotonin. *Brain Res.* **382**, 416–421.

Kirschbaum, C., Schommer, N., Federenko, I., Gaab, J., Neumann, O., Oellers, M., Rohleder, N., Untiedt, A., Hanker, J., Pirke, K-M. and Hellhammer, D.H. (1996). Short-term oestradiol treatment enhances pituitary-adrenal axis and sympathetic responses to psychosocial stress in healthy young men. *J. Clin. Endocrinol. Metab.*, **81**, 3639–3643.

Kling, M.A., Demitrack, M.A., Whitfield, H.J., Kalogeras, K.T., Listwak, S.J., Debellis, M.D., Chrousos, G.P., Gold, P.W. and Brandt, H.A. (1993). Effects of the glucocorticoid antagonist Ru-486 on pituitary-adrenal-function in patients with anorexia-nervosa and healthy-volunteers-enhancement of plasma Acth and cortisol secretion in underweight patients. *Neuroendocrinology*, **57**, pp. 1082–1091.

Kyriakis, S.C. and Andersson, G. (1989). Wasting pig syndrome (WPS) in weaners-treatment with amperozide. *J. Vet. Pharmacol. Therap.* **12**, 232–236.

Kyriakis, S.C., Olsson, N.G., Martinsson, K. and Bjork, A.K.K. (1991). Observations on the actions of amperozide: are there social influences on sow litter productivity. *Res. Vet. Sci.* **51**, 169–173.

Ladd, C.O., Owens, M.J. and Nemeroff, C.B. (1996). Persistent changes in corticotrophin releasing factor neuronal systems induced by maternal deprivation. *Endocrinology,* **137**, 1212–1218.

Lakowski, J.M. (1997). Oestrogen and the cellular physiology of serotonin neuronal systems: A key to the aging brain. *Biol. Psych.*, **42**, 7S.

Le Magnen A. (1985). *Hunger*. Cambridge University Press: Cambridge.

Lemieux, A.M. and Coe, C.L. (1995). Abuse related post traumatic stress disorder: evidence for chronic neuroendocrine activation in women. *Pseudosom. Med.* **57**, 105–115.

Leyton, M., Diksic, M., Yound, S.N., Ohazawa, H., Nishizawa, S., Paris, J., Mzengeza, S., and Benkelfat, C. (1997). Brain regional rates of serotonin synthesis in patients with borderline personality disorder: A PET study with alpha-11C methyl l tryptophan. *Biol. Psych.*, **42**, 16S.

Licinio, J., Wong, M. and Gold, P.W. (1996). The hypothalamic-pituitary-adrenal axis in anorexia nervosa. *Psychiat. Res.*, **62**, 75–83.

Liu, J.-P., Clarke, I.J., Funder, J.W. and Engler, D. (1994). Studies of the secretion of corticotrophin-releasing factor and arginine vasopressin into the hypophysial-portal circulation of the conscious sheep II. The central noradrenergic and neuropeptide Y pathways cause immediate and prolonged hypothalamic-pituitary-adrenal activation. Potential involvement in the pseudo-Cushing's syndrome of endogenous depression and anorexia nervosa. *J. Clin. Invest.*, **93**, 1439–1450.

Magarinos, A.M. and McEwan, B.S. (1995). Stress induced atrophy of apical dendrites of hippocampal CA3C neurons: Involvement of glucorticoid secretion and excitatory amino acid receptors. *Neuroscience*, **69**, 89–98.

McBride, P.A., Anderson, G.M., Khait, V.D., Sunday, S.R. and Halmi, K.A. (1991). Serotonergic responsivity in eating disorders. *Psychopharmacol. Bull.*, **27**, 365–372.

McKittrick, C.R., Blanchard, D.C., Blanchard, R.J., Mc Ewan B.S. and Sakai, R.R. (1995). Serotonin receptor binding in a colony model of chronic social stress. *Biol. Psych.*, **37**, 383–393.

Meijer, O.C. and De Kloet, E.R. (1995). A role for the mineralocorticoid receptor in a rapid and transient suppression of $5HT_{1A}$ receptor mRNA by corticosterone. *J. Neuroendocrinol.*, **7**, 653–657.

Morley, J.E., Levine, A.D. and Willenberg, M.L. (1986). Stress-induced feeding disorders. In: *Pharmacology of Eating Disorders: Theoretical and Clinical Developments* (eds M.A. Carruba and J.E. Blundell), pp. 71–99. Raven Press: New York.

Nemeroff, C.B. (1996). The cortocotrophin-releasing factor CRF hypothesis of depression: new findings and new directions. *Mol. Psych.*, **1**, 336–342.

Nemeroff, C.B., Owens, M.J. and Plotsky, P.M. (1997). Animal models of maternal separation: Evidence for persistent neurochemical defects. *Biol. Psych.*, **42**, 200 (S).

Nyberg, L., Lundstrom, K., Edfors.-Lilja, I. and Rundgren, M. (1988). Effects of transport stress on concentrations of cortisol, corticosteroid-binding globulin and glucocorticoid receptors in pigs with different halothane genotypes. *J. Anim. Sci.* **66**(5), 1201–1211.

O'Dwyer, A.M., Lucey, J.V. and Russell, G.F.M. (1996). Serotonin activity in anorexia nervosa after long-term weight restoration response to D-fenfluramine challenge. *Psychol. Med.*, **26**, 353–359.

Okamoto, Y., Okamoto, Y., Kagaya, A. *et al.* (1995). Serotonin-induced platelet calcium mobilization is enhanced in bulimia nervosa but not in anorexia nervosa. *Biol. Psychiatry*, **38**, 274–276.

Pecins-Thompson, M. and Bethea, C.L. (1997). The effect of oestrogen and progesterone on gene expression in serotonin neurons of rhesus macaques. *Biol. Psychiatry*, **42**, 6 (S).

Pecins-Thompson, M., Brown, N.A., Kohama, S.G. and Bethea, C.L. (1996). Ovarian steroid regulation of tryptophan hydroxylase mRNA expression in rhesus macaques. *J. Neurosci.*, **16**, 7021–7029.

Pijl, H., Cohen, A.F., Verkes, R.J., Koppescharr, H.P.F. *et al.* (1995). Plasma amino acid ratios related to brain-serotonin synthesis in response to food intake in bulimia nervosa. *Biol. Psychiatry*, **38**, 659–668.

Pirke, K.M., Kellner, M.B., Fries, E., Kreig, J.C. and Fichter, M.M. (1993). Satiety and cholecystokinin. *Int. J. Eat. Disorders*, **15**, 63–69.

Richard, D., Rivest, R., Naimi, N., Timofeeva, E. and Rivest, S. (1966). Expression of cortocotrophin releasing factor and its receptors in the brain of lean and obese Zucker rats. *Endocrinology*, **137**, 4786–4795.

Rohner-Jeanrenaud, F., Cusin, I., Sainsbury, A., Zakrzewska, K.E. and Jeanrenaud, B. (1996). The loop system between neuropeptide Y and leptin in normal and obese rodents. *Metab. Res.*, **28**, 642–648.

Romero, L. M. and Sapolsky, R. M. (1996). Patterns of ACTH secretagog secretion in response to psychological stimuli. *J. Neuroendocrinol.*, **8**, 243–258.

Routtenberg, A. and Kuznesoff, A.W. (1967). Self-starvation of rats living in activity wheels on a restricted feeding schedule. *J. Comp. Physiol. Psychol.*, **64**, 414–421.

Russell, G. F. M. (1995). Anorexia nervosa through time. In G. Szmukler, C. Dare, and J. L. Treasure (eds), *Handbook of Eating Disorders: Theory, Treatment and Research*. pp. 5–18. Wiley: Chichester.

Sapolsky, R.M. (1992). *Stress, the Aging Brain and the Mechanisms of Neuron Death*. MIT Press, Cambridge MA.

Sapolsky, R.M. (1996). Why stress is bad for your brain. *Science*, **273**, 749–750.

Schmidt, U.H., Tiller, J.M., and Treasure, J. (1993). Setting the scene for eating disorders: childhood care, classification and course of illness. *Psychol. Med.*, **23**, 663–672.

Schmidt, U.H., Tiller, J.M., Andrews, B., Blanchard, M. and Treasure, J.L. (1997). Is there a specific trauma precipitating the onset of anorexia nervosa? *Psychol. Med.*, **27**, 523–530.

Schwartz, M. W., Dallman, M. R. and Woods, S.T. (1995). Hypothalamic response to starvation: implications for the study of wasting disorders. *Amer. J. Physiol.*, **269** (*Regulatory Integrative Comp. Physiol.* **38**): R949–R957.

Shibasaki, T., Yamauchi, N., Kato, Y., Masuda, A., Imaki, T., Hotta, M., Demura, H., Oono, H., Ling, N. and Shizume, K. (1988). Involvement of corticotropin-releasing factor in restraint stress-induced anorexia and reversion of the anorexia by somatostatin in the rat. *Life Sci.* **43**(14), 1103–1110.

Smith, M.A., Davidson, J., Ritchie, J.C., Kudler, H., Lipper, S., Chappell, P. and Nemeroff, C.B. (1989). The corticotropin-releasing hormone test in patients with posttraumatic stress disorder. *Biol. Psychiatry*, **26**(4), 349–355.

Stanley, B. G., Kyrkouli, S. E., Lampert, S. and Leibowitz, S. F. (1986). Neuropeptide Y chronically injected into the hypothalamus; a powerful neurochemical inducer of hyperphagia and obesity. *Peptides*, **7**, 1189–1192.

Stephens, T.W., Basinski, M., Bristow, P.K. *et al.* (1995). The role of neuropepetide Y in the antiobesity action of the obese gene product. *Nature* **377**, 530–532.

Strack, A.M., Sebastian, R. J., Schwartz, M.W. and Dallman, M.F. (1995). Glucocorticoids and insulin: reciprocal signals for energy balance. *Am. J. Physiol.*, **268**, R142–R149.

Study Group on Anorexia Nervosa. (1995). Anorexia nervosa: directions for future research. *Int. J. Eating Dis.*, **17**, 235–241.

Suomi, S.J. (1991). Adolescent depression and depressive symptoms: Insights from longitudinal studies with rhesus monkeys. *J. Youth & Adolescence*, **20**, 273–287.

Suomi, S.J. (1997). Early determinants of behaviour: evidence from primate studies. *Brit. Med. Bull.*, **53**, 170–184.

Tecott, L.H., Sun, L.M., Akana, S.F. *et al.* (1995). Eating disorder and epilepsy in mice lacking 5-HT_{2C} serotonin receptors. *Nature*, **374**, 542–546.

Treasure, J. and Campbell, I. (1994). The case for biology in anorexia nervosa. *Psychol. Med.* **24**, 3–8.

Treasure, J.L. and Holland, A. (1995). Genetic factors in eating disorders. In: *Handbook of eating disorders: Theory, Treatment and Research*. (eds) G. Szmukler, C. Dare and J.L. Treasure. pp. 65–82. John Wiley & Sons: Chichester.

Treasure, J.L. and Owen J.B. (1997). What can animal models tell us about the aetiology of eating disorders? *Int. J. Eat. Dis.*, **21**, 307–311.

Treasure, J.L., Collier, D and Campbell, I.C. (1997). Ill fitting genes: The biology of weight and shape control in relation to body composition and eating disorders. *Lancet* **350**, 412.

Troop, N.A. and Treasure, J.L. (1997a). Psychological factors in the onset of eating disorders: Responses to severe events and difficulties. *Br. J. Med. Psychol.* **70**, 373–385.

Troop, N.A. and Treasure, J.L. (1997b). Setting the scene for eating disorders, II. Childhood helplessness and mastery. *Psychol. Med.*, **27**, 531–538.

Ur, E., Dinan, T.G., O'Keane, V., Clare, A.W., McLoughlin, L., Rees, L.H., Turner, T.H., Grossman, A. and Besser, G.M. (1992). Effect of metyrapone on the pituitary–adrenal axis in depression: relation to dexamethasone suppressor status. *Neuroendocrinology* **56**(4), 533–538.

Vamvakopoulos, N.C. and Chrousos, G.P. (1993). Evidence of direct oestrogenic regulation of human corticotrophin-releasing hormone gene expression. *J. Clin. Invest.*, **92**, 1896–1902.

Van Huijsduijnen, O.B., Rohner-Jeanrenaud, F. and Jeanrenaud, B. (1993). Hypothalamic neuropeptide Y messenger ribonucleic acid levels in pre-obese and genetically obese (*fa/fa*) rats: potential regulation thereof by corticotrophin releasing factor. *J. Neuroendocrinol.*, **5**, 381–386.

Waller, D.A., Sheinberg, A.L., Gullion, C. *et al.* (1996). Impulsivity and neuroendocrine response to buspirone in bulimia nervosa. *Biol. Psychiatry* **39**(5), 371–374.

Walsh, B.T., Roose, S.P., Katz, J.L. and Dyrenfurth, I. (1987). Hypothalamic–pituitary–adrenal–cortical activity in anorexia and bulimia. *Psychoneuroenocrinology*, **12**, 131–140.

Ward, A. *et al.*, in preparation.

Weltzin, T.E., Fernstrom, M.H., Fernstrom, J.D., Neuberger, S.K. and Kaye, W.H. (1995). Acute tryptophan depletion and increased food intake and irritability in bulimia nervosa. *Am. J. Psychiatry*, **152**, 1668–1671.

Yehuda, R., Teicher, M.H., Trestman, R.L., Levengood, R.A. and Siever, L.J. (1996). Cortisol regulation in posttraumatic stress disorder and major depression: a chronobiological analysis. *Biol. Psychiatry* **40**(2), 79–88.

Young, E.A., Haskett, R.F., Grunhaus, L., *et al.* (1994). Increased evening activation of the hypothalamic-pituitary-adrenal axis in depressed patients. *Arch. Gen. Psychiatry*, **51**(9), 701–707.

Zhang, Y., Procena, R., Maffei, M., Barone, M., Leopold, L. and Freidman, J.M. (1994). Positional cloning of the mouse obese gene and its human homologue. *Nature*, **372**, 425–432

10 The Neurobiology of Eating Behaviour and Weight Control

P. J. V. BEUMONT
Department of Psychological Medicine, University of Sydney, Sydney, Australia

ENERGY INTAKE, ENERGY EXPENDITURE AND BODY MASS

It is generally accepted that body mass is determined by the relationship between energy intake and energy expenditure:

$$\text{Energy in} - \text{Energy out} = \text{Energy stored.}$$

This simplistic equation is deceptive in that it ignores the many factors that affect eating, metabolism, and energy expenditure, ranging from the availability and palatability of food, to emotional and social influences, neurological and hormonal effects, and the presence of disease or illness. Moreover, it seems that total energy intake is only one aspect of the effect of food ingestion: the consumption of high-fat and concentrated sweet foods, independent of total caloric intake, induces obesity. Weight gain is more rapid on a high fat diet than on an equivalent high carbohydrate diet (Danforth 1985).

Energy expenditure, on the other hand, is also complex, involving various components. The *resting metabolic rate* is the amount of energy expended by a fasting person at rest in a comfortable situation. It represents the caloric cost of maintaining the body's functions and holding a normal, constant temperature, and it can be predicted for members of each sex from their weight and height. It accounts for about 60–70% of daily energy expenditure. *Thermogenesis* refers to the increase in energy expenditure that results from the effect of food eaten (diet-induced thermogenesis, normally about 10% of total energy expenditure) as well as other influences such as cold or heat exposure, or the effects of drugs and hormones. *Physical activity* is the most variable component of energy expenditure. Even in sedentary people, it accounts for 20–30% of total expenditure, and more in those who are very active. The energy cost of weight-bearing activities is proportional to body weight, and hence is higher in bigger persons.

For some decades, energy expenditure has been measured under sedentary conditions in a respiratory chamber by indirect calorimetry. This process provides data about energy output and fuel mix (substrate utilization) derived from oxygen consumption, carbon dioxide production, and nitrogen excretion. Its disadvantage is that its extension to unconfined subjects (those able to undertake their usual level of activity) is cumbersome and inaccurate. More recently, measuring energy expenditure in *unconfined* subjects has become relatively easy using the doubly

Neurobiology in the Treatment of Eating Disorders.
Edited by H.W. Hoek, J.L. Treasure and M.A. Katzman.

labelled water technique. The advent of this technique has resulted in a number of studies expanding our knowledge of weight control. The lowest 24-hour energy expenditure, found in very lean women, is in the vicinity of 1300 kilocalories a day, and consequently energy intakes below that range inevitably cause further weight loss. Moreover, under normal conditions, carbohydrate, protein and alcohol are not converted to fat because increasing the intake of non-fat nutrients simply stimulates oxidation rates proportionally, and hence cannot lead to obesity (Flatt 1993). (However, our own work has shown that this finding does not hold true for very low weight anorexia nervosa patients in whom we have observed evidence of lipogenesis and a respiratory quotient over one.) Under normal circumstances, an increase in fat stores indicates either a high fat diet or an impaired fat oxidation. Hence, a fat-balance equation is at least equally important to an energy-balance equation in the maintenance of a normal weight. The relevance of issues such as these to anorexia and bulimia nervosa are currently being studied by a number of groups, including our own in Sydney, and Pirke and his associates in Trier.

The basic regulation of energy intake and expenditure are described in standard textbooks of physiology (Guyton 1976). Mechanisms such as the action of glucoreceptors, the secretion of insulin, cholecystokinin, the gastrointestinal hormones, and many other factors, are involved. The interested reader is referred to a recent reviews by Liebowitz (1995). This chapter is not concerned with these issues, but rather with the neurobiology of eating behaviour *per se*, which is itself a key element influencing the control of energy balance. There is an immense literature pertaining to the subject, and my review must necessarily be brief and selective, referring to some interesting topics but neglecting many others. The greatest amount of attention in this area has been devoted to the hypothalamus.

THE HYPOTHALAMIC CONTROL HYPOTHESIS

A crucial role has been suggested for the hypothalamus in integrating neural and hormonal messages, controlling hunger and satiety, and influencing the deposition and utilization of energy stores. A clinical clue to this relationship is provided by Frohlich's syndrome: obesity and genital underdevelopment, arising from pathology in the region of the sella turcica, it was originally ascribed to pituitary hyposecretion. It is now recognized that the syndrome is caused by hypothalamic damage, because it can be induced in experimental animals by bilateral lesions in the medial hypothalamus without concomitant pituitary damage. The obesity results from hyperphagia—voracious overeating—and not from any associated metabolic disturbance (Anand and Brobeck 1961).

The hypothalamic hypothesis of weight control is based on experimental studies of rats undertaken about 50 years ago (Anand and Brobeck 1950; Stellar 1954) that showed that bilateral destruction of the ventromedial hypothalamus (VMH) led to hyperphagia and that lesions to the dorsolateral hypothalamus (DLH) produced aphagia and eventual death by starvation. Two centres concerned with feeding were proposed: a facilitatory centre in the lateral hypothalamus; and a satiety or inhibitory centre sited medially. The lateral centre was thought to be dominant, as its bilateral destruction leads to death by starvation irrespective of whether the medial centre is intact or not.

Lesions to the medial centre produce the effect of hyperphagia only in the presence of an intact lateral system. In the first few days after the trauma, VMH lesioned rats feed excessively, doubling their initial weight (the dynamic phase). Thereafter, food intake decreases to a level sufficient to maintain their new increased body weight (the static phase). If animals in this static phase are starved to lose this newly-acquired weight, and then again provided access to food, they feed excessively and return to the higher weight. On the other hand, if forced to overeat so as to gain further weight above their new plateau, they will reduce their intake when allowed to do so, and return to the level which had been set by the hypothalamic lesion.

On the other hand, rats with DLH lesions initially lose a large proportion of their body weight, even if fed by an intra-gastric tube. This response is reduced if the animal is subjected to starvation prior to the lesion. A few weeks after the lesion, the animal accepts only highly palatable food, but eventually progresses to a laboratory diet, so as to maintain its new decreased body weight. Unlike normal animals, its feeding does not increase in response to procedures that lower blood glucose or affect cellular glucose regulation. Food intake remains closely related to palatability, so that feeding appears to be influenced by hedonic factors, i.e. the appetite aroused by exposure to tasty foods. Two sorts of hypotheses have been proposed to account for these findings: (i) motor theories that suggest the lesions disrupt feeding by damage to specific motor systems involved in its co-ordination; and (ii) motivational theories that explain the behaviour as being caused by a loss of appetite or anorexia. In both, the gradual return of feeding that occurs eventually is seen to reflect a gradual recovery of normal functioning.

Advancing from this base, Powley and Keesey (1970) and Keesey *et al.* (1976) proposed a theory involving an alteration of the set-point for weight regulation. They suggested that, rather than abolish appetite or disrupt the motor control of feeding, lateral hypothalamic lesions lower set-point. Animals stop feeding and lose weight until they reach the level of the lowered set-point and it is this lag, rather than the gradual recovery of normal functions, that accounts for the animals' subsequent progress. Two experiments support this view. First, rats that have recovered normal feeding behaviour, after a phase of aphagia induced by lateral hypothalamic lesions, persist in maintaining weight levels substantially below those of control subjects, despite a relatively normal food intake. Second, reduction of the animals' weight by partial starvation prior to lesioning greatly reduces the periods of aphagia and anorexia that follow such operations. Nevertheless, these animals stabilize their weights at a level similar to those that have not been subjected to prior deprivation.

Keesey *et al.* (1978) went on to monitor food intake and utilization in animals with lateral hypothalamic lesions. Although control animals cannot be maintained at a reduced body weight without a substantial reduction in energy intake, those that have been lesioned continue to do. When lesioned rats and controls are subjected to progressive restrictions in food intake, both show equivalent falls in body weight. When given access to the same amounts of food that had been allowed before restriction, indexed to their reduced metabolic mass, both sets of animals regain weight rapidly and at an equivalent rate. Thus the lesioned animals, like the controls, appear to utilize food in a normal manner and to adapt to weight loss by increasing the efficiency of food utilization. However, the lesioned animals stabilize at a weight considerably below that of the control subjects, indicating that the adjustment, in their case, occurs around a set-point for body weight that has been reduced as a result of the trauma.

Electrical stimulation to the hypothalamus results in effects opposite to those of lesions. Stimulation by electrical probes of the DLH increases feeding and induces obesity, whereas stimulation to the VMH usually inhibits feeding. Similarly, micro-injections of noradrenaline and GABA (γ-aminobutyric acid) into the VMH elicits feeding, and injections of β-adrenergic and dopaminergic agonists and antagonists into the DLH produce the opposite effect on food intake (Liebowitz 1980).

Many hypothalamic neurons are influenced by local administration of glucose and insulin (Oomura 1976). Cells in the VMH increase their activity with glucose, and this increase is augmented when insulin is added, reflecting the situation that occurs in satiety when both are high. On the other hand, cells in the DLH decrease activity in response to glucose alone, and increase activity in response to insulin, perhaps reflecting the increased food intake which follows systemic injections of insulin. These findings accord with the glucostatic hypothesis of hunger.

Thus, a large number of consistent studies support the hypothalamic theory of food intake and weight control. Nevertheless, important questions have been raised in recent years that necessitate a change in its details and even question its ultimate validity. Re-interpretations of the results of various lesioning and stimulating experiments suggest that the concept of hypothalamic feeding centres is unwarranted, at least in as far as that term implies a nucleus of neurons concerned with a specific function. Thus, the effects of bilateral lesions of the VMH are not due to the destruction of the ventro-medial nuclei, but to areas near them which are connected to the amygdala and frontal cortex, and through which course sympathetic and parasympathetic fibres of the autonomic nervous system (Bray *et al.* 1981). Other lesions in the VMH induce a syndrome that was termed 'hypothalamic rage' (an inaccurate and unfortunate term) by earlier investigations. The state induced is that of general hyperactivity in response to all modalities of sensory input, presumably brought about by means of disinhibition of the affective reactors to hedonic stimuli. Hedonic disinhibition may underlie the changes in feeding, and this hypothesis (Grossman 1966) is supported by several different studies. VMH-lesioned rats become obese only when offered a palatable diet. If given completely unpalatable food, such as that to which quinine has been added, which is accepted by normal rats, they refuse it and starve. Drinking of ordinary water is not altered in the VMH lesioned animal, but if its taste is made more pleasant by adding sweetener, the rat drinks excessively. Evidence of this sort indicates that the regulation of feeding and weight is far more complex than would be expected from the original hypothalamic control hypothesis.

Lesion to the VMH elicits a hyperinsulinaemia that is associated with increased lipogenesis and fat deposition. The building up of energy stores is accompanied by a decrease in lipolysis so that Friedman and Stricker (1976) suggest that the animal is not so much gaining weight because it is overeating, but rather overeating because it is gaining weight. Perhaps the VMH function is lipo-regulatory, and not directly concerned with satiety or feeding (Le Magnen in Grossman 1995). The presence of some insulin is necessary for the VMH syndrome to occur, but hyperinsulinaemia, although usually a contributing factor, is not essential for the development of hyperphagia and obesity, suggesting that lesioned animals have disturbances of several different processes, renal, endocrine and metabolic, that regulate feeding and weight.

Only those lesions to the DLH that are relatively large and extend near to the major fibre tracts in the internal capsule and the lateral lemniscus induce aphagia and adipsia. The critical area has few neuronal bodies, but includes the pallido-fugal tract and much of the medial forebrain bundle. Lesions to the globus pallidus produce a similar picture to the DLH syndrome (Morgane 1961), which suggests that the latter is actually the result of interruption of the pallido-fugal fibre system. Further, the extreme lateral lesions of the lateral hypothalamus, which are most effective in producing aphagia, interrupt dopaminergic fibres coursing through the hypothalamus and lower dopamine concentrations in the forebrain (Stricker and Andersen 1980). Injecting the toxin 6-hydroxydopamine destroys the distant cell bodies of these fibres without causing local damage, and produces the same behavioural effects. Neurotoxin induces destruction of dopaminergic neurones in the substantia nigra region, produces acute coma, and major sensory, motor, and arousal defects, during which phase the animal neither feeds nor drinks (Ungerstedt 1971). As the animal's responsiveness and general arousal gradually return, feeding and drinking resume. However, specific deficits in the regulation of feeding, similar to those seen in the DLH syndrome, persist indefinitely. These various findings suggest that the feeding disturbance in DLH animals may be caused by as yet poorly understood sensori-motor and arousal deficits. It seems that damage to ascending dopaminergic tracts passing through the region is more important in the causation of the so-called lateral hypothalamic syndrome than is the destruction of local neurons.

Grossman (1990) surveys other studies that have challenged the hypothalamic control theory, and attempts to provide alternative interpretations to allow for the preservation of a basic tenet, namely DLH lesions affect ingestion and weight regulation because they disrupt the dopaminergic nigro-striatal fibre system. Although the evidence supporting the hypothesis that the VMH and DLH have specific and primary effects on food intake and body weight has never been completely refuted, he concedes that more recent research has established that the effects of brain lesions are greatly different to that originally envisaged in the hypothalamic theory.

NEUROTRANSMITTERS

Although the effect of hypothalamic lesions has not been as heuristic as was hoped previously, it has nevertheless drawn attention to the role of neurotransmitters in the regulation of feeding. From studies using a cannula to deliver drugs to discrete areas of brain in freely moving rats, Liebowitz (1983) proposed four distinct monoaminergic systems within the hypothalamus that modulate feeding and weight. First, an α-noradrenergic system within the medial hypothalamus stimulates feeding and is involved in the appetite-stimulating effects of drugs such as clonidine and the tricyclic antidepressants. Second, a serotonergic system, also within the medial hypothalamus, inhibits feeding and is associated with the appetite suppressant effect of fenfluramine which releases serotonin. Third, a β-adrenergic system in the lateral hypothalamus inhibits feeding and participates in the appetite suppressant effects of amphetamines. Fourth, and finally, a dopaminergic system in the lateral hypothalamus also inhibits feeding. The appetite stimulating action of phenothiazine antipsychotic drugs is caused by the blockade of dopamine receptors in this last system (Liebowitz 1983).

Liebowitz believes that the four hypothalamic monoaminergic systems she described also exist in humans, and that their disturbance is a factor in the pathogenesis of anorexia nervosa aand bulimia. Her own research has focused on the noradrenergic system in the medial hypothalamus. She proposes that anorexia nervosa is produced in part by a decrease in hypothalamic noradrenergic activity, a theory supported by the finding of a decreased level of the metabolite 3-methoxy-4-hydroxyphenylethylene glycol (MHPG) in the urine of anorexia nervosa patients (Halmi *et al.* 1978; Abraham *et al.* 1981). Food deprivation in turn has dramatic effects on noradrenergic activity within the medial hypothalamus which may account for the oscillating eating patterns associated with the reactive hyperphagia of bulimia patients.

Adopting a rather broader perspective, Morley (1980) proposed three neuroregulatory systems concerned with feeding: a *central feeding* system where the decision is made to forage for food; a *peripheral satiety* system involved in the termination of a phase of feeding, controlled by hormonal and neural signals generated from the gastrointestinal tract; and a *food choice* system, exposed for instance by the craving for salt of patients with Addison's disease. He postulated a cascade of neurotransmitter actions similar to other physiological cascades such as that involved in blood clotting, to integrate the multiple inputs and reach the result of whether or not to feed at any particular time. Endogenous opiates, cholecystokinin, thyroid releasing hormone, GABA and the diazepam receptor have roles in this cascade, and other substances such as members of the pancreatic polypeptide family (neuropeptide P), growth hormone releasing hormone, galanin, and corticotrophin releasing hormone are also involved (Morley and Gunion 1988). To review the evidence relating to each of these factors is beyond the scope of this chapter, so instead one example will be discussed as an illustration of the kind of actions envisaged.

CHOLECYSTOKININ AND GASTRIC EMPTYING (Robinson 1990)

The term cholecystokinin (CCK) refers to a group of related peptides produced by the proximal small intestine that inhibit feeding in rats and eating in man. Receptors for CCK occur in several body tissues, but only those in the brain, vagus nerve and pyloric sphincter are thought to mediate the satiety effect. Because relatively high doses are needed, it is unlikely that CCK plays a major physiological role in nutrient ingestion in normal subjects. Nevertheless, it may contribute to illnesses such as anorexia and bulimia nervosa.

A central nervous system (CNS) site of action for CCK is unlikely because most receptors within the brain, except those in the area postrema, the interpeduncular nuclei, and nucleus solitarius, are poorly accessed by it, and they have a lower relative affinity for the sulphated form of the hormone. Therefore, CCK's satiety action is probably exerted peripherally, involving receptors on the pylorus and vagal nerve. A relativity between gastric emptying and satiety is accepted. CCK inhibits gastric emptying in the rhesus monkey, and in man, acting via receptors in the circular muscle of the pyloric sphincter, and hence exerts a satiety effect. It also acts via receptors on the vagus nerve. Two mechanisms have been proposed for this effect. First, because CCK inhibits gastric emptying, food accumulates in the stomach, causing gastric distension. The sensory vagus conveys this information to the brain, evoking the termination of feeding. Second, CCK may itself stimulate terminals of the vagus.

Gastric emptying is a factor in the control of nutrient ingestion, and CCK influences this process, probably mainly by its effect on receptors in the pylorus. Delayed gastric emptying occurs in anorexia nervosa, and CCK would seem to be involved in this action. A role in bulimia nervosa is less likely. CCK does not reduce bulimia in bulimia nervosa patients, suggesting that CCK inhibition is not strong enough to overcome the bulimic binge, or that CCK sensitivity is abnormally low in these subjects.

RELEVANCE TO ANOREXIA NERVOSA

The original hypothalamic hypothesis provided two potential models for anorexia nervosa. The illness might result either from bilateral destruction of the lateral hypothalamus, or from chronic overstimulation of the medial hypothalamus.

Because lateral lesions inevitably lead to death by starvation, the second hypothesis was favoured at first. Later, when it was understood that recovery could take place from lateral lesions, it was the lateral hypothalamic syndrome that was usually proposed as the model of anorexia nervosa.

Stricker and Anderson (1980) discussed the comparison of anorexia nervosa with the lateral hypothalamic syndrome. They noted that the behavioural effects of the hypothalamic lesion are rather more diffuse than the original reports suggested. Although aphagia is a prominent feature, other alterations of behaviour are also present, such as loss of thirst, disinclination to seek warmth and inability to learn simple tasks. There appears to be a broad impairment of all voluntary activity, so that the animal is lethargic unless specifically provoked. In addition, neurological deficits such as akinesia, catalepsy, and sensory neglect are prominent. Rather than resemble anorexia nervosa with its hyperactivity, the behaviour of lesioned animals is reminiscent of patients with advanced Parkinson's disease, a known dopamine-deficiency condition.

The performance of lesioned animals can be improved by administering a number of pharmacological substances, all of which have a net dopaminergic effect. DOPA (dihydroxyphenylalanine), the precursor of dopamine, apomorphine and amphetamine, which are dopamine agonists, and drugs that augment the post-synaptic effects of dopamine such as theophylline and caffeine, have all been shown to be effective. The involvement of dopaminergic mechanisms in feeding, together with the observation that dopamine is important in controlling the secretion of luteinizing hormone releasing hormone (LHRH) and hence menstrual function, led to the suggestion that anorexia nervosa is a state of dopaminergic excess (Barry and Klawans 1976)! On the other hand, evidence of an adrenergic system concerned with satiety prompted the suggestion that increased activity of the satiety mechanism was important in the pathogenesis of the illness (Redmond *et al.* 1997).

IMPLICATIONS FOR CLINICIANS

Neurotransmitters and neuromodulators, as must be expected, are involved in the regulation of feeding and eating, and several relevant systems can be discerned. Similarly, several peripheral mechanisms, including the action of various neuropeptides, are also important, particularly in relation to satiety. There is much overlap with the mechanisms of glucose regulation, which have not been discussed in this chapter. Although it is possible that disturbances to these various systems may exert a causative influence in respect to obesity and to the dieting disorders, anorexia and bulimia nervosa, there is little direct evidence in favour of this view. A redirection of attention may be necessary if we are to understand the aetiology of eating disorders, and some tantalizing clues are given by studies of animal energy intake and energy expenditure behaviour.

SPONTANEOUS HYPOPHAGIA IN ANIMALS

Models are not accurate replicas, nor are they subject to tests of whether they are right or wrong. Rather they are analogies which reflect some aspects of the thing being modelled. A model aeroplane is not a real aeroplane, but it is similar to one in certain aspects e.g. aerodynamics, and different in others e.g. its means of propulsion. It is most unlikely that there will ever be a completely accurate animal model of human obesity—and if so, it ceases to be a model, and becomes an identical condition—and even more improbable that there will be a completely true model of anorexia or bulimia nervosa, those most human of illnesses. However, some animal models of human obesity and of dieting disorders are of interest because they contrast with these conditions, illustrating differences that exist between mechanisms that only appear to be similar. Other models accurately reflect some of the processes occurring in these human illnesses. In either instance, they add to our understanding. One model whose potential in the understanding of dieting disorders has not been adequately explored is that provided by the spontaneous hypophagias of some animal species (Beumont 1984).

People restrain their eating voluntarily for health or cosmetic reasons; they fast in response to religious dictates or as a means of protest; or they progress from the former to the latter under the influences of illnesses such as anorexia nervosa. Other animals also have phases during which their feeding decreases and they lose weight. These may be distinguished from the food refusal that arises from disease because they occur at specific periods in the life cycles. During the course of spontaneous hypophagias, there appears to be a true loss of appetite, hence the term 'animal anorexia' is more appropriate to them than is anorexia nervosa to the human illness, in which appetite is not so much lost as deliberately overridden.

Hibernation is a physiological state in which some animals spend the winter season, when food resources are scant, in a state of torpor, enabling them to conserve energy and survive. Hibernation of the ground squirrel, *Citellus lateralis*, was documented carefully in a laboratory setting (Mrosovsky and Sherry 1980). These animals become torpid and markedly decrease their food ingestion at the appropriate season, even if supplies of food are made available to them. If repeatedly aroused and forced to rewarm themselves so that they expend more energy, feeding increases correspondingly. However, irrespective of whether their energy output is high or low, they continue to lose weight at a constant rate throughout the winter. If they are deprived of food under these circumstances, weight loss accelerates. When food is again made available, they feed to regain weight to a level appropriate to their current stage in the hibernation cycle, not to predeprivation levels.

The incubation fast of the Emperor penguin, *Aptenodyte fosteri*, has some similarities to hibernation in the squirrel. The male bird has a long period of total fasting in very adverse climatic conditions. During this period it leaves the sea and travels across the Antarctic ice to its breeding site; selects its territory and couples with its mate; awaits the laying of the eggs; and then incubates the eggs while the female bird returns to the sea. By the time the female returns, the male has fasted for about 120 days, exposed to high winds and an average temperature of minus 48°C, and has lost approximately 40% of total body weight. However, if the female's return is delayed so that the male bird's weight falls below a critical level, he will abandon the egg and himself return to the sea. Presumably the parent birds wait faithfully until their lipid stores are depleted, but once catabolism of protein becomes necessary to sustain life they migrate back to the feeding grounds. Mrosovsky and Powley (1977) suggest that animal hypophagias such as these are caused by a programmed decline in the set point for body weight, or perhaps better body fat. They use the term set point to indicate the level at which a stable weight, or a programmed alteration of weight, is defended, and stress that this does not necessarily imply that a feedback system is involved. In fact, they state specifically that occurrences of this kind are probably controlled by different mechanisms in differing species.

At first sight, spontaneous animal hypophagias appear to be poor models of anorexia nervosa, because of the ways in which they differ from the human illness (Mrosovsky 1983). First, they provide a biological advantage to both individual and species (surviving an inhospitable season, helping to ensure reproduction) whereas anorexia nervosa has a significant mortality, and its persistent morbidity includes anovular infertility. Second, the animal conditions are assured to be associated with true anorexia or loss of appetite, whereas the anorexia nervosa patient often admits she is ravenously hungry, but will not allow herself to eat. Third, the weight loss in animals is regulated and part of a physiological stage, similar to the hormonal changes at puberty. The alteration in weight is gradual and each new value is defended as long as it is appropriate to the stage of the process. In anorexia nervosa, weight loss is usually insidious at first, but becomes precipitous later: to be ever thinner, to weigh less tomorrow than today. Fourth, activity is reduced during hibernation and incubation, but hyperactivity is a characteristic of many patients with anorexia nervosa. Fifth, when fat stores have been depleted the animal hypophagia ceases, hence there is little catabolism of protein tissue. In anorexia nervosa, it is principally energy reserves in fat tissue that are affected initially, but there is also a breakdown of protein leading to nitrogen depletion.

Because of these differences, Mrosovsky (1983) concluded that animal anorexias are of minimal value in understanding anorexia nervosa. However, this view is too simplistic; it ignores the many similarities between spontaneous animal hypophagias and the insidious development of anorexic behaviour, and it misrepresents the meaning of a model. Anorexia nervosa is a serious condition with a well-defined symptomatology and a predictable course, but it is also an extreme manifestation of the voluntary weight control behaviours that occur in most girls and young women following puberty, at least in Western societies. Almost all women diet, or have dieted, during the primary age of risk of 12–40 years. True, most do not go on to develop anorexia nervosa. It would be appropriate to see the anorexia nervosa patient as someone who is particularly vulnerable, and hence unable to cope with the food restriction that is part of the adolescent process for so many women in our culture. There are mechanisms operating in the spontaneous hypophagias that prevent the animal from going on to develop serious morbidity or even die from their food restraint. Similar mechanisms presumably operate in those many women who diet but do not go on to a dieting disorder. Their systematic study might clarify what goes wrong in those unfortunates who do not escape (Beumont 1984).

OVERACTIVITY AND FOOD DEPRIVATION

Whereas starvation is usually associated with increasing lethargy and inertia, the decreased food intake of anorexia nervosa patients is often coupled with extreme overactivity and excessive exercising that further deplete energy stores (Beumont *et al.* 1994). The picture is strongly reminiscent of the self-starvation observed in rats on a restricted diet with ready access to activity wheels (Routtenberg and Kuznezof 1967). Whereas, rats kept on a restricted diet, or alternatively exposed to activity wheels, quickly adapt and remain healthy, those exposed to both conditions simultaneously progress to a state of frenetic activity, with a paradoxical decrease in feeding, leading to inanition and eventual death. On the basis of research into this aspect of animal behaviour, and its reflection of the psychopathology of anorexia nervosa, Epling and Pierce (1996) have constructed a theory in which activity anorexia is a predominant factor in the pathogenesis of the human illness. Perhaps because of this putative relationship, activity anorexia in rats remains a topic of continuing research attention. The role of neurotransmitters and hormones in its genesis has been investigated (Pirke *et al.* 1993), and detailed analyses of the various factors contributing to its occurrence have been performed (Boakes and Dwyer 1997; Dwyer and Boakes 1997). The conclusion drawn from the latter studies is that the paradoxical behaviour results from an interaction between a number of dissociable processes, and has more to do with adaptation to new feeding schedules than to a basic mechanism applicable over a number of different species. Again, relevance of the model to anorexia nervosa in humans seems less assured than was thought at first. However, as was the case in respect to spontaneous animal hypophagias, this conclusion is biased by the poor understanding of the actual behaviour disturbance in anorexia patients that non-clinical scientists have. Thus, one of the reasons why Dwyer and Boakes (1997) discount the relevance of activity anorexia to anorexia nervosa is that they believe that anorexic patients increase their activity as they regain weight. In fact, increasing weight loss is more frequently associated with increasing levels of frenetic overactivity (Beumont *et al.* 1994). Again, this topic is one in which further exploration is likely to add to our understanding of the control of eating and of weight.

LEPTIN AND THE *ob* GENE

Because the amount of body fat appears to reflect the long-term difference between energy intake and energy expenditure, and because body weight and the size of adipose stores tend to remain constant, a lipostatic hypothesis for the negative feedback control of adiposity was proposed in the 1950s (Kennedy 1953). According to this theory, humoral signals generated in proportion to the organism's fat bulk exert an inhibitory influence on the areas of brain that control feeding. An increase in energy intake sufficient to effect an increase in the amount of body fat leads to a negative feedback on feeding, whereas food restriction suppresses the normal inhibitory feedback and results in increased food ingestion until the level of adiposity is restored to its previous value. Early evidence to support this theory was provided by experiments that used a technique known as parabiosis (Hervey 1952): when lean rats are joined to rats rendered obese by means of a VMH lesion, the lean rats undereat dramatically and eventually starve to death. Hence, the VMH lesioned animal appears to be generating a circulating message that crosses over to its lean partner and greatly inhibits its feeding. The VMH lesioned animal itself, however, appears to be unresponsive to this signal.

Two genetic models of obesity provide further clarification about the process: *ob/ob* and *db/db* mice. Both models manifest increased feeding and marked obesity as a result of single gene mutations. When a genetically normal mouse is joined to a *db/db* affected animal, the normal partner drastically reduces feeding and loses weight, again suggesting that it is reacting to a strong inhibiting signal from its affected partner. In contrast, parabiosis between a normal mouse and an *ob/ob* affected animal has opposite effects: the normal partner appears unaffected, but the *ob/ob* animal undereats and loses weight. These observations indicate that *db/db* mice produce large amounts of a substance related to obesity that has a negative feedback on feeding behaviour, but are themselves unable to respond to it, whereas *ob/ob* mice appear to produce inadequate quantities of this inhibitory substance, and hence are obese, but are able to respond adequately when exposed to it (Coleman 1973).

The lipostatic hypothesis has been confirmed dramatically by discoveries over the last 2 years (Schwartz and Seeley 1997): Zhang and his colleagues demonstrated that the *ob* gene is expressed only in adipose tissue, and various other workers, including Considine *et al.* Maffei *et al.* and Schwartz *et al.* (see Schwartz and Seeley 1997) showed that its encoded hormone product, leptin, is secreted into the circulation in proportion to the body's adiposity. Circulating leptin enters the central nervous system, prompting a search for neural targets for its action. There is evidence that the neuropeptide Y pathway is involved, but other effector pathways are also probably important. Leptin interacts with insulin as well: insulin has been known to contribute to the long-term regulation of adiposity for some decades (Woods *et al.* 1979). It too is produced from the islets of Langerhans in proportion to the extent of adiposity, enters into the CNS and, like leptin, appears to inhibit feeding by inhibiting the release or expression of hypothalamic neuropeptide Y. Thus, both insulin deficiency and leptin deficiency elicit increased feeding and subsequent obesity.

Leptin is known also to interact with CRH (corticotrophin releasing hormone), which itself inhibits feeding, increases energy expenditure, and depletes energy reserves. Low circulating levels of leptin inhibit hypothalamic CRH neurons, whereas high leptin levels activate catabolism by enhancing CRH pathways (Seeley *et al.* 1996).

The advent of leptin and the increasing understanding of its actions has brought a whole new understanding to the aetiology and pathogenesis of obesity, and promises to lead towards effective treatment from this most recalcitrant of conditions. It may also contribute substantially to the understanding and treatment of the dieting disorder group of illnesses, anorexia and bulimia nervosa.

CONCLUSIONS FOR CLINICIANS

Several experimental studies and animal models are apposite to our understanding of the eating disorders. The theory of hypothalamic control of eating and weight, albeit still unproven, is useful in that it leads to the concept of a set point controlling weight, or perhaps body fat composition. The questions of whether there is an alteration to this set point in cases of human over- or under-nutrition, and whether the new set point is preserved so as to impede the treatment of obesity or anorexia nervosa, needs further study. The role of neurotransmitters in weight regulation remains controversial, despite a wealth of studies. Because of the potential financial benefits, it is likely that pharmaceutical companies will continue to explore this area, and already some recent drugs, such as the serotonin selective reuptake inhibitor fluoxetine, are useful in treating bulimia nervosa and obesity. CCK and its influence on gastric emptying offers further potential for improving our treatment of eating disorder patients. Animal hypophagias warrant further attention from clinicians. Epidemiological research indicates that most girls and young women in our cultures voluntarily restrict their eating at one time or another. Why some are vulnerable and go on to anorexia nervosa, bulimia nervosa, or adolescent onset obesity, is unclear. It may well be that some ancient weight control mechanisms, that were originally entailed in situations such as the spontaneous hypophagias, are activated by dieting and lead to an aberrant progression from voluntary restriction to uncontrolled semi-starvation, or alternatively ravenous over-eating. Similarly, the hyperactivity and weight loss noted in animals on restricted diets with access to exercise is likely to be relevant to the excessive activity so commonly seen in dieting disorder patients, particularly those with anorexia nervosa. The discovery of leptin and its genetic control has opened a whole new area in research, and its implications for therapy may be enormous. This surely is where our understanding of eating and weight control shall be advanced most significantly over the next few years.

CLINICAL IMPLICATIONS

- Body mass is determined by the relation of energy intake and energy expenditure, but this equation needs to be understood in relation to the composition of food eaten, and the ways in which energy is utilized.
- The role of the hypothalamus in regulating eating and in determining the utilization of energy has been investigated vigorously over the last half-century. It is now accepted that the hypothalamus is not the prime centre of this control, but rather part of several integrated neural mechanisms.
- Research has elucidated the role of specific neurotransmitters and modulators in energy ingestion.
- Spontaneous variations in eating and in energy utilization in various species of animals provide useful models for understanding aspects of eating disorders in humans.
- A relationship between overactivity and food deprivation has been proposed, but recent findings suggest that the relationship may be less fundamental and less important than thought previously.
- The discovery of the *ob* gene and of the hormone leptin has opened a new chapter in the understanding of energy intake and utilization.

RESEARCH IMPLICATIONS

- The research priority of the next few years will be exploration of the actions and determinants of leptin, and its relationship to obesity, undernutrition, and eating and dieting disorders. This work should integrate biological research throughout the whole spectrum of dysfunctional eating.

REFERENCES

Abraham, S. F., Beumont, P.J.V. and Cobbin, D. M. (1981). Catecholamine metabolism and body weight in anorexia nervosa. *British Journal of Psychiatry*, **138**, 244–247.

Anand, B. K. and Brobeck J. R. (1950). Localization of a feeding centre in the hypothalamus of the rat. *Proceedings of the Society for Experimental Biology and Medicine*, **77**, 323–334.

Anand, B. K. and Brobeck J. R. (1961). Nervous regulation of food intake. *Physiology Reviews*, **41**, 677–708.

Barry, V. C. and Klawans, H. L. (1976). On the role of dopamine in the pathophysiology of anorexia nervosa. *Journal of Neural Transmission*, **38**, 107–122.

Beumont, P.J.V. (1984). A clinician looks at animal models of anorexia nervosa. In *Animal Models in Psychopathology*, edited by N. W. Bond. Sydney: Academic Press.

Beumont, P.J.V., Arthur, B., Russell, J. D. and Touyz S. W. (1994). Excessive physical activity in dieting disorder patients: proposals for a supervised exercise programme. *International Journal of Eating Disorders*, **15**, 21–36.

Boakes, R. A. and Dwyer, D. M. (1997). Weight loss in rats produced by running: effects of prior experience and individual housing. *Quarterly Journal of Experimental Psychology*, **50B(2)**, 129–148.

Bray, G. A., Inoue, S. and Nishizawa, Y. (1981). Hypothalamic obesity: the autonomic hypothesis and the lateral hypothalamus. *Diabetologia*, **20**, 366–378.

Brobeck, J. R. (1946). Mechanisms of the development of obesity in animals with hypothalamic lesions. *Physiological Review*, **26**, 541–559

Coleman, D. L. (1973). Effects of parabiosis of obese mice with diabetes and normal mice. *Diabetologia*, **9**, 294–298.

Danforth, E. (1985). Diet and obesity. *American Journal of Clinical Nutrition*, **41**, 1132–1145.

Dwyer, D. M. and Boakes, R. A. (1997). Activity-based anorexia in rats and failure to adapt to a feeding schedule. *Behavioural Neuroscience*, **111**, 195–205.

Epling, W. F. and Pierce, W. D. (1996). Activity Anorexia. Theory, Research and Treatment. Mahwah: Lawrence Erlbaum Associates.

Flatt, J. P. (1993). Dietary fat, carbohydrate balance and weight maintenance. *Annals of the New York Academy of Sciences*, **683**, 122–144.

Friedman, M. I. and Stricker, E. M. (1976). The physiological psychology of hunger: a physiological perspective. *Psychological Review*, **83**, 409–431.

Grossman, S. P. (1966). The VMH: a centre for affective reactions, satiety or both? *Physiological Behaviour*, **1**, 1–10.

Grossman, S. P. (1990). Brain mechanisms concerned with food intake and body weight regulation. In *Bulimia Nervosa. Basic Research, Diagnosis and Therapy*, edited by M. M. Fichter. Chichester: John Wiley & Sons.

Guyton, A. C. (1976). *Textbook of Medical Physiology*. Philadelphia: W.B. Saunders.

Halmi, K. A., Dekirmenjean, H., Davis, J. M., Casper, R. and Goldberg, S. (1978). Catecholamine metabolism in anorexia nervosa. *Archives of General Psychiatry*, **35**, 458–460.

Hervey, G. R. (1952). The effects of lesions in the hypothalamus in parabiotic rats. *Journal of Physiology*, **145**, 336–352.

Keesey, R. E., Boyle, P. C., Kemwitz, W. and Mitchell, J. S. (1976). The role of the lateral hypothalamus in determining the body weight set point. In *Hunger: Basic Mechanisms and Clinical Implications*, edited by D Novin, W. Wyrwicka and G. A. Bray. New York: Raven Press, pp. 243–256.

Keesey, R. E., Boyle, P. C. and Storlein, L. H. (1978). Food intake and utilization in lateral hypothalamus lesioned rats. *Physiology and Behaviour*, **21**, 265–268.

Kennedy, G. C. (1953). The role of depot fat in the hypothalamic control of food intake in the rat. Proceedings of the Royal Society, London. *Biology*, **140**, 579–592.

Liebowitz, S. F. (1980). Neurochemical systems of the hypothalamus: control of feeding and drinking behaviour and water-electrolyte excretion. In *Handbook of the Hypothalamus*, Vol. 3, edited by P. J. Morgane and J. Panksepp. New York: Marcel Dekker, pp. 299–437.

Liebowitz, S. F. (1983). Hypothalamic catecholamine systems controlling eating behaviour: a potential model for anorexia nervosa. In *Anorexia Nervosa, Recent Developments in Research*, edited by P. C. Darby, P. E. Garfinkel, D. M. Garner and D. V. Coscina. New York: Alan R. Liss, pp. 221–229.

Liebowitz, S. F. (1995). Central physiological determinants of eating behaviour and weight, pp. 3–7; Smith, G. P. and Gipps, J. (1995). Peripheral physiological determinants of eating and body weight, pp. 8–12; Berndell, J. E. (1995). The psychobiological approach to appetite and weight control, pp. 13-20; Ravussen, E. (1995). Energy expenditure and body weight, pp. 32–37. In *Eating Disorders and Obesity*, edited by K. D. Brownell and C. G. Fairburn. New York: Guildford Press.

Le Magnen, as reported by Grossman, S. P. (1995).

Morgane, P. J. (1961). Alterations in feeding and drinking behaviour of rats with lesions in the globi pallidi. *American Journal of Physiology*, **201**, 420–428.

Morley, J.E. (1980). The neuroendocrine control of appetite. *Life Science*, **2**, 335–368.

Morley, J. E. and Gunion, M. W. (1988). Central regulation of feeding: the role of neuropeptides. In *The Nutritional Modulation of Neural Function*, edited by J. E. Morley, M. B. Sterman and J. H. Walsh. San Diego: Academic Press Inc., pp. 125–134.

Mrosovsky, N. (1983). Animal anorexias, starvation and anorexia nervosa: Are animal models of anorexia nervosa possible? In *Anorexia Nervosa: Recent Developments in Research*, edited by P. L. Darby, P. E. Garfinkel, D. M. Garner and D. V. Coscina. New York: Alan R. Liss, pp. 199–205.

Mrosovsky, N. and Powley, T. L. (1977). Set points for body weight and fat. *Behavioural Biology*, **20**, 205–223.

Mrosovsky, N. and Sherry, D. F. (1980). Animal anorexias. *Science*, **207**, 837–842.

Oomura, Y. (1976). Significance of glucose, insulin and free fatty acids on the hypothalamic feeding and satiety neurons. In *Hunger: Basic Mechanisms and Clinical Implications.* edited by D. Novin, W. Wyrwicka and G. A. Bray. New York: Raven Press, pp. 145–157.

Pirke, K. M., Broocks, A., Wilckens, T., Marquard, R. and Schweiger U. (1993). Starvation induced hyperactivity in the rat: the role of endocrine and neurotransmitter changes. *Neurosciences and Behavioural Reviews*, **17**, 287–294.

Powley, T. L. and Keesey, R. E. (1970). Relationship of body weight to the lateral hypothalamic feeding syndrome. *Journal of Comparative and Physiological Psychology*, **70**, 25–36.

Redmond, D. E., Huang, Y. H., Snyder, D. R. and Maas, J. W. (1997). Norepinephrine and satiety in monkeys. In *Anorexia Nervosa*, edited by R. A. Vigersky. New York: Raven Press, pp. 81–96.

Robinson, P. (1990). Gastric control of food intake. In *Bulimia Nervosa. Basic Research, Diagnosis and Therapy,* edited by M. M. Fichter. Chichester: John Wiley and Sons, pp. 180–187.

Routtenberg, A. and Kuznezof, S. W. (1967). Self-starvation of rats living in activity wheels while on a restricted feeding schedule. *Journal of Comparative and Physiological Psychology*, **64**, 414–421.

Schwartz, M. W. and Seeley, R. J. (1997). The neurobiology of body weight regulation. *Journal of the American Dietetic Association*, **97**, 54–60.

Seeley, R. J., Chavez, M., Dallman, M. F., Matson, C. A., Woods, S. C. and Schwartz, M. W. (1996). Behavioural, endocrine and hypothalamic responses to involuntary overfeeding. *American Journal of Physiology*, **40**(3), R819–823.

Stellar, E. (1954). The physiology of motivation. *Psychological Reviews*, **61**, 5–22.

Stricker, E. M. and Andersen, E. A. (1980). The lateral hypothalamic syndrome: Comparison with the syndrome of anorexia nervosa. *Life Sciences*, **26**, 1927–1934.

Ungerstedt, U. (1971). Aphagia and adiposia after 60H dopamine induced degeneration of the nigro-striatal dopamine system. *Acta Physiologica Scandinavica* (Supplement) **367**, 97–122.

Woods, S. C., Steen, L. J., McKay, L. D. and Porte, D. (1979). Chronic intracerebroventricular infusion of insulin reduces food intake and body weight in baboons. *Nature*, **282**, 503–505.

11 Neuroimaging in Eating Disorders

Z. R. ELLISON AND J. FOONG
Maudsley Hospital, London, UK

INTRODUCTION

Over the last few decades there has been a growing interest in the use of neuroimaging techniques to investigate psychiatric disorders, including eating disorders. Early studies focused on structural brain imaging, using computed tomography (CT), and magnetic resonance imaging (MRI). In more recent years, it has become possible to investigate brain activity using functional neuroimaging techniques. Although the use of such techniques is growing rapidly, research using functional imaging in the investigation of eating disorders has been limited. Functional imaging may prove to be particularly valuable in the investigation of abnormal cognitive processes in anorexia nervosa and bulimia nervosa.

STRUCTURAL IMAGING TECHNIQUES

The development of non-invasive neuroimaging techniques has made possible the investigation of structural brain abnormalities in psychiatric disorders. As little is known about the pathophysiological processes in eating disorders, it has been important to determine their effects on the brain using these techniques.

COMPUTED TOMOGRAPHY (CT)

CT was the first non-invasive imaging technique used to examine brain structures. However, CT relies on ionizing radiation and concerns about exposure to radiation have been raised, especially when repeated investigations are performed in the same individual.

MAGNETIC RESONANCE IMAGING (MRI)

In recent years, MRI has become a major investigatory tool. It provides high resolution spatial images which are derived from the NMR signal of mobile protons (hydrogen nuclei) in water and fat. Spatial resolution of images is produced by applying a magnetic field gradient across the sample so that protons in different regions of the field will resonate at different frequencies, and thereby their location is established. MRI is thus able to differentiate between different tissues as they have different proton densities. MRI has a number of advantages over CT, the most

Neurobiology in the Treatment of Eating Disorders.
Edited by H.W. Hoek, J.L. Treasure and M.A. Katzman.

obvious being the safety implication of no exposure to radiation. Other advantages include the ability to generate images in three planes and in thinner slices, improved delineation of grey and white matter, more accurate volumetric measurements and greater resolution of small structures (Potts *et al.* 1993). However, the main disadvantage of MRI is that it uses a strong magnetic field, and therefore any patients who have metal in their bodies such as pacemakers, metallic prosthetic devices, or metal fragments, have to be excluded.

STRUCTURAL IMAGING INVESTIGATIONS OF EATING DISORDERS

Over the past two decades, there have been a number of studies using CT to investigate brain pathology in patients with eating disorders, particularly anorexia nervosa. The reports have included single case reports (Heinz *et al* 1977; Sein *et al.* 1981), small case series (Enzmann and Lane 1977; Datlof *et al.* 1986) and larger case controlled studies (Lankenau *et al.* 1985; Dolan *et al.* 1988). Most of the studies of anorexic patients have been conducted during the acute stages of their illness, that is, when they are at low body weight, and have generally reported cortical atrophy using indices such as sulcal widening and ventricular enlargement (Enzmann and Lane 1977; Lankenau *et al.* 1985; Datlof *et al.* 1986; Kohlmeyer *et al.* 1983). Sulcal widening appears to be the more frequently reported finding and studies which have examined both indices have tended to report ventricular enlargement less than sulcal widening (Dolan *et al.* 1988; Kohlmeyer *et al.* 1983).

The reversibility of cerebral atrophy was first reported in single case reports of anorexic patients who had repeat CT scans following weight gain (Heinz *et al.* 1977; Sein *et al.* 1981) which led to this structural abnormality being called 'pseudoatrophy'. These findings were extended by subsequent studies of larger samples of patients with anorexia nervosa who were found to have sulcal widening and ventricular enlargement on CT which decreased following weight gain (Kohlmeyer *et al.* 1983; Artmann *et al.* 1985). It has only been in more recent years that large case controlled studies have been performed to investigate structural brain changes after weight gain. Dolan *et al.* (1988) examined 25 anorexic patients and found that a significant number, that is, 15 of their 25 patients, had sulcal widening and ventricular enlargement on CT during the acute stages of their illness. There was a significant decrease in sulcal widening, although ventricular enlargement persisted, when these patients were re-scanned three months later following weight gain. The authors raised the possibility that ventricular enlargement may take a longer time to resolve or become irreversible with chronicity of the illness which may have accounted for the persistence of this abnormality in their group of patients. However, in another study by Kreig *et al.* (1988), 25 patients with anorexia nervosa were re-scanned following weight gain and found to have significant improvement in ventricular enlargement on CT, although mean ventricular size was still greater than for the control group.

There have only been a few studies which have attempted to investigate the structural brain abnormalities in patients with bulimia nervosa, and results to date have been conflicting. One study, which examined 21 patients with eating disorders only included five patients with bulimia, and these patients were found to have no difference in ventriculo-brain ratio (VBR) compared to a group of controls (Lankenau *et al.* 1985). In a larger series of patients with bulimia nervosa, Krieg *et al.* (1987) reported that nearly half of their patients (i.e. 13 of 28 patients) were found to have sulcal widening on CT, defined as the presence of at least six sulci measuring 3 mm or more in width. Five of these 13 patients were also found to have ventricular enlargement.

The MRI studies of eating disorders have generally confirmed the findings of earlier CT studies of anorexia nervosa, namely ventricular enlargement and sulcal widening (Hoffman *et al.* 1989a; Palazidou *et al.* 1990; Swayze *et al.* 1996). Hussain *et al.* (1992) examined 24 patients with eating disorders, of which half had anorexia nervosa and the others had bulimia, and found that the anorexic patients had significantly smaller thalamic and midbrain areas, indicative of subcortical atrophy, when compared to a group of controls and to the bulimic patients. In two separate studies, one of patients with anorexia nervosa and the other of patients with bulimia, Hoffman *et al.* (1989a,b) found that ventricular enlargement was present on MRI in both groups of patients.

More recently, Swayze *et al.* (1996), confirmed the findings of previous studies that structural abnormalities are reversible following weight gain. They used computerized volumetric measurements on MRI which were performed in 10 patients with eating disorders, eight with anorexia nervosa, one with bulimia nervosa and one with an atypical eating disorder. The patients were compared to 10 healthy controls and were found to have significant ventricular enlargement at low body weight. They were re-scanned when their weight had increased and a body mass index of 18 was reached. The results indicated that ventricular enlargement had decreased and total brain volume increased significantly. In another study, MRI was repeated in 12 female adolescents with anorexia nervosa following refeeding 11 months later (Golden *et al.* 1996). They found that ventricular enlargement had decreased significantly and there was a significant inverse correlation between body mass index and total ventricular volume. They concluded that ventricular enlargement correlates with the degree of malnutrition and is reversible following weight gain.

MRI has also allowed more accurate and detailed examination of the pituitary gland in patients with eating disorders. Doraiswamy *et al.* (1990) reported a significant decrease in the pituitary area on MRI in eight anorexic and ten bulimic patients compared to a group of healthy controls. In the absence of any macroscopic pituitary pathology, the authors have proposed that the decrease in pituitary size was most likely secondary to nutritional or endocrine dysfunction.

However, it is uncertain whether pituitary size is reversible as patients in this study were not re-examined following weight correction.

The techniques used in both CT and MRI studies of eating disorders to assess the indices of cortical atrophy have been limited. Early studies relied on visual inspection to provide global ratings or linear measures of sulci and ventricles. Other studies have used methods to calculate VBR either on a single slice or several thick slices. The accuracy and reliability of such measures has been questioned by Swayze *et al.* (1996). Furthermore, they have also emphasized that maintaining exact comparability of head positioning in re-scanning can be difficult and may have influenced the results in previous follow-up studies. It has been reported that any changes in the angle of the scanning plane or even variations as small as 1 mm in slice level can result in changes of more than 10% for VBR and ventricular measures (Woods *et al.* 1991). Swayze *et al.* (1996) have therefore recommended the use of more precise techniques with computerized volumetric analysis as described in their study.

The pathogenesis of the structural abnormalities observed on CT and MRI remains uncertain. A number of hypotheses have been suggested to explain these findings. One early suggestion was that the observed changes may be caused by underlying dehydration. However, this is unlikely as most studies have recruited patients admitted to hospital who have been re-fed for at least several days and screened for clinical and biochemical dehydration prior to their brain scans (Dolan *et al.* 1988; Kingston *et al.* 1996). Others have proposed that the observed changes reflect neuronal damage secondary to malnutrition with possible regeneration of myelin accounting for the reversibility of the CT changes (Artmann *et al.* 1985). Datlof *et al.* (1986) suggested that the ventricular dilatation found in their small number of anorexic patients could have been secondary to loss of lean body tissue mass. Other studies have reported that patients with anorexia nervosa who were found to have widening of cortical sulci had elevated cortisol levels compared to those who did not have any evidence of structural changes on CT (Krieg *et al.* 1986, 1988). This is not surprising as patients with Cushing's disease or those receiving long-term corticosteroid therapy have been observed to have ventricular dilatation, cortical atrophy and impairment of cognition (Bentson *et al.* 1978, Okuno *et al.* 1980; Mauri *et al.* 1993). More specifically, Starkman *et al.* (1992) reported a decrease in hippocampal formation volume in 12 patients with Cushing's syndrome which was negatively correlated with plasma cortisol levels and verbal memory tasks. However, in a recent review, O'Brien (1997) emphasized that the evidence for prolonged hypothalamic–pituitary axis activation causing neuronal damage, particularly in the hippocampal regions, with resultant cognitive impairment, is limited and requires further research. Another consideration is whether the brain changes observed may predate the onset of the eating disorder although this would not explain the reversibility of these changes, albeit partial, following weight gain. Interestingly, there have been reports that some patients recruited into studies have been found to have possible con genital or early brain abnormalities. Artmann *et al.* (1985) found that eight of their 35 patients with anorexia nervosa had ventricular asymmetry which they suggested may be secondary to perinatal hypoxic–ischaemic damage. Swayze *et al.* (1996) reported congenital anomalies, namely, cavum septi pellucidi, cavum vergae and lateral ventricular asymmetry, in three of their ten patients with anorexia nervosa.

A few studies have included male patients with eating disorders, but as the numbers are very small, most investigators have not attempted to make any comparisons on the basis of gender. Swayze *et al.* (1996) included three male patients in their sample of ten patients with anorexia nervosa and found that the male patients had less reversibility of changes in ventricular and brain size following weight gain, although this could have been related to their lower weight gain during treatment compared to the females. Nonetheless, this raises the possibility that there may be gender differences in the severity or reversibility of structural brain changes in patients with eating disorders and warrants further investigation.

There have been a few studies which have reported a correlation between structural abnormalities and clinical variables. Lankenau *et al.* (1985) reported that the rapidity of weight loss correlated significantly with VBR in their group of patients with anorexia nervosa. Hoffman *et al.* (1989a,b) reported that chronic self-induced vomiting correlated significantly with ventricular enlargement on MRI in both anorexic and bulimic patients. Datlof *et al.* (1986) found that ventricular enlargement was associated with loss of lean body mass in their small sample of patients with anorexia nervosa. Other studies (Kreig *et al.* 1989; Golden *et al.* 1996) have proposed that the structural abnormalities detected are associated with prolonged starvation or malnutrition and in one study (Golden *et al.* 1996), ventricular enlargement was reported to be reversible following weight gain. Some of these correlations have yet to be replicated. However, these clinical variables can be considered to be measures of illness severity and therefore the more severe the illness in terms of clinical symptomatology, the greater the likelihood of structural brain abnormalities being present. It is interesting to note that most studies have found no association between the duration of illness and structural abnormalities.

The functional significance of structural abnormalities in patients with eating disorders has yet to be clarified. The obvious question is whether the structural abnormalities are associated with cognitive impairment. Neuropsychological deficits have been reported in patients with anorexia nervosa as well as bulimia (Hamsher *et al.* 1981; McKay *et al.* 1986). Attempts have been made to characterize the nature of the neuropsychological deficits in anorexia nervosa and the findings in general have indicated that patients in the acute stages of their illness display deficits in attention, visuospatial ability, memory and problem solving (Pendleton-Jones *et al.* 1991; Szmukler *et al.* 1992). Attempts to correlate neuropsychological deficits with structural abnormalities have proved more difficult. In a study which included both anorexic and bulimic patients, no correlation between ventricular enlargement and performance on a vigilance task was found (Krieg *et al.* 1989). In contrast, Palazidou *et al.* (1990) reported that performance on the symbol digit test in 17 anorexic patients was inversely correlated with sulcal widening on CT.

More recently, Kingston *et al.* (1996) performed MRI scans and administered a battery of neuropsychological tests to a large group of patients with anorexia nervosa on two occasions, when they were first admitted to hospital and following weight gain of 10%, as well as to a control group. The patients performed worse on tasks of attention, visuospatial ability and memory and only improved on tests of attention following weight gain. There was some improvement in ventricular enlargement and sulcal dilatation but this did not correlate with neuropsychological performance. It is important to note that the patients in this study were re-tested and re-scanned after only a modest gain in weight (i.e. their mean BMI was 17.9 on the second testing which is still below the normal healthy range), which may have influenced the results. Lower weight was associated with increase in ventricular size and poorer performance on flexibility and memory tasks.

FUNCTIONAL IMAGING TECHNIQUES

Functional neuroimaging provides a powerful tool for research into psychiatric disorders for several reasons. Firstly, brain dysfunction may occur without evidence of any structural change, and functional imaging may detect regional brain abnormalities. Secondly, functional imaging can be used to investigate brain dysfunction associated with specific cognitive processes or phenomenology. Finally, brain abnormalities may result from abnormal connectivity between regions rather than dysfunction within one particular region, and this may be demonstrated by functional imaging (McGuire *et al.* 1996).

Functional neuroimaging in eating disorders may therefore be used to identify regional brain dysfunction (e.g. hypofunction of a particular brain region), to discover regional abnormalities associated with specific cognitive processes (e.g. limbic abnormalities associated with depressive symptoms in anorexia nervosa), or to indicate abnormal functional connectivity between brain regions. Eating disorder studies have mainly addressed the first of these three problems, with a few examining the second, and none, so far, the third.

There are however many potential methodological problems associated with functional neuroimaging studies (Nadeau and Crosson 1995; Woods, 1996). The choice of a suitable control group for studies of anorexia nervosa is problematic because of the difficulty of controlling for the effects of prolonged starvation and weight loss. Other potential confounding variables include sex, age, psychotropic drugs, and psychiatric comorbidity (such as depressive or obsessional symptoms). Some studies are carried out with the subject in the resting state, in which case cognitive processes may vary between subjects. Others involve subjects carrying out cognitive tasks, and this makes comparison of results difficult if patients and controls differ in their performance. Problems can also occur in the data acquisition (e.g. variation in signal to noise levels during a study) and analysis (e.g. spatial averaging of results from brains of different shape). Finally, the interpretation of results requires caution: for example, it may be difficult to decide whether changes in subjects with eating disorders reflect state or trait abnormalities.

SINGLE PHOTON EMISSION COMPUTED TOMOGRAPHY (SPECT)

In SPECT, a radioactive ligand is used. It binds to endothelial cell membranes and is rapidly transported across them and irreversibly altered so that it cannot diffuse back into the blood. An advantage is that if the ligand has a long half-life, the study can be carried out outside the scanner, and the subject moved into the scanner afterwards. This eliminates any effect of the scanner environment on the results. However, a drawback of the long half-life is that each subject can only have a maximum of three studies done per year. In its favour, SPECT is relatively cheap and easily available, although image-processing techniques are less advanced than in PET (positron emission tomography) (Nadeau and Crosson 1995). One potential disadvantage is that the physiology of tracers is unknown in malnutrition which makes the interpretation of the results of SPECT studies of eating disorders more difficult (Herholz 1996).

POSITRON EMISSION TOMOGRAPHY (PET)

PET measures cerebral blood flow by using radiotracers such as $H_2{}^{15}O$, which actively circulate in the cerebral vessels, and diffuse freely into cerebral tissue. The study must be conducted with the subject inside the scanner. Unfortunately its use is restricted by high cost, limited availability, and radiation exposure (Nadeau and Crosson 1995).

FUNCTIONAL MAGNETIC RESONANCE IMAGING (fMRI)

FMRI is the newest of the functional imaging techniques. Most fMRI studies use the BOLD (blood oxygen level dependent) technique, which depends on the small decrease in deoxyhaemoglobin in areas where there is increased synaptic activity. Images are mapped onto anatomical images. The spatial resolution of fMRI is better than SPECT and PET. Another major advantage of this method is the absence of radiation exposure. This is particularly important in the investigation of eating disorders, which primarily affect young women. Many PET and SPECT studies have been unable to use sex-matched controls for this reason. This also means that there is no limit to the number of studies a single subject can be involved in. Unfortunately the study must be carried out inside the scanner, a rather cramped and noisy environment (Nadeau and Crosson 1995).

MAGNETIC RESONANCE SPECTROSCOPY (MRS)

MRS has recently been used to investigate psychiatric disorders. It is a non-invasive technique capable of detecting the distribution of metabolites other than water in tissue such as *N*-acetyl aspartate, creatine or choline. MRS does not involve exposure to radiation as it is performed using an MRI scanner. Spectra obtained from MRS provide information about what chemicals are present and their concentration. This technique can therefore be used to examine biochemical processes or function in the brain and has already contributed to the evaluation of pathological states of the brain such as ischaemia, tumours, multiple sclerosis and epilepsy.

MRS studies have been performed in a number of psychiatric disorders including schizophrenia (Calabrese *et al.* 1992; Buckley *et al.* 1994; Fukuzako *et al.* 1995; Maier *et al.* 1995), bipolar affective disorder (Kato *et al.* 1994), and social phobia (Davidson *et al.* 1993), as well as in patients with cognitive impairment (Buckley *et al.* 1994; Meyerhoff *et al.* 1994), with interesting results. However, to date, there have been no such investigations of eating disorders. It remains to be determined whether MRS can be a valuable research tool in eating disorders, with its ability to examine brain biochemistry *in vivo*.

FUNCTIONAL IMAGING INVESTIGATIONS OF EATING DISORDERS

ANOREXIA NERVOSA

Several SPECT and PET studies of anorexia nervosa have been published, with variable findings. Some studies have found no functional differences between anorexic patients and controls, while others have found subcortical or cortical changes.

Krieg *et al.* (1989) investigated the relationship between structural and functional brain changes in anorexia nervosa. They performed CT and SPECT scans on 12 female anorexic patients with an older, mixed control group of five females and seven males. The CT findings were of enlarged extracerebral CSF spaces in eight of the 12 anorexic patients, six of whom also had enlarged ventricles. SPECT showed that there were no significant differences in regional cerebral blood flow (rCBF) between anorexic patients and controls. However, there was an inverse correlation between CBF and VBR in the anorexic patients which may have been caused by reduced rCBF measurements over areas of ventricular enlargement.

Several studies have examined basal ganglia activity in anorexia nervosa. Herholz *et al.* (1987) carried out a PET study scanning five female anorexic patients, when ill and recovered, and 15 male controls, all at rest. They found significant hypermetabolism in bilateral caudate nuclei in ill anorexic patients, compared to both controls, and the anorexic patients when recovered. There was no difference between the control and recovered anorexic groups. They hypothesized that this finding may be due to increased vigilance in patients with anorexia nervosa, or that since the caudate is involved in the initiation of eating behaviour (Rolls *et al.* 1983), hypermetabolism may indicate a pathophysiological role in anorexia. In their discussion they commented that although measurement of regional glucose metabolism depends to some extent on the size of brain structures, the brain shrinkage in anorexia would result in apparent hypometabolism, the opposite of this finding. Also, ketone bodies may be present in the plasma of anorexic patients, but again this would result in apparent hypometabolism. However, this finding of caudate hypermetabolism was not replicated by Delvenne *et al.* (1995) in their PET study of anorexia nervosa. They recruited 20 female anorexic patients and 10 female controls, and found that the metabolic rate was significantly reduced globally in anorexic patients. After normalization of regional glucose metabolism values for this global reduction, there was no difference in caudate or putamen regional glucose metabolism between anorexic patients and controls. It is possible that methodological differences might explain the different findings.

The presence of cortical abnormalities in anorexia nervosa is suggested by the results of Delvenne *et al.* (1995) who also found relative regional hypometabolism in frontal and parietal regions in the anorexic patients. They proposed several possible explanations for this global and regional hypometabolism. Firstly it may be due to the neurophysiological changes of anorexia, associated with prolonged starvation. Secondly it may be caused by associated symptoms of anxiety and depression. Higher levels of anxiety occurred in the anorexic patients than in controls. A functional imaging study of two groups of normal volunteers showed the group with higher anxiety to have reduced CBF with increasing anxiety (Gur *et al.* 1987). Reduced metabolism in the left inferior parietal region has also been described in panic disorder (Nordahl *et al.* 1990). Also, PET studies of depression have reported global and frontal hypometabolism (Martinot *et al.* 1990). Finally, Delvenne *et al.* (1995) speculated that the findings of parietal hypometabolism may represent a primary cerebral dysfunction in anorexia nervosa. Anorexic patients have been found to have difficulties with some mathematical tasks (Fox 1981), which are thought to involve the parietal lobe. The latter may also be involved in perception of body image (Trimble 1988).

Two studies have examined the effect of eating on rCBF in anorexic patients (Nozoe *et al.* 1993, 1995), which might be expected to cause rCBF changes in brain regions associated with the pathophysiology of anorexia. Nozoe *et al.* (1993) conducted a SPECT study on a group of seven females with anorexia nervosa, examining rCBF before and after a food stimulus (eating a piece of custard cake in 3 minutes), and before and after treatment. Their control group consisted of five healthy females. They found that prior to treatment, anorexic patients showed a significant increase in metabolism in the left inferior frontal cortex in response to food, compared to controls. Nozoe *et al.* (1995) used a similar SPECT protocol to study eight females with anorexia nervosa, five females with bulimia nervosa, and nine female controls. The rCBF response to feeding in the anorexic patients was significantly greater than in controls in the left parietal and occipital regions and right temporal and occipital regions, and was significantly greater than the bulimic patients in the left inferior frontal and right inferior frontal, parietal, and temporal regions. This seems to confirm that a food stimulus is a potent cause of rCBF increases in anorexic patients, although the regional specificity of this is unclear.

One approach to identifying brain abnormalities associated with relapse of anorexia is by comparing rCBF in anorexic patients before and after treatment. Nozoe *et al.* (1993) found that after treatment, the anorexic group showed a significantly increased resting metabolism in the temporal regions bilaterally compared to controls, which the authors thought might be due to physical change (i.e. weight gain) of the anorexic patients. Herholz *et al.* (1987) also found increased bilateral temporal metabolism in the anorexic patients, although this was before treatment compared to after. It is interesting that abnormalities of temporal function were seen in the small study of Drebit *et al.* (1992). They used SPECT to study six adolescents with eating disorders and found that two anorexic patients had temporal hyperperfusion on opposite sides and one bulimic patient had left temporal hyperperfusion. They noted that Trimble (1988) previously suggested that the temporal lobe may be important for the integration of sensory data related to body image. Temporal blood flow hypermetabolism has also been found in studies of bulimia nervosa (see below).

BULIMIA NERVOSA

Both SPECT and PET have also been used to investigate bulimia nervosa, some also using an anorexic group for comparison. Cortical changes in bulimia nervosa have been found by several research groups. Nozoe *et al.* (1995) found temporal hypermetabolism and frontal changes in bulimic patients. In their SPECT study of eight females with anorexia nervosa and nine female controls, they also scanned five female patients with bulimia nervosa. Blood flow before feeding was highest in bulimic patients, especially in the left temporal and right inferior frontal regions, and reduced after feeding in bilateral inferior frontal, left temporal, and right parietal regions in bulimic patients compared to controls. The authors suggested that bulimic patients may have temporal lobe hypermetabolism. They also proposed the frontal area changes may affect feeding control. Frontal damage leads to hyperphagia, indicating that the frontal lobe may contain a feeding suppression area, and Nozoe *et al.* (1995) suggested that reduced activity here after feeding may result in hyperphagia in bulimia nervosa. Andreason *et al.* (1992) using PET, also found temporal hypermetabolism. They compared 11 female bulimic patients and 18 female controls. They also screened for depressive and obsessive–compulsive symptoms. Hypometabolism in the left anterolateral prefrontal cortex was found in those with depressive symptoms.

There have been some reports of abnormal left lateralization of metabolism/rCBF in bulimia nervosa. Andreason *et al.* (1992) found temporal lobe metabolism to be greater on the left than right in bulimic patients, but not in controls, and this was independent of mood. Hagman *et al.* (1990) in their PET study, compared eight female bulimic patients, eight females with major affective disorder, and eight female controls. They found that in the bulimic patients there was a loss of the normal right lateralized temporal activations seen in the controls.

CONCLUSIONS

Neuroimaging techniques are now being used to investigate both structural and functional abnormalities in eating disorders. Structural studies have found enlarged ventricles and sulcal widening which appear to be partially reversible after recovery. These findings have generally been considered to be secondary to the malnutritional state (Herholtz 1996). The precision of techniques used in most studies to measure sulcal widening and ventricular enlargement has been questioned. It is evident that newer neuroimaging techniques such as volumetric analysis would provide more accuracy and could be valuable in extending the findings of previous studies. Serial investigations may assist in further elucidating the natural history of the structural deficits, their functional implications and long term outcome.

The area of functional neuroimaging is growing rapidly, and the few studies that have been carried out in eating disorders have produced interesting results. Unfortunately, studies to date have been small, and have often lacked a suitable control group. Functional imaging results are very sensitive to methodological differences between studies which may account for their variable results. We will summarize a number of findings which need further investigation. In anorexia nervosa, cerebral blood flow was inversely related to ventricular enlargement (Krieg *et al.* 1989). Regional cortical blood flow changes have been detected, although inconsistently, and related to feeding control (frontal lobe), integration of sensory information (temporal lobe), or body image (parietal lobe). If there are blood flow changes in anorexia, it needs to be established whether these result from starvation, associated psychiatric symptoms, or the primary pathophysiology of the disorder. Finally there seem to be profound rCBF changes in response to eating (Nozoe *et al.* 1993, 1995) although the regional specificity of this is unclear.

In bulimia nervosa, temporal hypermetabolism and some left lateralization (or loss of right lateralization) of blood flow have been found in some studies although the significance of these findings is uncertain. In addition, a reduction in bilateral inferior frontal blood flow has been found after eating which may be associated with a failure of feeding suppression (Nozoe *et al.* 1995).

Further developments in functional imaging techniques may help to investigate some of these results. These include: higher resolution scans, more powerful statistical methods for image analysis, and scanning modalities such as fMRI and MRS, which do not involve ionizing radiation. The latter may also allow the use of more suitable control groups, serial scans of patients during treatment, and more complex cognitive paradigms. In the future, an understanding of functional abnormalities in the brain in anorexia nervosa and bulimia nervosa may facilitate the evaluation of treatments for these disorders and the development of drugs targeted to particular neural systems.

CLINICAL IMPLICATIONS

- Brain structural changes can be detected in patients with eating disorders and are likely to be secondary to their nutritional state.
- Cognitive impairment can be observed in anorexic patients who are severely underweight.
- The brain structural changes and cognitive impairment appear to be reversible upon weight gain in most patients.

RESEARCH IMPLICATIONS

- Improvement in MR techniques (e.g. volumetric analysis) may be valuable in extending the findings of structural brain abnormalities.
- Serial investigations would assist in clarifying the long term outcome of structural brain abnormalities and cognitive impairment.
- Further MRI studies in examining the cognitive processes in patients with eating disorders may provide more insight into the psychological mechanisms involved.

DIFFICULTIES

- It would be difficult determine whether the structural or functional brain abnormalities detected are strictly secondary to the nutritional state or disease specific unless investigations done in the acute stages of illness are repeated upon normal weight gain.

ASSESSMENT

- Given the findings that cognitive impairment can occur in the acute stages, it would be important to obtain subjective reports from patients, corroborative information from their families or teachers and to include a cognitive assessment on mental state examination.
- Re-assessment should be considered upon recovery.

Continued

TREATMENT

- The neuroimaging findings in eating disorders to date suggest that early intervention or refeeding is indicated as brain abnormalities appear to correlate with the severity of illness and can be reversible.
- Educating patients and their families about the risks of cognitive impairment and the brain abnormalities would be important as they may improve compliance for treatment especially in those who are still in education or who are academic high achievers.
- There are also serious implications in determining whether patients who have cognitive impairment are able to give informed consent to treatment (e.g. refusing refeeding) as their judgement may be significantly impaired.

REFERENCES

Andreason, P.J., Altemus, M., Zametkin, A.J., King, A.C., Lucinio, J., and Cohen, R.M. (1992). Regional cerebral glucose metabolism in bulimia nervosa. *Am. J. Psychiatry*, **149**, 1506–1513.

Artmann, H., Grau, H., Adelmann, M., and Schleiffer, R. (1985). Reversible and non-reversible enlargement of cerebrospinal fluid spaces in anorexia nervosa. *Neuroradiology*, **27**, 304–312.

Bentson, J., Reza, M., Winter, J., and Wilson, G. (1978). Steroids and apparent cerebral atrophy on computed tomography scans. *J. Comput. Assist. Tomogr.*, **2**, 16–23.

Buckley, P.F., Moore, C., Long, H. *et al.* (1994). ^{1}H-magnetic resonance spectroscopy of the left temporal and frontal lobes in schizophrenia: clinical, neurodevelopmental and cognitive correlates. *Biol. Psychiatry*, **36**, 792–800.

Calabrese, G., Deicken, RF., Fein, G., Merrin, E.L., Schoenfeld, F., and Weiner, M.W. (1992). 31Phosphorus magnetic resonance spectroscopy of the temporal lobes in schizophrenia. *Biol. Psychiatry*, **32**, 26–32.

Datlof, S., Coleman, P.D., Forbes, G.B., and Kreipe, R.E. (1986). Ventricular dilation on CAT scans of patients with anorexia nervosa. *Am. J. Psychiatry*, **143**, 96–98.

Davidson, JRT., Krishnan, K.R.R., Charles, H.C. *et al.* (1993). Magnetic resonance spectroscopy in social phobia: preliminary findings. *J. Clin. Psychiatry*, **54** (suppl. 12), 19–25.

Delvenne, V., Lotstra, F., Goldman, S. *et al.* (1995). Brain hypometabolism of glucose in anorexia nervosa: a PET scan study. *Biol. Psychiatry*, **37**, 161–169.

Dolan R.J., Mitchell, J., and Wakeling, A. (1988). Structural brain changes in patients with anorexia nervosa. *Psychol. Med.*, **18**, 349–353.

Doraiswamy, P.M., Khrisnan, K., Figiel, G. *et al.* (1990). A brain magnetic resonance imaging study of pituitary gland morphology in anorexia nervosa and bulimia. *Biol. Psychiatry*, **28**, 110–116.

Drebit, R., Blackman, M., McEwan, A., and Chowdhury, T. (1992). Imaging and eating disorders. (letter). *J. Am. Acad. Child Adolesc. Psychiatry*, **31**, 990.

Enzmann, D.R., and Lane, B. (1977). Cranial computed tomography findings in anorexia nervosa. *J. Comput. Assist. Tomogr.*, **1**, 410–414.

Fox, C.F. (1981). Neuropsychological correlates of anorexia nervosa. *Int. J. Psychiatr. Med.*, **11**, 285–290.

Fukuzako, H., Takeuchi, K., Hokazono, Y. *et al.* (1995). Proton magnetic resonance spectroscopy of the left medial temporal and frontal lobes in chronic schizophrenia: preliminary report. *Psychiatry Res.*, **61**, 193–200.

Golden, N.H., Ashtari, M., Kohn, M.R. *et al.* (1996). Reversibility of cerebral ventricular enlargement in anorexia nervosa, demonstrated by quantitative magnetic resonance imaging. *J. Pediatr.*, **128**, 296–301.

Gur, R.C., Gur, R.E., Resnick, S.M., Skolnick, B.E., Alavi, A., and Reivich, M. (1987). The effect of anxiety and cortical cerebral blood flow and metabolism. *J. Cereb. Blood Flow Metab.*, **7**, 173–177.

Hagman, J.O., Buchsbaum, M.S., Wu, J.C., Rao, S.J., Reynolds, C.A., and Blinder, B.J. (1990). Comparison of regional brain metabolism in bulimia nervosa and affective disorder assessed with positron emission tomography. *J. Affect. Disord.*, **19**, 153–162.

Hamsher, K.S., Halmi, K.A., and Benton, A.l. (1981). Prediction of outcome in anorexia nervosa from neuropsychological status. *Psychiatry Res.*, **4**, 79–81.

Heinz, E.R., Martinez, J., and Haenggeli, A. (1977). Reversibility of cerebral atrophy in anorexia nervosa and Cushing's syndrome. *J. Comput. Assist. Tomogr.*, **1**, 415–418.

Herholz, K. (1996). Neuroimaging in anorexia nervosa. *Psychiatry Res.*, **62**, 105–110.

Herholz, K., Krieg, J.C., Emrich, H.M. *et al.* (1987). Regional cerebral glucose metabolism in anorexia nervosa measured by positron emission tomography. *Biol. Psychiatry*, **22**, 43–51.

Hoffman Jr, G.W., Ellinwood Jr., E.H., Rockwell, W.J.K., Herfkens, R.J., Nishita, J.K., and Guthrie, L.F. (1989a). Cerebral atrophy in anorexia nervosa: a pilot study. *Biol. Psychiatry*, **26**, 321–324.

Hoffman Jr, G.W., Ellinwood Jr., E.H., Rockwell, W.J.K., Herfkens, R.J., Nishita, J.K., and Guthrie, L.F. (1989b). Cerebral atrophy in bulimia. *Biol. Psychiatry*, **25**, 894–902.

Hussain, M.M., Black, K.J., Doraiswamy, P.M. *et al.* (1992). Subcortical brain anatomy in anorexia and bulimia. *Biol. Psychiatry*, **31**, 735–738.

Kato, T., Takahashi, S., Shioiri, T., Murashita, J., Hamakawa, H., and Inubushi, T. (1994). Reduction of brain phosphocreatine in bipolar II disorder detected by phosphorus-31 magnetic resonance spectroscopy. *J. Affect. Disord.*, **31**, 125–133.

Kingston, K., Szmukler, G., Andrewes, D., Tress, B., and Desmond, P. (1996). Neuropsychological and structural brain changes in anorexia nervosa before and after refeeding. *Psychol. Med.*, **26**, 15–28.

Kohlmeyer, K., Lemkuhl, G., and Potska, F. (1983). Computed tomography of anorexia nervosa. *Am. J. Neuroradiology*, **4**, 437–438.

Krieg, J.-C., Backmund, H., and Pirke, K.M. (1986). Endocrine, metabolic and brain morphological abnormalities in patients with eating disorders. *Int. J. Eat. Disord.*, **5**, 999–1005.

Krieg, J.-C., Backmund, H., and Pirke, K.M. (1987). Cranial computed tomography findings in bulimia. *Acta. Psychiatr. Scandanavia*, **75**, 144–149.

Krieg, J.-C., Pirke, K.M., Lauer, C., and Backmund, H. (1988). Endocrine, metabolic and cranial computed tomographic findings in anorexia nervosa. *Biol. Psychiatry*, **23**, 377–387.

Krieg, J.-C., Lauer, C., Leinsinger, G., Pahl, J., Schreiber, W., Pirke, K.-M., and Moser, E.A. (1989). Brain morphology and regional cerebral blood flow in anorexia nervosa. *Biol. Psychiatry*, **25**, 1041–1048.

Lankenau, H., Swigar, M.E., Bhimani, S., Luchins, D., and Quinlan, D.M. (1985). Cranial CT scans in eating disorder patients and controls. *Compr. Psychiatry*, **26**, 136–147.

Maier, M., Ron, M.A., Barker, G.J., and Tofts, P.S. (1995). Proton magnetic resonance spectroscopy: an *in vivo* method of estimating hippocampal neuronal depletion in schizophrenia. *Psychol. Med.*, **25**, 1201–1209.

Martinot, J-L., Hardy, P., Feline, A. *et al.* (1990). Left prefrontal glucose hypometabolism in the depressed state: a confirmation. *Am. J. Psychiatry*, **147**, 1313–1317.
Mauri, M., Sinforiani, E., Bono, G. *et al.* (1993). Memory impairment in Cushing's disease. *Acta Neurol. Scand.*, **87**, 52–122.
McGuire, P.K. and Frith, C.D. (1996). Disordered functional connectivity in schizophrenia. *Psychol. Med.*, **26**, 663–667.
McKay, S.E., Humphries, L.L., Allen, M.E., and Clawson, D.R. (1986). Neuropsychological test performance of bulimic patients. *Int. J. Neurosci.*, **30**, 73–80.
Meyerhoff, D.J., MacKay, S., Poole, N., Dillon, W.P., Weiner, M.W., and Fein, G. (1994). *N*-Acetylaspartate reductions measured by ^{1}H MRS in cognitively impaired HIV-seropositive individuals. *Magn. Reson. Imaging*, **12**, 653–659.
Nadeau, S.E. and Crosson, B. (1995). A guide to the functional imaging of cognitive processes. *Neuropsychiat., Neuropsychol., Behav. Neurol.*, **8**, 143–162.
Nordahl, T.E., Semple, W.E., Gross, M. *et al.* (1990). Cerebral glucose metabolic differences in patients with panic disorder. *Neuropsychopharmacology*, **3**, 261–272.
Nozoe, S., Naruo, T., Nakabeppu, Y., Soejima, Y., Najako, M., and Tanaka, H. (1993). Changes in regional cerebral blood flow in patients with anorexia nervosa detected through single photon emission tomography imaging. *Biol. Psychiatry*, **34**, 578–580.
Nozoe, S., Naruo, T., Yonekura, R. *et al.* (1995). Comparison of regional cerebral blood flow in patients with eating disorders. *Brain Res. Bull.*, **36**, 251–255.
O'Brien, J.T. (1997). The 'glucocorticoid cascade' hypothesis in man. *Br. J. Psychiatry*, **170**, 199–201.
Okuno, T., Ito, M., Konishi, Y., Yoshioka, M., and Nakano, Y. (1980). Cerebral atrophy following ACTH therapy. *J. Comput. Assist. Tomogr.*, **4**, 20–23.
Palazidou, E., Robinson, P., and Lishman, W.A. (1990). Neuroradiological and neuropsychological assessment in anorexia nervosa. *Psychol. Med.*, **20**, 521–527.
Pendleton-Jones, B., Duncan, C.C., Brouwers, P., and Mirsky, A.F. (1991). Cognition in eating disorders. *J. Clin. Exp. Neuropsychology*, **13**, 711–728.
Potts, N.L.W.S., Davidson, J.R.T., and Krishnan, K.R.R. (1993). The role of nuclear magnetic resonance imaging in psychiatric research. *J. Clin. Psychiatry*, **54** (suppl. 12), 13–18.
Rolls, E.T., Thorpe, S.J., and Maddison, S.P. (1983). Responses of striatal neurons in the behaving monkey. 1. Head of the caudate nucleus. *Behav. Brain Res.*, **7**, 179–210.
Sein, P., Searson, S., Nicol, A.R., and Hall, K. (1981). Anorexia nervosa and pseudoatrophy of the brain. *Br. J. Psychiatry*, **139**, 257–258.
Starkman, M.N., Gebarski, S.S., Berent, S., and Schteingart, D.E. (1992). Hippocampal formation volume, memory dysfunction and cortisol levels in patients with Cushings syndrome. *Biol. Psychiatry*, **32**, 756–765.
Swayze 2nd, V.W., Andersen, A., Arndt, S., Rajarethinam, R., Fleming, F., Sato, Y., and Andreasen, N.C. (1996). Reversibility of brain tissue loss in anorexia nervosa assessed with a computerized Talairach 3-D proportional grid. *Psychol. Med.*, **26**, 381–390.
Szmukler, G.I., Andrewes, D., Kingston, K., Chen, L., Stargatt, R. and Stanley, R. (1992). Neuropsychological impairment in anorexia nervosa: before and after refeeding. *J. Clin. Exp. Neuropsych.*, **14**, 347–352.
Trimble, M.R. (1988). Body image and the temporal lobes. *Br. J. Psychiatry*, **153** (Suppl 2), 12–14.
Woods, B.T., Douglass, A., and Gescuk, B. (1991). Is the VBR still a useful measure of changes in the cerebral ventricles? *Psychiatry Res. Neuroimaging*, **40**, 1–10.
Woods, R.P. (1996). Modeling for intergroup comparisons of imaging data. *Neuroimage*, **4**, S84–S94.

12 Emotional States and Bulimic Psychopathology

C. MEYER, G. WALLER and A. WATERS
Department of Psychology, University of Southampton, Southampton, UK

EMOTIONAL STATES AND BULIMIC PSYCHOPATHOLOGY

Bulimia nervosa and its symptoms have been known for many centuries (e.g. Parry-Jones and Parry-Jones 1991), but they have only received any significant level of attention over the past two decades. Russell (1979) systematically described bulimia nervosa, and thereafter it began to enter our diagnostic terminology and systems. It is clear that our understanding of the eating disorders is far from complete, as evidenced by the changes in diagnostic entities over the past decade. Similarly, we should not be surprised that there is considerable debate about the causes of bulimia nervosa. In this chapter, we will address different models of bulimic psychopathology, and then consider the evidence that physiological, biochemical and neurological factors might account for bulimic attitudes and behaviours (particularly emotionally-driven eating).

In such reviews, there is often a danger that models are perceived as competing. While it is our brief to address the relationship between emotional states and bulimic psychopathology, it should not be concluded that we are arguing for the exclusive role of emotional factors. However, it is important to take a historical perspective. Over the past decade, Fairburn and Cooper's (1989) starvation–bingeing model has been predominant, and has influenced our approach to the neurobiological facets of bulimia. Only more recently has the evidence for an emotion-led model begun to gain strength. Rather than suggesting that the emotional model is better than the starve–binge model, we will discuss how the two models might each explain bulimic psychopathology. Ultimately, we would hold that an integrative model is likely to be the most effective approach. Such a model has marked implications for understanding the potential role of biological factors in bulimic psychopathology.

Neurobiology in the Treatment of Eating Disorders.
Edited by H.W. Hoek, J.L. Treasure and M.A. Katzman.

HISTORICAL CONTEXT: THE STARVATION MODEL OF BULIMIA

Cognitive models of bulimia nervosa have long stressed the centrality of food-, shape- and weight-related concerns (e.g. Cooper 1997; Fairburn 1997). These models suggest that the individual develops concerns over weight and body shape as a result of poor self-esteem, and that compensatory efforts are made to modify body shape through restriction of food intake. Binge eating results from physiological and psychological susceptibility following such periods of starvation, and purging is used to reduce the impact of bingeing (e.g. Fairburn *et al.* 1993; Garner and Garfinkel 1997). This starvation–binge–purge model has strongly influenced the theory and practice of therapy for bulimia and related disorders (e.g. Fairburn and Cooper 1989).

Support for the starvation model comes from research indicating that women with bulimic attitudes and disorders have highly developed cognitive representations of food- and weight-related information (e.g. Channon *et al.* 1988; Ben-Tovim *et al.* 1989; Cooper *et al.* 1992; Cooper and Todd 1997; Long *et al.* 1994; Reiger *et al.* in press). However, while the evidence suggests that this model is necessary, there is considerable reason to doubt that it is sufficient to explain bulimic psychopathology. Perhaps most obviously, a large number of bulimics never go through an initial period of starvation, and bulimic behaviours can exist without starvation or purging (e.g. binge eating disorder). It is also clear that clients' descriptions of their reasons for binge eating often stress emotional antecedents, rather than appetitive ones (e.g. Cooper and Bowskill 1986; Davis *et al.* 1985; Grilo *et al.* 1994). More recently, a variety of empirical and experimental studies have emerged to support these clinical observations—that emotional factors seem to be important in understanding the aetiology and maintenance of overeating, bingeing and other bulimic behaviours.

EMOTIONAL ANTECEDENTS AND CORRELATES OF BULIMIC PSYCHOPATHOLOGY

Clinicians working with eating-disordered clients have long recognized the potential effects of emotional factors as antecedents to bulimic behaviours (e.g. Abraham and Beumont 1982; Garner and Bemis 1982; Lacey 1986; Arnow *et al.* 1992). However, little or no systematic research was carried out at the time to support these early observations. It is only more recently that substantial empirical investigation has been conducted, and has supported the hypothesis that certain emotions frequently precipitate binge eating.

EVIDENCE FOR THE ROLE OF EMOTION-DRIVEN BULIMIC BEHAVIOURS

In one strand of research, experimental studies have demonstrated that exposure to negative emotional cues can precipitate overeating. For example, Telch and Agras (1996) have demonstrated that women with binge eating disorder are more likely to binge in response to negative mood induction than in response to caloric deprivation. In a further set of studies on non-clinical women (Patton 1992; Waller and Mijatovich in press), it has been shown that subliminally presented emotional cues (particularly abandonment cues) can induce greater levels of eating, while appetitive cues do not have the same effect (Meyer and Waller in press).

A second paradigm in this empirical research is the naturalistic study, in which formal and systematic records are taken of the antecedents to bulimic behaviours. Grilo *et al.* (1994) found that either appetitive or emotional states can account for bulimics' bingeing. They found little consistency within individuals, suggesting that individuals binge for different reasons at different times (rather than neatly adhering to a single model). In a study of bulimics' responses to food cravings, Waters *et al.* (under consideration) explored the factors that determine whether or not women succumb to those cravings, and go on to binge. They found that cravings which resulted in binge eating were characterized by significantly lower hedonic tone (i.e. more feelings of sadness, dissatisfaction and depression) than those cravings which did not result in binge eating. It is also important to note that bingeing was associated with *lower* levels of hunger, emphasizing the importance of emotional antecedents where binges follow food cravings. Waters (1996) has concluded that the likelihood of bingeing in response to a negative affective state is far higher if one has the sensory experience of tasting a foodstuff, but that this relationship is unaffected by hunger *per se*. In a further naturalistic study, Davis *et al.* (1988) found that bulimics reported relatively negative mood states prior to binge eating, compared to their affective state prior to eating a normal meal.

The final strand in this research involves correlational studies. It has been shown that bulimia nervosa, bulimic eating attitudes and binge-eating behaviours are each associated with an attentional bias towards self-esteem threats (McManus *et al.* 1996; Waller *et al.* 1996) and negative emotions (Reiger *et al.* in press). There is also evidence that individuals with unhealthy eating-related characteristics are relatively slow to respond actively to such threats (Waller *et al.* 1995; Waller and Meyer 1997). These results demonstrate that bulimic psychopathology is associated with over-elaborated cognitive representations of threat and negative emotions (resulting in attentional biases), and with patterns of cognitive and behavioural avoidance when those representations are activated.

These experimental, naturalistic and correlational studies are important because they directly challenge the starve–binge model of bulimia. The Fairburn and Cooper (1989) model could only predict that the emotional factors would have their effects via inducing restrictive behaviour, which would be followed by overeating. However, the early studies in this field have clearly demonstrated a much more direct and immediate link between emotional state and eating behaviour. It is clear that there is a specific link between negative emotional states (including self-esteem threats) and bulimic behaviour, omitting the restrictive stage. Once again, it should be stressed that the emotional eating model is not intended to supplant the starve–binge model, but that the two should be integrated into a fuller understanding of bulimic psychopathology. Having provided evidence that emotional factors are important, it is necessary to understand how they affect eating.

THE FUNCTIONAL AND PSYCHOLOGICAL LINKS BETWEEN BULIMIC BEHAVIOUR AND EMOTIONAL DISTRESS

Two processes have been suggested that might explain why bulimic behaviours should be associated with negative emotional states and perceived self-esteem threats. One such model is the 'blocking' model (e.g. Lacey 1986; Root and Fallon 1989; Reiser 1990), which suggests that bulimic behaviours (particularly bingeing and vomiting) can serve the reinforcing function of focusing the individual's attention away from an emotional state that is both intolerable and unresolvable by any more adaptive means. This model is certainly compatible with the experiences of many of our clients, who describe finding themselves angry, lonely, anxious, bored or distressed immediately prior to bingeing, and who use purging behaviours as a means of controlling their panic about the consequences of their overeating.

The second suggestion is contained in Heatherton and Beaumeister's (1991) 'escape from awareness' model. These authors suggest that bingeing is a consequence of cognitive narrowing, which individuals use to escape from their awareness of negative emotional states and self-esteem threats. The cognitive narrowing involves focusing on the immediate, with the consequence that the individual reduces higher-order inhibitory functions. Such a reduction means that eating (and other related behaviours, such as alcohol consumption) will become disinhibited, resulting in overeating and bingeing.

While these models describe very different processes, they are not incompatible. Indeed, McManus and Waller (1995) have suggested that one might best understand the emotionally-driven strand of binge eating by an amalgam of the two (in combination with the starve–binge model). The initial onset of binge eating might be most easily explained by a combination of starvation effects and the 'escape from awareness' process. However, once the behaviour is established, there is the likelihood that the 'blocking' model will be the most potent explanatory construct underlying bingeing. Vomiting and purging may serve some of the same functions, reducing awareness of intolerable cognitive and affective states (e.g. Pitts and Waller 1993). Indeed, Tobin *et al.* (1997) have suggested that such vomiting and purging behaviours are more central to bulimic disorders than is usually acknowledged. However, it should be remembered that these behaviours are also clearly linked to the need to reduce the immediate panic that many bulimics experience after bingeing.

It is important to consider what psychological mechanisms might best account for these functional links. The 'blocking' model seems to be relatively easily understood as an example of negative reinforcement within an operant conditioning paradigm, where the behaviours of bingeing and purging reduce the experience of an aversive state (and thus are likely to be repeated in the same circumstances). However, Marlatt (1987) offers an alternative viewpoint, suggesting that bingeing may be a result of classical conditioning. In this model, food craving is 'a motivational state associated with a strong desire for an expected positive outcome'. Thus both classical and operant conditioning may be at work to produce the blocking effect.

In order to explain the 'escape from awareness' model, it is worth considering the construct of dissociation. Schulman (1991) equates the experience of bingeing to sensations of a 'mindless, vacant state' or 'blankness', which blocks out painful experiences and realities. This altered state of perception is very similar to the concept of dissociation (e.g. Speigel and Cardeña 1991), which is characterized by amnesia, derealization, depersonalization and absorption (e.g. Carlson and Putnam 1993). DSM-IV describes dissociation as 'a disruption in the usually integrated functions of consciousness, memory, identity or perception of the environment' (American Psychiatric Association 1994). Many previous studies have found links between dissociation and bulimia, and there is evidence that increased levels of dissociation are related to the severity and frequency of bingeing in those bulimics who report a history of abuse (e.g. Vanderlinden *et al.* 1993; Everill *et al.* 1995). The functional utility of dissociative experiences is such that they result in a narrowing of cognitive focus (Demitrack *et al.* 1990) and consequently lead to the disinhibition of otherwise inhibited behaviours (e.g. eating). This is clearly related to Heatherton and Beaumeister's (1991) 'escape from awareness' hypothesis.

Two final points should be borne in mind. First, emotional factors have been considered as antecedents so far in this chapter. However, it should be remembered that most bulimics find their behaviours to have negative emotional consequences. These consequences are likely to act as antecedents themselves at times, leading to the phenomenon of bingeing due to the distress of identifying oneself as bulimic. This effect should not be overlooked, as it contributes to the self-maintaining cyclical nature of bulimic psychopathology (better recognised in the starve–binge–purge–starve cycle). Second, it is important to consider the role of the individual's coping style. The use of emotional blocking behaviours (such as bingeing and vomiting) can be understood as a form of avoidant coping (e.g. Neckowitz and Morrison 1991). In the short term, this form of coping is reinforced by a reduction in the experience of intolerable cognitive and affective states. However, this is a relatively unproductive strategy in the long term, because it means that the stressors that initiated the negative emotional state remain at least as powerful. Thus, the bulimic behaviour is maintained, since no alternative means of coping are developed.

INTEGRATION OF EMOTIONAL EATING AND STARVATION THEORY

Despite the substantial evidence that emotional factors can be antecedents to binge eating, the starvation–bingeing–purging model should not be neglected. The theory and research base clearly indicates that bingeing often occurs during attempts at dietary restraint (e.g. Wardle 1980; Polivy and Herman 1985; Fairburn and Cooper 1989). Starvation can be an antecedent and a consequence of emotional distress, and both can influence binge eating (McManus and Waller 1995). While a fully integrated model of bulimic behaviours is beyond the scope of this chapter, it would be unreasonable to conclude that either starvation/restraint or affective state is sufficient to explain bulimic psychopathology in all cases.

COGNITIVE FACTORS THAT UNDERPIN EMOTIONAL EATING

As this literature has developed, it has become necessary to understand the cognitive processes and content that explain why emotional states should be linked to bulimic psychopathology.

COGNITIVE PROCESS

It is clear that the processing of emotional information occurs both consciously and preconsciously. Studies using subliminal processing tasks demonstrate the effects of preconscious threat cues upon eating behaviour (Patton 1992; Meyer and Waller in press; Waller and Mijatovich in press). Women with high levels of eating psychopathology eat significantly more following exposure to a subliminal threat cue (in particular an abandonment cue) than following a neutral cue, an appetitive or a positive emotion cue. Thus, it seems that one can provoke eating through activation of preconscious emotional structures, but there is no such effect of food and weight-related information (e.g. Schotte *et al.* 1990; Meyer and Waller in press). In summary, these findings are compatible with a cognitive model where overeating serves the function of reducing activation of threat-related schemata. They indicate that the earliest stage in this activation of overeating is triggered by emotional rather than appetitive material.

Once emotional and threatening material has entered cognitive awareness (i.e. conscious processing), individuals with bulimic attitudes and behaviours respond with two cognitive styles, depending on the nature of the response to be given. When the target responses are relatively automatic (e.g. in modified Stroop tasks), women with bulimic psychopathology show a strong attentional bias towards negative emotions and self-esteem threats (e.g. McManus *et al.* 1996; Waller *et al.* 1996; Reiger *et al.* in press). In contrast, when the response requires more purposeful behaviour (e.g. where the individual has to seek the threat cue), there is a pattern akin to cognitive avoidance of the material (e.g. Waller *et al.* 1995; Waller and Meyer 1997). While attentional bias and cognitive avoidance may appear to be independent processes, there is evidence that the two are linked (de Ruiter and Brosschot 1994). Future research might test models such as that of Beck and Clark (1997), which suggest that there will be a temporal sequence to the two processes, as automatic reactions give way to strategic responses.

COGNITIVE CONTENT

The links between threat processing and eating psychopathology are specific to certain types of threat. Preconscious processing of threats seems to be most highly linked to subsequent overeating when the threat is one of abandonment (Patton 1992; Meyer and Waller in press). In contrast, attentional biases and cognitive avoidance are more strongly shown in relation to self-esteem threats than to physical threats, both among bulimics and among women with unhealthy eating attitudes (e.g. McManus *et al.* 1996; Waller *et al.* 1996; Waller and Meyer in press). Studies of the core beliefs of bulimics (e.g. Waller and Ohanian 1997) demonstrate that they are characterized by feelings of defectiveness and shame, vulnerability, and fears of abandonment. Such findings are consistent with the notion that bulimic women binge eat as a means of escaping awareness of these negative emotions.

THE ORIGINS OF COGNITIVE PROCESSES UNDERLYING EMOTIONAL EATING

There has been considerable research detailing the aetiology and maintenance of bulimic psychopathology, much of which is likely to relate to emotionally-driven eating. It should be remembered that bulimia can best be seen as a disorder of multifactorial origin, where it is critical to understand distal and proximal antecedents as well as maintaining consequences (e.g. Lacey 1986). The factors outlined below can fit at a number of different points within such a framework.

PSYCHOSOCIAL ORIGINS OF THREAT PROCESSING CHARACTERISTICS

To date, this area has received relatively little attention in the field of eating disorders. However, three factors merit particular consideration. First, clinicians and researchers have reported links between bulimic symptomatology and reported abuse or neglect (e.g. Goldfarb 1987; Waller 1992; Rorty *et al.* 1994). Root and Fallon (1989) have described the functional role of bingeing in reducing the cognitive and affective consequences of traumatic childhood experiences. In addition, bulimic women who report a history of sexual abuse show an attentional bias towards abuse-related information, and the extent of that bias is proportional to the severity of their bulimic symptomatology (e.g. Waller and Ruddock 1995; Waller *et al.* 1995). Waller and Ruddock suggest that the abusive experience is over-represented cognitively, and that the bulimic behaviour serves to reduce awareness of it. When considering the content of the cognitions, this link between traumatic experiences and the onset of bulimia has been attributed to poor self-esteem and to self-denigratory beliefs (e.g. Silverstone 1990). For example, Andrews (1992) and Pitts and Waller (1993) found that women have self-denigratory cognitions (e.g. self-blame, self-criticism, shame) following abuse, and that such self-denigration is linked with high levels of bulimic behaviours (e.g. Swift and Letven 1984). However, abuse is a complex, multifaceted entity. Recent evidence (Kent and Waller in press) suggests that the critical factor in the association of traumatic experiences and eating psychopathology may be the victim's experience of emotional abuse, rather than sexual or physical trauma *per se*.

Second, certain types of parenting styles and family interaction have been found to be linked with eating disorders (e.g. Smolak *et al.* 1990; Pike and Rodin 1991; Hodes *et al.* 1997). Several models of bulimia have stressed the importance of abandonment-related schemata (e.g. Patton 1992; Meyer and Waller in press). The development of such schemata is likely to be related to life events such as loss or separation in the context of inflexible family structures, which are relatively common among bulimics (e.g. Pyle *et al.* 1981; Williams and Charmove 1990).

Finally, as outlined earlier, it is important to consider the role of coping mechanisms in maintaining bulimic psychopathology. Dissociation is a critical factor in the development of bulimia (e.g. Vanderlinden *et al.* 1993), assisting the individual in coping with the immediate aversive emotional state. However, such avoidant coping mechanisms do not resolve the emotional state, and are likely to be followed by the development of a cycle of avoidance of aversive emotions through bulimic behaviours (Fryer *et al.* 1997). Neckowitz and Morrison (1991) confirmed that bulimic women made greater use of escape-avoidant coping in stressful situations than a comparison group.

In summary, there is some preliminary evidence that the links between developmental life events and bulimic psychopathology can be understood as a result of the impact of those events upon the individual's cognitive and emotional development. It is clear that it is the cognitive and emotional consequences of such experiences (e.g. over-elaboration of schemata) that lead to bulimic psychopathology, rather than the event *per se*. However, it is also necessary to understand the individual's contribution to this process through the failure to employ positive coping mechanisms, which would resolve the aversive emotion or the situation that evoked them.

NEUROBIOLOGICAL FACTORS INVOLVED IN THE AFFECTIVE MODEL OF BULIMIC PSYCHOPATHOLOGY

As with any psychological disorder, there have been substantial efforts to understand the physical structures and processes that underpin the eating disorders. Perhaps more so than most other disorders, building a neurobiological model of anorexia and bulimia nervosa suffers from extraordinary problems of causal inference. These disorders involve such extreme abnormalities of nutritional intake that it is very difficult to establish causal direction. Such a problem is hard to overcome through the use of prospective studies with the eating disorders, because these disorders have a relatively low incidence rate and a point of onset that is so difficult to trace. It can be argued that many physical abnormalities could be either antecedents or consequences of the extreme dietary abnormalities. Similarly, many of the findings are inconsistent. For example, genetic studies to date have tended to suggest that there is some genetic predisposition to develop eating disorders, but the level of concordance among both monozygotic and dizygotic twins varies much more among bulimics than among anorexics (Treasure and Holland 1995). It is also clear that simply knowing that there is a genetic loading for an eating disorder tells us nothing about the carrier mechanisms, and that the mechanism might equally involve satiety, emotion or personality processes. For the moment, given the limited amount of reliable research that is available, it is best to consider a relatively small set of neurobiological systems.

NEUROLOGICAL STRUCTURE

Early biological models of the eating disorders focused on the aetiology of anorexia nervosa, and have generally proved impossible to substantiate. In general, the relatively gross physical changes that were cited (e.g. shrinkage of the hypothalamus; Hsu 1983; shrinkage of cortical mass relative to ventricular size) could more readily be explained as a consequence of starvation rather than as a causal factor. More recently, it has been suggested that prepubescent anorexics display a characteristic deficit in blood flow of the dorsal temporal lobe, although that deficit is not reliably located on a particular lobe (Lask 1997). It has been suggested that these preliminary findings are of interest because the deficit often does not revert to normal with weight gain, and because the area affected is part of the system that processes information about body shape, hunger and satiety. These conclusions should be treated with caution, because they do not establish any causal direction. However, even if there is a causal role for this aspect of brain structure, one should not forget that this part of the brain has a crucial role in the experience of emotion, and it may be that any deficit in this structure has an impact via emotional eating, rather than via satiety.

When considering bulimic disorders, there is almost no research suggesting deficits at this gross structural level. The physiological evidence to date suggests a number of *potential* links between brain structure and process and bulimia nervosa, but those links are found at the nutritional and biochemical levels.

NEUROBIOLOGICAL CORRELATES OF STARVATION AND THEIR INFLUENCE ON BULIMIA

Several researchers have found biological correlates of starvation among bulimics. Such relationships have led authors to suggest that the relationship may be causal, with prolonged starvation leading to a predisposition to bulimic behaviours (e.g. Laessle *et al.* 1996). Other theories suggest that those biological substrates that moderate appetitive behaviour are critical in the psychophysiology of bulimia. For example, Lydiard *et al.* (1993) found low levels of the neuroactive peptide cholecystokinin octapeptide in bulimic individuals. It is also worthy of note that binge eating often occurs following the consumption of 'forbidden' foods (e.g. Abraham and Beumont 1982). Thus, the mechanisms which control food cravings (particularly for high carbohydrate and sweet foods) may be important in explaining factors which precipitate binge eating. However, the evidence to date remains correlational, and many of the observed relationships might follow different causal paths. It is also important to understand that motivated behaviour will result only if the level of inhibition is low. It is possible that the consumption of 'forbidden' foods only becomes possible if one has gone through the emotionally-driven process of 'escape from awareness' (Heatherton and Beaumeister 1991) and the subsequent disinhibition of behaviour. Such a model would suggest that the neurobiological consequences of starvation can best be understood as a predisposing factor to bulimic behaviour, but not as a sufficient antecedent.

NUTRITIONAL HOMEOSTASIS

The craving of certain types of food is thought to result from a drive for homeostasis, where the desire to eat is aimed at redressing nutritional deficits. For example, cravings for chocolate by menstruating women have been described as an attempt to redress magnesium deficiencies (e.g. Weingarten and Elston 1990). However, no empirical evidence exists which matches the craved substance and nutritional deficit, and it is clear that nutritional deficiencies are not the best predictors of the types of food eaten (e.g. Hurst *et al.* 1982). Instead, it has been suggested that biological factors may influence the specific content of food intake only in extreme conditions of deficit (e.g. Spitzer and Rodin 1981). In conclusion, Gannon (1985) suggests that the homeostatic model of food craving (and hence overeating) is rather simplistic. Such conclusions underline the importance of considering other influences, such as the link between affect and craving.

BIOCHEMICAL FACTORS

There have been many studies of neuroendocrine and neurotransmitter function following periods of starvation (including restrictive anorexia), but fewer that address bulimia nervosa or its symptoms (e.g. Fichter and Pirke 1995). This literature is dogged by problems of causal direction and definition of recovery from restrictive states, and Fichter and Pirke point out the difficulties of teasing out the role of mood in such studies.

Recent research has focused on the role of serotonin in the regulation of bulimic behaviour. There has been considerable interest in the use of selective serotonin reuptake inhibitors (SSRIs) such as fluoxetine, which were originally developed as antidepressants (as is the case with many drugs that have some impact upon bulimia). These drugs have good efficacy in reducing symptomatology among a number of bulimics, although there is little evidence that these effects are sustained in the long term (e.g. Fairburn and Peveler 1990; Goldbloom and Olmsted 1993). The logic behind the use of these drugs with bulimics is that serotonin participates in the regulation of satiety, as well as the modulation of mood (e.g. Blundell 1991). Decreased levels of serotonin lead to an impaired perception of satiety, and therefore may to contribute to binge-eating behaviour (Leibowitz *et al.* 1988). In a causal argument, Jimerson *et al.* (1990) postulate that an abnormal regulation of serotonin provides a neurobiological vulnerability for eating disorders. Such vulnerability is thought to be caused by an impaired post-ingestive satiety, leading to concurrent or sequential patterns of binge eating (e.g. Halmi 1996).

Once one considers the role of emotional factors in bulimic psychopathology, this causal argument becomes much less clear. The evidence that we have cited clearly demonstrates that intolerable emotional states can be blocked from one's mind through the use of bulimic behaviours. Therefore, it can be argued that the use of antidepressants may have an impact on bulimic psychopathology because they do what they were originally intended to do—reduce negative affective states. This argument would account for the partial effectiveness of other antidepressants (e.g. desipramine, clomipramine), which have radically different biochemical effects. As is usual in such circumstances, an adequate explanation would probably involve a complex fusion of the two models—serotonin metabolism is likely to affect bulimic behaviour via both neurobiological satiety mechanisms and mood states. An important piece of research in this field would be to discover whether there are individual differences in the mechanisms via which the SSRIs have their impact upon bulimic behaviours, and why they appear to have no effect upon many bulimic individuals.

SUMMARY

To summarize, the neurobiological models of bulimia that have been proposed are still at a relatively undeveloped stage. They are in need of further evidence, particularly teasing apart the appetitive/starvation model and the emotional model. Until that evidence is forthcoming, one can only speculate on the links between neurobiology and cognitive process in the driving of emotional eating. For example, it is likely that the majority of the cognitive and emotional content associated with bulimia will be in the cortical and limbic structures. It is also likely that the (related) processes of attentional bias and cognitive avoidance will reflect largely cortical activity. However, the preconscious screening of emotional (but not appetitive) material may involve a different process and set of structures. Dixon (1981) claims that there are very plausible physiological bases for the unconscious discrimination of relevant stimuli. First, cortical receiving areas can respond to the meaning of sensory inflow before it achieves conscious representation. Second, the cortex can regulate its own level of activation by centrifugal control of the ascending reticular activating system. These two foregoing operations are made possible by the fact that transmission rates from the sensory receptors to the cortex are faster than those in the non-specific collateral pathways to the reticular system. Dixon concludes that the unconscious discrimination of emotional stimuli is predictable from what we know of the underlying neurophysiology. Finally, it is possible that some of the dissociative and 'escape from awareness' phenomena involve an unusual pattern of cortical processing of information (e.g. van der Kolk 1997).

There is more evidence of a link between neurobiological factors and the starvation model of eating and cravings, and there is strong evidence that the serotonergic system plays a part. However, these relationships are far from simple, and it may also be necessary to address other physiological factors, such as gastric emptying (Robinson and McHugh 1995). What is clear is that a fully informative model of the eating disorders will need to be able to account for the neurobiological factors cited here, as well as the integrated emotional/starvation model that has been outlined earlier in this chapter and elsewhere (McManus and Waller 1995).

CLINICAL IMPLICATIONS AND FUTURE RESEARCH

CLINICAL IMPLICATIONS

There is little evidence that a single psychotherapeutic approach is superior in the treatment of the eating disorders (e.g. Hartmann *et al.* 1992), although the majority of well-controlled studies that have demonstrated therapeutic gains have employed cognitive–behavioural therapies (Mitchell *et al.* 1996). In addition, some anti-depressants have at least a short-term impact upon bulimic behaviours. These findings have been used to support the starve–binge and neurobiological models of bulimia. However, recent studies have shown that other therapies can also be effective, including interpersonal therapy (Fairburn *et al.* 1995) and cognitive–analytic therapy (e.g. Treasure *et al.* 1995). These findings are more compatible with the emotional model of eating disorders, as such therapies are likely to address emotional factors and their antecedents.

The greatest challenge at present is to develop structured, effective therapies that are individual-centred. Where the aetiology of an individual's eating disorder centres on starvation–binge cycle, then the existing CBT model of Fairburn and Cooper (1989) seems likely to be sufficient. However, where the core problem is emotional, logic would suggest that the focus of the therapy should be the affective antecedents and consequences of the bulimic behaviours. Clinicians have suggested that it may be appropriate to use relatively complex therapies (such as schema-focused cognitive therapy or cognitive–analytic therapy: Bell 1996; Kennerley 1997) to address the eating disorders where emotional factors and associated antecedents are present. If one accepts the logic of targeting therapy on the central pathology, then it is vital that the assessment and formulation of the case should be appropriately informative, incorporating an understanding of cognitive, affective and neurobiological status.

FUTURE RESEARCH

In order to understand bulimic psychopathology, research to date has focused on starvation, affective and neurobiological factors in isolation. In future, it will be necessary to understand the interaction of these aspects of human functioning. It will also be important to consider the role of moderators (such as genetics, temperament and life events) and mediating factors. Central to the mediators (or 'carrier' mechanisms) will be the role of cognitive process and content, and the role of neurobiological mechanisms. For example, the role of serotonin has yet to be fully understood—does it have its impact via mood or satiety?

SUMMARY

Bulimic psychopathology involves a complex interaction of aetiological and maintaining factors. While early researchers have focused on the starve–binge process, this has been shown to be inadequate as an explanation, and it is clear that emotionally driven bulimic behaviours need to be incorporated into any model of bulimia nervosa. There is preliminary clinical and research evidence for the cognitive correlates of emotionally driven bulimic psychopathology. Future research and clinical work should build on this evidence base, but will need to incorporate and explain the role of neurobiological factors, in order to develop a fully integrated model of bulimia. Given this complexity of pathological routes, therapeutic developments will also need to be more complex, and geared to addressing the psychopathology of the individual case.

CLINICAL IMPLICATIONS

- The literature on the aetiology and maintenance of bulimia suggests that it is likely to involve a complex interplay of causes, including starvation, affective states, and associated neurobiological factors.
- However, there will be differences across individuals in the mixture of those causal factors that lead to bulimic psychopathology.

Continued

- Therefore, the most effective approach to the eating disorders will be to understand the aetiology and maintenance for the individual, and to use that information to allocate bulimics to the most appropriate therapy.
- Thus, it is important to focus on the individual case formulation in determining therapy, rather than relying on generic formulations of bulimic disorders.

RESEARCH IMPLICATIONS

- Within the eating disorders, research to date has focused on starvation, affective and neurobiological factors in isolation. It is now important to understand how these factors work interactively.
- Where this interaction is studied, it will be necessary to consider the role of cognitive process and content as potential mediators, or 'carrier' mechanisms.

REFERENCES

Abraham, S.F., & Beumont, P.J.V. (1982). How patients describe bulimia or binge eating. *Psychological Medicine*, **12**, 625–635.

American Psychiatric Association (1994). *Diagnostic and Statistical Manual of Mental Disorders* (4th edn). Washington: American Psychiatric Association.

Andrews, B. (1992). Shame as a mediating factor between early abuse and psychiatric disorder. Paper presented at the British Psychological Society Conference, London, December.

Arnow, B., Kenardy, J., & Agras, W.S. (1992). Binge-eating among the obese: a descriptive study. *Journal of Behavioral Medicine*, **15**, 155–170.

Beck, A.T., & Clark, D.A. (1997). An information processing model of anxiety: automatic and strategic processes. *Behaviour Research and Therapy*, **35**, 49–58.

Bell, L. (1996). Cognitive analytic therapy: its value in the treatment of people with eating disorders. *Clinical Psychology Forum*, **92**, 5–10.

Ben-Tovim, D.I., Walker, M.K., Fok, D., & Yap, E. (1989). An adaptation of the Stroop test for measuring shape and food-concerns in eating disorders: a quantitative measure of psychopathology? *International Journal of Eating Disorders*, **8**, 681–687.

Blundell, J.E. (1991). Pharmacological approaches to appetite suppression. *Trends in Pharmacological Sciences*, **12**, 147–157.

Carlson, E., & Putnam, F.W. (1993). An update on the Dissociative Experiences Scale. *Dissociation*, **6**, 16–27.

Channon, S., Helmsley, D., & de Silva, P. (1988). Selective processing of food words in anorexia nervosa. *British Journal of Clinical Psychology*, **27**, 259–260.

Cooper, M. (1997). Cognitive theory in anorexia nervosa and bulimia nervosa: a review. *Behavioural and Cognitive Psychotherapy*, **25**, 113–145.

Cooper, M.J., & Todd, G. (1997). Selective processing of three types of stimuli in eating disorders. *British Journal of Clinical Psychology*, **36**, 279–281.

Cooper, M.J., Anastasaides, P., & Fairburn, C.G. (1992). Selective processing of eating-, shape-, and weight-related words in persons with bulimia nervosa. *Journal of Abnormal Psychology*, **101**, 352–355.

Cooper, P.J., & Bowskill, R. (1986). Dysphoric mood and overeating. *British Journal of Clinical Psychology*, **25**, 155–156.

Davis, R., Freeman, R.J., & Solyom, L. (1985). Mood and food: an analysis of bulimic episodes. *Journal of Psychiatric Research*, **19**, 331–335.

Davis, R., Freeman, R.J., & Garner, D.M. (1988). A naturalistic investigation of eating behaviour in bulimia nervosa. *Journal of Consulting and Clinical Psychology*, **56**, 273–279.

Demitrack, M.A., Putnam, F.W., Brewerton, T.D., Brandt, H.A., & Gold, P.W. (1990). Relation of clinical variables to dissociative phenomenon in eating disorders. *American Journal of Psychiatry*, **147**, 1184–1188.

de Ruiter, C., & Brosschot, J.F. (1994). The emotional Stroop effect in anxiety: attentional bias or cognitive avoidance? *Behaviour Research and Therapy*, **32**, 315–319.

Dixon, N.F. (1981). *Preconscious Processing*. Chichester: John Wiley & Sons.

Everill, J.T., Waller, G., & Macdonald, W. (1995). Dissociation in bulimic and non-eating-disordered women. *International Journal of Eating Disorders*, **17**, 127–135.

Fairburn, C.G. (1997). Eating disorders. In: D.M. Clark & C.G. Fairburn (eds) *Science and Practice of Cognitive Behaviour Therapy*. Oxford: Oxford University Press.

Fairburn, C.G., & Cooper, P. (1989). Eating disorders. In K. Hawton, P.M. Salkozskis, J. Kirk. and D.M. Clark (eds), *Cognitive Behaviour Therapy for Psychiatric Problems* (pp. 227–314). New York: Oxford University Press.

Fairburn, C.G., & Peveler R.C. (1990). Bulimia nervosa and a stepped care approach to management. *Gut*, **31**, 1220–1222.

Fairburn, C.G., Marcus, M.D., & Wilson, G.T. (1993). Cognitive-behavioural therapy for binge-eating and bulimia nervosa: a comprehensive treatment manual. In C.G. Fairburn & G.T. Wilson (eds), *Binge-eating: Nature, Assessment and Treatment* (pp. 361–404). New York: Guilford Press.

Fairburn, C.G., Norman, P.A., Welch, S.L., O'Connor, M.E., Doll, H.A., & Peveler, R.C. (1995). A prospective study of outcome in bulimia nervosa and the long-term effects of three psychological treatments. *Archives of General Psychiatry*, **52**, 304–312.

Fichter, M.M., & Pirke, K.M. (1995). Starvation models and eating disorders. In G. Szmuckler, C. Dare, & J. Treasure (eds), *Handbook of Eating Disorders: Theory, Treatment and Research* (pp. 83–108). Chichester: Wiley.

Fryer, S., Waller, G., & Stenfert Kroese, B. (1997). Stress, coping and eating attitudes in teenage girls. *International Journal of Eating Disorders*. **22**, 427–436.

Gannon, L.R. (1985). *Menstrual Disorders and Menopause*. New York: Praeger.

Garner, D., & Bemis, K.M. (1982). A cognitive-behavioural approach to anorexia nervosa. *Cognitive Therapy and Research*, **6**, 123–150.

Garner, D.M., & Garfinkel, P.E. (1997). *Handbook of Treatment for Eating Disorders* (2nd edn). New York: Guilford Press.

Garner, D.M., Fairburn, C.G., & Davis, R. (1987). Cognitive-behavioural treatment of bulimia nervosa: a critical appraisal. *Behaviour Modification*, **11**, 398–431.

Goldbloom, D.S., & Olmsted, M.P. (1993). Pharmacotherapy of bulimia nervosa with fluoxetine: assessment of clinically significant attitudinal change. *American Journal of Psychiatry*, **150**, 770–774.

Goldfarb, L.A. (1987). Sexual abuse antecedent to anorexia nervosa, bulimia, and compulsive overeating: three case reports. *International Journal of Eating Disorders*, **19**, 423–433.

Grilo, C.M., Shiffman, S., & Carter-Campbell, J.T. (1994). Binge eating antecedents in normal-weight non-purging females: is there consistency? *International Journal of Eating Disorders*, **16**, 239–249.

Halmi, K.A. (1996). The psychobiology of eating behaviour in anorexia nervosa. *Psychiatry Research*, **62**, 23–29.

Hartmann, A., Herzog, T., & Drinkmann, D. (1992). Psychotherapy for bulimia nervosa: What is effective? A meta analysis. *Journal of Psychosomatic Research*, **36**, 159–167.

Heatherton, T.F., & Beaumeister, R.F. (1991). Binge eating as an escape from self-awareness. *Psychological Bulletin*, **110**, 86–108.

Hodes, M., Timimi, S., & Robinson, P. (1997). Children of mothers with eating disorders: a preliminary study. *European Eating Disorders Review*, **5**, 11–24.

Hsu, L.K.G. (1983). The aetiology of anorexia nervosa. *Psychological Medicine* **13**, 231–238.

Hurst, W.J., Martin, R.A., Zoumas, B.L. & Tarka, S.M. (1982). Biogenic amines in chocolate—a review. *Nutrition Reports International*, **26**, 1081–1086.

Jimerson, D.C., Lesem, M.D., Kaye, W.H., Hegg, A.P., & Brewerton, T.D. (1990). Eating disorders and depression: is there a serotonin connection? *Biological Psychiatry*, **28**, 443–454.

Kennerley, H. (1997). Managing complex eating disorders using schema-based cognitive therapy. Paper presented at the British Association of Behavioural and Cognitive Psychotherapy conference, Canterbury UK, July.

Kent, A., Waller, G., & Dagnan, D. A greater role of emotional than physical or sexual abuse in predicting disordered eating attitudes: the role of mediating variables. *International Journal of Eating Disorders*. in press.

Lacey, J.H. (1986). Pathogenesis. In L.J. Downey & J.C. Malkin (eds) *Current Approaches: Bulimia Nervosa* (pp 17–26). Southampton: Duphar.

Laessle, R.G., Platte, P., Schweiger, U., & Pirke, K.M. (1996). Biological and psychological correlates of intermittent dieting behaviour in young women. A model for bulimia nervosa. *Physiology and Behaviour*, **60**, 1–5.

Lask, B. (1997). Neuroimaging in young anorexia patients. Paper presented at the 14th World Congress on Psychosomatic Medicine, Cairns, August.

Leibowitz, S.F., Weiss, G.F., & Shor-Posner, G. (1988). Hypothalamic serotonin: pharmacological, biological, and behavioural analyses of its feeding-suppressive action. *Clinical Neuropharmacology*, **11**, S51–S71.

Long, C.J., Hinton, C., and Gillespie, N.K. (1994). Selective processing of food and body size words: application of the Stroop test with obese restrained eaters, anorexics and normals. *International Journal of Eating Disorders*, **15**, 279–283.

Lydiard, R.B., Brewerton, T.D., Fossey, M.D. *et al.* (1993). CSF cholecystokinin octapeptide in patients with bulimia nervosa and in normal comparison subjects. *American Journal of Psychiatry*, **150**, 1099–1101.

Marlatt, G.A. (1987). Craving notes. *British Journal of Addiction*, **82**, 42–43.

McManus, F., & Waller, G. (1995). A functional analysis of binge-eating. *Clinical Psychology Review*, **15**, 845–865.

McManus, F., Waller, G., & Chadwick, P. (1996). Biases in the processing of different forms of threat in bulimic and comparison women. *Journal of Nervous and Mental Disease*, **184**, 547–554.

Meyer, C., & Waller, G. The impact of emotion upon eating behaviour: the role of subliminal visual processing of threat cues. *International Journal of Eating Disorders*. in press.

Mitchell, J.E., Hoberman, H.N., Peterson, C.B., Mussell, M., & Pyle, R.L. (1996). Research on the psychotherapy of bulimia nervosa: half empty of half full. *International Journal of Eating Disorders*, **20**, 219–229.

Neckowitz, P., & Morrison, T.L. (1991). Interactional coping strategies of normal weight bulimic women in intimate and nonintimate stressful situations. *Psychological Reports*, **69**, 1167–1175.

Parry-Jones, B., & Parry-Jones, W.L. (1991). Bulimia—an archival review of its history in psychosomatic medicine. *International Journal of Eating Disorders*, **10**, 129–143.

Patton, C.J. (1992). Fear of abandonment and binge eating: a subliminal psychodynamic activation investigation. *Journal of Nervous and Mental Disease*, **180**, 484–490.

Pike, K.M., & Rodin, J. (1991). Mothers, daughters, and disordered eating. *Journal of Abnormal Psychology*, **100**, 198–204.

Pitts, C., & Waller, G. (1993). Self-denigratory beliefs following sexual abuse: association with the symptomatology of bulimic disorders. *International Journal of Eating Disorders*, **13**, 407–410.

Polivy, J., & Herman, C.P. (1985). Dieting and bingeing: a causal analysis. *American Psychologist*, **40**, 193–201.

Pyle, R.L., Mitchell, J.E., & Ekert, E.D. (1981). Bulimia: a report of 34 cases. *Journal of Clinical Psychiatry*, **42**, 60–64.

Reiger, E., Schotte, D.E., Touyz, S.W., Beumont, P.J.V., Griffiths, R., & Russell, J. Attentional biases in eating disorders: a visual probe detection procedure. *International Journal of Eating Disorders*. in press.

Reiser, L.W. (1990). The oral triad and the bulimic quintet—understanding the bulimic episode. *International Review of Psychoanalysis*, **17**, 239–248.

Robinson, P.H. & McHugh, P.R. (1995). A physiology of starvation that sustains eating disorders. In: *Handbook of Eating Disorders: Theory, Treatment and Research* (eds G. Szmuckler, C. Dare & J. Treasure), pp. 109–124. Chichester, Wiley.

Root, M.P.P., & Fallon, P. (1989). Treating the victimized bulimic. *Journal of Interpersonal Violence*, **4**, 90–100.

Rorty, M., Yager, J., & Rossotto, E. (1994). Childhood sexual, physical, and psychological abuse and their relationship to comorbid psychopathology in bulimia nervosa. *International Journal of Eating Disorders*, **16**, 317–334.

Russell, G.F.M. (1979). Bulimia nervosa: an ominous variant of anorexia nervosa. *Psychological Medicine*, **9**, 429–448.

Schotte, D.E., McNally, R.J., & Turner, M.L. (1990). A dichotic listening analysis of body weight concern in bulimia nervosa. *International Journal of Eating Disorders*, **9**, 109–113.

Shulman, D. (1991). A multitiered view of bulimia. *International Journal of Eating Disorders*, **10**, 333–343.

Silverstone, P.H. (1990). Low self-esteem in eating disordered patients in the absence of depression. *Psychological Reports*, **67**, 276–278.

Smolak, L., Levine, M., & Sullins, E. (1990). Are child sexual experiences related to eating-disordered attitudes and behaviours in a college sample? *International Journal of Eating Disorders*, **9**, 167–178.

Spiegel, D., & Cardeña, E. (1991). Disintegrated experience: the dissociative disorders revisited. *Journal of Abnormal Psychology*, **100**, 366–378.

Spitzer, L., & Rodin, J. (1981). Human eating behaviour: a critical review of studies in normal weight and overweight individuals. *Appetite*, **2**, 293–329.

Swift, W.J., & Letven, R. (1984). Bulimia and the basic fault: a psychoanalytic interpretation of the binge–vomiting syndrome. *Journal of the American Academy of Child Psychiatry*, **23**, 489–497.

Telch, C.F., & Agras, W.S. (1996). The effects of acute caloric deprivation and induced negative mood on binge-eating in subjects with binge eating disorder. Poster presented at the Eating Disorders Research Society meeting, Pittsburgh, November.

Tobin, D.L., Griffing, A., & Griffing, S. (1997). An examination of subtype criteria for bulimia nervosa. *International Journal of Eating Disorders*, **22**, 179–186.

Treasure, J., & Holland, A. (1995). Genetic factors in eating disorders. In G. Szmuckler, C. Dare, & J. Treasure. (eds), *Handbook of Eating Disorders: Theory, Treatment and Research* (pp 65–82). Chichester: Wiley.

Treasure, J., Todd, G., Brolly, M., Tiller, J., Nehmed, A., & Denman, F. (1995). A pilot study of a randomized trial of cognitive analytic therapy vs educational behaviour therapy for adult anorexia nervosa. *Behaviour Research and Therapy*, **33**, 363–367.

van der Kolk, B. (1997). The psychobiology of post-traumatic stress disorder. Paper given at the 14th World Congress on Psychosomatic Medicine. August.

Vanderlinden, J., Vandereycken, W., van Dyke, R., & Vertommen, H. (1993). Dissociative experiences and trauma in eating disorders. *International Journal of Eating Disorders*, **13**, 187–193.

Waller, G. (1992). Sexual abuse and the severity of bulimic symptoms. *British Journal of Psychiatry*, **161**, 90–93.

Waller, G., & Ruddock, A. (1995). Information processing correlates of reported sexual abuse in eating disordered and comparison women. *Child Abuse and Neglect*, **19**, 745–759.

Waller, G., & Meyer, C. (1997). Cognitive avoidance of threat cues: association with Eating Disorder Inventory scores among a non-eating disordered population. *International Journal of Eating Disorders*, **22**, 299–308.

Waller, G., & Ohanian, V. (1997). Core beliefs of women with eating disorders. Paper presented at Eating Disorders '97 Conference, London, April.

Waller, G., & Mijatovich, S. Preconscious processing of threat cues: impact on eating among women with unhealthy eating attitudes. *International Journal of Eating Disorders*. in press.

Waller, G., Quinton, S., & Watson, D. (1995). The processing of threat related information by women with bulimic eating attitudes. *International Journal of Eating Disorders*, **18**, 189–193.

Waller, G., Ruddock, A., & Cureton, S. (1995). Cognitive correlates of reported sexual abuse in eating-disordered women. *Journal of Interpersonal Violence*, **10**, 176–187.

Waller, G., Watkins, H., Shuck, V., & McManus, F. (1996). Bulimic psychopathology and attentional biases to ego-threats among non-eating-disordered women. *International Journal of Eating Disorders*, **20**, 169–176.

Wardle, J. (1980). Dietary restraint and binge eating. *Behaviour Analysis Modification* **4**, 201–209.

Waters, A. (1996). The experience of food cravings in bulimia nervosa. Doctoral thesis: University of Leeds.

Waters, A., Hill, A.J. & Waller, G. The role of food cravings in bulimia nervosa: Is binge-eating driven by emotions or hunger. *Journal of Abnormal Psychology*. Submitted.

Weingarten, H., & Elston, D. (1990). The phenomenology of food cravings. *Appetite*, **15**, 231–246.

Williams, G., & Charmove, A.S. (1990). Eating disorders, perceived control, assertiveness and hostility. *British Journal of Clinical Psychology*, **29**, 327–335.

13 Neurobiological Aspects of Early Onset Eating Disorders

D. CHRISTIE, R. BRYANT-WAUGH, B. LASK and I. GORDON*
*Department of Psychological Medicine and *Department of Radiology, Great Ormond Street Hospital, London, UK*

INTRODUCTION

This chapter describes advances in our understanding and knowledge of neurobiological aspects of eating disorders that develop in childhood and early adolescence. In order to set the scene we review the different types of eating disorder and eating difficulty that occur in children and adolescents between the ages of seven and fourteen. Children in this age range constitute an 'early onset' eating disorder population, which does not include infants and pre-school children. In our own clinic providing a service for such children and their families approximately one quarter of referrals are boys.

Children referred for treatment of an eating disorder tend to receive a diagnosis of either anorexia nervosa or eating disorder-not otherwise specified (EDNOS) using the DSM-IV classification system (American Psychiatric Association 1994), or of anorexia nervosa, atypical anorexia nervosa, or eating disorder unspecified using the ICD-10 system (World Health Organization 1992). In our experience children aged 12 and under very rarely present with bulimia nervosa and its variants, although this becomes more common in 13- and 14-year olds.

Well over half the children attending our eating disorders clinic fall into an 'unspecified' or 'atypical' category in formal diagnostic terms. This group of 'atypicals' includes those with subclinical anorexia nervosa and the majority of the boys—a few of whom have DSM-IV/ICD-10 anorexia nervosa, but they are more likely to present with unspecified disorders. Our clinical experience indicates that there are clear differences between the types of disturbance within the atypical and unspecified groups. For those not fulfilling formal diagnostic criteria for anorexia nervosa or bulimia nervosa our team currently uses the following terms (operational definitions and further description are given below):

- food avoidance emotional disorder
- selective eating
- functional dysphagia
- pervasive refusal syndrome

Neurobiology in the Treatment of Eating Disorders.
Edited by H.W. Hoek, J.L. Treasure and M.A. Katzman.

FOOD AVOIDANCE EMOTIONAL DISORDER (FAED)

This term was first used by Higgs *et al.* (1989) to describe a group of underweight children presenting with inadequate food intake and emotional disturbance who did not meet existing diagnostic criteria for anorexia nervosa. The original description indicated that food avoidance, food faddiness, or dietary restriction tended to be long-standing and that the food avoidance was a prominent feature at presentation. In children with this disorder the avoidance of food has an emotional basis and is not related to organic brain disease, psychosis or drug related causes. Girls seem to be affected more than boys, and children presenting with this type of eating problem tend to be physically unwell (Nicholls *et al.* 1997). They may also present with growth delay, and sometimes have a history of failure to thrive.

Our own operational definition has evolved from Higgs and colleagues' original description together with clinical experience and is as follows:

- weight loss
- food avoidance not accounted for by primary affective disorder
- mood disturbance not meeting criteria for primary affective disorder
- no abnormal cognitions about weight and shape
- no morbid preoccupation with weight or shape
- no organic brain disease or psychosis

SELECTIVE EATING

Selective eaters are a heterogeneous group of children who present with very restricted eating habits in terms of the range of foods they will accept. The majority of selective eaters that we see are boys. Our current operational definition is as follows:

- child has eaten a narrow range of foods for at least 2 years
- unwillingness to try new foods
- no abnormal cognitions about weight and shape
- no morbid preoccupation with weight or shape
- weight may be low, normal or high

Selective eaters do not generally represent a cause for concern in physical terms, but may become increasingly socially disadvantaged as they get older. Eating with peers is part of normal adolescent development and pressure to conform with peer eating habits in terms of food type can lead to increasing social difficulty for the selective eater. In some respects a number of these children share features with those with Asperger's syndrome, i.e. resistance to change, poor peer relationships and a degree of emotional aloofness, but this relationship requires further study.

FUNCTIONAL DYSPHAGIA

Children with functional dysphagia generally present with complaints of difficulty or pain on swallowing. Our operational definition is as follows:

- food avoidance
- fear of swallowing, choking or vomiting
- no abnormal cognitions about weight or shape
- no morbid preoccupation with weight or shape
- no organic brain disease or psychosis

In many cases it is possible to identify some event that is clearly linked to the fear of vomiting or choking. This may be either something that has happened to the child, for example a traumatic investigation of the gastrointestinal tract or witnessing someone else choking. Alternatively it may be related to parental fears about the child choking, for example following choking incidents in early childhood. Boys as well as girls may be affected.

PERVASIVE REFUSAL SYNDROME

This is a term first used by Lask *et al.* (1991) to describe a group of children with social withdrawal and a refusal to eat, drink, walk, talk or engage in any activity including self care. This original case series was based on only four children, but a further 21 children have since been described in the literature (Lask 1996; Nunn and Thompson 1996; Thompson and Nunn 1997). It appears that this type of disorder is more likely to be found in girls than in boys. Children with pervasive refusal syndrome may present to an eating disorders clinic because of their refusal to eat and drink. They have a potentially life-threatening condition that often requires lengthy treatment. They share some of the features of a number of different diagnoses (anorexia nervosa, selective mutism, school refusal, somatoform disorders, chronic fatigue syndrome, separation anxiety, depression, catatonic disorders and factitious disorder—see Thompson and Nunn 1997 for detailed discussion) but stand out by the presence of refusal across many aspects of normal functioning. At present our operational definition is as follows:

- profound refusal to eat, drink, walk, talk or self care
- determined resistance to efforts to help

More work needs to be done to determine whether pervasive refusal is a clinically useful term and whether this disorder has an identifiable aetiology. At present it appears to be an extreme response to trauma, although the type and extent of the trauma varies in case descriptions so far.

Finally, children may present for treatment of eating disorder when they in fact fulfil diagnostic criteria for other disorders. The most common are depression, obsessive–compulsive disorder and pain and/or vomiting not otherwise specified. Whilst there is often an element of comorbidity it is clearly important to distinguish those with a primary eating disorder (including atypical and unspecified) from those with other primary diagnoses. Many children with eating disorders are depressed (Fosson *et al.* 1987), whilst obsessive–compulsive symptoms are particularly common in boys with anorexia nervosa (Shafran *et al.* 1995). It should be evident from this introduction that the early onset eating disorder population is a mixed group, both in terms of gender and type of eating disorder.

It is this heterogeneity which makes understanding the aetiology of early onset eating disorders such a difficult task. The relatively recent identification of FAED as a separate group in children and the lack of formal diagnostic criteria means that there are no data on it's neurobiological features. Equally the tendency for selective eaters to be relatively healthy despite only eating a restricted range of foods means that there are few reasons for clinicians to do anymore than attempt to expand dietary repertoire. The majority of data on the neurobiology of eating disorders has focused on the relationship between weight loss and brain function and structure. Interest in the structure of the brain has been focused on several levels of explanation moving from chemical processing to cognitive processing. In order to avoid behaving like the blind men describing the elephant, this chapter aims to offer the reader an integrated and holistic view of all of these levels of understanding with a particular regard to children and adolescents.

NEUROENDOCRINOLOGY AND NEUROTRANSMITTERS

The roles of the neuroendocrine system and of the neurotransmitters in the eating disorders have been comprehensively discussed elsewhere e.g. Beumont Chapter 10; Connan and Treasure Chapter 9 and Carney and Andersen (1996). In this section we review what information, specific to early onset eating disorders, is available; regrettably there is little. Minimal such work has been done in this population because (a) the number of subjects is relatively low, particularly those with bulimia nervosa, (b) it is difficult to obtain a critical mass of subjects to investigate systematically, and (c) ethical concerns dictate that research should only be carried out on children if the findings are likely to be different from those in adults, or if the particular condition being investigated either occurs only in childhood or has an onset in childhood. Whilst each of these obstacles can be overcome, their totality does tend to obstruct research in this area.

The majority of physical findings are predominantly related to starvation, dehydration or the effects of bingeing and purging, with significant alterations occurring across a broad spectrum of physiological parameters. This makes the results of investigations difficult to interpret, at least in terms of their aetiological significance. As children and young adolescents normally have higher energy demands and lower levels of body fat, the physical findings associated with eating disorders may occur sooner with the starvation effects having a more rapid onset. Once weight loss and dehydration occur the usual mechanisms for the release and inhibition of various regulators of eating behaviour change, and a new set of regulating mechanisms is established (Weiner 1985).

In post-pubertal anorexia nervosa (AN) it has been firmly established that the illness is associated with a hypothalamic disorder, manifest by an endocrine disturbance involving the hypothalamic–anterior pituitary–gonadal axis (Russell

1992). The most widely accepted current view suggests that most endocrine changes in AN are a consequence of weight loss, increased exercise, changes in macronutrient content, and possibly anxiety (Carney and Andersen 1996). 'Primary endocrinological disorders may mimic the medical features of self-induced starvation but do not produce the core psychopathological features of a morbid fear of fatness and a relentless pursuit of thinness'. Experimental support for this view comes from the work of Fichter *et al.* (1983) who showed that the characteristic endocrine alterations seen in AN can be induced in normal individuals by voluntary semi-starvation and resolved with weight restoration alone. One of the most common endocrine events related to weight loss in post-pubertal AN is the cessation of menses. For pre-pubertal children significant weight loss can lead to delayed puberty with primary amenorrhoea. Pubertal onset is delayed until there has been sufficient weight gain (Russell 1992) although there is variation in the weight for height ratio or Body Mass Index at which menses recommences (Treasure *et al.* 1988; Lai *et al.* 1994). There has been controversy with regard to whether there is a minimum weight upon which the onset of puberty is dependent. Frisch and Revelle (1971) have maintained that there must be at least a critical body composition (17% as stored fat) whilst others have been dismissive of this view (e.g. Billewicz *et al.* 1981). The complex relationships between nutritional status, the hypothalamic–pituitary–adrenal axis and the reproductive organs are not fully understood. What is certain is that in the presence of malnutrition, growth and pubertal development are delayed or arrested (Russell 1992).

Russell (1992) has argued that the effects of weight loss on endocrine function can be surmised by following the stages of endocrine recovery as weight is restored.

> In post-pubertal subjects blood levels of gonadotrophins (LH and FSH) and oestrogen gradually rise. Early on the action of gonadotrophin-releasing hormone is restored to normal, indicating a return of the functional capacity of the anterior pituitary. Most significant is the return of hypothalamic responsiveness to administered oestrogen which in turn influences the release of LH.

In early childhood the ovaries are amorphous with very small follicles (micro-follicles) and the uterus is small and teardrop shaped. As weight increases at an age-appropriate rate the ovaries enlarge and demonstrate multiple small follicles, whilst the uterus also enlarges. As puberty is reached, the ovaries achieve their maximum volume and have a dominant or ovulatory follicle. The uterus becomes tubular in shape, also reaches its maximum volume and develops an endometrial lining. These changes are accompanied by a rise in follicle-stimulating hormone (FSH) and luteinizing hormone (LH) levels. With malnutrition, as seen in anorexia nervosa, the process goes into reverse, with an end-point of infantile ovaries and uterus and very low levels of FSH and LH. The use of pelvic ultrasound to monitor endocrine development and recovery in children with eating disorders was first described by

Lai *et al.* (1994). They described a cohort of 26 girls diagnosed with anorexia nervosa (age range 10.4–15.7). The mean weight for height for the group was 81%. The authors found a regression in pelvic organs which was reversible with weight gain. Uterine volume was a significant factor in the onset of menstruation. These findings suggest that the endocrine dysfunction in early anorexia nervosa is indeed secondary to weight loss rather than a primary phenomenon.

A further important aspect of endocrine dysfunction in children is the reduction in growth hormone levels. This can result in disruption to normal growth, in particular the speed and timing of the normal growth spurt being adversely affected. We have found that time of onset of the eating disorder in relation to pubertal development may be important to the attainment of projected final height. Those children who are most at risk appear to be those in whom the pubertal process has been already established but not completed.

The neuroendocrine system is but one component (albeit a very complex one) of an even more complex process involving interactions between multiple peptides, hormones and neurotransmitters. The modulation of eating is controlled by two separate but related systems, the central feeding system and the peripheral satiety system (Silver and Morley 1991). Food intake is regulated peripherally by the release of gastrointestinal peptides from the peripheral satiety system in the stomach and intestine. The chemicals involved include the cholecystokinins (CCKs), bombesin, glucagon, somatostatin, gastrin, secretin, gastric inhibitory polypeptide, and calcitonin. Whilst most of the intestinal peptides work peripherally, several are located in neurones and act as neurotransmitters with receptor sites in the brain (Lucas 1988).

CCK, somatostatin and glucagon summate leading to decreased food intake. Conversely it has been noted that lowered CCK levels lead to bingeing and that actively bulimic women secrete lower levels of CCK (Silver and Morley 1991). Thus, CCK at least appears to play an important part in appetite regulation and eating behaviour, with high levels correlating with diminished food intake and low levels correlating with increased food intake. The mechanisms are not understood but might include peripherally, high levels of CCK leading to delayed gastric emptying and centrally, stimulation of the satiety centre, and low levels of CCK doing the opposite. The process is however likely to be far more complex given that the role of some of the hormones is not yet understood and that there are many different forms of CCK. Nonetheless there is now good evidence to show that CCK does influence satiety and that abnormalities in plasma CCK concentrations occur in the eating disorders (Silver and Morley 1991; Phillip *et al.* 1991; Lamers *et al.* 1995).

The developmental variations in this system are yet to be determined, although it is clear that changes occur with time. Of particular interest is some evidence that although peripheral CCK receptors are present before birth, the central receptors may not develop for some years (Silver and Morley 1991). It is tempting to speculate how significant this may be in relation to the fact that anorexia nervosa and bulimia nervosa are relatively rare before puberty.

Finally, consideration needs to be given to serotonin activity. There is considerable evidence to suggest that serotinin activity is inhibitory and enables the organism to arrange or tolerate delay before acting (Kaye 1997). Low levels in contrast are associated with impulsivity. The possibility arises that there is a spectrum of serotonin activity with impulsive and aggressive behaviours at one end and obsessive, inhibited behaviours at the other. There is additional evidence for this hypothesis in childhood from a study which demonstrated high serotonin activity in children with OCD compared to low levels in those with aggressive disruptive behaviours (Kruesi *et al.* 1991).

Serotonin is also implicated in the aetiology and maintenance of affective disorders, particularly depression. Preventing the re-uptake of serotonin through the use of selective serotonin reuptake inhibitors (SSRIs) has significant therapeutic value although has been shown to be less effective in therapeutic trials in children (Simeon *et al.* 1990).

Secondary neuroendocrine dysfunction is also associated with cerebral insult caused by treatment for cancer (Leiper *et al.* 1987). Endocrine dysfunction, associated with psychological disturbance and symptoms of anorexia nervosa without neurological manifestation may also be presenting features of an early intracranial lesion. DeVile *et al.* (1995) describe three boys who initially presented with features of anorexia nervosa (from a series of 20 with eating disorders) who were found to have tumours affecting the hypothalamus, in two cases, and in the third a tumour impinging upon the brain stem.

How all these observations link together within the context of an eating disorder, particularly in children remains a major challenge to researchers.

NEUROIMAGING

Neuroimaging studies of individuals with anorexia nervosa have revealed alterations in both brain structure and function (Herholz 1996; Katzman *et al.* 1996; Krieg *et al.* 1991; Gordon *et al.* 1997; also see Foong and Ellison, Chapter 11). Most changes are currently interpreted as consequences of the anorectic state that are reversible, at least partially, after weight gain. In contrast a functional study (Gordon *et al.* 1997) has suggested that some abnormalities are not secondary responses to starvation.

Anatomical studies using computerized tomography (CT) and, more recently, magnetic resonance imaging (MRI) show similar features with enlargement of the cerebral spinal fluid (CSF) spaces, mainly of cortical sulci that resolves upon weight gain. This reversible shrinkage of brain tissue ('pseudoatrophy') also affects the pituitary gland (Herholz 1996). Katzman *et al.* (1996) showed, using MRI, that adolescent girls with AN had larger total CSF volumes in association with deficits in both total grey matter and total white matter volumes. Body mass index was inversely correlated with the total CSF volume and positively correlated with total grey matter volume.

One method used to examine the functioning of the brain is measuring metabolic activity levels. Krieg *et al.* (1991) measured regional cerebral glucose metabolism with ^{18}F-2-fluoro-2-deoxyglucose (18FDG) and positron emission tomography (PET) in nine patients with bulimia nervosa and in seven patients with anorexia nervosa. They showed that the ratio between caudate glucose metabolism and global cerebral glucose metabolism was significantly higher in anorexia nervosa than in bulimia nervosa. This relative hypermetabolism in the caudate suggests that caudate hyperactivity is characteristic of the anoretic state. Whether increased caudate function is a consequence of anorexic behaviour or whether it is directly involved in the pathogenesis of anorexia nervosa was not clear to these authors.

Other groups have reported different findings with 18FDG PET studies. Delvenne *et al.* (1995) compared glucose metabolism in 20 young female anorexics (age range 14–30) with a group of 10 normal weight controls (age range 18–30). The underweight anorexic patients showed a global hypometabolism and an absolute, as well as relative, hypometabolism of glucose in cortical regions, with the most significant differences found in the frontal and the parietal cortices, when compared to controls. This hypometabolism was not related to mood as there was no correlation between changes in the regional cortical metabolic rate of glucose (rCMRGlu) and measures of anxiety or depression in either the anorexic or control group (Delvenne *et al.* 1995). These changes were reported to normalize with weight gain (Delvenne *et al.* 1996). The authors argue that although there were no global differences between underweight anorexic patients and controls there is an observed trend toward parietal and superior frontal cortex hypometabolism associated with a relative hypermetabolism in the caudate nuclei and the inferior frontal cortex. After weight gain, all regions normalized for absolute and relative values. Here again though, there was a suggestion of a relative parietal hypometabolism and inferior frontal cortex hypermetabolism in anorexic patients who had gained weight. They suggest that absolute brain glucose hypometabolism might result from neuroendocrinological or morphological aspects of anorexia nervosa or might be the expression of altered neurotransmission following deficient nutritional state. The relative differences which have been demonstrated during low weight and which tend to persist following weight gain may support a model of abnormal cerebral functioning which requires a different reaction to starvation within several regions of the brain or possibly different rates of recovery within these different regions (Delvenne *et al.* 1996).

In a comparison of regional cerebral blood flow in patients with eating disorders Nozoe *et al.* (1995) reported rCBF changes in all areas of the brain except the left temporal region. They suggested that this may indicate a temporal lobe abnormality in anorexia nervosa. Our group has carried out a pilot study involving functional imaging of the brain using regional cerebral blood flow (rCBF) with single photon emission tomography (SPECT) (Gordon *et al.* 1997). Fifteen patients with anorexia nervosa between the ages of 8 and 15 years underwent an rCBF SPECT scan. Hypoperfusion in the temporal lobe was found in 13 of the group (87%). In eight this was on the left side and in five on the right. All children were reported to be right handed. Colleagues at the Children's Hospital in Sydney, Australia have also shown unilateral reduced temporal lobe rCBF in three out of four children with anorexia nervosa (Howman-Giles personal communication).

In a small follow-up study the unilateral hypoperfusion persisted in three out of four children who agreed to a repeat scan when they had regained a relatively normal weight for height. In one child there was a further reduction in rCBF in the basal ganglia on the same side as the temporal lobe abnormality. This child underwent magnetic resonance imaging which showed no abnormality. The fourth child who did not have the abnormal scan appearance after weight gain was the only one in whom distortion of body image had resolved.

The unilateral presentation of the decreased rCBF (Gordon *et al.* 1997) together with the persistence of an abnormality in three out of four patients re-scanned after weight restoration, suggest that the findings cannot be explained as secondary to starvation. Changes in rCBF which are purely secondary to starvation would be likely to produce global and symmetrical decreases in blood flow. The authors believe that the asymmetry may reflect an underlying primary neurological abnormality that is contributing to the development and/or maintenance of anorexia nervosa in these young patients (Gordon *et al.* 1997).

NEUROPSYCHOLOGY

The complex interaction between hormones, neurotransmitters, blood flow and structural changes associated with weight loss is given voice in anorexia nervosa by a determined refusal to eat and the expression of significant distress if made to do so. A preoccupation with shape and weight is justified by an absolute and unshakeable belief that an obviously skeletal body to observers is normal or even fat. An integrated neurobiological perspective requires us to try to add to this complexity by considering how the child with an eating disorder processes information at a cognitive as well as an emotional level.

Cravioto and Arrieta's work (1983) in malnourished children in the Third World suggests that starvation and low body weight have a selective effect on the development of cognitive skills in the developing brain. Deficits in visuospatial functions suggest a preferential sparing of verbal skills at the expense of visuospatial abilities. Functional reorganization in response to focal damage has been described by Isaacs *et al.* (1996) in children with early brain damage. The impact of global or specific insult to the developing brain is partly determined by the level of development of the underlying neural substrate. Different anatomical regions (related to different functional systems) develop at different times therefore resulting in a differential response to insult as a function of age. The consequence of structural changes described in the previous section may therefore be an alteration in information processing ability which adds another necessary level of description.

Emaciated patients with anorexia nervosa have been reported to have an abnormal neuropsychological profile. There is one study (Dally 1969) which reported above average IQs however more recently overall IQ and individual subsets are described as being within the average range (Witt *et al.* 1985; Casper and Heller 1991; Szmukler *et al.* 1992; Gilberg *et al.* 1996; Kingston *et al.* 1996). Dura and Bornstein (1989) also found average IQ with academic attainments (except for mathematics) above expected limits. None of these studies have looked exclusively at a younger, pre-pubertal population. Reported IQs were based on a selection of the subtests. As different subtests assess different facets of intellectual ability it is difficult to ascertain on the basis of estimated IQ scores which aspects of intelligence may be most vulnerable to long term starvation or alternatively may be making a contribution towards the onset of the illness.

Witt *et al.* (1985) reported a specific impairment in associative learning not attributable to problems with attention. This has not been found in other studies which have described difficulties in tasks requiring sustained attention (Laessle *et al.* 1989) and more general problems with attention and concentration (Hamsher *et al.* 1981; Szmukler *et al.* 1982; Pendleton-Jones *et al.* 1991; Kingston *et al.* 1996). Visuospatial processing is also reported to be impaired (Szmukler 1992; Kingston *et al.* 1996) although in a non-eating disordered sample of college students no relationship was found between visuospatial disturbances, body size estimation or bulimic disturbance (Thompson and Spana 1991). Inflexibility and poor planning are identified as a specific cognitive style in anorexic patients (Kingston *et al.* 1996) while other studies have described preferential use of concrete processing (Kowalski 1986) and difficulty shifting between abstract concepts for both anorexic and bulimic groups (Bowers 1994). As yet, no study has clearly demonstrated a clear and satisfactory link between the described cognitive deficits and structural changes.

Follow-up studies after weight gain suggest just as has been described in the section on neuroimaging that some deficits are reversible with weight gain (Szmukler *et al.* 1992; Kingston *et al.* 1996). Interestingly, Hamsher (1981) found that patients who continued to demonstrate neuropsychological deficits following weight gain had poorer long-term outcome than those who did not.

While the neuropsychological profiles are poorly characterized in the adolescent population there are no similar published reports in younger children with anorexia nervosa, in particular those who are pre-pubertal. Equally, there are no studies describing cognitive function in children with FAED or selective eating disorder.

While the plasticity of the developing brain affords greater scope for recovery of function following damage than is seen in adults the ability to regain certain cognitive functions seems to be at the expense of others. To date, there is no information about the long-term impact of low body weight associated with anorexic pathology on the development of intellectual functioning, school performance and cognitive processing in children whose brains are still developing.

GENETICS

Genetic studies of anorexia nervosa and bulimia nervosa are reported by Kaye elsewhere in this section, and need not be repeated here. There is a wide literature on familial patterns of eating disorder, affective disorder and weight and shape concerns. Much of this relates to studies of adults with eating disorders and their relatives. With regard to children and adolescents, family studies have focused primarily on investigating 'shared' weight and eating concerns in mothers and daughters, from both clinical and non-clinical populations. For example, Hill *et al.* (1990) looked at dieting concerns in 10-year-old girls and their mothers; Hall *et al.* (1986) conducted a study comparing a group of mothers of teenagers with eating disorders, with a group of mothers of eating disorder free teenagers; and Pike and Rodin (1991) looked at shared eating concerns in mothers and daughters. However, these studies describe environmental or generational interactive effects and do not clearly separate out the genetic aspects of familial transmission.

These aspects have been explored in a number of twin studies which provide support for the view that there is a genetic element in the development of anorexia nervosa (Scott 1986; Holland *et al.* 1988) and bulimia nervosa (Fichter and Noegel 1990; Hsu *et al.* 1990). Concordance rates in monozygotic twins are highest for anorexia nervosa, at around 50% indicating high heritability. Research continues into the nature of possible mechanisms relating to genetic predisposition.

Strober *et al.*'s (1990) statement that the manner in which genetic and environmental factors combine to produce illness remains uncertain, still applies, and to our knowledge there are no published studies of direct genetic effects with children as eating disorder probands.

In a more recent study attempting to further elucidate familial tendencies regarding eating concerns and psychopathological traits, Steiger *et al.* (1996) conclude that children may be exposed to parents' eating concerns and psychopathology, and that this may lead to similar concerns and psychopathological traits, but that some additional factor is necessary to explain the development of an eating disorder. They suggest that this 'vulnerability factor' might include some specific genetic vulnerability (i.e. a direct genetic effect), the interaction between family processes and other social experiences, some interaction between traits carried by each parent, or most likely a combination of these.

It is clear that there is still a way to go to clarify the relative importance of these different factors. In terms of our own clinical practice we have found it helpful to refer to the notion of 'individual vulnerability'. We describe this vulnerability as probably genetic in origin and probably involving a combination of biological predispositions and personality traits that make some people more likely to develop eating disorders than others. Given the present state of our knowledge regarding the aetiology of eating disorders, and the role of genetic effects, this seems a fair representation and certainly one that has been useful in trying to address a question often asked by parents ''Why our child?''.

IMPLICATIONS FOR CLINICAL PRACTICE

CURRENT PRACTICE

Whilst some children who develop eating disorders can be adequately treated by community services, there are those whose health is sufficiently compromised to require more intensive specialist support. In the UK children who prove resistant to first line treatment from their family doctor may get referred to a paediatrician or another child mental health professional. Some children can be successfully treated on an outpatient basis although a number fail to show a positive response and may require admission to an inpatient setting. This tends to be in a general adolescent psychiatric unit or on a paediatric ward. There are currently very few specialist eating disorder services for children, particularly for those who are pre-pubertal. Children and families referred to our childhood eating disorders team are first seen as a family. We consider this to be a crucial component of the initial assessment. The aim is to evaluate not only contributory factors to the child's illness but much more importantly whether any aspect of family functioning is perpetuating the problem. The child is also seen individually for an individual clinical assessment, a formal assessment of eating disorder pathology and a comprehensive physical assessment. All females will undergo a pelvic ultrasound to assess uterine and ovarian development. A measure of bone density is also obtained. Once the full assessment has been carried out, decisions are made regarding the child and family's treatment needs and how these can best be met.

The first stage of treatment involves emphasizing to the parents their role in their child's recovery. The message is not that they are to blame for the problem but that they are in a strong position to help their child recover.

Parental counselling will be offered on a regular basis while subsequent sessions will be paced depending in the child's physical state (e.g. weight for height ratio, cardiovascular status, electrolyte balance) and the persistence and intensity of the eating disorder psychopathology. Family therapy may also be offered. In addition to this first level of treatment parents may be invited to join a weekly parents' group while children also attend a childrens' group. Individual therapy may be offered to the child in some cases. A range of treatment techniques are offered depending upon the child's needs and stage of development (Christie 1998; Magagna 1998). At all times there are regular reviews of the treatment progress. The integration of knowledge about the neurobiology of early onset eating disorders has important implications for clinical practice.

DIAGNOSTIC ACCURACY

Accurate diagnosis is essential to exclude primary pathology e.g. brain tumours (DeVile *et al.* 1995) or Crohn's disease (Lask 1990). The integration of regular monitoring of physical and endocrine status also allows the detection and rapid treatment of concurrent illness.

MOTIVATION

Equally important is the degree to which concrete information about current, and future, physical state acts as a powerful motivator for both parents and children. Parents who find it difficult to acknowledge that their child is struggling with emotional difficulties may often be able to take physical aspects more seriously. Clinical experience suggests that the knowledge of possible long-term effect of endocrine changes associated with eating disorder on pubertal development and growth can have an impact upon the parents' commitment to treatment. These long-term risks, in some cases, seem to be more persuasive to parents than acute risks (e.g. heart failure). It is also our clinical experience that children who are given proof of the impact of their illness related behaviour on their physical functioning independent from physical appearance (i.e. 'your brain has shrunk and may not be working properly') may be helped at least to begin treatment, even if they do so grudgingly. Lai *et al.* (1994) also comment that pelvic ultrasound scanning is a better motivation for girls with anorexia nervosa than weight or weight for height targets. This focus may also be highly appropriate for individuals who have inflexible and concrete cognitive processing styles. Treatment works on reality based concrete issues rather than emotional distress. There are specific reasons why the child needs to put on weight rather than a general 'you have to or you'll die'. It also contributes to a 'hopeful' therapeutic stance. This acknowledges that weight gain alone does not mean recovery, and explicitly creates a future (Nunn and Thompson 1996) 'If you don't eat now, *when you get better* you may have all these other problems'.

PROFESSIONAL EDUCATION

The role of psycho-educational material is clearly essential in early onset eating disorders. Research and dissemination of knowledge about the neurobiological issue provides important information helping to emphasize the message that weight restoration is a priority in young patients. Sadly we are aware of cases where parents of children who have failed to progress normally along their weight and growth curves are told 'it's just a phase', while the illness becomes increasingly severe.

Awareness of the associated neurobiological factors highlights the dangers of treating the child by 'talking cure' alone. There must be continuing emphasis on associated physical monitoring. This information must be used by the clinician carefully and strategically.

SCHOOL PERFORMANCE

Including neuropsychological findings is a relatively new component to our clinical practice. Although there is little actual evidence (see above) it is believed by many that anorexics are 'super clever' and for many years AN was perceived as an illness seen mostly in over-achieving grade A students. Certainly many of the children who attend our clinic attend selective schools with a strong academic ethos. The research suggests however that many of these children are struggling to achieve levels of performance at the upper limits of their ability. One possible escape from mounting academic pressure may be starvation. This kind of pressure may be a contributory environmental trigger that can only be identified with the help of a comprehensive neuropsychological assessment. IQ testing may help determine what is a realistic expectation for both the child and parents as excessively high standards may be unrealistic. Knowledge of the child's cognitive strengths and weaknesses can also contribute towards decisions about an appropriate therapeutic style and ensure its delivery at an appropriate developmental level.

IMPLICATIONS FOR FUTURE RESEARCH

The clearest message in each of the sections in this chapter is the lack of data on children with eating disorders. While there is increasingly more research on early onset anorexia nervosa, detailed information on the immediate impact and long-term consequences of FAED are not known. The heterogeneous symptomatology of children with selective eating disorders is anecdotal at present and requires further study to determine if in fact there are separate subgroups of children within this diagnostic category.

For all early onset eating disorders the site and nature of an underlying biological substrate remains to be defined. This will require a combination of detailed neuroanatomical and functional imaging and neuropsychological profiling. These should be conducted at different stages of the disease process, including long-term follow-up, allowing us to understand whether any abnormalities are primary, or secondary to weight loss. Subgroups may exist such as those with and without obsessive–compulsive symptoms or with and without purging. It is possible also that differences exist between children and adults, and between males and females. Further studies of young people with eating disorders are clearly required to further our knowledge.

A FINAL THOUGHT

The preparation, serving, acceptance and enjoyment of food plays a central role in our cultural history. The enjoyment of eating is an experience associated with celebrations of life events (births, marriage and even death). Our language is rich with food related synonyms (e.g. hungry for experience, greedy for power, a glutton for punishment). Rejection of food is a rejection of both life and for children parental care.

About 9% of children who have early eating difficulties at the age of 3 continue to be selective eaters by the time they are 8 (Richman *et al.* 1982). Only a small number of these will be seen for treatment because of the low association with poor physical health. At present no-one has any idea what the long-term outcome for children with a limited range, carbohydrate-only diet is. The number of children who will develop an eating disorder which will cause life threatening physical symptoms is not known. The time, money and professional input offered to adults with eating disorders compared to children is exemplified by this book with just one chapter focusing on early onset eating disorders. Are children with anorexia nervosa and/or FAED the anorexics of the future? If the answer to this question is yes, the potential implications in terms of long-term physical and mental ill-health are substantial and thus represent a possible major strain in health resources. We do not have enough longitudinal data to know the answer for certain, but many adolescents with eating disorders describe early histories where early factors (cultural, social and familial) play a part in developing and establishing their anorexic thinking patterns. It may be that biological mechanisms in combination with these early circumstances create an 'anorexic-diathesis' model. If these thinking patterns are established early on it is incumbent upon professionals at all levels to consider mechanisms of secondary prevention. What messages need to be known?

1. Certainly in the UK (and most of the USA) for the first 2–3 years of life children are regularly monitored for weight and height to ensure adequate growth. We propose that this monitoring should ideally continue throughout development. The loss of the school nurse because of funding cuts in UK schools means that children are no longer given a yearly 'check up' and it is all too easy for children to make unilateral decisions about their weight and appearance and act upon those decisions. It is a matter of great concern that children who attend our clinic have been allowed to stop eating for a long enough period of time to lose more than 20% of their body weight. This weight loss may have even been monitored and documented by the primary care physician before a referral is finally made.
2. Primary care health professionals need to be given information about early onset eating disorders to help them recognize, diagnose and treat children under their care (Bryant-Waugh *et al.* 1992). One indicator of concern is children not progressing along their growth curve. Low weight children with primary amenorrhoea are also at risk if the delay in pubertal onset is not consistent with family history. Local paediatric services must be kept up to date with research developments on the long term physical consequences of low weight for height.
3. A thorough assessment of the child's physical condition is critical while the need for brain scans especially in young boys must be considered as an important tool in contributing to a differential diagnosis (DeVile *et al.* 1995). We believe that behavioural weight gain programmes are ineffective for anything other than pure weight gain, and even then may not be successful. Psychological treatment alone may help the child access their inner emotional

world but fail to address the real and dangerous physical consequences of refusal to gain weight.

Treatment is not about blaming parents or 'fixing' the child. Early onset eating disorders are complex and have multifactorial causality. They require an integrated approach to management and care which relies upon an integration of our knowledge at all levels of understanding—which is the only way we will ever really learn what the elephant looks like.

CLINCIAL IMPLICATIONS

- Comprehensive physical assessment must be completed to exclude a primary pathology disorder that may be
  - mimicking the symptoms
  - significantly interacting with psychological factors maintaining the condition
- Understanding the long-term physical effects of the endocrine dysfunction can motivate both parents and children to participate in the treatment process.
- Research and dissemination of knowledge about the neurobiological issues provides important information helping to emphasise the message that weight restoration is a priority in young patients.
- Awareness of the associated neurobiological factors highlights the dangers of treating the child by 'talking cure' alone.
- Knowledge of the child's cognitive strengths and weaknesses can also contribute towards decisions about an appropriate therapeutic style and ensure its delivery at an appropriate developmental level.

RESEARCH IMPLICATIONS

- Some of the most significant implications of the findings include
  1. Underlying mechanisms associated with control of satiety in adults may not be participating in early onset eating disorders
  2. There is preliminary evidence of a specific, focal and unilateral abnormality affecting the limbic system of children and young adolescents with anorexia nervosa
- Further studies of neuroanatomy, neurophysiology and cognitive functioning are required to ascertain whether there is a primary neurological abnormality in this population.

REFERENCES

American Psychiatric Association (1994). *Diagnostic and Statistical Manual of Mental Disorders*. Fourth Edition. American Psychiatric Association, Washington DC.

Billewicz, W., Fellowes, H. and Thomson, A. (1981). Pubertal changes in boys and girls in Newcastle upon Tyne. *Ann. Hum. Biol.* **8**, 211–219.

Bowers, W.A. (1994). Neuropsychological impairment among anorexia nervosa and bulimia patients. *Eating Disorders* **2**, 42–46.

Bryant-Waugh, R., Lask, B., Shafran, R. and Fosson, A. (1992). Do doctors recognise eating disorders in children. *Archives of Disease in Childhood* **67**, 103–105.

Carney, C. and Andersen, A. (1996). Eating disorders: guide to medical evaluation and complications. *Psychiatr. Clin. N. America* **19**, 657–678.

Casper, R.C. and Heller, W. (1991). 'La douce indifference' and mood in anorexia nervosa: neuropsychological correlates. *Biol. Psychiatry* **15**, 15–23.

Christie, D. (1998). Cognitive behavioural therapeutic techniques for children with eating disorders. In: *Anorexia Nervosa and Related Eating Disorders in Childhood*. R. Bryant-Waugh and B. Lask (eds) Lawrence Erlbaum Associates (UK).

Cravioto, J. and Arrieta, R. (1983). Malnutrition in children. In: *Developmental Neuropsychiatry*. M. Rutter (ed.) Churchill Livingstone, Edinburgh.

Dally, P. (1969). *Anorexia Nervosa*. Heinemann Medical Books, London (UK).

Dura, J.R. and Bornstein, R.A. (1989). Differences between IQ and school achievements in anorexia nervosa. *J. Clin. Psychol.* **45**, 433–435.

Delvenne, V., Lotstra, F., Goldman, S., *et al.* (1995). Brain hypometabolism of glucose in anorexia nervosa: a PET scan study. *Biol. Psychiatry* **37**(3), 161–169.

Delvenne, V., Goldman, S., De Maertelaer, V., Simon, Y., Luxen, A. and Lotstra, F. (1996). Brain hypometabolism of glucose in anorexia nervosa: normalization after weight gain. *Biol. Psychiatry* **40**(8), 761–768.

DeVile, C.J., Sofraz, R., Lask, B.D. and Stanhope, R. (1995). Occult intracranial tumours masquerading as early onset anorexia nervosa. *British Medical Journal* **311**, 1359–1360.

Fichter, M.M. and Noegel, R. (1990). Concordance for bulimia nervosa in twins. *Int. J. Eat. Disorders* **9**, 255–263.

Fichter, M., Weyerer, S., Sourdi, L. and Sourdi, Z. (1983). The epidemiology of anorexia nervosa. In: *Anorexia Nervosa. Recent Developments in Research*. P. Derby, P. Garfinkel, D. Garner, D. Coscina, (eds) New York: Alan R. Liss, pp. 95–106.

Fosson, A., Knibbs, J., Bryant-Waugh, R. and Lask, B. (1987). Early onset anorexia nervosa. *Arch. Dis. Childhood* **62**, 114–118.

Frisch, R. and Revelle, R. (1971). Heights and weight at menarche and a hypothesis of menarche. *Arch. Dis. Childhood* **46**, 695–701.

Gilberg, I.C., Gilberg, C., Råstam, M. and Johansson, M. (1996). The cognitive profile of anorexia nervosa: a comparative study including community-based sample. *Comp. Psychiatry* **37**, 23–30.

Gordon, I., Lask, B., Bryant-Waugh, R., Christie, D. and Timimi, S. (1997). Childhood onset anorexia nervosa—towards identifying a biological substrate. *Int. J. Eat. Disorders* **21**, 159–165.

Hall, A., Leibrich, J., Walkley, F. and Welch, G. (1986). Investigation of 'weight pathology' of 58 mothers of anorexia nervosa patients and 204 mothers of schoolgirls. *Psychol. Med.* **16**, 71–76.

Hamsher, K., Halmi, K.A. and Benton, A.L. (1981). Predictions of outcome of anorexia nervosa from neurological status. *Psychiatry Res.* **4**, 79–88.

Herholz, K. (1996). Neuroimaging in anorexia nervosa. *Psychiatry Res.* Apr 16; **62**(1) 105–110.

Higgs, J., Goodyer, I. and Birch, J. (1989). Anorexia nervosa and food avoidance emotional disorder. *Arch. Dis. Childhood* **64**, 346–351.

Hill, A.J., Weaver, C. and Blundell, J.E. (1990). Dieting concerns of 10 year old girls and their mothers. *Br. J. Clin. Psychol.* **29**, 346–348.

Holland, A.J., Sicotte, N. and Treasure, J. (1988). Anorexia nervosa: evidence for a genetic basis. *J. Psychosom. Res.* **32**, 561–572.

Hsu, L.K.G., Chesler, B.E. and Santhouse, R. (1990). Bulimia nervosa in eleven sets of twins: a clinical report. *Int. J. Eat. Disorders* **9**, 275–282.

Isaacs, E., Christie, D., Vargha-Khadem, F. and Mishkin, M. (1996). Effects of hemispheric side of injury, age at injury, and presence of seizure disorder on functional ear and hand asymmetries in hemiplegic children. *Neuropsychologia* **(34)** No 2: 127–137.

Katzman, D.K., Lambe, E.K., Mikulis, D.J., Ridgley, J.N., Goldbloom, D.S. and Zipursky R.B. (1996). Cerebral gray matter and white matter volume deficits in adolescent girls with anorexia nervosa. *J. Pediatr.* **129**(6), 794–803.

Kaye, W. (1997). Persistent alterations in behaviour and serotonin activity after recovery from anorexia and bulimia nervosa. In: M. Jacobson, J. Rees, N. Golden and C. Irwin (eds) *Adolescent Nutritional Disorders, Prevention and Treatment*. Annals of the New York Academy of Sciences, Vol. 817, pp. 162–178.

Kingston, K., Szmukler, G., Andrewes, D., Tress, B. and Desmond, P. (1996). Neuropsychological and structural brain changes in anorexia nervosa before and after refeeding. *Psychol. Med.* **26**, 15–28.

Kowalski, P.S. (1986). Cognitive abilities of female adolescents with anorexia nervosa. *Int. J. Eat. Disorders* **5**, 983–988.

Krieg, J.C., Holthoff, V., Schreiber, W., Pirke, K.M., Herholz, K. (1991) Glucose metabolism in the caudate nuclei of patients with eating disorders, measured by PET. *Eur. Arch. Psychiatry Clin. Neurosci.* **240**(6), 331–333.

Kruesi, M., Rapoport, S., Hamburger, *et al.* (1991). Cerebrospinal fluid monoamine metabolites, aggression, and impulsivity in disruptive behaviour disorders of children and adolescents. *Arch. Gen. Psychiatry* **47**, 419–426.

Laessle, R.G., Krieg, J.L. Fichter, M.M. and Pirke, K.M. (1989). Cerebral atrophy and vigilance performance in patients with anorexia nervosa and bulimia nervosa. *Neuropsychobiology* **21**, 187–191.

Lai, K., de Bruyn, R., Lask, B., Bryant-Waugh, R. and Hankins, M. (1994). Use of pelvic ultrasound in childhood onset anorexia nervosa. *Arch. Dis. Childhood* **71**, 228–231.

Lamers, C., Lieverse, R., Masclee, A. and Jansen, B. (1995). The role of cholecystokinin in appetite control. *Br. J. Hospital Med.* **53**, 113.

Lask, B. (1990). Anorexia nervosa and inflammatory bowel disease—commentary. *Arch. Dis. Childhood* **65**, 300.

Lask, B. (1996). Pervasive refusal syndrome. *ACCP Occasional Papers 12 Psychosomatic Problems in Children* 33–35.

Lask, B., Britten, C., Kroll, L., Magagna, J. and Tranter, M. (1991). Children with pervasive refusal. *Arch. Dis. Childhood* **66**, 866–869.

Leiper, A.D., Stanhope, R., Kitching P. and Chessells, J.M. (1987). Precocious and premature puberty associated with treatment of acute lymphoblastic leukaemia. *Arch. Dis. Child* **62**, 1107–1112.

Lucas, A. (1988). Gut hormones and the adaptation to extrauterine nutrition. In: P. Milla and D. Muller (eds), *Harries' Paediatric Gastroenterology* 2nd edition, pp. 302–317.

Magagna, J. (1998). Individual psychodynamic psychotherapy. In: R. Bryant-Waugh and B. Lask (eds) *Anorexia Nervosa and Related Eating Disorders in Childhood*. Lawrence Erlbaum Associates (UK).

Maxwell, J.K., Tucker, D.M. and Towes, B.D. (1984). Asymmetric cognitive function in anorexia nervosa. *Int. J. Neurosci.* **24**, 37–44.

Nicholls, D., Stanhope, R.G. and Lask, B. (1997). Food avoidance emotional disorder and early onset anorexia nervosa: differences in physical findings. In preparation.

Nozoe S., Naruo, T., Yoneukura, R. *et al.* (1995). Comparison of regional cerebral blood flow in patients with eating disorders. *Brain Res. Bull.* **36**, 251–255.

Nunn, K.P. and Thompson, S.L. (1996). The pervasive refusal syndrome: learned helplessness and hopelessness. *Clin. Child Psychol. Psychiatry* **1**, 121–132.

Pendleton-Jones, B., Duncan, C.C., Browers, P. and Mirsky, A.F. (1991). Cognition in eating disorders. *J. Clin. Exp. Neuropsychol.* **13**, 711–728.

Phillip, E., Pirke, K.-M., Kellner, M. and Krieg, J.-C. (1991). Disturbed CCK secretion in patients with eating disorders. *Life Sci.* **48**, 2443–2450.

Pike, K.M. and Rodin, J. (1991). Mothers, daughters, and disordered eating. *J. Abnormal Psychol.* **100**, 198–204.

Richman, N., Stevenson, J. and Graham, P.J. (1982). *Pre-school to School: A Behavioural Study*. Academic Press, London.

Russell, G. (1992). Anorexia nervosa of early onset and its impact on puberty. In: P. Cooper and A. Stein (eds) *Feeding Problems and Eating Disorders in Children and Adolescents.* Harwood Academic Publishers, Reading, UK.

Scott, D.W. (1986). Anorexia nervosa: a review of possible genetic factors. *Int. J. Eat. Disorders* **5**, 1–20.

Shafran, R., Bryant-Waugh, R., Lask, B. and Arscott, K. (1995). Obsessive compulsive symptoms in children with eating disorders: a preliminary investigation. *Eating Disorders: J. Treatment Prevention* **3**, 304–310.

Silver, A. and Morley, J. (1991). The role of CCK in the regulation of food intake. *Prog. Neurobiol.* **36**, 23–34.

Simeon, J.G., DiNicola, V.F., Fergerson, H.B. and Copping, W. (1990). Adolescent depression: a placebo controlled fluoxetine treatment study and follow up. *Prog. Neuropsychopharmacol. Biol. Psychiatry* **14**, 791–795.

Steiger, H., Stotland, S., Trottier, J. and Ghadirian, A.M. (1996). Familial eating concerns and psychopathological traits: causal implications of transgenerational effects. *Int. J. Eat. Disorders* **19**, 147–157.

Strober, M., Lampert, C., Morrell, W., Burroughs, J. and Jacobs, C. (1990). A controlled family study of anorexia nervosa: evidence of familial aggregation and lack of shared transmission with affective disorders. *Int. J. Eat. Disorders* **9**, 239–253.

Szmukler, G.I., Andrewes, D., Kingston, K., Chen, L., Stargatt, R. and Stanley, R. (1992). Neuropsychological impairment in anorexia nervosa before and after refeeding. *J. Clin. Exp. Neuropsychol.* **14**, 347–352.

Thompson, J.K. and Spana, R.E. (1991). Visuospatial ability, accuracy of size estimation and bulimic disturbance in a non eating disordered college sample; a neuropsychological analysis. *Perceptual and Motor Skills* **73**, 335–338.

Thompson, S.L. and Nunn, K.P. (1997). The pervasive refusal syndrome: the RAHC experience. *Clinical Child Psychology and Psychiatry* **2**, 145–165.

Treasure, J.L., Wheeler, M., King, E.A., Gordon, P.A.L. and Russell, G.F.M. (1988). Weight gain and reproductive function: ultrasonographic endocrine factors in anorexia nervosa. *Clin. Endocrinol.* **29**, 607–616.

Weiner, H. (1985). The physiology of eating disorders. *Int. J. Eat. Disorders* 4, 347–388.

Witt, E.D., Ryan, C. and Hsu, E. (1985). Learning deficits in adolescents with anorexia nervosa. *J. Nerv. Ment. Dis.* **173**, 182–184.

World Health Organization (1992). *The ICD-10 Classification of Mental and Behavioural Disorders: Clinical Descriptions and Diagnostic Guidelines*. World Health Organization, Geneva.

III Treatment

Introduction

M. KATZMAN
Institute of Psychiatry, London, UK and New York Hospital-Cornell Medical Center, New York, USA

Recovery from an eating problem requires, among many things, the reconstitution of self from many disparate pieces. The patient observing herself in the mirror may see an appalling jigsaw of fat thighs, droopy arms and sagging breasts. Turning the reflection inwards perhaps the image shatters around a wretched sense of self or an unsolvable matrix of roles. In contrast, the clinician's gaze may feast, depending on their bias and training, on neurotransmitter systems, nutritional deficits or neuroendocrine signals. Alternatively the practitioner may see cognitive distortions, critical family comments or cultural malaise. Seldom does the same person see all the variables, and perhaps they shouldn't or couldn't possibly.

The difficulty maintaining multiple perspectives is in part due to fractures in training and fights for our time. How can we expose ourselves quickly to the multitude of 'recent advances'? In the prior sections, eating disorders have been considered from modern day molecular to molar historical perspectives. Completing the mission of this volume requires the integration of these findings into our clinical practice. The chapters that follow are driven by the question, what does all this 'science' have to do with 'what I do'?

When I told friends and colleagues about my work on this book they asked, why would a feminist scholar be so interested in neurobiology? For me the link was obvious. Feminism is not just looking at the impact society has on women's sense of themselves, but also the impact our cultures of care have on how we make sense of women. Establishing respectful collaborations with our patients in which we relinquish our cloak of all knowing expert and work together to decode their bodily screams requires that we have the confidence in what we do and the willingness to share our information.

In the remaining section we hope to provide—in a highly encapsulated form—a lot of the information you meant to know but may not have had the time or easy access to acquire. The chapters address neurochemical markers and medical consequences of eating problems along with their clinical restoration through psychopharmacology, refeeding and therapy.

By including bullet-pointed summaries, duplicated in the Appendix in a handout form that can be distributed to patients and their families, we hope to add to your efforts to share your knowledge. The authors have been challenged with capturing the progress of the last two decades in treating eating disorders. You will see that in the chapters by Schmidt, Levine and Marcus, and Mayer and Walsh that the pertinent research has been carefully documented in clear tables while the gaps in our care are also elucidated. Quite importantly the authors discuss 'real life' in the treatment setting, given what we know from evidence based protocols, what can we realistically accomplish with our patients? While some authors summarize the literature, others like Wolf and Serpell, Van Furth, and Russell and Byrnes share specifically what they do on their programmes. Herzog makes sure we know every possible medical complication and can care for or refer our patients properly.

Evaluating the status quo, however, was not enough, we asked our authors to press us to contemplate the future. You will find that some contributors, like Van Furth, have taken us on a virtual time shuttle. It is my hope that by harnessing the advances in information distribution, we can empower ourselves and our patients with knowledge. In this way we can avoid the risk of seeing the women we treat as hapless victims and ourselves as sometimes helpless protectors.

The key to this goal is the examination of not simply what we know and do but *how we do it*. It is perhaps this later area that will be the focus of research in the next millennium. Quite notably, each of the chapters on psychological treatment of anorexia nervosa, bulimia nervosa, and binge eating disorder, all recognize that we must move beyond ritualistic recounts, preoccupied with weight and diet, to the examination of more complex mechanisms for change.

Wolf and Serpell, Van Furth and Schmidt all speak to the importance of examining the therapeutic alliance and offer suggestions to replace treatment hierarchies that proscribe 'solutions' with processes that allow patients to explore their sense of self.

Restoring a sense of wholeness to our understanding of the patient and her understanding of herself would perhaps be one of the most important advances in the integration of neurobiology in the treatment of eating disorders.

14 The Treatment of Anorexia Nervosa

E. F. VAN FURTH
Robert-Fleury Stichting, Eating Disorder Unit, Leidschendam, The Netherlands

When a therapist is confronted with a patient, the choice of a particular form of treatment for a specific illness is often governed by implicit motives. Among these are: the setting, the professional training of the therapist, the availability of beds, and the policy of the (local) government and health care insurance companies. Scientific evidence of the efficacy of a treatment is seldom considered. In the case of the treatment of anorexia nervosa we are faced with two problems: (1) There is very little scientific evidence on which to base rational treatment choices; and (2) In some countries, the choice of treatment options is drastically reduced by those organizations funding treatment.

In the Netherlands, neither the government, nor the health care insurance companies pose any limitations on psychiatric inpatient or day care treatment. Outpatient psychotherapeutic treatment is limited to 90 therapy sessions, which can be resumed after a 1-year rest period. At the Eating Disorder Unit of the Robert-Fleury Stichting, we were thus able to develop a broad range of psychiatric treatments for eating disorder patients, which focus on symptom reduction, on the underlying psychological problems and on social integration. The eating disorder unit comprises 30 inpatient beds of which six are substituted for intensive day care treatment, 10 primary day care 'chairs', and an outpatient unit which offers individual and family therapy and therapeutic groups for bulimia nervosa, obese binge eating disorder, chronic eating disorder patients, a psychomotor therapy group and a psychotherapy group along psychoanalytic lines. A flexible transition from inpatient care and day care to outpatient treatment (and vice versa) is possible. In the following paragraphs different aspects of treatment will be addressed.

WHAT HAVE BIOLOGICAL STUDIES TAUGHT US?

Anorexia nervosa is a result of sustained dieting behavior in response to a psychological conflict, stressful family relationships or psychological trauma, within the sociocultural context of pressures on young women. The *biological* regulation of appetite, eating behavior and satiety is complex. A dysregulation of one of the systems involved may directly threaten our survival. Only recently are we beginning to understand the physiologic basis of the neuroendocrine responses to starvation (Schwartz and Seeley 1997). Research in this area is important because it may provide empirical evidence of factors involved in the maintenance

Neurobiology in the Treatment of Eating Disorders.
Edited by H.W. Hoek, J.L. Treasure and M.A. Katzman.

of anorexia nervosa. A direct study of the brain in humans through the use of modern imaging techniques may give us insight into the function of specific sites in the brain (see Chapter 11). Both genetic studies (see Chapter 7) and neuroendocrine studies (see Chapter 9 and Chapter 10) may benefit from new animal models which have evolved from studies of disturbed eating behavior in animals (see Chapter 8).

The effects of prolonged starvation, such as amenorrhea, hyperactivity, delayed gastric emptying, an increase in sulci and ventricular volume in the brain, obsessive thoughts about food, and osteoporosis (see Chapter 20), underscore the importance of nutritional rehabilitation and weight restoration. Knowledge about the physiologic process underlying these signs and symptoms may, in the future, provide new additional forms of (pharmacological) treatment which may facilitate weight restoration.

WHAT CAN WE LEARN FROM FOLLOW-UP STUDIES?

The course of anorexia nervosa has been studied and reviewed quite extensively (Hsu 1980, 1988; Herzog *et al.* 1988; Steinhausen and Glanville 1933a,b; Steinhausen *et al.* 1991). Herzog *et al.* (1992a) reviewed a number of long-term follow-up studies of which most fulfilled minimal methodological criteria. In these studies, patients—most of whom had received inpatient treatment—were followed for an average duration of 12 years (mean duration of follow-up was 5–33 years). Approximately 70% of these patients improved, of which 40% recovered, with the highest proportion among the younger patients (cf. Steinhausen and Seidel 1993). However, 30% of the patients remain chronically ill. With an increase in duration of follow-up both the proportion of patients who recovered and the proportion of patients who died increased. Mortality in anorexia nervosa is estimated at 0.56% per year (Sullivan 1995), which is about four times higher than that of schizophrenia. About 50% of the deaths in anorexia nervosa are attributed to complications as a result of the eating disorder, approximately 30% to suicide.

A standardized assessment of co-morbidity was not commonplace when most long-term follow-up studies started. Nonetheless, serious co-morbid mental illness was reported in many studies. Besides marked depression, substance abuse and obsessive–compulsive disorder, acute schizophrenia, manic psychosis and, more frequently, personality disorders were diagnosed. Somatic co-morbidity after long-term follow-up was studied by Herzog *et al.* (1992b). At follow-up, on average 12.7 years after admission, 35% of the subjects alive had a somatic illness independent of their anorexia nervosa. Most common were renourogenitary, endocrine and neurological disorders. Terminal, dialysis-dependent renal failure, multiple pathological fractures due to severe osteoporosis and an increased risk of infection were among the conditions with the highest impact on prognosis.

The results of the follow-up studies of treated anorexia nervosa patients paint a somber picture. It is clear that anorexia nervosa follows a protracted course with a substantial proportion of patients relapsing after inpatient treatment. Chronicity accompanied by severe somatic and social handicap looms for many patients.

WHICH TREATMENT IS EFFECTIVE?

In search of an effective way to counteract this enigmatic mental illness, a great variety of treatments have been developed over the past decades. However, the number of controlled psychosocial treatment trials with anorexia nervosa patients is very limited. The lack of studies limit the reliability and generalization of the results and prevent the accumulation of knowledge on which rational treatment should be based. Why are there so few controlled trials for this challenging disease? This might be caused by: (a) the studies are very costly: the nature of the illness requires a prolonged treatment effort and extensive follow-up, which means longer staff involvement and more funding, which is difficult to obtain; (b) patient recruitment and drop-out: engaging and maintaining patients in treatment and research is difficult; (c) ethical concerns such as the comparison with a no treatment group; (d) a capitulation to the behavioral nursing model which leads to a lack of candidate treatments to serve as comparisons; (e) difficulty in establishing and assessing relevant outcome criteria. Because of the present hiatus in controlled psychosocial treatment trials it is still unknown what constitutes the optimal care for anorexia nervosa patients and which treatment (components) are most effective.

Despite the difficulties attached to conducting a controlled trial of psychosocial intervention some have succeeded. Crisp and colleagues compared three treatment groups to an 'assessment only' group ($N=90$) (Crisp *et al.* 1991; Gowers *et al.* 1994.). The treatment options were: (1) inpatient treatment of several months followed by 12 outpatient individual and family sessions; (2) 12 outpatient individual and family sessions spanned over several months; (3) 10 outpatient group sessions. All treatments focussed behaviorally on initial weight restoration, dietary counseling and dietary advice, the psychotherapies were directed at adolescent maturational problems.

Many methodological difficulties arose (Gowers *et al.* 1989; Crisp *et al.* 1991): 40% of the inpatient group did not comply to the treatment prescribed, and 30% of the 'assessment only' group were in treatment for almost the full duration of the follow-up period. Thus, many of these patients did receive some form of treatment. However, both at the 1-year and the 2-year follow-up, the three treatment groups did equally well on most outcome measures. The three treatment groups, inpatient treatment, outpatient individual/family therapy and outpatient group therapy, all gained significantly more weight than the assessment only group. When those patients who complied with their treatment were compared, the inpatient group gained the most weight in the shortest time. An interpretation of the results might be that despite the fact that patients did equally well on global measures of functioning, those patients who had received specialist care had restored their body weight to a higher level.

Russell *et al.* (1987) (see also Dare *et al.* 1990) conducted a controlled trial to assess the efficacy of family therapy in comparison to individual psychotherapy in the treatment of anorexia nervosa and bulimia nervosa. Eighty patients, of whom 57 suffered from anorexia nervosa, were hospitalized for on average 10 weeks to achieve weight restoration. Patients were then randomly assigned to outpatient family therapy or individual psychotherapy, which were offered for 1 year. At the 1-year follow-up only 23% of the anorectic patients had recovered. Further, the results showed that for anorexic patients, with an age of onset of the illness at 18 years or younger and a duration of illness less than 3 years, family therapy was superior to individual therapy, as assessed by both the General Outcome Categories and the Average Outcome Score on the Morgan and Russell Scales as well as by weight gain. The results were reversed for those anorexic patients with an age of onset at 19 years or older: patients in individual therapy had gained significantly more weight than those in family therapy. There was no difference on the other measures. The results were essentially confirmed at the 5-year follow-up (Russell *et al.* 1992; Dare and Eisler 1995). These studies underscore the importance of involving the family of the adolescent patient in treatment.

In a consecutive study Le Grange *et al.* (1992) compared conjoint family therapy with family counseling (patient and parents were seen separately). Eighteen adolescent eating disorder patients, with a short duration of illness, were randomly allocated to either one of the outpatient treatments. Both groups received nine therapy sessions on average. At follow-up, after 32 weeks, both groups had improved significantly, as assessed by various measures. A main aim of this study was to examine the changes in and predictive value of family measures. Importantly, the number of critical comments as rated on the Expressed Emotion (EE) scales *increased* for both fathers and mothers in the family therapy group, while it *decreased* in the family counseling group. Also, the number of critical comments of both parents was significantly higher in the poor outcome group than in the combined good/intermediate group, as classified by the General Outcome Categories on the Morgan and Russell Scales. Our own study (Van Furth *et al.* 1996) revealed low levels of emotional expression by mothers and fathers of adolescent eating disorder patients. However, specifically mother's critical comments predicted adolescent outcome at follow-up, on average 2.5 years later. A higher number of critical comments was associated with poorer outcome in the adolescent patient.

The efficacy of outpatient behavioral family systems therapy (BFST) was compared to ego-oriented individual therapy (EOIT) in a controlled trial reported by Robin *et al.* (1994). BFST combined behavioral, cognitive and family systems components, while working with both parents and the patient in weekly sessions. The weekly EOIT sessions with the adolescent focused on ego strength, coping skills, individuation and interpersonal issues. In the EOIT condition the parents were seen bimonthly. The purpose of these sessions was to educate the parents about anorexia nervosa and to engender a supportive, emphatic, nonjudgmental attitude towards their daughter. The duration of therapy was 16 months on average.

The amount of therapy was equalized over the two treatment conditions. At the post-treatment assessment, the 11 young anorexia nervosa patients in each of the two treatment conditions showed significant improvement on the EAT, EDI and CBCL subscales. However, the BFST group showed a significantly greater improvement on the BMI than the EOIT group. In the BFST group 67% and in the EOIT group 30% of the patients reached both the 50th percentile of the BMI and menstruated, a finding which did not reach statistical significance. The Parent Adolescent Relationship Questionnaire (PARQ) was used to assess family conflict. High levels of conflict over eating were reduced in both treatment groups. However, the authors report that the levels of perceived general conflict remained low over the treatment period. Follow-up data on this study have not been reported.

The process by which parental attitude influences outcome in adolescent anorexia nervosa is still unclear. One possible explanation is that critical and over involved attitudes arise when parents experience a lack of effectiveness in problem solving. An inability for effective emotional communication within the family may exacerbate these critical and overinvolved attitudes and behaviors. Conjoint family therapy sessions in these families may be highly charged and induce further feelings of guilt and shame in the patient and the parents. Seeing the parents separately from the child may help the parents cope with their feelings of ineffectiveness and restore adolescent and family development in a more matter-of-fact way.

Channon *et al.* (1989) reported a controlled trial which investigated the efficacy of 24 outpatient therapy sessions of cognitive-behavioral therapy (CBT) and behavioral therapy (BT) in comparison with a routine control treatment. Twenty-four young adult anorexic patients participated in this study. The number of patients who did not fulfill diagnostic criteria at the end of treatment or at follow-up is not reported. Despite the intensity of the two experimental therapies, all three groups did equally well on most clinical measures at the 1-year follow-up. However, compliance with treatment was significantly better in the CBT than the BT group. Also, treatment drop-out and hospital admissions were more frequent in the control group than in the BT or CBT group. These findings suggest that CBT was more acceptable to patients than BT or routine treatment.

In a study reported by Treasure *et al.* (1995) a group of 30 adult anorexia nervosa patients were randomly assigned to two forms of individual outpatient psychotherapy: educational behavior therapy (EBT) and cognitive analytic therapy (CAT). Each treatment comprised 20 weekly sessions. None of the patients required hospital admission, but treatment drop-out was notable: 29% in the CAT group and 38% in the EBT group. At 1-year follow-up 37% of the patients had recovered and both groups did equally well on most clinical outcome measures. The only difference between groups was that the CAT group rated significantly higher on self-rated improvement than the EBT group. This study shows that outpatient therapy for adult anorexia nervosa patients can lead to a sizeable improvement for at least a third of the patients. A study involving a greater number of patients is necessary to reveal possible differences between the two treatment modalities.

There are currently two controlled outpatient trials ongoing in which the efficacy of CBT and other forms of treatment, during the weight maintaining phase of treatment following hospitalization, are examined.

WHAT CONSTITUTES AN EFFECTIVE THERAPEUTIC ALLIANCE?

Many therapists consider anorexia nervosa patients among the most difficult to treat. These patients often evoke strong emotional responses from therapists (Vandereycken 1993), which may vary from utter frustration, anger and rejection to admiration and saviour fantasies. These feelings, if experienced often, can lead to a severe disruption of the therapeutic relationship as expressed by either an under- or overinvolved attitude. Discontinuation of treatment because the patient did not fulfill therapeutic goals or admitting the patient to the therapist's own home are extreme examples of possible ensuing behaviors.

Establishing and maintaining an effective therapeutic alliance is not an easy task (Bruch 1973). This process is greatly enhanced by working within a strong cohesive (multidisciplinary) team which propagates a shared philosophy. The cohesiveness of the team is essential to establish a therapeutic climate within an inpatient or day care setting and for solving problems within the ongoing process of therapeutic relationships. The team also helps to dissolve the burden of treatment which is often felt and helps to come to rational treatment decisions.

A single overall view of philosophy of treatment is also essential. In our eating disorder unit the patient's own responsibility within her treatment is emphasized throughout and attempts to control the patient during treatment are minimized as much as possible. The therapeutic attitude is one of respect for the individual's autonomy and right to self-determination, something which is extremely important since it touched on the core issues of the illness. Consequently, patients are invited to come into treatment and set their own goals, within the overall boundaries set by the team. We ask the patient: 'What would you like to come and work on with us?' Treatment goals are firstly put forth by the patient and then discussed with the therapist team. Treatment goals are evaluated every 6 weeks and progress is monitored through weight gain and psychotherapeutic progress. Nonnegotiable is the goal of weight restoration for anorexia nervosa patients. Within this framework, patients have a great deal of responsibility. The sociotherapeutic interventions aim at improving the patient groups' awareness of and responsibility for the therapeutic process within the group. Patients are stimulated to support each others goals for change and confront unwanted behaviour. Ideally, the therapists' team should be working alongside and not *for* or *against* the patient group. The balance between autonomy and control within the therapeutic setting is a delicate matter. An increase of control invites a retreat into (often) passive resistance leading to weight loss in anorexic patients, whereas a decrease of control may engender fear and avoidance of weight gain. Control in the form of peer pressure, within a homogeneous group of eating disorder patients, with the team as supervizing 'parents' looking after the patients' individual needs, requires a constant adjustment of therapeutic interventions. The treatment plan of the inpatient unit is set up in such a way that therapists' control rapidly decreases with an increase in body weight. The amount of supervision is adjusted to the severity of the malnutrition, the patient's somatic condition, and the patient's underweight. If necessary, firm limits are set to patient behavior. Examples are: standardized meal prescription, patients may eat alone in their room, limitations in physical activity, 'time-out' for the duration of week, and weighing twice a week. However, we do not check the amount of food eaten or the patient's toilet activities (e.g. purging), these remain his or her own responsibility.

THE PRE-TREATMENT PROCESS

The patients' ongoing 'battle for autonomy' is visible from the first contact onward. During the first assessment sessions clarity about the therapists' view on treatment should be provided. This is the time when the relationship between patient and therapist is defined. Given that the anorexic patients' motivation for change is by definition ambivalent, a relationship definition based on equality and clarity of goals can help form and strengthen the therapeutic relationship/bond. One of the main therapeutic aims at this stage is to establish a working relationship and to strengthen the patients' motivation for change. A psycho-educational approach may be beneficial to this process.

THE ROLE OF PSYCHO-EDUCATION

Psycho-education involves the transmission of knowledge with the aim of changing the patient's attitude and behavior (Garner *et al.* 1984). Psycho-education can be useful in both individual and family sessions. When used in early stages of treatment, involving both patient and family seems helpful. A knowledgeable therapist providing honest information about all aspects of the illness, can help the family to motivate the patient and can help the patient to analyse the pros and cons to change. Playing on the homeostasis of the ambivalent motivation to change is important to provide windows of opportunity for both the patient and her family. Unfortunately, the effects of a psycho-educational approach of anorexia nervosa have never been evaluated scientifically. This might be because it is unlikely that psycho-education alone will provide enough therapeutic impact to change the anorexic's behavior.

INVOLVING THE FAMILY IN TREATMENT

Ever since Minuchin's theorizing and research into the role of the family in anorexia nervosa (Minuchin *et al.* 1975; Minuchin *et al.* 1978), it has become common to involve the parents of an adolescent eating disorder patient in the assessment process. The practice of involving the parents and siblings of adult patients in treatment is, however, far less widespread. Many adult patients have very strong family ties despite an often long-standing history of illness and family burden. Notwithstanding difficulties with involving the families in treatment (Szmukler *et al.* 1985), family participation, from an early stage on, may provide the patient with extra motivation for treatment, and offer extra therapeutic possibilities for the therapist. However, in families where overinvolved or hostile attitudes prevail, a reduction of face-to-face contact seems warranted and family counseling may be beneficial. A family assessment session should provide some guidance.

In our clinic we try to involve the patients' family system in several ways. The most accessible form is the monthly parents' and partners' group meeting. From the time that patients are on the waiting list for treatment, parents and partners are invited for separate group meetings. This evening meeting is supervised by one of the psychotherapists and a nurse and relies heavily on self-help principles. Psycho-educational information is provided depending on the subject discussed. Participants are encouraged to speak of their experiences and to ask other participants about their solutions to encountered problems. The group supervisors will answer any questions about treatments offered and will involve participants in questions concerning family life. These meetings very often function as a reintroduction to therapy for disillusioned mothers and fathers. Parents greatly appreciate the opportunity to talk to other parents about continuing worries and frustrations. The group supervisors often grasp these occasions to encourage parents to contact their daughter's therapist and to intensify their involvement in treatment. Other forms of involving the family system are: family therapy, family counseling, sibling therapy, marriage therapy (see Vandereycken *et al.* 1989).

WEIGHT RESTORATION

Data presented by Hebebrand *et al.* (1996, 1997) revealed that patients presenting with a BMI of 13 kg/m^2 or less, at referral, had a much lower body weight at follow-up, on average 11.7 years later, than those with a BMI over 13. BMI at referral also predicted death of emaciation and chronic anorexia nervosa in this group. Following a group of 22 anorexia nervosa patients Baran *et al.* (1995) showed that patients who were still underweight (less than 85% of the recommended average body weight for age and height) at discharge had a worse clinical course than those discharged at a normal weight.

One of the few aspects of treatment on which there seems to be consensus between clinicians is the necessity of nutritional rehabilitation and weight restoration in anorexia nervosa patients. At the Robert-Fleury Stichting, inpatients are expected to gain, the arbitrary amount of, 1 kg per week and outpatients 0.5 kg per week on average up to at least BMI 19.5. Patients are then encouraged to continue weight restoration to their set point level.

Much is still unclear about the physiologic process and the management of weight restoration (see Chapter 19). For example, the physiologic optimal rate of and diet for weight restoration is not known. The number of times a week one weighs the patient does not seem to make a difference (Touyz *et al.* 1990). Research on this topic could provide some guidelines, since many clinicians tend to lower their expectations of the patient in this matter in response to the patient's obvious anxiety of weight gain.

INPATIENT TREATMENT

Most anorexia nervosa patients can be treated on an outpatient basis. Criteria for hospital admission for anorexia nervosa are:

1. Extreme low body weight (e.g. BMI < 13 kg/m^2)
2. Somatic co-morbidity

Criteria for admission to a specialized eating disorder unit would further include:

1. Psychiatric co-morbidity
2. Failed outpatient treatment

In many clinics inpatient treatment can only be utilized to achieve, important but limited, treatment goals such as somatic stability or weight restoration. These limitations are often posed by insurance companies. In the Netherlands, inpatient treatment can also include the treatment of underlying problems. The model for inpatient treatment at our clinic combines aspects of behavioral therapy with psychotherapeutic community principles within a homogeneous group of eating disorder patients. Patients function as co-therapists: they support each other to achieve therapeutic goals and challenge unwanted behavior in others. Recurrent therapeutic themes are physical and sexual abuse, identity problems, extremely low self-esteem and self hatred and conflicts concerning individuation and separation (cf. 'leaving home' problems). Not surprisingly, the mean duration of our inpatient treatment is 4 months, while 20% of our patients stay for a period of 6 months or longer.

IS INVOLUNTARY TREATMENT NECESSARY?

Treating patients against their explicit desire may only be necessary in case of a life-threatening situation (cf. Tiller *et al.* 1993). Spending several sessions to increase the patient's motivation for treatment, possibly with the help of her family, is much preferred. The number of anorexia nervosa patients treated under the Mental Health Act in the Netherlands seems to be very limited. The reason for this is unknown: it may be a result of the way in which our health care is organized or of a different referral pattern, leading to different interventions. General practitioners will refer severely emaciated patients to an internal medicine ward at a general hospital rather than to a psychiatric hospital. A referral to a somatic unit may be more acceptable to many patients and families.

MULTIDISCIPLINARY TREATMENT

Since there is no firm ground on which to base rational therapeutic strategies in the treatment of anorexia nervosa, many specialized clinics offer multiple therapies depending upon their focus in the etiology or illness perpetuating factors. Psychotherapeutic treatment often involves individual psychotherapy, group psychotherapy, family therapy and family counseling. Psychomotor therapy, art therapy and drama therapy have great advantages with these patients because of their nonverbal and symbolic intervention techniques. Other therapeutic activities we utilize are psycho-education, cooking activities, swimming and sports and for the inpatient and day care treatment, sociotherapeutic groups which focus on day-to-day group interactions and play an important role in the management of the therapeutic climate of the unit.

MEDICATION

The role of pharmacologic treatment for anorexia nervosa is very limited. There have been very few controlled medication trials. At this time there is no empirical evidence for any clinically significant use of medication in the treatment of anorexia nervosa (see Chapter 18 for a review).

CARE FOR THE CHRONIC ANOREXIC PATIENT

Unfortunately, many anorexia nervosa patients become chronic sufferers. Chronic anorexia nervosa can lead to severe handicap. Some of the medical problems which can arise are fractures due to osteoporosis, renal failure and neurological problems. Psychological disturbance can include depression and compulsiveness. Lacking an intimate relationship and social isolation can considerably limit the quality of life. Over the years, the chronic anorexia nervosa patient will be confronted with the death of her parents, lead an often childless life and she needs to cope with the difference between her youthful expectations of life and the reality of her day-to-day struggle with food and her body weight. Chronic anorexia nervosa patients are old at a young age. Their asceticism often denies them the most basic pleasures of life. The eating disorder has become ingrained in their personality. In contrast, many are successful in their profession, where their ambition and perfectionism serve their purpose.

Psychiatric and somatic care for these patients may lessen the chances of an exacerbation of the anorexia and prevent severe somatic disorders. Outpatient treatment may provide a long-term cost benefit, because of the expected medical consumption of these patients at old age. Three years ago we started an outpatient group for longstanding eating disorder patients. The group is supervised by a psychotherapist and a nurse and meets on a weekly basis. Patients need to have had several (unsuccessful) treatments which were specifically aimed at alleviation of their eating disorder symptomatology. The main aim of the group is to improve the quality of life of the participants. It is made explicit that the therapists do not expect the participants to work on weight restoration or cessation of bingeing and purging. Patients are of course free to work on these behaviors, but it is not a goal of treatment. The therapists work in close contact with the patient's GP. Patients are encouraged to take responsibility for their illness. For example, patients are informed of the risks and consequences of osteoporosis and are encouraged to arrange a bone density scan through their GP. The emotional problems which may arise around subsequent prescribed medication are then discussed in the group. Also, all somatic crises are handled though the GP. The participating patients' mean age is around 40 and most have had anorexia nervosa for 15 or more years. It is our experience that the patients are very involved in the group, all welcome the opportunity to speak freely about their life and the way in which their (not) eating or bingeing influences their life. However, the process of change is slow and the steps taken toward improvement of their everyday quality of life are small. Therapist expectations can exceed those of the patient and worries about patients who are very low in weight can be burdening for the therapists.

CONCLUSIONS

Treatment for anorexia nervosa has changed over the past decade from strict behavior therapy and psycho-analytic therapy to an eclectic mixture of behavioral and cognitive techniques, psycho-dynamic therapeutic attitude, combined with a family approach. There is however, little empirical evidence on which to base rational treatment decisions for anorexia nervosa. This is in contrast to bulimia nervosa, which has been studied extensively. There is some empirical support for the use of outpatient family therapy with younger anorectic patients, with a short duration of illness. This group of patients stands the best chance of recovery following specialized treatment. Follow-up studies of *treated* patients indicate that one-third of all patients remain chronically ill, with a high risk of developing somatic and psychiatric co-morbidity. There is a dire need for treatment effectiveness studies and controlled clinical trials in anorexia nervosa.

Treatment can also have adverse effects; one of the most obvious is the development of bulimia in response to refeeding. An increase in depression and in impulsive behaviors such as cutting and suicidal ideation are often seen in patients with traumatic experiences.

Research topics for the future are: possible harmful effects of treatment, the follow-up of untreated anorexia nervosa in the community, the efficacy of cognitive behavior therapy and interpersonal psychotherapy in anorexia nervosa, and research into the efficacy of the treatment of somatic co-morbidity, such as osteoporosis.

For most anorectic patients, weight restoration is not a difficult task to achieve, within a specialized inpatient treatment setting. However, subsequent weight stabilization and social integration are often difficult to accomplish. The generalization of treatment results is poor and relapse often imminent upon discharge. Treatment strategies dealing with these problems need to be developed. Short booster admissions to inpatient care, outpatient booster therapy and therapeutic hostels may be part of the answer.

FUTUROLOGY

If we could let our imagination wander, I would predict that in the next centennial, advances in molecular biology will help unravel the complex genotype of the phenotype restricting anorexia nervosa. The possibility of an extensive screening of young adolescents to identify individuals at risk will become available, but the ethical implications will remain heavily debated. Social–cultural pressures on males and females will become more and more similar, power struggles will no longer be gender based. Therefore, the number of males with anorexia nervosa will almost equal the number of females. Eating disorders will be endemic in eastern European and non-Western societies, such as the countries of the Far East.

The neuroendocrine regulatory pathways underlying hunger, satiety and eating behavior will be fully understood. Complete knowledge of the biological regulation of body weight and the response to starvation will lead to new pharmacological interventions. These new drugs will help the anorexia nervosa patient increase his or her food intake, optimizing the process of weight restoration.

New psychotherapeutic techniques involving computer-based interactive virtual reality will be developed to effectively treat the core intra-psychic issues in anorexia nervosa, such as identity problems, low self-esteem and problems relating to individuation and social integration. New diagnostic instruments will greatly increase the early detection of the illness. The availability of imminent specialist treatment upon detection will be regulated by law. Because of new intervention techniques and strategies, subsequent treatment will have a much higher degree of success: 95% of the anorexia nervosa patients will achieve complete recovery within one year of onset. Mortality as a consequence of anorexia nervosa will not exist.

ACKNOWLEDGMENTS

I would like to thank M.J. Bruna and M. van der Feltz for their critical review of the manuscript.

CLINICAL IMPLICATIONS

- Reviews of treatment studies and neurobiological literature converge in suggesting the following for anorexic patients:

1. Nutritional rehabilitation and weight restoration are essential to recovery
2. Many of the typical signs and symptoms of anorexia nervosa are a result of the malnutrition and emaciation
3. Patients need to learn to cope with perceived stress in their social environment

- A cohesive team aligned on a philosophy of treatment which emphasizes patient responsibility and the right to self-determination will help establish and maintain an effective therapeutic alliance. A multidisciplinary approach to the underlying problems is necessary to minimize the chances of relapse.

FORMULATION

- Given the finding that family therapy is beneficial for adolescent anorexia nervosa patients and that parental criticism predicts a poor outcome, case formulations should include the results of a family assessment session and strategies concerning the involvement of the family in treatment.

FUTURE RESEARCH

- Little is known about the natural course of untreated anorexia nervosa. Research should focus on treatment effectiveness and controlled clinical trials of anorexia nervosa. Harmful effects of treatment should be evaluated.

Continued

DIFFICULTIES

- Ethical, methodological and practical problems need to be overcome before treatment outcome studies are initiated.

REFERENCES

Baran, S.A., Weltzin, Th. E. and Kaye, W.H. (1995). Low discharge weight and outcome in anorexia nervosa, *Am. J. Psychiatry*. **152**, 1070–1072.

Bruch, H. (1973). *Eating Disorders: Obesity, Anorexia Nervosa, and the Person Within*. Basic Books, New York.

Channon, A., De Silva, P., Hemsley, D. and Perkins, S. (1989). A controlled trial of cognitive-behavioral and behavioral treatment of anorexia nervosa. *Behav. Res. Ther.*, **27**, 529–535.

Crisp, A.H., Norton, K., Gowers, S. *et al.* (1991). A controlled study of the effect of therapies aimed at adolescent and family psychopathology in anorexia nervosa, *Br. J. Psychiatry*, **159**, 325–333.

Dare, C. and Eisler, I. (1995). Family therapy, in *Handbook of Eating Disorders—Theory, Treatment and Research* (eds G. Szmukler, C. Dare and J. Treasure), pp. 333–349, Wiley, London.

Dare, C., Eisler, I., Russell, G.F.M. and Szmukler, G.I. (1990). The clinical and theoretical impact of a controlled trial of family therapy in anorexia nervosa, *J. Marital Family Therapy*, **16**, 39–57.

Garner, D.M., Rockert, W., Olmstead, M.P., Johnson, C. and Coscina, D.V. (1984). Psycho-educational principles in the treatment of bulimia and anorexia nervosa, in *Handbook of Psychotherapy for Anorexia Nervosa and Bulimia* (eds D.M. Garner and P.E. Garfinkel), pp. 513–572, Guilford Press, New York.

Gowers, S., Norton, K., Yeldham, D. *et al.* (1989). The St. George's prospective treatment study of anorexia nervosa: a discussion of methodological problems, *Int. J. Eat. Disorders*, **8**, 445–454.

Gowers, S., Norton, K., Halek, C. and Crisp, A.H. (1994). Outcome of outpatient psychotherapy in a random allocation treatment study of anorexia nervosa, *Int. J. Eat. Disorders*, **15**, 165–177.

Hebebrand, J., Himmelmann, G.W., Wewetzer, Chr. *et al.* (1996). Body weight in acute anorexia nervosa at follow-up assessed with percentiles for the body mass index: implications of a low body weight at referral, *Int. J. Eat. Disorders*, **19**, 347–357.

Hebebrand, J., Himmelmann, G.W., Herzog, W. *et al.* (1997). Prediction of low body weight at long-term follow-up in acute anorexia nervosa by low body weight at referral, *Am. J. Psychiatry*, **154**, 566–569.

Herzog, D.B., Keller, M.B. and Lavori, P.W. (1988). Outcome in anorexia nervosa and bulimia nervosa. A review of the literature, *J. Nerv. Ment. Dis.*, **176**, 131–143.

Herzog, W., Rathner, G. and Vandereycken, W. (1992a). Long-term course of anorexia nervosa: a review of the literature, in *The Course of Eating Disorders. Long-term*

Follow-up Studies of Anorexia and Bulimia Nervosa (eds W. Herzog, H.-C. Deter and W. Vandereycken), pp. 15–30, Springer-Verlag, Berlin.

Herzog, W., Deter, H.-C., Schellbert, D. *et al.* (1992b). Somatic findings at 12-year follow-up of 103 anorexia nervosa patients: results of the Heidelberg–Mannheim follow-up, in *The Course of Eating Disorders. Long-term Follow-up Studies of Anorexia and Bulimia Nervosa* (eds W. Herzog, H.-C. Deter and W. Vandereycken), pp. 85–108, Springer-Verlag, Berlin.

Hsu, L.K.G. (1980). Outcome of anorexia nervosa. A review of the literature (1954–1978), *Arch. Gen. Psychiatry*, **37**, 1041–1046.

Hsu, L.K.G. (1988). The outcome of anorexia nervosa: a reappraisal. *Psychol. Med.*, **18**, 807–812.

Le Grange, D., Eisler, I., Dare, C., and Russell, G.F.M. (1992). Evaluation of family treatments in adolescent anorexia nervosa: a pilot study, *Int. J. Eat. Disorders*, **12**, 347–357.

Minuchin, S., Baker, L., Rosman, B.L., Liebman, R., Milman, L. and Todd, T.C. (1975). A conceptual model of psychosomatic illness in children, *Arch. Gen. Psychiatry*, **32**, 1031–1038.

Minuchin, S., Rosman, B.L. and Baker, L. (1978). *Psychosomatic Families: Anorexia Nervosa in Context*, Harvard University Press, Cambridge (Mass.).

Robin, A.L., Siegel, P.T., Koepke, T., Moye, A.W. and Tice, S. (1994). Family therapy versus individual therapy for adolescent females with anorexia nervosa, *J. Dev. Behav. Pediatr.*, **15**, 111–116.

Russell, G.F., Szmukler, G.I., Dare, C., and Eisler, I. (1987). An evaluation of family therapy in anorexia nervosa and bulimia nervosa, *Arch. Gen. Psychiatry*, **44**, 1047–1056.

Russell, G.F.M., Dare, C., Eisler, I. and Le Grange, P.D.F. (1992). Controlled trials of family treatments in anorexia nervosa, in *Psychobiology and Treatment of Anorexia Nervosa and Bulimia Nervosa* (ed. K.A. Halmi), pp. 237–263, American Psychiatric Press, Washington, DC.

Schwartz, M.W. and Seeley, R. (1997). Neuroendocrine responses to starvation and weight loss, *New England J. Med.*, **336**, 1802–1812.

Steinhausen, H.C. and Glanville, K. (1983a). Retrospective and prospective follow-up studies in anorexia nervosa, *Int. J. Eat. Disorders*, **2**, 221–235.

Steinhausen, H.C. and Glanville, K. (1983b). Follow-up studies of anorexia nervosa: a review of research findings, *Psychol. Med.*, **13**, 239–249.

Steinhausen, H.C. and Seidel, R. (1993). Outcome in adolescent eating disorders, *Int. J. Eat. Disorders*, **14**, 487–496.

Steinhausen, H.C., Rauss-Mason, C. and Seidel, R. (1991). Follow-up studies of anorexia nervosa–a review of four decades of outcome research, *Psychol. Med.*, **21**, 447–454.

Sullivan, P.F. (1995). Mortality in anorexia nervosa. *Am. J. Psychiatry*, **152**, 1073–1074.

Szmukler, G.I., Eisler, I., Russell, G.F.M. and Dare, C. (1985). Anorexia nervosa, parental 'expressed emotion' and dropping out of treatment, *Br. J. Psychiatry*, **147**, 265–271.

Tiller, J., Schmidt, U. and Treasure, J. (1993). Compulsory treatment for anorexia nervosa: compassion or coercion?, *Br. J. Psychiatry*, **162**, 679–680.

Touyz, S.W., Lennerts, W., Freeman, R.J. and Beumont, P.J.V. (1990). To weight or not to weight? Frequency of weighing and rate of weight gain in patients with anorexia nervosa, *Br. J. Psychiatry*, **157**, 752–754.

Treasure, J., Todd, G., Brolly, M., Tiller, J., Nehmed, A. and Denman, F. (1995). A pilot study of a randomised trial of cognitive analytical therapy vs educational behavioural therapy for adult anorexia nervosa, *Behav. Res. Ther.*, **33**, 363–367.

Vandereycken, W. (1993). Naughty girls and angry doctor: eating disorder patients and their therapist, *Int. Rev. Psychiatry*, **5**, 13–18.

Vandereycken, W., Kog, E. and Vanderlinden, J. (1989). *The Family Approach to Eating Disorders: Assessment and Treatment of Anorexia Nervosa and Bulimia*, PMA Publishing, New York-Costa Mesa, CA.

Van Furth, E.F., Van Strien, D.C., Martina, L.M.L., Van Son, M.J.M., Hendrickx, J.J.P. and Van Engeland, H. (1996). Expressed emotion and the prediction of outcome in adolescent eating disorders, *Int. J. Eat. Disorders*, **20**, 19–32.

15 Treatment of Bulimia Nervosa

U. SCHMIDT
Maudsley Hospital, London, UK

INTRODUCTION

Treatment of bulimia nervosa has been extremely well researched given the recency of its first description (Russell 1979) and a research review on the psychotherapy of bulimia nervosa concluded that 'researchers in the area can be justifiably proud of the progress that has been made' and that many of the studies 'were highly complex, and clearly well designed, well executed, and carefully interpreted' (Mitchell *et al.* 1996). Similar comments could be made about the large number of studies of pharmacotherapy of bulimia nervosa. Yet the paper goes on to point out that many questions remain unanswered and there are severe limitations to the generalizability of existing research. Populations studied have varied considerably among studies due to different diagnostic criteria used and the subjectivity of some of the criteria used. Most studies have not included so-called atypical eating disorders, which constitute a large proportion of patients presenting for treatment. Nothing is known about the treatment of bulimia nervosa in adolescents, older patients or men, as research studies exclusively focus on the treatment of younger women. Subjects with comorbid depression or alcohol/drug abuse are often excluded, although many bulimics have these comorbid conditions. These patients are less likely to respond to research treatments than patients without comorbidity. Detailed assessments or having to wait for inclusion in a study may make it less likely that impulsive individuals are enrolled in research, biasing studies further in favour of less complex cases. Subjects may also be self-selecting for treatments they prefer, leading to differential dropout rates. In their data analysis most studies don't use carry-forward analysis and instead exclude or replace drop-outs thereby leading to an overoptimistic treatment outcome. Research treatments are often manualized and audio-taped and therapists highly trained and regularly supervised, to ensure treatment fidelity. Yet under real life conditions treatment is likely to be much more diluted. Follow-up periods are usually brief or non-existent and data may be exclusively reported in terms of percentage reductions of bingeing and vomiting rather than abstinence rates. This is worrying, especially in view of the recent drive towards evidence-based purchasing which increasingly uses 'research-derived norms for treatment decisions and practice guidelines, which may underestimate the treatment requirements of many patients' (Mitchell *et al.* 1996).

Neurobiology in the Treatment of Eating Disorders.
Edited by H.W. Hoek, J.L. Treasure and M.A. Katzman.

In the first part of what follows the status quo of psychological and pharmacological treatment research into bulimia nervosa will be summarized. In a second, more speculative part, some ideas are going to be put forward as to where to go from here in bulimia treatment research.

PSYCHOLOGICAL TREATMENT OF BULIMIA NERVOSA

COGNITIVE-BEHAVIOURAL TREATMENT

Cognitive-behavioural treatment (CBT) is now very much a first line treatment in bulimia nervosa (Wilson 1996). In the cognitive model of bulimia nervosa (Fairburn 1981; Fairburn *et al.* 1993b) extreme concerns about shape and weight are seen as both causative and maintaining factors in this disorder. It is thought that underlying these shape and weight concerns are long-standing feelings of ineffectiveness and negative self-evaluation (Fairburn *et al.* 1997). Weight and shape concerns are thought to trigger dieting, which in turn triggers bingeing, which leads to compensatory vomiting or purging in a cascade of interlocking vicious circles. Treatment attempts to tackle both the behavioural aspects of the disorder as well as the characteristic cognitive distortions. The apparent simplicity of this model is seductive, which is perhaps why it has gained so much prominence. However, it ignores the fact that a considerable proportion of individuals with the disorder do not have weight and shape concerns. Even in those bulimic individuals who do have prominent weight and shape concerns, an exclusive treatment focus on these issues can be said to be trivializing these individuals' difficulties which range far beyond superficial concerns about appearance.

A large number of controlled treatment studies have evaluated cognitive-behavioural treatment against other types of treatment (psychological and ϕ or drug treatments) administered both individually (see Table 15.1; Agras *et al.* 1989; Fairburn *et al.* 1986, 1991, 1993a, 1995; Freeman *et al.*, 1988; Wilson *et al.* 1991; Garner *et al.* 1993; Thackwray *et al.* 1993) or in groups (see Table 15.2; Yates and Sambrailo 1984; Kirkley *et al.* 1985; Lee and Rush 1986; Wilson *et al.* 1986; Wolchik *et al.* 1986; Mitchell *et al.* 1990; Wolf and Crowther 1992).

CBT in bulimia nervosa has been found to be more effective than supportive therapy, supportive–expressive therapy, behaviour therapy and interpersonal psychotherapy (Agras *et al.* 1989; Fairburn *et al.* 1991, 1993a; Garner *et al.* 1993; Kirkley *et al.* 1985; Thackwray *et al.* 1993; Walsh *et al.* 1997).

Drop-out rates for CBT (individual or groups) in bulimia nervosa vary from 0 to 47% with most studies of individual CBT giving drop-out rates between 10 to 30%. Kazdin and Mazurick (1994) emphasize that a distinction ought to be made between those patients who discontinue treatment at an early stage and those who leave treatment later in the therapeutic process. Coker *et al.* (1993) described a small number of patients with bulimia nervosa who 'failed to engage' with treatment. These patients had higher levels of eating pathology and borderline personality symptomatology than those who did engage with treatment. Waller (1997) studied 'failure to engage' separately from 'drop-out' in patients treated with individual CBT. Both groups of non-completers had higher levels of borderline psychopathology, with the 'failure to engage' patients surprisingly reporting more perceived family support.

Post-treatment abstinence rates with CBT range from 25 to 80% with most studies being somewhere between 30 to 60%. These rates can be maintained for up to 5 years (Fairburn *et al.* 1995). Treatment intensity ranges from 9–80 hours. When given individually, treatment intensity is usually in the range of approximately 20 sessions.

EXPOSURE TREATMENTS

In 1982, Rosen and Leitenberg proposed the anxiety reduction model of bulimia, in which vomiting is seen as a negative reinforcer of binge eating by removing the fear of weight gain. Based on this model they developed an exposure treatment, in which patients are required to consume binge foods up to the point where they would typically induce vomiting. They are then supervised for up to 2.5 hours to wait for the urge to be sick to subside (exposure plus prevention of vomiting = EPV). Wilson *et al.* (1986) and Leitenberg *et al.* (1988) compared EPV in combination with cognitive restructuring with a treatment in which only cognitive restructuring was used. Both studies found the combination treatment to be superior to cognitive restructuring alone. However, cognitive restructuring treatment is not comparable to the relatively more broad-based CBT treatment described by Fairburn (1981).

Three studies examined the effects of adding exposure and response prevention of vomiting to more conventional cognitive-behavioural treatment packages. Agras *et al.* (1989) found the combination of EPV and standard CBT techniques to be less successful than standard CBT alone, whereas Wilson *et al.* (1991) found similar effectiveness for the combined EPV plus CBT treatment compared with CBT alone. A third study (Cooper and Steere 1995) compared CBT without explicit exposure instructions with EPV without cognitive restructuring procedures. In the short term, both treatments led to substantial improvement, however, at 1-year follow-up whilst improvement was well maintained for those with CBT, many of those in the EPV condition had relapsed. Thus, in summary, there seems to be little advantage in using (either alone or in combination) what is a very time-consuming and potentially aversive treatment. Cooper and Steere (1995) also note that most conventional CBT packages contain an informal exposure element and that may be sufficient.

An alternative, less well studied approach involves exposure and prevention of bingeing (EPB). In this treatment small amounts of binge-foods are presented to patients who may touch it, smell it, taste it or even eat small amounts (Schmidt and Marks 1989; Jansen *et al.* 1992). Jansen *et al.* (1992) compared cue exposure with

Table 15.1. Controlled studies of individual psychotherapy of bulimia nervosa

Authors	Comparison	*n*	Completers (%)	Intensity (hours)	Abstinence post-R_x (%)	Abstinence at follow-up (%)	Comments
Ordman & Kirschenbaum 1985	Full CBT	10	100	15–36	20	Not reported	Full CBT > brief CBT
	Brief CBT	10	100	1.5	0		
Fairburn *et al.* 1986	CBT	12	92	19	36	Not reported	CBT > STP; gains maintained at FU
	STP	12	92		27		
Freeman *et al.* 1988	CBT	32	66	15	77 overall	Incomplete data	Active treatments > WL; CBT = BT
	BT	30	83				
	Group	30	63				
	WL	20	80				
Agras *et al.* 1989	SM	19	84	14	23	18	CBT > WL; CBT > SM and EPV at FU
	CBT	22	77		56	59	
	EPV	17	94		31	20	
	WL	19	95		6	–	
Wilson *et al.* 1991	CBT	11	73	20	46	42	CBT = CBT + EPV at post-R_x and FU
	CBT + EPV	11	82		55	86	
Fairburn *et al.* 1991, 1993a	CBT	25	84	19	42	34	At post-R_x: CBT > BT and IPT; at FU: IPT = CBT
	IPT	25	84		28	44	
	BT	25	72		38	20	
Jansen *et al.* 1992	EPB	7	86	15	100	100	EPB > self control
	Self control	7	86		50	33	
Garner *et al.* 1993	CBT	30	83	19	36	–	CBT > SET
	SET	30	83		12	–	
Thackwray *et al.* 1993	CBT	47	83	8	92	69	All 3 groups improved; gains maintained only in CBT group
	BT				100	38	
	Attention placebo Control				69	15	
Treasure *et al.* 1994	Manual	55	74	0	22	–	CBT and manual > WL
	CBT (8 sessions)	28	75	8	24		
	WL	27	70	0	11		

Cooper & Steere 1995	EPV	16	88	19	43	7	At post-R_x: CBT = EPV; at FU: CBT > EPV
	CBT	15	87		54	46	
Jaeger *et al.* 1996	Analytic inpatient treatment	37	95	2/12 inpatient treatment	34.4	65.6	Slight superiority for analytical R_x
	Systemic outpatient treatment	46	80	14–23 hours	25.6	43.6	
Treasure *et al.* 1996	Manual + ≤8 CBT sessions	55	84	≤8	30	40	Brief manual-assisted R_x = CBT
	16 CBT sessions	55	72	16	30	41	
Thiels *et al.* 1998	Manual + 8 CBT sessions	31	71	8	29	35	Guided self-care = CBT at FU
	16 CBT sessions	31	87	16	65	58	

BT: behaviour therapy; CBT: cognitive behavioural psychotherapy; IPT: interpersonal therapy; EPV: exposure and prevention of vomiting; EPB: exposure and prevention of bingeing; SET: supportive expressive therapy; SM: self-monitoring; STP: short-term focal psychotherapy; WL: waiting list. Abstinence rates: if abstinence from *both* bingeing and purging combined was given, this is reported here; if abstinence rates from bingeing and vomiting are given separately, abstinence from vomiting is reported as this is the more conservative measure.

Table 15.2. Controlled studies of group psychotherapy of bulimia nervosa

Authors	Comparison	*n*	Completers (%)	Intensity (hours)	Abstinence post-R_x (%)	Abstinence at follow-up (%)	Comments
Boskind-Lodahl & White 1978	Feminist-experiential + BT	13	not reported	28	Not reported	31	Treatment group > WL; study seriously flawed; gains not maintained beyond 3/12
	WL	13					
Lacey 1983	Eclectic	15	100	40	80	66	Eclectic R_x > WL; improvement maintained at FU
	WL	15			0		
Connors *et al.* 1984	CBT	26	77	24	Not reported	15	CBT > WL
	WL						
Yates & Sambrailo 1984	CBT	12	67	9	0	0	Both groups improved equally
	CBT + behavioural instruction	12	67		12.5	25	
Huon & Brown 1985	CBT	40	89	30	33	68	CBT? > WL at end of R_x; further improvement throughout FU
	WL						
Kirkley *et al.* 1985	CBT	14	93	24	Not reported	38	CBT > ND at end of R_x; not at FU
	Non-directive	14	64			11	
Wilson *et al.* 1986	CR	8	75	24	33	17	CR + EPV > CR at post-R_x and FU; the combined group maintained gains at FU
	CR + EPV	9	78		71	86	
Lee & Rush 1986	CBT	15	93	18	29	Not reported	CBT > WL; gains maintained at FU
	WL	15	93		7		
Wolchik *et al.* 1986	CBT	13	85	12.5	0	9	CBT > WL; gains maintained at FU
	WL	7	100				
Laessle *et al.* 1987	BT	8	100	–	36	75	BT > WL
	WL	9	100	–	38	–	

Leittenberg *et al.* 1988	CBT + EPV (ms)	12	2 early drop-outs were replaced, one additional drop-out in EPV-ss group	48	33	50	Active treatments > WL at post-R_x; exposure groups slightly superior to CBT at FU
	CBT + EPV (ss)	11			36	18	
	CBT	12			8	33	
	WL	12			0	–	
Olmsted *et al.* 1991	Psych.Ed. group	35	83	7.5	21	Not reported	CBT > Psych.Ed. group only for the most symptomatic subgroup of patients
	CBT (Individual)	30	83	19	36		
Laessle *et al.* 1991	Nutritional management	27	82	30	50	50	NM produced a more rapid improvement in eating behaviour and higher abstinence rates
	Stress management	28	93		27	20	
Wolf & Crowther 1992	CBT	15	100	20	Not reported	30% of subjects in active treatment	Both treatments > WL at post-R_x; BT showed better maintenance of reduction in binge eating at FU
	BT	15	100				
	WL	12	92				
Mitchell *et al.* 1993	CBT with high emphasis on abstinence/high intensity	33	88	45	64	Not reported	High intensity approach, early abstinence approach or combination of the two > low intensity + low abstinence approach
	high/low	41	88	22.5	68		
	low/high	35	86	45	68		
	low/low	34	82	22.5	21		

BT: behaviour therapy; CBT: cognitive behavioural psychotherapy; CR: cognitive restructuring; IPT: interpersonal therapy; EPV: exposure and prevention of vomiting; EPV (ss): exposure and prevention of vomiting (single setting); EPV(ms): Exposure and prevention of vomiting (multiple settings); Psych.Ed.: psychoeducation; WL: waiting lists. Abstinence rates: if abstinence from *both* bingeing and purging combined was given, this is reported here; if abstinence rates from bingeing and vomiting are given separately, abstinence from vomiting is reported as this is the more conservative measure.

self-control techniques in the treatment of 12 obese bulimics. All subjects in the EPB condition were abstinent from bingeing at post-treatment and follow-up, whereas only 33% of those in the self-control group achieved abstinence at follow-up. An open study (Kennedy *et al.* 1995) recently used EPB as an adjunct to the in-patient treatment of bulimic anorexics and bulimia nervosa patients. Significant within-session and pre-post treatment reductions in urges to binge, lack of control, feelings of guilt and tension were found especially in the bulimic anorexic groups, suggesting that this treatment deserves further study.

Carter and Bulik (1994) in a careful review of exposure techniques in bulimia nervosa conclude that 'despite being used for a decade in the treatment of BN exposure techniques remain controversial . . . ' and 'their ultimate value remains unclear'.

INTERPERSONAL THERAPY

Interpersonal therapy (IPT), a treatment developed at NIMH for depression (Klerman *et al.* 1984), was first used by Fairburn *et al.* (1991) in the treatment of bulimia nervosa as a control treatment to CBT. In this treatment no mention is made of eating problems or weight and shape concerns. To the authors' surprise, IPT—although not as effective at post-treatment—caught up with CBT over the 1-year follow-up period with patients in the CBT group making further gains (Fairburn *et al.* 1993a). These gains were maintained at 5-year follow-up (Fairburn *et al.* 1995). These findings challenge the dogma of the CBT model for bulimia nervosa. Jones *et al.* (1993) investigated further the different mechanisms involved in the three treatments in a subgroup of Fairburn's original sample. Patients in all three groups made early improvements (first 4 weeks of treatment), which could be attributed to unspecific treatment effects. Thereafter, those in the CBT and BT conditions continued to improve, which would suggest their direct effect on eating behaviour. The study gave no clues on the mechanism of action of IPT.

DYNAMIC AND SYSTEMIC PSYCHOTHERAPY

In contrast to the Anglo-American preference for CBT, in mainland Europe, many bulimics are treated with psychodynamic psychotherapy or other forms of conflict-oriented treatments. The rationale for this approach is that 'intrapsychic conflicts' and a 'psychological core pathology' are thought to be causing the symptomatology. Jaeger *et al.* (1996) compared analytic inpatient therapy with systemic out-patient therapy in patients with bulimia nervosa. The analytic regime consisted of a 2-month inpatient programme with 4 weekly psychodynamic groups sessions and additional structured and problem-oriented groups, creative therapy and the use of body-oriented techniques. Systemic therapy was based on the Milan family therapy model with 9 to 15 treatment outpatient treatment sessions given over 1 year. At 38 months follow-up 44% of the systemic therapy group and 65% of patients of the analytic therapy group were symptom free. This difference was significant and together with differences on a number of other variables pointed towards a slight superiority of analytic inpatient treatment. The problem with this study is that only about 50% of patients were randomized, the rest were allocated according to patient preferences. It is also unclear whether anyone had additional treatment. An evaluation of the cost of treatment was not included. No other comparative evaluations of dynamic or systemic therapies have been forthcoming.

INDIVIDUAL OR GROUP TREATMENT?

There are equally many studies evaluating psychological treatments given on an individual basis or in a group format (see Tables 15.1 and 15.2). Given the secretiveness of their disorder, for many bulimics, meeting other sufferers in a therapeutic context, can be a powerful way of helping them to address their problems and of reducing guilt, shame and social isolation. Additionally, group treatments may be more cost-effective in terms of requiring less therapist time. On the other hand drop-out rates may be higher (Freeman *et al.* 1988) and there may be logistical problems in getting together a sufficient number of patients to start a group. Only one study has so far compared directly group with individual treatment of similar intensity (Freeman *et al.* 1988) with comparable outcome for both treatment modalities. A further study is under way comparing a feminist–experiential treatment approach (Weiss *et al.* 1986) delivered in a group format with the same approach delivered individually (Mahon and Katzman, 1997).

An interesting quasi-experimental study examined whether additional sessions of group psychotherapy process would incrementally benefit bulimia nervosa subjects over and above what was achieved through a course of brief psychoeducation (Davis *et al.* 1997). Both treatments were associated with comparable levels of change on measures of specific and nonspecific psychopathology. However, subjects who received the opportunity to engage in psychotherapy process with other group members valued this more than their psychoeducational sessions. The study is limited by the absence of any follow-up data and it is possible that differences between the two treatments might yet emerge over the follow-up period.

A small study examined the reasons why some women drop out of group treatment (McKisack and Waller 1996). Poor attendance was related to the group not addressing the women's immediate concerns about weight loss and good attendance was associated with severe eating pathology.

Fettes and Peters (1992) in a meta-analysis of group treatments for bulimia nervosa found the weighted average effect size at post-treatment to be 0.75, suggesting moderate efficacy. This effect size was in-between the smaller post-treatment effect size of 0.60 for drug therapy and larger composite post-treatment effect for psychotherapy of 1.14 (based on both individual and group treatment studies) reported in another meta-analytic study, using somewhat different methodology

(Laessle *et al.* 1987). It is difficult to draw any firm conclusions about the relative effectiveness of group therapy and individual therapy for bulimia nervosa from this.

SELF-CARE, GUIDED SELF-CARE AND MINIMAL INTERVENTIONS IN BULIMIA NERVOSA

Increasingly, the cost-effectiveness of treatments is an important consideration (Koran *et al.* 1995). Several treatment manuals written for sufferers of bulimia nervosa are now available (Weiss *et al.* 1986; Cooper 1993; Fairburn 1995; Schmidt and Treasure 1993) and have been evaluated in open (Cooper *et al.* 1994, 1996; Schmidt *et al.* 1993) and controlled studies (Treasure *et al.* 1994, 1996; Thiels *et al.* 1998). Self-treatment with a book can lead to full recovery in 20% of bulimic patients (Treasure *et al.* 1994). Unsurprisingly, compliance with the self-care approach is associated with a better outcome (Troop *et al.* 1996). Thirty to 50% of patients become symptom free if a few therapist-guided sessions (up to 8) are added *after* self-treatment (sequential treatment) (Treasure *et al.* 1996) or *concurrently* (guided self-help) (Cooper *et al.* 1996; Thiels *et al.* 1998). Patients treated with a minimal intervention involving self-care continue to improve after the end of treatment with an abstinence rate comparable to that of full CBT (40% symptom free) at follow-up (Treasure *et al.* 1996, Thiels *et al.* 1998). These minimal interventions may be less useful for those with a shorter duration and greater severity of illness (Turnbull *et al.* 1997). A brief psychoeducational group programme (five 90 minute sessions over 5 weeks) was compared with a full CBT programme in a quasi-experimental design (Olmsted *et al.* 1991). As hypothesized the CBT treatment was generally more effective, but this could be explained by its effects on the most severely ill subgroup, whereas for less severely ill patients the two treatments were equally effective. At post-treatment, abstinence rates in the two groups did not significantly differ with 20.7% in the educational group and 36% in the CBT group.

A simplified form of CBT treatment has been developed for primary care (Waller *et al.* 1996) and seems to benefit a significant proportion of patients.

DRUG TREATMENT OF BULIMIA NERVOSA

A wide range of chemically heterogeneous substances have been used in the treatment of bulimia nervosa. Associations of bulimia nervosa with major depression and obsessive–compulsive disorder have provided the rationale for the use of antidepressants (tricyclics, atypical antidepressants, monoamine-oxidase inhibitors and selective serotonin re-uptake inhibitors (SSRIs)) and mood-stabilizers (lithium carbonate) in this disorder (see Chapter 17 by Mayer and Walsh). Antiepileptics (phenytoin) were tried following the observation that some bulimics have an abnormal EEG. Disturbance of hunger and satiety prompted the use of appetite suppressants (D-fenfluramine). The view that eating disorders are opioid-mediated addictions (Marazzi *et al.* 1995), whereby dieting triggers the release of endogenous opioids, led to the use of opioid-antagonists (naltrexone) in the treatment of bulimic disorders. Recently, in view of laboratory and clinical findings suggesting that impaired central nervous serotonergic responsiveness may be involved in the onset or maintenance of bulimia nervosa (Jimerson *et al.* 1992, 1997; Halmi 1997; Levitan *et al.* 1997) there has been particular interest in the study of those drugs which facilitate serotonergic neurotransmission (e.g. imipramine, fenfluramine, fluoxetine, desipramine). Open studies of fluvoxamine (Ayuso-Gutierrez *et al.* 1994) and of ipsapirone, a partial 5-HT_{1A} agonist have shown promising results (Geretsegger *et al.* 1995).

Twenty-two randomized placebo-controlled drug trials of bulimia nervosa have been reported using either parallel or cross-over designs (see Table 15.3). With the exception of three studies (Mitchell and Groat 1984; Sabine *et al.* 1983; Hsu *et al.* 1991) all others find active medication to be superior to placebo on eating symptomatology and other symptomatology, however, the observed abstinence rates are (if they have been reported at all) extremely variable. On the whole, short-term results only have been reported leaving open the question as to what happens when medication is discontinued and whether there might be any value in long-term medication. Pope *et al.* (1985) in a 2-year follow-up study of 20 bulimic patients treated with various antidepressants found that a substantial number relapsed when antidepressants were withdrawn. Interestingly, Agras *et al.* (1994) found that whilst early discontinuation after 16 weeks of desipramine treatment was associated with high relapse rates, at 1-year follow-up discontinuation after 24 weeks of desipramine was not. Walsh *et al.* (1991) set out to assess the long-term effects of imipramine. In the initial 8-week treatment phase superiority of desipramine over placebo in reducing binge frequency was demonstrated; however, less than half of the patients treated with desipramine met the criteria for entry into the maintenance phase (reduction of 50% or more in binge frequency in the last 2 weeks of the initiation phase). Twenty-nine percent of the patients who entered the maintenance phase relapsed in the following 4 months. Pyle *et al.* (1990) found a relapse rate of 67% for patients who in the short term had responded to imipramine only and were then switched to imipramine maintenance therapy, compared to a relapse rate of 83% for those who after responding to initial imipramine were switched to placebo. In contrast, relapse rates in those receiving imipramine in combination with CBT were only 22%.

One frequently used argument against drug treatment in bulimia nervosa is that it only suppresses eating symptoms, and does not change underlying psychopathology or induce attitudinal change, thereby making relapse on withdrawal of the drug more likely. However, contrary to this view, Goldbloom and Olmsted (1993) showed that fluoxetine was able to induce attitudinal improvements on a wide range of psychological measures, comparable to the changes seen in intensive psychological treatment. Concerns about the possibility of increased suicidality on fluoxetine have also been unfounded (Wheadon *et al.* 1992). A prospective, naturalistic longitudinal study of eating disorders (Herzog and Sacks 1993) found that

Table 15.3. Randomized placebo-controlled trials of drug treatment of bulimia nervosa

Authors	Drug/dosage	Duration	*n*	Completers (%)	Abstinence post-R_x (%)	Comments
Wermuth *et al.* 1997	Phenytoin (300 mg)	6 weeks; cross-over design	20	95	Not reported	Some evidence of positive effect of phenytoin
Pope *et al.* 1983	Imipramine (200 mg)	6 weeks	D = 11 P = 11	82 91	0 0	Imipramine > placebo in reducing binges and other eating symptoms
Sabine *et al.* 1983	Mianserine (60 mg)	8 weeks	D = 20 P = 30	70 73	Not reported	Mianserine = placebo
Mitchell & Groat 1984	Amitryptiline (150 mg)	8 weeks	D = 21 P = 17	76 94	19 19	Amitryptiline = placebo
Hughes *et al.* 1986	Desipramine (200 mg)	6 weeks	D = 10 P = 12	79 75	55	Desipramine > placebo; patients on placebo switched over to imipramine
Agras *et al.* 1987	Imipramine (mean = 176 mg; max = 300 mg)	16 weeks	D = 10 P = 12	100 83	30 10	Imipramine > placebo
Price & Babai 1987	Nomifensine (200 mg) Phenelzine (60 mg) Placebo	6 weeks; cross-over design	10	Not reported	Not reported	Nomifensine and phenelzine > placebo; Nomifensine = phenelzine
Walsh *et al.* 1987	Phenelzine (60–80 mg)	8 weeks	D = 31 P = 31	74 88	35 4	Phenelzine > placebo
Barlow *et al.* 1988	Desipramine (150 mg)	6 weeks cross-over design	47	51	4	Desipramine > placebo
Blouin *et al.* 1988	Desipramine (150 mg) Fenfluramine (60 mg)	6 weeks; cross-over design	36	61	Not reported	Both drugs > placebo; more patients responded to fenfluramine than to desipramine

Horne *et al.* 1988	Bupropion (225–450 mg)	8 weeks	D = 55 P = 26	68 46	30 None	Bupropion > placebo; but 3 subjects in bupropion group and 1 placebo subject had grand-mal seizures
Kennedy *et al.* 1988	Isocarboxide (60 mg)	6 weeks; cross-over design	29	62	35	Isocarboxazid > placebo
Russell *et al.* 1988	D-fenfluramine (15–30 mg)	12 weeks	D = 21 P = 21	62 57	Not reported	If drop-outs included in analysis: D-fenfluramine > placebo; if only completers were considered these differences disappeared
Mitchell *et al.* 1989	Naltrexone (50 mg)	6 weeks; cross-over design	18	89	Not reported	No significant differences between naltrexone and placebo
Pope *et al.* 1989	Trazodone (400–650 mg)	6 weeks	D = 23 P = 23	87 96	10 0	Trazodone > placebo
Hsu *et al.* 1991	Lithium carbonate (600–1200 mg)	8 weeks	D = 47 P = 44	81 68	17.6	Patients who completed the study showed a significant decrease in bulimic episodes. Lithium was not more effective than placebo.
Walsh *et al.* 1991	Desipramine (200–300 mg)	8 weeks	D = 40 P = 38	80 84	12.5 7.9	Desipramine > placebo
FBNC (1992)	Fluoxetine (60 mg) (20 mg)	8 weeks	D (60 mg) = 127 D (20 mg) = 128 P = 127	D(60) = 70 D(20) = 77 P = 62	25 15 10	Fluoxetine 60 mg > placebo in reducing binge eating and vomiting; with fluoxetine 20 mg being intermediate
Kennedy *et al.* 1993	Brofaromine	8 weeks	D = 19 P = 17	79 77	44 20	Brofaromine > placebo in terms of reduction of episodes of vomiting, but no differences *vis-à-vis* bingeing or on attitudinal measures
Rothschild *et al.* 1994	Phenelzine (≥ 45 mg) Imipramine (≥ 150 mg)	6 weeks	Phenelzine = 8 Imipramine = 6 Placebo = 10	100 100 100	Not reported	Subjects were patients with atypical depression plus bulimia; phenelzine > imipramine or placebo in terms of reducing depression and bulimic symptoms

Table 15.3 (*continued*)

Authors	Drug/dosage	Duration	*n*	Completers (%)	Abstinence post-R_x (%)	Comments
Goldstein *et al.* 1995	Fluoxetine (60 mg)	16 weeks	D = 296 P = 102	60 48	19 12	Fluoxetine > placebo
Marrazzi *et al.* 1995	Naltrexone (200 mg)	6 weeks; crossover design	13	Not reported	Not reported	Naltrexone > placebo

D, active drug; P, placebo.

bulimic patients who had drug treatment within the first 13 weeks were more likely to demonstrate sustained recovery over the course of the first year of the study than those who did not have pharmacotherapy. Whilst this might suggest that early drug treatment might have a differential effect on the outcome of bulimia nervosa, a possible alternative explanation is that selection bias existed in those prescribed medication and that the healthier, possibly more compliant patients were treated with drugs.

PSYCHOTHERAPY VERSUS ANTIDEPRESSANT TREATMENT

Several studies have now evaluated the effectiveness of psychological treatment (CBT) compared with medication or combinations of the two (see Table 15.4). Studies comparing CBT versus antidepressant medication alone have found CBT to be superior to desipramine and fluoxetine (Agras *et al.* 1992; Goldbloom *et al.* 1995 (quoted from Wilson 1996); Leitenberg *et al.* 1994). A combination of CBT and an antidepressant is superior to antidepressant alone (Mitchell *et al.* 1990; Agras *et al.* 1992; Leitenberg *et al.* 1994; Goldbloom *et al.* 1995; Walsh *et al.* 1997). Most studies—with the exception of Walsh *et al.* 1997 fail to find an advantage of the combined treatment (CBT plus antidepressant) over CBT combined with placebo (Fichter *et al.* 1991; Mitchell *et al.* 1990; Fahy *et al.* 1993a). The situation is more complex in the comparison of combined treatment with CBT alone, where Goldbloom *et al.* (1995) and Leitenberg *et al.* (1994) do not find any advantage of the combined treatment. However, Agras *et al.* (1992, 1994) found the combination of CBT plus 24 weeks of desipramine to be superior to CBT alone on measures of dietary preoccupation and emotionally driven eating. These results were maintained at 1-year follow-up.

OTHER TREATMENTS

Winter worsening of mood and eating symptoms akin to those in seasonal affective disorder have been reported in a substantial proportion of patients with bulimia nervosa (Lam *et al.* 1996). A controlled study of light therapy evaluated 17 bulimics who were treated with 2 weeks of bright white light exposure and 2 weeks of dim red light exposure (equivalent to office lighting; control treatment) in a counterbalanced, cross-over design (Lam *et al.* 1994). The bright white light condition was superior for all mood and eating outcome measures. Patients with seasonal bulimia had significantly greater improvement after the bright white light treatment than patients with non-seasonal bulimia. The mechanisms of action of light therapy are unknown. Prominent theories include correction of phase delays in circadian rhythm and effects on serotonergic receptor function.

Table 15.4. Randomized controlled trials of combined drug and psychotherapy in bulimia nervosa

Authors	Drug/dosage	Duration	*n*	Completers (%)	Abstinence post-R_x (%)	Comments
Mitchell *et al.* 1990	CBT + placebo	10 weeks	33	88	45	80 hours therapy! All three active treatments significantly superior to placebo; CBT > imipramine; CBT + imipramine ≥ CBT + placebo
	CBT + imipramine		48	81	56	
	imipramine (≤ 300 mg)		45	69	16	
	placebo		29	90		
Fichter *et al.* 1991	Fluoxetine (60 mg) + inpatient BT	35 days	40	100	Not reported	Significant improvements over time in both groups with no difference between them; ? ceiling effect
	Placebo + inpatient BT					
Agras *et al.* 1992	Desipramine (≤ 350 mg) 16/52	32 weeks	71	92	33	At 16 weeks: CBT and combined R_x > desipramine; at 32 weeks only combined 24-week R_x > 16/52 medication
	Desipramine 24/52			75	42	
	CBT + desipramine 16/52			83	64	intention to treat analysis
	CBT + desipramine 24/52			75	70	
	CBT			96	55	
Fahy *et al.* 1993a	D-fenfluramine (45 mg) + CBT	8 weeks	20	100	20.5	Carry forward analysis; both groups improved significantly with no difference between them
	placebo + CBT		23	83		
Leitenberg *et al.* 1994	CBT	20 weeks	7	86	71	Study terminated early because of high drop-out rate and lack of positive response in subjects in the desipramine condition. Significant pre-treatment to follow-up reductions in eating symptomatology in CBT and combined treatment. Combined treatment not superior to CBT alone.
	desipramine (≥ 150 mg)		7	43	0	
	CBT + desipramine		7	71	57	

Walsh *et al.* 1997	CBT + medication (desipramine → fluoxetine)	20 weeks	23	overall 66	48	CBT > supportive psychotherapy; psychological treatment plus medication > psychological treatment alone
	CBT + placebo		25		20	
	Supportive + medication		22		9	
	Supportive + placebo		22		14	
	Medication only		28		21	

PREDICTORS OF TREATMENT OUTCOME

A consistent finding from different psychological and drug treatment studies of bulimia nervosa is that those with a lower body mass index are less likely to respond to treatment as are those with more severe eating symptomatology (Garner *et al.* 1990; Bossert *et al.* 1992; Davis *et al.* 1992; Fahy and Russell 1993; Fahy *et al.* 1993b; Turnbull *et al.* 1996). Premorbid obesity may also predict a poorer outcome (Fairburn *et al.* 1995). Whilst Fahy and Russell (1993) found longer duration of illness to be related with a poorer outcome, Turnbull *et al.* (1997) found the opposite.

Low self-esteem has also been mentioned as a predictor of poor treatment outcome (Baell and Wertheim 1992; Fairburn *et al.* 1987, 1993b). Additionally, comorbid depression (Bossert *et al.* 1992) and personality disorders are negative prognostic factors (Fichter *et al.* 1992; Coker *et al.* 1993; Fahy *et al.* 1993b; Rossiter *et al.* 1993; Wonderlich *et al.* 1994); in particular those with so-called multi-impulse bulimia nervosa have a poor prognosis even with very intensive treatment (Fichter *et al.* 1994). Surprisingly, a history of prior substance abuse was not found to have an impact on outcome of pharmacological treatment (Strasser *et al.* 1992). One study mentions a highly controlled or discordant family environment as a predictor of poor outcome in group CBT of bulimia nervosa (Blouin *et al.* 1994).

An interesting study (Olmsted *et al.* 1996) attempted to tease out predictors for rapid or slow response, partial response and no response in the treatment of bulimia nervosa. Rapid responders tended to be older, less symptomatic and less preoccupied with bingeing; however, the differences between the groups were not large.

SUMMARY OF THE STATUS QUO

Recent advances in our understanding of the neurobiology of bulimia nervosa have stimulated research into treatment of the disorder with substances which facilitate serotonergic neurotransmission or with opioid antagonists. However, therapeutic effects of drug treatments are relatively modest even in the short term and often poorly sustained in the longer term. Despite the moderate effectiveness of antidepressant medication, primary care physicians and even some psychiatrists will use these drugs as a first line treatment, as this is often the course of least difficulty for the treating doctor. Interestingly, patients themselves are often reluctant to take antidepressant medication which may reflect their recognition that their problems go far beyond their eating disturbance.

Most reviewers agree that psychological treatments are preferable as a starting point and that based on current evidence CBT has to be seen as the first line treatment in bulimia nervosa (Wilson 1996). Milder disorders can be treated with one of the brief manualized treatments. Antidepressants should be considered as an option in all patients with bulimia nervosa who fail to respond to psychosocial treatments. Hudson *et al.* (1996) suggest that if antidepressants are used, an SSRI is used first, but these authors point out that one may need to be prepared if necessary to conduct a minimum of three trials of antidepressants in order to obtain an optimal response. It may be helpful to spell out to patients that SSRIs do not possess the unpleasant side effects so commonly associated with the older antidepressants (e.g. weight gain, sedation, dry mouth, blurred vision). Patients may also be relieved to know that low central serotonin leads to the reduced satiety that many patients experience post-prandially (Halmi 1997) and that SSRIs may be of help with this.

BEYOND THE STATUS QUO

As already pointed out at the beginning of this chapter, evidence-based protocols for the treatment of any disorder are likely to underestimate or to fail to address completely the treatment needs of many (Mitchell *et al.* 1996), especially if there are gaps in our knowledge (Schmidt *et al.* 1996), as is certainly the case in as far as our knowledge about the treatment of bulimia nervosa is concerned. Thus, to attempt to fit all our bulimic patients into the 'procrustean bed' of CBT may not be appropriate. The prevailing treatment model of CBT was developed on and for (childless) young Western women in their teens and twenties (mainly university students). Even if CBT is administered by specialists to the patients it was designed for, only 50% of patients fully recover. What to do with and for the other 50% remains an unanswered question.

With rising prevalences of BN it is recognized that BN does not just affect young Western women. It may affect older women, pre-pubertal or pre-menarchal children, those with obesity, those from ethnic minorities facing acculturation stress (Nasser 1986; Mumford and Whitehouse 1988; Crago *et al.* 1996; Davis and Katzman 1997), those from non-Western cultures (Pakistan: Choudry and Mumford 1992; Mumford *et al.* 1992; Hongkong: Lee *et al.* 1997) and those with metabolic disorders like insulin dependent diabetes (Steel *et al.* 1989) or thyroid disorder (Tiller *et al.* 1992) and men (Turnbull *et al.* 1987; Fichter and Hoffman 1990; Carlat and Camargo 1991). Whilst some of these may share the prevailing culture of slimness many do not and have very different explanatory models of what is wrong with them.

For example, young Muslim Asian women in the UK who develop bulimia nervosa often come from very traditional families and face considerable acculturation conflict. A desire to be slim is not often part of their presentation (Mumford and Whitehouse 1988). Based on their work with Chinese and American women with eating disorders and arguing from a feminist and transcultural perspective. Katzman and Lee (1997) have posited that problems of disconnection, transition and oppression may be much more important than weight and shape concerns.

Men with bulimia nervosa also often have minimal weight or shape concerns (Schneider and Agras 1987; Fichter and Hoffman 1990). It is possible that a drive for fitness, rather than a drive for thinness plays a role in the development of their eating disorders (Carlat and Camargo 1991). Interestingly, a recent comparison of men and women with binge eating disorder found no differences with regards to eating-related psychopathology or behaviour (Tanofsky *et al.* 1997). However, the men were more likely to have Axis I comorbidity and less likely than women to report eating in response to negative emotions.

An additional problem for younger children is the question whether their cognitive development has progressed far enough to allow them to use cognitive treatment strategies effectively. Adolescents may rebel against the idea of homework and dietary monitoring as this 'smacks too much of school'.

Patients with histories of abuse and those with severe (often multi-impulsive) comorbidity also require particular attention. Treatment which exclusively focuses on structured management of eating symptomatology and which does not address the abuse may make these women feel ignored or silenced, or may be experienced as irrelevant (Wooley 1994; Schmidt *et al.* 1997a).

Thus considerable problems may occur in trying to 'socialize' these 'atypical' patients to the prevailing CBT model and treatment may need adapting or may not be valid at all.

PUTTING SOME THOUGHT BACK INTO CBT

Hollon and Beck (1994) and Waller (1997a) criticize some of the earlier forms of cognitive behavioural treatment for eating disorders with their focus on weight, shape and dieting concerns and suggest that there needs to be a shift onto more central issues such as deeper concerns about the self. Vitousek and Hollon (1990) draw attention to the role of self-schemata (absolute beliefs about the self) in eating disorders, and newer forms of CBT very much move away from a discussion of superficial weight and shape-related cognitions (Kennerley 1997) into an examination of the underlying schemata. Newer forms of CBT also take into account motivational issues and the therapeutic alliance (Pike *et al.* 1996) as well as interpersonal issues and women's reactivity to emotional threats (Waller 1997b), and may be much more meaningful and appropriate forms of treatment, especially for those patients with personality difficulties or complicating 'atypical' features.

DEVELOPING ALTERNATIVES TO CBT

Alternative forms of treatment also need further development and study. Anecdotally, many patients enjoy and benefit from experiential therapies, yet evaluations of these are not forthcoming and they are often seen as 'cranky therapies' or as a 'fringe' activity. With the advent of more sophisticated multi-level models of meaning and emotion (e.g. Teasdale and Barnard 1993; Brewin *et al.* 1996; Power and Dalgleish 1997) it is likely that these therapies will attract greater attention (and perhaps some grant money for study!). There are also a number of established forms of psychotherapy, which with some adaptation may add much to our therapeutic repertoire.

Interpersonal therapy has already been demonstrated to be a useful alternative to CBT in bulimia nervosa, with follow-up results as good as those of CBT (Fairburn *et al.* 1993). These findings make intuitive sense as many bulimics' problems are triggered and maintained by interpersonal events and difficulties (Schmidt *et al.* 1997b). The findings of the study by Fairburn and colleagues are in urgent need of replication.

It has been suggested that IPT might be used as a second line treatment in those cases where CBT has failed. However, in binge eating disorder those who had not responded to CBT fared no better when subsequently given interpersonal therapy (Agras *et al.* 1995).

COGNITIVE ANALYTIC TREATMENT

This is a form of therapy developed by Anthony Ryle (1990), which combines some aspects of cognitive behavioural therapy with an additional focus on interpersonal relationships in particular the therapist–patient relationship. This form of treatment has been adapted for use in anorexia and bulimia nervosa (Treasure and Ward 1997) and has been evaluated and found to be effective in the treatment of anorexia nervosa (Treasure *et al.* 1995).

DIALECTICAL BEHAVIOUR THERAPY

Wilson (1996) suggested that comorbid personality disorders in bulimia nervosa patients might be treated by using Linehan's (1993) dialectical behaviour therapy, which was developed for chronically suicidal borderline patients. Telch (1997) used skills training based on Linehan's approach—not to treat personality disorder—but to improve affect regulation in a woman with binge eating disorder. The central assumption underlying this endeavour was that binge eating functions for these patients in the same way that impulsive behaviours like deliberate self-harm functions for borderline individuals, i.e. by affording temporary relief from painful negative affect. The patient was taught core mindfulness skills, distress tolerance skills, emotion regulation skills and interpersonal effectiveness skills. By the end of treatment the patient had overcome her eating disorder. This approach might also show promise for individuals with bulimia nervosa, irrespective of whether there is underlying personality disorder.

MULTIFACETED PROGRAMMES

Lacey and Read (1993) describe a multifaceted inpatient treatment programme for severely disturbed multi-impulsive bulimics. In this programme focal-interpretative and cognitive techniques are used in both group and individual sessions. Major use is made of creative and reality-oriented techniques. Pilot results suggest that patients respond well to this programme and that the improvement in symptomatology is maintained during follow-up. This approach certainly deserves further study.

MOTIVATIONAL ENHANCEMENT THERAPY (MET)

This hybrid therapy was developed originally for individuals with alcohol problems treated in Project Match (1997). Four sessions of MET were as effective in the treatment of these patients as twelve sessions of CBT. MET is designed to produce rapid, internally motivated change. It does not 'attempt to guide and train the client, step by step, through recovery, but instead employs motivational strategies to mobilize the client's own change resources' (Miller *et al.* 1992). The therapeutic style is that of Motivational Interviewing (Miller and Rollnick 1991) which is a non-directive client-centred approach, designed to avoid confrontation, overcome ambivalence and minimize resistance. The MET approach is further grounded in research on the processes of natural recovery, described by Prochaska and DiClemente (1992) in their transtheoretical model. Within this model the questions of the 'when, how and what to change' are addressed. Different stages of change (precontemplation, contemplation, preparation, action, maintenance and relapse) have been defined and depending on an individual's stage of change certain tasks need to be accomplished and certain processes to be used in order to achieve change. MET has now been adapted for use in eating disorders (Schmidt and Treasure, 1997; Treasure and Ward, 1997) and a study evaluating it in bulimia nervosa is now underway (Mahon and Katzman 1997; Treasure 1997).

OTHER RESEARCH QUESTIONS

Beyond the questions of what kind of therapy for what patient at what stage there is the question of the 'how' of change, which has so far received very little attention. Additionally, questions of 'therapy dose' and intensity are important. In a meta-analytic study (Hartman *et al.* 1992) the average effect size of studies with 15 or more sessions was high (1.367), whereas the average effect size for treatment with less than 15 sessions was significantly lower with an effect size of 0.792. Mitchell *et al.* (1993) found that a high intensity group treatment, or treatment with an emphasis on early abstinence or a combination of the two were superior to low intensity group treatment or an approach which did not emphasize early abstinence.

A FINAL NOTE

Only twenty years ago therapists and doctors were totally helpless *vis-à-vis* bulimia nervosa, a disorder which initially was seen strictly as an 'ominous' variant of anorexia nervosa (Russell 1979). The advent of CBT contributed greatly to reducing the helplessness of therapists, by for the first time providing a specific model to conceptualize the disorder. With its focus on eating symptoms and weight and shape concerns it helped to raise the profile of the disorder as a distinct entity and to give sufferers a voice.

The limitations of this kind of treatment have become clearer in recent years and research into other therapeutic approaches—psychological and pharmacological—used as alternative first-line or second-line treatments, is urgently needed, in order to offer something to the 50–60% of patients who do not recover with conventional treatments.

Whatever we do there will be some patients who will fail to improve. As therapists we may often feel that we should not and cannot give up on those patients who have failed to respond to treatment. However, a salutary note is injected by Wilson (1996) who points out that some patients may be intractable and there is evidence that some patients improve following treatment, even if they have not improved during treatment (Fairburn *et al.* 1995). Despite our best efforts we may not be able to reach out to all our patients.

CLINICAL IMPLICATIONS

- CBT is the most widely evaluated psychological treatment for bulimia nervosa and leads to abstinence rates of 40–60%.
- Standard CBT may not address adequately the treatment needs of atypical (in terms of age, sex, culture, weight) patients or those with co-morbidity.
- Cognitive behavioural self-help manuals or guided self-help are effective in a proportion of sufferers.
- IPT is promising but needs further evaluation.
- The value of exposure treatment is uncertain.
- Medication is not usually a first-line treatment for bulimia nervosa.

RESEARCH IMPLICATIONS

- Promising new approaches to treatment which need further evaluation include: Schema-focused CBT, dialectical behaviour therapy, cognitive analytic therapy, motivational enhancement therapy, experiential therapies and multi-faceted day or in-patient programmes.

REFERENCES

Agras, W.S., Dorian, B., Kirkley, B.G., Arnow, B. and Bachman, J. (1987). Imipramine in the treatment of bulimia: a double-blind controlled study. *International Journal of Eating Disorders* **6**, 29–38.

Agras, W.S., Schneider, J.A., Arnow, B., Raeburn, S.D. and Telch, C.F. (1989). Cognitive behavioural and response prevention treatments for bulimia nervosa. *Journal of Consulting and Clinical Psychology* **57**, 215–221.

Agras, W.S., Rossiter, E.M., Arnow, B. *et al.* (1992). Pharmacologic and cognitive-behavioral treatment for bulimia nervosa: a controlled comparison. *American Journal of Psychiatry* **149**, 82–87.

Agras, W.S., Rossiter, E.M., Arnow, B. *et al.* (1994). One-year follow-up of psychosocial and pharmacologic treatments for bulimia nervosa. *Journal of Clinical Psychiatry* **55**, 179–183.

Agras, W.S., Telch, C.F., Arnow, B. *et al.* (1995). Does interpersonal therapy help patients with binge eating disorder who fail to respond to cognitive-behavioural therapy. *Journal of Consulting and Clinical Psychology* **63**, 356–360.

Ayuso-Gutierrez, J.L., Palazon, M., Ayuso Mateos, J.L. (1994). Open trial of fluvoxamine in the treatment of bulimia nervosa. *International Journal of Eating Disorders* **15**, 245–249.

Baell, W.K., and Wertheim, E.H. (1992). Predictors of outcome in the treatment of bulimia nervosa. *British Journal of Clinical Psychology* **31**, 330–332.

Barlow, J., Blouin, J., Blouin, A. and Perez., E. (1988). Treatment of bulimia with desipramine: A double-blind crossover study. *Canadian Journal of Psychiatry* **33**, 129–133.

Blouin, A.G., Blouin, J.H., Perez, E.L., Bushnik, T., Zuro, C. and Mulder, E. (1988). Treatment of bulimia with fenfluramine and desipramine. *Journal of Clinical Psychopharmacology* **8**, 261–269.

Blouin, J.H., Carter, J., Blouin, A.G. *et al.* (1994). Prognostic indicators in bulimia nervosa treated with cognitive behavioural group therapy. *International Journal of Eating Disorders* **15**, 113–123.

Boskind-Lodahl, M. and White, W.C. (1978). The definition and treatment of bulimarexia in college women—a pilot study. *JACHA* **27**, 85–86,87.

Bossert, S., Schmolz, U., Wiegand, M., Junker, M. and Krieg, J.C. (1992). Predictors of short-term treatment outcome in bulimia nervosa inpatients. *Behaviour Research and Therapy* **30**, 193–199.

Brewin, C.R. (1989). Cognitive change processes in psychotherapy. *Psychological Review* **96**, 379–394.

Brewin, C.R., Dalgleish, T. and Joseph, S. (1996). A dual representation theory of post traumatic stress disorders. *Psychological Review* **103**, 670–686.

Carlat, D.J. and Camargo, C.A. (1991). Review of bulimia nervosa in males. *American Journal of Psychiatry* **148**, 831–843.

Carter, F. A. and Bulik, C.M. (1994). Exposure treatments for bulimia nervosa. Procedure, efficacy and mechanisms. *Advances in Behaviour Research and Therapy* **16**, 77–129.

Choudry, I.Y. and Mumford, D.B. (1992). A pilot study of eating disorders in Mirpur (Pakistan) using an Urdu version of the Eating Attitudes Test. *International Journal of Eating Disorders* **11**, 243–251.

Coker, S., Vize, C., Wade, T. and Cooper, P.J. (1993). Patients with bulimia nervosa who fail to engage in cognitive behavioural therapy. *International Journal of Eating Disorders* **13**, 35–40.

Connors, M.E., Johnson, C.L. and Stuckey, M.K. (1984). Treatment of bulimia with brief psychoeducational group therapy. *American Journal of Psychiatry* **141**, 1512–1516.

Cooper, P. (1993). *Bulimia Nervosa. A Guide to Recovery*. Robinson Publishing, London.

Cooper, P.J. and Steere, J. (1995). A comparison of two psychological treatments for bulimia nervosa: implications for models of maintenance. *Behaviour, Research and Therapy* **33**, 875–885.

Cooper, P.J., Coker, S. and Fleming, C. (1994). Self-help for bulimia: a preliminary report. *International Journal of Eating Disorders* **16**, 401–404.

Cooper, P.J., Coker, S. and Fleming, C. (1996). An evaluation of the efficacy of supervised cognitive behavioural self-help for bulimia nervosa. *Journal of Psychosomatic Research* **40**, 281–287.

Crago, M., Shisslak, C.M. and Estes, L.S. (1996). Eating disturbances among American minority groups: a review. *International Journal of Eating Disorders* **19**, 239–248.

Daris, C. and Katzman, M.A. (1998). Chinese men and women in the United States and Hong Kong: body and self-esteem ratings as a prelude to dieting and exercise. *International Journal of Eating Disorders* **23**, 99–102.

Davis, R., Olmsted, M.P. and Rockert, W. (1992). Brief group psychoeducation for bulimia nervosa. II Prediction of clinical outcome. *International Journal of Eating Disorders* **11**, 205–211.

Davis, R., Olmsted, M., Rockert, W., Marques, T. and Dolhanty, J. (1997). Group psychoeducation for bulimia nervosa with and without additional psychotherapy process sessions. *International Journal of Eating Disorders* **22**, 25–34.

Fahy, T.A., and Russell, G.F. (1993). Outcome and prognostic variables in bulimia nervosa. *International Journal of Eating Disorders* **14**, 135–145.

Fahy, T. A., Eisler, I. and Russell, G.F. (1993a). A place-controlled trial of D-fenfluramine in bulimia nervosa. *British Journal of Psychiatry* **162**, 597–603.

Fahy, T.A., Eisler, I. and Russell, G.F.M. (1993b). Personality disorder and treatment response in bulimia nervosa. *British Journal of Psychiatry* **162**, 765–770.

Fairburn, C.G. (1981). A cognitive behavioural approach to the management of bulimia nervosa. *Psychological Medicine* **11**, 707–711.

Fairburn, C.G. (1995). *Overcoming Binge Eating*. Guilford Press, New York.

Fairburn, C.G., Kirk, J., O'Connor, M. and Cooper, P.J. (1986). A comparison of two psychological treatments for bulimia nervosa. *Behaviour Research and Therapy* **24**, 629–643.

Fairburn, C.G., Kirk, J., O'Connor, M., Anastasiades, P. and Cooper, P.J. (1987). Prognostic factors in bulimia nervosa. *British Journal of Clinical Psychology* **26**, 223–224.

Fairburn, C.G., Jones, R., Peveler, R.C. *et al.* (1991). Three psychological treatments for bulimia nervosa. *Archives of General Psychiatry* **48**, 463–469.

Fairburn, C.G., Jones, R., Peveler, R.C., Hope, R.A. and O'Connor, M.E. (1993a). Psychotherapy and bulimia nervosa: the longer term effects of interpersonal psychotherapy, behaviour therapy and cognitive behavior therapy. *Archives of General Psychiatry* **50**, 419–428.

Fairburn, C.G., Marcus, M.D. and Wilson, G.T. (1993b). Cognitive behavioural therapy for binge eating and bulimia nervosa: a comprehensive treatment manual. In: C.G. Fairburn, and Wilson, G.T. (eds). *Binge Eating: Nature, Assessment and Treatment.* (pp. 361–404). Guilford Press, New York.

Fairburn, C.G., Peveler, R.C., Jones, R., Hope, R.A. and Doll, H.A. (1993c). Predictors of 12-month outcome in bulimia nervosa and the influence of attitudes to shape and weight. *Journal of Consulting and Clinical Psychology* **61**, 696–698.

Fairburn, C.G., Norman, P.A., Welch, S.L., O'Connor, M.E., Doll, H.A. and Peveler, R.C. (1995). A prospective study of outcome in bulimia nervosa and the long-term effects of three psychological treatments. *Archives of General Psychiatry* **52**, 304–312.

Fairburn, C.G., Welch, S.L., Doll, H.A., Davies, B.A. and O'Connor, M.E. (1997). Risk factors for bulimia nervosa. A community-based case–control study. *Archives of General Psychiatry* **54**, 509–517.

Fettes, P.A. and Peters, J.M. (1992). A meta-analysis of group treatments for bulimia nervosa. *International Journal of Eating Disorders* **11**, 97–110.

Fichter, M.M. and Hoffman, R. (1990). Bulimia (nervosa) in the male. In: Fichter, M.M. (ed.). *Bulimia Nervosa: Basic Research, Diagnosis and Therapy*. John Wiley, Chichester.

Fichter, M.M., Leibl, K., Rief, W., Brunner, E., Schmidt-Auberger, S. and Engel, R.R. (1991). Fluoxetine versus placebo: a double-blind study with bulimic inpatients undergoing intensive psychotherapy. *Pharmacopsychiatry* **24**, 1–7.

Fichter, M.M., Quadflieg, N. and Rief, W. (1992). The German Longitudinal Bulimia Nervosa Study I. In: Herzog, W., Deter, H.C. and Vandereycken, W. (eds). *The Course of Eating Disorders*. Springer Verlag, Berlin.

Fichter, M.M., Quadflieg, N. and Rief, W. (1994). Course of multi-impulsive bulimia. *Psychological Medicine* **24**, 591–604.

Fluoxetine Bulimia Nervosa Collaborative (FBNC) Study Group (1992). Fluoxetine in the treatment of bulimia nervosa. A multicenter, placebo-controlled, double-blind trial. *Archives of General Psychiatry* **49**, 139–147.

Freeman, C.P.L., Barry, F., Dunkeld-Turnbull, J. and Henderson, A. (1988). Controlled trial of psychotherapy for bulimia nervosa. *British Medical Journal* **296**, 521–525.

Garner, D.M., Olmsted, M.P., Davis, R., Rockert,W., Goldbloom, D. and Eagle M. (1990). The association between bulimic symptoms and reported psychopathology. *International Journal of Eating Disorders* **9**, 1–15.

Garner, D.M., Rockert, W., Davis, R., Garner, M.P. and Eagle, M. (1993). Comparison of cognitive behavioural and supportive expressive therapy for bulimia nervosa. *American Journal of Psychiatry* **150**, 37–46.

Geretsegger, C., Greimel, K.V., Roed, I.S. and Hesselink, J.M. (1995). Ipsapirone in the treatment of bulimia nervosa: an open pilot study. *International Journal of Eating Disorders* **17**, 359–363.

Goldbloom, D.S. and Olmsted, M.P. (1993). Pharmacotherapy of bulimia nervosa with fluoxetine: assessment of clinically significant attitudinal change. *American Journal of Psychiatry* **150**, 770–774.

Goldbloom, D., Olmsted, M., Davis, R. and Shaw, B. (1995). A randomized controlled trial of fluoxetine and individual cognitive behavioural therapy for women with bulimia nervosa: short term outcome. Unpublished manuscript, Department of Psychiatry, University of Toronto.

Goldstein, D.J., Wilson, M.G., Thompson, V.L., Potvin, J.H. and Rampey, A.H. Jr. (1995). Long-term fluoxetine treatment of bulimia nervosa. Fluoxetine Bulimia Nervosa Research Group. *British Journal of Psychiatry* **166**, 660–666.

Halmi, K.A. (1997). Models to conceptualize risk factors for bulimia nervosa. *Archives of General Psychiatry* **54**, 507–508.

Hartman, A., Herzog, T. and Drinkmann, A. (1992). Psychotherapy of bulimia nervosa: What is effective? A meta-analysis. *Journal of Psychosomatic Research*, **36**, 159–167.

Herzog, D.G. and Sacks, N.R. (1993). Bulimia nervosa: comparison of treatment responders vs nonresponders. *Psychopharmacology Bulletin* **29**, 121–125.

Hollon, S.D. and Beck, A.T. (1994). Cognitive and cognitive behavioural therapies. In: Bergin, A.C. and Garfield, S.L. (eds) *Handbook of Psychotherapy and Behaviour Change*, 4th Edn, pp. 428–466. Wiley, New York.

Horne, R.L., Ferguson, J.M., Pope, H.G. *et al.* (1988). Treatment of bulimia with bupropion: a multicenter controlled trial. *Journal of Clinical Psychiatry* **49**, 262–266.

Hsu, L.K.G., Clement, L., Santhuse, R. and Ju, E.S.Y. (1991). Treatment of bulimia nervosa with lithium carbonate: a controlled study. *Journal of Nervous and Mental Disease* **179**, 351–355.

Hudson, J.I. Carter, W.P. and Pope, H.G. Jr (1996). Antidepressant treatment of binge eating disorder: research findings and clinical guidelines. *Journal of Clinical Psychiatry* **Suppl 8**, 73–79.

Hughes, P.L., Wells, L.A., Cunningham, C.J. and Ilstrup, D.M. (1986). Treating bulimia with desipramine, *Archives of General Psychiatry* **43**, 182–186.

Huon, G.F. and Brown, L.B. (1985). Evaluating a group treatment for bulimia. *Journal of Psychiatric Research* **19**, 479–483.

Jaeger, B., Liedtke, R., Kunsebeck, H.W., Lempa, W., Kersting, A. and Seide, L. (1996). Psychotherapy and bulimia nervosa: evaluation and long-term follow-up of two conflict-oriented treatment conditions. *Acta Psychiatrica Scandinavica* **93**, 268–278.

Jansen, A., Broekmate, J. and Heymans, M. (1992). Cue exposure versus self-control in the treatment of binge eating: a pilot study. *Behaviour Research and Therapy* **30**, 235–241.

Jimerson, D.C., Lesem, M.D., Kaye, W.H. and Brewerton, T.D. (1992). Low serotonin and dopamine metabolic concentrations in cerebrospinal fluid from bulimic patients with frequent binge episodes. *Archives of General Psychiatry* **49**, 132–138.

Jimerson, D.C., Wolfe, B.E., Metger, E.D., Finkelstein, D.M., Cooper, T.B. and Levine, J.M. (1997). Decreased serotonin function in bulimia nervosa. *Archives of General Psychiatry* **54**, 529–534.

Jones, R., Peveler, R.C., Hope, R.A. and Fairburn, C.G. (1993). Changes during treatment for bulimia nervosa: a comparison of three psychological treatments. *Behaviour Research and Therapy* **31**, 479–485.

Katzman, M.A. and Lee, S. (1997). Beyond body image: the integration of feminist and transcultural theories in the understanding of self starvation. *International Journal of Eating Disorders*. **22**, 385–394.

Kazdin, A.E. and Mazurick, J.L. (1994). Dropping out of child psychotherapy: distinguishing early and late dropouts over the course of treatment. *Journal of Consulting and Clinical Psychology* **62**, 1069–1074.

Kennedy, S.H., Piran, N., Warsh, J.J. *et al.* (1988). A trial of isocaboxazid in the treatment of bulimia nervosa. *Journal of Clinical Psychopharmacology* **8**, 391–396.

Kennedy, S.H., Goldbloom, D.S., Ralevski, E., Davis, C., D'Souza, J.D. and Lofchy, J. (1993). Is there a role for selective monoamine oxidase inhibitor therapy in bulimia nervosa? A placebo-controlled trial of brofaromine. *Journal of Clinical Psychopharmacology* **13**, 415–422.

Kennedy, S.H., Katz, R., Neitzert, C.S., Ralevski, E. and Mendlowitz, S. (1995). Exposure with response prevention treatment of anorexia nervosa-bulimic subtype and bulimia nervosa. *Behaviour Research and Therapy* **33**, 685–689.

Kennerly, H. (1997). *Managing complex eating disorders using schema-based cognitive therapy*. Paper presented at the BABCP Meeting, Canterbury 8–12 July 1997.

Kirkley, B., Schneider, J.A., Agras, W.S. and Bachman, J.A. (1985). Comparison of two group treatments for bulimia. *Journal of Consulting and Clinical Psychology* **53**, 43–48.

Klerman, G.L., Weissman, M.M., Rounsaville, B.J. and Chevron, E.S. (1984). *Interpersonal Therapy of Depression*. Basic Books, New York.

Koran, L.M., Agras, W.S., Rossiter, E.M. *et al.* (1995). Comparing the cost effectiveness of psychiatric treatments: bulimia nervosa. *Psychiatry Research* **58**, 13–21.

Lacey, H. (1983). Bulimia nervosa, binge eating, and psychogenic vomiting: a controlled treatment study and long term outcome. British Medical Journal **286**, 1609–1613.

Lacey, J.H. and Read, T.R.C. (1993). Multi-impulsive bulimia: description of an inpatient eclectic treatment programme and a pilot follow-up study of its efficacy. *Eating Disorders Review* **1**, 22–31.

Laessle, R.G., Waadt, S. and Pirke, S.J. (1987). A structured behaviorally oriented group treatment for bulimia nervosa. *Psychotherapy Psychosomatics* **48**, 141–145.

Laessle, R.G., Beumont, J.P.V., Butow, P. *et al.* (1991). A comparison of nutritional management with stress management in the treatment of bulimia nervosa. *British Journal of Psychiatry* **159**, 250–261.

Lam, R.W., Goldner, E.M., Solyom, L., Remick, R.A. (1994). A controlled study of light therapy for bulimia nervosa. *American Journal of Psychiatry* **151**, 744–750.

Lam, R.W., Goldner, E.M. and Grewal, A. (1996). Seasonality of symptoms in anorexia and bulimia nervosa. *International Journal of Eating Disorders* **19**, 35–44.

Lee, N.F. and Rush, A.J. (1986). Cognitive-behavioral group therapy for bulimia. *International Journal of Eating Disorders* **5**, 599–615.

Lee, S., Leung, T., Lee, A.M., Yu, H. and Leung, C.M. (1997). Body dissatisfaction among Chinese undergraduates and its implications for eating disorders in Hong Kong. *International Journal of Eating Disorders*. In press.

Leitenberg, H., Rosen, J., Gross, J., Nudelman, S. and Vara, L.S. (1988). Exposure plus response-prevention treatment of bulimia nervosa. *Journal of Consulting and Clinical Psychology* **56**, 535–541.

Leitenberg, H., Rosen, J.C., Wolf, J., Vara, L.S., Detzer, M.J. and Srebnik, D. (1994). Comparison of cognitive behavioural therapy and desipramine in the treatment of bulimia. *Behaviour Research and Therapy* **32**, 37–48.

Levitan, R.D., Kaplan, A.S., Joffe, R.T., Levitt, A.J. and Brown, G.M. (1997). Hormonal and subjective responses to intravenous meta-chlorophenylpiperazine in bulimia nervosa. *Archives of General Psychiatry* **54**, 521–527.

Linehan, M. (1993). *Cognitive-Behavioural Treatment of Borderline Personality Disorder*. Guilford Press, New York.

Mahon, J. and Katzman, M. (1997). Group work and eating disorders: turning guilty secrets into good psychology. Paper presented at 'Eating Disorders 97'. The third London international conference on eating disorders. London, UK, April 15th to 17th 1997.

Marrazzi, M.A., Bacon, J.P., Kinzie, J. and Lubie, E.D. (1995). Naltrexone use in the treatment of anorexia nervosa and bulimia nervosa. *International Clinical Psycho-pharmacology* **10**, 163–172.

McKisack, C. and Waller, G. (1996). Why is attendance variable at groups for women with bulimia nervosa? *International Journal of Eating Disorders* **20**, 205–209.

Miller, W. and Rollnick, S. (1991). *Motivational Interviewing. Preparing People to Change Addictive Behaviours*. Guilford Press, New York.

Miller, W.R., Zweben, A., DiClemente, C.C. and Tychtarik, R.G. (1992). *Motivational Enhancement Therapy Manual. A Clinical Research Guide for Therapists Treating Individuals with Alcohol Abuse and Dependance*. Project Match Monograph Series, Vol 2., US Department of Health, Washington DC.

Mitchell, J.E. and Groat, R. (1984). A placebo-controlled, double-blind trial of amitryptiline in bulimia. *Journal of Clinical Psychopharmacology* **4**, 186–193.

Mitchell, J.E., Christenson, G., Jennings, J. *et al.* (1989). A placebo-controlled, double-blind crossover study of naltrexone hydrochloride in outpatients with normal weight bulimia. *Journal of Clinical Psychopharmacology* **9**, 94–97.

Mitchell, J.E., Pyle, R.L., Eckert, E.D., Hatsukmi, D., Pomery, C. and Zimmerman, R. (1990). A comparison study of antidepressants and structured intensive group psychotherapy in the treatment of bulimia nervosa. *Archives of General Psychiatry* **47**, 149–157.

Mitchell, J.E., Pyle, R.L., Pomery, C. *et al.* (1993). Cognitive-behavioural group psychotherapy of bulimia nervosa: importance of logistical variables. *International Journal of Eating Disorders* **14**, 277–287.

Mitchell, J.E., Hoberman, H.N., Peterson, C.B., Mussell, M. and Pyle, R.L. (1996). Research on the psychotherapy of bulimia nervosa: half empty or half full. *International Journal of Eating Disorders* **20**, 219–229.

Mumford, D.B. and Whitehouse, A.M. (1988). Increased prevalence of bulimia nervosa among Asian schoolgirls. *British Medical Journal* **297**, 718.

Mumford, D.B., Whitehouse, A.M. and Choudry, I.Y. (1992). Survey of eating disorders in English-Medium Schools in Lahore, Pakistan. *International Journal of Eating Disorders* **11**, 173–184.

Nasser, M. (1986). Comparative study of the prevalence of abnormal eating attitudes among Arab female students of both London and Cairo Universities. *Psychological Medicine* **16**, 621–625.

Olmsted, M.P., Davis, R., Garner, D.M., Eagle, M., Rockert, W. and Irvine, M.J. (1991). Efficacy of a brief group psychoeducational intervention for bulimia nervosa. *Behaviour Research and Therapy* **29**, 71–83.

Olmsted, M.P., Kaplan, A.S., Rockert, W. and Jacobsen, M. (1996). Rapid responders to intensive treatment of bulimia nervosa. *International Journal of Eating Disorders* **19**, 279–285.

Ordman, A.M. and Kirschenbaum, D.S. (1985). Cognitive behavioural therapy for bulimia: an initial outcome study. *Journal of Consulting and Clinical Psychology* **53**, 305–313.

Peveler, R.C. and Fairburn, C.G. (1992). The treatment of bulimia nervosa in patients with diabetes mellitus. *International Journal of Eating Disorders* **11**, 45–53.

Pike, K.M., Loeb, K. and Vitousek, K. (1996). Cognitive behavioural therapy for anorexia nervosa and bulimia nervosa. In: Thompson, K (ed.) *Body Image, Eating Disorders and Obesity*. American Psychological Association, Washington DC.

Pope, H.G., Hudson, J.I., Jonas, J.M. and Yurgelun-Todd, D. (1983). Bulimia treated with imipramine: A placebo-controlled, double-blind study. *American Journal of Psychiatry* **140**, 554–558.

Pope, H.G., Hudson, J.I., Jonas, J.M. and Yurgelun-Todd, D. (1985). Antidepressant treatment of bulimia: a two-year follow-up study. *Journal of Clinical Psychopharma-cology* **5**, 320–327.

Pope, H.G., Keck, P.E., McElroy, S.L. and Hudson, J.I. (1989). A placebo-controlled study of trazodone in bulimia nervosa. *Journal of Clinical Psychopharmacology* **9**, 254–259.

Power, M. and Dalgleish, T. (1997). *Cognition and Emotion. From Disorder to Order*. Psychology Press, Hove.

Price, W.A. and Babai, M.R. (1987). Antidepressant drug therapy for bulimia current status revisited. *Journal of Clinical Psychiatry* **48**, 385.

Prochaska, J.O. and DiClemente, C.C. (1992). The transtheoretical model of change. In: Norcross, J.C. and Goldfried, M.R. (eds) *Handbook of Psychotherapy Integration*. Basic Books, New York.

Project Match Research Group (1997). Matching alcoholism client heterogeneity: post treatment outcomes. *Journal of Studies on Alcohol* **58**, 7–25.

Pyle, R.L., Mitchell, J.E., Eckert, E.D., Hatsukami, D., Pomeroy, C. and Zimmerman, R. (1990). Maintenance Treatment and 6-month outcome for bulimic patients who respond to initial treatment. *American Journal of Psychiatry* **147**, 871–875.

Russell, G.F.M. (1979). Bulimia nervosa an ominous variant of anorexia nervosa. *Psychological Medicine* **9**, 429–448.

Russell, G.F.M., Checkley, S.A., Feldman, J. and Eisler, I. (1988). A controlled trial of D-fenfluramine in bulimia nervosa. *Clinical Neuropharmacology* **11**, S146–159.

Rosen, J.C. and Leitenberg, H. (1982). Bulimia nervosa: treatment with exposure and response prevention. *Behavior Therapy* **13**, 117–124.

Rossiter, E.M., Agras, W.S., Telch, C.F. and Schneider, J.A. (1993). Cluster B personality disorder characteristics predict outcome in the treatment of bulimia nervosa. *International Journal of Eating Disorders* **13**, 349–358.

Rothschild, R., Quitkin, H. M., Quitkin, F.M. *et al.* (1994). A double-blind placebo-controlled comparison of phenelzine and imiprarnine in the treatment of bulimia in atypical depressives. *International Journal of Eating Disorders* **15**, 1–9.

Ryle, A. (1990). *Conitive Analytical Therapy——Active Participation in Change.* Wiley, Chichester.

Sabine, E.J., Yonace, A., Farrington, A.J., Barratt, K.H. and Wakeling, A. (1983). Bulimia nervosa: a placebo controlled double-blind therapeutic trial of mianserin. *British Journal of Clinical Pharmacology* **15**, 195S–202S.

Schmidt, U. and Marks, I. (1989). Exposure and prevention of binges versus exposure plus prevention of vomiting: a crossover study. *Journal of Nervous and Mental Disease* **177**, 259–266.

Schmidt, U. and Treasure, J. (1993). *Getting Better Bit(e) by Bit(e)*. Lawrence Erlbaum Associates, London.

Schmidt, U. and Treasure, J. (1997). *Clinician's Guide. Getting Better Bit(e) by Bit(e)*. Psychology Press, Hove, East Sussex.

Schmidt, U., Tiller, J. and Treasure, J. (1993). Self-treatment of bulimia nervosa—a pilot study. *International Journal of Eating Disorders*, **13**, 273–277.

Schmidt, U., Dent, J. and Tanner, M. (1996). Evidence-based medicine. Pride and prejudice. *Bulletin of the British Journal of Psychiatry*.

Schmidt, U., Humfress, H. and Treasure, H. (1997a). The role of general family environment and sexual and physical abuse in the origins of eating disorders. *European Eating Disorders Review*. **5**, 184–207.

Schmidt, U., Tiller, J., Blanchard, M., Andrews, B. and Treasure, J. (1997b). Is there a specific trauma precipitating anorexia nervosa? *Psychological Medicine*. in press.

Schneider, J.A. and Agras, W.S. (1987). Bulimia in males: a matched comparison with females. *International Journal of Eating Disorders* **2**, 235–242.

Steel, J.M., Young, R.J., Lloyd, G.G. and MacIntyre, C.C. (1989). Abnormal eating attitudes in young insulin-dependent diabetics. *British Journal of Psychiatry* **155**, 515–521.

Strasser, T.J., Pike, K.M. and Walsh, B.Y. (1992). The impact of prior substance abuse on treatment outcome for bulimia nervosa. *Addictive Behaviour* **17**, 387–395.

Tanofsky, M.B., Wilfley, D.E., Spurrell, E.B., Welch, R. and Brownell, K.D. (1997). Comparison of men and women with binge eating disorders. *International Journal of Eating Disorders* **21**, 49–54.

Teasdale, J. and Barnard, P. (1993). *Affect, Cognition and Change*. Psychology Press, Hove.

Telch, C.F. (1997). Skills training treatment for adaptive affect regulation in a woman with binge-eating disorder. *International Journal of Eating Disorders*, **22**, 77–81.

Thackwray, D.E., Smith, M.C., Bodfish, J.W. and Meyers, A.W. (1993). A comparison of behavioral and cognitive-behavioral interventions for bulimia nervosa. *Journal of Consulting and Clinical Psychology* **61**, 639–645.

Thiels, C., Schmidt, U., Treasure, J., Garthe, R. and Troop, N. (1998). Guided self-change for bulimia nervosa incorporating a self-treatment manual. *American Journal of Psychiatry*. In press.

Tiller, J., Treasure, J., Schmidt, U., Macrae, A. and Bloom, S.R. (1992). Eating disorders in patients attending a thyroid clinic: a pilot study. *Journal of Psychosomatic Research* **38**, 609–616.

Treasure, J. (1997). *Motivational interviewing and eating disorders*. Paper given at the BABCP Meeting, Canterbury, 8–12 July, 1997.

Treasure, J. and Ward, A. (1997). A practical guide to the use of motivational interviewing in anorexia nervosa. *European Eating Disorders Review* **5**, 102–114.

Treasure, J., Schmidt, U., Troop, N., Tiller, J. and Todd, G. (1994). First step in managing bulimia nervosa a controlled trial of a therapeutic manual. *British Medical Journal* **308**, 686–689.

Treasure, J., Todd, G., Brolly, M., Tiller, J., Nehmed, A. and Denman, F. (1995). A pilot study of a randomized trial of cognitive analytical therapy versus educational behavioural therapy for adult anorexia nervosa. *Behaviour Research and Therapy* **33**, 363–367.

Treasure, J., Schmidt, U., Troop, N., Tiller, J., Todd, G. and Turnbull, S. (1996). Sequential treatment for bulimia nervosa incorporating a self-care manual. *British Journal of Psychiatry* **68**, 94–98.

Troop, N., Schmidt, U., Tiller, J., Todd, G., Keilen, M. and Treasure, J. (1996). Compliance with a self-directed treatment manual for bulimia nervosa: predictors and outcome. *Journal of Clinical Psychology* **35**, 435–438.

Turnbull, J.D., Freeman, C.P.L. and Annandale, K. (1987). Physical and psychological characteristics of five male bulimics. *British Journal of Psychiatry* **150**, 25–29.

Turnbull, S., Treasure, J., Schmidt, U., Troop, N., Tiller, J. and Todd, G. (1997). Predictors of short- and long-term outcome of bulimia nervosa. *International Journal of Eating Disorders* **21**, 17–22.

Vitousek, K.B. and Hollon, S.D. (1990). The investigation of schematic content and processing in the eating disorders. *Cognitive Therapy and Research* **14**, 191–214.

Waller, D., Fairburn, C.G., McPherson, A., Kay, R., Lee, A. and Nowell, T. (1996). Treating bulimia nervosa in primary care—a pilot study. *International Journal of Eating Disorders* **19**, 99–103.

Waller, G. (1997a). The cognitive and affective characteristics of bulimics: recent research and its implications for treatment. Paper presented at the BABCP Meeting, Canterbury, 8–12 July 1997.

Waller, G. (1997b). Drop-out and failure to engage in individual outpatient cognitive behavior therapy for bulimic disorders. *International Journal of Eating Disorders* **22**, 35–41.

Walsh, T.B., Gladis, M., Roose, S.P., Stewart, J.W. and Glassman, A. (1987). A controlled trial of phenelzine in bulimia. *Psychopharmacology* **23**, 49–51.

Walsh, B.T., Hadigan, C.M., Devlin, M.J., Gladis, M. and Roose, S.P. (1991). Long-term outcome of antidepressant treatment for bulimia nervosa. *American Journal of Psychiatry* **148**, 1206–1212.

Walsh, B.T., Wilson, G.T., Loeb, K.L. *et al.* (1997). Medication and psychotherapy in the treatment of bulimia nervosa. *American Journal of Psychiatry* **154**, 523–531.

Weiss, L., Katzman, M. and Wolchik, S. (1986). *You Can't Have Your Cake & Eat it Too: A Program for Controlling Bulimia*. R & E Publishers, Saratoga, California.

Wermuth, B.M., Davis, K.L., Hollister, L.E. and Stunkard, A.J. (1977). Phenytoin treatment of the binge-eating syndrome. *American Journal of Psychiatry* **134**, 1249–1253.

Wheadon, D.E., Rampey, A.H. Jr, Thompson, V.L., Potvin, J.H., Masica, D.N. and Beasley, C.M. Jr (1992). Lack of association between fluoxetine and suicidality in bulimia nervosa. *Journal of Clinical Psychiatry* **53**, 235–241.

Wilson, D.G.T., Rossiter, E., Kleinfels, E.I. and Lindholm, L. (1986). Cognitive behavioral treatment of bulimia nervosa: a controlled evaluation. *Behaviour Research and Therapy* **214**, 277–288.

Wilson, D.G.T., Eldredge, K.L., Smith, D. and Niles, B. (1991). Cognitive behavioural treatment of bulimia nervosa: a controlled evaluation. *Behaviour Research and Therapy* **29**, 575–583.

Wilson, T.G. (1996). Treatment of bulimia nervosa: when CBT fails. *Behaviour Research and Therapy* **34**, 197–212.

Wolchik, S.A., Weiss, L. and Katzman, M.A. (1986). An empirically validated, short-term psychoeducational group treatment program for bulimia. *International Journal of Eating Disorders* **5**, 21–34.

Wolf, E.M. and Crowther, J.H. (1992). An evaluation of behavioral and cognitive-behavioral group intervention for the treatment of bulimia nervosa in women. *International Journal of Eating Disorders* **11**, 3–16.

Wonderlich, S.A., Fullerton, D., Swift, W.J. and Klein, M.H. (1994). Five year outcome from eating disorders: relevance of personality disorders. *International Journal of Eating Disorders* **15**, 233–243.

Wooley, S.C. (1994). Sexual abuse and eating disorders: the concealed debate. In: Fallon, P., Katzman, M.A. and Wooley, S.C. (eds). *Feminist Perspectives on Eating Disorders*, pp. 171–211. Guilford Press, New York.

Yates, A.J. and Sambrailo, F. (1984). Bulimia nervosa: a descriptive and therapeutic study. *Behaviour Research and Therapy* **5**, 503–517.

16 The Treatment of Binge Eating Disorder

M. D. LEVINE and M. D. MARCUS
University of Pittsburgh School of Medicine, Pittsburgh, PA, USA

INTRODUCTION

Binge eating, the consumption of a large amount of food in a defined period of time with an accompanying perception of losing control over eating, is a hallmark of both bulimia nervosa (BN) and binge eating disorder (BED). In BN, the binge eating is accompanied by the regular use of inappropriate compensatory behaviors (e.g. vomiting, laxative abuse, or strict dieting). In contrast, individuals with BED engage in frequent binge eating without regular compensatory behaviors. Binge eating in the absence of compensatory behavior originally was described among obese individuals (Stunkard 1959), and the recent inclusion of binge eating disorder in the Fourth Edition of the Diagnostic and Statistical Manual of Mental Disorders (DSM-IV; American Psychiatric Association 1994), as a proposed diagnosis, has helped to accelerate research on the nature and treatment of recurrent binge eating in the absence of regular compensatory behavior. In comparison to the amount of research on the treatment of bulimia nervosa, however, the amount of research evaluating the effectiveness of treatments for BED is limited.

The majority of individuals with BED are obese (Marcus 1993; Yanovski 1995). Data from a large, multi-site community survey has indicated that approximately 2% of individuals in the community meet criteria for BED. In contrast, 30% of individuals seeking obesity treatment meet BED criteria (Spitzer *et al.* 1992). Early investigations of binge eating included normal weight patients with non-purging BN (e.g. McCann *et al.* 1991). However, because individuals with non-purging BN, by definition, must engage in some form of compensatory behavior, it is not likely that these findings would apply to obese BED patients. Moreover, there is considerable overlap in the features associated with both the purging and non-purging forms of BN (Garfinkel *et al.* 1996). Accordingly, research on BED has focused predominantly on obese individuals, and little is known about normal weight individuals with BED.

Thus, patients with BED share characteristics with both BN and other obese individuals. There also, however, are significant differences in the behaviors and biological correlates associated with BED and those of BN and obesity. Throughout this chapter, we will highlight the similarities and differences among obesity, BN, and BED, and the manner in which they may affect the treatment of BED.

Neurobiology in the Treatment of Eating Disorders.
Edited by H.W. Hoek, J.L. Treasure and M.A. Katzman.

Following a brief review of current biological findings and treatment outcome data, we will discuss the application of these findings to the treatment of BED, and conclude with areas for future work.

REVIEW OF BIOLOGIC AND TREATMENT OUTCOME FINDINGS

BIOLOGY OF BINGE EATING DISORDER

In general, the biological correlates of BED have been studied in comparison to those of BN, obesity and mood disorders. Among individuals with BN, a number of neuroendocrine abnormalities have been observed, including alterations in the serotonergic, noradrenergic and endogenous opiate systems, as well as abnormal glucose and insulin responses (e.g. Fava *et al.* 1989; Kaye *et al.* 1990). Recent data also have suggested differences in the pain detection thresholds of individuals who binge eat and those who do not, and a relationship between stimulation of the vagal nerve and the perpetuation of binge eating has been postulated (Faris *et al.* 1996; Raymond *et al.* 1996). Although there are data to support alterations in the neuroendocrine and metabolic functioning of individuals with disordered eating, most of this research has been conducted using individuals who engage in a number of aberrant eating and compensatory behaviors in addition to binge eating (Yanovski 1995). Moreover, the direction of the relationship between these biological abnormalities and disordered eating behaviors is unclear. It is not known if the observed neuroendocrine and metabolic changes are causally related to binge eating or other eating disorder behaviors such as purging, or if they are a consequence of the aberrant eating behaviors.

Studies comparing biological correlates of obese BED patients and equally overweight individuals without binge eating problems have failed to find differences in measures of metabolic rate, 24-hour energy expenditure or body composition (Adami *et al.* 1995; Alger *et al.* 1995; Wadden *et al.* 1993). Thus, to date, there are no data to suggest biological differences between obese binge eaters and non-binge eaters. Other research has compared BED patients with BN patients. Biological markers of depression, such as perturbations in the activity of the hypothalamic–pituitary–adrenal (HPA) axis, have been commonly reported among BN patients (Halmi 1985). Initial data from studies of BED samples, however, have not found such abnormalities of dexamethasone suppression or other markers of HPA activity (Yanovski 1995).

Studies comparing the eating behaviors and attitudes of BED patients with those of obese and BN individuals also have been inconclusive. Some laboratory studies have found that obese binge eaters consume significantly more calories and a greater percentage of fat intake than non-binge eaters (Yanovski *et al.* 1992), while others have reported no differences in daily caloric or macronutrient intake (Alger *et al.* 1995).

Recently, research focusing on genetic factors in the development of obesity and other disorders has proliferated. Future work should examine the relationship among the genetic risks for obesity, BN, and the development of BED. It is possible that a predisposition toward obesity precipitates early efforts to diet, and may initiate a cycle of weight loss and regain that is etiologically related to BED. Alternatively, the genetic propensity to obesity may drive overeating, or there may be genetic factors that specifically predispose individuals to the attitudes and behaviors of binge eaters.

In summary, as Yanovski (1995) concluded in a recent comprehensive review of the biological abnormalities in binge eating, few biological correlates of binge eating in the absence of purging have been identified. In addition, because many of the studies of BED patients to date have been conducted on small samples with poorly defined groups and methods, conclusions about the biology of BED remain premature. Additional work using larger, well defined samples and sound methodology that is derived from clearly formulated hypotheses may reveal clinically significant biological correlates of BED.

TREATMENT OUTCOME STUDIES

Not surprisingly, treatments for BED have been adapted from those that have been shown to be effective in reducing binge eating in individuals with BN or producing weight loss among obese individuals. Both psychological and pharmacological interventions for BN and obesity have been evaluated and will be described below.

Psychological treatments for binge eating

Cognitive-behavioral therapy (CBT) is the most extensively studied treatment for BN, and consistently has been shown to be an effective treatment for BN (Fairburn *et al.* 1992; Wilson and Fairburn 1993). Interpersonal psychotherapy (IPT) also has received preliminary support as an efficacious treatment for binge eating in individuals with BN, although the time course of the effects may differ from those of CBT (Fairburn *et al.* 1993a). In addition, antidepressant medications have been shown to result in modest, short-term reductions in the frequency of binge eating in BN patients (Fluoxetine Bulimia Nervosa Collaborative Study Group [FBNCSG] 1992; Mitchell *et al.* 1993), and the combination of CBT and antidepressant medication may be associated with greater reductions in bingeing and vomiting than medication alone (Walsh *et al.* 1997). Since the development of empirically supported diagnostic criteria for BED (Spitzer *et al.* 1992), a handful of clinical trials have been conducted to evaluate CBT, IPT, and pharmacologic interventions in patients with BED.

Initial evidence indicated that a cognitive-behavioral approach was acceptable among women with BED (Telch *et al.* 1990; Smith *et al.* 1992), and to date, four controlled clinical trials (Telch *et al.* 1990; Wilfley *et al.* 1993; Agras *et al.* 1994; Porzelius *et al.* 1995) have been conducted in which CBT has been evaluated in

BED patients. These studies are summarized in Table 16.1. Because a majority of individuals with BED are obese (Marcus 1993; Yanovski 1995), and because obesity and disordered eating are associated with long-term difficulties, it is important to evaluate the efficacy of interventions in addressing both disordered eating and overweight. As seen in Table 16.1, CBT is more effective than no treatment (Telch *et al.* 1990; Wilfley *et al.* 1993) in decreasing the frequency of binge eating, but generally has not resulted in significant weight loss by the end of treatment. However, it appears that individuals who are abstinent from binge eating post-treatment are more likely than those who are not to have lost weight during treatment (Agras *et al.* 1994). Moreover, recent evidence suggests that those who maintain abstinence 1-year post-treatment lose weight, whereas a relapse to binge eating is associated with a small weight gain (Agras *et al.* 1997).

IPT may also be effective in women with BED, but these findings should be regarded as preliminary. Wilfley and colleagues (1993) provided group treatment for women with BED using IPT. In this study, IPT led to significant reductions in the average number of binges per week both at post-treatment and 1 year following the end of treatment. Compared to CBT, women who received IPT treatment also reported significant increases in their level of dietary restraint. Despite this increase in dietary restraint, however, IPT treatment did not have significant effects on body weight. A pilot study from our research group also has provided evidence that individual IPT can be effective in reducing binge eating in obese women with BED (Marcus *et al.* in preparation).

Weight control and binge eating

Although some studies have found that BED patients, in contrast to non-BED patients, lose less weight (Keefe *et al.* 1984) or regain weight more rapidly (Marcus *et al.* 1988) in weight loss programs, the preponderance of the evidence suggests that BED and non-BED patients benefit equally from obesity treatment (see Table 16.2). Moreover, in contrast to initial speculation, obesity treatment does not exacerbate binge eating (Telch and Agras 1993), and behavioral treatment for obesity appears to be useful in ameliorating binge eating in BED patients (Marcus *et al.* 1995a). Nonetheless, because binge eaters are characterized by marked fluctuations in body weight over time (Marcus *et al.* 1992), additional studies of weight maintenance in BED patients are needed. Maintenance of weight loss is one of the most pressing difficulties in the field of obesity in general, and interventions to promote weight maintenance are being tested (e.g. Agras *et al.* 1996; Wing *et al.* 1996). Individuals with BED, however, may require specialized interventions to deal with exacerbations of binge eating and associated periods of weight gain.

Pharmacological treatments for BED

Based on the moderate efficacy of antidepressant medication in the treatment of BN (e.g. Mitchell *et al.* 1993), and the substantial comorbidity of major depressive

Table 16.1. Studies comparing psychological treatments for obese binge eaters

Reference	Subjects (*N*)	Treatments compared	Attrition rate	Outcome: binge eating	Outcome: weight loss
Telch *et al*. 1990	Obese women with non-purging BN (44)	Group CBT, 10 sessions vs waiting list (WL)	17% from CBT	CBT less binge episodes than WL (79% abstinent)	Not assessed
Wilfley *et al*. 1993	Obese women with non-purging BN (56)	Group CBT, 16 weeks vs group IPT vs waiting list (WL)	33% CBT 11% IPT; not significant	CBT = IPT > WL. 28% abstinent CBT vs. 44% IPT, ns At 1 year follow up, 50% reduction in binge eating that is not different between CBT IPT. No data on abstinence rates at follow-up	Small change in IPT (3 kg, not significantly different from CBT)
Agras *et al*. 1994	Obese women meeting criteria for BED (108)	Group treatment: behavioral weight control (WC) vs CBT + WC vs CBT + WC + desipramine	No difference 27% vs 17% vs 23%	Initially, CBT > Weight Control in decreasing binge eating. At the end of treatment, there were no differences in binge eating frequency or percent abstinent from binge eating	Initially, WC > CBT. At end of treatment no significant differences, but desipramine increased weight loss during active treatment
Porzelius *et al*. 1995	Obese women (70)	Group SBT vs obese binge eating treatment (OBET)	4 from each	No difference between treatments. BES decreased in all groups	Trend for severe binge eaters to lose more in OBET than SBT

BED = binge eating disorder; BES = binge eating scale; CBT = cognitive behavioral therapy; IPT = interpersonal psychotherapy.

Table 16.2. Studies comparing the outcome of obese binge eaters and non-binge eaters in weight loss treatments[a]

Reference	Subjects (criteria)[b]	Treatment (weeks)	Attrition rate[c]	Weight loss post-treatment (kg)[c]	Follow-up	Weight regained (kg)[c]
Keefe *et al.* (1984)	23 BE[d,f] (DSM-III) 21 NBE	BT (9)	Not available (retrospective study)	BE < NBE (1.9 vs 4.4)	6 months	BE > NBE (5.50 vs 3.05)
Marcus *et al.* (1988)	35 BE[c] 33 NBE (Interview, DSM-III)	BT (10)	BE > NBE (9% vs 3%)	BE = NBE	6 & 12 months	At 6 months: BE < NBE; At 1 year: BE = NBE
LaPorte (1992)	25 BE[f] 24 NBE (BES)	BT + VLCD (10)	BE = NBE (17% vs 32%)	BE = NBE (18.7 vs 20.2)	No follow-up	No follow-up
Wadden *et al.* (1992)	29 BE[c] 180 NBE (Self-report, DSM-III-R)	BT + VLCD (26)	BE = NBE (52.7% vs 62.8%)	BE + NBE (21.5 vs 21.7)	12 months (7 BE compared to 73 NBE)	BE = NBE
Telch & Agras (1993)	20 BE[c] 71 NBE (Interview, DSM-III-R)	BT + VLCD (52)	Not compared	BE = NBE	3 months	BE = NBE (94.4 vs 89.7)
Yanovski *et al.* (1994)	21 BE[c] 17 NBE (Self-report, DSM-IV)	BT + VLCD (26)	BE = NBE[f] (10% vs 0)	BE = NBE (19.6 vs 21.3)	3,6,9, & 12 months (16 BE compared to 17 NBE)	BE = NBE at all four follow-up assessments

BE = Binge eater; NBE = Non-binge eater; BES = binge eating scale; BT = behavioral weight control treatment; VLCD = very-low calorie diet.
[a]Only studies in which behavioral treatments for obesity were compared are tabulated. [b]Criteria used to determine binge eating status. [c]<, >, = refers to statistical significance of comparisons of weight or attrition rates. [d]Used definite and probable diagnosis of bulimia; assessed following the end of treatment. [e]Subjects were all females. [f]Male and female subjects.

disorders and BED (Marcus 1993), the efficacy of antidepressant medication for binge eating among patients with BED has been examined. Theoretically, the effect of serotonergic, antidepressant agents has been attributed to the role of serotonin in the regulation of appetite and mood. Serotonergic agents, such as fluoxetine (Marcus *et al.* 1990a; McCann and Agras 1990; Greeno and Wing, 1996), and the combination of psychotherapy and antidepressant medications (Agras *et al.* 1994) have proven to be moderately effective in reducing the frequency of binge eating in individuals with BED during active treatment (see Table 16.3). Although antidepressant medications are superior to placebo, they do not appear to enhance the effectiveness of CBT, or relate to long-term changes in eating behavior. Agras and his colleagues (1994) examined the efficacy of the combination of desipramine and a behavioral weight loss treatment subsequent to CBT for binge eating. At the end of the nine months of treatment, the group that received desipramine had lost more than the group receiving weight loss treatment alone (6.0 kg versus 1.6 kg); however, these weight loss differences were not statistically significant.

One study has investigated the use of a serotonergic anorectic agent, D-fenfluramine, in the treatment of BED (Stunkard *et al.* 1996). Obese binge eaters treated with D-fenfluramine experienced a significantly greater reduction in the number of binges per week while taking the medication than did those given placebo. Four months following the end of treatment, however, binge frequency no longer differed between placebo- and drug-treated (Stunkard *et al.* 1996). Thus, serotonergic agents appear to be associated with modest, short-term reductions in binge eating, but not with weight loss.

Another neurochemical system that has been implicated in the pathophysiology of binge eating is the endogenous opiate system (Drewnoski *et al.* 1995), and preliminary data have suggested that the opiate antagonist, naltrexone, may be useful in reducing binge eating symptoms in overweight women with BED (Marrazzi *et al.* 1995). Although theories about the relationship between opiate peptides and preferences for sweet and/or high-fat foods have been postulated (Drewnoski *et al.* 1995), additional treatment studies are needed.

Summary: treatments for BED

In summary, both CBT and IPT have been associated with statistically significant reductions in the frequency of binge eating in women with BED, and, in comparison to other behavioral treatment programs (e.g. for smoking cessation or weight loss), the rate of attrition appears to be less problematic. Moreover, a modest proportion of women receiving these treatments achieve abstinence from binge eating by the end of treatment. Importantly, abstinence post-treatment appears to either be maintained or associated with considerably lower rates of binge eating 1 year later (Agras *et al.* 1997), and may therefore represent a more clinically significant improvement.

In addition, pharmacological interventions, involving both the opiate and serotonergic systems, have been found to reduce the frequency of binge eating in

Table 16.3. Studies comparing pharmacological treatments for obese binge eaters[a]

Reference	Subjects (*N*)	Study design (weeks)	Attrition rate	Outcome: eating behavior[b]	Outcome: weight loss (kg)[b]
McCann & Agras (1990)	Obese women with non-purging BN (23)	Randomized to desipramine vs placebo (12)	5 drug vs 2 placebo	D > P 63% vs 16% reduction in binge eating, and 60% vs 15% abstinent from binge eating	D = P (3.5 vs 1.2)
Marcus *et al.* (1990a,b)	Obese men and women: BE (22) c and NBE (23)	All received BT and randomly assigned to fluoxetine vs placebo (52)	Not related to drug or binge status	Not evaluated	D > P for all subjects; No significant difference in weight loss between binge eaters and non-binge eaters taking fluoxetine (17.1 vs 8.4)
Greeno & Wing (1996)	Obese women BED (40) and NBE (39)[d]	Randomized to fluoxetine or placebo (1)[e]	Not related to binge status	D > P in overall intake; Women with and without BED responded similarly to drug treatment	Not evaluated[e]

[a]Only placebo-controlled studies using obese binge eaters are tabulated.
[b] <, >, = refers to statistical comparisons of weight or attrition rates.
[c]Groups were determined according to scores on the BES.
[d]Diagnosis was made according to clinical interview (EDE).
[e]This report concerns the first 6 days on drug or placebo-treatment prior to dietary intervention.
D = drug treatment, P = placebo; BT = behavioral weight control treatment; BED = binge eating disorder, BES = binge eating scale.

women with BED. Antidepressant medications are associated with short-term reductions of binge eating during treatment, but do not appear to contribute to additional weight loss or continued decreases in binge eating. Initial work has also tested serotonergic anorectic agents, such as D-fenfluramine, in treating BED. However, conclusions about the use of anorectic agents in obesity are limited by the lack of methodologically sound, long-term studies, and additional research is needed. One particular question about the use of these anorectic drugs in BED patients is the potential relationship between the use of anorectic agents and the development of depressive episodes. The development of depression during treatment with serotonergic agents has been observed among obese individuals (National Task Force on Obesity 1996), and clinical observations have indicated that the same potential adverse effect of anorectic agents is possible among BED patients.

A number of important gaps in our understanding of both the application of available treatments and their mechanisms of action in individuals with BED remain. First, current theories about the development, maintenance and treatment of binge eating for BED patients have been derived, without significant modification, from theories of binge eating in BN. However, as noted, the biological correlates of BED and BN differ. Second, BED is associated with obesity and available data suggest that BED patients are similar to their non-binge eating peers in metabolism, body composition, and other biologic correlates. We will highlight the impact of these differences on the delivery of treatment in BED in the following section.

TREATING BINGE EATING DISORDER: INTEGRATING DATA AND TREATMENT

TREATMENT GOALS FOR BINGE EATING DISORDER

There are three general areas to consider in formulating treatment plans for individuals with BED: disordered eating, obesity, and associated psychopathology. These three areas appear to be interrelated. Therefore, until research is available to inform clinical decision making, decisions about the order in which to target these behaviors and the design of an intervention are best made on an individual basis.

Binge eating

Aberrant eating behaviours are a clear commonality between BED and BN. However, in BED patients, the binge eating differs from that in BN as the episodes of binge eating are not punctuated by compensatory behaviors. Compared to other obese individuals, BED patients eat more at both meals and binges (Yanovski *et al.* 1992), and have significantly wider variation in daily caloric intake (Alger *et al.* 1995). Clinical observations also have suggested a tendency for BED patients to eat frequently both at and between regular meals throughout the course of a day. Therefore, one important goal of treatment is to normalize eating and ameliorate the binge eating episodes.

The cognitive-behavioral model of binge eating, developed to explain the maintenance of binge/purge behaviors in individuals with BN, posits that binge eating often develops in response to restrictive food intake. Repeated efforts to diet are thought to promote feelings of deprivation and hunger that lead to binge eating. Cognitive-behavioral treatments for binge eating often focus first on normalizing eating, and eliminating efforts to diet (Fairburn *et al.* 1993b). Importantly, however, several lines of evidence suggest that the nature of dietary restraint in BED patients differs from that observed in patients with BN.

First, on average, patients with BED do not exhibit the high level of dietary restraint endorsed by patients with BN (Marcus *et al.* 1992; Rossiter *et al.* 1992). Using a semi-structured, clinical interview, the Eating Disorder Examination (EDE; Cooper and Fairburn 1987; Fairburn and Cooper, 1993), Marcus and colleagues (1992) found the level of dietary restraint in a group of overweight women with BED to be significantly lower than the level of dietary restraint in both a group of normal weight bulimia nervosa patients and normal weight restrained eaters.

Second, considerable evidence supports the assertion that dieting does not always precede the onset of binge eating in individuals with BED (Marcus *et al.* 1995b; Mussell *et al.* 1995; Spurrell *et al.* 1997). Moreover, patients for whom the onset of binge eating problems precedes first attempts at dieting, appear to have more eating disorder psychopathology than their peers who began to binge at an older age (Marcus *et al.* 1995b). The finding that not all women with BED are restrained eaters suggests that there are multiple pathways to the development of binge eating problems. For example, women with BED may experience fluctuations in their levels of restraint, alternating between periods of dieting, or high restraint and periods of low restraint. It is possible that these women only binge eat during periods of low restraint, not during periods of high restraint, a pattern opposite of that used to explain the cycle of dieting and binge eating in women with BN.

That binge eating has its onset both before and after the initiation of attempts to diet also runs counter to established theories about the relationship between dietary restraint and the development of binge eating (Polivy *et al.* 1984; Polivy and Herman 1985; Ruderman 1986). For example, eating in response to negative emotional states appears to be particularly problematic among BED patients (Eldredge and Agras 1996), and negative emotionality may trigger a binge in the absence of previous dieting behaviors. With each individual patient, it is therefore important to identify and discuss the various triggers for binge episodes.

Certainly, dysfunctional thoughts contribute to the maintenance of binge eating in BED. However it appears that the nature of these thoughts may differ from those of BN patients. One particular group of cognitions that may need to be specifically targeted with BED patients are those relating to large body size. Overweight individuals with BED may be helped to accept their larger than average body size and to restructure maladaptive thoughts about weight loss that may perpetuate binge eating. Although modest weight loss, as discussed below, may relate to improvements in binge eating, for the majority of BED patients a 5 or 10 kg weight loss may not correspond with their desired weight loss. It is therefore important that cognitions about acceptable body sizes be targeted.

Weight loss

The prevalence of binge eating increases with the level of obesity (Telch *et al.* 1988), and approximately 30% of individuals who seek treatment for weight control in tertiary care centers have significant binge eating problems (Spitzer *et al.* 1992). Yet, the most effective way to target the related problems of obesity and binge eating remains unknown. Because the medical risks associated with obesity are serious (Pi-Sunyer 1991), addressing the obesity is a potentially important aim of treatment with BED patients. Although much previous theorizing has stressed the role of restraint in precipitating binge episodes, patients with BED do not necessarily binge in response to restraint or hunger, and the preponderance of evidence suggests that dieting is not contraindicated for these patients. In fact, increasing the level of dietary restraint or dieting may help to ameliorate binge eating (Marcus *et al.* 1995a).

A number of serotonergic agents have been associated with weight loss among obese individuals both alone (Stunkard *et al.* 1996), and in conjunction with behavior modification interventions (Marcus *et al.* 1990a; McCann and Agras 1990; Greeno and Wing 1996). Because between one third and one half of obese individuals with BED endorse lifetime rates of mood disorders (Marcus *et al.* 1990b; Mitchell and Mussell 1995), and BED patients seeking treatment endorse high rates of depressive symptomatology, antidepressant therapy may be particularly helpful.

It is important to note that the efficacy of drug treatment of obesity has been examined only for short-term use, and the long-term use of these anorectic agents has yet to be well established. Based on a review of the current data, members of the National Task Force on the Prevention and Treatment of Obesity (1996) concluded that 'SSRIs (selective serotonin reuptake inhibitors) do not appear to be efficacious for long-term treatment of obesity and are not recommended for this indication alone (p. 1911)'. It is not reasonable to expect that obese individuals with BED will be more likely than obese individuals who do not binge eat to benefit from drug therapy for weight loss, and the effectiveness of these agents on the urge to binge eat and related eating disorder symptoms is not known. Moreover, potential adverse consequences, such as the development of depressive episodes during drug treatment, need to be balanced with the possible benefits of moderate weight loss.

Mood disorders and other associated psychopathology

Mood fluctuations and periods of depression may be associate with weight gain among individuals with BED. Kendler and colleagues (1996) have recently reported a relationship between overweight and a tendency to experience atypical episodes of depression, characterized by weight gain. Because episodes of depression are known to affect changes in body weight (DiPietro *et al.* 1992), the vulnerability to increased eating when depressed, suggests that BED patients may be at increased risk for repeated cycles of depression and weight gain. Overall, these data support the importance of addressing problems which affect regulation and mood disorders in BED. It is possible that prophylactic antidepressant medication following the normalization of eating habits may help prevent repeated cycles of depression and weight gain. Alternatively, it may be necessary to address psychosocial factors (e.g. using IPT) that may contribute to the aberrant eating habits prior to attempting to ameliorate binge eating.

A final area to consider in the treatment of BED patients is the associated psychiatric disorders apparent in these individuals. As many as 32% of binge eaters reported a history of mood disorder (Marcus *et al.* 1990b), and the rates of anxiety disorders are also higher than in a comparable population sample (Yanovski 1993). Personality disorders are also prevalent among individuals with BED. For example, Yanovski (1993) reported that 14% of obese binge eaters met criteria for borderline personality disorder. These diagnoses may not only complicate the treatment of BED, but may also affect tendency to relapse, and therefore additional weight gain. It is possible that alternative treatment modalities, such as dialectical behavior therapy (Linehan 1993), may be useful in addressing these related problems.

DIRECTIONS FOR THE FUTURE

Prevention: targeting younger, non-psychiatric populations

One area for future research is the identification and treatment of binge eating problems in younger patients and ethnic minority populations. Recently, our research group has been evaluating eating disorder symptoms and behaviors in a group of adolescent women ($N=153$; ages 14–19) presenting to an urban, primary health care clinic (Wisniewski *et al.* 1996). In this setting, nearly one half (44%) of young women had a body mass index (BMI; weight in kilograms divided by the square of height in meters) above the ideal for their height and weight, and a small but surprising percentage (4%) of young girls endorsed difficulties with binge eating. In addition, an alarming proportion of young women in this setting (28%) reported significant difficulties with depression. These data indicate that mood and eating problems can be successfully identified in a primary care setting, and suggest that it may be important to develop treatments for subclinical eating and mood problems at younger ages.

Carter and Fairburn (1995) have described an adaptation of short-term CBT for binge eating that may be applied in a primary care setting. They also discuss a treatment focused around a self-help book, either using the book alone or in conjunction with brief contact with a clinician. One preliminary evaluation has suggested that it may be possible to address eating disorders in a primary care setting (Waller *et al.* 1996). The effectiveness of interventions for binge eating that target subclinical patients delivered in a primary care setting need to be further evaluated. Further research using younger samples in primary care settings may help to elucidate the relationship between subclinical disordered eating and the development of BED, as well as the relationship between mood and eating.

Applications in diverse populations: males and older patients

Although BED affects both men and women, and occurs in older and younger age groups, the theories of binge eating have been adapted from those of a disorder that most commonly affects younger, female clients. Moreover, each of the treatment outcome studies to date have evaluated the effectiveness of CBT only among women. Although BED is somewhat more common among women than men, males also have difficulties with binge eating (Spitzer *et al.* 1992; Harvey *et al.* 1994; Olivardia *et al.* 1995).

Differences in the attitudes toward body shape (Wilfley *et al.* 1996), tolerance for overweight (Brown *et al.* 1995) and eating disorder behaviors (Wing *et al.* 1993) have been shown among women in different ethnic backgrounds. Males and females also differ in their attitudes and behaviors around food and eating (e.g. Grunberg and Straub 1992; Rolls *et al.* 1991). Thus, future research is needed to determine how these different populations respond to treatment for BED.

Finally, it is remarkable that the majority of treatments for BED have been delivered in groups. Our research group has conducted the only comparison of individual CBT for BED. Initial results from this investigation have shown that a modification of CBT resulted in marked reductions in binge eating. Interestingly, the standard behavioral weight loss treatment to which CBT was compared also produced a similar reduction in binge eating (Marcus *et al.* 1995a). It is possible that treatment delivered in an individual context may be better able to address the psychopathology associated with the eating disorder and thereby promote greater behavior change than those delivered in groups.

CONCLUSIONS

In conclusion, findings to date have indicated that patients with BED are similar in biology and behavior to both those with BN and obesity. Therefore, it is important that treatments for BED incorporate aspects from the treatment of both BN and obesity. In addition, given the apparent vulnerability of BED patients to mood disorders and problems which affect regulation, effective treatment for BED may need to address comorbid psychopathology. Specifically, treatments for individuals with BED must work to eliminate binge eating, prevent future weight gain, address associated psychopathology, and potentially promote modest weight loss.

Importantly, available evidence suggests that, counter to some current theories of binge eating, increasing dietary restraint for this population is not contraindicated. In fact, BED patients may benefit from weight control interventions. Cognitive-behavior therapy is effective in decreasing binge eating, but is not associated with significant weight loss. Serotonergic drugs and opiate antagonists also have been associated with modest, short-term improvements in binge eating. However, additional studies involving the combinations of aspects from these and other interventions are needed. Future research should help to elucidate the mechanisms of action in the different approaches to treating BED, and may lead to the development of more effective interventions for BED.

CLINICAL IMPLICATIONS

- Although neuroendocrine and metabolic abnormalities have been associated with disordered eating, few biological correlates of binge eating in absence of purging have been identified.
- The biological correlates of obese BED patients are similar to those of equally obese non-binge eaters.
- Genetic factors have been implicated in development of obesity and may relate to onset or maintenance of BED.
- The treatment of BED must target *both* obesity and disordered eating.
- Cognitive-behavior therapy (CBT) is effective in decreasing binge eating frequency, but is not associated with significant weight loss.
- Abstinence from binge eating post-treatment appears to prevent further weight gain.
- Contrary to initial speculations, BED patients may benefit from weight control interventions.
- Pharmacological interventions including antidepressant medication, anorectic agents, and opiate antagonists have been evaluated in the treatment of BED. Antidepressants and opiate antagonists are associated with modest, short-term reductions in binge eating.
- Conclusions about the efficacy of pharmacological interventions in BED are limited by the lack of studies.

RESEARCH IMPLICATIONS

- Future, hypothesis-driven work needs to examine biological correlates of BED, and explore the direction of the association between the neurochemical and metabolic perturbations associated with binge eating and the onset and maintenance of BED.
- The relationship between repeated episodes of depression that are associated with weight gain and obesity, and the role of genetic risks for BN, mood disorders, and obesity merit attention in understanding the etiology and treatment of BED.
- Additional research that includes men, younger patients, ethnic minorities and subclinical BED patients is needed to understand BED and its treatment.

REFERENCES

Adami, G.F., Gandolfo, P., Campostano, A., Cocchi, F., Bauer, B. and Scopinaro, N. (1995). Obese binge eaters: metabolic characteristics, energy expenditure and dieting. *Psychological Medicine*, **25**, 195–198.

Agras, W.S., Telch, C.F., Arnow, B. *et al.* (1994). Weight loss, cognitive-behavioral, and desipramine treatments in binge eating disorder: an additive design. *Behavior Therapy*, **25**, 225–238.

Agras, W.S., Berkowitz, R.I., Arnow, B.A. *et al.* (1996). Maintenance following a very-low calorie diet. *Journal of Consulting and Clinical Psychology*, **64**, 610–613.

Agras, W.S., Telch, C.F., Arnow, B., Eldredge, K. and Marnell, M. (1997). One-year follow-up of cognitive-behavioral therapy for obese individuals with binge eating disorder. *Journal of Consulting and Clinical Psychology*, **65**, 343–347.

Alger, S., Seagle, H. and Ravussin, E. (1995). Food intake and energy expenditure in obese female bingers and non-bingers. *International Journal of Obesity*, **19**, 11–16.

American Psychiatric Association (1994). *Diagnostic and statistical manual of mental disorders*. (4th edn.). Washington, D.C.: American Psychiatric Association.

Brown, K.M., Schreiber, G.B., McMahon, R.P., Crawford, P. and Ghee, K.L. (1995). Maternal influences on body satisfaction in black and white girls aged 9 and 10: the NHLBI growth and health study (NGHS). *Annals of Behavioral Medicine*, **17**, 213–220.

Carter, J.C. and Fairburn, C.G. (1995). Treating binge eating problems in primary care. *Addictive Behaviors*, **20**, 765–772.

Cooper, Z. and Fairburn, C.G. (1987). The eating disorder examination: a semi-structured interview for the assessment of the specific psychopathology of eating disorders. *International Journal of Eating Disorder*, **6**, 1–8.

DiPietro, L., Anda, R.F., Williamson, D.F. and Stunkard, A.J. (1992). Depressive symptoms and weight change in a national cohort of adults. *International Journal of Obesity*, **16**, 745–753.

Drewnoski, A., Krahn, D.D., Demitrack, M.A., Nairn, K. and Gosnell, B.A. (1995). Naloxone, an opiate blocker, reduces the consumption of sweet high-fat foods in obese and lean female binge eaters. *American Journal of Clinical Nutrition*, **61**, 1206–1212.

Eldredge, K.L. and Agras, W.S. (1996). Weight and shape overconcern and emotional eating in binge eating disorder. *International Journal of Eating Disorders*, **19**, 73–82.

Fairburn, C.G. and Cooper, Z. (1993). The Eating Disorder Examination (twelfth edition). In C.G. Fairburn and G.T. Wilson (eds), *Binge Eating: Nature, Assessment and Treatment*. (pp. 1–40). New York: Guilford Press.

Fairburn, C.G., Agras, W.S. and Wilson, G.T. (1992). The research on the treatment of bulimia nervosa: practical and theoretical implications. In G.H. Anderson and S.H. Kennedy (eds), *The Biology of Feast and Famine: Relevance to Eating Disorders* (pp. 318–340). San Diego, CA: Academic Press.

Fairburn, C.G., Jones, R., Peveler, R.C., Hope, R.A. and O'Connor, M. (1993a). Psychotherapy and bulimia nervosa: longer-term effects of interpersonal psychotherapy, behavior therapy and cognitive behavior therapy. *Archives of General Psychiatry*, **50**, 419–428.

Fairburn, C.G., Marcus, M.D. and Wilson, G.R. (1993b). Cognitive-behavioral therapy for binge eating and bulimia nervosa: a comprehensive treatment manual. In C.G. Fairburn and G.T. Wilson (eds), *Binge Eating: Nature, Assessment and Treatment*. (pp. 361–404). New York: Guilford Press.

Faris, P.I., Hartman, B.K., Kim, S.W., Meller, W.H., Raymond, M.D. and Eckert, E.D. (1996). Vagal involvement in the pathophysiology of bulimia nervosa: II: Relationship of pain thresholds, disease symptoms and vagal activity. Paper presented at the Seventh International Conference on Eating Disorders, New York, NY.

Fava, M., Copeland, P.M., Schweiger, U. and Herzog, D.B. (1989). Neurochemical abnormalities of anorexia nervosa and bulimia nervosa. *American Journal of Psychiatry*, **146**, 963–971.

Fluoxetine Bulimia Nervosa Collaborative Study Group. (1992). Fluoxetine in the treatment of bulimia nervosa: a multicenter, placebo-controlled, double-blind trial. *Archives of General Psychiatry*, **49**, 139–147.

Garfinkel, P.E., Lin, E., Goering, P. *et al.* (1996). Purging and nonpurging forms of bulimia nervosa in a community sample. *International Journal of Eating Disorders*, **20**, 231–238.

Greeno, C.G. and Wing, R.R.(1996). A double-blind, placebo-controlled trial of the effect of fluoxetine on dietary intake in overweight women with and without binge-eating disorder. *American Journal of Clinical Nutrition*, **64**, 267–273.

Grunberg, N.E. and Straub, R.O. (1992). The role of gender and taste class in the effects of stress on eating. *Health Psychology*, **11**, 97–100.

Halmi, K.A. (1985). Relationship of the eating disorders to depression: biological similarities and differences. *International Journal of Eating Disorders*, **4**, 667–680.

Harvey, E.M., Rawson, R.A., Alexander, E. and Bachar, K.J. (1994). Binge eating in males: A sample description and treatment outcome study. *Eating Disorders: The Journal of Treatment and Prevention*, **2**, 215–230.

Kaye, W.H., Berrettini, W., Gwirtsman, H. and George, D.T. (1990). Altered cerebrospinal fluid neuropeptide Y and peptide YY immunoreactivity in anorexia and bulimia nervosa. *Archives of General Psychiatry*, **43**, 548–556.

Keefe, P.H., Wyshogrod, D., Weinberg, E. and Agras, W.S. (1984). Binge eating and outcome of behavioral treatment of obesity. *Behavior Research and Therapy*, **22**, 319–321.

Kendler, K.S., Eaves, L.J., Walters, E.E., Neale, M.C., Heath, A.C. and Kessler, R.C. (1996). The identification and validation of distinct depressive syndromes in a population-based sample of female twins. *Archives of General Psychiatry*, **53**, 391–399.

LaPorte, D.J. (1992). Treatment response in obese binge eaters: preliminary results using a very low calorie diet (VLCD) and behavior therapy. *Addictive Behaviors*, **17**, 247–257.

Linehan, M.M. (1993). *Cognitive behavioral treatment of borderline personality disorder*. New York: Guilford Press.

Marcus, M.D. (ed.). (1993). Binge eating in obesity. In C.G. Fairburn and G.T. Wilson (eds), *Binge Eating: Nature, Assessment and Treatment* (pp. 77–96). New York: Guilford Press.

Marcus, M.D. (in preparation). Interpersonal psychotherapy in obese women with binge eating disorder.

Marcus, M.D., Wing, R.R. and Hopkins, J. (1988). Obese binge eaters: affect, cognitions and response to behavioral weight control. *Journal of Consulting and Clinical Psychology*, **56**, 433–439.

Marcus, M.D., Wing, R.R., Ewing, L., Kern, E., McDermott, J. and Gooding, W. (1990a). A double-blind placebo-controlled trial of fluoxetine plus behavior modification in the treatment of obese binge eaters and non-binge eaters. *American Journal of Psychiatry*, **147**, 876–881.

Marcus, M.D., Wing, R.R., Ewing, L., Kern, E.,Gooding, W. and McDermott, M. (1990b). Psychiatric disorders among obese binge eaters. *International Journal of Eating Disorders*, **9**, 69–77.

Marcus, M.D., Smith, D., Santelli, R. and Kaye, W. (1992). Characterization of eating disordered behavior in obese binge eaters. *International Journal of Eating Disorders*, **12**, 249–255.

Marcus, M.D., Wing, R.R. and Fairburn, C.G. (1995a). Cognitive treatment of binge eating versus behavioral weight control in the treatment of binge eating disorder. *Annals of Behavioral Medicine*, **17**, S090.

Marcus, M.D., Moulton, M.M. and Greeno, C.G. (1995b). Binge eating onset in obese patients with binge eating disorder. *Addictive Behaviors*, **20**, 747–755.

Marrazzi, M.A., Marknam, K.M., Kinzie, J. and Luby, E.D. (1995). Binge eating disorder: response to naltrexone. *International Journal of Obesity*, **19**, 143–145.

McCann, U.D. and Agras, W.S. (1990). Successful treatment of nonpurging bulimia nervosa with desipramine: a double-blind, placebo-controlled study. *American Journal of Psychiatry*, **147**, 1509–1513.

McCann, U.D., Rossiter, E.M., King, R.J. and Agras, W.S. (1991). Nonpurging bulimia: a distinct subtype of bulimia nervosa. *International Journal of Eating Disorders*, **10**, 679–687.

Mitchell, J.E., Raymond, N. and Specker, S. (1993). A review of the controlled trials of pharmacotherapy and psychotherapy in the treatment of bulimia nervosa. *International Journal of Eating Disorders*, **14**, 229–247.

Mitchell, J.E. and Mussell, M.P. (1995). Comorbidity and binge eating disorder. *Addictive Behavior*, **20**, 725–732.

Mussell, M.P., Mitchell, J.E., Weller, C.L., Raymond, N.C., Crow, S.J. and Crosby, R. (1995). Onset of binge eating, dieting, obesity and mood disorders among subjects seeking treatment for binge eating disorder. *International Journal of Eating Disorders*, **17**, 395–401.

National Task Force on the Prevention and Treatment of Obesity (1996). Long-term pharmacotherapy in the management of obesity. *Journal of the American Medical Association*, **276**, 1907–1915.

Olivardia, R., Pope, H.G., Mangweth, B. and Hudson, J.I. (1995). Eating disorders in college men. *American Journal of Psychiatry*, **152**, 1279–1285.

Pi-Sunyer, F.X. (1991). Health implications of obesity. *American Journal of Clinical Nutrition*, **53**, 1595–1603.

Polivy, J. and Herman, C.P. (1985). Dieting and bingeing. *American Psychologist*, **40**, 193–201.

Polivy, J., Herman, C.P., Olmstead, M.P. and Jazwinski, C. (1984). Restraint and binge eating. In R.C. Hawkins, W.J. Fremouw and P.F. Clement (eds), *The Binge-Purge Syndrome: Diagnosis, Treatment and Research* (pp. 104–122). New York: Springer.

Porzelius, L.K., Houston, C., Smith, M., Arfken, C. and Fisher, E. (1995). Comparison of a standard behavioral weight loss treatment and a binge eating weight loss treatment. *Behavior Therapy*, **26**, 119–134.

Raymond, N.C., Faris, P.I., Hartman, B.K., Kim, S. W., Evanson, P.D., Thuras, P.D. and Eckert, E.D. (1996). Vagal involvement in the pathophysiology of bulimia nervosa: III: Acute changes in pain thresholds over the binge/vomit cycle. Paper presented at the Seventh International Conference on Eating Disorders, New York, NY.

Rolls, B.J., Fedoroff, I.C. and Guthrie, J.F. (1991). Gender differences in eating behavior and body weight regulation. *Health Psychology*, **10**, 133–142.

Rossiter, E.M., Agras, W.S., Telch, C.F. and Bruce, B. (1992). The eating patterns of non-purging bulimic subjects. *International Journal of Eating Disorders*, **11**, 111–120.

Ruderman, A.J. (1986). Dietary restraint: a theoretical and empirical review. *Psychological Bulletin*, **99**, 247–262.

Smith, D.E., Marcus, M.D. and Kaye, W. (1992). Cognitive-behavioral treatment of obese binge eaters. *International Journal of Eating Disorders*, **12**, 257–262.

Spitzer, R.L., Devlin, M., Walsh, T.B. *et al.* (1992). Binge eating disorder: a multisite field trial of the diagnostic criteria. *International Journal of Eating Disorders*, **11**, 191–203.

Spurrell, E.B., Wilfley, D.E., Tanofsky, M.B. and Brownell, K.D. (1997). Age of onset for binge eating: Are there different pathways to binge eating? *International Journal of Eating Disorders*, **21**, 55–65.

Stunkard, A.J. (1959). Eating pattern and obesity. *Psychiatric Quarterly*, **33**, 284–292.

Stunkard, A., Berkowitz, R., Tanrikut, C., Reiss, E. and Young, L. (1996). D-Fenfluramine treatment of binge eating disorder. *American Journal of Psychiatry*, **253**, 1455–1459.

Telch, C.F. and Agras, W.S. (1993). The effects of a very low calorie diet on binge eating. *Behavior Therapy*, **24**, 177–193.

Telch, C.F., Agras, W.S. and Rossiter, E.M. (1988). Binge eating increases with increasing adiposity. *International Journal of Eating Disorders*, **7**, 115–119.

Telch, C.F., Agras, W.S., Rossiter, E.M., Wilfley, D. and Kenardy, J. (1990). Group cognitive-behavioural treatment for the nonpurging bulimic: an initial evaluation. *Journal of Consulting and Clinical Psychology*, **58**, 629–635.

Wadden, T.A., Foster, G.D. and Letizia, K.A. (1992). Response of obese binge eaters to treatment by behavior therapy combined with very low calorie diet. *Journal of Consulting and Clinical Psychology*, **60**, 808–811.

Wadden, T.A., Foster, G.D., Letizia, K.A. and Wilk, J. E. (1993). Metabolic, anthropometric and psychological characteristics of obese binge eaters. *International Journal of Eating Disorders*, **14**, 17–25.

Waller, D., Fairburn, C.G., McPherson, A., Kay, R., Lee, A. and Nowell, T. (1996). Treating bulimia nervosa in primary care: a pilot study. *International Journal of Eating Disorders*, **19**, 99–103.

Walsh, B.T., Wilson, G.T., Loeb, K.L. *et al.* (1997). Medication and psychotherapy in the treatment of bulimia nervosa. *American Journal of Psychiatry*, **154**, 523–531.

Wilfley, D.E., Agras, W.S., Telch, C.F. *et al.* (1993). Group cognitive-behavioral therapy and group interpersonal psychotherapy for the nonpurging bulimic individual: a controlled comparison. *Journal of Consulting and Clinical Psychology*, **61**, 296–305.

Wilfley, D.E., Schreiber, G.B., Pike, K.M., Streigel-Moore, R.H., Wright, D.J. and Rodin, J. (1996). Eating disturbance and body image: a comparison of a community sample of adult black and white women. *International Journal of Eating Disorders*, **20**, 377–387.

Wilson, G.T. and Fairburn, C.G. (1993). Cognitive treatments for eating disorders. *Journal of Consulting and Clinical Psychology*.

Wing, R.R., Adams-Campbell, L.L., Marcus, M.D. and Janney, C.A. (1993). Effect of ethnicity and geographical location on body weight, dietary restraint and abnormal eating attitudes. *Obesity Research*, **1**, 193–198.

Wing, R.R., Jeffery, R.W., Hellerstedt, W.L. and Burton, L.R. (1996). Effect of frequent phone contacts and optional food provision on maintenance of weight loss. *Annals of Behavioral Medicine*, **18**, 172–176.

Wisniewski, L., Marcus, M.D., Levine, M.D. and Greeno, C.G. (1996). Binge eating, depression and obesity in adolescent women presenting to a primary health care facility. Paper presented at the 2nd meeting of the Eating Disorder Research Society, Pittsburgh, PA.

Yanovski, S.Z. (1993). Binge eating disorder: current knowledge and future directions. *Obesity Research*, **1**, 306–318.

Yanovski, S.Z. (1995). Biological correlates of binge eating. *Addictive Behaviors*, **20**, 705–712.

Yanovski, S.Z., Leet, M., Yanovski, J.A. *et al.* (1992). Food selection and intake of obese women with binge eating disorder. *American Journal of Clinical Nutrition*, **56**, 975–980.

Yanovski, S.Z., Gormally, J.F., Leser, M.S., Gwirtsman, H.E. and Yanovski, J.A. (1994). Binge eating disorder affects outcome of comprehensive very-low calorie diet treatment. *Obesity Research*, **2**, 205–212.

17 Pharmacotherapy of Eating Disorders

L. E. S. MAYER and B. T. WALSH
College of Physicians and Surgeons, Columbia University, New York, USA

ANOREXIA NERVOSA

INTRODUCTION

The currently recommended treatments for anorexia nervosa rely predominantly on an eclectic, multidisciplinary approach. Combinations of individual and family psychotherapies with cognitive-behavioral components are the mainstays, with pharmacotherapy often used as an adjunct. Recent advances afford us increasing avenues to study and understand the biologic underpinnings of this disorder; however, the etiology of anorexia nervosa remains elusive. Therefore, despite these recent advances, behavioral and psychosocial treatments remain the standard, and there are only hints about effective pharmacological interventions for anorexia nervosa.

Many of the recent biologic studies in anorexia nervosa have focused on various neurotransmitter systems including serotonin, dopamine and norepinephrine, and neuroendocrine signals, such as corticotropin releasing hormone, neuropeptide Y, and, more recently, leptin. It is hoped that these studies will provide insights into the biology underlying this enigmatic disorder, which, in turn, will lead to the development of successful pharmacological interventions. However, the conundrum which has bedeviled much research on anorexia nervosa continues to be a problem; are the biological disturbances simply a consequence of the self-induced starvation, or do they play a more fundamental etiological role in the development or perpetuation of the disorder. In any case, because of the profound effects of weight loss, it is worthwhile to review recently derived knowledge of the physiological and neuroendocrine responses to starvation.

NEUROENDOCRINE RESPONSES TO STARVATION

Feeding behaviors appear to be influenced by multiple hormones and peptides, both central and peripheral, working in concert with each other to maintain energy homeostasis. Critical neuroendocrine factors include, but are not limited to, insulin, leptin, neuropeptide Y, corticotropin releasing hormone and the glucocorticoids

Neurobiology in the Treatment of Eating Disorders.
Edited by H.W. Hoek, J.L. Treasure and M.A. Katzman.

(Jimerson *et al.* 1996). Although feedback from the periphery is clearly important, the locus of control seems to be central, involving the hypothalamus and its connections.

CORTICOTROPIN RELEASING HORMONE

Corticotropin releasing hormone (CRH) and the hypothalamic–pituitary–adrenal axis (HPA) appear to play a role in the regulation of energy balance, although this role continues to be clarified. Starvation induces activation of the HPA axis and a rise in serum glucocorticoids, and CRH is the primary controller of this axis (Schwartz and Seeley 1997). Curiously, animal studies have shown reduced synthesis of CRH in response to food deprivation (Brady *et al.* 1990; Suemaru *et al.* 1986), while elevated levels of CRH are found in patients with anorexia nervosa (Gold *et al.* 1986). The meaning of this apparent discrepancy awaits further investigation.

NEUROPEPTIDE Y

Neuropeptide Y (NPY), a 36 amino acid peptide discovered in 1983 (Allen *et al.* 1983), appears to be involved in promoting feeding, particularly the consumption of carbohydrate-rich foods (Stanley *et al.* 1985). NPY injected intracerebroventricularly into experimental animals strongly stimulates feeding behaviors (Clark *et al.* 1984). This response occurs even in satiated animals, and repeated injection causes weight gain and obesity (Stanley *et al.* 1986). In response to caloric restriction, the neurons of the arcuate nucleus secrete NPY via projections to the paraventricular nucleus of the hypothalamus. In addition to stimulating food intake, NPY also inhibits sympathetic outflow (Bray 1992), thus reducing energy expenditure. Central administration of NPY also appears to have the peripheral effect of promoting fat synthesis and storage (Billington *et al.* 1991), although the exact mechanism responsible for this effect remains unclear.

Curiously, genetically altered mice lacking the NPY gene, so-called 'knockout' mice, appear phenotypically normal: they are neither underweight nor overweight, and except for a tendency to seizures, appear unremarkable (Erickson *et al.* 1996). In addition, knockout mice that are food restricted for 2 days, have little difficulty in regaining weight. This suggests that feeding pathways are redundant, so absence of one does not disable the system, and/or that compensatory pathways develop, or are recruited, to accommodate the deficiency (Schwartz and Seeley 1997).

Cerebrospinal fluid (CSF) levels of NPY have been measured in patients with anorexia nervosa. In underweight patients, levels are elevated and remain elevated even in short-term (less than 2 months) weight-recovered patients (Kaye *et al.* 1990b). It is possible that the elevation in NPY is a compensatory mechanism to stimulate feeding in response to decreased caloric intake, albeit an apparently ineffective one in patients with anorexia nervosa. With long-term maintenance of normal weight, CSF NPY levels return to normal, except in patients who have persistent menstrual irregularities. Such patients continue to have higher levels of

NPY despite the return to and maintenance of a normal weight (Kaye *et al.* 1990b). Further investigation into the relationship between NPY and the amenorrhea of anorexia seems warranted.

LEPTIN

Leptin, the recently discovered protein product of the *ob* gene, appears to work in concert with NPY to control eating. Whereas NPY promotes caloric intake, leptin limits food intake. It is the first hormone known to link the central control of feeding behaviors directly with peripheral body fat regulation (Campfield *et al.* 1995). Leptin is produced by the fat cells, and its circulating level is directly proportional to body fat mass (Considine *et al.* 1996; Rosenbaum *et al.* 1996). Weight loss is associated with reductions in serum levels of leptin (Considine *et al.* 1996). Obese patients have elevated leptin levels (Considine *et al.* 1996), whereas patients with anorexia nervosa have low levels (Grinspoon *et al.* 1996).

Mice genetically deficient in leptin (*ob/ob*) are obese and infertile, and exogenous replacement of the missing leptin leads to weight loss (Campfield *et al.* 1996). Although leptin's mechanism of action is currently being investigated, it appears to both decrease appetite and increase energy usage, possibly by promoting physical activity or accelerating metabolism (Campfield *et al.* 1996). These speculations are derived from animal data, and their application to humans is as yet untested. However, if leptin has direct links to activity and metabolic rate, it might play an interesting role in anorexia nervosa, a disorder in which changes in activity and metabolism are common.

Although discovered through its connection to obesity, leptin also appears to play a role in the response to starvation and weight loss. During acute weight loss, leptin concentrations fall in excess of body fat loss (Boden *et al.* 1996). This suggests that acute negative energy balance alters the quantum of leptin secreted from the adipocytes, perhaps in a way different than chronic negative energy balance. To extrapolate, perhaps the neurobiology that precipitates anorexia nervosa is different than the neurobiology that maintains it.

The relationship between leptin and reproductive function also adds to its potential relevance in eating disorders. The administration of leptin to immature mice (Chehab *et al.* 1997) and rats (Cheung *et al.* 1997) hastens the onset of reproductive maturity. In addition, administering leptin to food-deprived mice reverses the starvation-induced suppression of the reproductive cycle (Ahima *et al.* 1997). It therefore seems possible that leptin may be an important neuroendocrine signal which serves to mediate some of the weight-loss associated changes in reproductive function noted in anorexia nervosa.

SUMMARY OF NEUROENDOCRINOLOGY

To summarize a proposed pathophysiology of the starvation response in anorexia nervosa: Caloric restriction leads to negative energy balance and reduced fuel stores, and leptin concentrations fall. As leptin levels fall, its inhibitory effects on

NPY and weight control are released. Neuropeptide Y is secreted and stimulates CRH production. In addition, increased release of neuropeptide Y leads to decreased sympathetic outflow which reduces energy expenditure, thus attempting to restore the energy balance. The increased production of NPY would also be expected to increase food consumption, and perhaps, the binge eating and increased consumption of low calorie foods evidenced by a significant fraction of patients with anorexia nervosa are reflections of NPY's influence. However, whatever effects NPY may have on increasing food consumption are obviously not sufficient in persistent cases to restore weight to normal.

NEUROTRANSMITTERS

In addition to the neuroendocrine control of feeding, the role of neurotransmitters has also been investigated. Serotonin has been the most intensively studied, in part because changes in central nervous system (CNS) serotonin function clearly affect feeding behavior. Experimental manipulations which enhance serotonergic function, such as the administration of serotonin agonists, reliably decrease food intake in animals. Conversely, administration of serotonin antagonists results in increases in caloric consumption. Thus, one would predict that human eating disorders associated with weight loss, such as anorexia nervosa, might result in low serotonergic function. In fact, the CSF levels of the serotonin metabolite 5-hydroxyindoleacetic acid (5-HIAA) are low in underweight patients with anorexia nervosa, which may be part of a compensatory physiological shift intended to increase food intake. With refeeding (Kaye *et al.* 1988) and even partial weight restoration (Gerner *et al.* 1984), CSF 5-HIAA increases to normal or near normal levels. Interestingly, weight recovered patients (those who maintain ±1 kg within at least 85% ideal body weight (IBW) for a minimum of 6 months) are reported to have elevated 5-HIAA levels (Kaye *et al.* 1991). This raises the question whether, at normal weights, patients with anorexia nervosa are subject to physiological influences to restrict their food intake predisposing them to relapse.

Another reason to consider a link between disturbances in serotonin function and eating disorders is that many of the symptoms exhibited by patients with eating disorders, such as anxiety, depression, and obsessionality, also occur in other psychiatric illnesses which respond to treatment with agents which affect serotonin function. It is well established that many of these symptoms develop in psychologically normal individuals during starvation (Keys 1950). It is not clear whether disturbances in serotonin are responsible for the development of such symptoms both during starvation and in non-weight-related psychiatric illnesses, or whether similar symptoms develop via differing mechanisms under these different nutritional circumstances.

REVIEW OF CLINICAL TRIALS

There are a limited number of controlled trials of the utility of medications in anorexia nervosa, and, with rare exception, they have been conducted in low weight patients, during the weight gain phase of treatment. The methodological limitations of such studies have been discussed elsewhere (see Jimerson *et al.* 1996) and will not be reviewed here, except for one. There is substantial clinical and biologic 'heterogeneity' among patients with anorexia nervosa. Given the limited, albeit expanding, knowledge about the neurobiology of anorexia nervosa, it is possible that only patients with specific, currently unidentified characteristics will respond to pharmacological intervention. The inclusion of patients without these characteristics will obscure the benefits of the medication. Thus, it may be helpful, in future studies, to focus on subgroups, such as patients with the restricting or binge/purge subtypes, patients with short duration of illness, or patients who have already attained a certain level of weight restoration.

ANTIPSYCHOTIC MEDICATION

Dally and Sargant (1960, 1996) performed the earliest systematic studies on the use of medications in the treatment of anorexia nervosa. Using large doses of chlorpromazine, up to 1600 mg per day, often in combination with insulin, they compared the rate of weight gain in 30 hospitalized patients who received this regimen to 27 patients who had been treated previously on the same unit without medication. Those who received chlorpromazine gained weight faster and were discharged sooner than those who did not, but also experienced significantly more side effects, including seizures (5 of 30 patients). The authors noted that purging developed in 45% of those who had received medication, whereas only 12% of non-medicated began to purge. On long-term follow-up, there was no significant difference in the two groups' weights.

The next studies of the efficacy of antipsychotic medication were not conducted until almost 20 years later. Vandereycken and Pierloot (1982), prompted by a theory put forth by Barry and Klawans (1976), postulated that the physical activity often seen in anorexia nervosa might reflect increased dopamine transmission. They therefore conducted a double-blind, placebo-controlled, cross-over design study of the dopamine antagonist, pimozide. They divided 17 subjects into two groups: eight received pimozide (4 or 6 mg per day) for 3 weeks and then crossed over to placebo; nine received placebo first, followed by pimozide. All subjects were hospitalized and participated in a behaviorally oriented treatment program. There was a trend for patients to have higher mean daily weight gain in pimozide than on placebo ($P = 0.07$), but staff ratings of patients' attitudes showed small and inconsistent differences. A similarly designed study by the same group using the antipsychotic medication sulpiride showed no difference in either weight gain or patients' eating attitudes and behaviors (Vandereycken 1984).

Therefore, the controlled studies of the use of antipsychotic medications are few in number and provide little evidence that these agents substantially assist treatment. Given their potential for disturbing side effects, antipsychotic medications are not recommended for the standard treatment of anorexia nervosa.

ANTIDEPRESSANT MEDICATION

The controlled trials of antidepressant medications are almost as disappointing. Lacey and Crisp (1980) examined the effect of clomipramine on the rate of weight gain. Using a low dose of 50 mg per day, they found that the eight patients on active medication reported significantly increased appetite, but manifested slower weight gain compared to the placebo-treated patients. Long-term follow-up at 1 and 4 years showed no persisting differences between the groups.

Biederman *et al.* (1985) conducted a double-blind, placebo-controlled trial of another tricyclic antidepressant, amitriptyline. Twenty-five subjects were divided into three groups: 11 were randomly assigned to receive amitriptyline, and 14 were randomly assigned to receive placebo; 18 patients refused to take medication, and served as an additional comparison group. Although unable to account for the high refusal-to-participate response, the authors could find no significant difference among the three groups with respect to mood, weight gain or body perception, except for increased side effects in the amitriptyline group.

Halmi and colleagues (1986) were also interested in the efficacy of amitriptyline, and compared it to cyproheptadine (a serotonin antagonist) and placebo. Using doses of up to 60 mg of amitriptyline per day, they found that patients were able to tolerate side effects, but they noted a need to closely monitor for medical complications. While there appeared to be no major benefit to amitriptyline, one analysis showed a significant reduction in the number of days needed to reach target weight (32 ± 17 days for amitriptyline vs 36 ± 20 days for cyproheptadine vs 45 ± 18 days for placebo). Of note, while there was a decrease in depressive symptoms, this improvement appeared to be more closely related to weight gain than to medication.

Since the introduction of the selective serotonin reuptake inhibitors (SSRIs), clinical practice has shifted to using these medications as first line treatment of depression largely because of their minimal side effects compared to older antidepressant medications. The use of SSRIs in the treatment of anorexia nervosa is only now being studied. An open trial of fluoxetine in six patients showed improvement in depressive symptoms and an apparent increase in weight (Gwirtsman *et al.* 1990). Our group is currently conducting a controlled trial of fluoxetine combined with an inpatient treatment program; unfortunately, the preliminary results of this trial are not encouraging. On the other hand, a recent report suggests that fluoxetine may be of benefit to patients with anorexia nervosa once weight gain has been achieved. Kaye *et al.* (1997) found that patients beginning fluoxetine at the conclusion of an inpatient program had a lower rate of relapse compared to similar patients treated with placebo.

CYPROHEPTADINE

Controlled trials of cyproheptadine have been reported in anorexia nervosa. This medication was noted to be associated with weight gain when used to treat allergic conditions, and investigators wondered if this property could be usefully applied to patients with anorexia nervosa. Additionally, cyproheptadine is a centrally acting serotonin antagonist. As such, it should effectively reduce central serotonergic activity and stimulate food intake.

The first controlled trial studied 24 patients (Vigersky and Loriaux 1977). For 8 weeks, thirteen patients received 12 mg/day of cyproheptadine and were compared to 11 patients who received placebo. There was no significant difference between the groups.

A second study of cyproheptadine was that of Halmi *et al.* (1986), mentioned above. In addition to examining amitriptyline and placebo, these investigators placed a third group of patients on a higher dose of cyproheptadine (32 mg/day). Again, there was no significant difference in weight gain between patients receiving cyproheptadine and patients receiving placebo. Of note, however, there was a suggestion that those patients who were severely ill did receive some benefit. In addition, the authors noted a provocative relationship between binge/purge subtype and response to medication. For restricting patients, cyproheptadine enhanced weight gain, whereas for patients with binge eating and/or purging, cyproheptadine slowed weight gain. These results are consistent with the notion that restricting behavior is associated with a relatively hyperserotonergic state, which is counteracted by a serotonin antagonist, while binge eating behavior is associated with a hyposerotonergic state, which is worsened by a serotonin antagonist.

LITHIUM

Because of its mood-stabilizing effects and its commonly noted side effect of weight gain, the use of lithium for anorexia nervosa was examined in a single controlled trial (Gross *et al.* 1981). Although sample size was small ($N = 16$), limiting the power of the study, it appears that, in the second half of a 4-week, double-blind trial, the average weight gain in the lithium-treated group may have been greater than in the placebo group. Further study with a larger sample size and longer duration of treatment might be of interest.

TETRAHYDROCANNABINOL

The same group (Gross *et al.* 1983) conducted an interesting study testing the benefit of daily tetrahydrocannabinol (THC) use, given its potent appetite stimulating and anti-emetic properties. In a 4-week, double-blind, crossover study, 11 patients were evaluated for the effects of oral THC vs diazepam on caloric intake, daily weight gain, and psychiatric assessments. Significant differences were found on measures of somatization, interpersonal sensitivity and sleep disturbance, with the THC group reporting more symptoms than the diazepam group. Three patients receiving THC experienced severe dysphoric mood, paranoia and a feeling of being out of control, and dropped out of the study prematurely. There was no significant effect on food intake or weight, and the conclusion was THC is not helpful as a short-term treatment for weight gain in anorexia nervosa.

CISAPRIDE

Hoping that relieving the complaints of gastric distention, fullness and bloating would lead to increased food intake and more rapid weight gain, two groups have conducted double–blind studies of the gastrointestinal prokinetic agent, cisapride. The results are mixed, and overall, not encouraging. Stacher *et al.* (1993) measured gastric emptying, gastric symptoms and weight gain in 12 hospitalized patients with anorexia nervosa. There was a statistically significant decrease in gastric emptying time in those patients treated with cisapride, and it appeared that at the end of the first 6 weeks, those that had received cisapride had fewer gastric complaints and greater increases in weight when compared to placebo. However, at the end of 12 weeks, medication offered no additional benefit on weight gain over time. The effect on weight gain of cisapride vs placebo was not directly compared, and this study was further limited by its very small sample size.

In an 8-week trial, Szmukler *et al.* (1995) conducted a similar study with a larger sample size ($N=29$) comparing the effect of cisapride on gastric emptying time, gastrointestinal symptoms and weight gain. Comparing cisapride to placebo, they found no differential effect of cisapride on gastric emptying time, physical symptoms (except hunger) or weight gain. The effect of cisapride on the rate of gastric emptying in anorexia nervosa is, surprisingly, uncertain, and there is no convincing evidence its use substantially enhances the rate of weight gain. Cisapride may, however, be of some benefit to patients with severe gastrointestinal symptoms.

BULIMIA NERVOSA

INTRODUCTION

Advances in the pharmacological treatment of bulimia nervosa have been more rapid than for anorexia nervosa. Several factors have probably contributed to the comparatively successful development of these interventions. First, bulimia nervosa is roughly 10-fold more prevalent than anorexia nervosa, and most patients can be treated without need for hospitalization. Both of these facts make the conduct of treatment studies of bulimia nervosa much simpler logistically and less costly than similar studies of anorexia nervosa. In addition, serious metabolic derangements are far less frequent among patients with bulimia nervosa. Conceivably, this more normal physiological state may be conducive to the therapeutic impact of the psychotropic medications which have been examined. Understanding of the neurobiology of bulimia nervosa has also progressed, spurred, in part, by the success of pharmacological treatments. Much of the neurobiological research has focused on serotonin, because of the established role of this neurotransmitter in the control of feeding behavior and because of the widespread use of the SSRI, fluoxetine, in the treatment of this disorder. In addition, research has examined

CNS pathways involving norepinephrine, endogenous opiates and the neuropeptides including peptide YY, and the peripheral satiety signal, cholecystokinin (CCK).

A similar caveat to the one noted before the description of the neurobiology of anorexia nervosa seems appropriate here. In the studies conducted on the neuroendocrine changes of bulimia nervosa, it is difficult to assess which abnormalities predate the symptoms and which are results of the disorder. Studies observe patients either when they are actively bingeing and purging or soon after they have stopped. Evidence (for example, Pirke *et al.* (1985)) suggests that, even at a normal weight, patients with bulimia nervosa may exhibit some of the metabolic manifestations of starvation. Despite weight being normal, peculiar dietary practices may contribute to neurobiological disturbances. Thus, studies of the psychobiology of bulimia nervosa presumably encompass the sequellae of binge eating, purging, and intermittent caloric deprivation.

SEROTONIN

Use of serotonin antagonists in animals stimulates increased food intake, while serotonin agonists produce the opposite effect, a decrease in food intake. These results are consistent with the idea that the synaptic release of serotonin in the hypothalamus during a meal induces satiety, and thereby limits meal size.

An accumulating body of evidence suggests that women with bulimia nervosa have altered CNS serotonergic function. For example, two groups have documented that patients with bulimia nervosa exhibit a blunted prolactin response to an mCPP (a serotonin agonist) challenge (Brewerton and Jimerson (1990); Levitan *et al.* (1997)), and Jimerson *et al.* (1997) reported a blunted prolactin response to another serotonin agonist, D-fenfluramine. Jimerson also found an inverse correlation between the frequency of binge eating episodes in the 4 weeks preceding the testing and magnitude of the prolactin response. While CSF 5-HIAA levels have been reported as normal in patients with bulimia nervosa (Jimerson *et al.* 1989; Kaye *et al.* 1990a), further analysis by Jimerson *et al.* (1989) yielded a similar inverse correlation between higher binge frequency (at least twice per day) and CSF 5-HIAA levels.

NOREPINEPHRINE

When injected into the paraventricular nucleus of the hypothalamus of animals, even immediately after they have eaten, norepinephrine promotes feeding (Liebowitz *et al.* 1985). Kaye *et al.* (1990c) measured both plasma and CSF norepinephrine levels in hospitalized patients with bulimia nervosa at three points in time: on admission (attempting to assess the effects of chronic bingeing and purging), immediately following a binge, and at the end of a 30 day binge/purge-free period. On admission, patients with bulimia nervosa appeared to have normal levels of norepinephrine concentrations in both plasma and CSF. Immediately following a binge, peak plasma norepinephrine levels were significantly higher in patients than in normal controls eating a large meal. Most surprising, however, was the finding that central and peripheral norepinephrine levels were substantially reduced compared to admission levels, when patients were binge/purge free for 30 days. Patients with bulimia nervosa also have signs of depressed sympathetic nervous system activity (e.g. lower resting pulse), consistent with decreased noradrenergic activity (Kennedy and Heslegrave 1989; Kaye *et al.* 1990a). Heufelder *et al.* (1985) reported increased α_2-receptor activity on the platelets of patients with bulimia nervosa, but Kaplan *et al.* (1989) found no significant difference in the response to a low dose of the α_2 noradrenergic agonist clonidine between patients with bulimia nervosa and normal controls. Thus, while evidence suggests dysregulation of the noradrenergic system in patients with bulimia nervosa, such a disturbance has not been unequivocally established, and, certainly, its nature is unclear.

PEPTIDE YY

Peptide YY (PYY) is a protein found in the CNS which is similar to neuropeptide Y, and, when injected either intracerebroventricularly or directly into the paraventricular nucleus of the hypothalamus, elicits feeding behavior. One difference between PYY and NPY seems to be that, while PYY concentrations are lower than NPY, PYY stimulates feeding more robustly than NPY (Kaye 1992b). Studies of PYY levels in the CSF of bulimic patients yielded interesting results (Kaye *et al.* 1990b). PYY levels appear normal when measured in patients with active bulimia nervosa. However, when levels were measured 30 days after the last binge/purge episode, normal-weight bulimic patients showed significantly higher levels of PYY than normal controls and patients with anorexia nervosa. NPY levels were within normal ranges both during active bingeing and 30 days post-binge. The meaning of this PYY elevation is unclear. One explanation is that stopping the binge/purge behavior causes a rebound effect of PYY, thus leading to higher levels and predisposing the patient to relapse. It is also conceivable that the binge eating and purging of patients with bulimia serve in some way to normalize a pre-existing elevation in the level of PYY (Kaye 1992a).

CHOLECYSTOKININ

Cholecystokinin (CCK) is a hormone released by the proximal intestine in response to the presence of nutrients and is considered to be important in the regulation of satiety. The release of CCK triggers a number of physiological events related to the post-ingestive handling of food, such as relaxation of the stomach, contraction of the gallbladder, and the release of digestive enzymes from the pancreas. In addition, via stimulation of vagal afferent fibers, CCK is thought to transmit satiety signals to the CNS. Thus, exogenously administered CCK reduces food intake in both humans and animals, and, in experimental animals, vagotomy abolishes the effect of CCK on satiety (Smith and Gibbs 1994).

Patients with bulimia nervosa have been shown to have abnormal responses to CCK. Geracioti and Liddle (1988) assessed plasma levels of CCK and subjective satiety before and after a liquid meal in 14 women with bulimia and 10 non-eating disorder controls. While pre-meal, CCK levels were comparable in both groups, postprandial CCK levels and subjective satiety were significantly depressed in patients with bulimia nervosa. Two subsequent studies (Pirke *et al.* 1994; Devlin *et al.* 1997) have confirmed that patients with bulimia nervosa release less CCK following a standard meal than do controls.

These data lend support to the hypothesis that peripheral mechanisms related to the development of satiety, such as the release of CCK and, possibly, stomach function (Devlin *et al.* 1997) are abnormal in bulimia nervosa, and contribute to the persistence of the disorder. Conceivably, such abnormalities could provide targets for focused pharmacological interventions, but none has been seriously explored as yet.

OPIOIDS

In both animals and humans, alterations in endogenous opioid activity are associated with changes in food intake. In animals, administration of opioid agonists increase food intake, whereas administration of opioid antagonists decrease food intake (Morley and Blundell 1988). Abnormalities in opioid levels have been described in patients with bulimia nervosa. Brewerton *et al.* (1992) reported reduced β-endorphin levels in CSF, although dynorphin levels were within normal limits, as had been reported previously (Lesem *et al.* 1991). Plasma levels of β-endorphin have been reported to be both increased (Fullerton *et al.* 1986) and decreased (Waller *et al.* 1986). The relationship between peripheral concentrations of endogenous opiates and opioid activity in the CNS, which is presumably more relevant to eating behavior, is unclear. Furthermore, clinical trials of naltrexone, an opiate antagonist, in patients with bulimia nervosa have met with mixed success (Mitchell *et al.* 1986, 1989; Jonas and Gold 1988). Thus, the role of endogenous opiates in the pathophysiology of bulimia nervosa remains uncertain.

SUMMARY OF NEUROBIOLOGY

In summary, numerous biological abnormalities have been found in patients with bulimia nervosa, some more provocative than others, suggesting the presence of neurobiologic disturbances underlying bulimia nervosa. Evidence of a disturbance in the regulation of CNS serotonin is most compelling, and fits neatly with the treatment utility of fluoxetine (see below). Suggestions that peripheral signals related to the development of satiety, such as the release of CCK, are intriguing, and may lead to novel therapeutic interventions.

REVIEW OF CLINICAL TRIALS

Trials of medications in bulimia nervosa have been based on a variety of clinical models, distantly related to the pathophysiological investigations just reviewed. With the notable exception of studies of antidepressant medications, discussed below, trials of most medications have been few in number, small in sample size, and equivocal in outcome. For example, over 20 years ago, the idea that patients with bulimia were suffering from a form of seizure disorder (Green and Rau 1974) prompted controlled studies of phenytoin (Wermuth *et al.* 1977) and carbamazepine (Kaplan *et al.* 1983). A robust response was not found, although there was a suggestion that a small number of patients might benefit.

FENFLURAMINE

On the premise that bingeing reflected an unrestrained appetite, trials of the appetite suppressant D-fenfluramine have been conducted. Blouin *et al.* (1988), in a double-blind, placebo-controlled, cross-over design, compared treatment of bulimia nervosa with desipramine to D-fenfluramine. While both drugs had an effect on bingeing and purging, those who received fenfluramine tended to fare slightly better. Russell *et al.* (1988) reported no significant benefit of D-fenfluramine over placebo, in their randomized trial, but their results were limited by a high dropout rate. In a study from the same group, Fahy *et al.* (1993) examined the role of fenfluramine in patients receiving cognitive-behavioral therapy, and reported little additional benefit from fenfluramine. Given the role of other serotonin-enhancing agents in the treatment of bulimia nervosa (see below) and the role of fenfluramine in the treatment of both obesity and binge eating disorder (Stunkard *et al.* 1996), it is surprising that fenfluramine has such a limited impact on the treatment of bulimia nervosa.

Trials of antidepressants, however, have been far more fruitful. Prompted initially by the observation of the high frequency of depressive symptoms among patients with bulimia nervosa, investigators began to examine the potential utility of antidepressant medication in the early 1980s. Initial open trials of imipramine and phenelzine led to a series of double-blind, controlled trials of various antidepressants, including parallel and cross-over design studies (see Figure 17.1) (Pope *et al.* 1983, 1989; Mitchell and Groat 1984; Hughes *et al.* 1986; Agras *et al.* 1987; Horne *et al.* 1988; Walsh *et al.* 1988, 1991; Freeman *et al.* 1989; Fluoxetine Bulimia Nervosa Collaborative Study Group 1992). These studies are impressively consistent and, taken together, clearly document that antidepressant medication is superior to placebo in the treatment of bulimia nervosa. However, a number of important theoretical and clinical issues regarding the use of such agents for this disorder remain unresolved.

The duration of treatment in most of these studies was 6 to 8 weeks, leaving uncertain the optimal length of the treatment and the outcome of treatment over longer intervals. Pope *et al.* (1985) reported a 2-year follow-up study of patients initially treated with imipramine. While most patients remained improved at follow

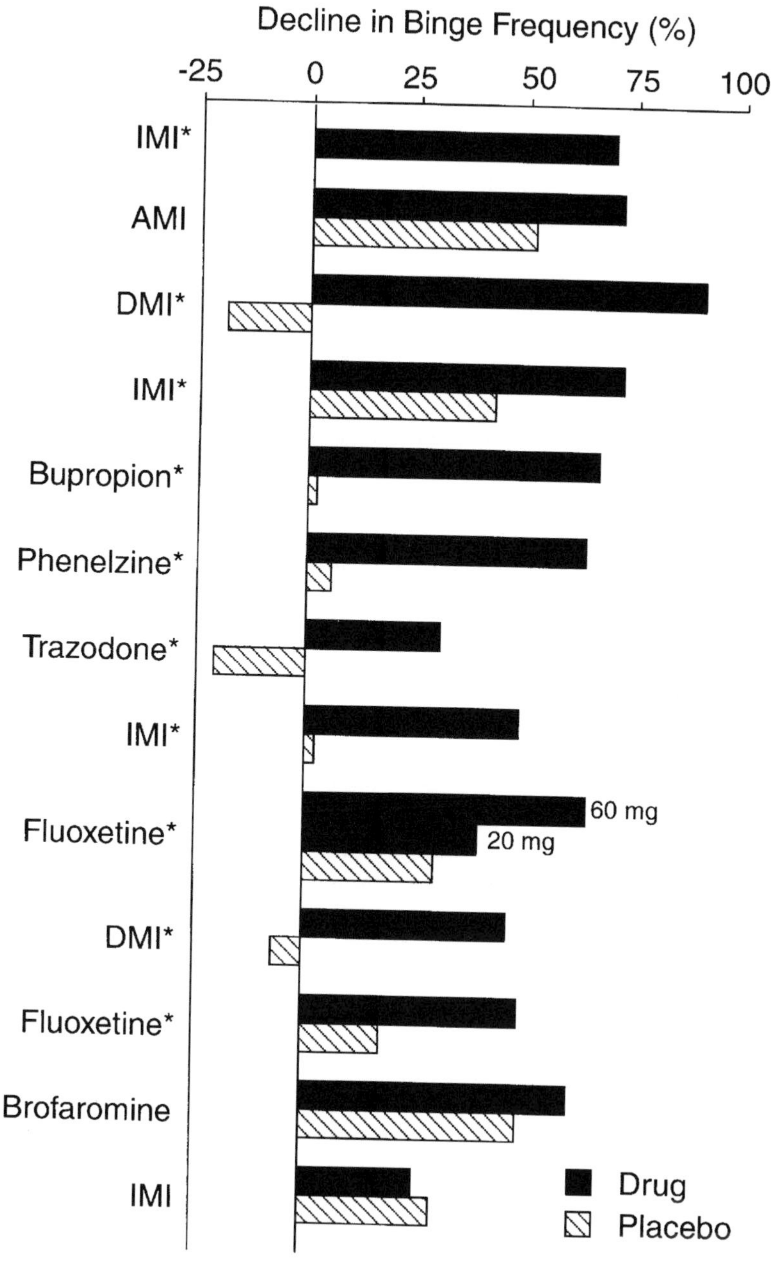

Figure 17.1. Controlled trials of antidepressants in bulimia nervosa (parallel design). *Indicates statistically significant difference between drug and placebo. Reproduced by permission of Walsh, B.T. and Devlin, M.J. The pharmacologic treatment of eating disorders. *Psychiatric Clinics of North America* **15**(1) p 151, 1992

up, many had required several changes of their pharmacological intervention to maintain their response. A study by our own group (Walsh *et al.* 1991) which attempted to examine long-term outcome of desipramine treatment found that despite continued medication treatment, after 4 months, almost half the patients who had initially responded, relapsed. Thus, while medication can quickly induce a significant reduction in binge/purge frequency in most patients, it does not necessarily lead to lasting remission.

Generally, the dose of medication utilized in these studies was the 'standard' dose for the treatment of major depression; it is possible that different dosing strategies would be superior for bulimia nervosa. The single study which addressed this issue directly was the first multi-site examination of the SSRI fluoxetine (Fluoxetine Bulimia Nervosa Collaborative Study Group 1992). In this trial, one group of patients received 20 mg/day, a second group received 60 mg/day, and a third, placebo. Although 20 mg/day is often adequate to treat depression, this dose was marginally superior to placebo in the treatment of bulimia nervosa, whereas the dose of 60 mg/day of fluoxetine was clearly superior. Subsequent studies of fluoxetine in bulimia nervosa have tended to use 60 mg/day, which is generally tolerated with minimal side effects.

A surprising and provocative finding is that, while depressive symptoms and bulimia tend to co-occur, the presence of depressive symptoms does not predict the degree of improvement in bulimic symptoms with antidepressant treatment (Hughes *et al.* 1986; Agras *et al.* 1987; Walsh *et al.* 1988). That is, with respect to the eating disorder symptoms, patients with bulimia nervosa and depression do not respond better to antidepressant medication than do patients with bulimia nervosa who are not depressed. This may suggest that the mechanism of action of antidepressants in bulimia nervosa may be different than that in depression.

Study populations have usually been restricted to normal weight adult women with bulimia nervosa who purge through vomiting, and the results may not be generalizable to other populations including men, overweight bulimic patients, or patients with bulimia nervosa who use alternate methods of purging such as fasting or exercise. It also remains unclear whether these results generalize to a younger, adolescent population.

The questions left unresolved by the studies so far conducted, particularly concerns regarding the long-term outcome of medication treatment, leave the precise place of antidepressant medication in the treatment of bulimia nervosa unclear. Given the sustained success of psychotherapeutic interventions, particularly cognitive behavioral treatment, many clinicians believe it is best to initiate treatment with such psychotherapy and augment secondarily with antidepressants if the response is not satisfactory.

Recent studies have begun to explore the role of combined treatments, psychotherapy and pharmacotherapy, and results are mixed. As this section has focused primarily on the pharmacological interventions for bulimia nervosa, for a more in depth discussion of the utility of combined treatments, the reader is referred to Walsh *et al.* (1997).

CONCLUSION

Advances in the field of neurobiology have greatly enhanced our basic knowledge about the regulation of feeding and weight, and we are beginning to explore the importance of these abnormalities in anorexia and bulimia nervosa. Studies of the role of neurotransmitters in controlling food intake have been very productive, and provide a basis, especially in the case of the serotonergic system, for understanding the success of antidepressants in the treatment of bulimia nervosa. Additionally, leptin's role in linking central signals to peripheral fat regulation, as well as to the metabolic and reproductive systems holds much promise for understanding some of the medical complications of anorexia nervosa. It remains unclear, however, how these biological abnormalities are related to patients' symptoms, and how we can capitalize on our knowledge of these biologic abnormalities to design more effective pharmacologic interventions.

ACKNOWLEDGMENTS

This work was supported in part by grants MH 903-1406E, MH 5-36884 and from National Institutes of Health.

ANOREXIA NERVOSA

CLINICAL IMPLICATION OF RESEARCH TRIALS

No medication has been clearly shown to be effective in accelerating weight gain or altering the disturbed thinking about shape and weight.

- Studies do not support the efficacy of neuroleptic agents as standard treatment for anorexia nervosa.
- Antidepressant medications have not been shown to be useful when patients are underweight.
- Fluoxetine may be helpful in preventing relapse once a normal weight has been restored.
- Other medications including cyproheptadine, lithium, THC and cisapride have not been shown to be helpful.

Therefore, the standard treatment of anorexia nervosa should be an eclectic, multidisciplinary approach with pharmacological intervention only as an adjunct.

Continued

Difficulties:

- There is clinical and biologic 'heterogeneity' among patients with anorexia nervosa. It may be that patients with specific behavioral forms of the disorder, such as binge/purge or restricting subtypes, or patients with as yet unidentified biological characteristics will respond to medication.

RESEARCH IMPLICATIONS

Multiple neuroendocrine and neurotransmitter abnormalities occur in underweight patients with anorexia nervosa. Among the abnormalities described in recent research are:

- Decreased levels of plasma leptin.
- Increased levels of CSF neuropeptide Y, corticotropin releasing hormone and plasma glucocorticoids.
- Decreased levels in the CSF of the serotonin metabolite, 5-HIAA.

Future research is needed to clarify the role of these disturbances in anorexia nervosa. That is,

- Are they precursors or consequences of the illness?
- If they are consequences, are they specifically associated with anorexia nervosa, or are they non-specific manifestations of food restriction, weight loss and starvation?
- How can we translate the knowledge of these abnormalities into effective treatment strategies?

Difficulties answering these questions arise in that:

- It is difficult to study a complex physiological system, such as the regulation of feeding, without confounding variables.
- Our knowledge of normal physiology is limited, which further constrains our understanding of what and how things become abnormal.

BULIMIA NERVOSA

Pharmacologic agents are helpful in the treatment of bulimia nervosa, and their presumed mechanism of action is consistent with the current knowledge about the associated neurobiology.

Continued

CLINICAL IMPLICATIONS

Clinical trials repeatedly confirm the utility of antidepressant agents in reducing the binge/purge cycle and the treatment of bulimia nervosa.

- Virtually all classes of antidepressants (e.g. tricyclic, monoamine oxidase inhibitors (MAOI), SSRI) have been shown to be effective treatments in reducing binge eating and/or purging behaviors in bulimia nervosa.
- Fluoxetine, 60 mg/day, has been shown to be more effective than 20 mg/day of fluoxetine and placebo in curbing binge eating and purging.
- Cognitive-behavioral therapy has also been shown to be an effective treatment for bulimia nervosa.

There is a significant co-morbidity of bulimia nervosa and depressive symptoms, however:

- Antidepressant medication is effective regardless of the presence and/or severity of depressive symptoms.
- The therapeutic mechanism of action of antidepressant medication may be different for depression and bulimia nervosa.

Future research is needed to determine how to match patients to various types of treatment (e.g. medication vs psychotherapy vs combination), and to develop interventions for patients who fail to respond to CBT and antidepressant medication.

RESEARCH IMPLICATIONS

Studies confirm abnormalities in major neurotransmitter systems and neuroendocrine signals.

- Alterations in serotonin appear to play a significant role in the neurobiology of bulimia nervosa.
- Norepinephrine (NE) disturbances also exist. During active bingeing and purging, NE levels are normal, but are significantly reduced following a 30 day binge/purge-free period.
- CSF peptide YY levels are normal in patients with active bulimia nervosa, but are elevated following a 30 day binge/purge-free period.
- Postprandial plasma CCK levels and subjective satiety are reduced in patients with bulimia nervosa.

REFERENCES

Agras, W.S., Dorian, B., Kirkley, B.G., Arnow, B. and Bachman, J.A. (1987). Imipramine in the treatment of bulimia: a double-blind controlled study. *Int. J. Eat. Dis.*, **6**, 29–38.

Ahima, R.S., Dushay, J., Flier, S.N., Prabakaran, D. and Flier, J.S. (1997). Leptin accelerates the onset of puberty in normal female mice. *J. Clin. Invest.*, **99**, 391–395.

Allen, Y.S., Adrian, T.E., Allen, J.M. *et al.* (1983). Neuropeptide Y distribution in the rat brain. *Science*, **221**, 877–879.

Barry, V.C. and Klawans, H.L. (1976). On the role of dopamine in the pathophysiology of anorexia nervosa. *J. Neur. Trans.*, **38**, 107–122.

Biederman, J., Herzog, D.B., Rivinus, T.M. *et al.* (1985). Amitriptyline in the treatment of anorexia nervosa: a double-blind, placebo-controlled study. *J. Clin. Psychopharmacol.*, **5**, 10–16.

Billington, C.J., Briggs, J.E., Grace, M. and Levine, A.S. (1991). Effects of intracerebroventricular injection of Neuropeptide Y on energy metabolism. *Am. J. Physiol.*, **260**, R321–R327.

Blouin, A.G., Blouin, J.H., Perez, E.L., Bushnik, T., Zuro, C. and Mulder, E. (1988). Treatment of bulimia with fenfluramine and desipramine. *J. Clin. Psychopharmacol.*, **8**, 261–269.

Boden, G., Chen, X., Mozzoli, M. and Ryan, I. (1996). Effect of fasting on serum leptin in normal human subjects. *J. Clin. Endocrinol. Metab.*, **81**, 3419–3423.

Brady, L.S., Smith, M.A., Gold, P.W. and Herkenham, M. (1990). Altered expression of hypothalamic neuropeptide mRNAs in food-restricted and food-deprived rats. *Neuroendocrinology*, **52**, 441–447.

Bray, G. (1992). Peptides affect the intake of specific nutrients and the sympathetic nervous system. *Am. J. Clin. Nutr.*, **55**, Suppl: 265S–271S.

Brewerton, T.D. and Jimerson, D.C. (1990). Studies of serotonin function in anorexia nervosa. *Psychiatry Res.*, **62**, 31–42.

Brewerton, T.D., Lydiard, R.B., Laraia, M.T., Shook, J.E. and Ballenger, J.C. (1992). CSF β-endorphin and dynorphin in bulimia nervosa. *Am. J. Psychiatry*, **149**(8), 1086–1090.

Campfield, L.A., Smith, F.J., Guisez, Y., Devos, R. and Burn, P. (1995). Recombinant mouse OB protein: evidence for a peripheral signal linking adiposity and central neural networks. *Science*, **269**, 546–549.

Campfield, L.A., Smith, F.J. and Burn, P. (1996). The OB protein (leptin) pathway—a link between adipose tissue mass and central neural networks. *Horm. Metab. Res.*, **28**, 619–632.

Chehab, F.F., Mounzih, K., Lu, R. and Lim, M. (1997). Early onset of reproductive function in normal female mice treated with leptin. *Science*, **275**(5296),
88–90.

Cheung, C.C., Thornton, J.E., Kiujper, J.L., Weigle, D.S., Clifton, D.K. and Steiner, R.A. (1997). Leptin is the metabolic gate for the onset of puberty in the female rat. *Endocrinology*, **138**(2), 855–858.

Clark, J.T., Kalra, P.S., Crowley, W.R. and Kalra, S.P. (1984). Neuropeptide Y and human pancreatic polypeptide stimulate feeding behavior in rats. *Endocrinology*, **115**, 427–429.

Considine, R.V., Sinha, M.K., Heinman, M.L. *et al.* (1996). Serum immunoreactive-leptin concentrations in normal-weight and obese humans. *N. Engl. J. Med.*, **334**, 292–295.

Dally, P. and Sargant, W. (1960). A new treatment of anorexia nervosa. *BMJ*, **1**, 1770–1773.

Dally, P. and Sargant, W. (1966). Treatment and outcome of anorexia nervosa. *BMJ*, **2**, 793–795.

Devlin, M.J., Walsh, B.T., Guss, J.L., Kissileff, H.R., Liddle, R.A. and Petkova, E. (1997). Postprandial cholecystokinin release and gastric emptying patients with bulimia nervosa. *Am. J. Clin. Nutr.*, **65**(1), 114–120.

Erickson, J.C., Clegg, K.E. and Palmiter, R.D. (1996). Sensitivity to leptin and susceptibility to seizures of mice lacking neuropeptide Y. *Nature*, **381**, 415–421.

Fahy, T.A., Eisler, I. and Russell, G.F.M. (1993). A placebo-controlled trial of D-fenfluramine in bulimia nervosa. *Br. J. Psychiatry*, **162**, 597–603.

Fluoxetine Bulimia Nervosa Collaborative Study Group (1992). Fluoxetine in the treatment of bulimia nervosa: a multicenter placebo-controlled double-blind trial. *Arch. Gen. Psychiatry* **49**, 139–147.

Freeman, C.P.L., Davies, F., Morris, J., Cheshire, O. and Hampson, M. (1989). A double-blind controlled trial of fluoxetine versus placebo for bulimia nervosa. Unpublished manuscript.

Fullerton, D.T., Swift, W.J., Getto, C.J. and Carlson, I.H. (1986). Plasma immunoreactive beta-endorphin in bulimics. *Psychol. Med.*, **16**, 59–63.

Geracioti, T.D. and Liddle, R.A. (1988). Impaired cholecystokinin secretion in bulimia nervosa. *N. Engl. J. Med.*, **319**, 683–688.

Gerner, R.H., Cohen, D.J., Fairbanks, L. *et al.* (1984). CSF neurochemistry of women with anorexia nervosa and normal women. *Am. J. Psychiatry*, **141**, 1441–1444.

Gold, P.W., Gwirtsman, H., Avgerinos, P.C. *et al.* (1986). Abnormal hypothalamic–pituitary–adrenal function in anorexia nervosa pathophysiologic mechanisms in underweight and weight-corrected patients. *N. Engl. J. Med.*, **314**, 335–1342.

Green, R.S. and Rau, J.H. (1974). Treatment of compulsive eating disturbances with anticonvulsant medication. *Am. J. Psychiatry*, **131**, 428–432.

Grinspoon, S., Gulick, T., Askari, H. *et al.* (1996). Serum leptin levels in women with anorexia nervosa. *J. Clin. Endocrinol. Metab.*, **81**(11), 3861–3863.

Gross, H.A., Ebert, M.H., Faden, V.B. *et al.* (1981). A double-blind controlled trial of lithium carbonate in primary anorexia nervosa. *J. Clin. Psychopharmacol.*, **1**, 376–381.

Gross, H.A., Ebert, M.H., Faden, V.B. *et al.* (1983). A double-blind trial of d9-tetrahydrocannabinol in primary anorexia nervosa. *J. Clin. Psychopharmacol.*, **3**(3), 165–171.

Gwirstman, H.E., Guze, B.H., Yager, J. *et al.* (1990). Fluoxetine treatment of anorexia nervosa: An open clinical trial. *J. Clin. Psychiatry*, **51**, 378–382.

Halmi, K.A., Eckert, E.D., LaDu, T.J. and Cohen, J. (1986). Anorexia nervosa: treatment efficacy of cyproheptadine and amitriptyline. *Arch. Gen. Psychiatry*, **43**, 177–181.

Heufelder, A., Warnoff, M. and Pirke, K.M. (1985). Platelet α-2 adrenoceptor and adenylate cyclase in patients with anorexia nervosa and bulimia. *J. Clin. Endocrinol. Metab.*, **61**, 1053–1060.

Horne, R.L., Ferguson, J.M., Pope, H.G. *et al.* (1988). Treatment of bulimia with bupropion: a multicenter controlled trial. *J. Clin. Psychiatry*, **49**, 262–266.

Hughes, P.L., Wells, L.A. and Cunningham, C.J. (1986). The dexamethasone suppression test in bulimia before and after successful treatment with desipramine. *J. Clin. Psychiatry*, **47**, 515–517.

Jimerson, D.C., Lesem, M.D., Kaye, W.H. *et al.* (1989). Symptom severity and neurotransmitter studies in bulimia. *Psychopharmacology*, **96**, S124.

Jimerson, D.C., Wolfe, B.E., Brotman, A.W. and Metzger, E.D. (1996). Medications in the Treatment of Eating Disorders. *Psych. Clin. N. Am.*, **19**(4), 739–754.

Jimerson, D.C., Wolfe, B.E., Metzger, E.D., Finkelstein, D.M., Cooper, T.B. and Levine, J.M. (1997). Decreased serotonin function in bulimia nervosa. *Arch. Gen. Psychiatry*, **57**, 529–534.

Jonas, J.M. and Gold, M.S. (1988). The use of opiate antagonists in treating bulimia: A study of low-dose versus high-dose naltrexone. *Psychiatry Res.*, **24**, 195–199.

Kaplan, A.S., Garfinkel, P.E., Darby, P.L. and Garner, D.M. (1983). Carbamazepine in the treatment of bulimia. *Am. J. Psychiatry*, **140**, 1225–1226.

Kaplan, A.S., Garfinkel, P.E., Warsh, J.J. *et al.* (1989). Clonidine challenge test in bulimia nervosa. *Int. J. Eating Disord.*, **8**, 425–435.

Kaye, W.H. (1992a). Neuropeptide abnormalities. In Halmi, K.A. (ed.): *Psychobiology and Treatment of Anorexia Nervosa and Bulimia Nervosa.* Washington, DC, American Psychiatric Press, Inc, pp. 169–192.

Kaye, W.H. (1992b). Neurotransmitter abnormalities in anorexia nervosa and bulimia nervosa. In Anderson, G.H., Kennedy, S.H. (eds) *The Biology of Feast and Famine. Relevance to Eating Disorders.* San Diego, Academic Press, Inc, pp. 105–134.

Kaye, W.H., Gwirtsman, H.E., George, D.T. *et al.* (1988). CSF 5-HIAA concentrations in anorexia nervosa: reduced values in underweight subjects normalize after weight gain. *Biol. Psychiatry*, **23**, 102–105.

Kaye, W.H., Ballenger, J.C., Lydiard, B. *et al.* (1990a). CSF monoamine levels in normal-weight bulimia: evidence for abnormal adrenergic activity. *Am. J. Psychiatry*, **147**, 225–229.

Kaye, W.H., Berrettini, W.H., Gwirtsman, H.E. *et al.* (1990b). Altered cerebrospinal fluid neuropeptide Y and peptide YY immunoreactivity in anorexia and bulimia nervosa. *Arch. Gen. Psychiatry*, **47**, 548–556.

Kaye, W.H., Gwirtsman, H.E., George, D.T. *et al.* (1990c). Disturbances of noradrenergic systems in normal weight bulimia: Relationship to diet and menses. *Biol. Psychiatry*, **27**, 4–21.

Kaye, W.H., Gwirtsman, H.E., George, D.T. *et al.* (1991). Altered serotonin activity in anorexia nervosa after long-term weight restoration: does elevated CSF 5-HIAA correlate with rigid and obsessive behavior? *Arch. Gen. Psychiatry*, **48**, 556–562.

Kaye, W.H., Weltzin, T.E., Hsu, G., Sokol, M., McConaha, C. and Plotnicov, K.H. (1997). Relapse prevention with fluoxetine in anorexia nervosa: a double-blind placebo-controlled study. 150th APA Meeting, **178** (May 17).

Kennedy, S.H. and Heslegrave, R.J. (1989). Cardiac regulation in bulimia nervosa. *J. Psychiatric Res.*, **23**, 267–273.

Keys, A. (1950). *The Biology of Human Starvation*. Minneapolis, MN, University of Minnesota Press.

Lacey, J.H. and Crisp, A.H. (1980). Hunger, food intake and weight: the impact of clomipramine on a refeeding anorexia nervosa population. *Postgrad. Med. J.*, **56**-Suppl 1, 79–85.

Leibowitz, S.F., Brown, O., Treetter, J.R. *et al.* (1985). Norepinephrine, clonidine, and tricyclic antidepressants selectively stimulate carbohydrate ingestion through noradrenergic system of the paraventricular nucleus. *Pharmacol. Biochem. Behav.*, **23**, 541–550.

Lesem, M.D., Berrettini, W.H., Kaye, W.H. and Jimerson, D.C. (1991). Measurement of CSF dynorphin A 1-8 immunoreactivity in anorexia nervosa and normal-weight bulimia. *Biol. Psychiatry*, **29**(3), 244–252.

Levitan, R.D., Kaplan, A.S., Joffe, R.T., Levitt, A.J. and Brown, G.M. (1997). Hormonal and subjective responses to intravenous *meta*-chlorophenylpiperazine in bulimia nervosa. *Arch. Gen. Psychiatry*, **54**, 521–527.

Mitchell, J.E. and Groat, R. (1984). A placebo-controlled, double-blind trial of amitriptyline in bulimia. *J. Clin. Psychopharmacol.*, **4**, 186–193.

Mitchell, J.E., Laine, D.E., Morley, J.E. and Levine, A.S. (1986). Naloxone but not CCK-8 may attenuate binge-eating behavior in patients with the bulimia syndrome. *Biol. Psychiatry*, **21**, 1399–1406.

Mitchell, J.E., Christenson, G., Jennings, J. *et al.* (1989). A placebo-controlled, double-blind crossover study of naltrexone hydrochloride in outpatients with normal weight bulimia. *J. Clin. Psychopharmacol.*, **9**, 94–97.

Morley, J.E. and Blundell, J.E. (1988). The neurobiological basis of eating disorders: some formulations. *Biol. Psychiatry*, **23**, 53–78.

Pirke, K.M., Pahl, J., Schweiger, U. *et al.* (1985). Metabolic and endocrine indices of starvation in bulimia: a comparison with anorexia nervosa. *Psychiatry Res.*, **15**, 33–39.

Pirke, K.M., Kellner, M.B., Friess, E., Krieg, J. and Fichter, M.M. (1994). Satiety and cholecystokinin. *Int. J. Eat. Dis.*, **15**(1), 63–69.

Pope, H.G., Hudson, J.I., Jonas, J.M. and Yurgelun-Todd, D. (1983). Bulimia treated with imipramine: a placebo-controlled, double-blind study. *Am. J. Psychiatry*, **140**, 554–558.

Pope, H.G. Jr., Hudson, J.I., Jonas, J.M. and Yurgelun-Todd, D. (1985). Antidepressant treatment of bulimia: A two-year follow-up study. *J. Clin. Psychopharmacol.*, **5**, 320–327.

Pope, H.G. Jr., Keck, P.E.J., McElroy, S.L. and Hudson, J.I. (1989). A placebo-controlled study of trazodone in bulimia nervosa. *J. Clin. Psychopharmacol.*, **9**, 254–259.

Rosenbaum, M., Nicolson, M., Hirsch, J. *et al.* (1996). Effects of gender, body composition, and menopause on plasma concentrations of leptin. *J. Clin. Endocrinol. Metab.*, **81**, 3424–3427.

Russell, G.F.M., Checkley, S.A., Feldman, J. and Eisler, I. (1988). A controlled trial of D-fenfluramine in bulimia nervosa. *Clin. Neuropharmacol.*, **11**, Suppl. 1, S146–S159.

Schwartz, M.W. and Seeley, R.J. (1997). Neuroendocrine responses to starvation and weight loss. *N. Engl. J. Med.*, **336**(25), 1802–1811.

Smith, G.P. and Gibbs, J. (1994). Satiating effect of cholecystokinin. *Ann. N. Y. Acad. Sci.*, **713**, 236–241.

Stacher, G., Abatzi-Wenzel, T.A., Wiesnagrotzki, S., Bergmann, H., Schneider, C. and Gaupman, G. (1993). Gastric emptying, body weight and symptoms in primary anorexia nervosa. Long term effects of cisapride. *Br. J. Psychiatry*, **162**, 398–402.

Stanley, B.C., Daniel, D.R., Chin, A.S. *et al.* (1985). Paraventricular nucleus injections of peptide YY and neuropeptide Y preferentially enhance carbohydrate ingestion. *Peptides*, **6**, 1205–1211.

Stanley, B.C., Kyrkouli, S.E., Lampert, S. and Leibowitz, S.F. (1986). Neuropeptide Y chronically injected into the hypothalamus: a powerful neurochemical inducer of hyperphagia and obesity. *Peptides*, **7**, 1189–1192.

Stunkard, A., Berkowitz, R., Tanrikut, C., Reiss, E. and Young, L. (1996). D-Fenfluramine treatment of binge eating disorder. *Am. J. Psychiatry*, **153**(11), 1455–1459.

Suemaru, S., Hashimoto, K., Hattori, T., Inoue, H., Kageyama, J. and Ota, Z. (1986). Starvation-induced changes in rat brain corticotropin-releasing factor (CRF) and pituitary-adrenocortical response. *Life Sci.*, **39**, 1161–1166.

Szmukler, G.I., Young, G.P., Miller, G., Lichtenstein, M. and Binns, D.S. (1995). A controlled trial of cisapride in anorexia nervosa. *Int. J. Eat. Dis.*, **17**(4), 347–357.

Vandereycken, W. (1984). Neuroleptics in the short-term treatment of anorexia nervosa: a double-blind placebo-controlled study with sulpiride. *Br. J. Psychiatry*, **144**, 288–292.

Vandereycken, W. and Pierloot, R. (1982). Pimozide combined with behavior therapy in the short-term treatment of anorexia nervosa. *Acta Psychiatr. Scand.*, **66**, 445–450.

Vigersky, R.A. and Loriaux, D.L. (1977). The effect of cyproheptadine in anorexia nervosa: a double-blind trial. In Vigersky, R.A. (ed.) *Anorexia Nervosa*. New York, Raven Press, pp. 349–356.

Waller, D.A., Kiser, R.S., Hardy, B.W. *et al.* (1986). Eating behavior and plasma β-endorphin in bulimia. *Am. J. Clin. Nutr.*, **44**, 20–23.

Walsh, B.T., Gladis, M., Roose, S.P. *et al.* (1988). Phenelzine vs placebo in 50 patients with bulimia. *Arch. Gen. Psychiatry*, **45**, 471–475.

Walsh, B.T., Hadigan, C.M., Devlin, M.J., Gladis, M. and Roose, S.P. (1991). Long-term outcome of antidepressant treatment for bulimia nervosa. *Am. J. Psychiatry*, **148**, 1206–1212.

Walsh, B.T., Wilson, G.T., Loeb, K.L. *et al.* (1997). Medication and psychotherapy in the treatment of bulimia nervosa. *Am. J. Psychiatry*, **154**(4), 523–531.

Wermuth, B.M., Davis, K.L., Hollister, L.E. and Stunkard, A.J. (1977). Phenytoin treatment of the binge-eating syndrome. *Am. J. Psychiatry*, **134**, 1249–1253.

18 A Cognitive Model and Treatment Strategies for Anorexia Nervosa

G. WOLFF AND L. SERPELL
Eating Disorders Unit, Maudsley and Bethlem (NHS) Trust, and Institute of Psychiatry, London, UK

INTRODUCTION

'What I really need to do is make my life bigger' anorexic patient

Since it was first described, anorexia nervosa has been one of the most enigmatic of the neuroses. William Gull (1874), for example stated: 'The want of appetite is, I believe, due to a morbid mental state . . . we might call the state hysterical without committing ourselves to the etymological values of the word . . . '.

It took nearly a century for observers to draw attention to the 'disturbed experience (of the) body' (Bruch 1966), 'weight phobia' (Crisp 1967) and 'morbid fear of fatness' (Russell 1970). Indeed, cognitive distortions around weight and body image are now considered 'core' features of the disorder (although some authors disagree with this view, e.g. Katzman and Lee 1997). However, this paper describes evidence for the presence of other, more general features of the psychopathology of anorexia nervosa, including abnormalities in aspects of self esteem and the presence of relatively stable, deep-seated dysfunctional beliefs or schemata. It is proposed that these aspects of eating disorders are as important as those concerned directly with body image.

In view of the success with which cognitive-behavioural approaches have been used in the understanding and treatment of bulimia nervosa (Fairburn *et al.* 1991, 1993), it seems surprising that anorexia nervosa, which appears to present such a feast of cognitive dysfunction, has been one of the last of the neuroses to succumb to a satisfactory cognitive model and cognitive treatment strategy. Two related reasons for this may be the 'egosyntonic' nature of the disorder and the tendency toward 'resistance' to treatment: the illness is often cherished and the psychopathology jealously guarded by the patients.

There is a small amount of literature dealing with cognitive conceptualizations of the disorder, notably work by Garner and Kelly Bemis and Vitousek (Garner and

Neurobiology in the Treatment of Eating Disorders.
Edited by H.W. Hoek, J.L. Treasure and M.A. Katzman.

Bemis 1985; Vitousek and Hollon 1990; Vitousek 1997). Myra Cooper has also provided a comprehensive review of work in this area (Cooper 1997).

In support of the current model, evidence from studies concerned with family background, personality and cognitive and emotional dysregulation in anorexia nervosa are reviewed. These are interpreted in the light of both clinical experience and recent developments in cognitive conceptualizations of neurotic disorders. A tentative cognitive model is outlined, and finally, suggestions are made for treatment strategies within a cognitive framework.

REVIEW OF THE LITERATURE

FAMILY FACTORS

Early work on anorexia nervosa stressed the importance of family environment in both the development and maintenance of the disorder. Indeed, a major element of early twentieth century treatments was the removal of the anorexic patient from her family environment (e.g. Ryle 1936). More recently, the family systems approach (Selvini-Palazzoli 1974; Minuchin *et al.* 1975) has highlighted the importance of what Minuchin calls the 'psychosomatic family' characterized by enmeshment, emotional over-involvement/overprotectiveness, rigid structure and lack of conflict resolution. In recent years, many studies have assessed the evidence for and against elements of Minuchin's model (e.g. Minuchin *et al.* 1978; Gupta 1990; Dare *et al.* 1994; Blair *et al.* 1995) and also for the view that inhibition of emotionality is an important aspect of these families (Casper 1990; Casper *et al.* 1992; Telerant *et al.* 1992; Waller 1994).

The principal criticism of much of this work is based on the problem of inferring causation from correlation. Indeed, there is an increasing awareness that family factors may be produced both *in response to* and *as a result of* the presence of an anorexic in the family. This point is well illustrated by Lawrence (1984):

> The families who are seen in treatment when their daughters or sisters have already become anorexic are families under almost unbearable stress. Any observations about them and their behaviour must be evaluated in this light (p. 60).

Several studies give support to the notion that family dynamics are not simply a *result* of the presence of a sick family member. Blair and colleagues (Blair *et al.* 1995) compared families in which one child was anorexic with families in which a child had cystic fibrosis. The authors found few differences between the two types of families on self-report measures of family functioning and on the Expressed Emotion measure of emotional over-involvement. However, the families of anorexics showed more elements of enmeshment and over-protectiveness and were poorer at problem solving than the cystic fibrosis families.

A second study (Le Grange *et al.* 1992) examined elements of Minuchin's model using measures of Expressed Emotion and the Family Adaptability and Cohesion

Scales (FACES). Partial support for the model came from evidence of enmeshment from the FACES scales as well as evidence for very *low* levels of EE Critical Comments, which might be taken as evidence of conflict avoidance. There is little evidence from this study for the idea that anorexic families are universally overprotective.

From the current research in this area, it is difficult to come to any definite conclusions about the contribution of family factors to the causation or maintenance of anorexia nervosa. However, the model described in this chapter incorporates certain speculative suggestions about interactions between environment (including family structure) and premorbid personality which may be important in these patients.

PERSONALITY FACTORS

Much of the clinical literature describes particular personality traits as being characteristic of the anorexic, including elements of perfectionism, external locus of control (Shisslak *et al.* 1990; Williams *et al.* 1997, 1990; Casper *et al.* 1992; Srinivasagam *et al.* 1995), narcissism (Simpson and Ramberg 1992), obsessionality (Simpson and Ramberg 1992; Vitousek and Manke 1994), low novelty seeking and conflict avoidance (e.g. Guidano and Liotti 1983; Bruch 1978). However, it has proved difficult to demonstrate either the generality or specificity of many of these traits experimentally. For example, perfectionism is almost universally accepted as a clinical feature of anorexia, but experimental evidence for its presence is equivocal (Hewitt *et al.* 1995; Terry-Short *et al.* 1995).

There is clearly a need in this area for more longitudinal work. Prospective studies are generally impracticable due to the relatively low base rate of anorexia nervosa in the general population; however, it may be possible to reach tentative conclusions about premorbid personality by administering measures after recovery as well as during acute phases of illness (Vitousek and Manke 1994). This type of approach has proved useful in depression research (e.g. Sheppard and Teasdale 1996).

COGNITIVE SCHEMATA

The existence of unconditional negative schemata in relation to the self is generally accepted to be characteristic of anorexia nervosa (Vitousek and Hollon 1990). Conditional schemata are likely to include elements of over-control (Casper *et al.* 1992; Turnbull and Treasure submitted), black-and-white or dichotomous thinking and a tendency to evaluate self-worth almost entirely in terms of self-control (Butow *et al.* 1993).

EMOTIONAL DYSREGULATION

Several aspects of emotion regulation have been suggested to be abnormal in anorexia. Leon and colleagues (Leon *et al.* 1993) found, in a population study, that eating disorder sufferers were more likely than normals to show a tendency to negative emotionality (a feeling of being at the mercy of an 'emotional maelstrom') and a lack of emotional discrimination (an inability to label emotions).

Furthermore, a lack of awareness of the role played by inner sensations in regulating weight and behaviour is suggested in a repertory grid study by Butow *et al.* (1993). This is illustrated by an example from our own clinical practice:

> I was always confused and panicked by emotional extremes because I did not know how to express myself. Anger always choked me. I would lose all contact with my vocabulary, feel hot and get palpitations and then cry. I know I showed how angry I was through my body. I hit, hurt, punished my body instead of shouting or screaming but I had no vocabulary to express these feelings with.

This pervasive emotional dysregulation is really the other side of the coin to cognitive dysfunction. Indeed, Laird (1989), among others have suggested that 'feelings are cognitions'.

ELEMENTS OF THE COGNITIVE MODEL

When a patient presents to a doctor, there are three questions of fundamental importance which need to be asked. These are as follows:

1. What sort of illness does the patient have?
2. What sort of patient does the illness have?
3. What does the illness mean to the patient?

In formulating a cognitive model of anorexia nervosa (see Figures 18.1 and 18.2), these three questions, respectively, will address:

1. The 'core' anorexic beliefs;
2. The 'general' cognitive psychopathology (anorexics' beliefs);
3. Beliefs about anorexia.

The following account addresses each of these aspects. The discussion starts with beliefs about anorexia because it is these which initially colour the therapeutic interaction and which need to be addressed earliest in therapy. Next, the general and core beliefs are discussed, followed finally by perpetuating and maintaining factors.

BELIEFS ABOUT ANOREXIA: WHAT DOES THE ILLNESS MEAN TO THE PATIENT?

Recently, several authors have highlighted the importance of metacognitions in the maintenance of emotional disorders (Teasdale 1985; Wells 1997). Metacognitions are beliefs and actions concerned with the regulation and interpretation of a person's own cognitions (Metcalfe and Shimamura 1994). In the case of the

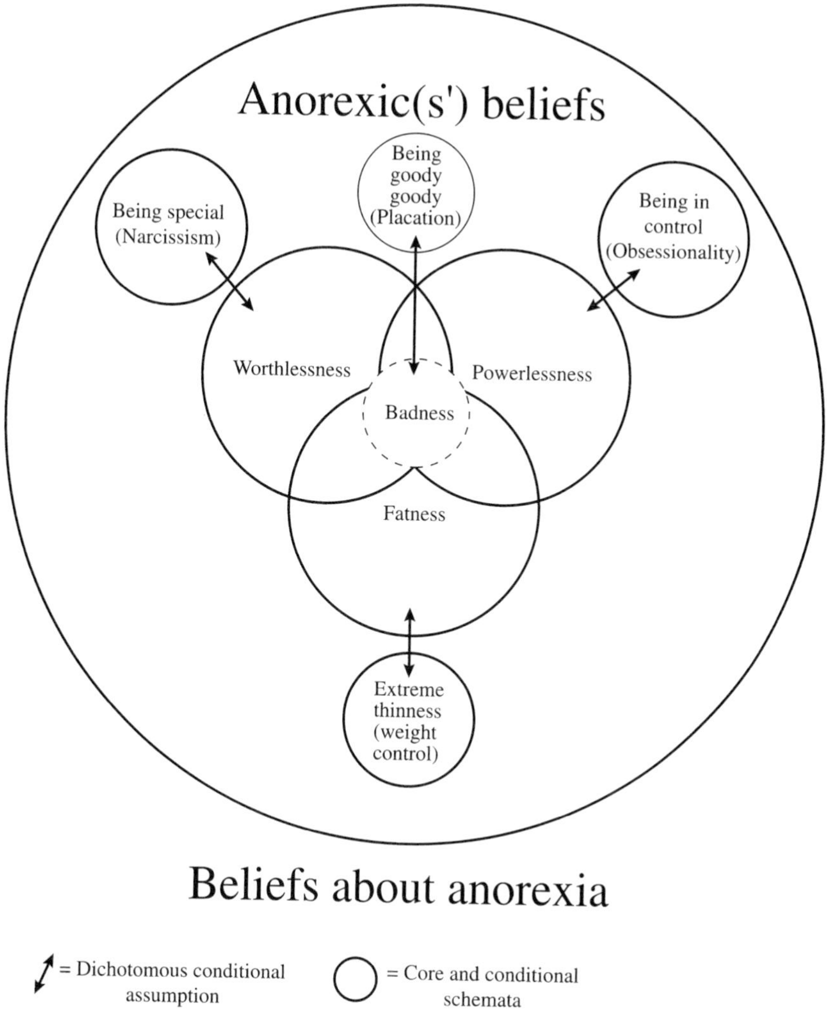

Figure 18.1. Schematic beliefs in anorexia

emotional disorders the term is used to describe the beliefs a patient may have about his or her illness. In generalized anxiety disorder, Wells (1997) has described how patients see worrying as a useful and beneficial activity and that this needs to be addressed early in treatment. In his work on depression, Teasdale (1985) proposes that depression can be exacerbated by negative meta-cognitions, or 'depression about depression'.

Similarly, we propose that metacognitions in the form of pro-anorexia beliefs, are implicated in maintenance of the disorder. In particular, they may account for one of the more striking features of anorexic patients, their ambivalent approach to treatment.

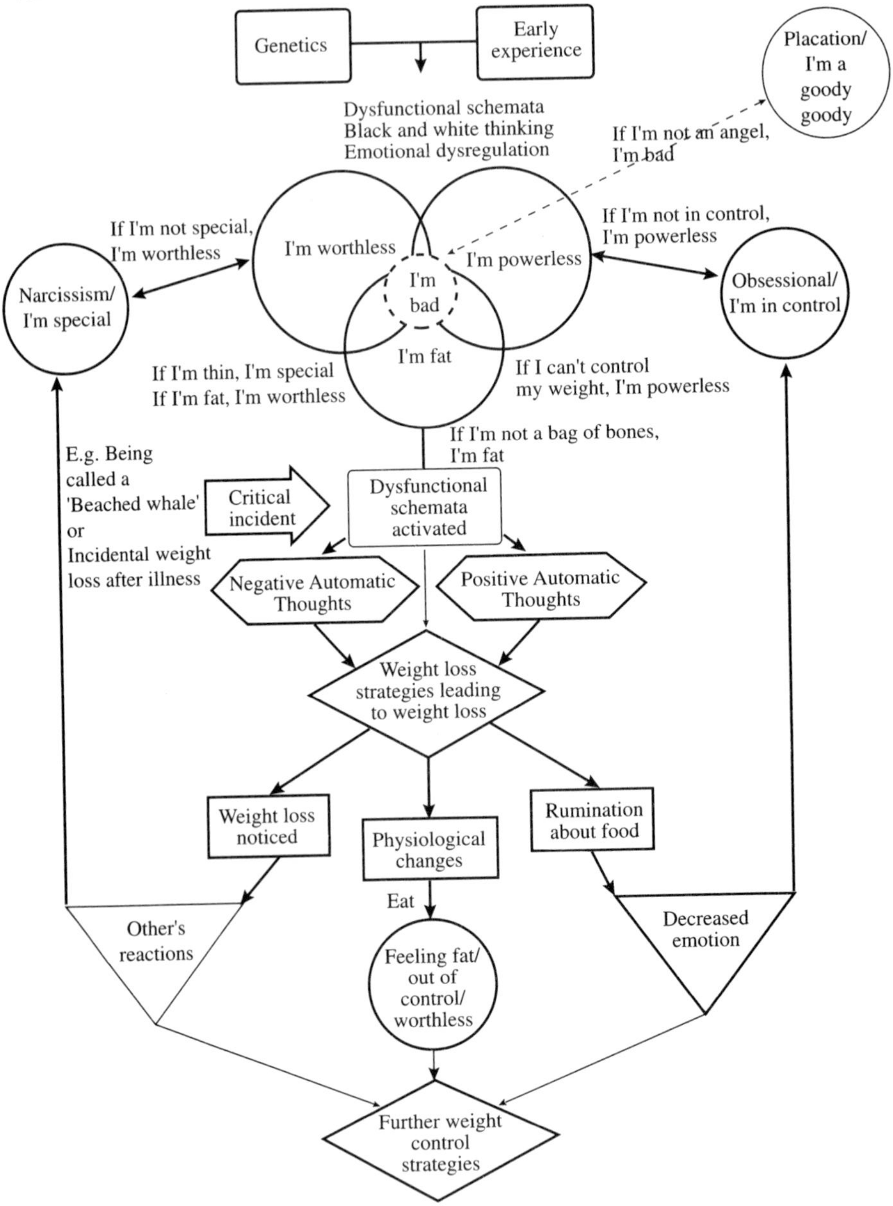

Figure 18.2. A cognitive model of anorexia

Pro-anorexia meta-cognitions, (such as 'if I didn't have anorexia, my whole world would fall apart, I wouldn't be able to cope') enhance resistance to treatment, whilst anti-anorexia meta-cognitions, (such as 'anorexia stops me from having a life') can enhance motivation to change.

ANOREXICS' BELIEFS: WHAT SORT OF PATIENT DOES THE ILLNESS HAVE?

These include the general pre-morbid psychopathology which provides the 'soil' for the illness to flourish (see Figure 18.1). Firstly, there are various sets of core beliefs or unconditional schemata concerned with the self which are extreme. These include both low self-worth (e.g. worthlessness, badness) and lack of self-efficacy (e.g. powerlessness) (e.g. Troop and Treasure 1997). These beliefs derive mainly from the interaction between the individual and their early environment and are often idiosyncratic.

These schemata may be linked to perceived or actual criticism, rejection or enmeshment. This view is supported by clinical experience, as illustrated by this extract from a heartfelt letter written by an anorexic patient to her parents: 'I felt over-criticized, over-disciplined, dominated and controlled. I could never be my own person. You can't expect to keep me wrapped up in cotton wool for the rest of my life'. The authors propose that these schemata are extreme, and are characterized by black-and-white or dichotomous thinking (represented in Figure 18.1 by arrows).

The extreme nature of distressing unconditional schemata within these domains lead the patient to develop compensatory conditional schemata. In black-and-white terms, there is only one place to go from the intolerable position of worthlessness or badness and that is to the opposite extreme. Hence the patient may 'state-shift' from worthlessness to a position of specialness and narcissism; from badness to 'goody-goody-ness' and placation; or from powerlessness to overcontrol and obsessionality. This shifting from one state to another has much in common with the 'reciprocal roles' described in Ryle's cognitive analytic therapy (Ryle *et al.* 1990; Ryle 1995) These address the interpersonal dimension of the schemata. Because of the extreme nature of these schemata, contradictory evidence is commonly encountered, and even ambiguous events tend to be interpreted negatively.

Examples of dichotomous dysfunctional assumptions which are associated with this shift include: 'If I'm not special, I'm worthless', 'If I'm not liked by everybody, not just people, but animals and things, I'm bad' and 'If I'm not in complete control, I'm powerless' (see Figure 18.2). These defences are, however, imperfect. The patient therefore repeatedly shifts back to the core cognitive-emotional state. This cognitive-emotional dysregulation makes the patient feel out of control or at the mercy of an emotional maelstrom.

ANOREXIC BELIEFS: WHAT SORT OF ILLNESS DOES THE PATIENT HAVE?

In our culture, thinness is highly valued and has links with self esteem (including specialness, goodness and power) (e.g. Wolf 1992). However, in anorexia nervosa, these become excessively cemented together (see Figures 18.1 and 18.2). In other words, core beliefs concerning thinness overlap with core beliefs concerned with self-esteem. Some of the compensatory anorexic assumptions reflect this: 'If I'm thin, I'm special; if I'm fat, I'm worthless', 'If I can't control my weight, I'm powerless' and 'If I'm fat, I'm bad'.

The interlinking of cognitive schemata has also been described in depression in the Interacting Cognitive Subsystems model (Teasdale 1997a; Teasdale and Barnard 1993). This model suggests that mood effects operate not at the level of individual constructs but a more generic level of higher order interrelationships. It is not 'fatness' *per se* which causes distress, but the intimacy of its link with self-esteem.

Indeed, once anorexia has developed, patients do not necessarily think they are fat. Patients may say they know they are a 'bag of bones' but they also fear being fat, with dichotomous thinking leaving nothing in between. Their dichotomous conditional assumption may be: 'If I am not a bag of bones, I'm fat'.

These assumptions are exacerbated and re-enforced by dichotomous thinking ('I know I'm a bag of bones but I'm terrified of being fat' and 'I thought I'd be the size of a house at my first custard cream'). Part of the work of therapy is to restructure the dichotomous thinking and to dissolve some of the anorexic glue which binds body-image schemata to self-esteem schemata'.

PRECIPITATING FACTORS

Precipitating events can often be identified in patients with anorexia nervosa (see review by Troop, submitted). In many cases, a link can be made between these events and underlying schemata.

The following are examples from clinical practice:

- A patient who comes from an enmeshed family feels even more powerless when she leaves home and struggles with independence issues, hence begins to diet in an attempt to regain control.
- A borderline patient with a particular fear of abandonment due to an underlying 'badness schema' is rejected by a boyfriend who calls her a 'beached whale' and she begins to diet.
- A patient who feels worthless loses weight as a result of a viral illness, and then begins to diet when people comment favourably on her initial weight loss.

MAINTAINING FACTORS

Positive automatic thoughts (PATs)

In contrast to most neurotic illness, anorexia nervosa is strongly egosyntonic. Especially in the early stages, the disorder is fuelled by feelings of mastery and cheerfulness as well as depression and anxiety. Whereas dysphoric states are related to negative automatic thoughts (NATs), we propose that these euphoric states are related to positive automatic thoughts (PATs) which have the same qualities of automaticity and distortion but induce positive mood. In the case of the

Table 18.1. The dysfunctional thoughts record in anorexia nervosa

Situation	Emotion	Automatic thoughts
Friend says: 'You've lost weight'	Pleased	'I look more attractive' (PAT)
Resist doughnut	Euphoric	'I'm in control (of my weight/feelings)' (PAT)
Eat doughnut	Anxious	'I'll get fat' (NAT)

patient described above who lost weight after a viral illness, and then started dieting, each 3 kg lost led to a tremendous sense of accomplishment with thoughts such as 'I look more attractive', 'I'm in control', 'I'll be more popular' and this led to further weight loss strategies. These thoughts were related to underlying linked body-image/self-esteem schemata as described above. The standard dysfunctional thoughts record (DTR) for recording dysfunctional thoughts can also be used for recording both negative and positive mood states, with associated NATs and PATs. Therapists should guard against the common error of focusing on the NATs but neglecting the PATs and therefore missing the opportunity to work on egosyntonic issues. An example of a dysfunctional thoughts record from clinical practice is as follows (see Table 18.1).

Physiological (and physical) change

Increased fullness and bloating (starvation effects) make the patient feel out of control and fat when she eats even small amounts and, as the patient may well rely mostly on interoceptive awareness to make her judgment, these feelings reinforce the dichotomous assumption: 'I'll be the size of a house at my first custard cream' or 'I'll blow up like a balloon if I eat a biscuit'. (Similarly, a reliance on interoceptive awareness has been implicated in social phobia (Wells 1997).) Physical effects such as hair loss may further reinforce feelings of worthlessness and powerlessness.

Safety behaviours

Safety behaviours have been recognized as an important maintaining factor in anxiety disorders (Clark 1997) and obsessive–compulsive disorder (Salkovskis 1996). This concept can also be a useful way to characterize certain anorexic behaviours. For example, avoidance of 'dangerous' foods may be seen as a safety behaviour to prevent the patient 'blowing up like a balloon'. The patient may attribute her 'success' in extreme weight control to the complete avoidance of such foods. She never gets the chance to disconfirm beliefs such as: 'one custard cream, and I'll be the size of a house'. A further example of safety behaviour is illustrated by a patient who believed that having a dessert would make her put on 3 kg in weight. She would either avoid dessert or vomit immediately afterwards. Again, she never gave herself the chance to disconfirm her dysfunctional belief.

Identifying and helping the patient to challenge the beliefs implicated in these safety behaviours is an important element of therapy with these patients.

REACTIONS OF OTHERS

Attention from family, friends and health care workers can all support the patient's belief that 'if I'm thin I'm special'. After an initial period of weight loss this attention may be in the form of compliments about the thinner figure, but severe weight loss is normally greeted with concern, care giving and worry. The response to this attention is often ambivalent; the anorexic may initially beg to be left alone with the insistence that 'everything is fine', but later admit that she is concerned that if she gains weight she will lose the special attention she gains as a result of her anorexia and be abandoned.

Rumination about food

It is recognized that in generalized anxiety disorder, anxious rumination may be a mechanism for inhibiting processing of emotionally charged information (Wells 1997). This hunger driven rumination may dampen down the emotional dysregulation because it fills the mind with food related thought at the expense of even more distressing emotionally charged rumination (see Figure 18.3). That is, 'If I'm thin, I'm in control' is reinforced by the dampening down of emotional processing consequent upon starvation driven rumination about food (and consequent PATs). An example from clinical practice is as follows: a patient who feels powerless and humiliated by a bowel disease which requires treatment with steroids (which lead to weight gain) tries to control her weight. When she begins to starve, her emotions are suppressed and she feels more in control.

TREATMENT

Freud's metaphor for therapy as archaeology provides an illustration of a common problem in treating anorexia—resistance. Imagine waking up one morning to find a team of archeologists trampling over your garden, digging up the rose-beds. Would you be 'resistant'? So it is with the anorexic patient. You need to demonstrate to the patient, or help them see, that the dig is worthwhile and to get their permission—engagement (Vitousek *et al.* in press).

WORKING ON META-BELIEFS ABOUT ANOREXIA

Engagement and therapeutic alliance

Engagement is the vital first phase of treatment. Time and time again, research has shown that so called non-specific factors, such as the *therapeutic alliance*, are the best predictors of outcome. This is particularly important in anorexia nervosa as it is easy to get into a *confrontation–denial trap* with the clinician trying to prove to the patient what a terrible state she is in, and the patient insisting she does not have a problem (see Figure 18.3). Miller and Rollnick's (1990) motivational interviewing style is helpful here (Treasure and Ward 1997).

After the initial assessment, it is useful for the therapist to write a feedback letter to the patient, detailing the patient's main concerns about how the illness has affected her, how it has developed and what treatment options are available. The patient is encouraged to discuss the feedback with the therapist and to correct any misunderstandings between them and the therapist. As therapy progresses, further feedback letters are sent to the patient and the patient is encouraged to write letters back to the therapist about what has been learned.

These letters can be very powerful devices for both building therapeutic alliance and for cognitive restructuring. One patient for example burst into tears on reading the letter in front of the therapist and said: 'Nobody has ever understood me like this' and 'reading this, I realize just how much anorexia has affected my life'.

Working on the ambivalence

Ideas from Prochaska and DiClemente's (1982, 1986) transtheoretical *stages of change* model are helpful here. What this therapist needs is an understanding of the patient's position in the cycle of change (see Figure 18.4) and use strategies appropriate to this stage. Patients with anorexia nervosa are unlikely to present in the *action stage* (Blake *et al.* 1997). If they are in the *precontemplation* or

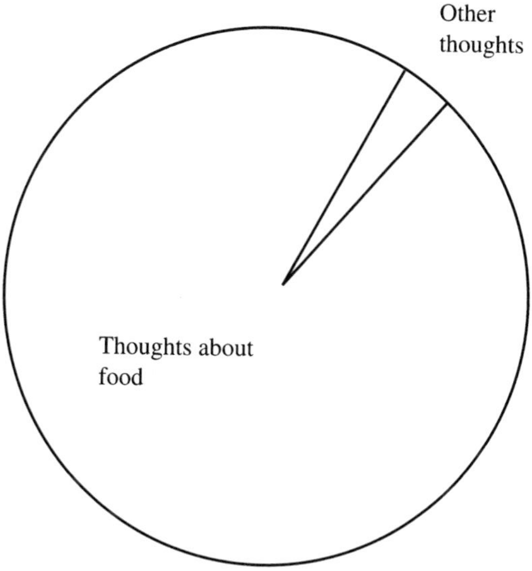

Figure 18.3. Thought chart

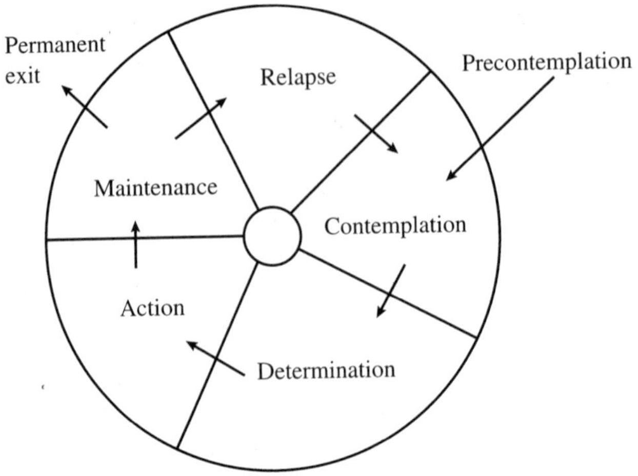

Figure 18.4. Prochaska and DiClemente's stages of change

contemplation stages for example, the therapist must deal with the beliefs about anorexia, that is the meta-beliefs.

Although they are strongly held, these beliefs can be challenged by the patient. This process is facilitated by an understanding of the fact that by nature, people are inconsistent and may already hold a conflicting range of attitudes at the same time. This kind of paradox was observed by Somerset Maugham (1938) who wrote: 'What has chiefly struck me in human beings is their lack of consistency. I have never seen people all of a piece. It has amazed me that the most incongruous traits should exist in the same person and for all that yield a plausible harmony. I have often asked myself how characteristics, seemingly irreconcilable, can exist in the same person.' Jung (1935) also noted: 'In the psychology of our unconscious there are typical figures that have a definite life of their own. The so-called unity of consciousness is an illusion. We like to think we are one; but we are not, most decidedly not.' People may have limited awareness of these conflicting inner states, and an important element of therapy is to raise this awareness.

Such conflicts are also evident in the work of George Brown and colleagues on self-esteem (Brown *et al.* 1990a–d). They measured both positive and negative evaluation of self independently, and found that both could co-exist. Furthermore, negative evaluation of self appears to predict vulnerability to depression and positive evaluation of self predicts recovery. Recovery may depend upon the ability to access these positive schemata. Ornstein, in *The Evolution of Consciousness*, describes the concept of 'the mind-in-place' whereby such differing states are accessed at different times by different stimuli. Teasdale (1997a) suggests that in depression, patients become 'stuck' in one mind. If one assumes that patients with anorexia get stuck in an anorexic mind-in-place, then one early object in therapy is to help the patient to start to let go of this mind-set and to access healthier ones.

As the anorexic mind-set is related to power and control, it is important not to inadvertently reinforce its dominance by strategies which make the patient feel powerless and out of control (cf. Aesop's fable of the sun and the wind competing to get a man to take his coat off. The harder the wind blew, the more he grabbed onto the coat. It was only the gentle sun warming the man which made him decide to take the coat off himself).

To start to shift patients along, the therapist needs to draw attention to these conflicting 'Jungian' figures thus creating *cognitive dissonance* which facilitates *cognitive restructuring*, as, hopefully, the anorexia is reframed by the patient as an imperfect pseudo-solution worthy of attempts at change. It is only when the patient enters the action phase that therapist will be able to work at the level of anorexic beliefs.

It is essential to the task of developing a good therapeutic alliance that the therapist accepts and understands the powerful beliefs patients almost invariably hold about the benefits of their illness. As Hilde Bruch describes in *Conversations with Anorexics*, '[They believe that] they have found, in their extreme thinness, the perfect solution to all their problems' (Bruch 1988).

Once the patient is engaged with the therapist, work can begin on cognitive restructuring of this belief. Various techniques can be used in this process.

SPECIFIC TECHNIQUES

It is often useful to ask patients to list and explore the pros and cons of anorexia (see Table 18.2). It is important to begin with the pros before moving onto the cons, thereby indicating to the patient your acceptance of the good things anorexia provides for her, as well as the costs. Work can then begin to help the patient to find activities or ways of being which can begin to replace the anorexia by fulfilling some of its functions. They may also be asked to examine the difference in their enjoyment of various activities pre and post onset of their anorexia (see Table 18.3).

These techniques are a useful starting point but they often fail to access higher order emotional meaning, the importance of which has been recognized (Clark 1996). In patients with personality disorders such as many of those with anorexia, it is important to use more emotion based strategies (Young 1994; McGinn and Young 1996).

Table 18.2. Exploring the pros and cons of anorexia

The good things about anorexia	The bad things about anorexia
People notice me, so don't feel ignored or lonely.	Health affected.
Make parents feel guilty.	Cannot socialize as much.
Don't think about feelings and no depression.	Forgetful, lack concentration.
No one will be able to cope with or understand my true feelings.	Feel isolated, lonely and unhappy.

Table 18.3. Examining change in enjoyment pre/post anorexia

Activity you enjoy	Past (Rate: 0–10)	Present (Rate: 0–10)	Reason for change in level of enjoyment
Visiting friends	8	2	Worry they'll see how fat I am
Going to pub	7	1	Feel too tired
Studying	6	2	Can't concentrate
Eating out	8	1	Self-conscious

Patients are asked, as homework, to write letters to their anorexia as if it were their friend, then their enemy, and also a letter to a friend describing their lives as if it were five years on, first as though they still had the illness, then as if they were well. Examples of extracts of letters from clinical practice are as follows:

> Dear Friend, I'm so pleased I have you . . . You make me feel in control and I can keep all my feelings and emotions locked up inside so I don't have to cope and deal with them. If I let them out, I think everything will explode so it's great to keep them in a safe and hidden place. When I'm in hospital being looked after, I don't feel lonely as there are lots of people to look after me. I can get lots of attention so that I feel wanted . . .

> Dear Enemy, I hate you . . . You control my thoughts . . . I feel abnormal and self-conscious, I feel tired and lack energy. I feel scared of eating with others and so I have to restrict where I go so I feel isolated, lonely and unhappy . . .

> Dear Sally, It is five years since I saw you . . . I still have anorexia and I feel miserable and lonely most of the time. I don't go out much . . .

> Dear Sally, It is five years since I saw you . . . I have beaten the anorexia. I am happily married now and have two children . . .

Ideas about the benefits of anorexia which commonly emerge from these tasks include feeling looked after, feeling more self-controlled, the disorder giving sense of safety or a sense of achievement to the patient (Serpell *et al.* 1997; Serpell *et al.* submitted). Each of these can be related to aspects of the cognitive model we have presented. For example, the anorexic who expresses her sense of achievement in being able to lose weight, 'my anorexia makes me feel I can do something other people cannot do' is expressing the way in which anorexia allows her to gain a sense of personal power and control, and a feeling of specialness or narcissism in relation to others. On the other hand, the letter to anorexia as an enemy may express some of the negative aspects of the dichotomies depicted in Figure 18.1, such as the sense of worthlessness expressed by a patient who wrote: 'sometimes I think I am nothing without you, anorexia'.

The letter writing tasks can also give clues to particular dichotomous dysfunctional assumptions held by a patient. For example, a patient who wrote (in her letter to anorexia as a friend) that anorexia enabled her to control herself and others, and (in her letter 5 years into the future without anorexia) about her sad, lonely, out of control life feeling fat and useless. We could characterize one of this patient's dichotomous assumptions as 'either I'm anorexic and perfectly in control or I'm not anorexic and a lonely fat blob'.

WORKING ON ANOREXIC BELIEFS

The principles used to work with anorexic beliefs draw on cognitive therapeutic techniques used in depression and anxiety. The key points are that the patient needs to answer both negative and positive automatic thoughts, and conduct behavioural experiments. Intellectual challenging alone, however, usually isn't sufficient because of the existence of a neurotic logic which can sabotage any attempts at rationalization. By way of illustration, there's a tradition in Middle Eastern Sufi philosophy of fables about a mulla (or spiritual teacher) called Nasrudin. In one of these, a man was passing by the mulla Nasrudin's house. The mulla was on the roof shouting and jumping and clapping his hands loudly. When the man asked the reason for this strange behaviour, Nasrudin replied 'It's to chase away the tigers'. 'Tigers?' said the man, perplexed, 'But there aren't any around here'. Whereupon the mulla replied 'Ah, you see, it works'.

In the treatment of anorexia, as with other neurotic disorders, behavioural experiments are used to get the patient to predict and then actually check out what would happen if they didn't cling on to their safety strategies: Would the tigers appear or not?

There are a number of other specific techniques which have also been found to be useful in this group of patients. These are described below.

Dealing with individual negative schemata

One-dimensional continua can be used as described by Christine Padesky (1994) (see Figure 18.5). In the case of one-dimensional schemata the patient first defines her negative schema (e.g. 'I'm a bad person') in terms of its positive dimension (e.g. 'goodness'). She then plots herself on the positive dimension of 'goodness'. She may well put herself very close to the 'no good' end of the spectrum. When she adds in other people (including infamous people such as the serial killer, Fred West), she often finds that she decides to shift herself up the scale. This technique helps to moderate dichotomous thinking about the self. There are various other techniques which can be employed to modify these negative schemata, including: the use of a positive data log (Padesky 1994), imagery techniques and the use of metaphor (Young 1994).

Dealing with linked schemata

Both two-dimensional continua (Padesky 1994) and pie-charts can be used. In the case of the two-dimensional continua (see Figure 18.6), linked schemata (such as being liked by virtue of being thin) are represented on the two dimensions and the patient is asked to plot herself and other important figures from her life (famous or fictitious figures may also be included). The patient may well be surprised to see that there is less of a direct relationship between the two dimensions than she had assumed. One perfectionist patient was surprised to find that often perfectionists are not well liked and 'scatty' people are loved.

In the case of pie-charts (see Figure 18.7), the patient is asked how much being thin makes her a special person and to represent this on the pie-chart. The remaining segment represents all the other factors. The patient is then asked to brainstorm all these other factors and put them into the second pie chart one by one. The segment remaining for thinness is usually then much smaller than at first thought and this is discussed. Finally, a third chart can be completed with what other people think makes the patient special. Usually thinness will not be a major

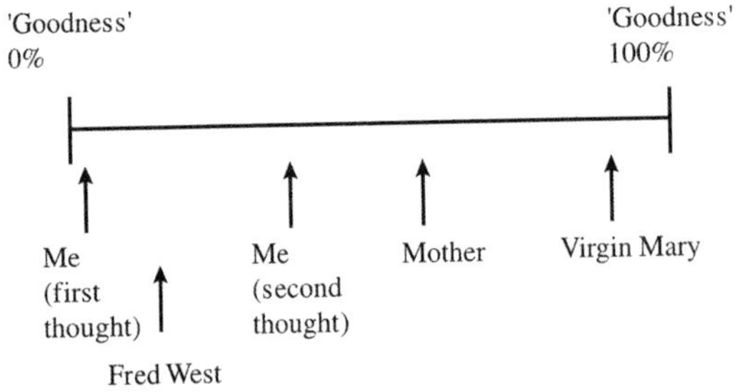

Figure 18.5. One-dimensional continuum

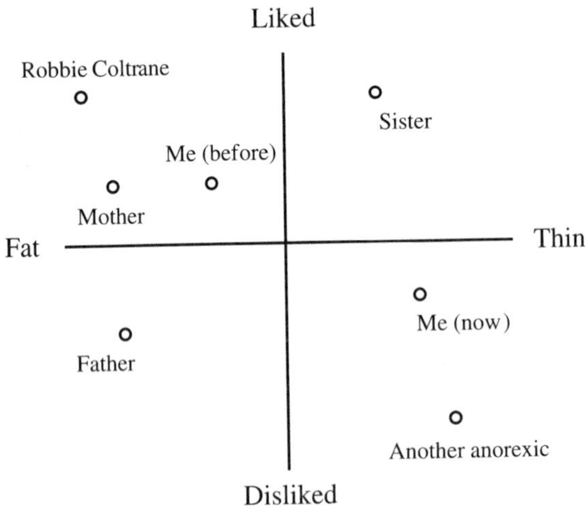

Figure 18.6. Two-dimensional continuum

segment of this pie chart and the implications of this can be discussed in relation to the patient's anorexia.

Dealing with interpersonal schemata

There is a growing awareness of the importance of interpersonal issues in the aetiology and maintenance of neurotic illness such as generalized anxiety disorder (Borkovec 1997), panic disorder (van Rijsoort and Arntz 1997) and the eating disorders (Fairburn *et al.* 1991). Cognitive models of these disorders often fail to incorporate any interpersonal element. Interpersonal issues may be particularly significant for patients who fail to respond to therapies based on these models. We would suggest that dealing with the interpersonal dimension of dichotomous schemata is one of the most important aspects of cognitive therapy with anorexic patients. Dichotomous reciprocal roles (Ryle *et al.* 1990; Ryle 1995) need to be identified and addressed. For example, anorexic patients are often placatory. They may have beliefs such as: 'either I'm a brute or a martyr (secretly blaming the

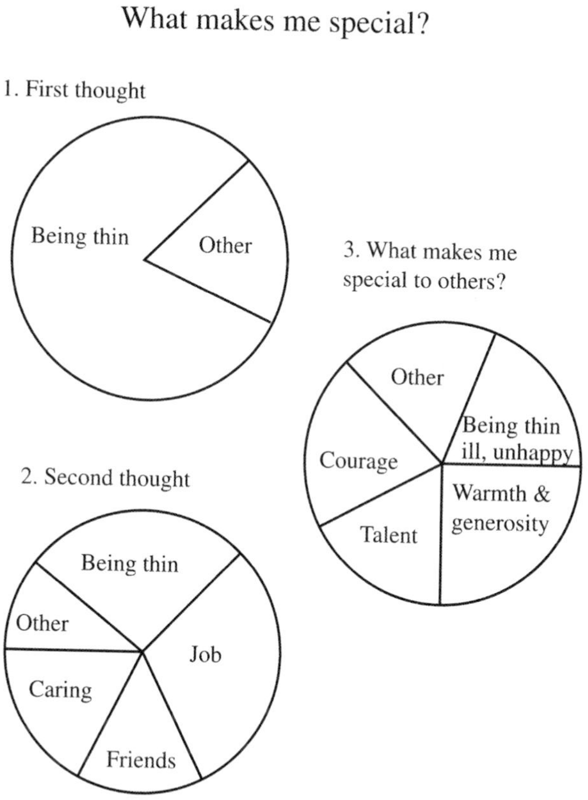

Figure 18.7. Pie charts of 'What makes me special?'

other)' or 'either I look down on other people, or they look down on me'. Once such beliefs are identified, they can be challenged. The patient can be encouraged to look for evidence for and against these beliefs and begin to set up behavioural experiments to test them out. Interpersonal issues are particularly important when addressing the issue of termination of therapy, as dysfunctional schemata may be strongly activated at this stage.

SUMMARY AND CONCLUSIONS

Teasdale (1982) asks the question (in relation to depression) 'What kind of theory will improve psychological treatment?' Since the early 1980s, the interaction between research and treatment in conditions such as depression, anxiety and PTSD, especially in the cognitive-behavioural domain, has enabled a shared conceptual framework to develop between clinicians and researchers (Teasdale 1997b). However, in the eating disorders, this collaborative, hypothesis testing approach has been much less apparent, despite calls for more work in this interface, principally by Vitousek (Vitousek and Hollon 1990; Vitousek 1997). This paper presents a model which, although grounded in previous research, is necessarily speculative. The authors not only recognize the need for, but positively encourage, the experimental evaluation of its various components.

It is suggested that the model can be used as a framework to begin to test specific low-level hypotheses between variables (an approach to experimental methods which has been found to be more fruitful than attempting to fully test more ambitious models (Gelder 1997)).

Cognitive-behavioural therapy needs to be adapted to meet the needs of the various disorders for which it is used. In particular, in anorexia nervosa, emphasis needs to be placed on dealing with the following: meta-beliefs; dichotomous thinking; linked body-image/self-esteem schemata; and interpersonal schemata. Some of the clinical treatment strategies described have been drawn directly from the cognitive therapy literature, others have been adapted from other therapies for use in a cognitive framework. All have been found to be clinically useful in the management of such patients but research needs to be conducted to test their efficacy.

CLINICAL IMPLICATIONS

- The model provides a rationale for a cognitive behavioural therapy strategy with an initial emphasis on engagement, and on working through ambivalence by exploring and restructuring anorexic meta-beliefs.
- A focus on the function of anorexia as a solution to other underlying problems enhances therapeutic alliance and facilitates collaborative work on egodystonic issues, such as dichotomous self-esteem schemata.
- The emphasis on the importance of the linking of weight/shape schemata to self esteem schemata gives a rationale for helping the patient to loosen these connections without directly confronting body image issues which may be egosyntonic, culturally entrenched and may not be realistically amenable to significant modification.

THEORETICAL/RESEARCH IMPLICATIONS

- The model integrates elements of Motivational Enhancement Therapy and Stages of Change Theory into a cognitive framework.
- The model opens up a new area of research which is focused on fundamentally important issues other than weight and shape, such as the issue of meta-beliefs in anorexia.
- This model has not yet been subject to rigorous evaluation, but can be used as a framework to test specific low-level hypotheses.

REFERENCES

Blair, C., Freeman, C. and Cull, A. (1995) The families of anorexia nervosa and cystic fibrosis patients. *Psychological Medicine*, **25**(5), 985–993.

Blake, W., Turnbull, S. and Treasure, J. (1997) Stages and processes of change in eating disorders: implications for therapy. *Clinical Psychology and Psychotherapy* **4**, 188–197.

Borkovec, T. (1997) The insufficiency of current cognitive behavioural therapy for GAD: failure to address maintaining interpersonal problems. Paper presented at the British Association of Behavioural and Cognitive Psychotherapies 25th Anniversary Conference, Canterbury, 8th–12th July 1997.

Brown, G.W., Andrews, B., Bifulco, A. and Veiel, H. (1990a) Self-esteem and depression: Measurement issues and prediction of onset. *Social Psychiatry and Psychiatric Epidemiology*, **25**, 200–209.

Brown, G.W., Bifulco, A., Veiel, H. and Andrews, B. (1990b) Self-esteem and depression: 2. social correlates of self-esteem. *Social Psychiatry and Psychiatric Epidemiology*, **25**, 225–234.

Brown, G.W., Bifulco, A. and Andrews, B. (1990c) Self-esteem and depression: 3. aetiological issues. *Social Psychiatry and Psychiatric Epidemiology*, **25**, 235–243.

Brown, G.W., Bifulco, A. and Andrews, B. (1990d) Self-esteem and depression: 4. effect on course and recovery. *Social Psychiatry and Psychiatric Epidemiology*, **25**, 244–249.

Bruch, H. (1966) Anorexia nervosa and its differential diagnosis. *Journal of Nervous and Mental Disease*, **141**, 556–566.

Bruch, H. (1978) *The Golden Cage: The Enigma of Anorexia Nervosa*. Open Books, UK.

Bruch, H. (1988) *Conversations with Anorexics*. Basic Books, Inc., New York.

Butow, P., Beumont, P. and Touyz, S. (1993) Cognitive processes in dieting disorders. *International Journal of Eating Disorders*, **14**(3), 319–329.

Casper, R.C. (1990) Personality features of women with good outcome from restricting anorexia nervosa. *Psychosomatic Medicine*, **52**(2), 156–170.

Casper, R.C., Hedeker, D. and McClough, J.F. (1992) Personality dimensions in eating disorders and their relevance for subtyping. *Journal of the American Academy of Child and Adolescent Psychiatry*, **31**(5), 830–840.

Clark, D.M. (1996) Panic disorder: from theory to therapy. In: Salkovskis, P.M. (ed.), *Frontiers of Cognitive Therapy*. The Guilford Press, London.

Clark, D.M. (1997) Panic disorder and social phobia. In: Clark, D.M. and Fairburn, C.G. (eds), *Science and Practice of Cognitive Behaviour Therapy*. Oxford Medical Publications, Oxford, UK.

Cooper, M.J. (1997) Cognitive theory in anorexia nervosa and bulimia nervosa: a review. *Behavioural and Cognitive Psychotherapy*, **25**, 113–145.

Crisp, A. (1967) Anorexia nervosa. *Hospital Medicine*, **1**, 713–718.

Dare, C., Le-Grange, D., Eisler, I. and Rutherford, J. (1994) Redefining the psychosomatic family: Family process of 26 eating disorder families. *International Journal of Eating Disorders*, **16**(3), 211–226.

Fairburn, C. G., Jones, R., Peveler, R. C. *et al.* (1991) Three psychological treatments for bulimia nervosa: a comparative trial. *Archives of General Psychiatry*, **48**, 463–469.

Fairburn, C. G., Jones, R., Peveler, R. C., Hope, R. A. and O'Connor, M. (1993) Psychotherapy and bulimia nervosa. Longer-term effects of interpersonal psychotherapy, behaviour therapy and cognitive behaviour therapy. *Archives of General Psychiatry*, **50**, 416–428.

Garner, D.M. and Bemis, K.M. (1985) Cognitive therapy for anorexia nervosa. In: Garner, D.M. & Garfinkel, P.E. (eds) *Handbook of Psychotherapy for Anorexia Nervosa and Bulimia*, pp. 107–146. Guilford Press, New York.

Gelder, A. (1997) The scientific foundations of cognitive behaviour therapy. In: Clark, D.M. and Fairburn, C.G. (eds), *Science and Practice of Cognitive Behaviour Therapy*. Oxford Medical Publications, Oxford, UK.

Guidano, V.F. and Liotti, G. (1983) *Cognitive Processes and Emotional Disorders: A Structural Approach to Psychotherapy*. Guilford Press, New York.

Gull, W.W. (1874) Anorexia nervosa (apepsia hysterica, anorexia hysterica). *Transactions of Clinical Society of London*, **7**, 22–28.

Gupta, M.A. (1990) Fear of aging: a precipitating factor in late onset anorexia nervosa. *International Journal of Eating Disorders*, **9**(2), 221–224.

Hewitt, P.L., Flett, G.L. and Ediger, E. (1995) Perfectionistic traits and perfectionistic self presentation in eating disorder attitudes. *International Journal of Eating Disorders*, **18**(4), 317–326.

Jung, C.G. (1935) The Tavistock Lectures. In: Read, H., Fordham, M. and Adler, G. (eds), *The Collected Works of C.G. Jung*, **Vol 18**, Routledge, London.

Katzman, M.A. and Lee, S. (1997) Beyond body image: the integration of feminist and transcultural theories in the understanding of self-starvation. *International Journal of Eating Disorders* **22**(4), 385–394.

Laird, J.D. (1989) Mood affects memory because feelings *are* cognitions. *Journal of Social Behaviour and Personality*, **4**, (special issue), 33–38.

Lawrence, M. (1984) *The Anorexic Experience*. The Womens Press, London.

Le-Grange, D., Eisler, I., Dare, C. and Hodes, M. (1992) Family criticism and self-starvation: A study of expressed emotion. *Journal of Family Therapy*, **14**(2), 177–192.

Leon, G.R. *et al.* (1993) Personality and behavioural vulnerabilities associated with risk status for eating disorders in adolescent girls. *Journal of Abnormal Psychology*, **102**,-.

Maugham, S. (1938) *The Summing Up*. Pan, 1976. (p. 40).

McGinn, L.K. and Young, J.E. (1996) Schema-focused therapy. In: Salkovskis, P.M. (ed.), *Frontiers of Cognitive Therapy*. The Guilford Press, London.

Metcalfe, J. and Shimamura, A.P. (eds) (1994) *Metacognition: Knowing about Knowing*. MIT Press, Cambridge, MA.

Miller, W.R. and Rollnick, S. (1991) *Motivational Interviewing: Preparing People to Change Addictive Behaviour.* Guilford Press, New York, NY.

Minuchin, S., Baker, L., Rosman, B.L., Liebman, R., Milman, L. and Todd, T.C. (1975). A conceptual model of psychosomatic illness in children. Family organisation and family therapy. *Archives of General Psychiatry*, **32**, 1031–1038.

Minuchin, S., Rosman, B.L. and Baker, L. (1978) *Psychosomatic Families: Anorexia Nervosa in Context*. Harvard University Press, Cambridge, MA.

Ornstein, R. (1992) *The Evolution of Consciousness*. Simon & Schuster, New York.

Padesky, C.A. (1994) Schema change processes in cognitive therapy. *Clinical Psychology and Psychotherapy*, **1**(5), 267–278.

Prochaska, J.O. and DiClemente, C.C. (1982) Transtheoretical therapy: Towards a more integrative model of change. *Psychotherapy: Theory, Research, and Practice*, **19**, 276–288.

Prochaska, J.O. and DiClemente, C.C. (1986) Toward a comprehensive model of change. In: W.R. Miller and N. Heather (eds), *Treating Addictive Behaviours: Processes of Change*. pp. 3–27. Plenum Press, New York.

Russell, G.F.M. (1979) Anorexia nervosa: its identity as an illness and its treatment. In: Price, J.H. (ed.) *Modern Trends in Psychological Medicine*. pp. 131–164. Butterworths, London.

Ryle, A. (ed.) (1995) *Cognitive Analytic Therapy: Developments in Theory and Practice*. Wiley, Chichester.

Ryle, A., Poynton, A.M. and Brockman, B.J. (1990) *Cognitive-analytic therapy: Active Participation in Change: A New Integration in Brief Psychotherapy*. Wiley, Chichester.

Ryle, J.A. (1936) Anorexia nervosa. *Lancet* (**ii**) 893–899.

Salkovskis, P.M. (1996). The Cognitive Approach to Anxiety: Threat Beliefs, Safety-Seeking Behaviour and the Special Case of Health Anxiety and Obsessions. In: Salkovskis, P.M. (ed.) *Frontiers of Cognitive Therapy.* The Guilford Press, London.

Selvini-Palazzoli, M. (1974). *Self-starvation: From Individual to Family Therapy in the Treatment of Anorexia Nervosa*. Chaucer Human, London.

Serpell, L., Treasure, J. and Teasdale, J. (1997). Anorexia: Friend or Foe? Paper presented at ED '97, The Third London International Conference on Eating Disorders: London, UK. 15th–17th April 1997.

Serpell, L., Treasure, J., Teasdale, J. and Sullivan V. Anorexia: friend or foe? A qualitative analysis of the themes expressed in letters written by anorexia nervosa patients. *International Journal of Eating Disorders* (in press).

Sheppard, L.C. and Teasdale, J.D. (1996) Depressive thinking—changes in schematic mental models of self and world. *Psychological Medicine*, **26**, 1043–1051.

Shisslak, C.M., Pazda, S.L., Crago, M. (1990) Body weight and bulimia as discriminators of psychological characteristics among anorexic, bulimic, and obese women. *Journal of Abnormal Psychology*, **99**(4), 380–384.

Silverstone, P.H. (1990) Low self-esteem in eating disordered patients in the absence of depression. *Psychological Reports*, **67**(1), 276–278.

Simpson, W.S. and Ramberg, J.A. (1992) Sexual dysfunction in married female patients with anorexia and bulimia nervosa. *Journal of Sex and Marital Therapy*, **18**(1), 44–54.
Srinivasagam, N.M., Kaye, W.H., Plotnicov, K.H., Greeno, C., *et al.* (1995) Persistent perfectionism, symmetry, and exactness after long-term recovery from anorexia nervosa. *American Journal of Psychiatry* **152**(11), 1630–1634.
Teasdale, J.D. (1982) What kind of theory will improve psychological treatment? In: Boulougouris, J.E. (ed.) *Learning Theory Approaches to Psychiatry*, pp. 57–66. Wiley, Chichester.
Teasdale, J.D. (1985) Psychological treatments for depression – how do they work? *Behaviour Research and Therapy* **23** (2), 157–165.
Teasdale, J.D. (1997a) The relationship between cognition and emotion: the mind-in-place in mood disorders. In: Clark, D.M. and Fairburn, C.G. (eds), *Science and Practice of Cognitive Behaviour Therapy*. Oxford Medical Publications, Oxford, UK.
Teasdale, J.D. (1997b) Clinically relevant theory: integrating clinical insight with cognitive science. In: Salkovskis, P.M. (ed.), *Frontiers of Cognitive Therapy*. Guilford Press, New York.
Teasdale, J.D. and Barnard, P.J. (1993) *Affect, Cognition And Change: Re-Modelling Depressive Thought*. Lawrence Erlbaum Associates, Hove.
Telerant, A., Kronenberg, J., Rabinovitch, S. *et al.* (1992) Anorectic family dynamics. *Journal of the American Academy of Child and Adolescent Psychiatry*, **31**(5), 990–991.
Terry-Short, T., Owen, R.G., Slade, P. D. and Dewey, M. E. (1995). Positive and negative perfectionism. *Personality and Individual Differences*, **18**, 663–668.
Treasure, J.L. and Ward, A. (1997) Cognitive Analytic Therapy in the treatment of anorexia nervosa. *Clinical Psychology and Psychotherapy*, **4**, 62–71.
Troop, N.A. (in preparation) Precipitating factors in anorexia nervosa: A review of the literature.
Troop, N.A. and Treasure, J.L. (1997) Psychosocial factors in the onset of eating disorders: Responses to life-events and difficulties. *British Journal of Medical Psycology*, **70**, 373–385.
Turnbull, S. and Treasure, J. (submitted) The relationship between eating disorder diagnosis, early maladaptive schema, and childhood adversity.
van Rijsoort, M. and Arntz, A. (1997) Interpersonal psychotherapy as a treatment for panic disorder. Paper presented at the British Association of Behavioural and Cognitive Psychotherapies 25th Anniversary Conference, Canterbury, 8th–12th July, 1997.
Vitousek, K. and Bemis, K. (1997) The current status of cognitive behavioural models of anorexia nervosa and bulimia nervosa. In: Salkovskis, P.M. (ed.) *Frontiers of Cognitive Therapy*. Guilford Press, New York.
Vitousek, K. and Hollon, S. (1990). The investigation of schematic content and processing in eating disorders. *Cognitive Therapy and Research*, **14**, 191–214.
Vitousek, K. and Manke, F. (1994) Personality variables and disorders in anorexia nervosa and bulimia nervosa. Special Issue: Personality and psychopathology. *Journal of Abnormal Psychology*, **103**(1), 137–147.
Vitousek, K., Watson, S. and Wilson, G.T. (in press) *Clinical Psychology Review.*
Waller, G. (1994) Borderline personality disorder and perceived family dysfunction in the eating disorders. *Journal of Nervous and Mental Disease*, **182**(10), 541–546.
Wells, A. (1996) Generalised anxiety disorder. In: Salkovskis, P.M. (ed.), *Frontiers of Cognitive Therapy*. Guildford Press, New York.
Wells, A. and Butler, G. (1997) Generalised anxiety disorder. In: Clark, D.M. and Fairburn, C.G. (eds), *Science and Practice of Cognitive Behaviour Therapy*. Oxford Medical Publications, Oxford, UK.

Williams, G.J., Power, K.G., Millar, H.R. *et al.* (1993) Comparison of eating disorders and other dietary/weight groups on measures of perceived control, assertiveness, self-esteem, and self-directed hostility. *International Journal of Eating Disorders*, **14**(1), 27–32.
Williams, G.J., Chamove, A.S. and Millar, H.R. (1997) Eating disorders, perceived control, assertiveness and hostility. *British Journal of Clinical Psychology,* **29**(3), 327–335.
Wolf, N. (1992). *The Beauty Myth*. Vintage.
Young, J.E. (1994) *Cognitive Therapy for Personality Disorders: A Schema Focused Approach*. Professional Resource Press, Sarasota, Florida.

19 Nutritional Management

J. RUSSELL and S. BYRNES
Eating Disorders Unit, Northside Clinic, Greenwich, NSW, Australia

Never was the Hippocratic axiom 'let your food be your medicine and your medicine be your food' more true than in the treatment of the eating or more properly the dieting disorders. Nutritional management begins with reinstitution of fluid and nutrient intake and cessation of weight losing behaviours. Restoration of body weight and composition to normal levels is the next objective followed by establishment of regular, balanced 'good enough' eating and healthy exercise patterns (Rock and Curran-Celentano 1996). All of this is much more easily said than done and can rarely be accomplished without major psychotherapeutic input. Eating disorders have become burdensome to Western health economies and the question has arisen as to how much treatment is necessary or whether treatment is needed at all in conditions which are self induced and where the patient's motivation is seen to be ambivalent. Alternatively, treatment and hence nutritional management is all about dealing with this challenge.

TO REFEED OR NOT TO REFEED

Eating disorders have a remittent course of long duration. The essential problem is the patient's sustained attempt to lose weight or to maintain a physiologically suboptimal weight by engagement in weight losing behaviours. The body might fight back as happens in bulimia nervosa or weight losing might become a vicious cycle with major physical and psychological consequences as in anorexia nervosa which represents the other end of the spectrum. Here the relapse rate in the year following hospital refeeding approaches 50% (Eckert *et al.* 1995) which makes refeeding sound to be a futile exercise. Studies from patients who have had at least some contact with treating agencies indicate that as many as 1% die each year from anorexia nervosa or its effects (Ratnisuriya *et al.* 1991; Sullivan 1995). Standardized mortality rates over 20 years in anorexic patients treated in a specialized inpatient unit where refeeding to premorbid i.e. normal weights was the rule, was shown to be one-third of that in patients treated on a general psychiatric hospital unit (Crisp *et al.* 1992). In the study of Baran *et al.* (1995), anorexic patients who remained in hospital long enough to reach their designated target weights did better over a 2-year period and required fewer hospitalizations than those who failed to do so. Unfortunately there are, to date, no other clinical outcome studies of suitable duration (although some are in progress) which address

Neurobiology in the Treatment of Eating Disorders.
Edited by H.W. Hoek, J.L. Treasure and M.A. Katzman.

the issue of whether or not anorexia nervosa patients ultimately benefit from standard inpatient refeeding regimes. Nevertheless there is now enough biological data to suggest that it is unethical not to attempt to restore weight to normal or near normal levels however this might be defined, in an anorexic patient.

Studies of total body nitrogen (Russell *et al.* 1983, 1994) demonstrate that total body protein (total body nitrogen multiplied by 6.25) is depleted by weight loss in anorexia nervosa and effectively replenished with weight gain. Patients with bulimia nervosa are usually within 10% of the normal weight range so total body protein is effectively maintained. Anorexia nervosa patients can be distinguished from those in whom weight loss has occurred because of medical illness. Here, protein repletion is impaired by the primary disease process so fat is replenished preferentially with refeeding. Because protein depletion has been associated with complications and premature demise in medical patients (Allen *et al.* 1995) the loss and replenishment of protein/nitrogen in anorexia nervosa would seem relevant to long term morbidity and mortality. This includes cardiac complications caused by loss of heart muscle and osteoporosis which might be determined by depletion of protein matrix of bone, although definitive evidence is still lacking because of the length of the requisite study period and the relatively recent availability of appropriate technology. Areas of uncertainty include the length of time necessary for irretrievable brain, organ and bone changes to occur and the protective influence of constitutional, genetic and other factors.

WHAT WEIGHT IS THE RIGHT WEIGHT?

Driven by cost containment imperatives, the denial symptomatic of the illness and a paucity of treatment efficacy data, the necessity for full weight restoration in patients with anorexia nervosa has been questioned along with the ethics and benefits of making this compulsory (Russell 1995). In our experience, a number of patients who do not reach target weight and maintain this at their index admission, return for treatment at progressively lower weights. On subsequent admissions they leave hospital even more prematurely and finally refuse admission altogether until, in extremis, require rescucitation and prolonged admission, often medicolegally enforced. Some of these patients (though by no means all) have emerged from this period of adequate refeeding to complete recovery and have expressed gratitude that matters were taken out of their hands.

It has been stated that the right weight has been reached in females when normal menstrual function has been restored or when the patient has returned to premorbid weight. However as these events are influenced by a variety of other factors including exercise, diet, stressors, growth patterns, heredity and ethnicity, newer techniques must be used in combination to provide a more dynamic assessment of weight restoration in terms of normalization of body structure, metabolism and function. Approaches to this problem include the use of pelvic ultrasound (Treasure *et al.* 1988), total body potassium, nitrogen and other parameters of body composition (Russell *et al.* 1994), indirect calorimetry, isotopic measurement of total daily energy expenditure (Casper *et al.* 1991; Pirke *et al.* 1991) and markers of bone turnover. Irreversible changes in grey matter have been found in weight recovered patients (Lambe *et al.* 1997) as has osteopenia (Ward *et al.* 1997) suggesting that brain imaging and bone densitometry be used earlier to gauge adequacy of refeeding.

Patient resistance to sophisticated investigations is likely to prove a stumbling block, however good our attempts at persuasion and education. Clinical and laboratory parameters such as heart rate, blood pressure, serum potassium, blood glucose, haemoglobin, white cell count and specific nutritional markers such as albumin, prealbumin, retinol binding prealbumin and transferrin will often remain the only practical objective measures of weight restoration despite their lack of precision and relatively early normalization (Russell *et al.* 1983, 1994; Ward *et al.* 1997). What is needed is a way, preferably simple and nonintrusive, in which the functional and biochemical correlates of irreversible brain and bone changes or better still their precursors, can be identified (Lambe *et al.* 1997; Ward *et al.* 1997) whilst remediation is still possible.

HOW FAST SHOULD REFEEDING BE?

It is usual to set weekly weight targets in refeeding programmes which our patients usually protest are excessive, particularly when leave and other privileges are contingent. Length of stay is determined by many things other than clinical need, financial constraints and educational requirements heading the list. The fact remains that the optimal rate of refeeding has not been established. As weight is gained more energy must be consumed so as to achieve a steady rate of weight gain and the patient usually needs to eat substantially more than a 'normal' diet to maintain the newly regained weight. This has been shown in females, to consist of almost equal proportions of fat and lean tissue, and to contain 13.4% protein (Russell *et al.* 1983, 1994). The fact that regained weight is not composed entirely of fat should be reassuring for patients.

The rate of replenishment of total body nitrogen and hence protein is influenced solely by weight gain. No correlation has been shown with aerobic and nonaerobic exercise levels, dietary protein, biochemical status or psychological parameters (Russell 1993; Russell *et al.* 1995). The disappointing truth for patients is that the need to eat more so as to gain weight is not obviated by weight training. Muscle size and strength as a biological 'luxury', will only increase when full replenishment of nitrogen has occurred i.e. at 100% of premorbid body weight. Attempts at muscle building will not hasten the process.

Rapid refeeding early on can be dangerous and leads to rapid fluid expansion and alarming increases in weight. Even where weight is gained at the usual rate of 1 kg per week, there appears to be a state of energy wasting as evidenced clinically by patients' complaints of feeling overheated as they approach target weight and their increasing energy requirements. This would make relapse likely even with good dietary compliance and modest activity levels. The need to prevent long-term bone and brain changes and the development of entrenched behaviours and attitudes must be balanced against an understanding of homeostatic mechanisms, practical considerations and the patient's fragile self acceptance.

HOW DO WE DETERMINE TARGET WEIGHT RANGE?

In children and pre-pubertal adolescents, it is easy enough to determine weight matched for height using percentile charts if height is appropriate for age (Fosson *et al.* 1993). Even where stunting has occurred, projected height can be determined by bone age and a weight appropriate to this can be designated. It is with post-pubertal patients that the real difficulty arises. Ideally the patient should be required to reach a weight within 10% of premorbid weight and this is usually the case with male patients. Such advice inevitably meets with strong resistance in females and our usual practice is to set target weight range around an arbitrary minimum body mass index (BMI) of 18.5 for those younger than 16 and 20 for older patients.

Most patients insist that their premorbid weight, if this is known, is much higher than their natural weight because they were eating more, exercising less, or taking the oral contraceptive pill. However they may have grown if not in linear height (and this is unlikely in girls of over 13.5 or 14 years) then in weight of bones and muscles which continues to increase into the second decade. Thus a higher weight or at least the premorbid weight is most often appropriate. Some patients, however, have been premorbidly obese or at least at the upper part of the normal weight range and it would then be reasonable to aim for a somewhat lower weight with much education as to the breadth of the normal weight range, the relative unimportance of weight *per se*, the desirability of concentrating on healthy eating and exercise habits and the need to maintain at a weight where it will not be necessary to diet.

At 85% of premorbid weight, when most patients leave hospital after refeeding, their mental state is not conducive to maintaining this. A minimum healthy weight is often as much as 10 kg less than what might be deemed physiologically appropriate. This was reflected by a mean depletion of 10% for total body protein/nitrogen and 20% for fat in patients whose mean post-refeeding BMI was 19 (Russell *et al.* 1994). Depression, anxiety scores and abnormal attitudes to weight, shape and food were shown to have improved though not to control levels and amennorrhoea, hyperactivity and rigid, perseverative thought patterns were likely to persist (Russell 1993). Thus anorexic preoccupations might still be intense at a time when weight has increased substantially, albeit not quite sufficiently even if the amount seems uncomfortably excessive to the patient. It should be stated that patients might need to remain in a hospital refeeding programme for as long as 12 weeks to reach and maintain target weight. Clinical experience has shown that if the extra weight is gained and maintained, the preoccupations not infrequently lessen.

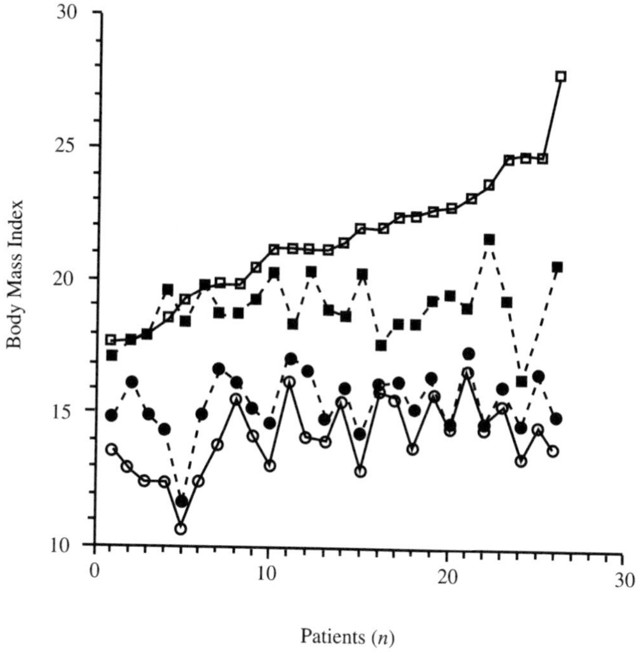

Figure 19.1. Body mass index (weight/height squared) before (●) and after (■) refeeding compared to the highest (□) and lowest (○) BMI lifetime ($n = 26$). Patients were sorted by their highest BMI ever achieved (an indication of premorbid weight). Although some patients achieved their premorbid weight after being refed for this episode (e.g. first 10 patients), several others did not. Six patients were not used in this analysis because their highest BMI could not be calculated

Figure 19.1 shows data from a group of 26 anorexia nervosa patients (ranked according to weights) who participated in a study of body composition and the effects of refeeding and in whom premorbid weight was known (Russell 1993). A marked discrepancy can be seen between the premorbid or highest ever weights (mean BMI approximately 21) of the majority of the patients and the weights achieved after hospital refeeding (mean BMI approximately 19). All patients described themselves as 'fat' at their premorbid or highest ever weights, yet these were all within the normal BMI range for post-pubertal females and not significantly different to that of a group of matched controls.

In Figure 19.2 it can be seen that in six of the eight of these patients who were followed up 6 to 12 months later, a similar discrepancy remained between their post-refeeding and follow up weights and their premorbid weights (Russell 1993). Although four of the patients had already lost weight, one had remained at and another had returned to her premorbid weight. The latter remains well 6 years later. Our group has embarked upon a study in which the 10-year outcome of all patients in whom total body nitrogen was measured will be assessed along with changes in

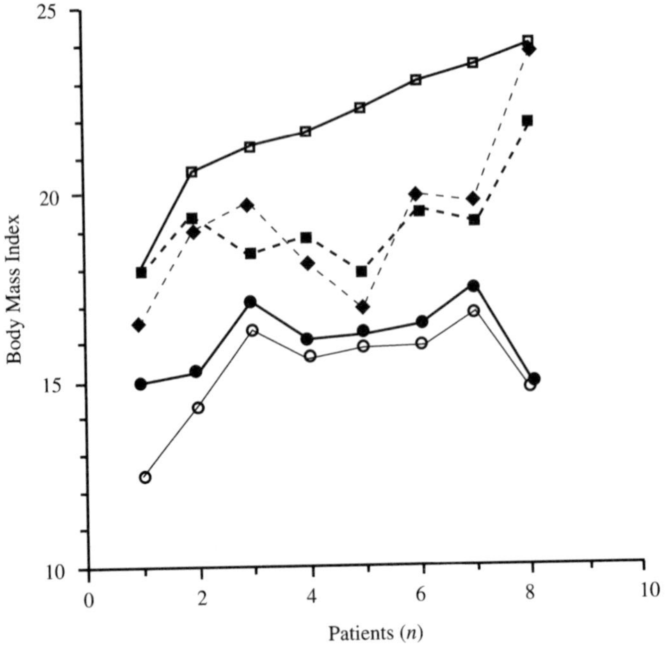

Figure 19.2. Body mass index before refeeding (●), after refeeding (■) and at 6–12 months follow-up (◆) compared to the highest (□) and lowest (○) BMI lifetime ($n = 8$). The dotted line indicates BMI in controls (21.5 kg m^{-2}). Patients were sorted by their highest BMI ever achieved (an indication of premorbid weight). Only two patients reached their premorbid weights. The first patient achieved her premorbid weight after refeeding and the last patient reached hers 6–12 months after discharge

total body nitrogen and current bone density. A comparison will be made between patients who reached a BMI of 19 or more at index refeeding and those who failed to do so.

CHRONIC ANOREXIA NERVOSA AS AN ACCEPTABLE LIFESTYLE

An increasingly popular view is that patients with anorexia nervosa should be allowed to remain at very low weights provided that they are stable and that they should be afforded whatever therapy they desire, be this general support, medical care or intensive psychotherapy with no expectation of weight gain. This conflicts with the observation that at very low weights meaningful attitudinal or behavioural change is almost impossible whilst social detriment and physical deterioration will inevitably progress to premature demise if the patient cannot be induced to gain weight. Brain imaging and bone density studies support the latter contention and the period of time necessary for irretrievable changes to occur may be relatively short (Lambe *et al.* 1997; Ward *et al.* 1997). When the situation deteriorates, palliative care or euthanasia have been seen as acceptable alternatives to refeeding.

However, knowing what we do about the effects of anorexia nervosa on brain function and mental state, we must ask ourselves whether it is ever responsible to allow such a patient to make decisions of this nature (Russell 1995).

Nevertheless, a decision to recover or to partly recover can still occur in ostensibly chronic patients and it would seem best to keep the therapeutic door open. Accepting limited goals in nutritional management is frustrating but who are we to say that the patient's choice is unreasonable given the circumstances? Although we clinicians may see ourselves as having a mandate to save life or offer a means of improving its quality, we are sometimes forced to accept that patients know themselves better than we do.

WHEN THE BODY FIGHTS BACK

In bulimia nervosa the body normalizes weight via the mechanism of binge eating, in spite of its owner's wishes and the most strenuous efforts to oppose what is experienced as shameful, out of control behaviour. The higher body weight appears to confer a biological advantage and the outcome although less well elucidated owing to the relatively recent definition of the syndrome (Russell 1979), looks better in terms of long-term mortality rate. In a 10-year study of treated patients, it was reported that only 5% of participants had not improved, almost 2/3 were symptom free and no patients had died (Abraham *et al.* 1983).

Nutritional rehabilitation is the objective of treatment and this entails establishment of dietary balance, regular eating patterns and adequate energy intake. With good compliance, the result is a gratifying reduction in the urge to binge eat and as a consequence, less urge to purge. Normalization of weight is an important objective in those bulimics who maintain weights that are suboptimal albeit within the normal range. However, this is of lower priority than normalizing eating. Patients with bulimia nervosa and binge eating disorder also engage in bingeing and purging in order to manage various uncomfortable psychological states which require treatment in their own right as part of the strategy to secure abstinence. Most bulimics fear weight gain even more than they want to be rid of their shameful behaviours and improved eating will be powerfully reinforced if it leads not only to a reduction in bingeing and purging but to stabilization or modest reduction in weight. Unfortunately patients with bulimia nervosa form a heterogeneous group diagnostically and their comorbid problems make management considerably less simple.

THE VICIOUS CYCLES OF ANOREXIA NERVOSA AND BULIMIA NERVOSA

As mentioned earlier, a chain of events ensues when weight is lost to a critical level and again when weight is regained as a result of reinstitution of nutrition. This was shown conclusively by the seminal studies of Keys and coworkers (1950). From a group of conscientious objectors from military service, a cohort of young men, chosen for their physical and psychological fitness, were induced by dietary restriction, to lose 25% of their former body weight. Abnormal eating behaviours, attitudes and weight, hyperactivity and food preoccupations supervened along with other disturbances of mood, behaviour, physiological and endocrine function. Physical changes were also similar to those seen in eating disordered patients. During the refeeding phase which was closely supervised for the first 3 months, some subjects binge ate and mean weight temporarily exceeded the premorbid weight returning to this 6 months later. Despite the gender difference, interesting parallels can be seen with the development of eating/dieting disorders in that at least 50% of patients with bulimia nervosa have previously suffered from anorexia nervosa and arguably the rest have lost substantial amounts of weight. The fact that eating disordered patients might also be seen as conscientious objectors makes the study all the more relevant.

GASTRIC STASIS AND 'TRUE' ANOREXIA

Following loss of 15% or more of body weight, patients complain of early satiety along with bloating and abdominal distension after eating small amounts of food or even drinking water. It is known that the stomach empties more slowly (Robinson *et al.* 1988) and there may be a functional pyloric stenosis which contributes to a state of true 'anorexia'. This becomes a real impediment to refeeding particularly in view of patients' typical food choices. Other components of the vicious cycle of self starvation include constipation, increased exercise salience (Beumont *et al.* 1994), high endorphins, low levels of insulin and sex steroids, ketosis, and the characteristic obsessive, perseverative thinking (Russell and Beumont 1987; Russell 1993; Rock and Curran-Celentano 1996).

TASTE ACUITY AND FOOD PREFERENCES

In anorexia nervosa taste acuity is often reduced—hence the tendency of patients to use strongly flavoured condiments and seasonings e.g. tomato sauce, chilli and in Australia, the highly salty spread Vegemite. Zinc deficiency has been implicated but not conclusively proven to be the cause although therapeutic benefit from supplementation has been reported (Birmingham *et al.* 1994). Anorexic patients often demonstrate fat and protein avoidance, although this may be a relatively recent phenomenon influenced by nutritional fashion. Anecdotal reports suggest that a decade or so ago they avoided carbohydrate with the same vigour. In the process of losing weight many patients eschew meat claiming to dislike the taste and the development of vegetarianism is not unusual (Rolls *et al.* 1992). This both increases the bulk and diminishes the energy density of the diet.

APPETITE AND BULIMIA NERVOSA

In bulimia nervosa appetite is often good, and even ravenous, following a long period of starvation or vigorous purging. It is experienced as something to be opposed. Eating is often normal in rate, as are table manners and food preferences in observed situations, although the appreciation of hunger and fullness becomes blunted and social constraints are overturned by emotional forces. There may be craving for carbohydrates or other palatable food items such as chocolate and food restriction or frank fasting between binges. Consumption of carbohydrate and fat has been shown to increase in certain 'preload' situations where it is uncertain whether this is due to perception (conscious or unconscious), of having eaten something 'forbidden' and usually avoided or neurochemical disinhibition induced by certain macronutrients (Huon and Wootton 1991; Rolls *et al.* 1992; Sunday *et al.* 1992). This raises the question of whether bulimic patients would be best advised to avoid high fat and carbohydrate food items or whether restraint perpetuates the observed phenomenon.

CARBOHYDRATES AS SELF MEDICATION

It is known that ingestion of a high carbohydrate load increases the transport of L-tryptophan in preference to other large neutral amino acids, across the blood–brain barrier with a subsequent increase in serotonin (5-hydroxytryptamine; 5-HT) synthesis. Goodwin's group (1987) demonstrated an increase in 5-HT sensitivity (as shown by prolactin levels in response to L-tryptophan) after dieting. This effect was more marked in females than in males and has been postulated to account for the antidepressant effect of binge eating. The frequent coexistence of depressive mood disorder with dieting disorders, the female preponderance and the salutary effects of serotinergic antidepressants in bulimia nervosa and binge eating disorder would be consistent with this view (Russell 1996; Russell *et al.* 1996).

PERPETUATING FACTORS IN BINGE EATING

Other putative perpetuating factors in binge eating include hypoglycaemia (Johnson *et al.* 1994) following purging and hyperinsulinaemia after bingeing (Russell *et al.* 1996a). Hypoglycaemia can be detected in both anorexia nervosa patients and those with bulimia nervosa. In anorexia nervosa sudden death has been associated with hypoglycaemia (Zalin and Lant 1984) and nadir blood sugar levels occur during sleep and in the early morning. As emaciated patients are sympathetically downregulated and in a state of true 'anorexia' they are usually asymptomatic. Most do not increase their food intake even if they experience hunger unless they are suffering from the bulimic or purging subtype of anorexia nervosa.

When weight is gained anorexic patients may be surprised to experience hunger usually before breakfast. Insulin levels are initially low in anorexia nervosa hence the reports of impaired glucose tolerance (Stordy *et al.* 1977), but increase with weight gain (Stordy *et al.* 1977; Russell and Beumont 1987; Johnson *et al.* 1994). As nutritional rehabilitation proceeds, some patients may engage in frank binge eating (as Keys' subjects did) or at least experience the urge to continue eating or to eat highly palatable energy dense food items. This is anxiety provoking and the patient must be reassured that this should be seen as a sign of recovery and the need to increase intake. The development of bulimia nervosa following recovery from weight loss can be readily understood in this context.

NUTRITIONAL DEPRIVATION IN BULIMIA NERVOSA

The situation in bulimia nervosa differs as a result of the more normal body weight and nutritional status. Prolonged engagement in a repertoire of bulimic behaviours has been shown to result in hyperinsulinaemia in response to a glucose load which is probably a mechanism whereby the body maintains a stable weight through the lipotrophic effect of insulin in promoting appetite, instigating and perpetuating binge eating. Compliance with treatment and abstinence from starving, bingeing and vomiting returns the insulin response to normal. Patients who vomit frequently and whose weights are unstable are in the most marked state of nutritional deprivation and have been shown to have a blunted insulin response more akin to that seen in anorexia nervosa (Stordy *et al.* 1977; Russell *et al.* 1996a). This is further evidenced by the demonstration of elevated levels of ketones such as β-hydroxy butyric acid and other markers of intermittent starvation in normal weight bulimia nervosa patients (Pirke *et al.* 1985).

ANOREXIA NERVOSA AS AN 'ENERGY WASTING' DISORDER OR WHY NUTRITIONAL MANAGEMENT IS SO DIFFICULT

Energy requirements in anorexia nervosa are initially low (indicating energy conservation) and increase disproportionately during the course of refeeding. Schebendach's group showed that in the first 4 days of hospital treatment, mean measured resting energy expenditure was only 62% of predicted values (1995) and a much earlier study reported that the average metabolic rate of anorexia nervosa patients was lower on admission than the metabolic rate of control subjects (Stordy *et al.* 1977). This has been shown elsewhere and attributed to reduced lean body mass and endocrine changes such as lowered triiodothyronine and reduced norepinephrine secretion (Heufelder *et al.* 1985). Krahn and coworkers examined the usefulness of the Harris–Benedict equation in anorexia nervosa patients at four sequential time phases throughout hospital treatment, reporting that it overestimated the basal metabolic rate (BMR) by a mean of 14% in the earliest phase, yet underestimated this in the later phases by as much as 24% (Krahn *et al.* 1993).

While BMR has been consistently reported to be 20–30% below that of controls, the total daily energy expenditure has been shown to be similar or increased in anorexia nervosa. Using the doubly labelled water technique, Pirke's group (1991) reported increased total daily energy expenditure in eight low weight stable chronic anorexia nervosa patients when compared to controls. The difference persisted after correction for lean body mass and was attributed to higher activity levels in anorexic patients. These findings have been replicated using the same technique and a comparable patient group (Casper *et al.* 1991).

As in a number of other studies, mean BMR in these chronic anorexia nervosa patients was reported to be 24% less than that of controls. In the same study Casper's group (1991) also measured the diet induced thermogenesis (DIT) of a mixed liquid meal by indirect calorimetry and reported no difference between these stable low weight patients and controls. This contrasted with the early demonstration of elevated DIT in anorexic patients, compared to controls, after a 100 g glucose load (Stordy *et al.* 1977) and our own group has recently shown greater increases in post-glucose thermogenesis in anorexia nervosa patients at low weight compared to the same patients as their own controls, after a mean 8 kg weight gain (Russell *et al.* 1996b). It might then be inferred that ingestion of glucose and possibly other carbohydrates, promotes energy wasting whereas a balanced mixture of substrates containing fat and protein, does not. This would refute the possibility that the increased DIT after glucose is solely an effect of heat dysregulation because of lower body weight. Alternatively it may be that the chronic anorexia nervosa patients studied by Casper's group (1991) were metabolically adapted to their low body weights. If the first inference is correct, anorexic patients' preferred diets which are most often high in carbohydrate and avoidant of fat and protein, might enhance their difficulties in gaining and maintaining weight by causing relative metabolic inefficiency.

SUBSTRATES, RESPIRATORY QUOTIENT AND LIPOGENESIS

In anorexia nervosa active lipogenesis is indicated by a high respiratory quotient (the ratio of carbon dioxide produced divided by oxygen consumed)—an indicator of the mix of fuels being consumed versus the utilization or laying down of body components. A normal weight subject consuming a normal diet will have a respiratory quotient (RQ) of 0.83 which will rise to unity after a glucose load in accordance with the biochemical equation for the metabolism of glucose (White *et al.* 1994). The RQ was thought never to exceed unity in humans but this has been reported by three other groups (Vaisman *et al.* 1991; Krahn *et al.* 1993; Kubata *et al.* 1993) before our own and always in refeeding anorexic patients following a glucose load. Thus, as soon as nutrients are available the malnourished body of the patient with anorexia nervosa avidly engages in fat synthesis and the RQ exceeds unity in accordance with the biochemical equation for the synthesis of palmitic acid, the main component of human adipose tissue (White *et al.* 1994). As RQ is inversely correlated with BMI it would seem to be an indicator of fat stores. However, at the time patients were discharged from hospital when they were on average still 15% below a normal weight and at least 20% depleted in fat (Russell *et al.* 1994), mean post glucose RQ was similar to that of controls (Russell *et al.* 1996b). This suggests some problem with fat synthesis which might enhance the propensity to relapse.

POST-REFEEDING AND RELAPSE

After nutritional rehabilitation and return to an ostensibly normal weight, the BMR has been reported to return to a normal value. Platte's group (1994) reported this to be significantly lower in six low weight anorexia nervosa patients when compared to six weight recovered patients and 12 healthy age-matched controls. No significant difference in BMR was observed between the weight recovered patients and the control group. This finding is consistent with that of Dempsey *et al.* (1984) who showed that in anorexic patients with similar degrees of malnutrition, metabolic rate on admission averaged 70% of that predicted by the Harris–Benedict equation and at time of discharge metabolic rate had increased to 102% of the predicted rate (although it is unclear exactly how long these patients had maintained their weight).

It is not known how the BMR returns to a normal value over the course of refeeding, weight gain and maintenance. In the earlier mentioned study of Krahn *et al.* (1993) this issue was addressed by measuring the BMR of 10 anorexic patients over four different phases of refeeding, the fourth being a maintenance period. The BMR progressively increased in the second and third phases and was sustained at the maximum level during maintenance. This observation could not be explained by the increase in lean body mass alone but is consistent with the finding that, early in refeeding, the empiric Calorie prescription necessary for weight gain was on average 276% of the measured value (Schebendach *et al.* 1995). However the contribution made by secret engagement in such behaviours as food disposal, overexercise and purging was not stated.

While BMR is reported to return to normal over the course of refeeding in anorexia nervosa, total daily energy expenditure has been shown to be elevated. Studies based on dietary records (Falk *et al.* 1985) demonstrated that energy requirements were increased as target weight was approached and during the first 6 months after refeeding. Increased energy requirements were related to increased physical activity which is in agreement with the finding of other studies demonstrating high exercise levels in weight recovered patients 6–12 months after discharge from hospital (Falk *et al.* 1985; Russell 1993; Beumont *et al.* 1994). Another factor in the increased energy requirement is altered body composition after partial refeeding when fat mass remains relatively more depleted than protein. Thus lean body mass would be disproportionately high and this too would be expected to increase energy requirements and the instability of newly gained weight.

ENERGY REQUIREMENTS IN BULIMIA NERVOSA OR WHY NUTRITIONAL MANAGEMENT SHOULD BE EASIER

It has been consistently shown that basal metabolic rate and energy requirements in patients with bulimia nervosa are reduced. In one indirect calorimetric study of 22 normal weight bulimia nervosa patients and 19 matched controls, the BMR of the patient group was shown to be 8% lower than that of controls, a small but significant difference, suggesting a greater metabolic efficiency (Dempsey *et al.* 1984). This is consistent with the finding that bulimic (purging) anorexia nervosa patients had reduced energy requirements for weight maintenance compared with restricting (non-bulimic) anorexia nervosa patients and that normal weight bulimia nervosa patients had reduced energy requirements for weight maintenance compared with weight recovered anorexia nervosa patients (Kaye *et al.* 1986; Weltzin *et al.* 1991).

THE CASE FOR INDIRECT CALORIMETRY

Clinically the weights of patients with bulimia nervosa are ostensibly normal i.e. within 10% of average (however this is defined). Nevertheless, the physiological adequacy might be seen to vary widely given that some bulimia nervosa patients are maintaining weights which are too low as evidenced by persisting amennorrhoea and osteopenia whilst those in the upper part of the normal weight range or above might be medically disadvantaged. This is of particular relevance in older sufferers of bulimia nervosa and binge eating disorder where comorbid conditions such as non-insulin dependent diabetes mellitus are not uncommon (Russell 1996). Although Shebendach's group showed the mean BMR of their bulimia nervosa subjects to be only 83% of the Harris–Benedict predicted value, measured BMR was extremely variable ranging from 55 to 118% (Schebendach *et al.* 1995). Unlike the situation in anorexia nervosa, no correlation was seen between measured and predicted values. Indirect calorimetry then provides a practical means of determining energy requirements in bulimia nervosa and binge eating disorder as a basis for appropriate dietary recommendations.

HYPOMETABOLISM IN BULIMIA NERVOSA

Binge eating, followed by purging and/or periods of severely restricted food intake have been proposed to account for the hypometabolic state seen in bulimia nervosa. Although the degree of reduction in mean BMR is minor, it has been suggested that this might incur cumulative effects over time (Devlin *et al.* 1990). If bulimia nervosa patients have an abnormally efficient metabolism, they may need to restrict their intake to avoid weight gain. Such a restriction would be expected to lead to increased hunger, preoccupation with food and vulnerability to binge eating (Newman *et al.* 1987). It is not known whether BMR returns to normal with treatment and recovery.

ANOREXIA NERVOSA AND THE REFEEDING PROGRAMME

Basic refeeding programmes are usually multimodal combining lenient behavioural reinforcement (Touyz *et al.* 1984) and eclectic psychotherapy with nutritional rehabilitation. The aim is to encourage and facilitate weight gain and in the process help identify and understand psychological, physical, family and social issues which may adversely affect eating patterns. Core elements include nutritional counselling, facilitating active changes in eating patterns, supervision and support at meals with planned rest and exercise.

GOALS

The goals of nutritional management in anorexia nervosa as outlined by Abraham and Llewellyn-Jones (1992) include:

- increasing weight by up to 1 kg per week and stabilizing in the desirable range
- ceasing weight-losing behaviours and continuing to resist these
- learning normal eating patterns
- developing healthy exercise patterns
- developing confidence in implementing the above
- decreasing preoccupation with weight, food and shape.

THE NUTRITIONAL HISTORY

Shortly after admission the dietitian takes a comprehensive nutritional history where a typical 24-hour food and fluid intake is reconstructed. In this interview information is collected regarding the development of patients' beliefs and fears about food, the level of nutritional knowledge, behaviours used to reduce energy intake and increase energy output, exercise type and level, exercise 'debting', weight loss methods including purging, binge eating and anorexigenic agents or supplements. This provides a guide for dietary alterations necessary to initiate weight gain and identifies specific topics requiring nutritional counselling (Beumont *et al.* 1987).

THE MEAL PLAN

If patients are to return to a healthy varied diet they need to learn to eat normal everyday food with a regular meal pattern. Our menu plan consists of three main meals and three or four mid-meals or snacks. The late evening snack has an important function in preventing early morning asymptomatic hypoglycaemia with ketonuria (Zalin and Lant 1984). The proportions of nutrients in the diet have until recently conformed to the standard nutritional recommendations of 50% energy from carbohydrate, 30% from fat and 20% from protein. Efforts have been made to increase the energy content from fat during refeeding and maintenance towards 45% with proportional reduction of carbohydrate content on the basis of clinical observations of better weight gain and reduced levels of gastrointestinal discomfort, ankle oedema and daytime sleepiness.

The energy content of our prescribed menu plan varies from levels as low as 6300 kJ/day initially to 17 000 kJ/day as target weight is approached. Energy content will depend on the size of the patient, the stage of weight gain, activity level and the food intake prior to admission. If a patient has consumed only fruit and water for 3 months prior to admission, a large food intake will not only cause discomfort but may precipitate hypophosphataemia. This is associated with delirium, heart failure and sudden death and is a particular risk when the emaciated patient is given large carbohydrate feeds (Beumont and Large 1991). A low-energy (but appropriately balanced) menu plan is appropriate as long as weight gain can be achieved. The preferred mode of refeeding is the consumption of food, although oral nutrition can be reinstituted using liquid supplements which may continue to be a useful adjunct. Patients whose BMIs are below 17.5 may be commenced on a supplement preferably one with higher fat content in place of main meals until these can be managed.

BEDREST AND EXERCISE

Patients in whom BMI is less than 14 or those in whom there are medical reasons for concern i.e. ECG changes, severe bradycardia, symptomatic hypotension, are placed on medical bedrest. All patients in our refeeding programme are required to rest on their beds for a prescribed period after meals. Non-aerobic exercise (stretching and toning) is introduced early but aerobic activity is contingent on weight gain and compliance (Beumont *et al.* 1994). Poor progress may be managed by a lenient bedrest programme (Touyz *et al.* 1984) usually instituted after a period of negotiation and bargaining with the patient and often preceded by individual meal supervision and nutritional supplements. The aim with the lenient bedrest programme is not only to conserve energy but to offer more rather than less support, and to individualize the regime as far as possible. Contrary to our expectations, patients experienced lenient bedrest as boring rather than persecutory, and there was a steady reduction in anxiety and depression scores during this time (Griffiths *et al.* in press).

PROGRESS AND POLICIES

Initial gains are due to fluid repletion whilst blood biochemistry stabilizes. Haemoglobin levels can fall alarmingly from already low levels when total body water reaches its maximum somewhere between the end of the first and the third weeks (Vaisman *et al.* 1988). As treatment progresses and weight increases, a greater energy intake is required for continued weight gain. Further food items are incorporated into the menu plan at a rate and quantity determined by the patient's progress. Food or drink may not be brought into the ward and diet products are discouraged.

Avoidance of red meat and vegetarianism are popular trends in the eating habits of anorexic patients. Due to the high risk of nutritional deficiencies (particularly calcium, iron, zinc) and relatively low energy content of vegetarian foodstuffs, this behaviour is discouraged, as is the use of laxatives and bulky high fibre supplements. Phosphate, iron and zinc are given where levels are low and calcium is advised in patients with osteopenia on densitometry. Good arguments can be mounted for giving nutritional supplements routinely in accordance with the expectation of increased requirements necessitated by organ and tissue repletion.

PROBLEMS WITH FLUID INTAKE

In addition to food restriction, anorexia nervosa patients particularly those in the younger age group, may refuse to take fluids which can rapidly lead to dehydration (Bryant-Waugh and Kaminski 1993). Feelings of fullness after drinking fluids are misinterpreted as feeling fat and the risk is magnified in those who induce vomiting or abuse laxatives or diuretics. The patient's intake and output of fluid must be monitored and an intake of 1.5–2.0 l per day encouraged. This will be sufficient to promote normal hydration although fluid replacement should be guided by clinical assessment.

Patients with long-standing emaciation can develop central diabetes insipidus (Russell and Beumont 1987). There will be an inability to concentrate urine and the patient will be noted to be drinking large amounts of fluid and passing large volumes of urine particularly at night. This may be difficult to distinguish from compulsive water drinking which can occasionally be a problem with older patients who use this behaviour to deal with emotional discomfort or obsessional and overvalued nutritional beliefs. Deliberate water loading may be a form of non-compliance based on falsification of weight. Whereas fluid restriction increases urinary osmolality and causes no ill effects in this situation, it will cause thirst, dehydration and no increase in urinary osmolality in central diabetes insipidus. These patients must be permitted to drink as much as their thirst dictates until the problem abates with continued weight gain. With water loading weight gain is not maintained and the problem will be detected upon 'spot weighing'.

NUTRITIONAL CHALLENGES

As patients progress they are challenged with 'fear foods'. Commonly these are foods of high fat content and high palatibility such as chocolate bars, full cream dairy foods, fried foods, and take-away meals which have been often avoided since the onset of the eating disorder. Patients are encouraged and supported to include these in their eating as a 'short cut' to weight restoration and later, on an occasional basis, as part of a normal eating pattern.

Special weekly outings are incorporated into our programme at main and mid-meal times so patients can practise normal social eating and take-away meals are organized on a regular basis. Guidance for these activities are provided in weekly education sessions with the nutritionist which incorporate a variety of learning topics. These also provide a forum for discussion in which patients are encouraged to take an active role in presenting ideas and information on topics ranging from basic nutrition and nutritional deficiencies to metabolism, normal eating, food myths and fear foods. Given the long periods of time patients sometimes need to stay in a refeeding programme, keeping the content novel and interesting is a constant challenge.

SUPPLEMENTS

Some patients continue to have difficulty consuming the amount of food recommended. Where rate of weight gain is low or maintenance of target weight is difficult to achieve despite a large menu, the continued use of dietary supplements in the form of a readily available brand may be indicated. This might offer a practical and relatively inconspicuous means whereby increased energy intake can be sustained after the patient has left hospital.

THE MAINTENANCE PHASE

At completion of refeeding there is ideally a closely supervised maintenance period of at least 3 weeks in which weight is kept within 2 kg above target weight which is most often set at minimum healthy weight for height and age. In pre-pubertal patients target weight is designated at 95% of that predicted from height. Frequent adjustments of food and exercise are necessary at this time and patients are expected to take on the sort of challenges likely to be faced at home and in social, work and educational situations. Ideally, this phase of hospital refeeding should be considerably longer if it cannot be managed in a less restrictive setting.

As discussed earlier, weight appears to be unstable for the initial 6 months after refeeding and the maintenance period should probably be seen to include this entire period during which time frequent contact with members of the treatment team will be necessary. Although a small reduction in food intake may be appropriate, this is usually not the case due to increased activity levels after leaving hospital and the patient may need to eat quantities of food which are both uncomfortable and socially awkward. Not surprisingly, energy intake is often further reduced to perceived ‘normal levels’ along with a return to old weight losing behaviours. The triggers for this should be sought and relapse may be averted thereby. Understanding the biological impediments to maintaining weight should enable the clinican to put aside feelings of frustration and make it easier to engage the patient as a collaborator.

NUTRITIONAL STRATEGIES IN BULIMIA NERVOSA

Many components of the programme previously discussed are incorporated into the treatment regime for bulimia nervosa. However, in contrast to anorexia nervosa where a structured eating plan is designed (rather than a controlled diet prescribed) to result in weight gain, in bulimia nervosa our eating plan is even more flexible with the expressed aim of initially stabilizing body weight. Despite normal or excess body weight, bulimic patients often present with a history of dietary chaos and more often than not personal crisis. Medical complications such as hypokalaemia or haematemesis might be another reason for hospital admission. The programme offers a safe, supportive environment and time out to break the vicious cycle and resolve the crisis. A brief admission may suffice and the effect can often, though not always, be continued using a variety of less restrictive treatment options but with the emphasis on nutritional counselling (Laessle *et al.* 1991) and containment.

GOALS

The goals of nutritional management in bulimia nervosa include the following (Abraham and Llewellyn-Jones 1992):

- normalize eating patterns appropriate to lifestyle
- decrease preoccupation with weight and food
- eat at regular frequent intervals over the day
- cease weight loss and stabilize weight in desirable target range
- cease the weight losing behaviours.

EATING ENOUGH

For patients with bulimia nervosa the programme is designed to facilitate changing unhealthy attitudes towards eating and weight control and to substitute healthy patterns. The basis of the bulimia nervosa syndrome (and probably binge eating disorder) is the persistent dieting which invariably precedes its onset (Beumont *et al.* 1987). The gorging episodes are a reaction to chronic restrictive eating, with vomiting and purging as compensatory behaviours to prevent weight gain. This behaviour sequence disrupts eating patterns and overrides the control mechanisms of appetite and satiety. It is possible to reverse these processes, and the aim of the treatment programme is therefore to restore a healthy eating pattern. Regular, structured meals and snacks are prescribed which consist of a wide variety of foods and provide an energy content sufficient to maintain weight.

Engaging in vomiting, diuretic or laxative abuse or excessive exercising is prevented and after meals there is a compulsory period of bed rest with supervision. This utilizes the principal of 'response behaviour', encourages postprandial relaxation and helps to break unhealthy habits. Regular exercise is factored into the programme after consultation with the exercise counsellor and nutritionist. Links between disturbed emotional states, eating and weight losing behaviours are identified and alternate ways are sought for handling the triggers.

PROGRESS AND RECOVERY

With cessation of bingeing and vomiting patients usually gain 2 kg simply as a result of rehydration. Gradual weight gain may occur and should be tolerated as long as the patient remains in the healthy weight range (BMI 20–25). If the patient is overweight and binge eating and weight-losing behaviours have ceased, 'sensible' dieting (i.e. relatively low fat content) may be attempted. However, upon recovery, a slow and consistent weight loss occurs over a period of months or years and dieting is usually unnecessary (Abraham and Llewellyn-Jones 1992). Even where there is a medical indication for weight reduction, it is often wiser to be patient than to risk further binge eating by precipitous weight loss. When eating is under control and the bingeing and purging have ceased the patient must be encouraged to learn to be spontaneous and flexible enough to cope with eating in different social situations.

FOOD RECORDS

Food records are a useful tool for the bulimic patient who is unaware of the connection between eating behaviour, mood and feelings. By recording the thoughts and feelings associated with the eating episode a patient can identify how consumption of food is used as an emotional coping mechanism. Food records allow the identification of certain physical and emotional environments or events which can trigger the bingeing episode. Thus they serve as powerful self disclosing instruments as well as forcing a patient to be more accountable for previously secret behaviours. Useful strategies can then be designed to avoid, distract from or handle a situation differently. There is the possibility that food records may foster a preoccupation with food and eating for some patients and in such instances their use should be discontinued.

A MODEL OF 'GOOD ENOUGH' EATING

As discussed by Beumont *et al.* (1987), one of the most challenging aspects of the nutritional education is to guide patients back to normal i.e. not excessively perfectionistic, eating. This implies a reasonable degree of flexibility and allows socially appropriate indiscretion. If healthy eating habits are to be re-established then it is necessary to provide a model of normal eating from which the patients can learn. To this end all members of the treatment team have daily meals with patients in a relaxed setting. Patients' food choices and eating behaviours are observed and unhealthy or unusual eating practices noted and discussed with the patient later. Eating behaviours do not improve automatically with weight gain but often need to be specifically addressed using a variety of strategies including video recording meals. By this means patients can work with the nutritionist to identify and manage disordered eating behaviours. Prior to discharge the patient's living situation should be assessed to ensure that a safe and suitable eating environment is provided. The patient's family and peer group often welcome support and education as to normal eating practices and nutritional principles.

WORKING WITH FAMILIES

As most patients, particularly those who are younger, will return to their families, efforts must be made to foster involvement in practical aspects of the patient's recovery. Parents are encouraged to meet with the nutritionist and are often given a copy of the patient's menu plan. Patients are encouraged to have selected family members, particularly those with whom they share or prepare meals, eat with them in the hospital cafeteria and to make meals for family members in the ward kitchen. The family context may be widened to include spouses, flat-mates and work colleagues as those most likely to be affected by the patient's eating disorder and most able to assist.

OUTPATIENT TREATMENT AND PARTIAL HOSPITALIZATION

Adequate levels of containment can be achieved in a well structured outpatient setting or a day programme (partial hospitalization) so that many patients can achieve adequate weight restoration without recourse to inpatient. This mode of management is probably not appropriate for patients whose BMI is lower than 14 and in our experience, for patients with major medical problems, a particulary adverse home situation or those who have been ill for more than a few years. Outpatient follow up of sufficient frequency and with suitable expertise is mandatory to maintain weight gains after full or patial hospitalization and if weight plateaus well below 85% of premorbid level a short inpatient stay should be considered. In our particular programme, outpatients would be offered regular appointments with psychiatrist/psychotherapist, psychologist, family therapist and nutritionist and they would be encouraged to return to their general practitioner for medical assessment and any investigations deemed necessary. A relapse prevention support programme is also offered.

TASKS FOR THE FUTURE

Early intervention at the primary care level, and particularly provision of suitably skilled nutritional counselling, is already changing the referral profile of eating disorders in our own clinical situation which is probably not unique. Specialist facilities must be ready for the challenge of increasingly difficult patients with increasingly challenging comorbidity. Tertiary prevention is also coming to the fore as patients with long-standing illness present for treatment—albeit on their own terms. This will include managing the long-term health complications and devising nutritional regimes and supplements which these patients will find acceptable.

Clinicians will need to adjust to different treatment goals particularly if the number of chronic anorexia nervosa patients increases substantially—which might be the case if effective hospital-based treatment becomes less accessible. Work must continue on the myriad psychological factors which impinge on or conversely can be used to facilitate nutritional management. Attention also needs to be directed towards eating disorders in demographic groups other than those most commonly affected. This includes post-pubertal males, different racial groups and older patients where basic information pertaining to weight norms, energy and exercise requirements is still not readily available.

As a public health problem, eating disorders will not go away and there will be a continued demand for treatment, lengthy and expensive as it often is and in spite of its detractors who might be seen to collude with the patients' nihilism and denial. Questions are being asked about the efficacy of treatment of which nutritional management is its mainstay. Newer technologies and some of the older ones must be used to answer these as authoritatively as possible. The real challenge is to provide the evidence to prove conclusively what we have observed clinically (Russell 1996). Namely that given the time and the resources, nutritional management does work—not just in the short term but in the long haul. We must continue to strive to make this increasingly efficient, user friendly, portable and above all empowering for our patients.

CLINICAL AND RESEARCH IMPLICATIONS

The issue of nutritional management in the eating disorders is beset by a number of important questions.

- The first of these is whether patients with these conditions need treatment at all given their questionnable level of motivation.
- The relapse rate in anorexia nervosa is unacceptably high but there is sufficient evidence to suggest that weight should be restored sooner rather than later judging by brain and bone changes which appear not to be reversible.
- In bulimia nervosa the normal or near normal body weight appears to confer a biological advantage but normalizing eating patterns remains paramount.
- It is unclear exactly what weight is the right weight and a number of approaches including assessment of ovarian activity and of body composition might be used in order to gauge the adequacy of nutritional rehabilitation.
- How fast refeeding should be accomplished is also not known nor is the best method in which to elucidate the target weight range in view of the variablility of our patients' patterns of recovery.
- Anorexia nervosa and bulimia nervosa both represent vicious cycles which ultimately become self perpetuating.

Continued

- Bulimia nervosa, however, represents a state in which the body fights back, despite its owner's attempts to oppose the process.
- Here the metabolic rate is highly variable although in general, lower than would be expected, whilst in anorexia nervosa, although energy conservation occurs at low weight, there is a relative metabolic inefficiency during refeeding.
- This appears to be the case with carbohydrate as a substrate and may account for the instability of recently regained weight. The high respiratory quotient following a glucose load indicates lipogenesis and early on serves as measure of fat stores.

REFERENCES

Abraham, S. and Llewellyn-Jones, D. (1992) *Eating Disorders: The Facts*, Oxford University Press, Oxford, UK.

Abraham, S.F., Mira, M. and Llewellyn-Jones, D. (1983) Bulimia nervosa: a study of outcome. *Int. J. Eat. Disord.*, **2**, 175–180.

Allen, B.J., Pollock, C.A., Russell, J., Oliver, C. and Smith, R. (1995) Role of body protein as a prognostic indicator in wasting disease. *Asia Pacific J. Clin. Nutr.*, **4**, 31–33.

Baran, S.A., Weltzin, T.E. and Kaye, W.H. (1995) Low discharge weight and outcome in anorexia nervosa. *Amer. J. Psychiatry*, **152**, 1070–1072.

Beumont, P.J.V. and Large, M. (1991) Hypophosphatemia, delirium and cardiac arrhythmia in anorexia nervosa. *Med. J. Aust.*, **155**, 519–522.

Beumont, P.J.V., Chambers, T.C., Rouse, L. and Abraham, S.F. (1981) The diet composition and nutritional knowledge of patients with anorexia nervosa. *J. H. Nutr.*, **35**, 265–273.

Beumont, P.J.V., O'Connor, M., Touyz, S. and Williams, H. (1987) Nutritional counselling in the treatment of anorexia and bulimia nervosa. In Beumont, P.J.V., Burrows, G. and Casper, R. (eds) *Handbook of Eating Disorders*. Elsevier Science Publishers.

Beumont, P.J.V., Arthur, B., Russell, J.D. and Touyz, S. (1994) Excessive physical activity in dieting disorder patients: proposals for a supervised exercise program. *Int. J. Eat. Disord.*, **1**, 21–36.

Birmingham, C.L., Goldner, E.M. and Bakan, R. (1994) Controlled trial of zinc supplementation in anorexia nervosa. *Int. J. Eat. Disord.*, **15**, 251–255.

Bryant-Waugh, R. and Kaminski, Z. (1993) Eating disorders in children: an overview. In Lask, B. and Bryant-Waugh, R. (eds) *Childhood Anorexia Nervosa and Related Eating Disorders*, Lawrence Erlbaum Associates Ltd., East Sussex.

Casper, R.C., Schoeller, D.A., Kushner, R., Hnilicka, J., and Gold, S.T. (1991) Total daily energy expenditure and activity level in anorexia nervosa. *Am. J. Clin. Nutr.*, **53**, 1143–1150.

Crisp, A., Callender, J.S., Halek, C. and Hsu, L.K.G. (1992) Long term mortality in anorexia nervosa. *Brit. J. Psychiatry*, **161**, 104–107.

Dempsey, D.T., Crosby, L.O., Pertschuk, M., Feurer, I.D., Buzby, G. and Mullen, J.L. (1984) Weight gain in and nutritional efficacy in anorexia nervosa. *Am. J. Clin. Nutr.*, **39**, 236–242.

Devlin, M.J., Walsh, T., Kral, J.G., Heymsfield, S.B., Pi-Sunyer F.X. and Dantzic, S. (1990). Metabolic abnormalities in bulimia nervosa. *Arch. Gen. Psychiatry*, **47**, 144–148.

Eckert, E.D., Halmi, K.D., Marchi, P., Grove, W. and Crosby, R. (1995) Ten-year follow-up of anorexia nervosa: clinical course and outcome. *Psychol. Med.*, **25**, 143–156.

Falk, J.R., Halmi, K.A. and Tyron, W.W. (1985) Activity measures in anorexia nervosa. *Arch. Gen. Psychiatry*, **42**, 811–814.

Fosson, A., de Bruyn, R. and Thomas, S. (1993) Physical aspects. In Lask, B. and Bryant-Waugh, R. (eds), *Childhood Anorexia Nervosa and Related Eating Disorders*. Lawrence Erlbaum Associates Ltd., East Sussex.

Goodwin, G.M., Fairburn, C.G. and Cowen, P.J. (1987) Dieting changes serotinergic function in women, not men: implications for the aetiology of anorexia nervosa. *Psychol. Med.*, **17**, 839–842.

Griffiths, R., Gross, G., Russell, J., Thornton, C., Schotte, D., Touyz, S. and Beumont, P. (in press) Patients' perceptions of strict bed rest programs. *Int. J. Eat. Disord.*

Heufelder, A., Warnhoff, M. and Pirke, K.M. (1985) Platelet alpha-2-adrenoreceptor and adenylate cyclase in patients with anorexia nervosa and bulimia. *J. Clin. Endocrinol.*, **61**, 1053–1060.

Huon, G.F. and Wootton, M. (1991) The role of dietary carbohydrate and of knowledge of having eaten it in the urge to eat more. *Int. J. Eat. Disord.*, **10**, 31–42.

Johnson, W.G., Jarrell, M.P., Chupurdia, K.M. and Williamson, D.A. (1994) Repeated binge/purge cycles in bulimia nervosa: role of glucose and insulin. *Int. J. Eat. Disord.*, **15**, 331–341.

Kaye, W.H., Gwirtsman, H.E., Ozbarzanek, E., George, D.T., Jimerson, D.C. and Elbert, M.H. (1986) Caloric intake necessary for weight maintenance in anorexia nervosa: nonbulimics require greater caloric intakes than bulimics. *Am. J. Clin. Nutr.*, **22**, 1253–1263.

Kaye, W.H., Gwirtsman, H.E., Ozbarzanek, E. and George, D.T. (1988) Relative importance of calorie intake needed to gain weight and level of physical activity in anorexia nervosa. *Am. J. Clin. Nutr.*, **47**, 989–994.

Keys, A., Brozek, J., Henschel, A., Mickelson, U. and Taylor, H. (1950) *The Biology of Human Starvation*. University of Minnesota Press, Minneapolis.

Krahn, D.D., Rock, C., Dechert, R.E., Nairn, K.K., and Hasse, S.A. (1993) Changes in resting energy expenditure and body composition in anorexia nervosa patients during refeeding. *J. Am. Diet Assoc.*, **93**, 434–438.

Kubata, S., Tamai, H., Ishimoto-Matsubayashi, S., Nakagawa, T. and Aoki, T. (1993) Carbohydrate oxidation rates in patients with anorexia nervosa. *Metabolism*, **42**, 928–931.

Laessle, R.G., Beumont, P.J., Butow, P. *et al.* (1991) A comparison of nutritional management with stress counselling in the treatment of bulimia nervosa. *Br. J. Psychiatry* **159**, 250–261.

Lambe, E.K., Katzman, D.K., Mikulis, D.J., Kennedy, S.H. and Zipursky, R.B. (1997) Cerebral gray matter volume deficits after weight recovery from anorexia nervosa. *Arch. Gen. Psychiatry*, **54**, 537–542.

Newman, M.M., Halmi, K.A. and Marchi, P. (1987) Relationship of clinical calorie requirements in subtypes of eating disorders. *Biol. Psychiatry*, **22**, 1253–1263.

Pirke, K.M., Pahl, J., Schweiger, U. and Warnhoff, M. (1985) Metabolic and endocrine indices of starvation in bulimia: a comparison with anorexia nervosa. *Psychiatry Res.*, **15**, 33–39.

Pirke, K.M., Trimborn, P., Platte, P. and Fichter, M. (1991) Average total energy expenditure in anorexia nervosa, bulimia nervosa and healthy young women. *Biol. Psychiatry*, **30**, 711–718.

Platte, P., Pirke, K.M., Trimborn, P., Pietsch, K., Krieg, J.C. and Fichter, M. (1994) Resting metabolic rate and total energy expenditure in acute and weight recovered patients with anorexia nervosa and in healthy young women. *Int. J. Eat. Disord.*, **16**, 45–52.

Ratnisuriya, R.H., Eisler, I., Szmukler, G.I. and Russell, G.F.M. (1991) Anorexia nervosa: outcome and prognostic factors after 20 years. *Brit. J. Psychiatry*, **158**, 495–502.

Robinson, P.H., Clarke, M., Clark, A. and Berrell, J. (1988) Determinants of delayed gastric emptying in anorexia nervosa and bulimia nervosa. *Gut*, **29**, 458–464.

Rock, C.L. and Curran-Celentano, J. (1996) Nutritional management. *Psychiatric Clin. Nth Amer. Eating Disorders* **19**, 701–714.

Rolls, B.J., Anderson, A.E., Moran, T.H., McNelis, A.L., Baier, H.C. and Federoff, I.C. (1992) Food intake, hunger, and satiety after preloads in women with eating disorders. *Amer. Soc. Clin. Nutr.*, **55**, 1093–1103.

Russell, D.McR., Prendergast, P.J., Darby, P.L., Garfinkel, P.E., Whitwell, J. and Jeejeebehoy, K.N. (1983) A comparison between muscle function and body composition: The effect of refeeding. *Amer. J. Clin. Nutr.*, **38**, 229–237.

Russell, G. (1979) Bulimia nervosa: an ominous variant of anorexia nervosa. *Psychol. Med.*, **9**, 429–448.

Russell, J.D. (1993) Body composition in anorexia nervosa. MD thesis, University of Sydney.

Russell, J. (1995) Treating anorexia nervosa. Humbling for doctors. *Brit. Med. J.*, **311**, 584.

Russell, J. (1996) Clinical Perspectives. Update in eating disorders. *Aust. NZ. J. Med.*, **26**, 819–823.

Russell, J. and Beumont, P.J.V. (1987) The endocrinology of anorexia nervosa. In Beumont, P.J.V., Burrows, G.D. and Casper, R.C. (eds) *The Handbook of Eating Disorders, part 1: Anorexia and Bulimia Nervosa.* Elsevier, Amsterdam.

Russell, J.D., Mira, M., Allen, B.J., Stewart, P., Vizzard, J., Arthur, B. and Beumont, P.J.V. (1994) Protein repletion and treatment in anorexia nervosa. *Amer. J. Clin. Nutr.*, **59**, 98–102.

Russell, J.D., Allen, B.J., Vizzard, J., Arthur, B., Mira, M., Stewart, P.J. and Beumont, P.J.V. (1995a) Body composition in anorexia nervosa—changes with treatment, determinants and techniques. *Asia Pacific J. Clin. Nutr.*, **4**, 113–115.

Russell, J., Beumont, P., Touyz, S. *et al.* (1996) The effects of fluoxetine in patients receiving nutritional counselling for bulimia nervosa. *Eur. Neuropsychopharmacol.* (special issue), **5**, 291–292.

Russell, J.D., Hooper, M. and Hunt, G.E. (1996a) Insulin levels as a marker of nutritional deficit in bulimia nervosa. *Int. J. Eat. Disord.*, **20**, 307–313.

Russell, J., Beumont, P., Buckley, C. *et al.* (1996b) Energy expenditure in anorexia nervosa, *Poster presentation at 7th International Conference on Eating Disorders*, New York, April 1996.

Schebendach, J., Golden, N.H., Jacobson, M.S. *et al.* (1995) Indirect calorimetry in the nutritional management of eating disorders. *Int. J. Eat. Disord.*, **17**, 59–66.

Stordy, B.J., Marks, V., Kalucy, R.S. and Crisp, A.H. (1977) Weight gain, thermic effect of glucose and resting metabolic rate during recovery from anorexia nervosa. *Am. J. Clin. Nutr.*, **30**, 138–146.

Sullivan, P. (1995) Mortality in anorexia nervosa. *Amer. J. Psychiatry*, **152**, 1073–1074.

Sunday, S.R., Einhorn, A. and Halmi, K.A. (1992) Relationship of perceived macronutrient and caloric content to affective cognitions about food in eating disordered, restrained, and unrestrained subjects. *Am. J. Clin. Nutr.*, **55**, 362—371.

Touyz, S.W., Beumont, P.J.V., Glaun, D., Phillips, T. and Cowie, I. (1984) Comparison of lenient and strict operant conditioning programmes in refeeding patients with anorexia nervosa. *Am. J. Psychiatry*, **144**, 512–520.

Treasure, J.L., Wheeler, M., King, E.A., Gordon, P.A.L. and Russell, G.F.M. (1988) Weight gain and reproductive function: ultrasonographic and endocrine features in anorexia nervosa. *Clin. Endocrin.*, **29**, 607–616.

Vaisman, N., Rossi, M., Goldberg, E., Dibden, L.J., Wykes, L.J. and Pencharz, P.B. (1988) Energy expenditure and body composition in patients with anorexia nervosa. *J. Paediatr.*, **113**, 919–924.

Vaisman, N., Rossi, M., Corey, B., Clarke, R., Goldberg, E. and Pencharz, P.B. (1991) Effect of refeeding on the energy metabolism of adolescent girls who have anorexia nervosa. *Europ. J. Clin. Nutr.*, **45**, 527–537.

Ward, A., Brown, N. and Treasure, J. (1997) Persistent osteopenia after recovery from anorexia nervosa. *Int. J. Eat. Disord.*, **22**, 71–75.

Weltzin, T.E., Fersnstrom, M.H., Hansen, D., McConaha, C. and Kaye, W. (1991) Abnormal calorie requirements for weight maintenance in patients with anorexia and bulimia nervosa. *Am. J. Psychiatry*, **148**, 1675–1682.

White, A., Handler, P. and Smith, E. (1994) *Principles of Biochemistry*. McGraw-Hill, New York.

Zalin, A.M. and Lant, A.F. (1984) Anorexia nervosa presenting as a reversible hypoglycemic coma. *J. Royal Soc. Med.*, **77**, 193–195.

20 Medical Complications of Eating Disorders

S. ZIPFEL, T. SPECHT and W. HERZOG
Medizinische Klinik und Poliklinik, Universität Heidelberg, Heidelberg, Germany

INTRODUCTION

Besides the investigation of psychiatric comorbidity in anorexia nervosa (AN) and bulimia nervosa (BN) (Halmi *et al.* 1991), increasing interest is being taken in somatic comorbidity (Herzog *et al.* 1997a). In a 12-year catamnesis Herzog *et al.* (1992) have shown that even after treatment in a specialized center, only 40% of the patients could be regarded as cured: in addition one-third still had severe psychic disorders and one-third showed distinct physical changes. One-third of the latter group had already died. The prevalence of AN being 1% of the female risk population between 15 and 25 years (and about 5% for BN) (Engel 1989), these protracted and chronic cases constitute about 15% of all inpatient cases in psychiatric hospitals (Herzog *et al.* 1996). These figures show that besides severe psychic and psychiatric disorders, extreme somatic changes due to self-induced malnutrition may often determine the clinical picture.

In the following, we will deal with the somatic complications of acute and chronic eating disorders. In AN, the consequences of massive malnutrition represents the outstanding problem. The clinical picture of BN is determined by the consequences of purging behavior (self-induced vomiting as well as the abuse of laxatives and diuretics), such as hypokalemic alkalosis or disorders of the electrolyte and water balance (Mitchell *et al.* 1987).

There is no real difference between cachexia due to AN and the consequences of semi-starvation. The neuroendocrine system adjusts the organism to a new balance, with an economization of all body functions (Scalfi *et al.* 1993; Platte *et al.* 1994). Many of the acute changes are fully reversible after the body weight has been normalized again. Distinct somatic changes of the acute phase such as hypokalemia and bradycardia are often surprisingly well tolerated by the patients. It is important, however, that somatic complications occur not only when the body weight falls below a critical minimal value, but also when the gradually obtained balance in malnutrition is abruptly disturbed. This is often the case in the refeeding period (Beumont *et al.* 1993). Because of the numerous possible complications (e.g. disorders of the water and electrolyte balance, fat overloading syndrome, hyperglycemia, thrombosis) particularly in cachectic patients, parenteral nutrition should be avoided if possible (Sharp and Freeman 1993).

Neurobiology in the Treatment of Eating Disorders.
Edited by H.W. Hoek, J.L. Treasure and M.A. Katzman.

Table 20.1. The most common medical complications in eating disorders

Acute phase	Chronic phase
Disturbances in electrolyte and acid–base balance, exsiccosis, edema	Chronic renal insufficiency
Acute renal failure	
Amenorrhea	Amenorrhea, infertility
	Osteoporosis, incl. vertebral fractures
Cardiac arrythmia	Cardiac arrythmia
Impaired gastric emptying, constipation, gastric dilatation, ileus	Constipation
Gastroduodenal ulcers, upper gastrointestinal bleeding	
Anemia, leukopenia	Anemia, leukopenia
Opportunistic infections, sepsis	Dental defects
General muscular weakness, headaches, seizures	
Hypothermia	

ACUTE COMPLICATIONS

Because patients with eating disorders tend to deny their disease and the resulting physical damage, acute somatic complications are often the reason they receive medical treatment for the first time.

Even if in most cases the diagnosis is obvious, according to clear criteria (ICD-10, DSM-IV), an exact recording of physical findings is necessary. This helps on the one hand, to describe the potential somatic consequences (Brown 1985; Hall and Beresford 1989) and on the other hand, to differentiate between eating disorders and other internal diseases, e.g. malabsorption syndromes, chronic inflammatory bowel diseases, chronic consumptive diseases (McClain *et al.* 1993). As, in most cases, young women are affected, eating disorders in older or male patients are easily overlooked (Touyz *et al.* 1993a). Male patients in particular may not present until massive somatic changes have developed (Siegel *et al.* 1995).

One of the most important aims of the physical examination is the early recognition of potentially fatal somatic complications, which require immediate hospitalization (Beumont *et al.* 1995). In the following, we will describe in detail the possible complications of the acute phase (see Table 20.1).

ELECTROLYTE BALANCE

Hypokalemia (< 3.5 mmol/l)

Hypokalemia is found in about one-third of all patients with eating disorders treated in the hospital and is in most cases a consequence of chronic, in some cases of acute purging behavior. Some of the patients adapt even to very low values (< 2.0), and therefore in these patients symptoms may be missing (Bonne *et al.* 1993). Hypokalemia may have fatal consequences: typically tachyarrhythmias, paralytic ileus, adynamia/pareses or nephropathy. Substitution should be done slowly, whereby administration with oral effervescent tablets is definitely preferable to intravenous administration.

Hyponatremia (< 135 mmol/l)

Hyponatremia is usually the result of hypotonic dehydration because of chronic purging (Challier and Cabrol 1995). The symptoms are disorientation, myasthenia, and circulatory disorders.

Hypophosphatemia (< 0.8; severe: < 0.3 mmol/l)

A quick decrease in the phosphate levels typically occurs during the refeeding period ('nutritional recovery syndrome', especially in cases of parenteral refeeding) (Van Dissel *et al.* 1992; McClain *et al.* 1993), but also as a result of diuretic abuse and renal failure (Palla and Litt 1988). Severe hypophosphatemia can be fatal (Beumont and Large 1991). It can result in cardiopulmonary decompensation (Cariem *et al.* 1994), arrhythmia (Beumont and Large 1991), metabolic acidosis, polyneuropathia, delirium, as well as disorders of erythrocyte and leukocyte function or rhabdomyolysis (Wada *et al.* 1992). As a preventive or supplementary measure, milk powder (which contains phosphate) should be given preferably to intravenous administration.

Hypomagnesemia (< 0.7 mmol/l)

Severe magnesium deficiency can lead to muscle cramps, intestinal spasms, hypokalemia, and arrhythmias (Hall *et al.* 1988; Palla and Litt 1988).

Hypocalcemia (< 2.15 mmol/l)

Hypocalcemia can be a symptom of calcium deficiency, but also of alkalosis, and may be associated with ECG changes (Beumont *et al.* 1993). In the differential diagnosis, possible hypocalcemic tetany should be distinguished from hyperventilation syndrome.

Zinc deficiency/hypercarotenemia

So far there has been no clear evidence that an alteration in zinc and carotene levels, which is frequently seen in eating disorders, is of any relevance with regard to the diagnosis, therapy or course of the condition (Curran-Celentano *et al.* 1985; Lask *et al.* 1993; Rickards *et al.* 1994; Roijen *et al.* 1991; Sherman *et al.* 1994). One study describes a favorable effect of zinc supplementation on weight gain (Birmingham *et al.* 1994); another study has found an association between α-carotene levels and eating pathology (Rock *et al.* 1996).

WATER BALANCE

Exsiccosis

Exsiccosis occurs as a result of reduced fluid supply or of chronic purging behavior and is often associated with circulatory disorders and electrolyte imbalances (hypokalemia, hypotonic dehydration, see above), which have to be considered in rehydration.

Edema

Edema can be a result of hypoalbuminemia (< 2.5 g/dl), but can also occur in cases of secondary hyperaldosteronism due to diuretic or laxative abuse. Why ‘rebound edemas’ typically develop during the initial weeks of refeeding is unclear, but their effect on body weight should be considered (Mitchell *et al.* 1988; Bihun *et al.* 1993; Beumont *et al.* 1993). Pericardial effusions may develop in connection with edema, but rare isolated cases may also occur (Beumont *et al.* 1993).

ACID–BASE BALANCE

Metabolic alkalosis

Generally metabolic alkalosis occurs in association with the loss of gastric acid from self-induced vomiting (McClain *et al.* 1993). However, it can also be caused by hypokalemia, which leads to the loss of renal acid. About one quarter of BN patients are affected by this disorder (Mitchell *et al.* 1983). The pseudo-Bartter syndrome, which consists of metabolic alkalosis, hypokalemia, hypochloremia, polyuria, and exsiccosis, is a typical result of massive purging behavior (Mitchell *et al.* 1988; Fujita *et al.* 1991). In the differential diagnosis the syndrome of inadequate ADH secretion (Schwartz–Bartter syndrome) should be taken into consideration (Challier and Cabrol 1995).

Metabolic acidosis

Metabolic acidosis affects about 8% of BN patients and is a result of enteral bicarbonate loss in case of laxative abuse (Mitchell *et al.* 1987). Possible additional causes are a markedly increased endogenous acid formation in AN as well as reduced acid excretion in connection with renal insufficiency.

CARDIOVASCULAR COMPLICATIONS

Cardiac complications are the most common cause of immediate/premature death in AN patients (Beumont *et al.* 1993). Low blood pressure and bradycardia are typical findings in AN (Herzog *et al.* 1992), and both are thought to be caused by the volume depletion. Many patients have adapted to very low blood pressure and heart rate values; decompensation is possible, however (Alvin *et al.* 1993; Kreipe *et al.* 1994; Palla and Litt 1988).

ECG alterations/arrhythmias

ECG alterations occur in more than 80% of these patients (Alvin *et al.* 1993). Besides sinus bradycardia, which is frequently seen, indications of ST depressions and abnormal U waves may be found on the ECG. They are often associated with electrolyte imbalances and are considered to be warning signals for arrhythmias. These are responsible for a considerable number of deaths in eating disorders (Campanini *et al.* 1991; Cooke *et al.* 1994; Schocken *et al.* 1989). In this context, special emphasis is placed on the extension of the QT interval, which is seen in 15% (Cooke *et al.* 1994) to 40% (Durakovic *et al.* 1994) of cases. This QT extension is considered to be a decisive predictor of ventricular tachyarrhythmias (Isner *et al.* 1985) or of sudden cardiac death.

In general, cardiac complications occur mostly in patients with purging behaviour (Sharp and Freeman 1993; Comerci 1990; Hall *et al.* 1989), but are not always associated with manifest hypokalemia. Kreipe *et al.* (1994) investigated a possible dysfunction of the autonomic nervous system using the heart rate power spectrum analysis. His results indicate that there is a decrease in sympathetic modulation of the heart rate, evident by a deficit in low frequency (0.01–0.15 Hz). In further recent investigations in this field the issue of the extent to which a supplementary evaluation of heart rate variability could provide additional diagnostic possibilities for assessing the risk of fatal arrhythmias in patients with eating disorders has been addressed. Changes in repolarization, such as an extension of the corrected QT interval in AN patients, showed a significant tendency to reverting to normal after refeeding (Cooke *et al.* 1994).

Morphological changes

The weight loss in AN is associated with a loss in heart muscle mass. Echocardiographic studies of AN patients reported on a decreased left ventricular mass and an increased incidence of mitral valve prolapse (Kaplan *et al.* 1991; Cooke and Chambers 1995; de Simone *et al.* 1994; Schocken *et al.* 1989). In 62% of the patients abnormalities of mitral valve motion were found which occur as a result of an imbalance between valve size and ventricle volume and can lead to a mitral valve prolapse (Alvin *et al.* 1993).

Disorders of the pumping action, however, can also occur as a complication during refeeding (Kahn *et al.* 1991; Foster 1994), and probably in cases of simultaneous hypophosphatemia in particular (Schocken *et al.* 1989). Malnutrition, electrolyte imbalance, and ipecac abuse (Mitchell *et al.* 1987) can result in a—possibly irreversible—secondary cardiomyopathy. Particularly in male AN patients with an increased heart rate, the possibility of congestive heart failure should be taken into account (Siegel *et al.* 1995).

Studies of victims suffering from malnutrition have also shown that in the course of weight loss there is a decrease in heart size and a rotation of the heart's axis into a vertical position. These changes were reversible in the refeeding period.

Only few studies exist on cardiovascular disorders in BN. The increased incidence of arrhythmias reported in some studies was usually directly associated with hypokalemia due to massive vomiting (Ferguson 1985). In arrhythmic patients a detailed drug anamnesis is especially important in order to record any side effects of, for example tricyclic antidepressants.

GASTROINTESTINAL SYSTEM

Hyperamylasemia/enlargement of the parotid gland/pancreatitis

An increase in serum amylase levels is found in about 50% of patients treated in the hospital. In most cases it is due to vomiting and is not a result of pancreatitis (Mitchell *et al.* 1983). Correspondingly, this increase is caused by the iso-amylase of the parotid gland (McClain *et al.* 1993; Humphries *et al.* 1987). A distinct enlargement of the parotid gland is often observed especially in BN (Mitchell *et al.* 1987). Acute pancreatitis can be assumed if the increase in the serum amylase level is more than threefold above normal and is associated with abdominal pain (Pieper-Bigelow *et al.* 1990). If in doubt, it may be helpful to measure the lipase levels. Pancreatitis as a complication of eating disorders is rare; it can, however, develop as a result of refeeding or binge eating (Treasure and Szmukler 1995).

Impaired gastric emptying/constipation/ileus

An impairment of gastric emptying is a typical consequence of malnutrition and is fully reversible after weight gain (Szmukler *et al.* 1990; McClain *et al.* 1993; Ravelli *et al.* 1993). It manifests itself as a sensation of fullness after food ingestion, which can make refeeding difficult (Robinson *et al.* 1988; Kamal *et al.* 1991). Megaduodenum and duodenal immobility are also secondary complications and are reversible (Buchman *et al.* 1994). Obstipation is frequent and in most cases a result of false nutrition and hypokalemia (laxative abuse). The possibility of obstipation due to antidepressant medication, however, should be considered. Deaths from paralytic ileus have been described (Herzog *et al.* 1992).

Gastric dilation/perforation

Gastric dilation typically occurs after binge eating (Spigset 1990) and becomes manifest in spontaneous vomiting and upper abdominal pain (Alvin *et al.* 1993). Conservative therapy is usually sufficient (Stheneur *et al.* 1995); in rare cases, however, circulation disorders of the gastric wall occur, leading to necrosis and gastric perforation (Abdu *et al.* 1987). In these cases immediate surgery is required

(Willeke *et al.* 1996). Five of the 60 cases with spontaneous gastric rupture described since 1960 have been AN patients (Schou *et al.* 1994). Diagnosis may be difficult as more than 50% of the patients suffer from vomiting, upper abdominal pain, and gastrointestinal disorders (McClain *et al.* 1993).

Gastroduodenal ulcers/upper gastrointestinal bleeding

Ulcers develop in about one-sixth of the patients (Hall *et al.* 1989). They can cause bleedings, which may lead to anemia and circulatory decompensation; however, bleeding can also occur as a result of tears of the esophagus when vomiting. A rare, but serious, complication is pneumomediastinum (Alvin *et al.* 1993; Foster 1994). One case in conjunction with necrotizing colitis has been described (Sakka *et al.* 1994).

Hepatitis

Elevated liver function parameters are found in about one-third of patients treated in the hospital ('nutritional hepatitis'). If there is no infectious or autoimmune cause, additional treatment is not necessary (Mira *et al.* 1987; Sherman *et al.* 1994; Colombo *et al.* 1995). If the indirect bilirubin levels are elevated, one should consider the manifestation of Gilbert's syndrome (5% of the total population is affected) in the starving period. Hypercholesterolemia is a result of a reduced bile acid requirement (Mira 1987; Richter *et al.* 1991).

RENAL SYSTEM

Acute renal failure/renal insufficiency

Acute renal failure (ARF) can be caused by (transitory) impaired perfusion in hypovolemia or cardiac decompensation (pre-renal ARF), but can also occur as a result of persisting electrolyte imbalance (e.g. hypokalemic nephropathy). One case of ARF due to rhabdomyolysis in hypophosphatemia has been described (Wada *et al.* 1992). Often the concentrating function of the kidney is reduced as a result of its impaired sensibility to ADH (anti-diuretic hormone). If there is considerable weight loss, a marked impairment in creatinine clearance may occur, the reversibility of which is decisively dependent on weight gain (Boag *et al.* 1985). Further renal manifestations may be hematuria, pyuria, and proteinuria (Palla and Litt 1988).

HEMATOLOGICAL SYSTEM

Bone marrow hypoplasia

A frequent consequence of malnutrition is a reversible, reactive bone marrow hypoplasia (Alloway *et al.* 1988; Larrain 1989; Alvin *et al.* 1993; Beumont *et al.* 1993). It leads to anemia in about 25%, to leukopenia in about 30%, and to thrombopenia in about 10% of the patients. Only two of 67 AN patients showed pancytopenia (Devuyst 1993). The bleeding risk is increased if thrombocyte values fall below 30/nl. Anemia may be accompanied by iron deficiency, rarely by vitamin B12 or folic acid deficiency (Larrain *et al.* 1989). In severe anemia, gastrointestinal bleeding should also be considered.

IMMUNOLOGIC SYSTEM

(Bacterial) infections

Although leukocyte counts and immunoglobulin and complement factor levels are often reduced, the immunologic competence is intact in most cases, and serious or opportunistic infections are quite rare (Larrain *et al.* 1989; Alvin *et al.* 1993). Devuyst *et al.* (1993), however, reports a 9% rate of serious infections in AN patients, occurring in particular in those individuals with neutropenia or very low weight on admission. In any case, infection as a complication of AN has to be taken seriously, because as a result of hypothermia and leukopenia it can take a course without fever or leukocytosis (Tenholder and Pike 1991). Therefore, weekly controls of the blood sedimentation rate or C-reactive protein are recommended in serious cases.

CENTRAL NERVOUS SYSTEM

Imaging methods such as computerized tomography (CT) or magnetic resonance imaging (MRI) play a secondary role in the basic diagnostics of patients with eating disorders; therefore the routine use of these methods is not recommended in the guidelines for eating disorders of the American Psychiatric Association (Yager *et al.* 1993). In individual cases, however, the use of these methods may be indicated for example to exclude a brain tumor or if there is suspicion of a compressive intracerebral process.

Seizures

About 5% of the patients are affected by seizures (Patchell *et al.* 1994). Disturbances in calcium, sodium and glucose metabolism as well as uremia due to renal failure can be responsible for myoclonic and generalized tonoclonic seizures. Nevertheless, neurological affections of the brain besides metabolic changes should be taken into account for differential diagnosis. Therefore, patients suffering from seizures should be examined by EEG and, if necessary, CT.

Morphological and functional cerebral changes

Systematic studies on brain changes in AN patients show dilated lateral ventricles and/or enlarged cortical sulci (Dolan *et al.* 1988; Krieg *et al.* 1988; Kornreich *et al.* 1991; Golden *et al.* 1996). Kingston *et al.* (1996) tested neuropsychological and structural brain changes in AN before and after refeeding. The AN group performed significantly worse than the controls on tasks measuring attention, visuospatial ability, and memory. This group could also demonstrate enlarged lateral ventricles and sulci on both cortical and cerebellar surfaces. In this study the correlations between morphological brain changes and cognitive impairment were weak. Lower weight was associated with greater ventricular size on MRI, but not with the duration of illness. However, there are contradictory results as to whether the cognitive deficits occurring in the acute phase were directly connected to the morphological changes (Kohlmeyer *et al.* 1983; Laessle *et al.* 1989; Palazidou *et al.* 1990). Interestingly, ventricle enlargements have also been found in patients with BN; thus, they are not only connected with malnutrition (Krieg *et al.* 1987).

In a series of further studies (Schlegel and Kretschmar 1997) it was shown that during weight normalization there is an increase of brain parenchyma of up to 25 vol.% compared to the time of minimum weight.

Additional findings

Unspecific EEG changes in terms of abnormal background activity are often found in AN as a result of the effect of starvation on cerebral metabolism (Hughes 1996). Although these atypical EEG findings were seen in a number of studies measuring EEG and sleep-EEG, it was found, compared to other disease groups, that these changes were not specific for eating disorders (Rothenberger *et al.* 1991). Moreover, there were no significant correlations to the body mass index (Delvenne *et al.* 1995).

It was the aim of recent studies using MRI spectroscopy and positron emission tomography (PET) in patients with eating disorders to get additional evidence on alterations, for example, of membrane properties or of the cerebral metabolism in addition to the known cerebral structural changes already known to facilitate the evaluation of possible functional cerebral impairments. The glucose metabolism in the nucleus caudatus measured by PET is significantly higher in AN than in controls (Herholz *et al.* 1987) and in BN (Krieg *et al.* 1991). In contrast, in BN there is a higher metabolic activity in the left hemisphere as assessed by PET (Wu *et al.* 1990). Abnormal auditory evoked potentials (AEP) have only been found in cases of massive underweight; however these changes were fully reversible and showed no correlation to CCT alterations (Rothenberger *et al.* 1991). Doraiswamy *et al.* (1991) found the pituitary glands of patients with eating disorder to be smaller than those of controls.

Neuromuscular abnormalities

Nearly 50% of the patients are affected by neuromuscular abnormalities. Main symptoms are general muscular weakness, peripheral neuropathy, and headaches (Alloway *et al.* 1988; Patchell *et al.* 1994). Pulmonary function can be severely disturbed because of an impairment of diaphragmatic contractility—which is reversible after malnutrition is compensated (Murciano *et al.* 1994).

METABOLISM AND ENDOCRINE SYSTEM

Glucose metabolism

In most cases of AN, glucose levels are low and glucose tolerance is reduced (Fukushima *et al.* 1993; Koffler and Kisch 1996). Insulin stimulates glucose oxidation rather than glucose storage (Franssila-Kallunki *et al.* 1991). Hypoglycemic coma may develop (Ratcliffe and Bevan 1985).

Hypothermia

Hypothermia is a typical side effect of malnutrition and probably the result of the neuroendocrinal adaptation (Palla and Litt 1988).

Hypothalamo–pituitary axes

The hormonal changes of the gonadal, adrenal, and thyroidal axes, as measured in the laboratory, probably can be considered as secondary. They are caused by the adaptation of the neuroendocrine system to the condition of malnutrition and are fully reversible after weight normalization. They do not play a role in the acute treatment of patients with eating disorders in so far as they do not help to distinguish eating disorders from primary endocrine diseases (Newman and Halmi 1988; Beumont *et al.* 1993; Foster 1994). Their relevance for the long-term course is described under 'chronic complications' (see below).

CHRONIC COMPLICATIONS (see Table 20.1, page 458)

ENDOCRINE SYSTEM AND REPRODUCTIVE FUNCTION

Amenorrhea

The impairment of the hormonal axes is a main symptom of AN and was included as a diagnostic guideline in the ICD-10 as well as in the DSM-IV. Involvement of the hypothalamo–pituitary–gonadal axis is associated with primary or secondary amenorrhea, depending on the age of the patient at first manifestation. Although endocrine disorders are not a part of the diagnostic criteria of BN, 20 to 50% of BN patients are found to be amenorrheic. Menstruation disorders are reported by 40% of BN patients (Fairburn and Cooper 1984; Pirke *et al.* 1985). Studies by Pirke (1989) have shown, however, that self-reports often underestimate the rate of menstrual cycle disorders, especially in BN. He showed by repeated measurements of plasma estradiol levels that the rate of patients with levels of $<120\,pg/ml$ was considerably higher, follicle maturation thus being rather unlikely. Moreover, in 50% of the patients the progesterone levels measured in the subsequent luteal phase, were too low as well due to an insufficient pulsatile gonadotropin release. For AN too it could be shown that persisting hypothalamic amenorrhea does not require permanent inhibition of the GnTH pulse generator (Allouche *et al.* 1991). At least for some patients in their study they were able to demonstrate that a transient inhibition of pulsatility and qualitative abnormalities of the gonadotropins might be involved in the pathomechanism of amenorrhea. In experiments, a comparably short fasting period has led to a pre-pubertal pattern of gonadotropin levels, especially LH levels (Schweiger *et al.* 1987; Pirke *et al.* 1989). This suggests that the disorders of the menstrual cycle are a secondary phenomenon caused by malnutrition, and it might explain why amenorrhea in AN often precedes a massive weight loss and may continue even if there is an increase in weight again. Nevertheless, it is still not known whether factors other than malnutrition and weight loss are involved in the development of hormonal disorders.

Eating disorders and pregnancy

Hormonal changes also affect fertility. Thus, a reduced fertility and increased abortion rate was found because of disturbances of the follicular and luteal phase (Horta *et al.* 1977; Bates *et al.* 1982). There is evidence that even in successful pregnancy, the infants are clearly underweight. Brinch *et al.* (1988) carried out a catamnesis study on 140 patients with AN after 10–12 years. This study showed that 50 former patients had children; meanwhile, 10% had problems with infertility and 20% became pregnant while they continued to be anorectic. In this sample, the rate of premature births was twice as high as in an age matched population. Perinatal mortality was increased by a factor of 6. A miscarriage rate increased by a factor of 2 was reported in a controlled study by Willis and Rand (1988). There is evidence that in patients with BN there is an increased rate of malformations from the additional intake of laxatives and diuretics and the increased incidence of simultaneous alcohol and drug abuse.

Nonreproductive endocrinal abnormalities

In most cases hormonal changes associated with the eating disorders are directly associated with insufficient energy intake. Beumont (1992) reported on an increased basal growth hormone (GH) level in about 50% of patients with AN. The elevated GH level is probably an adaptation to the low energy intake and it is necessary to combat the accompanying hypoglycemia by mobilizing fat tissue. A low T3 syndrome is also usually found which helps to conserve energy in the presence of undernutrition. The circulating levels of cortisol are often elevated. Fichter and Pirke (1990) show that patients with AN have an abnormal 24-hour cortisol secretion, an impaired suppression by dexamethasone, reduced catabolism, and greater hypothalamic effect on cortisol production. In the Munich fasting experiment they could demonstrate similar patterns in healthy fasting people.

THE SKELETON AND TEETH

Bone metabolism

Disorders of bone metabolism are a frequent and serious complication in the long-term course of these diseases. In a long-term catamnesis (Herzog *et al.* 1993), 17% of the AN patients had distinct osteoporosis 12 years after the first treatment. This finding was confirmed by other teams (Rigotti *et al.* 1991; Maugars and Proust 1994). Thus, osteoporosis has been the most frequent somatic diagnosis, especially in chronically anorectic patients. Apart from a reduced bone density as is typical for osteoporosis (Treasure *et al.* 1986; Newman and Halmi 1989; Joyce *et al.* 1990; Herzog *et al.* 1993; Poet *et al.* 1993), patients with an unfavorable course showed pathological fractures in up to 44% of all cases (Herzog *et al.* 1993). These spontaneous fractures can lead to early invalidism and essentially contribute to the suffering of the patients. A considerable part of the hospitalization rate, which with 70 days per year is 50-fold higher than in the normal population, is because of the consequences of osteoporosis. A reduction in bone density has also been reported in patients with BN (Newton *et al.* 1993). The BN subgroup with long-lasting secondary amenorrhea has been especially described as a risk group. The developing osteopenia can be characterized by two mechanisms that supplement and reinforce each other. For one, because of the early onset of the disease, which in most cases is already in puberty, there is a reduced peak bone mass (Biller *et al.* 1989; Bachrach 1993). That means that the maximum bone substance will not be reached. Secondly, there is premature and increased bone destruction (Matthews *et al.* 1985; Ruegsegger *et al.* 1988). Loss of bone mass is a manifestation of a chronification process in AN and in some of the BN patients. Rigotti *et al.* (1991) found a sevenfold increased annual fracture rate in the second and third decade of life and after an average duration of the disease of 5.8 years in patients with AN, compared to healthy women of the same age. The initially measured mean density of the corticalis at the shaft of the radius was significantly reduced, depending on the individual duration of amenorrhea. Herzog *et al.* (1993) reported that after an interval of 12 years, the lumbar bone density was strongly determined by the relative duration of the exposure to estrogen. The cortical bone density was influenced more by the duration of the disease. Altogether, the patients with an unfavorable course showed a marked reduction in the lumbar (z-value -2.18) and the radial (z-value -1.73) bone density, the reduction in the trabecular bone of the lumbar vertebrae being stronger than that of the radial bone which is built up from a more compact substance. All authors agree that, besides the weight course and the duration of the disease, the duration of the secondary amenorrhea, which is found in nearly all cases as a result of the estrogen deficit, can be held responsible for the development of the osteopenia (Rigotti *et al.* 1984; Biller *et al.* 1989; Newman and Halmi 1989; Herzog *et al.* 1993; Newton *et al.* 1993; Poet *et al.* 1993). Studies on further endocrinologic risk factors for the development of osteoporosis in these patients gave inconsistent results regarding the vitamin D metabolism (Aarskog *et al.* 1986; Fonseca *et al.* 1988; Olmos *et al.* 1991). Hypercortisolism (Salisbury and

Mitchell 1991; Maugars and Proust 1994) which is found in some of the patients and a disturbed calcium metabolism (Abrams *et al.* 1993) are described as additional factors. Studies on osteogenetic parameters such as osteocalcin (Fonseca *et al.* 1988) have not given definite results so far. Recent studies (Klibansky *et al.* 1995) have shown a direct connection between the food-dependent hormonal markers (internal growth factor-1; IGF-1 and triiodothyronine; T3) and the trabecular bone mass. Iketani *et al.* (1995) described the connection between weight gain, recurring of menstruation, and the effects on bone metabolism.

Malabsorption caused by possible secondary diseases such as colitis ulcerosa or massive laxative abuse also has to be considered. Heavy nicotine, alcohol, and caffeine abuse are known to be additional noxae. Apart from laxatives, the use of thiazide diuretics, glucocorticoids, anticonvulsive drugs, and heparins has to be taken into account in the drug anamnesis. Prolonged periods of immobilization only seldom play a role in patients with eating disorders. In addition to osteodensitometry, there is great interest in the laboratory parameters that allow further evaluation of the bone metabolism even at short intervals (Seibel *et al.* 1993). In this regard hydroxypyridinium crosslinks seem to be of special interest as osteoclastic parameters (Hassager *et al.* 1993; Seibel *et al.* 1993, 1994). Furthermore, ultrasound methods for the measurement of bone density at the calcaneus (Baran 1995; Sakata *et al.* 1997) and the phalanges (Ventura *et al.* 1996) will play an increasing role in bone screening in the future.

Therapeutic approaches in osteoporosis

There is evidence that weight gain can prevent further loss of bone mass and may even lead to an increase in bone density (Bachrach *et al.* 1991; Rigotti *et al.* 1991). Regarding a combined estrogen/progesterone replacement therapy, up to now there has been only one controlled, prospective study in a group of 48 amenorrheic patients with AN (Klibansky *et al.* 1995). This intervention study showed a therapeutic effect of the hormone replacement at least for AN patients with a body weight of less than 70% of the ideal weight. The treatment could at least prevent further bone destruction. The optimal estrogen and gestagen dosage is still unclear, as the known dosage regimens have only been proven for postmenopausal women so far. The same is true for the duration of the replacement therapy. Furthermore, a sufficient intake of vitamin D and calcium is essential. There have been no controlled studies on the use of calcitonin or bisphosphonates as of yet. The same is true for substances such as sodium fluorides, which are meant to stimulate bone formation, and therapeutic models using growth factors such as IGF-1 are still in the phase of clinical testing.

THE FEMALE ATHLETE TRIAD

Eating disorders and the development of osteoporosis are not only relevant for patients with AN and BN. An increasing number of publications have been dealing with the so-called 'female athlete triad' (Skolnick 1993), including eating disorders, secondary amenorrhea, and osteoporosis. Competitive athletes, especially long-distance runners or those in expression sports such as gymnastics, ballet, or dancing, represent a high-risk group. Studies on the female athlete triad have shown that in some disciplines, such as gymnastics, up to 62% (Skolnick 1993) of the athletes suffer from a primary or secondary amenorrhea and a massive eating disorder. Supplementary studies (Nativ *et al.* 1994; Putukian 1994) have shown a significant connection between this triad and manifest osteoporosis, in some cases even with detectable pathologic fractures. The borderline between preclinical risk groups and manifestly affected patients is fluid (Hannan *et al.* 1995).

DENTAL COMPLICATIONS

Dental defects in patients with eating disorders have increasingly been the focus of attention in the past years, oral changes often being the first indication that an eating disorder is present. The effect of acid regurgitation on the teeth is well appreciated (Bishop *et al.* 1994; Robb *et al.* 1995). Besides they demonstrated that a history of vomiting may have far-reaching consequences for the condition of the teeth. Apart from deterioration, vomiting increases the need for dental work and increased loss of teeth. Simmons *et al.* (1986) showed that a common sign of frequent and long-term vomiting is erosion of the dental enamel. Enamel was lost from the lingual and palatal surfaces of the anterior teeth. Touyz *et al.* (1993b) showed that patients with both AN and BN revealed changes indicative of gingivitis and gingival recession but not of periodontitis.

RENAL SYSTEM

In a recent study, Herzog *et al.* (1997a) showed that serum creatinine levels at first admission showed a robust main effect on the likelihood of first recovery which was not confounded by other variables. High serum creatinine levels were indicators of reduced renal function and may be due to fluid loss. Serum creatinine levels correlated significantly with the frequency of vomiting. In addition, increased creatinine levels were seen in those patients who demonstrated purging behaviour but concealed this information. Finally, an increase in creatinine levels may be a sign of permanent kidney damage after a chronic course of disease and in individual AN patients may even cause death (Fichter 1985; Beumont *et al.* 1993; Deter and Herzog 1994).

COMORBIDITY

The possibility of a secondary somatic disease developing should not be overlooked, especially if the incidence of eating disorders is increased, as is the case in chronic diseases which are associated with the need for special diets or changes in body weight and intestinal motility (Kaplan 1990). These are, in particular type I insulin-dependent diabetes mellitus (IDDM) (Robertson and Rosenvinge 1990;

Nieuwenhuijzen-Kruseman 1991; Cantwell and Steel 1996; Koffler and Kisch 1996), Crohn's disease (Meadows and Treasure 1989; Ainley *et al.* 1991; Rickards *et al.* 1994), or hyperthyroidism (Tiller *et al.* 1994). In IDDM it is significant that some of the affected patients induce vomiting in order to control their body weight and to reduce the insulin dose (Biggs *et al.* 1994). As a consequence, the control of glucose metabolism is impaired and ketoacidosis and an accelerated development of secondary changes may occur (Steel *et al.* 1989; Peveler *et al.* 1992; Vila *et al.* 1994; Herpertz *et al.* 1995).

MEDICAL OUTCOME

Theander (1985) as well as Morgan and Russell (1975) were able to demonstrate that one of the central criteria for a favorable outcome is the spontaneous recurrence and regular onset of menstruation (see Beumont 1992). However, the recurrence of menstruation should not be regarded independently of the nutritional state (Pirke *et al.* 1995). Frisch (1988) reported on a connection between body fat content and menstruation in a series of studies.

Herzog *et al.* (1997b) studied the significance of somatic factors as predictors for the long-term physical outcome in patients with AN. In a follow-up study 12 years after first admission to a specialized eating disorder center they found that an abnormally low serum albumin level (< 36 g/l) and a low weight (< 60% of average body weight) at the initial examination were the variables which best predicted a lethal course. In addition, high serum creatinine and uric acid levels predict a chronic course. Most of their initial abnormal laboratory findings were reversible with normal food intake.

In a discrete-time survival analysis of this AN population Herzog *et al.* (1997a) demonstrated that low serum creatinine levels were predictors for earlier recovery. One specific aspect was that AN patients who show purging behavior in combination with additional social disturbances have a lower chance of recovering.

Russell *et al.* (1994) showed that clinical outcome was positively correlated with depletion of total body nitrogen and therefore of body protein. They found a high correlation ($r = -0.80$) between nitrogen index and the number of hospitalizations. In addition, the depletion of body nitrogen/protein might be an indicator for chronicity in AN.

MORTALITY

The main causes of death in AN patients are suicide and ventricular tachyarrhythmias. Further important causes, however, are disorders of the electrolyte balance (including hypophosphatemia), infections (pneumonia, sepsis), terminal renal failure, shock, ileus and gastric perforation (Patton 1988; Herzog *et al.* 1992; Foster 1994). The mortality in AN patients of the binge eating/purging type is about twice as high as that of the restricting type (Norring and Sohlberg 1993).

Table 20.2. Examinations recommended on admission or in the course of refeeding

Obligatory	Optional
Blood count, differential blood count	In anemia: reticulocytes, iron, ferritin, transferrin, vitamin B_{12}
Blood sedimentation rate, or C-reactive protein (CRP)	
Sodium, potassium, calcium, phosphate, chloride, magnesium	Arterial or capillary blood gas analysis
	Creatinine-clearance, uric acid
Creatinine, urea	Diurnal profile of blood glucose
Blood glucose	Creatine kinase, alkaline phosphatase
Liver enzyme profile	Lipase
Amylase	Total protein, protein electrophoresis
Albumin	Thyroid hormones, estradiol
Body mass index	Body composition measurement (skinfold, BIA, DEXA)
Heart rate, blood pressure, temperature	
Electrocardiography	Echocardiography, Holder ECG
	Chest X-ray
	Abdominal ultrasound
	Osteodensitometry (DEXA scan) in patients with long-term course
	Abdominal X-ray (in suspected ileus or gastric dilatation)
	In case of seizures or for differential diagnosis EEG and neuroimaging (CT, MRI)

NEW APPROACHES

Patient care in acute cases of AN includes a number of examinations (Table 20.2) to assess the nutritional status or the extent of the malnutrition better than has previously been possible with the clinically established body mass index (BMI [kg/m^2]). Especially in view of the typical fluctuations in fluid balance (including weight manipulations by the patients), which are typical for the acute phase, the BMI has its disadvantages. DXA (dual energy X-ray absorptiometry) has been used as a noninvasive standard for the measurement of the body fat content; however, it is unsuitable as regular follow-up. Procedures such as the measurement of skin thickness or bioimpedance analysis have not been generally accepted for clinical use so far. Moreover, their superiority to the BMI has not been proven, at least for scientific purpose. Of special interest are laboratory parameters, which are suitable for the assessment of the nutritional status, as they are easy to obtain and probably independent of the water balance.

LEPTIN AS A MEASUREMENT FOR BODY FAT

Leptin, a protein that is only expressed by adipocytes (Zhang *et al.* 1994), is supposed to inform the central nervous system of the present amount of adipose tissue in an endogenous feedback mechanism (Considine *et al.* 1996). It possibly also has a direct effect on the adaptation of the neuroendocrine system to fasting periods (Ahima *et al.* 1996). From a sample of 25 patients with eating disorders it could be shown that the leptin value is superior to the BMI with regard to the assessment of the amount of body fat. DXA served as a reference method (Zipfel *et al.* 1997). Moreover, there seem to be connections between leptin levels and reproductive functions, which will be further described elsewhere and which suggest that leptin is an interesting parameter for eating disorder research.

THE ROLE OF LEPTIN IN THE FEMALE CYCLE

While the most attention to the biological effects of leptin has been given to the hypothalamus, the leptin receptor was also identified in other nonneuronal tissues such as liver, kidney, fat, and especially in the reproductive organs (Lee *et al.* 1996). Barash *et al.* (1996) showed a direct effect on the reproductive organs in infertile mice. Obese (*ob/ob*) female mice treated with leptin for 14 days had significantly elevated serum levels of LH, increased ovarian and uterine weights, and stimulated aspects of ovarian and uterine histology compared to controls. In normal female mice treated with leptin the group of Chehab *et al.* (1997) showed that this group of leptin-treated mice reproduced earlier than controls and also showed an earlier maturation of the reproductive tract. In this case leptin acts as a signal triggering puberty.

These results demonstrate that leptin stimulates the reproductive endocrine system of the obese mice and may serve as a permissive signal to the reproductive systems of normal animals (Rosenbaum *et al.* 1996). So it may be supposed that leptin expressed by adipocytes not only plays a central role in the feedback of total body fat mass, but also has a direct connection to the reproductive organs. This may be another key to the adaptation of the female organism in periods of fasting and starvation. A positive effect on the reproductive organs by direct administration of leptin has already been demonstrated in an animal model. It is being discussed whether there might be a critical threshold.

ANOREXIA NERVOSA

CLINICAL IMPLICATIONS

- Medical complications play an important role in the course of anorexia nervosa. It is important to keep in mind that the stage and the dynamic course of the illness, the subtype of AN, the possible abuse of drugs (e.g. laxatives, diuretics) and an additional medical comorbidity (e.g. diabetes) will effect presenting medical complications. Each stage of the illness demands a different focus to assessment and treatment:

Continued

1. *Acute phase:* Nutritional status, electrolyte and acid–base imbalance should be checked. In addition a basic cardiovascular diagnostic should be administered.
2. *Refeeding phase:* Parenteral nutrition should be avoided if possible, particularly in cachectic patients because of numerous possible complications (e.g. hypophosphatemia, water and electrolyte imbalance, fat overloading, high risk of infections).
3. *Chronic phase:* It should be considered that patients with a long-term course run a high risk of getting severe osteoporosis, chronic renal failure and several other kinds of structural organ damage.

RESEARCH IMPLICATIONS

- To prevent medical complications it is important to develop cost-effective, minimal invasive methods that are sensitive and valid. Some of the most significant implications in this field of research are:

1. New techniques for the measurement of body composition and nutritional status (e.g. DEXA, BIA, leptin).
2. Biochemical markers of bone resorption and new ultrasound techniques which give a new perspective for noninvasive assessment of bone mineral density and structure.
3. Leptin, a hormone secreted by adipocytes is a promising approach for a new neuroendocrine perspective in anorexia nervosa patients.
4. In the field of neuroimaging, new techniques like functional MRI or PET give a broader insight in the pathology and pathogenesis of this illness and the structural alterations.

BULIMIA NERVOSA

CLINICAL IMPLICATIONS

- In patients with bulimia nervosa (BN), unlike those with AN, malnutrition and its implications are not the major factors affecting medical complications. Nevertheless, because of the fact that one-third of BN patients develop amenorrhea, there is still a significant risk of problems, like osteoporosis. But the most dangerous medical complications are caused by the massive binge eating and purging behavior that characterizes this illness.

1. Patients with BN, especially those with a high frequency of vomiting and an additional intake of laxatives or diuretic pills run a risk of electrolyte and acid–base disturbances.

Continued

2. A combination of metabolic alkalosis, hypokalemia, hypochloremia, polyuria and exsiccosis, is a typical result of massive purging behavior.
3. Cardiac complications occur mostly in patients with purging behavior but are not necessarily associated with hypokalemia.
4. In the gastrointestinal system gastric dilation (particularly after binge eating) and gastroduodenal ulcers (sometimes in combination with upper gastrointestinal bleeding) can occur.
5. BN patients with the comorbidity of diabetes mellitus run a high risk of hypoglycemia and of early onset vascular complications due to impaired glucose metabolism.

RESEARCH IMPLICATIONS

- To prevent medical complications it is important to develop cost-effective, minimal invasive methods that are sensitive and valid. Some of the most significant implications in this field of research are:

1. New techniques for the measurement of body composition and nutrition status (e.g. DEXA, BIA, leptin).
2. In BN patients with amenorrhea biochemical markers of bone resorption and new ultrasound techniques which give a new perspective for noninvasive assessment of bone mineral density and structure.
3. Leptin, a hormone secreted by adipocytes is a promising approach for a new neuroendocrine perspective in bulimia nervosa, especially in those patients with large fluctuations in weight. Further, a number of recently detected, highly potent appetite stimulating neurohormones (e.g. neuropeptide Y, urocortin) could broaden our understanding of the illness.
4. In the field of neuroimaging, new techniques like functional MRI or PET give a broader insight to the underlying central nervous disturbances, particularly in phases of acute bulimic symptomatology.

REFERENCES

Aarskog, D., Aksens, L., Markestad, T. and Trygstad, O. (1986). Plasma concentrations of vitamin D metabolites in pubertal girls with anorexia nervosa, *Acta Endocrin. Suppl. Copenh.*, **279**, 458–467.

Abdu, R.A., Garritano, D. and Culver, O. (1987). Acute gastric necrosis in anorexia nervosa and bulimia. Two case reports, *Arch. Surg.*, **122**(7), 830–832.

Abrams, S., Silber, T., Esteban, N. *et al.* (1993). Mineral balance and bone turnover in adolescents with anorexia nervosa, *J. Pediatr.*, **123**, 326–331.

Ahima, R.S., Prabakaran, D., Mantzoros, C. *et al.* (1996). Role of leptin in the neuroendocrine response to fasting, *Nature*, **382**, 250–252.

Ainley, C., Cason, J., Slavin, B.M. *et al.* (1991). The influence of zinc status and malnutrition on immunological function in Crohn's disease, *Gastroenterology*, **100**(6), 1616–1625.

Allouche, J., Bennet, A., Barbe, P. *et al.* (1991). LH pulsatility and in vitro bioactivity in women with anorexia nervosa-related hypothalamic amenorrhea, *Acta Endocrinol. Copenh.*, **125**(6), 614–620.

Alloway, R., Shur, E., Obrecht, R. *et al.* (1988). Physical complications in anorexia nervosa. Haematological and neuromuscular changes in 12 patients, *Br. J. Psychiatry*, **153**, 72–75.

Alvin, P., Zogheib, J., Rey, C. *et al.* (1993). Severe complications and mortality in mental eating disorders in adolescence. On 99 hospitalized patients, *Arch. Fr. Pediatr.*, **50**(9), 755–762.

Andersen, A.E., Woodward, P.J. and LaFrace, N. (1995). Bone mineral density of eating disorder subgroups, *Int. J. Eat. Disorders*, **18**(4), 335–342.

Bachrach, L.K., Katzmann, D.K., Litt, I., Guido, D. and Marcus, R. (1991). Recovery from osteopenia in adolescent girls with anorexia nervosa, *J. Clin. Endocrinol. Metab.*, **72**, 602–606.

Bachrach, L.K. (1993). Bone mineralization in childhood and adolescence, *Curr. Opin. Pediatrics*, **5**, 7–573.

Baran, D.T. (1995). Quantitative Ultrasound: a technique to target women with low bone mass for preventive therapy. *Am. J. Med.*, **98** (suppl. 2a), 48–51.

Barash, I.A., Cheung, C.C., Weigle, D.S. *et al.* (1996). Endocrinology, **137**(7), 3144–3147.

Barbe, P., Bennet, A., Stebenet, M. *et al.* (1993). Sex-hormone-binding globulin and protein-energy malnutrition indexes as indicators of nutritional status in women with anorexia nervosa, *Am. J. Clin. Nutr.*, **57**(3), 319–322.

Bates, G.W., Bates S.R. and Whitworth, N.S. (1982). Reproductive failure in women who practice weight control, *Fertil. Steril.*, **37**, 373–378.

Beumont, P.J.V. (1992). Menstrual disorder and other hormonal disturbances In: *The Course of Eating Disorders*, (eds. W. Herzog, H.C. Deter and W. Vandereycken), pp. 257–272.

Beumont, P.J. and Large, M. (1991). Hypophosphataemia, delirium and cardiac arrhythmia in anorexia nervosa, *Med. J. Aust.*, **155**(8), 519–522.

Beumont, P.J.V., Russell, J.D. and Touyz, S.W. (1993). Treatment of anorexia nervosa, *Lancet*, **341**, 1635–1640.

Beumont, P.J., Kopec-Schrader, E.M. and Lennerts, W. (1995). Eating disorder patients at a NSW teaching hospital: a comparison with state-wide data, *Aust. N.Z. J. Psychiatry*, **29**(1), 96–103.

Biggs, M.M., Basco, M.R., Patterson, G. *et al.* (1994). Insulin withholding for weight control in women with diabetes, *Diabetes Care*, **17**(10), 1186–1189.

Bihun, J.A., McSherry, J. and Marciano, D. (1993). Idiopathic edema and eating disorders: evidence for an association, *Int. J. Eat. Disorders*, **14**(2), 197–201.

Biller, B.M. *et al.* (1989). Mechanism of osteoporosis in adult and adolescent women with anorexia nervosa, *J. Clin. Endocrin. Metab.*, **68**, 548–554.

Birmingham, C.L., Goldner, E.M. and Bakan, R. (1994). Controlled trial of zinc supplementation in anorexia nervosa, *Int. J. Eat. Disorders*, **15**(3), 251–255.

Bishop, K., Briggs, P. and Schmidt, E. (1994). Identification and immediate management of the oral changes associated with eating disorders, *Br. J. Hosp. Med.*, **326**, 329–334.

Boag, F., Weerakoon, J., Ginsburg, J. *et al.* (1985). Diminished creatinine clearance in anorexia nervosa: reversal with weight gain, *J. Clin. Pathol.*, **38**(1), 60–63.

Bonne, O.B., Bloch, M. and Berry, E.M. (1993). Adaptation to severe hypokalemia in anorexia nervosa: a plea for conservative management, *Int. J. Eat. Disorders*, **13**(1), 125–128.

Brinch, M., Isager, T. and Tolstroop, K. (1988). Anorexia nervosa and motherhood; reproduction pattern and mothering behavior of 50 women. *Acta Psychiat. Scand.*, **77**, 98–104.

Brown, N.W. (1985). Medical consequences of eating disorders, *South. Med. J.*, **78**(4), 403–405.

Buchman, A.L., Ament, M.E., Weiner, M. *et al.* (1994). Reversal of megaduodenum and duodenal dysmotility associated with improvement in nutritional status in primary anorexia nervosa, *Dig. Dis. Sci.*, **39**(2), 433–440.

Campanini, M., Cusinato, S., Airoldi, G. *et al.* (1991). Heart involvement in anorexia nervosa: an electrocardiographic, functional and morphological study, *Ann. Ital. Med. Int.*, **6**(2), 210–216.

Cantwell, R. and Steel, J.M. (1996). Screening for eating disorders in diabetes mellitus, *J. Psychosom. Res.*, **40**(1), 15–20.

Cariem, A.K., Lemmer, E.R., Adams, M.G. *et al.* (1994). Severe hypophosphataemia in anorexia nervosa, *Postgrad. Med. J.*, **70**(829), 825–827.

Challier, P. and Cabrol, S. (1995). Severe hyponatremia associated with anorexia nervosa: role of inappropriate antidiuretic hormone secretion, *Arch. Pediatr.*, **2**(10), 977–979.

Chehab, F.F., Mounzih, K., Lu, R. *et al.* (1997). Early onset of reproductive function in normal female mice treated with leptin, *Science*, **275**, 88–90.

Colombo, L., Altomare, S., Castelli, M. *et al.* (1995). Kinetics of hepatic enzymes in anorexia nervosa, *Recenti. Prog. Med.*, **86**(5), 204–207.

Comerci, G.D. (1990). Medical complications of anorexia nervosa and bulimia nervosa, *Med. Clin. North Am.*, **74**(5), 1293–1310.

Considine, R.V., Madhur, K.S., Heiman, M.L. *et al.* (1996). Serum immunoreactive-leptin concentrations in normal-weight and obese humans, *N. Engl. J. Med.*, **334**, 292–295.

Cooke, R.A. and Chambers, J.B. (1995). Anorexia nervosa and the heart, *Br. J. Hosp. Med.*, **54**(7), 313–317.

Cooke, R.A., Chambers, J.B., Singh, R. *et al.* (1994). QT interval in anorexia nervosa, *Br. Heart J.*, **72**(1), 69–73.

Curran-Celentano, J., Erdman, J.W. Jr., Nelson, R.A. *et al.* (1985). Alterations in vitamin A and thyroid hormone status in anorexia nervosa and associated disorders, *Am. J. Clin. Nutr.*, **42**(6), 1183–1191.

Delvenne, V., Lotstra, F., Goldman, S. *et al.* (1995). Brain hypometabolism of glucose in anorexia nervosa: a PET scan study, *Biol. Psychiatry*, **37**(3), 161–169.

de Simone, G., Scalfi, L., Galderisi, M. *et al.* (1994). Cardiac abnormalities in young women with anorexia nervosa, *Br. Heart J.*, **71**(3), 287–292.

Deter, H.C. and Herzog W. (1994). Results of the Heidelberg–Mannheim Study. *Psychosom. Med.*, **56**, 20–27.

Devuyst, O., Lambert, M., Rodhain, J. *et al.* (1993). Haematological changes and infectious complications in anorexia nervosa: a case-control study, *Q. J. Med.*, **86**(12), 791–799.

Dolan, R.J., Mitchell, J. and Wakeling, A. (1988). Structural brain changes in patients with anorexia nervosa, *Psychol. Med.*, **18**(2), 349–353.

Doraiswamy, P.M., Krishnan, K.R., Boyko, O.B. *et al.* (1991). Pituitary abnormalities in eating disorders: further evidence from MRI studies, *Prog. Neuropsychopharmacol. Biol. Psychiatry*, **15**(3), 351–356.

Durakovic, Z., Durakovic, A. and Korsic, M. (1994). Changes in the corrected Q-T interval in the electrocardiogram of patients with anorexia nervosa, *Int. J. Cardiol.*, **45**(2), 115–120.

Engel, H.D. (1989) Prävalenz anorektischen Verhaltens in einer Normalpopulation. *Zeitschr. Psychosomatische Medizin*, **34**, 117–129.

Fairburn, C.G. and Cooper, P.J. (1984). The clinical features of bulimia nervosa, *Br. J. Psychiatry*, **144**, 268–269.

Ferguson, J.M. (1985). Bulimia: A potentially fatal syndrome, *Psychosom.*, **26**, 252–253.

Fichter, M.M. (1985). *Magersucht und Bulimia*. Springer, Berlin.

Fichter, M.M. and Pirke, K.M. (1990). Endocrine dysfunctions in bulimia nervosa: In: *Bulimia Nervosa*, (ed. Fichter, M.M.) Wiley, Chichester.

Fonseca, V.A., D'Souza, V., Houlder, S., Thomas, M. and Wakeling, A. (1988). Vitamin D deficiency and low osteocalcin concentration in anorexia nervosa, *J. Clin. Pathol.*, **41**, 195–197.

Foster, D.W. (1994). Anorexia nervosa and bulimia, In: *Harrison's Principles of Internal Medicine* (eds. K. J. Isselbacher *et al.*) 13th Edn, pp. 452–455, McGraw-Hill, New York.

Franssila-Kallunki, A., Rissanen, A., Ekstrand, A. *et al.* (1991). Fuel metabolism in anorexia nervosa and simple obesity, *Metabolism*, **40**(7), 689–694.

Frisch, R.E. (1977). Food Intake, Fatness and Reproductive Ability. In: *Anorexia Nervosa*, (ed. Vigersky, R.A.), pp. 149–161, Raven Press, New York.

Frisch, R.E. (1988). Fatness and fertility, *Sci. Am.*, **258**, 88–95.

Fujita, M., Tamai, H., Mizuno, O. *et al.* (1991). Secretory function of the renin aldosterone system in patients with anorexia nervosa, *Nippon Naibunpi Gakkai Zasshi.*, **67**(1), 50–55.

Fukushima, M., Nakai, Y., Taniguchi, A. *et al.* (1993). Insulin sensitivity, insulin secretion, and glucose effectiveness in anorexia nervosa: a minimal model analysis, *Metabolism*, **42**(9), 1164–1168.

Garcia-Rubira, J.C., Hidalgo, R., Gomez-Barrado, J.J. *et al.* (1994). Anorexia nervosa and myocardial infarction, *Int. J. Cardiol.*, **45**(2), 138–140.

Golden, N.H., Ashtari, M., Kohn, M.R. *et al.* (1996). Reversibility of cerebral ventricular enlargement in anorexia nervosa, demonstrated by quantitative magnetic resonance imaging, *J. Pediatr.*, **128**(2), 296–301.

Greenfeld, D., Mickley, D., Quinlan, D.M. *et al.* (1995). Hypokalemia in outpatients with eating disorders, *Am. J. Psychiatry*, **152**(1), 60–63.

Hall, D.E., Kahan, B. and Snitzer, J. (1994). Delirium associated with hypophosphatemia in a patient with anorexia nervosa, *J. Adolescent Health*, **15**(2), 176–178.

Hall, R.C. and Beresford, T.P. (1989). Medical complications of anorexia and bulimia, *Psychiatr. Med.*, **7**(4), 165–192.

Hall, R.C., Hofman, R.S., Beresford, T.P. *et al.* (1988). Hypomagnesemia in patients with eating disorders, *Psychosomatics*, **29**(3), 264–272.

Hall, R.C., Hoffman, R.S., Beresford, T.P. *et al.* (1989). Physical illness encountered in patients with eating disorders, *Psychosomatics*, **30**(2), 174–191.

Halmi, K.A., Eckert, E., Marchi. P., Sampugnaro, V., Apple, R. and Cohen, J. (1991). Comorbidity of psychiatric diagnosis in anorexia nervosa. *Arch. Gen. Psychiat.*, **48**, 712–718.

Hannan, W.J., Wrate, R., Cowen, S. and Freeman, C. (1995). Body mass index as an estimate of body fat, *Int. J. Eat. Disorder*, **18**, 91–97.

Hassager, C., Colwell, A. and Assiri, A. (1993). Effect of menopause and replacement therapy on urinary excretion of pyridinium crosslinks: a longitudinal and cross-sectional study, *Clin. Endocrinol.*, **37**, 45–50.

Herholz, K., Krieg, J.C., Emrich, H.M. *et al.* (1987). Regional cerebral glucose metabolism in anorexia nervosa measured by positron emission tomography, *Biol. Psychiatry*, **22**(1), 43–51.

Herpertz, S., von Blume, B. and Senf, W. (1995). Eating disorders and diabetes mellitus, *Zeitschr. Psychosomatik und Psychoanalyse*, **41**(4), 329–343.

Herzog, W., Deter, H.C., Schellberg, D. *et al.* (1992). Somatic findings at 12-year follow-up of 103 anorexia nervosa patients: Results of the Heidelberg–Mannheim follow-up, In: *The Course of Eating Disorders*, (eds W. Herzog, H.C. Deter and W. Vandereycken), pp. 85–107, Springer, Berlin.

Herzog, W., Minne, H., Deter, H. *et al.* (1993). Outcome of bone mineral density in anorexia nervosa patients 11.7 years after first admission, *J. Bone Miner. Res.*, **8**, 597–605.

Herzog, W., Munz, D. and Kächele, H. (1996). *Analytische Therapie bei Esstörungen*. Schattauer Verlag, Stuttgart.

Herzog, W., Schellberg, D. and Deter, H.C. (1997a). First recovery in anorexia nervosa patients in the long-term course: a discrete-time survival analysis, *J. Consult. Clin. Psychol.*. Vol. **65**, No.1, 169–177.

Herzog, W., Deter, H.C., Fiehn, W. and Petzold, W. (1997b). Medical findings and predictors of long-term physical outcome in anorexia nervosa: a prospective, 12-year follow-up study, *Psychol. Med.*, **27**, 269–279.

Horta, J.L., Fernandez, J.G., Soto de Leon, B. and Cortes-Gallegos, A. (1977). Direct evidence of luteal insufficiency in women with habitual abortion, *Obst. Gyn.*, **49**, 705–708.

Hughes, J.R. (1996). A review of the usefulness of the standard EEG in psychiatry, *Clin. Electroencephalogr.*, **27**(1), 35–39.

Humphries, L.L., Adams, L.J., Eckfeldt, J.H. *et al.* (1987). Hyperamylasemia in patients with eating disorders, *Ann. Intern. Med.*, **106**(1), 50–52.

Iketani, T., Kiriike, N., Nakanisihi, S. *et al.* (1995). Effect of weight gain and resumption of menses on reduced bone density in patients with anorexia nervosa, *Biol. Psychiatry*, **37**(8), 521–527.

Isner, J.M., Roberts, W.C., Heymsfield, S.B. *et al.* (1985). Anorexia nervosa and sudden death, *Ann. Intern. Med.*, **102**(1), 49–52.

Jarman, F.C., Rickards, W.S. and Hudson, I.L. (1991). Late adolescent outcome of early onset anorexia nervosa, *J. Paediatr. Child Health*, **27**(4), 221–227.

Jones, B.P., Duncan, C.C., Brouwers, P. *et al.* (1991). Cognition in eating disorders, *J. Clin. Exp. Neuropsychol.*, **13**(5), 711–728.

Joughin, N.A., Crisp, A.H., Gowers, S.G. *et al.* (1991). The clinical features of late onset anorexia nervosa, *Postgrad. Med. J.*, **67**(793), 973–977.

Joyce, J.M., Warren, D.L., Humphries, L.L., Smith, A.J. and Coon, J.S. (1990). Osteoporosis in women with eating disorders: comparison of physical parameters, exercise and menstrual status with SPA and DPA evaluation, *J. Nucl. Med.*, **31**, 325–331.

Kahn, D., Halls, J., Bianco, J.A. *et al.* (1991). Radionuclide ventriculography in severe underweight anorexia nervosa patients before and during refeeding therapy, *J. Adolescent Health*, **12**(4), 301–306.

Kamal, N., Chami, T., Andersen, A. *et al.* (1991). Delayed gastrointestinal transit times in anorexia nervosa and bulimia nervosa, *Gastroenterology*, **101**(5), 1320–1324.

Kaplan, A.S. (1990). Biochemical variables in the eating disorders, *Can. J. Psychiatry*, **35**(9), 745–753.

Kaplan, A.S., Goldbloom, D.S., Woodside, D.B. *et al.* (1991). Mitral valve prolapse in eating and panic disorder: A pilot study, *Int. J. Eat. Disorders*, **10**, 531–537.

Kingston, K., Szmukler, G.I., Andrewes, D. *et al.* (1996). Neuropsychological and structural brain changes in anorexia nervosa before and after refeeding, *Psychol. Med.*, **26**(1), 15–28.

Klibansky, A., Beverly, M., Biller, K., Schoenfeld, D., Herzog, D.B. and Saxe, V. (1995). The effect of estrogen administration on trabecular bone loss in young women with anorexia nervosa, *J. Clin. Endocrinol. Metab.*, **80**, 898–904.

Koffler, M. and Kisch, E.S. (1996). Starvation diet and very-low-calorie diets may induce insulin resistance and overt diabetes mellitus, *J. Diabetes Compl.*, **10**(2), 109–112.

Kohlmeyer, K., Lehmkuhl, G. and Poutska, F. (1983). Computed tomography of anorexia nervosa, *Am. J. Neuroradiol.*, **4**(3), 437–438.

Kornreich, L., Shapira, A., Horev, G., Danzinger, Y., Tyano, S. and Mimouni, M. (1991). CT and MR evaluation of the brain in patients with anorexia nervosa, *Am. J. Neuroradiology*, **12**, 1213–1216.

Kreipe, R.E., Goldstein, B., DeKing, D.E. *et al.* (1994). Heart rate power spectrum analysis of autonomic dysfunction in adolescents with anorexia nervosa, *Int. J. Eat. Disorders*, **16**(2), 159–165.

Krieg, J.C. (1991). Eating disorders as assessed by cranial computerized tomography (CCT, dSPECT, PET), *Adv. Exp. Med. Biol.*, **291**, 223–229.

Krieg, J.C., Backmund, H. and Pirke, K.M. (1987). Cranial computed tomography findings in bulimia, *Acta Psychiatr. Scand.*, **75**(2), 144–149.

Krieg, J.C., Pirke, K.M., Lauer, C. *et al.* (1988). Endocrine, metabolic, and cranial computed tomographic findings in anorexia nervosa, *Biol. Psychiatry*, **23**(4), 377–387.

Krieg, J.C., Holthoff, V., Schreiber, W. *et al.* (1991). Glucose metabolism in the caudate nuclei of patients with eating disorders, *Eur. Arch. Psychiatry Clin. Neurosci.*, **240**(6), 331–333.

Laessle, R.G., Krieg, J.C., Fichter, M.M. *et al.* (1989). Cerebral atrophy and vigilance performance in patients with anorexia nervosa and bulimia nervosa, *Neuropsychobiology*, **21**(4), 187–191.

Larrain, C., Ampuero, R. and Pumarino, H. (1989). Hematologic changes in anorexia nervosa, *Rev. Med. Chil.*, **117**(5), 534–543.

Lask, B., Fosson, A., Rolfe, U. *et al.* (1993). Zinc deficiency and childhood-onset anorexia nervosa, *J. Clin. Psychiatry*, **54**(2), 63–66.

Lee, G.H., Proenca, R., Montez, J.M. *et al.* (1996). Abnormal splicing of the leptin receptor in diabetic mice, *Nature*, **379**, 632–635.

Matthews, B.J., Lacey J.H. and Cleeve, H. (1985). Premature loss of bone in chronic anorexia nervosa. *Br. Med. J. Clin. Res. Ed.*, **290**, 1431.

Maugars, Y. and Proust, A. (1994). Osteoporosis in anorexia nervosa, *Presse Med.*, **23**, 156–158.

McClain, C.J., Humphries, L.L., Hill, K.K. *et al.* (1993). Gastrointestinal and nutritional aspects of eating disorders, *J. Am. Coll. Nutr.*, **12**(4), 466–474.

Meadows, G. and Treasure, J. (1989). Bulimia nervosa and Crohn's disease: two case reports, *Acta Psychiatr. Scand.*, **79**(4), 413–414.

Mira, M., Stewart, P.M., Vizzard, J. *et al.* (1987). Biochemical abnormalities in anorexia nervosa and bulimia, *Ann. Clin. Biochem.*, **24**(Pt 1), 29–35.

Mitchell, J.E., Pyle, R.L., Eckert, E.D. *et al.* (1983). Electrolyte and other physiological abnormalities in women suffering from eating disorders, *Psychol. Med.*, **13**(2), 273–278.

Mitchell, J.E., Seim, H.C., Colon, E. *et al.* (1987). Medical complications and medical management of bulimia, *Ann. Intern. Med.*, **107**(1), 71–77.

Mitchell, J.E., Pomeroy, C., Seppala, M. *et al.* (1988). Pseudo-Bartters syndrome, diuretic abuse, idiopathic oedema and eating disorders, *Int. J. Eat. Disorders*, **6**, 557–560.

Morgan, H.G. and Russell, G. F.M.(1975). Value of family background and clinical features as predictors of long-term outcome in anorexia nervosa, *Psychol. Med.*, **5**, 355–371.

Murciano, D., Rigaud, D., Pingleton, S. *et al.* (1994). Diaphragmatic function in severely malnourished patients with anorexia nervosa. Effects of renutrition, *Am. J. Respir. Crit. Care Med.*, **150**(6 Pt 1), 1569–1574.

Nativ, A., Agostint, R., Drinkwater, B. and Yeager, K. (1994). The Female Athlete Triad, *Clin. Sports*, **13**2, 405–418.

Newman, M.M. and Halmi, K.A. (1988). The endocrinology of anorexia nervosa and bulimia nervosa, *Endocrinol. Metab. Clin. North Am.*, **17**(1), 195–212.

Newman, M.M. and Halmi, K.A. (1989). Relationship of bone density to estradiol and cortisol in anorexia nervosa and bulimia, *Psychiat. Res.*, **9**, 105–112.

Newton, R., Freeman, C., Hannan, W. and Cowen, S. (1993). Osteoporosis and normal weight bulimia nervosa—which patients are at risk? *J. Psychosom. Research*, **37**, 239–247.

Nieuwenhuijzen-Kruseman, A.C. (1991). Anorexia and bulimia nervosa in diabetic subjects: more than coincidental, *Neth. J. Med.*, **38**(1-2), 1–3.

Norring, C.E. and Sohlberg, S.S. (1993). Outcome, recovery, relapse and mortality across six years in patients with clinical eating disorders, *Acta Psychiatr. Scand.*, **87**(6), 437–444.

Olmos, J.M., Riancho, J., Amado, J., Freijanes, J., Menendez-Arango, J. and Gonzales-Macias (1991). Vitamin D metabolism and serum binding proteins in anorexia nervosa, *Bone*, **12**, 43–46.

Palazidou, E., Robinson, P. and Lishman, W.A. (1990). Neuroradiological and neuropsychological assessment in anorexia nervosa, *Psychol. Med.*, **20**(3), 521–527.

Palla, B. and Litt, I.F. (1988). Medical complications of eating disorders in adolescents, *Pediatrics*, **81**(5), 613–623.

Patchell, R.A., Fellows, H.A. and Humphries, L.L. (1994). Neurologic complications of anorexia nervosa, *Acta Neurolog. Scand.*, **89**(2), 111–116.

Patton, G.C. (1988). Mortality in eating disorders, *Psychol. Med.*, **18**(4), 947–951.

Peveler, R.C., Fairburn, C.G., Boller, I. *et al.* (1992). Eating disorders in adolescents with IDDM. A controlled study, *Diabetes Care*, **15**(10), 1356–1360.

Pieper-Bigelow, C., Strocchi, A. and Levitt, M.D. (1990). Where does serum amylase come from and where does it go? *Gastroenterol. Clin. North Am.*, **19**(4), 793–810.

Pirke, K.M. (1989). Menstruation und neuroendocrine Stoerungen in der Gonadenachse bei Bulimia nervosa. In: *Bulimia nervosa* (ed. Fichter, M.M.). Enke, Stuttgart.

Pirke, K.M. and Platte, P. (1995). Zur Neurobiologie von Esstörungen im Jugendalter, In: *Eating Disorders in Adolescence. Anorexia and Bulimia Nervosa.* (ed. H. Steinhausen), pp. 171–189, de Gruyter, Berlin.

Pirke, K.M., Pahl, J., Schweiger, U. and Warnoff, M. (1985). Metabolic and endocrine indices of starvation in bulimia: a comparison with anorexia nervosa. *Psychiatr. Res.*, **15**, 33–37.

Platte, P., Pirke, K.M., Trimborn, P. *et al.* (1994). Resting metabolic rate and total energy expenditure in acute and weight recovered patients with anorexia nervosa and in healthy young women, *Int. J. Eat. Disorders*, **16**(1), 45–52.

Poet, J.L., Galinier-Pujol, A., Tonolli-Serabian, I., Conte-Devoix, B. and Roux, H. (1993). Lumbar spine mineral density in anorexia nervosa, *Clin. Rheumatol.*, **12**, 236–239.

Putukian, M. (1994). The female triad. Eating disorders, amenorrhea and osteoporosis, *Sports Med.*, **782**, 345–356.

Ratcliffe, P.J. and Bevan, J.S. (1985). Severe hypoglycaemia and sudden death in anorexia nervosa, *Psychol. Med.*, **15**(3), 679–681.

Ravelli, A.M., Helps, B.A., Devane, S.P. *et al.* (1993). Normal gastric antral myoelectrical activity in early onset anorexia nervosa, *Arch. Dis. Child.*, **69**(3), 342–346.

Richter, W.O. and Schwandt, P. (1991). Anorexia nervosa, In: *Innere Medizin* (eds M. Classen, V. Diehl and K. Kochsiek), p. 669, Urban and Schwarzenberg, München.

Rickards, H., Prendergast, M. and Booth, I.W. (1994). Psychiatric presentation of Crohn's disease. Diagnostic delay and increased morbidity, *Br. J. Psychiatry*, **164**(2), 256–261.

Rigotti, N.A., Nussbaum, S.R., Herzog, D.B. and Neer, R.M. (1984). Osteoporosis in women with anorexia nervosa, *N. Engl. J. Med.*, **311**, 1601–1605.

Rigotti, N.A., Neer, R.M., Ridgway, L., Skates, S.J., Herzog, D.B. and Nussbaum, S.R. (1991). The clinical course of osteoporosis in anorexia nervosa, *J. Am. Ass.*, **265**, 1133–1138.

Robb, N.B., Schmith, B.G. and Geidrys, L.E. (1995). The distribution of erosion in the dentitions of patients with eating disorders, *Br. Dent. J.*, **178**(5), 171–175.

Robertson, P. and Rosenvinge, J.H. (1990). Insulin-dependent diabetes mellitus: a risk factor in anorexia nervosa or bulimia nervosa? An empirical study of 116 women, *J. Psychosom. Res.*, **34**(5), 535–541.

Robinson, P.H., Clarke, M. and Barrett, J. (1988). Determinants of delayed gastric emptying in anorexia nervosa and bulimia nervosa, *Gut*, **29**(4), 458–464.

Rock, C.L., Gorenflo, D.W., Drewnowski, A. *et al.* (1996). Nutritional characteristics, eating pathology, and hormonal status in young women, *Am. J. Clin. Nutr.*, **64**(4), 566–571.

Roijen, S.B., Worsaae, U. and Zlotnik, G. (1991). Zinc in patients with anorexia nervosa, *Ugeskr. Laeger.*, **153**(10), 721–723.

Rosenbaum, M., Nicolson, M., Hirsch, J. *et al.* (1996). Effects of gender, body composition, and menopause on plasma concentrations of leptin, *J. Clin. Endocrinol. Metab.*, **81**(9), 3424–3427.

Rothenberger, A., Blanz, B. and Lehmkuhl, G. (1991). What happens to electrical brain activity when anorectic adolescents gain weight? *Eur. Arch. Psychiat. Clin. Neurosci.*, **240**(3), 144–147.

Ruegsegger, P., Müller, A., Dambacher, M.A., Ittner, J., Willi, J. and Kopp, H.G. (1988). Knochenabbau bei Patientinnen mit Anorexia nervosa, *Schweiz. Med. Zsch.*, **118**, 233–238.

Russell, J., Allen, B., Mira, M., Vizzard, J, Stewart, P. and Beumont, P.J. (1994). Total body nitrogen as a predictor of clinical status in anorexia nervosa, *Int. J. Eat. Disorder*, **15**, 275–278.

Sakata, S., Kushida, K., Yamazaki, K. *et al.* (1997). Ultrasound bone densitometry of os calcis in elderly Japanese women with hip fracture, *Calcif. Tissue Int.*, **60**, 2–7.

Sakka, S., Hurst, P. and Khawaja, H. (1994). Anorexia nervosa and necrotizing colitis: case report and review of the literature, *Postgrad. Med. J.*, **70**(823), 369–370.

Salisbury, J.J. and Mitchell, J.E. (1991). Bone mineral density and anorexia nervosa, *Am. J. Psychiat.*, **148**, 768–774.

Scalfi, L., Di Biase, G., Coltorti, A. *et al.* (1993). Bioimpedance analysis and resting energy expenditure in undernourished and refeed anorectic patients, *Eur. J. Clin. Nutr.*, **47**(1), 61–67.

Schlegel, S. and Kretschmar, K. (1997). Stellenwert von CT und NRT in der psychiatrischen Diagnostik, *Nervenarzt*, **68**, 1–10.

Schocken, D.D., Holloway, J.D. and Powers, P.S. (1989). Weight loss and the heart. Effects of anorexia nervosa and starvation, *Arch. Intern. Med.*, **149**(4), 877–881.

Schou, J.A., Lund, L. and Sandermann, J. (1994). Spontaneous ventricular rupture in adults, *Ugeskr. Laeger.*, **156**(22), 3299–3302.

Schweiger, U., Laessle, R., Pfister, H. *et al.* (1987). Diet induced menstrual irregularities: effect of age and weight loss. *Fertil. Steril.*, **48**, 746–751.

Seibel, M., Cosman, F., Shen, V., Gordon, S., Dempster, D., Ratcliffe, A. and Lindsay, R. (1993). Urinary hydroxypyridinium crosslinks of collagen as markers of bone resorption and estrogen efficacy in postmenopausal osteoporosis, *J. Bone Miner. Res.*, **8**, 881–889.

Seibel, M., Zipf, A. and Ziegler, R. (1994). Pyridinium-Crosslinks im Urin. Spezifische Marker der Knochenresorption bei metabolischen Knochenerkrankungen, *Dtsch. Med. Wochenschr.*, **119**, 923–929.

Sharp, C.W. and Freeman, C.P. (1993). The medical complications of anorexia nervosa, *Br. J. Psychiatr.*, **162**, 452–462.

Sherman, P., Leslie, K., Goldberg, E. *et al.* (1994). Hypercarotenemia and transaminitis in female adolescents with eating disorders: a prospective, controlled study, *J. Adolescent Health*, **15**(3), 205–209.

Siegel, J.H., Hardoff, D., Golden, N.H. *et al.* (1995). Medical complications in male adolescents with anorexia nervosa, *J. Adolescent Health*, **16**(6), 448–453.

Simmons, M.S., Grayden, S.K. and Mitchell, J.E. (1986). The need for psychiatric–dental liaison in the treatment of bulimia, *Am. J. Psychiat.*, **143**, 783–784.

Skolnick, A. (1993). Female athlete triad risk for women, *JAMA*, **2708**, 921–922.

Spigset, O. (1990). Somatic and biochemical complications in bulimia, *Tidsskr. Nor. Laegeforen.*, **110**(11), 1349–1353.

Steel, J.M., Young, R.J., Lloyd, G.G. *et al.* (1989). Abnormal eating attitudes in young insulin dependent diabetics, *Br. J. Psychiatr.*, **155**, 515–521.

Stheneur, C., Rey, C., Pariente, D. *et al.* (1995). Acute gastric dilatation with superior mesenteric artery syndrome in a young girl with anorexia nervosa, *Arch. Pediatr.*, **2**(10), 973–976.

Swayze, V.W., Andersen, A., Arndt, S. *et al.* (1996). Reversibility of brain tissue loss in anorexia nervosa assessed with a computerized talairach 3-D proportional grid, *Psychol. Med.*, **26**(2), 381–390.

Szmukler, G.I., Young, G.P., Lichtenstein, M. *et al.* (1990). A serial study of gastric emptying in anorexia nervosa and bulimia, *Aust. N.Z. J. Med.*, **20**(3), 220–225.

Tenholder, M.F. and Pike, J.D. (1991). Effect of anorexia nervosa on pulmonary immunocompetence, *South. Med. J.*, **84**(10), 1188–1191.

Theander, S. (1985). Outcome and prognosis in anorexia nervosa and bulimia nervosa: some results of previous investigations compared with those of a Swedish long-term study. *J. Psychtr. Res.*, **9**, 493–508.

Tiller, J., Macrae, A., Schmidt, U. *et al.* (1994). The prevalence of eating disorders in thyroid disease: a pilot study, *J. Psychosom. Res.*, **38**(6), 609–616.

Tomova, A., Kumanov, P. and Kirilov, G. (1995). Factors related to sex hormone binding globulin concentrations in women with anorexia nervosa, *Horm. Metab. Res.*, **27**(11), 508–510.

Touyz, S.W., Kopec-Schrader, E.M. and Beumont, P.J. (1993a). Anorexia nervosa in males: a report of 12 cases, *Aust. N.Z. J. Psychiatry*, **27**(3), 512–517.

Touyz, S.W., Liew, V.P., Tseng, P. *et al.* (1993b). Oral and dental complications in dieting disorders, *Int. J. Eat. Disorders*, **14**(3), 341–347.

Treasure, J. and Szmukler, G. (1995). Medical complications of chronic anorexia nervosa, In: *Handbook of Eating Disorders: Theory, Treatment and Research*. (eds. G. Szmukler, C. Dare and J. Treasure), John Wiley & Sons Ltd., Chichester.

Treasure, J.L., Fogelman, I. and Russell, G.F. (1986). Osteopenia of the lumbar spine and femoral neck in anorexia nervosa, *Scott. Med. J.*, **31**, 206–207.

Van Dissel, J.T., Gerritsen, H.J. and Meinders, A.E. (1992). Severe hypophosphatemia in a patient with anorexia nervosa during oral feeding, *Miner. Electrolyte Metab.*, **18**(6), 365–369.

Ventura, V., Mauloni, M., Mura, M. *et al.* (1996). *Osteoporosis-Int.*, **6**, 368–375.

Vila, G., Robert, J.J. and Mouren-Simeoni, M.C. (1994). Eating disorders and insulin dependent diabetes: a current issue, *Ann. Med. Psychol. Paris*, **152**(9), 577–588.

Vogel, G. (1996). Neuroscience meeting brief 2: Leptin: a trigger for puberty? *Science*, **29**(274), 1466.

Wada, S., Nagase, T., Koike, Y. *et al.* (1992). A case of anorexia nervosa with acute renal failure induced by rhabdomyolysis; possible involvement of hypophosphatemia or phosphate depletion, *Psychiatr. Res.*, **31**(4), 478–482.

Willeke, F., Riedl, S., von Herbay, A. *et al.* (1996). Decompensated acute gastric dilatation caused by a bulimic attack in anorexia nervosa, *Deutsch. Med. Wochenschr.*, **121**(40), 1220–1225.

Willis, J. and Rand, P. (1988). Pregnancy in bulimic women, *Obstet. Gynecol.*, **71**, 708.

Wu, J.C., Hagman, J., Buchsbaum, M.S. *et al.* (1990). Greater left cerebral hemispheric metabolism in bulimia assessed by positron emission tomography, *Am. J. Psychiatry*, **147**(3), 309–312.

Yager, J., Andersen, A., Devlin, M. *et al.* (1993). Practice guideline for eating disorders. American Psychiatric Association Practice Guidelines, *Am. J. Psychiatry*, **150**, 207–228.

Zipfel, S., Specht, T., Herzog W. *et al.* (1997). Leptin—a new parameter for the body fat measurement in patients with eating disorders, *Eur. Eat. Dis. Rev.* (in press).

Zhang, Y., Proneca, R., Maffei, M. *et al.* (1994). Positional cloning of the mouse obese gene and its human homologue. *Nature*, **372**, 425–479.

APPENDIX

Biting the Bullet: Concise Summary Charts to Share our Knowledge

1 Concepts of Eating Disorders: A Historical Reflection

R. A. GORDON

CLINICAL IMPLICATIONS

- Eating disorders have a long history, and it is only within the past 100 years or so that they have been approached in exclusively medical terms. The expression and construction of eating disorders has always been heavily influenced by sociocultural factors, and the present is no exception.
- To remain sensitive to the human complexities of our patients, clinicians need to maintain an awareness of the wider social contexts that give rise to eating disorders. A focus on critical biological factors in the eating disorders need not and should not preempt such an awareness.
- Contemporary eating disorders are strongly colored by norms of weight and their impact on body image experience. It is important for clinicians to maintain an awareness about how such norms influence patients, as well as how public representations and discussion of eating disorders may influence patients's own perceptions of themselves, both positive and negative.
- Gender, and particularly female experience, plays a critical role in the genesis of eating disorders. In fact, issues in female identity and role expectations may well be more fundamental than 'cosmetic' concerns about body image. Clinician awareness of such factors are key to an effective therapeutic relationship.

RESEARCH IMPLICATIONS

- Ongoing research into the epidemiology of disordered eating behaviour and particularly to how changes in symptomatology are correlated with changes in dieting practices, body image norms and related factors.
- Further cross-cultural research is needed, especially into the emergence of eating disorders in non-Euro/American cultural contexts as well the changing body image ideals and altered expectations and aspirations of women.
- It would be extremely useful to have further studies of the public imagery of eating disorders and particuarly on how such imagery affects patient self concept or identity.

Neurobiology in the Treatment of Eating Disorders.
Edited by H.W. Hoek, J.L. Treasure and M.A. Katzman.

2 The Behavioural Disturbance, Psychopathology, and Phenomenology of Eating Disorders

P. J. V. BEUMONT

CLINICAL IMPLICATIONS

- The eating disorders can be categorised into two clusters: one in which behaviours to lose weight are prominent (anorexia nervosa and bulimia nervosa) and another in which attempts to lose weight are less of a focus (binge eating disorder and obesity).
- One must understand the individual with a diet disorder fully, simply insisting that a person eats more will be inadequate.
- Issues such as low self esteem, depression, obsessionality, and prior sexual abuse all require appropriate therapy.
- Keeping up to date with clinical observations is as important as keeping up with the research developments as the eating disorders are pathoplastic and evolving.

RESEARCH IMPLICATIONS

- There is a need for more research on the psychopathology of binge eating disorder, because it is less understood than that of anorexia nervosa or bulimia nervosa.

Neurobiology in the Treatment of Eating Disorders.
Edited by H.W. Hoek, J.L. Treasure and M.A. Katzman.

3 Psychological and Physical Assessment of Persons with Eating Disorders

J. S. NATHAN and D. B. ALLISON

CLINICAL IMPLICATIONS

- Assesments play an integral role in the development of individualized treatment plans.
- The age of the patient, comfort level and degree of rapport with the assessor must be taken into consideration when designing a multi-dimensional approach to assessment.
- The evaluator should be clear on the goal of the assessment and how the data can be used to develop effective interventions.
- Available tools are rarely designed for males, as a result men go undiagnosed with our current instruments.
- Although eating disorders exist in non-western populations, in older persons and in African-American populations, there are limited numbers of valid measures available.
- Diagnoses of eating disorders in the elderly may be compounded by physical ailments and must be done with caution.
- Age specific measures must be used with children who exhibit different cognitive development than adolescents.

RESEARCH IMPLICATIONS

- More culturally sensitive assessment techniques are needed for all minority populations.
- There is a need for tools which identify children at risk for eating disorders.

Neurobiology in the Treatment of Eating Disorders.
Edited by H.W. Hoek, J.L. Treasure and M.A. Katzman.

4 Epidemiology

D. VAN HOEKEN, A. R. LUCAS and H. W. HOEK

CLINICAL IMPLICATIONS

- Clinicians in secondary and tertiary care should be aware that they see only a selected minority of all persons with a clinically significant eating disorder.
- There is a tendency for those in treatment to have comorbid conditions.
- Although an eating disorder is usually preceded by dieting, not all dieters develop an eating disorder.
- There has been an enormous increase in the 'treated' incidence of eating disorders. However, from epidemiological studies there is no convincing evidence that eating disorders in general are on the rise; there does seem to be an increase for the most vulnerable group of females 15–24 years old over the past 50 years.
- General practitioners detect only about 12% of all bulimia nervosa cases, and about 45% of all anorexia nervosa cases. As they often serve as gate keepers to specialized care, they should receive better training in the recognition of eating disorders, particularly of bulimia nervosa.

RESEARCH IMPLICATIONS

- It is time to move beyond the study of the occurrence of eating disorders, and to undertake studies which focus on risk factors.
- This requires prospective follow-up studies on carefully chosen, initially healthy at-risk populations of sufficient size.
- In the search for etiological factors, it seems wise to adopt a 'broad-spectrum' approach to the assessment of eating disorder symptomatology, including a wide definition of atypical and/or subclinical criteria. This might result in specific risk factors of more narrowly defined subgroups of eating disorders.

Neurobiology in the Treatment of Eating Disorders.
Edited by H.W. Hoek, J.L. Treasure and M.A. Katzman.

5 Etiology of Anorexia Nervosa

C. GILLBERG and M. RÅSTAM

CLINICAL IMPLICATIONS

- Anorexia is associated with strong genetic determinants in some cases.
- It appears that in some cases AN can be triggered by life events.
- In many cases of AN the aetiology is still unknown, yet it appears to be multifactorially determined and therefore should be interpreted from a biopsychosocial perspective.
- There is no support for the once widely held belief that family dysfunction is a major causative factor.
- It is important to begin an assessment of a new case with no preconceived notion about underlying causes.

RESEARCH IMPLICATIONS

- Singularly biological, psychosocial, or family based models will probably only provide partial explanations.
- Subgroups of individuals with AN will have aetiologies that partly overlap.

Neurobiology in the Treatment of Eating Disorders.
Edited by H.W. Hoek, J.L. Treasure and M.A. Katzman.

6 Aetiology of Bulimia Nervosa

R. L. PALMER

CLINICAL AND RESEARCH IMPLICATIONS

Personal versions of prevalent beliefs about weight and eating provide the motivation for eating restraint which is the usual first step on the pathway to the disorder.

- Primary prevention of bulimia nervosa would need to involve successful challenge of the widespread overvaluing of slimness and the belief that weight reduction can be easily achieved by dieting.
- Treatment requires that the sufferer lessens or abandons such restraint.

Restraint of eating leads to psychological and biological consequences.

- Further research should investigate the nature and range of these consequences. It is possible that relevant drugs might be produced if the biological consequences were better understood.

Such consequences may be different or be interpreted differently by people who are in some ways vulnerable.

- Such vulnerability includes low self esteem and a range of developmental experiences which have promoted it. Treatment needs to address such wider issues.
- There may be biological variation in response to eating restraint. Genetic research may help to elucidate this.
- There is certainly psychological variation. Research should examine further the risk factors and mechanisms that determine whether or not an individual develops disorder in the presence of a sustained attempt at eating restraint.

As the disorder develops the sufferer comes to have more unusual ideas linking weight and eating with wider personal issues. These tend to be exaggerated versions of the beliefs which prompted the eating restraint in the first place. Such ideas constitute the specific psychopathology of the disorder.

- Treatments which address directly this specific psychopathology (e.g. CBT) may be especially efficacious.

It is possible that a minority of bulimia nervosa sufferers and perhaps a majority of those with binge eating disorders have a disorder which is not based in restraint. They may have some primary problem of eating regulation.

- Future research needs to further define, describe and study this subgroup.

Neurobiology in the Treatment of Eating Disorders.
Edited by H.W. Hoek, J.L. Treasure and M.A. Katzman.

7 Genetic Studies of Anorexia and Bulimia Nervosa

L. R. LILENFELD and W. H. KAYE

CLINICAL IMPLICATIONS

- An understanding of genetically determined premorbid personality traits, which may be etiologically related to the development of eating disorders, may influence the approach of clinicians in what potential areas of behavior and personality are targeted for change during treatment.
- An understanding of familial personality and behavioral traits which may be relevant in the etiology of eating disorders may influence the targets of change in family intervention approaches used by clinicians.
- The likelihood of genetically determined personality traits playing a role in the development of eating disorders may influence the assessment of such patients, both when gathering information about the patient as well as her family members.
- The convergence in the literature that eating disorders aggregate in families suggests that clinicians should assess for a history of these disorders in the families of these patients, as it may potentially influence the conceptualization and understanding of a particular case.
- The convergence in the literature that anxiety and mood disorders aggregate in families should encourage clinicians to be sure to assess for a history of such disorders in the families of eating disorder patients, as it may potentially influence the conceptualization and understanding of a particular case.

RESEARCH IMPLICATIONS

- Future genetic research on personality and temperamental traits, such as harm avoidance and emotional restraint in anorexia nervosa and emotional lability and impulsivity in bulimia nervosa, is needed to further our understanding of the personality traits that may function as risk factors in eating disorders.
- Evidence of familial aggregation of anxiety and mood disorders among the relatives of eating disordered probands exists and requires further study with larger family study samples in order to develop a greater understanding of potentially common underlying mechanisms which may explain the relationship between these disorders and eating disorders.
- The finding that anorexia nervosa and obsessive–compulsive personality disorder may share a similar underlying vulnerability is particularly worthy of future family and genetic methodological study.
- The relationship between bulimia nervosa and impulsive behavior is also worthy of future family and genetic methodological study.

Neurobiology in the Treatment of Eating Disorders.
Edited by H.W. Hoek, J.L. Treasure and M.A. Katzman.

8 Models of Eating Disturbances in Animals

J. B. OWEN

CLINICAL AND RESEARCH IMPLICATIONS

- Evidence from animal models together with that on human patients, indicate that vulnerability to anorexia nervosa (AN) and several obesity syndromes show a significant genetic component.
- The degree of expression of the genetic predisposition depends on environmental triggers or stress factors that influence the timing and/or severity of the symptoms.
- This finding is consistent with the fact that both appetite control and stress response are subject to hypothalamus control.
- Both AN and obesity appear to stem from a mis-setting or mis-reading by the brain of the body composition target for different growth-stages, resulting in overshooting (obesity) or undershooting (emaciation as in AN).
- Animal models are increasingly suggesting suitable candidate genes by which these basal errors are compounded.

FUTURE RESEARCH

- Search for candidate genes influencing the range of body composition from emaciation to obesity across a number of appropriate animal species.
- Further elucidation of stress responses acting as triggers in animal models.

DIFFICULTIES

- Getting sufficient multiply affected families to carry out powerful linkage studies (QTLs) in humans and animal models.
- Distinguishing the results of primary genetic defects from secondary physio-logical effects of emaciation in AN subjects (vice versa in obese subjects).

Continued

Continued

FORMULATION

- These findings from animal models strengthen the need for more comprehensive case formulation procedures.
- These should include, in addition to routine measures of weight, height etc., as full a family history as possible of degree of leanness, stress susceptibility as well as related conditions such as alcohol abuse.

TREATMENT

- The indication of a significant genetic basis from animal models has several implications for treatment and establishing open communication with the patient.
- Patients will benefit from being classified as suffering from a basic metabolic dysfunction rather than an ill-defined, primarily psychiatric mental, condition. This will enable clinicians and patients to better understand and to cope with the secondary 'psychiatric' phenomena, minimising any possible guilt feeling by the patient.
- Animal models present an opportunity in the near future to identify genetic markers that will enable individuals to be classified as 'at risk'. This will allow targeted preventative measures to avoid potential risk factors (triggers), including extreme caution in indulgence in wilful 'dieting' that could trigger a catabolic spiral.
- Candidate genes from animal model work could also help to identify the lack of, or miscoded, proteins. These basic deficiencies could be rectified by direct administration of replacements or by somatic gene therapy.

OTHER EATING DISORDERS

- Bulimia nervosa and bingeing: There are as yet no reported direct equivalents of these conditions in animal models. Even if there were, they would be observable only in non-ruminant models, because of similarity to humans in their digestive anatomy. At first sight this could strengthen the argument that AN and Bulimia are distinctly separate entities, even though they coincide in a proportion of sufferers. However, there are many indirect evidential features that point to the possibility of a common aetiology, possibly genetic. If this is so then we may be observing a rather different degree and symptoms of closely related genetic disorders.
- Obesity: Many of the points made for AN above apply in some measure to the other side of the coin and the *ob* gene is one candidate for both conditions.

Neurobiology in the Treatment of Eating Disorders.
Edited by H.W. Hoek, J.L. Treasure and M.A. Katzman.

9 Stress, Eating and Neurobiology

F. CONNAN and J. L. TREASURE

CLINICAL IMPLICATIONS

- The prolonged exposure to high levels of cortisol in anorexia nervosa may lead to damage of hippocampal neurons.
- It will be important in psychotherapeutic work to encourage effective problem solving and coping strategies so that the stress and strain caused by any difficulty is rapidly resolved. This will prevent the over-sensitive HPA system from perpetuating the catabolic spiral.
- SSRI drugs may be able to ameliorate the hyper-reactive stress response which is a vulnerability factor for the development of bulimia nervosa. However, psychotherapeutic work will be necessary to counteract the effect of maintaining factors such as prolonged emotional stress and strain.
- It may be possible to monitor the effectiveness of psychotherapy by measuring the level of cortisol. We might hypothesize a biphasic response in anorexia nervosa, involving an increase in cortisol release when the issues surrounding the psychosocial conflict are first addressed and a decrease in cortisol levels when these issues are resolved.

RESEARCH IMPLICATIONS

- There may be heterogeneity in bulimia nervosa: those with developmental stress may have persistent abnormalities in the HPA and 5-HT system. Those with a family history of obesity may have reduced central leptin.
- It may be possible to screen for vulnerability to anorexia nervosa by measuring plasma cortisols.
- The genetic vulnerability may involve components of the 5-HT system, and/or HPA axis.

Neurobiology in the Treatment of Eating Disorders.
Edited by H.W. Hoek, J.L. Treasure and M.A. Katzman. © 1998 John Wiley & Sons Ltd.

10 The Neurobiology of Eating Behaviour and Weight Control

P. J. V. BEUMONT

CLINICAL IMPLICATIONS

- Body mass is determined by the relation of energy intake and energy expenditure, but this equation needs to be understood in relation to the composition of food eaten, and the ways in which energy is utilized.
- The role of the hypothalamus in regulating eating and in determining the utilization of energy has been investigated vigorously over the last half-century. It is now accepted that the hypothalamus is not the prime centre of this control, but rather part of several integrated neural mechanisms.
- Research has elucidated the role of specific neurotransmitters and modulators in energy ingestion.
- Spontaneous variations in eating and in energy utilization in various species of animals provide useful models for understanding aspects of eating disorders in humans.
- A relationship between overactivity and food deprivation has been proposed, but recent findings suggest that the relationship may be less fundamental and less important than thought previously.
- The discovery of the *ob* gene and of the hormone leptin has opened a new chapter in the understanding of energy intake and utilization.

RESEARCH IMPLICATIONS

- The research priority of the next few years will be exploration of the actions and determinants of leptin, and its relationship to obesity, undernutrition, and eating and dieting disorders. This work should integrate biological research throughout the whole spectrum of dysfunctional eating.

Neurobiology in the Treatment of Eating Disorders.
Edited by H.W. Hoek, J.L. Treasure and M.A. Katzman.

11 Neuroimaging in Eating Disorders

Z. R. ELLISON AND J. FOONG

CLINICAL IMPLICATIONS

- Brain structural changes can be detected in patients with eating disorders and are likely to be secondary to their nutritional state.
- Cognitive impairment can be observed in anorexic patients who are severely underweight.
- The brain structure changes and cognitive impairment appear to be reversible upon weight gain in most patients.

RESEARCH IMPLICATIONS

- Improvement in MR techniques (e.g. volumetric analysis) may be valuable in extending the findings of structural brain abnormalities.
- Serial investigations would assist in clarifying the long term outcome of structural brain abnormalities and cognitive impairment.
- Further MRI studies in examining the cognitive processes in patients with eating disorders may provide more insight into the psychological mechanisms involved.

DIFFICULTIES

- It would be difficult to determine whether the structural or functional brain abnormalities detected are strictly secondary to the nutritional state or disease specific unless investigations done in the acute stages of illness are repeated upon normal weight gain.

ASSESSMENT

- Given the findings that cognitive impairment can occur in the acute stages, it would be important to obtain subjective reports from patients, corroborative information from their families or teachers and to include a cognitive assessment on mental state examination.
- Re-assessment should be considered upon recovery.

TREATMENT

- The neuroimaging findings in eating disorders to date suggest that early intervention or refeeding is indicated as brain abnormalities appear to correlate with the severity of illness and can be reversible.
- Educating patients and their families about the risks of cognitive impairment and the brain abnormalities would be important as they may improve compliance for treatment especially in those who are still in education or who are academic high achievers.
- There are also serious implications in determining whether patients who have cognitive impairment are able to give informed consent to treatment (e.g. refusing refeeding) as their judgement may be significantly impaired.

Neurobiology in the Treatment of Eating Disorders.
Edited by H.W. Hoek, J.L. Treasure and M.A. Katzman.

12 Emotional States and Bulimic Psychopathology

C. MEYER, G. WALLER and A. WATERS

CLINICAL IMPLICATIONS

- The literature on the aetiology and maintenance of bulimia suggests that it is likely to involve a complex interplay of causes, including starvation, affective states, and associated neurobiological factors.
- However, there will be differences across individuals in the mixture of those causal factors that lead to bulimic psychopathology.
- Therefore, the most effective approach to the eating disorders will be to understand the aetiology and maintenance for the individual, and to use that information to allocate bulimics to the most appropriate therapy.
- Thus, it is important to focus on the individual case formulation in determining therapy, rather than relying on generic formulations of bulimic disorders.

RESEARCH IMPLICATIONS

- Within the eating disorders, research to date has focused on starvation, affective and neurobiological factors in isolation. It is now important to understand how these factors work interactively.
- Where this interaction is studied, it will be necessary to consider the role of cognitive process and content as potential mediators, or 'carrier' mechanisms.

Neurobiology in the Treatment of Eating Disorders.
Edited by H.W. Hoek, J.L. Treasure and M.A. Katzman.

13 Neurobiological Aspects of Early Onset Eating Disorders

D. CHRISTIE, R. BRYANT-WAUGH, B. LASK and I. GORDON

CLINCIAL IMPLICATIONS

- Comprehensive physical assessment must be completed to exclude a primary pathology disorder that may be
  - mimicking the symptoms
  - significantly interacting with psychological factors maintaining the condition
- Understanding the long-term physical effects of the endocrine dysfunction can motivate both parents and children to participate in the treatment process.
- Research and dissemination of knowledge about the neurobiological issues provides important information helping to emphasise the message that weight restoration is a priority in young patients.
- Awareness of the associated neurobiological factors highlights the dangers of treating the child by 'talking cure' alone.
- Knowledge of the child's cognitive strengths and weaknesses can also contribute towards decisions about an appropriate therapeutic style and ensure its delivery at an appropriate developmental level.

RESEARCH IMPLICATIONS

- Some of the most significant implications of the findings include
  1. Underlying mechanisms associated with control of satiety in adults may not be participating in early onset eating disorders
  2. There is preliminary evidence of a specific, focal and unilateral abnormality affecting the limbic system of children and young adolescents with anorexia nervosa
- Further studies of neuroanatomy, neurophysiology and cognitive functioning are required to ascertain whether there is a primary neurological abnormality in this population.

Neurobiology in the Treatment of Eating Disorders.
Edited by H.W. Hoek, J.L. Treasure and M.A. Katzman.

14 The Treatment of Anorexia Nervosa

E. F. VAN FURTH

CLINICAL IMPLICATIONS

- Reviews of treatment studies and neurobiological literature converge in suggesting the following for anorexic patients:

  1. Nutritional rehabilitation and weight restoration are essential to recovery
  2. Many of the typical signs and symptoms of anorexia nervosa are a result of the malnutrition and emaciation
  3. Patients need to learn to cope with perceived stress in their social environment

- A cohesive team aligned on a philosophy of treatment which emphasizes patient responsibility and the right to self-determination will help establish and maintain an effective therapeutic alliance. A multidisciplinary approach to the underlying problems is necessary to minimize the chances of relapse.

FORMULATION

- Given the finding that family therapy is beneficial for adolescent anorexia nervosa patients and that parental criticism predicts a poor outcome, case formulations should include the results of a family assessment session and strategies concerning the involvement of the family in treatment.

FUTURE RESEARCH

- Little is known about the natural course of untreated anorexia nervosa. Research should focus on treatment effectiveness and controlled clinical trials of anorexia nervosa. Harmful effects of treatment should be evaluated.

DIFFICULTIES

- Ethical, methodological and practical problems need to be overcome before treatment outcome studies are initiated.

Neurobiology in the Treatment of Eating Disorders.
Edited by H.W. Hoek, J.L. Treasure and M.A. Katzman.

15 Treatment of Bulimia Nervosa

U. SCHMIDT

CLINICAL IMPLICATIONS

- CBT is the most widely evaluated psychological treatment for bulimia nervosa and leads to abstinence rates of 40–60%.
- Standard CBT may not address adequately the treatment needs of atypical (in terms of age, sex, culture, weight) patients or those with co-morbidity.
- Cognitive behavioural self-help manuals or guided self-help are effective in a proportion of sufferers.
- IPT is promising but needs further evaluation.
- The value of exposure treatment is uncertain.
- Medication is not usually a first-line treatment for bulimia nervosa.

RESEARCH IMPLICATIONS

- Promising new approaches to treatment which need further evaluation include: Schema-focused CBT, dialectical behaviour therapy, cognitive analytic therapy, motivational enhancement therapy, experiential therapies and multi-faceted day or in-patient programmes.

Neurobiology in the Treatment of Eating Disorders.
Edited by H.W. Hoek, J.L. Treasure and M.A. Katzman.

16 The Treatment of Binge Eating Disorder

M. D. LEVINE and M. D. MARCUS

CLINICAL IMPLICATIONS

- Although neuroendocrine and metabolic abnormalities have been associated with disordered eating, few biological correlates of binge eating in absence of purging have been identified.
- The biological correlates of obese BED patients are similar to those of equally obese non-binge eaters.
- Genetic factors have been implicated in development of obesity and may relate to onset or maintenance of BED.
- The treatment of BED must target *both* obesity and disordered eating.
- Cognitive-behavior therapy (CBT) is effective in decreasing binge eating frequency, but is not associated with significant weight loss.
- Abstinence from binge eating post-treatment appears to prevent further weight gain.
- Contrary to initial speculations, BED patients may benefit from weight control interventions.
- Pharmacological interventions including antidepressant medication, anorectic agents, and opiate antagonists have been evaluated in the treatment of BED. Antidepressants and opiate antagonists are associated with modest, short-term reductions in binge eating.
- Conclusions about the efficacy of pharmacological interventions in BED are limited by the lack of studies.

RESEARCH IMPLICATIONS

- Future, hypothesis-driven work needs to examine biological correlates of BED, and explore the direction of the association between the neurochemical and metabolic perturbations associated with binge eating and the onset and maintenance of BED.
- The relationship between repeated episodes of depression that are associated with weight gain and obesity, and the role of genetic risks for BN, mood disorders, and obesity merit attention in understanding the etiology and treatment of BED.
- Additional research that includes men, younger patients, ethnic minorities and subclinical BED patients is needed to understand BED and its treatment.

Neurobiology in the Treatment of Eating Disorders.
Edited by H.W. Hoek, J.L. Treasure and M.A. Katzman.

17 Pharmacotherapy of Eating Disorders

L. E. S. MAYER and B. T. WALSH

ANOREXIA NERVOSA

CLINICAL IMPLICATION OF RESEARCH TRIALS

No medication has been clearly shown to be effective in accelerating weight gain or altering the disturbed thinking about shape and weight.

- Studies do not support the efficacy of neuroleptic agents as standard treatment for anorexia nervosa.
- Antidepressant medications have not been shown to be useful when patients are underweight.
- Fluoxetine may be helpful in preventing relapse once a normal weight has been restored.
- Other medications including cyproheptadine, lithium, THC and cisapride have not been shown to be helpful.

Therefore, the standard treatment of anorexia nervosa should be an eclectic, multidisciplinary approach with pharmacological intervention only as an adjunct.

Difficulties:

- There is clinical and biologic 'heterogeneity' among patients with anorexia nervosa. It may be that patients with specific behavioral forms of the disorder, such as binge/purge or restricting subtypes, or patients with as yet unidentified biological characteristics will respond to medication.

RESEARCH IMPLICATIONS

Multiple neuroendocrine and neurotransmitter abnormalities occur in underweight patients with anorexia nervosa. Among the abnormalities described in recent research are:

- Decreased levels of plasma leptin.
- Increased levels of CSF neuropeptide Y, corticotropin releasing hormone and plasma glucocorticoids.

Continued

- Decreased levels in the CSF of the serotonin metabolite, 5-HIAA.

Future research is needed to clarify the role of these disturbances in anorexia nervosa. That is,

- Are they precursors or consequences of the illness?
- If they are consequences, are they specifically associated with anorexia nervosa, or are they non-specific manifestations of food restriction, weight loss and starvation?
- How can we translate the knowledge of these abnormalities into effective treatment strategies?

Difficulties answering these questions arise in that:

- It is difficult to study a complex physiological system, such as the regulation of feeding, without confounding variables.
- Our knowledge of normal physiology is limited, which further constrains our understanding of what and how things become abnormal.

Neurobiology in the Treatment of Eating Disorders.
Edited by H.W. Hoek, J.L. Treasure and M.A. Katzman.

17 Pharmacotherapy of Eating Disorders

L. E. S. MAYER and B. T. WALSH

BULIMIA NERVOSA

Pharmacologic agents are helpful in the treatment of bulimia nervosa, and their presumed mechanism of action is consistent with the current knowledge about the associated neurobiology

CLINICAL IMPLICATIONS

Clinical trials repeatedly confirm the utility of antidepressant agents in reducing the binge/purge cycle and the treatment of bulimia nervosa.

- Virtually all classes of antidepressants (e.g. tricyclic, monoamine oxidase inhibitors (MAOI), SSRI) have been shown to be effective treatments in reducing binge eating and/or purging behaviors in bulimia nervosa.
- Fluoxetine, 60 mg/day, has been shown to be more effective than 20 mg/day of fluoxetine and placebo in curbing binge eating and purging.
- Cognitive-behavioral therapy has also been shown to be an effective treatment for bulimia nervosa.

There is a significant co-morbidity of bulimia nervosa and depressive symptoms, however:

- Antidepressant medication is effective regardless of the presence and/or severity of depressive symptoms.
- The therapeutic mechanism of action of antidepressant medication may be different for depression and bulimia nervosa.

Future research is needed to determine how to match patients to various types of treatment (e.g. medication vs psychotherapy vs combination), and to develop interventions for patients who fail to respond to CBT and antidepressant medication.

Continued

Neurobiology in the Treatment of Eating Disorders.
Edited by H.W. Hoek, J.L. Treasure and M.A. Katzman.

RESEARCH IMPLICATIONS

Studies confirm abnormalities in major neurotransmitter systems and neuroendocrine signals.

- Alterations in serotonin appear to play a significant role in the neurobiology of bulimia nervosa.
- Norepinephrine (NE) disturbances also exist. During active bingeing and purging, NE levels are normal, but are significantly reduced following a 30 day binge/purge-free period.
- CSF peptide YY levels are normal in patients with active bulimia nervosa, but are elevated following a 30 day binge/purge-free period.
- Postprandial plasma CCK levels and subjective satiety are reduced in patients with bulimia nervosa.

Neurobiology in the Treatment of Eating Disorders.
Edited by H.W. Hoek, J.L. Treasure and M.A. Katzman.

18 A Cognitive Model and Treatment Strategies for Anorexia Nervosa

G. WOLFF AND L. SERPELL

CLINICAL IMPLICATIONS

- The model provides a rationale for a cognitive behavioural therapy strategy with an initial emphasis on engagement, and on working through ambivalence by exploring and restructuring anorexic meta-beliefs.
- A focus on the function of anorexia as a solution to other underlying problems enhances therapeutic alliance and facilitates collaborative work on egodystonic issues, such as dichotomous self-esteem schemata.
- The emphasis on the importance of the linking of weight/shape schemata to self esteem schemata gives a rationale for helping the patient to loosen these connections without directly confronting body image issues which may be egosyntonic, culturally entrenched and may not be realistically amenable to significant modification.

THEORETICAL/RESEARCH IMPLICATIONS

- The model integrates elements of Motivational Enhancement Therapy and Stages of Change Theory into a cognitive framework.
- The model opens up a new area of research which is focused on fundamentally important issues other than weight and shape, such as the issue of meta-beliefs in anorexia.
- This model has not yet been subject to rigorous evaluation, but can be used as a framework to test specific low-level hypotheses.

Neurobiology in the Treatment of Eating Disorders.
Edited by H.W. Hoek, J.L. Treasure and M.A. Katzman.

19 Nutritional Management

J. RUSSELL and S. BYRNES

CLINICAL AND RESEARCH IMPLICATIONS

The issue of nutritional management in the eating disorders is beset by a number of important questions.

- The first of these is whether patients with these conditions need treatment at all given their questionnable level of motivation.
- The relapse rate in anorexia nervosa is unacceptably high but there is sufficient evidence to suggest that weight should be restored sooner rather than later judging by brain and bone changes which appear not to be reversible.
- In bulimia nervosa the normal or near normal body weight appears to confer a biological advantage but normalizing eating patterns remains paramount.
- It is unclear exactly what weight is the right weight and a number of approaches including assessment of ovarian activity and of body composition might be used in order to gauge the adequacy of nutritional rehabilitation.
- How fast refeeding should be accomplished is also not known nor is the best method in which to elucidate the target weight range in view of the variability of our patients' patterns of recovery.
- Anorexia nervosa and bulimia nervosa both represent vicious cycles which ultimately become self perpetuating.
- Bulimia nervosa, however, represents a state in which the body fights back, despite its owner's attempts to oppose the process.
- Here the metabolic rate is highly variable although in general, lower than would be expected, whilst in anorexia nervosa, although energy conservation occurs at low weight, there is a relative metabolic inefficiency during refeeding.
- This appears to be the case with carbohydrate as a substrate and may account for the instability of recently regained weight. The high respiratory quotient following a glucose load indicates lipogenesis and early on serves as measure of fat stores.

Neurobiology in the Treatment of Eating Disorders.
Edited by H.W. Hoek, J.L. Treasure and M.A. Katzman.

20 Medical Complications of Eating Disorders

S. ZIPFEL, T. SPECHT and W. HERZOG

ANOREXIA NERVOSA

CLINICAL IMPLICATIONS

- Medical complications play an important role in the course of anorexia nervosa. It is important to keep in mind that the stage and the dynamic course of the illness, the subtype of AN, the possible abuse of drugs (e.g. laxatives, diuretics) and an additional medical comorbidity (e.g. diabetes) will effect presenting medical complications. Each stage of the illness demands a different focus to assessment and treatment:

1. *Acute phase:* Nutritional status, electrolyte and acid–base imbalance should be checked. In addition a basic cardiovascular diagnostic should be administered.
2. *Refeeding phase:* Parenteral nutrition should be avoided if possible, particularly in cachectic patients because of numerous possible complications (e.g. hypophosphatemia, water and electrolyte imbalance, fat overloading, high risk of infections).
3. *Chronic phase:* It should be considered that patients with a long-term course run a high risk of getting severe osteoporosis, chronic renal failure and several other kinds of structural organ damage.

RESEARCH IMPLICATIONS

- To prevent medical complications it is important to develop cost-effective, minimal invasive methods that are sensitive and valid. Some of the most significant implications in this field of research are:

1. New techniques for the measurement of body composition and nutritional status (e.g. DEXA, BIA, leptin).
2. Biochemical markers of bone resorption and new ultrasound techniques which give a new perspective for noninvasive assessment of bone mineral density and structure.
3. Leptin, a hormone secreted by adipocytes is a promising approach for a new neuroendocrine perspective in anorexia nervosa patients.
4. In the field of neuroimaging, new techniques like functional MRI or PET give a broader insight in the pathology and pathogenesis of this illness and the structural alterations.

20 Medical Complications of Eating Disorders

S. ZIPFEL, T. SPECHT and W. HERZOG

BULIMIA NERVOSA

CLINICAL IMPLICATIONS

- In patients with bulimia nervosa (BN), unlike those with AN, malnutrition and its implications are not the major factors affecting medical complications. Nevertheless, because of the fact that one-third of BN patients develop amenorrhea, there is still a significant risk of problems, like osteoporosis. But the most dangerous medical complications are caused by the massive binge eating and purging behavior that characterizes this illness.

1. Patients with BN, especially those with a high frequency of vomiting and an additional intake of laxatives or diuretic pills run a risk of electrolyte and acid–base disturbances.
2. A combination of metabolic alkalosis, hypokalemia, hypochloremia, polyuria and exsiccosis, is a typical result of massive purging behavior.
3. Cardiac complications occur mostly in patients with purging behavior but are not necessarily associated with hypokalemia.
4. In the gastrointestinal system gastric dilation (particularly after binge eating) and gastroduodenal ulcers (sometimes in combination with upper gastrointestinal bleeding) can occur.
5. BN patients with the comorbidity of diabetes mellitus run a high risk of hypoglycemia and of early onset vascular complications due to impaired glucose metabolism.

RESEARCH IMPLICATIONS

- To prevent medical complications it is important to develop cost-effective, minimal invasive methods that are sensitive and valid. Some of the most significant implications in this field of research are:

1. New techniques for the measurement of body composition and nutrition status (e.g. DEXA, BIA, leptin).
2. In BN patients with amenorrhea biochemical markers of bone resorption and new ultrasound techniques which give a new perspective for noninvasive assessment of bone mineral density and structure.

Continued

3. Leptin, a hormone secreted by adipocytes is a promising approach for a new neuroendocrine perspective in bulimia nervosa, especially in those patients with large fluctuations in weight. Further, a number of recently detected, highly potent appetite stimulating neurohormones (e.g. neuropeptide Y, urocortin) could broaden our understanding of the illness.
4. In the field of neuroimaging, new techniques like functional MRI or PET give a broader insight to the underlying central nervous disturbances, particularly in phases of acute bulimic symptomatology.

Neurobiology in the Treatment of Eating Disorders.
Edited by H.W. Hoek, J.L. Treasure and M.A. Katzman.

Index

Index compiled by Liz Granger